# Andrew Salmon

# TO THE LAST ROUND

## *The Epic British Stand on the Imjin River, Korea 1951*

Aurum

First published in Great Britain
2009 by Aurum Press Ltd
7 Greenland Street, London NW1 0ND
www.aurumpress.co.uk

This paperback edition published in 2010 by Aurum Press

A catalogue record for this book is available from the British Library.

ISBN 978 1 84513 533 1

1 3 5 7 9 10 8 6 4 2
2010 2012 2014 2013 2011

Text designed and typeset by Robert Updegraff
Printed by CPI Bookmarque, Croydon

# CONTENTS

List of Maps                                                        vi

Acknowledgements and Sources                                       vii

Introduction  Battle, Tragedy, Legend                               xi

Prologue     Ambush Patrol: Prelude to Battle                        1

Chapter 1    Lack of the Morning Calm: The Korean War                8

Chapter 2    To Korea                                               23

Chapter 3    Catastrophe                                            43

Chapter 4    At War in Winter                                       67

Chapter 5    Valley of the Water Dragon                            111

Chapter 6    Onslaught: 22 April                                   136

Chapter 7    St George's Day: 23 April                             159

Chapter 8    Crescendo: 24 April                                   185

Chapter 9    Fortress in the Clouds: The Glosters' Last Stand      200

Chapter 10   Death Ride: Breakout Down Route 11                    224

Chapter 11   Flags and Body Bags                                   253

Chapter 12   In Enemy Hands: The Camps                             269

Chapter 13   In Retrospect                                         301

Appendix     Where Are They Now?                                   329

Glossary                                                           341

List of Sources                                                    344

Notes                                                              349

Index                                                              365

# List of Maps

Korea and 29th Brigade Battles, November 1950 – April 1951    11

Happy Valley – Royal Ulster Rifles Battlefield    71

Happy Valley – Royal Northumberland Fusiliers Battlefield    75

Valley of the Water Dragon – Imjin Front, April 1951    122

Onslaught – 22 April    143

St George's Day – Battle of the Imjin River, 23 April    175

Crescendo – Eastern Sector, 24 April    192

The Glosters' Last Stand    220

Death Ride: Breakout on Eastern Sector, 25 April    236

The Armageddon North of Seoul – Chinese Fifth Offensive    263

# Acknowledgements and Sources

I have elected, both below and in the text, to list brigade units in alphabetical order (i.e. Belgians first, Royal Ulster Rifles last). My first thanks must go to veterans who granted interviews. Ranks are given at time of battle. From the Belgian Battalion: Sergeant Armand Philips, Sergeant André VanDamme, Sergeant Lucien Senterre and Lieutenant Henri Wolfs. From the Glosters: Private Morris 'Brassy' Coombes, Private Tony Eagles, the late Captain Mike Harvey, Private Sam Mercer, the late Medical Orderly George Newhouse, the late Lance-Corporal Albert Perkins, Lance-Corporal Charles Sharpling, Second Lieutenant Guy Temple and Private Ben Whitchurch. From the 8th King's Royal Irish Hussars: Lieutenant David Boyall, Lieutenant Bernard Dowling, Lieutenant Ted Paul and Cornet John Preston-Bell. From the Republic of Korea 1st Infantry Division: General Paik Sun-yup and Colonel Kim Chum-kon. From the Royal Artillery: Lance-Bombardier Tom Clough, Gunner Bob Nicholls and Lieutenant George Truell. From the Royal Northumberland Fusiliers: Fusilier John Bayliss, Sergeant William Beattie, Lieutenant Malcolm Cubiss, Fusilier Derek Kinne, the late Major Robbie Leith-MacGregor, Lieutenant Tony Perrins, Lieutenant Sam Phillips, Fusilier David Strachan, Corporal Joe Thompson, Fusilier Stan Tomenson and Fusilier Vick Wear. From the Royal Ulster Rifles: Captain Robin Charley, Lance-Corporal Joe Farrell, Sergeant William 'Doc' Holliday, Interpreter Lee Kyung-sik, Second Lieutenant Mervyn McCord, Lieutenant John Mole, Corporal Michael O'Leary, CQMS Tommy Sturgeon and Corporal Norman Sweetlove. From the US Air Force: pilot officers Robert Moxley and Carl Schneider.

At museums, I must thank: Geoff Crump, Researcher at the Cheshire Military Museum, for biographical data and photograph of Brigadier Tom Brodie. At the Soldiers of Gloucestershire Museum: Historian David Read for opening his archive, and Graham Gordon and his wife Mary for driving me around the Cotswolds, to James Carne's home village of Cranham. At the Royal Northumberland Fusiliers Museum: Lesley Frater, and veteran Sam Phillips for driving me to and from Alnwick. At the Royal Ulster Rifles Museum: Captain Jackie Knox for arranging interviews and opening her archive. And at the National War Memorial of Korea, Dr Nam Jeong-ok, Lieutenant-Colonel Lee Wang-woo and Private Choi Seung-bee. I owe a heavy debt to the Imperial War Museum, London, where audio recordings with veterans, mostly undertaken by Dr Conrad Wood, are invaluable. (The most useful ones for this work were Denis Whybro, Peter Ormrod and Frank Carter.) Thanks to Chris Hunt in the IWM's Reading Room for various kindnesses.

I could not have asked for better co-operation from the US 8th Army in Korea. I must thank Lieutenant-Colonel (ret.) Steve Tharp,* who handles public affairs for the 8th Army and teaches graduate-level courses on the Korean War (and is a barbecue artist par excellence), for introducing me to 8th Army historian Lieutenant-Colonel (ret.) Ronney Miller, who permitted use of his office's Korean War library, took me on an Imjin battlefield tour with US Special Operations Command Korea in 2007, and discussed the battle over beers. Thanks also to Command Historian Dr Lewis Bernstein for information on Chinese tactics. At the British Embassy, Seoul, thanks to Military Attaché, Brigadier Matt O'Hanlon, Royal Irish Regiment, for granting long-term loan of the British official history, and for accompanying the author on a drive over the battlefield in April 2008.

For reading sections of the manuscript, and/or making various useful suggestions, I must credit Commandant (ret.) Jan Dillen, Fusilier (ret.) Derek Kinne, Brigadier (ret.) Mervyn McCord, Captain (ret.) Tony Perrins, Sergeant (ret.) Lucien Senterre, Lieutenant-Colonel (ret.) Guy Temple, Lieutenant-Colonel (ret.) Steve Tharp, Major-General (ret.) David Thomson and Brigadier (ret.) Dick Webster. Any mistakes, naturally, are my own. Particular thanks go to Dick and Captain Barry De Morgan, who, preparing a DVD on the Hussars in the Korean War, generously shared with me their materials, both textual and visual; to Tony Perrins, for putting me in touch with so many sources; to Jan Dillen, who served in the Belgian battalion later in the war, and who introduced me to Belgian veterans; to Bill Hall of the Fusiliers' All Ranks Club for putting me in contact with several ex-Fusiliers; to Mervyn McCord, John Preston-Bell and the appropriate museums for granting use of their fine photographs; and to Jan Dillen for letting me use his collection of Padre Vander Goten's shots. Thanks also to General (ret.) Sir Peter de la Billière for his insights on how the Imjin and his own Korean experiences affected his command in Gulf War I. Others: Mark Godsman, an ex-gunner in 45 Field, who assisted with various sources and contacts,

---

* Tharp has his own Imjin tale. As a Ranger NCO in 1979, he was deployed below the DMZ in 29th Brigade's old sector when South Korean President Park Chung-hee was assassinated. Amid suspicions that North Korea was behind the killing, fears rose of an invasion. Tharp's commander took him to the Gloster Memorial and stated dramatically: 'Tharp! I expect nothing less of you!' Tharp's pleas that his squad lacked live ammunition were ignored. In fact, Park had been shot by his own intelligence chief; North Korea made no move.

and who put me on to the Royal Artillery Institute when the MOD's PR team could not. Brian Kennedy, an expert on Chinese martial culture, gave valuable insights into some of the more bizarre sights of the Imjin battlefield. Online, I must thank various posters on military history site www.armchairgeneral.com (you know who you are), who answered many arcane enquiries. I also tip my hat to the http://rokdrop.com/ blog, which features various Korean War-related articles and links. Thanks to Jeremy Bigwood and David List for research at, respectively, the US and UK national archives in Washington and Kew. Cheers to my agent, Chelsey Fox at Fox and Howard for placing me in front of Piers Burnett of Aurum Press, and to Piers for remaining civil as deadlines drifted by.

\* \* \*

A full List of Sources appears at the end of the book, but I must acknowledge critical sources up front.

While there is no single, definitive history of the brigade battle, there are many personal accounts. The Glosters have produced the most. The only British Korean War book to attain classic status is Anthony Farrar-Hockley's account of battle and captivity: *The Edge of the Sword*; no other work records the struggle for Hill 235 with such immediacy. David Green's *Captured at the Imjin River* is a personal reminiscence, contrasting humorous with shocking experiences. A searing account of B Company's annihilation appears in Lofty Large's career autobiography *Soldier Against the Odds* (and thanks to his widow, Ann, for filling me in on her husband's later years). Denys Whatmore's *One Road To Imjin* is the most vivid account of a platoon commander's battle in Korea that I know of. Mike Harvey's *At War in Korea: The Battle Decides All* is uneven, but provides compelling detail on that unconventional officer's approach to warfare. Digby Grist's *Remembered With Advantage* tells the story of the Glosters' tragedy from the second in command's perspective. *Blowing Our Bridges* by Tony Younger, the commander of 55 Field Squadron Royal Engineers, is a fine account of war by one of 29th Brigade's most humane officers. The Fusiliers were underrepresented in libraries until 2002, when the battalion's intelligence officer, Anthony Perrins, published *A Pretty Rough Do Altogether: The Fifth Fusiliers in Korea 1950–51*. Merging the personal (letters home from officers) with the organizational (the Fusiliers' war diary and official accounts of engagements), Perrins provides a benchmark for regimental historians. The Royal Ulster Rifles have the benefit of a regimental history written by the battalion's adjutant immediately after the war, Hugh Hamill's *The RUR in Korea*. More personal is Rifleman Henry O'Kane's *O'Kane's Korea*; like

Green's work, it deserves a wider readership. Then there is P.J. Kavanagh's autobiographical *The Perfect Stranger*; his account of the Battle Patrol's drive into annihilation is masterly. The Imjin features in general Korean War histories from both sides of the Atlantic. Among British historians, Max Hastings' *The Korean War*, Michael Hickey's *The Korean War: The West Confronts Communism* and Tim Carew's *Korea: The Commonwealth at War* offer well-sourced, vivid accounts of the battle. The most accurate, taken from regimental histories, is Bryan Perret's, in his collection *Last Stand*. Farrar-Hockley's two-volume official history, *The British Part in the Korean War*, is indispensable for any British historian of the war. From the United States, the official US Army history, Billy Mossman's *Ebb and Flow*, and Roy Appleman's *Ridgway Duels for Korea* both showcase the detailed research at which American historians are so capable. Perhaps the most popular overall Korean War history, Clay Blair's *The Forgotten War*, offers valuable information on the American commanders. For the Chinese view, Zhang Shu-guang's *Mao's Military Romanticism* is fascinating. And no historian of the war should start work without Spencer C. Tucker's mammoth *Encyclopedia of the Korean War* at his elbow.

\* \* \*

Finally, an apology to my wife Ji-young and my daughter Hannah. For a year and a half, they suffered a husband and father whose body was in Seoul, but whose mind was on the Imjin.

# Introduction

....................

# BATTLE, TRAGEDY, LEGEND

*I am a soldier, and unapt to weep*
*Or to exclaim on fortune's fickleness.*

Shakespeare

IT WAS A SUNNY WEEKEND afternoon in April 2001.
After a light lunch, I and several friends were slogging up a dirt
track to the summit of a low hill. Although we were all in our twenties and thirties and the weather was mild, it was a sweaty climb:
jackets were slung over shoulders, lungs were tested.

Passing in clouds of dust, South Korean army jeeps were rattling up
to the hilltop a couple of hundred metres ahead of us. Driven by young
Korean troops, they were conveying to the summit old British soldiers –
men in their seventies and eighties, survivors of a war that had sputtered to an uneasy halt half a century previously.

Every April Seoul's little British community joins visiting veterans on
their annual visits to this site. It is forty minutes' drive north of Seoul
and a mile south of the Imjin River. It lies among artillery emplacements, dug-in armoured vehicles and military bases, for just beyond the
river is the so-called 'Demilitarized Zone' – actually, one of the world's
most heavily armed strips of real estate – which divides capitalist South
Korea from the communist North. This border, the 38th Parallel, is the
Cold War's last front line.

Even so, it is a pleasant occasion: diplomats, businesspeople and their
families meeting for a picnic in the countryside. It is also a sombre one. The
event commemorates the most tragic action fought by British troops in that
distant, savage conflict: the Battle of the Imjin River, fought from 22 to 25
April 1951. This year was special. It was the fiftieth anniversary, and, in
addition to veterans, the VIPs had descended in force: generals, ambassadors, South Korea's Defence Minister – even Prince Andrew, Duke of York.

As the dust thrown up by the last jeep dissipated, I noticed ahead of
us a tall, solitary figure working his way painstakingly up the steepest
part of the track. He was wearing a dark blazer and a beret – the unofficial uniform of visiting veterans. I noticed a badge on the rear of his
beret. The only regiment in the British Army with a back badge is the

Glosters; it was this battalion which had been wiped out in the battle. I caught up with the old soldier.

'You know, there are jeeps for veterans,' I told him. 'You don't have to walk.'

'I know,' he replied. 'But I feel I have to walk up this hill.'

We fell into conversation. His name was Sam Mercer. As a twenty-two-year-old private he had fought on the hill we were now climbing. He had, in fact, taken part in the close-quarters action in which his platoon commander, Lieutenant Philip Curtis, won a Victoria Cross at the cost of his life. And Sam had not escaped unscathed. Despite his erect posture, one of his legs was a prosthetic; one of his eyes was glass.

At the summit, we paused for breath and surveyed the landscape. Around us, the rolling countryside was sprouting green. Behind us the craggy granite hills rose higher. Just below the lip of the hill we were standing on were fresh trenches: the old Gloster position is, to this day, occupied by South Korean troops. As the eye lifted, the lazy bends of the Imjin River could be made out, glittering in the sun. Beyond, the blue hills of North Korea shimmered mysteriously in the haze.

Sam pointed out where Curtis's desperate counter-attack had taken place, and told me a bit of his own part in the battle. It was sobering stuff. Night assaults by overwhelming numbers. A suicidal attack on an enemy bunker. A withdrawal under fire. Survivors whittled down. A last stand on a napalm-scorched hilltop. In the bright, peaceful afternoon, I wondered what it must have been like for the man at my side. He had survived that first night of battle, but lost an eye to shrapnel on the Glosters' final position. Left behind with the wounded as survivors attempted to break out, his leg had been shot out by an enemy soldier. Then he had spent two bleak years in the POW camps in North Korea's mountains. Given these experiences, he must be as bitter as hell, presumably?

He looked into my two eyes with his one.

'I joined the army for travel and adventure and I got my fair share of both,' he said. 'I don't regret a moment.'

I was impressed. 'I don't regret a moment.' He was no curmudgeon, whining at the injustices of life. Nor was he a loudmouth, declaiming his courage to all and sundry. He could legitimately have been either. Or both. Instead, he was modest, understated: he had no complaints, but took a quiet pride in talking of what he, his mates and his regiment had done.

Here, I thought, was the representative of a dying breed of Britons, men for whom duty and the concept of the 'stiff upper lip' were not material for mocking comedy. I would later learn of an officer from the Glosters – and would meet a private from the Royal Northumberland Fusiliers – who had taken these concepts to the limit. Both were young men. The former died; the latter survived . . . just. Both won the George Cross. They would not have found jokes about such things amusing.

Other veterans I spoke to that day, from various units, impressed me for similar reasons. Most had undergone what are, by the comfortable standards of twenty-first-century Britain, extraordinarily traumatic experiences. Many were still haunted by the sights they had seen in the terrible winter retreat of 1950/51. They had fought in nightmarish battles. The closest friendships are forged in the trenches, and all had lost friends. The previous day they had visited some. A key point on the itinerary for returning veterans is a visit to the UN Cemetery in the city of Pusan. There, 886 British soldiers lie under the grass.

Yet almost every veteran, astonished at the peace and prosperity they found, felt their sacrifices had been worthwhile. 'In Korea, the people say "thank you" to us, more than in any other nation where British troops have fought,' one said. Clearly, these old soldiers had achieved some kind of closure.

At the time I was writing a story about the veterans' and VIPs' visit for a local newspaper. Easy enough: sketch in background, add a splash of local colour, round it out with a few quotes. But the more I heard, the more I wanted to discover about this legendary battle in which young Sam Mercer had been so horribly wounded, but was still so proud to have taken part.

* * *

I knew about the Glosters; anyone with an interest in military history had heard of their lonely stand. But they had not been the only ones who had held China's entire 63rd Army – three divisions of men, or odds of around 7:1 – on the Imjin.

The Glosters had been part of 29th Infantry Brigade, and the other battalions – the infantrymen of the Belgian Battalion, the Royal Northumberland Fusiliers, the Royal Ulster Rifles and the tank crews of the 8th King's Royal Irish Hussars, even a group of engineers shoved into the line as the brigade ran out of infantry and the battle grew ever more intense – had had an equally desperate time. However, as these units had narrowly escaped annihilation – after a death ride down a four-mile enfilade – they never achieved the recognition accorded the doomed Glosters.

It rankled with some. On a previous battlefield visit, an embassy staff member told me, *sotto voce*, that some veterans from another battalion had had to be restrained from assaulting a senior Gloster officer who had lectured on the battle without giving them what they believed was due credit. Even after half a century, the tribal structures of British fighting regiments engendered fierce loyalties.

Regardless of which battalion won the lion's share of the honours, it was clear that the brigade had put up one hell of a fight. How had they managed to cling on for three nights? Why had they been forced to stand against such fearful odds? Why was an entire battalion written off? Had there been mistakes?

To my surprise, I found that, while regimental histories and general Korean War histories covered the battle, as did various privately published personal chronicles, there was no single, detailed account available. There was certainly no film about it. And yet the Imjin remains the costliest, most desperate battle fought by British forces since World War II.

Take the lost battalion, the Glosters. At no other time since World War II has a unit of this size been written off. Or take the rifle companies of the surviving infantry battalions, which lost around half their strength. In fighting as murderous as this, rank was no defence. Of the commanders of the four infantry battalions engaged, one was wounded, one captured and one killed; only one made it out in one piece. The encounter was no less intense for the artillery. The gun positions themselves came under infantry attack. Each gun fired off approximately a thousand rounds: twice as many as were fired in the entire Falklands War, and approximately the same number as were fired at the battle of El Alamein.

All within less than three days.

Here was a tale up there with Hastings, Rorke's Drift or Arnhem: a stand against monumental odds by men whose orders were simply to hold fast – the Thermopylae of the Korean War. Why had this epic fight gone largely unrecorded?

\* \* \*

Perhaps because it took place in Korea. Although over a thousand Britons lost their lives on the peninsula – a longer butcher's bill than those paid in Malaya, Borneo, Suez, Northern Ireland, the Falklands, Iraq or Afghanistan – the 'Forgotten War' is almost dead to popular culture. Few films cover it. Military history is a popular genre, but in bookshops, it is rare to find a single volume devoted to it. In the popular consciousness, Korea (1950–1953) is filed away in an uneasy slot between World War II (1939–1945) and Vietnam (1965–1975).

World War II continues to generate fascination. It was the greatest clash of arms in history, a struggle in which our national survival was at stake. Korea – fought on the opposite side of the earth, over a peninsula that few had heard of – was not. With the trans-Atlantic ties engendered by a common language and mass communications, Vietnam is probably a better-known war in Britain than is Korea, although no British troops served in it. Vietnam was fought by men who watched

TV and listened to rock music, rather than by those who listened to jazz over the 'wireless': the GIs in the jungles may not have been British, but they were recognisably modern – like us.

Korea was not solely a British war; it was the first UN war. The United States and South Korea provided far and away the largest contingents, overshadowing Britain's contribution. Moreover, Korea lacked the tactical innovations or iconic images that define World War II and Vietnam. World War II was the war of *blitzkrieg*, of massed tanks and bomber fleets, of parachute landings and amphibious assaults, of Churchill's V sign, concentration camps and the fascist salute. Vietnam was the war of the helicopter and the guerrilla, the jungle and live colour coverage. These elements were reflected in the films of those wars: classics such as *The Longest Day*, *The Battle of Britain* and *Saving Private Ryan* for World War II; *Apocalypse Now*, *The Deer Hunter* and *Platoon* in the case of Vietnam.

Few Korean War movies made an impact. *Pork Chop Hill* (1959) is a good film, but little remembered. A former Royal Fusilier and Korean veteran, Maurice Micklewhite, got his start on the screen with *A Hill in Korea* (1956) but went on to greater things – today he is better known as Sir Michael Caine. The film was not a highlight of his career. And of course, there was *MASH*, the US television series. Though supposedly set in Uijongbu – the ruined township some fifteen miles south of 29th Brigade's battle sector – the 1970s/1980s series was more about Vietnam than about Korea, albeit set in a Korea which looked suspiciously like Malibu, California (where it was filmed).

Korea was fought using largely World War II-era weapons, in a harsh landscape bleached of colour. Quite who we were fighting was unclear: the enemy leaders, Mao Tse-tung and Kim Il-sung, were neither as recognisable nor as demonisable as Hitler and Tojo. And why were we fighting? War was never declared: Korea remains officially a 'conflict', or a 'police action'. The description is derided by those who fought. As one veteran put it: 'A thousand men dead, artillery, Centurion tanks – a police action?!'

Finally, the war – for the men who fought, that is what it was – never really ended. This was the first 'limited' war, a war concluded by armistice, not victory. The British public, exhausted by World War II, lost interest in the indecisive struggle. Today, North Korea is even more mysterious than in 1950 – and, possessing nuclear arms, perhaps as dangerous.*

---

* To this day, nearly 30,000 US troops are still based in South Korea. The last American combat division on the peninsula is positioned just two miles east of 29th Brigade's positions, underscoring the strategic importance of the ground the British soldiers held in 1951.

Yet the Korean War was not lacking in drama. Ferocious drama. This was the first 'hot' war of the Cold War; a to-the-death struggle in an ancient land against a brave and overwhelming, but frighteningly alien, enemy. It was a civil war (North Korea versus South Korea) that expanded to become a clash of both ideology (communism versus capitalism) and culture (East versus West). It was a cruel fight.

The names the soldiers gave their battlefields tell their own tales: Hellfire Ridge, The Bloody Hook, Massacre Valley. Viewed through a rifle sight, the Korean War was a mosaic of confusing, terrifying snapshots. It was a war of freezing temperatures and searing heat . . . of burning cities and refugees perishing in freezing wastelands . . . of terrible atrocities and midnight 'human-wave' assaults . . . of hilltop perimeters and last-minute retreats down valleys overlooked by the enemy to escape annihilation.

Moreover, this was the coldest campaign fought by the British Army since the Crimea, and the last one fought against an enemy who, like the Zulus, favoured close-range, mass attack. That first, see-saw year – when the contesting armies raged up and down the devastated peninsula – was, for the soldiers on the ground, probably more akin to the German experience on the World War II Russian front than to any other British action fought before or since. Central to this drama is the greatest attack of the war: the Chinese 'Fifth Offensive' of April 1951. In the path of that offensive, occupying a critical hinge in the line, stood 29th Infantry Brigade.

\* \* \*

Over the years I gathered material – books, logs, documents – and gleaned much from taped interviews with 29th Infantry Brigade veterans in the collections of London's Imperial War Museum. In the summer of 2007 I spent a month interviewing veterans, and followed up with written and telephone interviews in 2008. Many felt the media had passed them by, and that their war – their stories – were being lost. 'Old soldiers don't die, they just fade away'; indeed.

All are retired now. In their twilight years, they were keen to speak. In some cases I spent only an hour with them – in other cases, we spoke for an entire day. Adding poignancy to the interviews was the timing. We spoke while British soldiers were once again heavily engaged, alongside American allies, on another barren battleground, against another culturally incomprehensible enemy.

In their homes, or among the faded battle memorabilia of regimental museums, these old soldiers told me of incidents horrific and comical, of decisions good and bad, of exhilaration and desperation, of friends made and lost. They were not boastful; their pride was a quiet kind.

This, perhaps, was another reason that their battle had not been accorded greater acclaim. They were unfamiliar with PR; they did not beat breasts or 'create a buzz'. They came from a stoic generation; one bred to control emotions, to speak modestly and to both expect and endure adversity.

Many were still haunted by what they had done or witnessed in Korea. On several occasions, men broke down. While others downplayed the war's psychological impact, one fact spoke volumes: arguably the bravest man who fought on the Imjin would, years later, spend time in a mental institution. Another veteran, discussing post-traumatic stress, told me a tale so chilling that it reversed my long-held disbelief in ghosts.

But, still, there were few complainers.

The result of this research you hold now. It is military history. It deals with strategy and tactics, weapons and equipment, weather and terrain. It deals with luck, good and ill. But, above all, it deals with men. Tested in the crucible of battle in the most demanding of circumstances – massive attack – few soldiers of 29th Brigade were found wanting.

With regret, I only present half the story. I had hoped to interview surviving 'Chinese People's Volunteers', those men who fought with such apparent disregard for their lives that many British veterans are convinced they were drugged. However, I was writing at a sensitive time. China, despite its surging economy and rising standard of living, remains communist. With North Korean denuclearisation talks under way, sources in Beijing and Seoul made clear that this would be a difficult task. Moreover, I lacked the resources – time and finances – to garner their accounts. The story of the Chinese fighting man on the Imjin must await another author.

This, then, is the story of one of the two contestants in that legendary struggle of April 1951: the story of defiance against towering odds, the story of the Battle of the Imjin River.

## NOTE TO THE READER

First, a word on spellings. Although The Gloster Regiment is more correctly spelled The Gloucestershire Regiment, and shortened to The Gloucester Regiment, the former, phonetic usage has passed into common currency. This is the spelling used.

Korean and Chinese are more problematic. In 2000 the South Korean government changed its official romanisation system. Henceforth, 'Pusan' became 'Busan', 'Inchon' became 'Incheon', 'Taegu' became 'Daegu' and so on. Given that the older spellings continue to be reproduced in Korean War literature, those are the spellings I have opted for. For consistency's sake, I have stuck with the pre-Pinyin spellings of Chinese: hence 'Mao Zedong' appears here as 'Mao Tse-tung', and his capital is spelled 'Peking' not 'Beijing'.

To the Last Round is written chronologically – as far as possible – but, given that fighting was under way simultaneously on different sectors of the battlefield, I have chosen to focus on units rather than timings. So, for example, the fighting on the night of 24/25 April on the eastern and western flanks, while it happened at the same time, is covered in two separate chapters (8 and 9 respectively). Likewise, some events in Chapters 2 and 3 are not presented strictly in a linear timeline. I suggest the reader approach this work, then, as primarily a chronological, but secondarily, a thematic one.

There is a Glossary at the back of the book that I hope will elucidate unfamiliar military terminology, acronyms and slang.

Lastly, a note on notes. I have used footnotes to expand on certain points, or insert items of interest that would interrupt the narrative flow if included in the main text; I suggest the reader follow these while reading. Endnotes are reserved for references/sources. Where no endnote is appended, the information comes from an author interview with the participant.

*Andrew Salmon*
*Seoul*
*Winter 2009*

## Prologue

·············

# AMBUSH PATROL:
# PRELUDE TO BATTLE

*April is the cruellest month.*

T.S. Eliot

LAST LIGHT, 22 APRIL 1951. Imjin River Front.

As the moon rose, a group of heavily laden men dropped from their armoured vehicles, spread into tactical formation and moved noiselessly down towards the Imjin. With their blackened faces and khaki battledress, the patrol from C Company, 1st Battalion, the Glosters blended into the dust and darkness of the Korean landscape.

Ahead of them the river glinted in the cool darkness. Behind them, the outlines of their hilltop positions faded into the black sky. There, the men could take comfort in the safety of numbers and prepared defences. Here, on the river bank, they were in no man's land, a mile forward of the rest of their battalion. Somewhere north of the river, invisible, lay the enemy.

How close? Unknown. How many? Unknown. Intentions? Unknown.

With the two Oxford armoured troop carriers rumbling back to battalion through the ruined hamlet and across the bare, brown plain, the 17 men of the patrol were on their own. Tension and suppressed excitement was in the air: the men had heard ominous tales – for days now, rumours of a Chinese offensive had circulated. Tonight, they knew there was something afoot: they had been issued with an unusual amount of ammunition. What they didn't know was that their patrol commander had exceeded his orders.

Three hours earlier Second Lieutenant Guy 'Guido' Temple[1] had been summoned to headquarters. There he was briefed by Lieutenant-Colonel James Carne, Commanding Officer of the Glosters' 1st Battalion, which was holding this section of the front. The colonel – a man who, Temple thought, 'seemed to ration himself to twenty words a day' – was characteristically terse.

US intelligence had indicated that an enemy party would cross the Imjin under cover of darkness. Temple was to take a 'small patrol' down to the river ford, intercept the enemy and snatch a prisoner. Two South Korean military policemen would accompany the patrol to interrogate him. The patrol was to break contact if enemy numbers exceeded thirty. No questions? Good. That is all.

Temple, a twenty-one-year-old West Countryman with an easygoing manner and a near-permanent grin, was well liked in the battalion – he was nicknamed, inevitably, 'the Good Guy' – but seen as something of a dilettante by his men. Two years earlier, when the battalion had been posted to the rather more agreeable location of Jamaica, he was noted for racing round the island in a Rolls-Royce packed with party-going subal-terns.* But the insouciant manner – adopted by many highly professional British officers – was misleading. A fellow officer, hearing Temple's name, stabbed his finger in the air and exclaimed, 'Guy Temple is a very brave man!'[2] Previously the battalion signals officer, Temple had yearned to get to the sharp end and had requested command of a rifle platoon. The request was granted. Temple's father was a major-general, and two relations were archbishops – which could explain why the youngster had acquired the kind of sixth sense that soldiers and priests learn to trust. While being briefed, his internal 'crystal ball' flickered into action. Somehow, Temple knew immediately: 'It was not going to be small number of enemy – it was going to be a mass. But of course, a lieutenant does not say to a colonel, "I think the Americans have got it wrong; I think it's going to be thousands of them!"'[†]

Returning to his platoon, Temple draped canvas bandoliers of .303 ammunition over his chest and stuffed his parachute smock with hand grenades. Then he gathered a nine-man section – a seven-man rifle group and a two-man Bren light machine-gun group. So far, he was acting according to orders. But he also stripped the platoon of its remaining two Brens, its 2-inch mortar and a radio operator. Each machine-gun was pro-vided with 4,000 rounds, and the mortar team took as many bombs as they could carry. This was far more firepower than would be required for

* Sam Mercer, Gloster private (author interview). Temple explained that ownership of the car was the result of a fortuitous combination of circumstances. When he was travelling on a refrigerated 'banana boat' from the UK to join the battalion on Jamaica, his luggage had been stowed in the cork-lined hold. A fire broke out there, damaging the ship ('the sharks were circling'), which, listing, limped into Port of Spain. There the first official Temple met on the dock was from Lloyd's, with whom he had insured his luggage. Some days later, a wad of cash in hand, he was scanning the 'for sale' column of the local newspaper; this happened to be next to the 'liquidation' column, where he spotted a Rolls Royce for sale. He immediately called and made a bid for £50 – which was accepted. As for the partying: 'The infantry is not as well-off as all that,' Temple said. 'But in Jamaica you could spend a whole night dancing with as much rum and Coke as you wanted for one shilling and sixpence!'
† Many writers have applauded Colonel Carne's tactical prescience in setting an ambush on the river. In fact, it was Temple's initiative to fight a denial action, not Carne's; the colonel had ordered a simple prisoner snatch, to gauge the enemy's intentions. When small listening patrols were sent out upriver from Temple on the same night, the results were far less impressive, as we shall see.

a prisoner snatch. 'I had no plan to take any prisoners at all,' Temple recalled. 'You could say I did not follow orders, but everyone can have his own opinion as to what a "small patrol" means!'

Now, on the fifteen-foot-high river bank, Temple positioned his men around the top of the earthen cutting that led down from the steep banks to the shingle beach and the river itself. As so often in this see-saw war up and down the ravaged peninsula, there were already slit trenches dug. Below and to the front of them, the broad Imjin drifted gently by. Although the river was approximately 150 metres wide, here it was only a few feet deep. A line of oil drums, placed by the engineers, marked the underwater ford, or, as the British troops called it, 'Gloster Crossing'.*

It was a beautiful spring evening, if chilly. The full moon, shimmering on the black water, gave the mission a 'romantic' ambience, Temple thought. It also provided a perfect hunter's moon. 'Look at that!' he whispered to his second in command, Corporal Manley. 'We'll see everything!'

In fact, they wouldn't. Even with binoculars, neither man would see a sign of the enemy forces closing on them. As the patrol settled down to watch and listen, Temple's 'crystal ball' clicked on again, telling him that nothing would happen until 22:00. He told his corporal to take first watch, then curled up at the bottom of his trench. On operations, wise soldiers seize any chance to sleep. At 22:00 Temple was shaken awake. 'There are voices in the river,' Manley hissed. They peered into the darkness. Nothing. Vision is restricted at night, but sound carries further than in daytime. There it came again – voices from the water. Chinese voices.

The men clicked off safety catches, took up first trigger pressure, but still they could see nothing. Temple aimed his Verey pistol skyward to shoot a flare. *Click*. The round was a dud. The voices were getting closer. Urgently, he ordered his mortar man to send up a para-illuminating round. There was a 'thunk' as the weapon fired, then the flare burst and hung, swaying over the ford. Below, frozen in the fizzing white circle of light, were around a hundred shocked Chinese soldiers, caught in the act of wading the river.

'Fire!' Temple roared.

A .303 Bren gun has a 30-round magazine; its rate of fire is 500 rounds a minute. A .303 short-muzzle Lee Enfield bolt-action rifle, which all other members of the patrol carried, can fire 15–20 aimed rounds a minute; its locking mechanism makes it the fastest-shooting bolt-action rifle in the world. Moreover, British troops had devised a technique that upped its rate of fire to the equivalent of a semiautomatic. Conventionally, when working the bolt, it is held in the fist; only

---

* The ford had something of a dog-leg in it, and the drums were navigational markers for the vehicles of 29th Brigade that had been driving to and fro across the river over the previous two weeks. They would also prove useful indicators for the attacking Chinese.

after it is snapped home does the hand move from the bolt down to the stock and squeeze the trigger with the forefinger. In Korea the bolt was worked with the little finger extended. This finger pulled the trigger as soon as the round was chambered, while the others continued to grip the bolt. This technique – the 'mad minute' – enabled well-trained infantrymen to unload 30 rapid shots a minute.[3]

A .303 bullet travels at around 2,400 feet per second. Fired on a straight line, a high-velocity round at 200 yards will rip through two men, even three, and the bullet is a stopper: as one infantryman put it, a target hit by a .303 'stays hit'. The patrol was positioned above the Chinese, so its fire was less effective – 'plunging fire' usually only passes through one or two – and it had not been possible to site the Brens to achieve crossfire. But in those first ten seconds, the patrol poured around 200 rounds into the illuminated Chinese force. A trained infantryman changes magazines in seconds, and then the process was repeated, the Glosters snap-shooting as fast as they could. In mid-stream, under the swaying flare light, the Chinese were sitting ducks. Up to their chests in water, they had no cover and could not run. The water churned into a maelstrom.

The hammering of the Brens and the crackling of the rifles made 'a hell of a lot of noise'. Above the din of firing, the Glosters could hear shouting and screaming, could see their targets flopping into the water as their bullets tore into and through them. After some thirty seconds the flare guttered out, and the firing, too, died down: the Glosters' night vision had been ruined by the light. Another flare went up from the mortar. The withering fire resumed.

There was little or no return fire from the river. From their low position the Chinese probably could not see their attackers due to the steep banks – moreover, anyone returning fire would have become an immediate target. But from the opposite bank a machine-gun, presumably set up to cover the assault troops' crossing, opened up. Its green tracer zipped over the Glosters without effect; the gunner was too low in his trench.

Temple shouted the cease-fire order . . . Sudden silence . . . Clouds of cordite drifted across the water. Approximately half a platoon's worth of survivors could just be seen splashing back to the far bank. Of the dead, there was no sign: the Imjin's swift undercurrent whirled them down towards the Yellow Sea. In those first, furious moments, Temple estimated his little patrol had accounted for around seventy men.

In the absence of flare light the Imjin was again cloaked in darkness. There was a pause: perhaps five minutes, perhaps ten, but no let-up in tension. Then, again, voices from the river. Another parachute flare was launched; this time, it revealed what looked like a crowd of men wading towards the tiny patrol.

Again the British soldiers opened up with everything they had – then Temple remembered what he had forgotten in the excitement of the first contact. Artillery was on standby; he had a pre-set DF (Defensive Fire) SOS task for the river. Ducking into his trench, he radioed the battery of eight 25-pounder field guns supporting the Glosters and gave the word: 'DF SOS! Now!'

Within seconds came the 'whoofle' of shells over head, then multiple 'crumps' and flashes as they impacted. The shells were hitting the far shore, rather than the masses in the river. Temple radioed, 'Drop 100!' to bring the fire 100 yards closer to the south bank. Realising that this would be 'uncomfortably close', he shouted to his men to keep low as the next rounds hurtled in.

The white light of the flares showed the huge splashes of shells smashing into the water; in the darkness between flares, all that could be seen were flashing white detonations. Down in the river the high-explosive blasts ruptured internal organs, and shrapnel scythed down the compressed Chinese ranks.

Temple called off the firing to see the effect. Again, nothing was visible. After the smoke cleared, the roiled water of the river was empty. The current had dragged the bodies downstream. The machine-gun on the far bank had also ceased firing.

Again, there was a pause – 'perhaps minutes, I am not sure; there was a lot going on' – and then, again, voices from the river. Another parachute flare was sent up. This time the river was literally jammed with enemy, all splashing urgently towards the Glosters. The Chinese commanders were determined to force the Imjin – at any price.* Seeing that mass approaching, Temple requested a 'Mike Target', the maximum concentration of fire; this would bring the weight of an entire artillery regiment – the full three batteries, or 24 guns, of 45 Field Regiment – in a 'Time on Target' strike. Every shell would hit at the same moment.

An express-train shriek over the heads of the patrol heralded a thunderous series of explosions as the barrage impacted. Then the guns reloaded and fired again and again: ten rounds each from 24 guns.† 'It was quite impressive,' said Temple, who was orchestrating the destruction

---

* In his detailed report on the Chinese in Korea, *A Historical Perspective on Light Infantry* (Fort Leavenworth, KS: US Army Command and General Staff College, Combat Studies Institute), p. 59, Maj. Scott R. McMichael wrote: 'Rivers and streams were no barrier to the Chinese. They used existing bridges and fords where possible and, at other times, improvised bridges and rafts, which they could hide or dismantle by day. Typically, CCF *chose the easiest crossing sites, not the tactically best positioned ones*' (my italics). At 'Gloster Crossing' on 22 April 1951, they suffered for taking the 'easiest crossing'.

† Queen's Royal Hussars Historical Society, seminar. At this seminar David Wilcox, a 45 Field Regiment officer, confirmed the number of rounds fired on that Mike Target on the Imjin River crossing – and Temple expressed his belated gratitude, fifty-five years after the action.

from his slit trench. 'I have always found fireworks displays terribly boring after that!' The river was a pandemonium of flashes, splashes and tracers.

Throughout the bombardment, the patrol continued firing. Although soldiers are trained to fire a three- or four-round 'squirt' with a Bren, the gun crews were shooting off entire magazines in sustained bursts – few depot weapons instructors could ever have imagined such magnificent targets – and the barrels of the three machine-guns, the patrol's chief killing instruments, were glowing pinkish-orange in the night. 'In peace time it would have mattered – the barrels would have worn out,' Temple noted. 'In war, it didn't.' Again the bombardment ceased. But by now, battle had been joined elsewhere along the Imjin front. Competing demands were coming in for the artillery.* There would not be another Mike Target. Crouched over the hot metal of their smoking weapons, the patrol strained to see into the darkness.† Then they heard voices in the cutting below them.

The Chinese were across the river.

Due to the intensity of their fire, most of the patrol were either running out of ammunition or already empty. It was time to get out: 'There was no point getting cut off when we had had no casualties.' Temple ordered his men to move – fast. This was no phased, step-by-step withdrawal, with rifles covering Bren guns and vice versa. The patrol vaulted out of their slit trenches and took off at the double. All were much lighter than when they had arrived: 'We were not carrying a hell of a lot of ammunition by that time!' After about 500 metres, they slowed to a walk, and Temple radioed C Company to expect their arrival. As they pulled back, Temple remembered his colonel's instruction to withdraw if they encountered more than thirty enemy. Half jokingly, the exhilarated young officer whispered to his panting corporal, 'You might have reminded me!' 'I thought you were enjoying it as much as I was!' Corporal Manley replied.

Back in the C Company position, the men climbed the hill to their trenches and bivouacs. The company was entrenched in a reserve position covering the Glosters' Battalion HQ (according to normal procedure, C Company had provided the river patrol, so as not to weaken the companies on the forward hills). Temple ordered Manley to get the men 'ammoed up' while he headed to the battalion command post for a

---

* 45 Field Regiment had three batteries, one each to support the three battalions of 29th Brigade, i.e. the Glosters, the Royal Northumberland Fusiliers and the Royal Ulster Rifles. The attachment of an added unit to the brigade, the Belgian Battalion, put additional strain on the gunners.
† Most accounts of the battle state that Temple's patrol repelled four separate thrusts over the river. Temple himself says it was three. Presumably, different men counted the different advances over the river differently.

debrief. It was even terser than the briefing. By this time, his taciturn colonel had other matters to occupy him.

The battalion intelligence officer, who joined the debrief, commented that the young lieutenant, with his cap comforter pulled down over his head, looked 'Byronesque' and was 'fairly fizzing'. By any standard of soldiering, the massacre at the river had been a good night's work.* Another Gloster, crossing the Imjin ford in an ambulance days later, would have the chilling feeling that he was driving over the broken bodies of dead Chinese soldiers.[4] And half a century later a British brigadier, surveying the ground Temple had fought on, observed, 'to spring that ambush, then to bring all his men back over that billiard table [the riverside plain] without a single casualty is as fine a piece of small-unit soldering as any I have heard of'.[5]

But, despite their losses, the enemy had forced the Imjin. The shock phase of the greatest communist offensive of the Korean War – hurling almost a third of a million men against the UN lines – was under way. As Temple returned to his platoon trenches, waves of Chinese attackers were storming up and into the forward positions of the Glosters, their sister battalions in 29th Brigade, the brigade's parent, US 3rd Division, and higher command, I Corps. Across a forty-mile front, battle was joined.

Even the young lieutenant's 'crystal ball' could not predict that within fifty-eight hours, the Chinese would be flooding south, his mangled brigade would be desperately fighting its way through a closing trap, and his decimated battalion, cut off and surrounded, would be poised on the brink of annihilation.

* Temple won a Military Cross for the action.

**Chapter 1**

# LACK OF THE MORNING CALM: THE KOREAN WAR

*Borders are scratched across the hearts of men*
*By strangers with a calm, judicial pen,*
*And when the borders bleed we watch with dread*
*The lines of ink across the map turn red.*

Marya Mannes

NIGHT, SUNDAY, 25 JUNE 1950. Under the curved grey tiles of a cottage near East Gate Market in Seoul, the capital of South Korea, Lee Chun-hee, a ten-year-old schoolgirl, tossed and turned on her mattress. A strange thunder from the north was disturbing her sleep. Eventually, she drifted off.

On Monday morning she headed to school as usual. She was delighted when, around mid-morning, her teacher told the children that all classes were cancelled. Gaily, the little girl skipped off to spend the day with her parents, North Korean refugees who ran a profitable shoe shop. Heading to the market, she noticed something odd: the streets were bustling with people, many running, with bundles of possessions on their heads.

Chun-hee had not been told the reason for her dismissal. She didn't know that – after five years of national division, years of guerrilla fighting and a summer of border skirmishing – Kim Il-sung, North Korea's leader, had launched a full-scale invasion of the capitalist south before dawn on Sunday. Nor did she know that Seoul's 2,000 American residents were already being evacuated along the Han River. She was unaware that enemy armoured spearheads were bearing down on the capital; the thunder that had disturbed her sleep had been artillery.

Had the child had any idea of the events to come, her cheerful mood would have evaporated. The cruellest wars are civil or ideological, and the Korean War would be both. Kim's invasion had summoned a terrible demon. For three harrowing years, it would stalk the land, creating a vortex that sucked in soldiers from eighteen nations, laid waste the peninsula, and littered it with the corpses of millions.

\* \* \*

The land where this savage drama played out is an austere peninsula that projects from China's north-east corner some 500 miles southwards into the Pacific. Due to its mountainous backbone – like that of a spiny prehistoric beast – Korea is sometimes likened to a dragon's back.

Most waterways run east–west, most tracks run north–south, and there are four distinct seasons: a freezing winter from December to March, a brisk spring from April to June, a steamy monsoon from July to September, and a cool autumn from September to November. In many ways, Korea is beautiful – a corrugated land of jagged peaks tumbling towards blue horizons, of postage-stamp rice paddies reflecting the skies, of thatched farming villages tucked into valleys, of white sand beaches and rocky coastlines. It is also harsh. The mountains are high, cultivatable space is limited, and the seas are lashed by typhoons. Lying at the crossroads of north-east Asia, Korea was the conduit through which Chinese culture reached Japan, but its location between larger, stronger neighbours – China, Japan and Russia – has also made the peninsula strategically vital. The Korean proverb 'when whales fight, shrimps are crushed' alludes to the fact that metaphorically the land has frequently been swept by ill winds.

According to myth, the first state on the peninsula was Chosun, 'The Land of Morning Calm', established in 2333 BC. But its recorded history begins in the first century BC, when the 'Three Kingdoms' of Shilla, Paekje and Koguryo began a prolonged struggle for mastery: the eventual winner was Shilla, which united the peninsula in AD 668. Aspects of this heroic period echoed down to the twentieth century. First, the peninsula's division into competing kingdoms. Secondly, the role played by powerful outside forces – for it was only with China's aid that Shilla had emerged victorious.

In 918 Shilla was succeeded by Koryo ('high mountains, sparkling waters'), which gave the nation its modern name, but in 1231 Koryo was subjugated by the greatest military force of the East, Kublai Khan's Mongols, who used the peninsula as a launch pad for two disastrous invasions of Japan. However, Koryo endured until 1392, when an ambitious general, Yi Song-gye, seized the throne in a military coup – not Korea's last – establishing his own Yi Dynasty. His seat was a mountain-ringed capital set in a broad valley in the heart of the peninsula: Seoul. Yi dubbed his kingdom Chosun, after the legendary kingdom of yore. Under Chosun, Korea suffered its most devastating attack when, in 1592, Japanese warlord Hideyoshi Toyotomi launched his samurai armies against China – through Korea. Help came from Ming China, and the Japanese withdrew in 1598, leaving Korea a wasteland. There was more to come. In 1636 the Manchus attacked, taking the kingdom and forcing it into a tributary relationship with the Ching Dynasty that the Manchus subsequently established in China. After these disasters Korea turned inward, isolating herself and gaining a new name, 'The Hermit Kingdom'. But far to the west, aggressive new powers were stirring. While the Hermit Kingdom slumbered, the age of colonialism was awakening.[1]

* * *

In summer 1866 an American steamship, *General Sherman*, entered the estuary of the Taedong River and set course for Pyongyang, deep inside the mysterious Hermit Kingdom. The vessel had been hired by a Peking-based British company, Meadows and Co., to force trade with Korea. The merchant adventurers planned to trade their cargo of tin, cotton and glass for Korea's fabled ginseng, gold, paper and leopard skins. We can imagine the black ship thumping upriver in the haze, its funnel trailing smoke as its twenty crew – Americans, British, Chinese and Malays – squinted across the paddies towards the distant blue mountains. But we can only imagine, for no survivors of the first Anglo-American penetration of the peninsula lived to tell the tale.

The *General Sherman* crossed the rapids below Pyongyang and dropped anchor before the walled city. When locals refused to trade, the crew kidnapped an official. Fighting broke out. The ship's cannon gave her crew an early advantage, and they beat off all attacks. But the monsoon rains had ceased, and when the river dropped, the steamer was trapped deep in hostile territory. The Koreans launched fire boats, the ship caught alight, and the crew leapt overboard, where they were hacked down in the shallows. Parts of their bodies were reportedly cut off, pickled, and used for medicine.[2]

In 1871 the US Navy's Asiatic Squadron appeared off the Korean coast to take retaliatory action, focusing its attention on the fortress island of Kangwha, in the Han River estuary, that guarded the route to Seoul. US Marines carried the forts but made no attempt to advance inland and withdrew, leaving the forts heaped with white-clad Korean dead. The French had made similar raids following a massacre of Catholics in 1866.* Like the Americans, they had lacked the strength or the patience to force significant change.

The nation which would force open Korea's gates lay much closer to home. In the 1850s Japan had radically modernised in the Meiji Restoration. By the 1880s she was a rising power seeking overseas markets and the

---

* The low hill overlooking the Han, where the Catholics were slaughtered and the river is said to have run red with blood, can still be visited in Seoul. Choltusan ('Beheading Rock') is now a Catholic shrine.

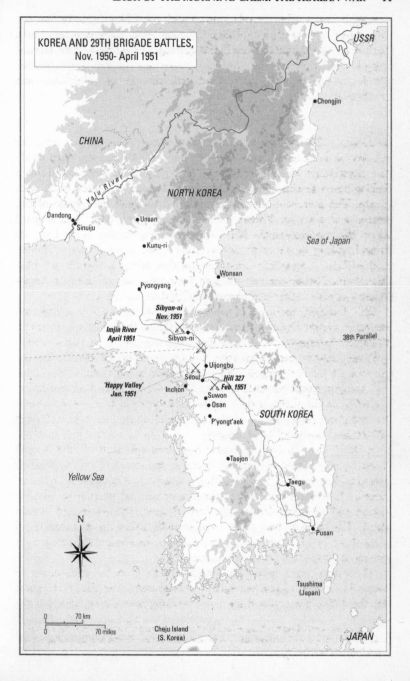

opportunity to establish foreign colonies, like the Western nations she sought to emulate. The US and French raids had been pinpricks; Japan had staying power. In 1876 Tokyo's gunboat diplomacy forced open three Korean ports – Inchon, Pusan and Wonsan. The Hermit Kingdom had been prised open.

Foreigners who arrived in the early 1880s found themselves entering a medieval Asian kingdom. But it was a weak, bewildered kingdom. Korea's revenue collection was outdated, her bureaucracy corrupt, her gentry (a slave-owning class) parasitic, her military powerless. Transport was rudimentary, education hidebound, industry non-existent. For centuries Korea had seen China as a big brother, but by the late nineteenth century China, 'the Sick Man of Asia', was in decline. Western powers were forcing concessions and winning treaty ports, and Tokyo was ready to challenge Peking. In 1895 the first Sino-Japanese war (much of it fought in Korea) ended with Chinese defeat, and in 1905 Tokyo's victory in the Russo-Japanese war established Japan as master of the East. Korea was the prize; with nods from London and Washington, Tokyo declared the peninsula a protectorate. Annexation followed in 1910. The Land of the Morning Calm had been eclipsed by the Land of the Rising Sun.

The next thirty-five years of Japanese colonial rule would be marked by a mix of modernisation and repression, development and exploitation. Japan established communications, financial markets and industries. She modernised education; culture and business flourished; Korea was jerked into the modern era. At the same time, the Japanese brutally suppressed dissidents. By 1937 Japan was, again, at war with China. Korea was harnessed to the cause and began to be squeezed to support Japan's war effort. Tens of thousands of women were enlisted, tricked or coerced into the Imperial Army's military brothels ('comfort stations'); other Koreans were recruited as forced labourers or into military units.

One such recruit was Kim Chum-kon. Born in 1923 he had taken advantage of educational opportunities available to the colonised, and enlisted at Japan's Waseda University, only to find himself, as part of the student cadet force, dispatched to the battlefields in China. 'I had no choice,' he said. 'I was sent by the government.' In northern China he tasted combat: 'The Chinese guerrillas were strong, but not enough to beat the Japanese.' Soon, as a platoon commander, he was guarding supply lines against hundreds of guerrillas.

Japan was also heading for war with the West. After Pearl Harbor, Tokyo's forces rampaged across the Pacific, but America's industrial might and manpower sealed her fate. By 1945, with her armies defeated, her battle fleets rusting beneath the Pacific and her supply routes severed, Japan was on her knees. In Japan's grip, Korea had been powerless to control her own fate; in 1943, at the Cairo Conference, the Western allies had agreed on a post-war Korean 'trusteeship' to which Stalin consented at Yalta in February 1945. Details, however, were left vague.

On 10 August 1945, after atomic and fire bombing of her cities, and the Soviet invasion of Manchuria, Japan requested an armistice. Around midnight, in the Office of the Navy, two American colonels were given a map and told they had thirty minutes to choose a demarcation line in Korea to divide the Soviet and US occupation zones; they decided on the 38th parallel.* The Soviet Union agreed – somewhat to American surprise, for the Red Army had boots on the ground in Korea a month before any American landed. Thus was the division of Korea decided upon. No Korean was present at the relevant meetings.

Under Japanese rule Korea had been a political vacuum. After August 1945 this was filled by those who, in one form or another, had opposed the Japanese occupation Various groups had resisted Japan – disbanded soldiers, student demonstrators, exiled nationalists, communist guerrillas. In terms of achieving independence, none achieved success, nor did they co-operate with each other. By 1945 they had become starkly polarised, like the wider world around them as it now entered the Cold War era. In this charged climate, the powers that controlled the two halves of Korea would choose champions who best fitted their own political outlooks.

South of the 38th parallel US occupation forces overturned locally installed 'Peoples' Committees' and instituted a US Military Government. In the absence of any other bureaucratic infrastructure, the USMG maintained much of the apparatus of Japanese rule – including the detested police. North of the line the Soviet Union backed the establishment in 1946 of a de facto government, the North Korean People's Committee, headed by Kim Il-sung, 34, a good-looking but ruthless former guerrilla leader. Kim had fought the Japanese in Manchuria and northern Korea in the 1930s but sat out World War II as a major in the Red Army in Russia's Far East. Following Soviet–US meetings on the Korea in 1946 and 1947 which reached no agreement, the US referred the peninsula to the United Nations. But the UN's proposals for elections were unsatisfactory to the Soviet Union, and in 1948 elections were held only in the South. On 15 August 1948, the Republic of (South) Korea, or ROK, was established with Rhee Syngman, 73, as its president. Rhee was rather less dynamic than Kim; an exiled right-wing nationalist who had spent most of the Japanese imperium in the US, he held a PhD from Princeton and spoke English,

* One of those colonels, Dean Rusk, went on to become Assistant Secretary of State for Far Eastern Affairs during the Korean War. Accounts differ over the kind of map they used in choosing the 38th parallel: some say a National Geographic map, others a school atlas.

but would have a stormy relationship with Washington. Kim and Rhee never met, and Korea's division hardened. Both stated their ambitions to reunify the peninsula, but their backers would take very different approaches to that issue.

Amid the upheavals of colonisation, war, peace, the end of colonisation, civil war in China and Korean division, ordinary Koreans, members of a diaspora spread across Japan's former empire, strove to control their destinies. Among them was the family of Lee Chun-hee. In the 1930s and 1940s the Lees had run a profitable business, the Heung-A Trading Co., a grain-supply store in Japanese-controlled Shanghai with some forty workers, importing and exporting from Korea. The wily Madam Lee – 'She was better at business than my father,' remembered Lee Chun-hee – profited by selling opium on the side. But, like many Koreans who had left their homeland, the Lees pined for home. When they heard news of independence, and with China's civil war in its final stages, they returned to northern Korea, resettling and acquiring a rice store. Life proved dull: Kim's communism was leaching all colour from the nation. 'We had money, but could not eat or buy anything interesting,' remembered Chun-hee. 'I kept saying, "Let's go back to Shanghai."' The direction that the Kim regime's politics were taking was obvious to merchants like the Lees; already landlords and Christians were being targeted. After just a year in the North the family decided to make for Seoul, so they contacted a courier to take them across the 38th parallel. 'We were pretty fearless,' said Chun-hee. 'We had dealt with bandits and rebels in North China.' One night, the family joined a fifty-strong group creeping south.

'It was exciting, like a picnic,' remembered Chun-hee. Her parents fastened US dollars around her stomach. Tension increased as they approached the parallel; there were no wire or minefields yet, but there were patrols. Cloths were tied around the mouths of young children, so they would not cry out, and the group moved stealthily across moonlit paddies. Suddenly a whistle sounded – the escapees had been spotted. Everyone broke into a run. Chun-hee held her mother's hand tightly; her younger brother was on her father's back. Shots were fired into the air. Running soldiers closed in. Her father thrust his son at his wife before being seized by North Korean troops. The rest of the group tumbled across the border and the pursuit ceased. The refugees arrived in a processing camp in the south. There was dysentery, and Chun-hee queued for rice gruel for her sick mother. 'This is reality,' she thought. 'Families are separated.' To Lee's relief, her father arrived three days later, having bribed his guards to release him. The Lees moved to Seoul, buying a house and establishing a shoe shop near East Gate market.

South Korean police brutally interrogated her father on suspicion that he might be a communist spy, but after that life in Seoul was good.

Another returner was student-soldier Kim Chum-kon. He was unimpressed by the US Military Government. 'If I had a pill to make Americans smart, I'd make a fortune!' he said. 'They made huge mistakes.' Kim, suffering from post traumatic stress disorder after his China experiences – 'I had nightmares, I heard the sound of gunshots' – hoped to return to school, but his experience was valuable, and he was persuaded to join the nascent ROK Army as a lieutenant. Dispatched to the parallel, he created border checkpoints, and his unit drafted some of the first intelligence reports on North Korea after interrogating southbound refugees. By 1948 he was a lieutenant-colonel – in the ROK Army, youth was no barrier to rank – when he volunteered for the guerrilla war now raging in the southern mountains.

Outside Seoul turmoil had increased. In 1948 tens of thousands of alleged communists were massacred by government forces on Cheju-Do, an island off the south coast, following a popular uprising. By 1950 guerrilla conflict flickered among the mountains, and border clashes between ROK and North Korean People's Army (NKPA) forces flared along the 38th parallel. In the Chinese zodiac 1950 was the Year of the Tiger: a volatile year, one in which tumult was to be anticipated. The Tiger Year is considered a propitious one for soldiers.

* * *

At 04:00 on Sunday, 25 June 1950, the bulk of the North Korean People's Army (NKPA) massed in the darkness along North Korea's southern border. This was no border raid. Kim Il-sung had mustered 130,000 men in seven divisions, with 151 tanks. His armour would prove decisive, for the southern forces had nothing to match it. President Truman had refused the belligerent Rhee offensive weapons, but Stalin had equipped Kim with the T-34, the outstanding tank of World War II. Artillery lined up as watches ticked towards H-Hour. The attack was to be an all-arms assault, patterned after the armoured penetrations that Soviet forces had learned from the *Wehrmacht* in World War II. At 04:40 there was a sound like thunder, then white flashes detonated all along the parallel. As Yak fighter-bombers zoomed overhead, the NKPA stormed into South Korea along three axes.[3]

At the time, many pundits assumed the attack had been ordered by Stalin as part of a worldwide communist plot, but documents from Soviet archives have revealed that it was Kim who pressed invasion plans for more than a year in the face of Soviet reluctance. Stalin only gave his approval in April 1950, after he had established that Mao Tse-tung, who had just won his own civil war, agreed.* With communism triumphant in China, thousands of highly experienced Koreans who had fought with Mao in Manchuria returned home to bolster Kim's forces. Kim, the former guerrilla leader, could now fulfil his ambition of reunifying the peninsula.[4]

The communists had reason to believe that Washington would not intervene. In January 1950 US Secretary of State Dean Acheson ill-advisedly outlined a US defence perimeter in Asia that omitted Korea. Nations beyond that perimeter, Acheson said, would have to rely on the United Nations.[5]

Even so, Kim's attack was not unexpected. Many had been predicting war, but the timing caught ROK forces on the back foot. 'We thought the North would some day invade,' said Paik Sun-yup, a thirty-year-old general who, like Kim, had fought communist guerrillas as a member of the Japanese Imperial Army in China. 'But 25 June 1950 . . . that general attack was a complete shock.' That Sunday Paik, hearing the news at 08:00, dashed to Army HQ. 'We knew the North Koreans had tanks and heavy artillery. They were well-trained, they had aircraft. We did not have a single tank. We had little artillery and not enough training. We had been too busy chasing guerrillas.'

Months earlier Paik had summoned one guerrilla-chaser, Kim Chum-kon, an old acquaintance, back to Seoul because of the increasing violence of the border clashes. 'That was the process of training the NKPA and testing the south,' Kim said of the border fighting. 'But few people considered it a prelude to war.' Kim himself had been predicting all-out hostilities, but few listened. The night of the invasion he watched people dancing. Early reports indicated just another skirmish, but Kim was uneasy. When he reached the War Room, he was told enemy tanks had reached Uijongbu, just fifteen miles to the north. Paik and Kim departed for their unit, the ROK 1st Division, north-west of Seoul: Paik was divisional commander, Kim headed its 12th Regiment. The two China veterans were plunged immediately into desperate combat.

Kim Il-sung's attack was going according to plan. An NKPA battalion had taken a train into the station of the old Koryo capital of Kaesong, on the 38th parallel, disembarked and assaulted directly from the platform. Armoured columns were spearing south. Two ROK divisions – Paik's 1st and the 6th – put up determined resistance: Paik sent suicide troops

---

* Both Seoul and Pyongyang have instilled fierce nationalism in their populations in the last fifty years. In North Korea, alleged independence from foreign interference is embodied in Kim Il-sung's *juche*, or self-reliance philosophy. Yet, as the Korean War shows, Kim was totally reliant upon Stalin to equip him, Mao to save him, and both to consent to his plans. Today the bankruptcy of Kim's philosophy is evident: few countries in the world, if any, are more reliant upon outside aid to feed their people.

with explosives strapped to their bodies against the T-34s. But other ROK units crumbled. By the evening of 27 June, residents of Seoul's northern suburbs heard a strange, clattering squeak: tanks nosing into the city. Thousands of citizens fled south, towards the Han. The kilometre-wide river was crossed by four bridges, and in the early hours of the 28th their iron spans were crawling with refugees. At 02:30 all bridges were blown by ROK engineers.* Hundreds – perhaps thousands – perished in the black waters.[6]

When she returned home from school on 26 June, Lee Chun-hee's parents had told her that North Korea had invaded, but the family had no intention of fleeing. Her father did not think North Korea would prevail for long, and her mother considered invasion a business opportunity: fleeing people need shoes! So it proved – the Lees had to stuff their earnings into potato and rice sacks. On the 28th Seoul fell. The invaders proved disciplined. Parades were held. Portraits of Stalin and Kim appeared on buildings. Some Seoulites chuckled to hear of Northern soldiers, unfamiliar with modern plumbing, drinking from the toilet bowls in Seoul's finest hotel, the Chosun.† For Chun-hee, the early days of the occupation were not bad (especially as school was cancelled). But before long, she began to fear going outside; groups of parentless children were roaming the streets, and as the days passed, the gangs became aggressive. While Kim's forces regrouped in Seoul for a week before striking south to complete their conquest, the non-communist world was reacting.

\* \* \*

The United States had come out of World War II with a strong economy and full of self-confidence, firmly established as the free world's leader. At cinemas in 1950 people thrilled to Walt Disney's *Cinderella* and John Wayne in *The Sands of Iwo Jima*. Al Jolson sang 'Are You Lonesome Tonight?' and Ray Bradbury published *The Martian Chronicles*. Yet international developments were ominous. In 1946 Churchill had noted that an 'Iron Curtain' had fallen across Europe. A Soviet attempt to starve West Berlin into submission in 1948 had been defeated only after the US and UK had mounted a massive airlift, and the same year Moscow detonated an atomic device. In 1949 in China – the huge country at the centre of Asia, recipient of vast amounts of US aid and focus of so many vain American hopes – the last nationalist

---

\* The officer responsible for blowing the bridges was later court-martialled and executed. He was rehabilitated fourteen years later, when it was discovered that he was acting under the orders of the Chief of Staff, who was himself killed in action soon after the bridges were destroyed.
† This story is still told in the Westin Chosun Hotel today.

troops surrendered to Mao's communists. In February 1950 a Sino-Soviet Friendship Treaty was signed.

China was gone. Now, Korea, the last line of defence before Japan, was tottering. Washington reacted swiftly. The United States put the Korean crisis before the United Nations on 27 June. Here the US was inadvertently assisted by the Soviet Union, whose ambassador to the UN was boycotting the international body due to its refusal to admit China, and was therefore unable to wield his veto.* The UN Security Council passed a resolution calling for assistance to the ROK. The steadfast response won media approval: a *New York Times* headline blared 'Democracy Takes Its Stand',† and Republicans supported President Harry Truman in his determination to resist further communist advances.[7] On 30 June Truman committed US troops to ground war. On 7 July, the UN called for member states to provide military forces and asked the US to lead the UN contingent in Korea.

The man who would head the UN Command in Korea was already a legend. General Douglas MacArthur, son of a Civil War hero, had won a chestful of decorations in World War I. In World War II, he had fled the collapsing Philippines, fought back across the Pacific, liberated the country he had lost, and in 1945, on the great battleship USS *Missouri* in Tokyo Bay, presided over Japan's surrender.** As Supreme Commander, Allied Forces Japan, he oversaw the remoulding of that shattered nation as a democracy. He had the ego of a prince, the style of an actor and a personal charisma and gift for rhetoric that some found near-hypnotic. Seventy years old in 1950, his plans for a new Japan were coming to fruition. There seemed no challenge left. Then, from Korea came news of the invasion. MacArthur had visited South Korea only once when, on 15 August 1948, he had casually assured Rhee Syngman that he would defend Korea 'as if it were California'. On 28 June he flew to the embattled peninsula, where he decided only US combat troops could restore the situation.[8]

Some 8,872 kilometres west of Seoul in Westminster, Britain's Labour government under Prime Minister Clement Attlee was more concerned with nationalisation, the building of a welfare state and disengagement

---

* More recent theories suggest that Soviet absence from the UN had a purpose: Stalin wanted the US to enter the Korean War, prompting China's intervention, which would lead to Mao's manpower grinding up America's soldiers. See Chang Jung, and John Halliday, *Mao: The Unknown Story* (London, 2005), pp. 438–9.

† The undemocratic – not to mention venal, corrupt and cruel – nature of Rhee's government was at this stage of the war not yet evident to reporters and editors, who had little or no familiarity with the obscure Far Eastern nation.

** Delighted at the fall of Japan, Koreans yet retained a taste for their former colonial masters' cuisine. One of the most popular Korean-run Japanese restaurants in Seoul after the colonial period took the very un-Japanese name of Missouri.

from Empire than in distant foreign adventures. Britain's economy was still fractured from World War II, the country was grey and threadbare, and food rationing remained in force. Moreover, unlike America, which had governed South Korea from 1945 until 1948, the UK had no attachment to the peninsula. Korea was far beyond India, and unnecessary as a way-station for China trade. Anglo-Korean contacts had therefore been brief and desultory. The Korean coast was first surveyed by Royal Navy Captain William Broughton in 1797;* some British ships had raided Korean islands for supplies during the Opium Wars; a British missionary in China had been the first to translate the gospel into Korean in the 1870s; a bilateral treaty had been signed in 1883; and in 1885, during a period of tense Anglo-Russian relations, the Royal Navy had occupied the tiny island of Komun-do ('Port Hamilton') for a year. Otherwise, apart from visits by a handful of Victorian travellers and the operation of a small consulate and bishopric, British interaction with Korea had been minimal. Few Britons had even heard of the country: those who had, most likely knew it as the birthplace of some of Japan's most brutal prison camp guards.[†]

But, despite their left-wing DNA, Attlee and his Foreign Secretary, Ernest Bevin, distrusted Moscow and were convinced that aggression must be challenged. Just three days after the T-34s had clanked across the 38th parallel Attlee made clear that Britain, like America, was prepared to pick up the gauntlet Kim had thrown down. On 28 June he addressed the House of Commons. Calling the North Korean attack 'naked aggression' he stated that Britain would live up to its UN obligations.[9] On the same day Royal Navy units in the Far East set course for Korea.[10] Aircraft from the carrier HMS *Triumph* were in action within days, and the war claimed its first British victims when the cruiser HMS *Jamaica* was hit by North Korean coastal batteries on 8 July.[11]

By then young Americans were already rotting in Korean paddies. Troops from the 24th Infantry Division, part of the Japan-based 8th US Army, had landed in Korea on 1 July. Its first combat unit, 'Task Force Smith', deployed at Osan, south of Seoul – but these were not the men who had won World War II. America's post-war army had been run down; Japan-based GIs were softened by half a decade of occupation duties, poorly led and lacked anti-tank weapons. They were brushed aside on 5 July as T-34s drove right through their line.[12] Other American units were forced to retreat or overrun; American prisoners were found shot in

---

* The captain is memorialised in Seoul today, in the form of the British Embassy's 'Broughton Bar'.
† Colonial Japan had used Koreans the same way the Nazis used the Ukrainians: for their dirtiest jobs.

the back of the head. On 19 July the 24th Division dug in to defend Taejon; a day later the city fell, and divisional commander General William Dean was taken. Panic set in. The term 'bug-out' – a fast retreat with neither delaying action nor thought for flanking units – gained currency. In the heat and stink of the sultry Korean summer, down dusty tracks amid streams of refugees, US and ROK troops fell back, the NKPA in hot pursuit.

On 15 July, with humiliation, if not disaster, looming, London's ambassador to Washington, Sir Oliver Franks, wrote to Attlee that pressure was building in America's media and among politicians for her allies to provide troops on the ground. He suggested expediting Britain's commitment. Beyond the British naval contribution, London had already been considering sending RAF units, but Attlee knew that if Britain committed anything less than a ground force, the 'special relationship' with Washington was in danger. On the 24th, the Imperial General Staff proposed sending an army brigade, acknowledging that, though this move was 'militarily unsound, they recognised the strong political arguments'. Britain was now committed to ground combat in Korea.[13] In a national broadcast on 31 July Attlee outlined why an attack on a far-off land that most Britons could not place on a map had to be repulsed. 'Here is a case of aggression,' he said. 'If the aggressor gets away with it, aggressors all over the world will be encouraged. The same results which led to the Second World War will follow; and another world war may result.' With memories of Chamberlain's appeasement of Hitler uncomfortably fresh, Attlee aimed his rhetoric directly at his listeners. 'That is why what is happening in Korea is of such importance to you. The fire that has been started in distant Korea may burn down your house.'[14]

Britain's 'Imperial Strategic Reserve' was the Colchester-based 29th Infantry Brigade, but the earliest it could arrive was November. The British liaison officer at MacArthur's headquarters was told that speed was critical: 'a little got in fast was better than a lot later on'.[15] On 18 August the 27th Infantry Brigade based in Hong Kong, composed of 1st Battalion the Middlesex Regiment and 1st Battalion, the Argyll and Sutherland Highlanders, was deployed post-haste to Korea as a stop-gap measure.[16]

By the end of August, demoralised and near-defeated, ROK and US forces had been pressed back to a defensive ring around Korea's southern port: 'The Pusan Perimeter'. The American 8th Army commander in Korea, General Walton 'Bulldog' Walker exhorted his men to 'stand or die'. With desperate fighting under way, few noticed that the balance of forces was shifting as American troops flooded in. The NKPA, still in headlong assault mode, had been ground down to around

68,000 men, of whom 20,000 were untrained recruits impressed in the South. US forces were topping 35,000, while the ROK Army could boast 73,000.[17] On 29 August, as 27th Infantry Brigade landed in Pusan, MacArthur was moved to comment on the 'historic unity of the Anglo-Saxon peoples'.[18] Meanwhile, the 'Arsenal of Democracy' was gearing up. Massive piles of materiel were trucked from Pusan harbour to the nearby front. Battle raged. The NKPA strove to drive UN forces into the sea. But Kim's army, at the end of a long, tenuous supply line and under heavy attack from the USAF, which had won air superiority in a matter of days, was breaking its teeth on the solidifying defences.

* * *

Fifteen miles to the west of Seoul, Inchon on the Yellow Sea had been the gateway to Korea since the days of gunboat diplomacy and treaty signings. It is the port serving Seoul – itself the peninsula's key road and rail hub. As early as July MacArthur, one of World War II's premier amphibious warriors, had fantasised about putting men ashore there. If he did, he could cut the NKPA off from its supplies, compromise its divisions besieging Pusan and retake Seoul. But the US 8th Army opposed weakening its defensive lines at Pusan, and all key Navy and Marine commanders were firmly against what was dubbed 'Operation Chromite'. For Inchon was no South Pacific island: its approach channel was narrow; there were no beaches, but instead sea walls that would have to be scaled; its tidal range was dramatic, 32 feet, and at low tide the harbour drained into mud flats. Only two dates, 15 September and 11 October, were practical.[19]

Events reached a head on 23 August, when MacArthur faced his critics in his Tokyo HQ. Navy and Marine officers briefed in detail, fluently expressing objections. Then MacArthur stood. The great orator spoke for forty-five minutes. Korea, he asserted, was where communism had made its play for global domination. He praised the Navy's history, he evoked the spirit of audacity that had delivered Quebec to General Wolfe. Then his finale: 'I can almost hear the ticking of the second hand of the clock of destiny,' he intoned. 'We must act now, or we will die. We shall land at Inchon, and I shall crush them.' . . . Silence. MacArthur's words had wrought their magic. The chief of naval operations climbed to his feet and declared: 'General, the Navy will get you to Inchon!' Operation Chromite was a go.[20]

At dawn on 15 September, from out of a typhoon, a mighty armada appeared off Inchon with 70,000 fighting men embarked. Warships and aircraft pounded the port and its offshore islands. Great columns of smoke rose. At 06:45 the first US Marines went in. (Probably not one knew that their forefathers had stormed ashore on another island just off Inchon 79 years earlier.) The bombardment had done its work, and resistance was light. On D-Day +1, the marines thrust towards Seoul. The same day Walker's 8th Army broke out of the Pusan Perimeter and went onto the offensive. The NKPA was trapped in a closing vice. MacArthur spun the handle.

On 25 September, the two jaws of the UN pincer closed south of Seoul. The NKPA was resisting fiercely in the city, but Marines, backed by tanks and air strikes, battled their way through roadblocks and fortified buildings. Four days later MacArthur presided over a dramatic handover ceremony in the bullet-scarred Capitol Building, returning Seoul to an emotional Rhee Syngman.[21] The NKPA was on the run.

In the smoking capital, schoolgirl Lee Chun-hee had been lucky. The street fighting which devastated much of Seoul had bypassed her district. The Lees trudged through the rubble to see the handover. She watched the flag-raising, listened to the speeches. 'President Rhee told the people not to worry,' she said. 'We believed him.' Meanwhile, ROK units were roaming the streets, grabbing suspected communists. 'They dragged them to the rice fields and the lettuce fields and shot them,' Chun-hee recalled. As South Korean forces had retreated down the peninsula they had executed thousands of leftists; now, with Seoul back in UN hands, gruesome evidence was found of communist score-settling – trenches piled with massacred civilians. The brutality of the war was upped another notch.

Yet MacArthur's Inchon gamble had paid off. Kim's had ruined him. His army was shattered. His troops were dead, fleeing north or taking to the hills. Except for a pursuit and the mopping up of guerrillas, the UN's war seemed as good as won. By late October, British troopships carrying 29th Infantry Brigade were at last nearing their destination. The question was, would they have a mission once they landed?

## Chapter 2

..................

# TO KOREA

*Quo Fata Vocant**
Regimental motto, Royal Northumberland Fusiliers

O N 27 JULY a group of British staff officers returned to the UK after a tour of the Normandy battlefields. Docking in the Solent, they were greeted with news that their unit – the Colchester-based 29th Independent Infantry Brigade Group – was being mobilised for war in Korea.[1] Its commander, Brigadier Tom Brodie, 46, a stoutly built, aggressive infantry officer who had commanded Chindits behind Japanese lines, was ordered to be ready to move on 1 November.[2]

As an organisation, the brigade was not unfamiliar with the Far East: in World War II Burma – the first air-mobile campaign in warfare – its sleeve patch, a black circle on a white background, had been dubbed 'the flying arsehole'.† However, though tasked with responding to any contingency that might arise outside the UK or Germany, the brigade was far from ready for immediate action: its constituent units were at only half to two-thirds the strength of war establishment.[3] Given the commitments the British Army faced in 1950, this was not surprising. Troops were deployed across the globe – fighting communist insurgents in Malaya, garrisoning war-scarred Germany and Austria, and manning bases in a crumbling Empire which still stretched from South America to Singapore. Moreover, it had been decided that the National Service conscripts, who provided the bulk of the Army's manpower, were only to be deployed to Korea if they volunteered. More men were needed. Directives flew from Whitehall. Regulars who wished to extend their service or who volunteered to return to the colours were dubbed 'K Volunteers'. But this was still not enough; reservists who had originally signed up for 'seven 'n five' (seven years with the regular army and five years in the reserve) were recalled.

Reluctantly, the reservists, many of whom had started families or businesses, flocked in. Some had done well in civilian life: one arrived in Colchester in a Bentley.[4] A sentry at the barracks gate was taken aback

* Literally, 'Whither the fates call.'
† Once winter descended upon Korea, it was rebranded 'the frozen arsehole'.

when a woman appeared, thrust a baby at him and said, 'You've got my husband, you'd better take this as well.'[5] A popular story doing the rounds concerned the taxi driver ferrying reservists from the railway station to the garrison. He had expressed some *schadenfreude* at his passengers' expense – until he, too, received call-up papers and was driven to camp by an erstwhile colleague.[6] In barracks, for the old sweats it was back to the old regimen of listening to the 'rumour mill', 'hurry up and wait', and the endless routine of 'blanco' (webbing cleaner), 'Brasso' (brass polish) and 'bullshit' (the endless series of orders and counter-orders that have been part and parcel of military life since Caesar).

It is worth pausing here to examine what a brigade is.* During the two World Wars the smallest unit that was considered self-sufficient in terms of weapons and other equipment was a division, about 15,000 men, which had its own field artillery, engineers and logistical back-up. But in the British Army, a small, professional force with far-flung commitments, brigades (one third of a division) had often been deployed independently, particularly on the fringes of empire. Indeed, 27th Infantry Brigade, which had already been rushed to Korea, had been deployed in this way in Hong Kong. The 'teeth' of an infantry brigade consist of its three rifle battalions, but in the case of 29th Brigade, which was intended to operate independently, these were supplemented by resources that would normally be provided at divisional level. The most critical of these were its artillery and tank regiments, but there were also various other 'odds and sods': field workshops, hospitals, field postal and pay offices, NAAFI tea-sellers, PR staff, dental teams, a legal affairs section, a mobile laundry and even a field bath unit.[7] Even so, 29th Brigade would be small fry in a war where the basic formation was already the division.

An infantry battalion of 1950 had a paper strength of 38 officers and 945 other ranks[8] but, due to casualties, replacements, postings and leave, few battalions fielded more than 750 at any one time in Korea. A battalion was commanded by a lieutenant-colonel, assisted by his regimental sergeant major. Its core was its HQ Company, containing a transport platoon, a signals platoon, a medical detachment, field kitchens and intelligence and administrative personnel. Its Support Company operated the battalion's 3-inch mortars, 17-pounder† anti-tank guns and Vickers medium machine-guns and included an engineer ('Assault Pioneer') platoon. Its core strength, its four rifle companies, each fielded around 130 men. Each company was commanded by a major with his own HQ detachment of signallers and a medical orderly.

---

* In Korea, the US equivalent of a brigade was designated a regiment or regimental combat team.
† Refers to the weight of the shell it fired.

Each company was composed of three platoons of 35 men, headed by a lieutenant with his own small HQ consisting of a sergeant, a signaller and two men with a small, hand-carried 2-inch mortar. The men at the 'sharp end' were the rifle sections, usually commanded by a corporal. A rifle section was divided into two: the gun group – two men with a Bren light machine-gun – and the rifle group – six to eight riflemen.

The basic tactic in assault is fire and manoeuvre: covered by machine-gun fire, riflemen leapfrog forward. The basic tactic in defence is to hold fast, breaking the enemy's will by inflicting casualties, and retaking lost ground by counter-attack. At this level of battle, orders are either verbal – by shouting – or by hand signal. Here, machine-gun teams do the real killing. Not only do their weapons fire faster and longer, but amid the chaos of action, while a lone rifleman may cease firing to take cover (or simply hide), a two-man team will reinforce each other's courage, and continue shooting. 29th Brigade's weapons were of World War II vintage. The Vickers medium machine-gun, the key infantry support weapon, was famed for its utter reliability and was effective to over 700 metres; firing on fixed lines, a pair of Vickers could dominate ground with a cone of bullets. However, its rate of fire was a relatively sedate 400 rounds per minute. The Bren, the portable (23-lb) light machine-gun, was respected for its reliability and accuracy. With its curved, 30-round magazine, it fired at 500 rounds per minute to a range of over 500 metres, and, although it was usually served by two men, a strong soldier could use a Bren at close range like a submachine-gun. For personal weapons, the British soldiers carried the solid, 9-lb Lee-Enfield. This weapon, developed in 1907, was ideal for accurate daytime shooting at medium or long ranges, out to around 500 metres. The Vickers, Bren and Lee-Enfield all fired the heavy .303 round. Sten submachine-guns were also carried by officers, NCOs and signallers, but, being mass-produced – they cost under four pounds apiece – were unreliable and fired 9mm pistol rounds that lacked range, velocity and stopping power. Finally, officers were issued .38 revolvers, a weapon of minimal utility on the battlefield. The most effective weapon at close range was the hand grenade, in its fragmentation and white phosphorus variants.

29th Brigade's bayonets were provided by 1st Battalion the Gloucestershire Regiment, 1st Battalion the Royal Northumberland Fusiliers* and 1st Battalion the Royal Ulster Rifles.† All these regiments

---

* The Fusiliers replaced a battalion of the Bedfordshire Regiment, which had too few regular soldiers, in the brigade.

† Of the three battalions assigned to the brigade, each was its parent regiment's 1st Battalion. In the British Army at the time, regiments were based in, and recruited from, regional depots, which were the regiments' permanent homes. Each regiment's 1st Battalion was its front-line unit; its 2nd or 3rd Battalions might be territorial, training or under-strength units.

were similarly trained, organised and equipped, yet each had a proud history that was inculcated into every member of the regiment; each was recruited from a different part of the country; each was a warrior tribe with its own distinct character.

## 1ST BATTALION, THE GLOSTER REGIMENT

Recruited chiefly from south-west England, the Glosters could claim more battle honours than any other regiment. Raised in 1694 as the 28th Regiment of Foot, they fought with Wolfe at Quebec, where they acquired the bloodthirsty nickname 'The Slashers' after members of the regiment allegedly cut the ear off an unpopular local magistrate in a Montreal brawl in 1764. Other notable actions took place during the Peninsular and Crimean wars, at Gallipoli and Dunkirk and in India and Burma, but their most famous exploit had been in Egypt in 1801, at Alexandria, when the 28th were deployed in the key position in the British line, a ruined castle. French infantry assaulted their front and both flanks, and cavalry charged their rear. The order was given, 'Rear rank! About face!' and, back-to-back, the 28th held. From that time on, the regiment has been permitted to wear a badge on the back, as well as the front, of its headdress.[9]

In 1950 the 1st Battalion's commanding officer was Lieutenant-Colonel James 'Fred' Carne. During World War II he had served in the King's African Rifles, where he had perhaps discovered something in the empty silence of the bush. He was tall, ascetic, Christian – and strikingly taciturn. 'I would occasionally ask him a question and I'd wait for an answer and realise it was a pretty silly question,' recalled Guy Temple. 'He was not a loner, but he was a reticent type. When he talked, you listened,' remembered Private Sam Mercer. There was an old-fashioned quality to the man. 'Not much imagination; probably lacking slightly in brainpower,' was the verdict of a brigade officer who believed that, had Carne not led the Glosters in Korea, he would have retired into obscurity.[10] But that he was a dedicated foot soldier who led by example, there was no doubt. 'He was very fit,' Temple found. 'If there was any question of going uphill, he led from the front.'[11] He had another quality essential in a combat commander. This tall, silent man with his ever-present pipe was 'pretty unflappable';[12] his nickname was 'Cool Carne'. These qualities made him a leader his men had confidence in. 'If Carne said, "Fix bayonets" we'd have followed him – to a man,' Mercer reckoned.

Another key personality was the Glosters' adjutant, Captain Anthony Farrar-Hockley. He was a keen pipe-smoker like his commander, but there the similarities ended. Stocky, pugnacious, aggressive, he had lied about his age to join the Glosters during the war, but was discovered and discharged. He subsequently joined the nascent Parachute Regiment and fitted perfectly into that unit, with its aggressive ethos. Promotion was fast, and as a company commander he won a Military Cross in 1944. He engendered strong reactions. Temple considered him 'a brilliant chap'; another brigade officer thought him 'a genuine man, intensely loyal, with the highest moral standards . . . a very good soldier indeed'.[13] Royal Artillery officer George Truell, who supported the Glosters, found him 'strong-minded and determined, very full of his own opinions'. The soldiers respected but feared him. Some found him overbearing and arrogant, calling him 'Horror-Fuckley' behind his back.[14]

A very different kind of officer again was Lieutenant Maurice 'Mike' Harvey. Unusually for a British officer, he was 'humourless; rather serious . . . not an easy chap to get to know, or get on with'.[15] In a day when it was a very exotic pastime Harvey held a judo black belt, and his fascination with things Eastern influenced his approach to tactics. Harvey's unorthodox leanings reminded Mercer of Orde Wingate, the unconventional officer who founded and led the Chindit Brigades.

The only Gloster not trained to fight was Padre Sam Davies. Davies was an active, mobile padre who visited as many soldiers as he could, as often as he could. 'He used to go around improving morale and drinking about fifteen cups of tea a day,' said Temple. 'He was very good at talking to the soldiers.'[16]

The soldiers who made up the Glosters' non-commissioned ranks were that mix of keen, green young volunteers and dour but experienced reservists common to the brigade. Mercer was in the former category. A Londoner living in Gloucester, he joined up at seventeen. He had served for two years in the West Indies, then a year in Colchester. Among the battalion's National Servicemen was David Green. Like many Glosters, he was a poor countryman – his father was a jobbing gardener, the grandson of a poacher. Young Green was a 'scrapper' and had had a troubled youth, including time in a remand home and a spell in jail.[17] Called up, he was determined to make the best of the army, and in basic training was unconsciously infused with regimental spirit. Absent from the Passing Out Parade due to illness, he watched from the sick bay. As his comrades marched past, bayonets fixed, while the band crashed out 'To Be a Farmer's Boy', Green found, to his astonishment, that tears were rolling down his face.[18]

One reservist distinctly displeased with his lot was medic George Newhouse. He had served as a stretcher-bearer in Burma – widely considered the worst combat posting for British soldiers in the war – and had fought in the Battle of the Admin Box, where a surrounded British garrison, supplied by air, held off a superior Japanese force in a jungle siege. When he got his recall papers he felt an ominous foreboding. 'I had got through World War II with no wounds, just a few tropical diseases,' he said. 'In Korea, I knew something bad would happen.'*

The Glosters were not, by nature, aggressive. Temple found them 'country chaps, pleasant to meet. Our strong point was defence: "If this hill is mine, it's mine." That's it.' They were easy to command, Temple thought – unlike a Cockney or Northern regiment.[19] His men agreed. 'I don't think we were gung-ho,' Mercer mused. 'We were stoical. If we accepted that there was a job to do, we'd do it.'[20]

## 1ST BATTALION, THE ROYAL NORTHUMBERLAND FUSILIERS

The Royal Northumberland Fusiliers – 'The Fighting Fifth', from the days when line regiments were numbered – had as long and bloody a history as the Glosters. The men were chiefly recruited among the 'Geordies' of north-eastern England, and the regiment's cap badge was appropriate for the war they would soon be fighting: St George slaying the dragon. Nicknamed the 'Old and Bold', 'Wellington's Bodyguards' and 'The Shiners', they traced their origins back to 1674, when they served against France in the Low Countries. The regiment was heavily engaged in both the American War, where it fought at Bunker Hill, and in the Peninsula against Napoleon. In Spain in 1836 it was armed with fusils (smooth-bore muskets), and so took the name the Northumberland Fusiliers. It raised more battalions than any other regiment in World War I, and in World War II served in the Western Desert, Sicily and Italy. Returning to the UK in 1950 after a Gibraltar posting, its 1st Battalion was chosen as demonstration battalion at the School of Infantry at Warminster – indicative of high tactical skill – before joining 29th Brigade.[21]

The Fusiliers' CO was Lieutenant-Colonel Kingsley Foster. With his jowly face and military moustache, he looked the stereotypical 'Colonel Blimp' but was a highly professional officer. His father had also commanded a Fusilier battalion, and the son turned down a full colonelcy in Singapore to lead the battalion into action.[22] Foster had spent much of World War II in staff postings, which perhaps explains why in Korea he would seek to get close – too close, some officers thought – to the thick of the fighting. Although wealthy, Foster was not distant, taking a strong interest in his soldiers' welfare, often writing to their families.[23] 'He was a dedicated Fusilier and very good on his feet, talking to the troops,' said Lieutenant Tony Perrins, the Fusiliers' intelligence officer. If Carne's leadership gift was his coolness, Foster's was his likeability, that paternal side

---

* While the rationally minded reader might put Newhouse's forebodings down to hindsight, and so take them with a pinch of salt, many soldiers do – as we shall see – have antennae acutely attuned to an ill wind.

that built trust. One corporal, Joe 'Tommo' Thompson, first met Foster in 1948. 'My father died when I was six,' Thompson said. 'Colonel Foster was like a father to me.'[24]

The Fusiliers were an aristocratic regiment: 'second echelon, after the Household Cavalry and the Guards', thought Perrins. 'We were all young men, chasing girls, jumping into cars, driving helter-skelter to London, then hightailing it back in time for duty.' Beagling was a popular pastime; some officers were planning falconry. 'It was a cushy life – albeit you weren't paid much – and there were long periods of playing,' Perrins said. Z Company* commander, Major John Winn, was a very traditional British officer. A colleague found him 'extremely cultured, an extremely laid-back person who was absolutely natural. He appeared sleepy but wasn't; he had a remarkable sense of humour.'[25] Like many courageous soldiers, the affable Winn was a quiet man. Y Company was commanded by Robbie Leith-MacGregor, a strong character who had won a Distinguished Flying Cross with the RAF during the war. 'He was outstandingly good as a company commander, though pretty firm,' said Lieutenant Sam Phillips, one of Leith-MacGregor's platoon commanders. 'He was respected, but not necessarily liked; he could frighten you.' Many junior officers in the reserve were keen to get back into harness. Malcolm Cubiss, a diminutive but enthusiastic lieutenant who had left the army in 1949, was delighted to be recalled. 'I'd always wanted to stay in, so when I was called back, I was quite pleased,' he said. 'I'd been working in a bank, but you only live once!'

Many of the men came from heavy industrial or mining backgrounds. 'We were self-supportive, clannish, a close mix, excellent morale,' thought Fusilier Vick Wear. 'The Geordie likes his sport – keen on football – but can become aggressive when roused.' 'They had a great sense of humour and they were tough,' Phillips thought of his platoon. 'When you got to know them, they were extremely nice.' The battalion was beefed up with reservists from the North-east and the Midlands, many of whom were highly experienced soldiers with 'chests full of medals', but the Fusiliers' training in tactical skills at Warminster paid off: 'As the demonstration battalion, we were very well trained,' said Wear. 'We revered the reservists when they first came but it turned out that they were not as professional as we were.'

One Fusilier with significant experience was mortar man John Bayliss. A regular, he had fought through World War II, having been an anti-tank gunner on D-Day, at Nijmegen during operation Market Garden, and one of the first to enter Belsen concentration camp. He was unconcerned by

---

* While the Glosters and the Rifles identified their rifle companies from the beginning of the alphabet – i.e. A, B, C and D – the Fusiliers used W, X, Y and Z.

the prospects ahead. 'With a Geordie behind you, you felt safe,' he said. David Strachan had joined up at 17, inspired by war stories from German and Italian POWs who worked on his farm. 'I was proud to join the "Fighting Fifth" – they were very renowned,' he said. 'I wanted to be a fighting soldier and I got that wish!' Bill Beattie, a mortar sergeant, had just started courting and was in a cinema in Trowbridge when the order for all Fusiliers to report to base flashed on screen. He and his fiancée married on 12 September, but he had no qualms about going. 'Soldiers are always keen to go – that is what you train for.' Not all shared that spirit. One man in Phillips's platoon was the son of the Leeds Communist Party chairman. Phillips took him aside. 'I said, "You may think you are fighting on the wrong side, but if you step out of line, you will be dealt with."'

## 1ST BATTALION, THE ROYAL ULSTER RIFLES

The most distinctive of the brigade's battalions was the Royal Ulster Rifles. For one thing, the Rifles were light infantry, meaning they marched at double the pace of other troops; to those unfamiliar with it, the spectacle looks comical, like film of a quick march speeded up. Instead of berets they wore baggy green caubeens, and their band played Irish pipes and drums. And there were the accents: in contrast to the slow drawl of the Glosters and the northern staccato of the Fusiliers, among the Rifles dialects ranged from the musical lilt of the Emerald Isle to the guttural bark of back-street Belfast.

The regiment had been founded in 1793, when the British Army was expanded due to war with France. It fought against Napoleon in Egypt and Réunion, at Talavera and Badajoz and later in the Indian Mutiny. Being a rifle regiment was an honour: rifles were more accurate than muskets, but required greater skill.[26] In World War I, the Irish regiments forged a legend at the Somme, and in World War II, the Rifles' crack status was confirmed when its first battalion was converted to the airborne glider assault role, where it fought in Normandy, at the Battle of the Bulge and the Rhine crossing.

The Rifles' commander in 1951 was another tall, slim and quietly spoken officer, Lieutenant-Colonel Hank Carson, but he was to be plagued by ill-health in the Far East. The second in command, Major Tony Blake, a member of an old Anglo-Norman family from Galway, was fluent in Russian and Polish, had been attached to the Polish Parachute Brigade and was one of only three Parachute Regiment officers to escape from Arnhem.[27]

One of the battalion's toughest officers was Major John Shaw, Support Company commander. Shaw had fought with special forces in

Yugoslavia in World War II, and, thought one of his subordinates, Lieutenant John Mole, was 'rather taciturn, rather frightening, very strict. He would always ask "Why?" when you wanted to do something.' But Mole also found him, like many of the 'tremendous characters' in the Rifles' mess who had done well during the war, 'a splendid chap'. The lure of action in Korea was strong, even (or perhaps particularly) for officers in cushy billets. The laid-back Captain Robin Charley was a general's aide-de-camp when he heard that the Rifles were heading for Korea. He immediately volunteered. With no vacancy for a captain, he took a pay cut to lieutenant.

As in the other regiments, many officers had family ties. Mole had lost his father with the regiment at Nijmegen, so felt himself 'destined to be a soldier almost from birth'. Second Lieutenant Mervyn McCord's father had also served in the Rifles. The younger McCord, a keen athlete who trained with four-minute-miler Roger Bannister, had done a year at Queen's University Medical School in Belfast, but felt trammelled. 'I couldn't stand five years of that and took the regular commissions board in 1947,'[*] he said. 'I just felt that it was what I wanted to do.' Lieutenant Peter Whitamore, a native of Kent, was serving in the Loyal North Lancashire Regiment in Trieste and volunteered for Korea; he requested a posting to the Rifles, with whom he had done his basic training. When he rejoined them he was impressed. 'They were firstclass. Their spirit was high: good fighting spirit, keen. The Irish are always fighting: if not someone else, then each other! They were more aggressive than the Loyals.'[28]

In the ranks were 'a lot of good men – a lot of hard men!' said Sergeant William 'Doc' Holliday, a machine-gunner. One of the regiment's legendary characters kept a lion in his yard, and it was rumoured he could not be dragged home on a Saturday night by less than six policemen. One man who was perhaps born to be a soldier was Lance-Corporal Joe Farrell. Even before signing up, he had already seen active service on the streets of his native Belfast – as a light welterweight boxer. Signals Corporal Norman Sweetlove, a regular whose uncle had served with the regiment, was equally proud of it: 'in action, we carried less; we got to the objective quicker'.

The Rifles included a strong contingent from the Irish Republic. For centuries, Irish soldiers have served widely in British regiments, and the mess included some eccentric Irish officers who, on occasions like St Patrick's Day, encouraged the flying of the Irish Tricolour. Due to the battalion's effectiveness, such activities were ignored by higher authorities.[29]

---

[*] The board was (and is) the entry-level leadership test for potential army officers.

'There were Southern Irish – quite a few of them. They were good men – the best!' reckoned Farrell. 'We punched the hell out of each other in the canteen, but there was no animosity the next day. We drank the peace together.' The regiment's Catholic and Protestant contingents were demarcated on Church Parades. One Sunday, the men formed up and the RSM bawled: 'Catholics on the right! Protestants on the left! Fall out!' As the soldiers fell into the appropriate ranks, one man was left standing alone. 'What are you doing standing there?' the RSM thundered. 'I'm . . . I'm Jewish, sir!' quavered the unfortunate. The sergeant major proved equal to this conundrum. 'Protestant Jew or Catholic Jew?' he demanded.[30]

As in other regiments, disparate groups of men were bonded by loyalty to the unit. One young Rifleman, Henry O'Kane, returned to the depot one evening after a route march in 1948. It was sunset. Martial sounds were born on the breeze; something was under way on the parade ground. In the twilight, flags cracked on their poles as the pipes and drums beat retreat. Watching silently were ranks of immobile onlookers: bemedalled officers and senior NCOs, veterans of countless actions across the globe. O'Kane was deeply moved.[31]

## 8TH KING'S ROYAL IRISH HUSSARS

29th Brigade's armoured component was provided by one of the army's most dashing regiments: the 8th King's Royal Irish Hussars. During the Napoleonic wars the term 'Hussar' became almost a byword for reckless courage: General Antoine Charles Louise Lasalle, arguably Bonaparte's finest leader of light horse, defined it by declaring: 'Any hussar who is not dead by the time he is thirty is a useless layabout!'* Ireland has always produced fine horsemen, and the 8th Hussars were formed there in 1693. They would fight in the Low Countries, India and Afghanistan, but their most famous action came at Balaclava, where 144 of them charged with the Light Brigade into the 'mouth of hell'; 66 were lost, and one survivor was a terrier named Jemmy, the regimental mascot. In World War I the combination of war and industry introduced a grim new reaper to the battlefield: the machine-gun, against which horsed swordsmen were no longer viable. In 1935 the Hussars held their last mounted parade, then exchanged horseflesh for internal combustion engines. If World War I had been the war of the trench, World War II would be the war of the tank, and on their tracked steeds, the Hussars won battle honours at Bir Hachim, Alamein and Normandy, and in the closing days of the war liberated Belsen.[32]

---

* In fact Lasalle, despite his courage (in one famous action he broke seven swords and had two horses killed under him), lived to thirty-four before succumbing to the inevitable at Wagram. See his Wikipedia entry: http://en.wikipedia.org/wiki/Antoine_Charles_Louis_Lasalle

Many 1950s cavalry officers owned horses and maintained an aristo-cratic air. 'There was a classic saying* in the British Army – "He was a cavalry officer who was so stupid, that even his peers noticed it,"' said John Preston-Bell, the regiment's greenest officer. 'But the squadron leaders, adjutant and colonel were all highly professional soldiers.' The man who would command the Hussars for most of their service in Korea was Lieutenant-Colonel Sir Guy Lowther. 'He was cheerful, bluff – absolutely characteristic of the huntin', shootin' and fishin' man,' said Preston-Bell. The Hussars' motto – *Pristinae Virtutis Memores* ('Mindful of former valour') – is perhaps the perfect expression of the regimental system, and Lowther was a keen promoter of military heritage. When 29th Brigade was folded into the Commonwealth Division later in the war, he strode into the Royal Australian Regiment's mess, hurled a lance into the ground and declared, 'As of now, we are affiliated!'[33] But this robust bonhomie masked a thoughtful professionalism. In Korea, he urged his men to push their tanks to the limits and sent detailed reports back to the War Office, relating operational and technical lessons.[34]

Few men in 29th Brigade were as liked and respected as C Squadron's leader, Major Henry Huth. Described as 'brave as a lion',[35] he was a big, lean professional; just one of his exploits, after capture in the Western Desert, was escaping via a latrine. Quiet, humorous and relaxed in person, he was one of those rare warriors who seemed to actually enjoy combat, and possessed a keenly honed battle sense and the critical cavalry quality of fast decision. 'He was a charming bachelor, very good company – a typical cavalry officer,' thought McCord. His leadership was low-key. 'I remember once he called us together for a briefing and I shambled up. He said, "I'm a little browned off at the lack of proper military discipline among some officers,"' recalled Preston-Bell. 'He didn't shout or scream, but one felt terrible.'

Huth's second in command, Captain Peter Ormrod, was already battle-scarred: approaching the beaches in his tank on D-Day, he was hit, and lost an eye, but this did not prevent his returning to the front for the closing stages of World War II, nor his volunteering for Korea. Due to manpower pressures facing 29th Brigade, the doctor conducting medicals was ordered to OK as many volunteers as possible. Ormrod had previously been classed as unfit, but on his second medical, when asked to read a list of letters, he placed his palm over his glass eye, read with his good eye, and was passed 'fit for action'.[36] Some junior officers found Ormrod stand-offish, but his bravery was unquestioned, as was his skill at the cavalry officer's customary pursuit: cross-country riding to hounds.

---

* Or, as a senior cavalry officer indignantly commented to the author, 'a tired old joke'.

Among the Hussars' English accents was a note of broad Strine. Lieutenant David Boyall, an adventurous Australian, had completed National Service but on a trip round the world was 'rolled' in Panama and landed in London penniless, so joined the Coldstream Guards 'to get something to eat'. He was commissioned and transferred to the cavalry, taking command of a troop under Huth. True to the fire-eating Hussar tradition, many cavalry officers were keen for war. In the mess of the 14th/20th Hussars three officers put their names into the hat for one billet with the undermanned 8th in Korea, and the recently commissioned Ted Paul, who joined the cavalry because he 'didn't like walking', was the lucky one. Yet not everyone was a *beau sabreur*. Cornet* John Preston-Bell was a sensitive and impressionable young National Serviceman: his brother had served in the Queen's Bays, which had led him to select cavalry; he volunteered for the 8th Hussars after being taken by the dashing 'tent cap' of the adjutant – an 8th Hussar – at Mons Officer Cadet Training School.

One man with a better idea of the realities of warfare was reservist Trooper Denis Whybro. After serving in armour in north-west Europe, he had found a career and was making it in civvy street when he was recalled as a radio operator in the Hussars. 'It was a bit traumatic,' he said. 'I was just beginning to get back on my feet.'[37]

In Korea the regiment would consist of a headquarters element, a reconnaissance ('recce') element of fast Cromwell tanks and Oxford Bren-gun carriers and its own echelon of trucks and recovery vehicles. Fighting power was concentrated in its three 'Sabre Squadrons' – A, B and C – each commanded by a major. All consisted of a headquarters element and four troops, each led by a lieutenant, with the troop consisting of four tanks, each with a crew of four. The Hussars' mount was the British Army's most advanced fighting vehicle and still on the 'top secret' list: the Mk III Centurion.

Although Britain invented the tank, it had fielded none of the top models of World War II. The German and Soviet armies, in their titanic clashes on the Eastern front, had the strongest incentives to develop ever bigger, deadlier tanks. The Centurion, ironically, was the peak of these developments. The Soviet T-34, with its sloped armour (giving exceptional protection), and its double-wheeled, broad tracks (providing rough-country performance) had shocked the *Wehrmacht* in 1941. Outmatched, German troops demanded a panzer to face it, and many suggested copying the T-34. Hitler's designers came up with the Panther; this deadly cat copied the T-34's key features, but added a high-velocity

* 'Cornet' is the lowest commissioned rank in cavalry, equivalent to Second Lieutenant.

75mm gun and an electrically operated turret. Impressed with the Panther – clearly superior to their own tanks – British designers copied its key features for a new vehicle, the Centurion. Germany surrendered before the Centurion saw action, so Korea was the first battleground on which this soon-to-be-legendary tank was deployed.

Each one cost £38,000, weighed 50 tons, was nearly 25 feet long and 11 feet wide. Its Meteor petrol engine – based on the famous Rolls-Royce Merlin, of Spitfire fame – delivered 650 horsepower, for a road speed of 20 m.p.h. and a cross-country speed of 15 m.p.h. Its armour was 76mm thick on the glacis and 150mm on the turret; it also had steel 'skirt plates' hanging down to protect its vulnerable suspension and thin hull armour.[38]

The driver sat forward of the turret, between two steering levers. When driving opened up, with his head sticking out of a hatch in the frontal armour, he was protected to some extent by the long, metal equipment bins on either side and by the turret behind him. This made him vulnerable to enemy fire only from the front – though few enemy soldiers would dare face the business end of a charging Centurion – or from above – more problematic in Korea's hilly terrain.[39] Closed down, the driver looked through two periscopes with greatly reduced vision.[40] The remaining crew – commander, radio operator/loader and gunner – sat crammed in the turret, the 'fighting compartment'. Here, the men could talk above the whining engine and gun-stabiliser equipment; the commander communicated to the driver via an intercom worn around the neck. The commander usually stood in his turret for maximum visibility; when the turret hatch was closed, he looked outside via a ×10-magnification periscope, or through the vision cupola – rectangular blocks of reinforced glass built into the turret hatch. However, the tank lacked infrared optics, meaning it could not operate after dark. On the left sat the radio operator with two radios, a 19 set and a 38 set, usually tuned into the inter-squadron and the wider regimental radio nets. The radio operator loaded the main armament and machine-gun. One feature the crews especially appreciated was an on-board water boiler.

The turret contained the Centurion's 20-pounder (83.4mm) main gun and its co-axial BESA .303 (7.92mm) machine-gun. The 20-pounder was both deadly and accurate. On the range in England each tank was required to fire three consecutive shells into a two-foot square at 1,000 yards, meaning it could post a high-explosive package through a bunker's slit.[41] The tank carried 65 20-lb rounds – in Korea, usually high-explosive shells – most in lockers under the deck. There was also a clutch of six launchers, attached to either side of the turret, which projected white phosphorus grenades 60 yards to the front to create a smoke-screen.[42]

Not only was the Centurion accurate, it could fire on the move (a massive advantage over World War II tanks, which had to halt to shoot accurately). This was thanks to a gyroscopic gun stabiliser, the reason for the tank's 'top secret' designation. The Hussars awed the infantry with a demonstration in which a Centurion in a valley, with its hull spinning on its axis, fired its main armament onto a fixed target.[43] With its low profile, bevelled armour and long, stabilised gun, the Centurion was the prototypical modern tank, arguably the world's finest in 1950. Whybro was amazed. 'There was no comparison to the tanks we'd had in the Second World War. If we'd had a regiment of them in 1944 . . .'[44]

## THE GUNNERS: 45 FIELD REGIMENT AND 170 INDEPENDENT MORTAR BATTERY

Infantry seize or hold ground; cavalry undertake reconnaissance, shock and exploitation; and the artillery supports them with fire. It is the deadliest arm. Most casualties on modern battlefields are caused by blast (which ruptures internal organs) or shrapnel (which shreds bodies).

29th Brigade's senior gunner was Lieutenant-Colonel Maris Young, who had led three regiments during World War II. A tall, broad man and a keen jazz pianist, he immediately impressed one of his officers, Lieutenant George Truell. Truell, a trim and typically enthusiastic young officer, had been commissioned in 1946 and had served in the Middle East before joining 66th Parachute Gunners. When the 66th was disbanded he was at a loose end and having a pre-lunch beer in the Royal Artillery mess at Larkhill when he was summoned to the CO's office. Apprehensively ('I thought I was being called up for boozing at 11:00!') he went in. To his surprise, he was not chastised for loose living but asked if he would like to join 45 Field Regiment, then preparing to mobilise with 29th Brigade. There could be only one answer. Truell jumped into his 'clapped out' MG and sped to Colchester where, mounting the steps to the Mess, a 'funny little one-eyed officer' thrust the second pint of the day into Truell's hand and boomed, 'Welcome to 45!' The officer was Captain Dennis O'Flaherty, a highly decorated ex-commando. Morale at 45 was high. Young had been given *carte blanche* to select his officers, so went about forming his own band of brothers, booting out anyone who didn't fit. 'He chucked out some officers, and new chaps like myself appeared; some would be there for breakfast, but wouldn't be there for lunch.' Truell gelled. He found Young 'progressive . . . and a very nice chap'.

45 Field, approximately 500 men strong, was composed of a regimental HQ and three batteries, one to support each infantry battalion. Each battery was divided into two troops of four guns each, commanded by a lieutenant. The battery commander, usually a captain, was

embedded with the battalion he was supporting as a Forward
Observation Officer (FOO), co-ordinating fire by radio.* The artillery
are sometimes known by infantry as 'drop shorts',[45] a grim nickname
indicating that tired artillery officers, or those with incorrect information about position, time or distance can – and do – kill their own
troops. With the amount of information squawking over the different
wireless nets, adding to the confusion of battle, radio discipline was crucial. Young made sure that no signallers were 'rabbiting on – he wanted
short, sharp orders'.[46]

45 Field's gun was a classic: the 25-pounder entered service just before
World War II and combined the functions of a direct-fire gun and a how-
itzer (a gun that fires shells up in a parabola). It had an eight-mile range,
and fired primarily high-explosive (HE) shells: on impact, the shell casing
breaks up into 2-inch squares, filling the air with scything shrapnel for a
radius of 70–80 yards. The 25-pounders also fired smoke shells, used
when the guns were ranging, or to create smoke-screens. Each gun was
served by a crew of six. One outstanding design feature of the 25-pounder
was the fact that it sat on a circular rail, meaning it could be easily traversed through a full 360° arc. The 1.4-ton guns were towed by trucks.

Once a fire order was given – 'Time on Target!† 15:25! Three rounds, all
guns! Fire!' – the battery would fire and reload with maximum speed. The
25-pounder was one of the fastest-firing guns in the world: 45 Field's
crews could fire five shells a minute, so the full regiment could drop 120
shells onto a target in 60 seconds. In action, a 25-pounder is an impressive
sight. The barrel hammers back with recoil, and flame spouts from the
muzzle followed by a cloud of acrid smoke. Its boom is considerable:
many old artillerymen suffer hearing problems. Yet, for all their speed,
accuracy and reliability, the 25-pounders were dated; in 1950 the US
Army standard field artillery piece was a 105mm gun – the 25-pounder's
calibre, by contrast, was a mere 87.6mm. By these standards, 29th
Brigade was undergunned.

Also joining 29th Brigade was 170 Independent Mortar Battery, Royal
Artillery. The battery comprised three troops of 4.2-inch mortars, one
attached to each infantry battalion. A mortar is simple: a four-foot-long,
smooth-bore barrel (a 'stovepipe') with a fixed pin in the bottom,

---

* The British practice of embedding battery commanders with units was the opposite of the
US system, where battery commanders were with the guns. The latter system has an
inbuilt problem Truell encountered in Korea. Truell was with an American artillery
lieutenant when they came under machine-gun fire. The American officer said, 'Don't
worry George, I'll deal with this!' and called his battery. His superior officer, with the
guns, came back and said, 'There ain't no enemy there, and you ain't getting no shells!' In
the British Army, FOOs could *order* their guns to fire.
† 'Time on Target': a barrage calculated so that all rounds impact at the same time.

standing on a heavy baseplate. The bomb is dropped down the tube, where its propellant is detonated; it then flies in a steep parabola before exploding on impact with the ground. Mortars are ideal among hills, as they fire in a high trajectory, and are faster than guns. 'We were a fast-deploying unit: we could dismount from vehicles and do a "crash action" in minutes,' said Bob Nicholls, a gunner with 170, who had served with airborne artillery before volunteering for Korea. Once one tube had the range, the rest fired on its mark. The bombs landed with a crump, a puff of smoke and a spray of invisible shrapnel. Although a mortar impact did not dig the crater of an artillery shell, a 4.2-inch mortar bomb had a killing radius of twenty-five yards. Moreover, it made no sound and left no smoke trail.[47] 'A 25-pounder was more effective against a bunker, but when we caught the Chinese in the open, a mortar was the deadliest thing they could walk into,' Nicholls said. Each infantry battalion also had six 3-inch mortars. By their nature, mortars are extremely fast-firing – all a loader has to do is drop the bomb down the mouth of the tube. A decent mortarman could have 12 bombs in the air before the first one landed.

\* \* \*

As the units bulked up, the brigade began working together, and Brigadier Brodie made himself known. 'He was a soldier's soldier; he had the knack of getting to know people,' according to McCord. 'You thought you could trust him. He was great, one-to-one, but wasn't a great cocktail-party communicator.' Cubiss found Brodie terse: 'He couldn't really hold a conversation; before you gave him the answer, he had lost interest.' His no-nonsense nature became apparent. At Colchester he briefed the Glosters about Korea, then unexpectedly ordered the entire battalion to muster on the ranges in twenty minutes. The men scrambled. It was discovered that range staff were absent, and all targets were locked up. Brodie, impatient, ordered the men to sling their helmets on the target frames – contravening every safety rule about hard targets – and let fly. The Glosters rapidly knocked the targets down, apparently satisfying their brigadier.[48]

Training was stepped up to brigade-level exercises.[49] As the units got to know each other, key figures began to stand out. Rifles Captain Robin Charley learned that, 'If I wanted a decision from the Glosters, I was to call Anthony Farrar-Hockley; he was the adjutant, but he ran the show. If I wanted a decision from the Rifles, call the second in command, Tony Blake. And from the Fusiliers, you called the CO, Kingsley Foster.'

Colchester – a garrison town since Roman times – might have greeted the brigade's departure with relief. Before the Fusiliers arrived, the

Glosters and Rifles had frequently been at each other's throats while in their cups, so that one or the other battalion was usually banned from local pubs and cafés.[50] Although the brigade's destination was an unknown to most – Truell knew 'Sweet Fanny Adams' about Korea – some officers were delighted to be heading for the exotic Orient. For Perrins, 'It was wonderful: Here was His Majesty paying for me to go to the Far East! All the officers and regulars had the same reaction. The only negatives were those who were married – but I wasn't!' After the excitement of the deployment announcement died down, the Fusilier officers dug out an atlas to find where Korea was. When Nicholls showed it to his father on a map, he said, 'That is the end of the world – that is as far as you can go without coming back.' Even so, Nicholls, who had followed World War II closely, was keen to go. 'I lie to say I went to Korea for anything more than excitement. I didn't like communists, but I didn't go there to fight communists, I went to fight with the army.' More thoughtful men looked at politics. 'I knew there was a war on and was delighted to go off and practise my profession, though I had no idea what it was like,' said Whitamore. 'We were fighting for the UN. We were very conscious of the UN, because we were a founder member.'

The brigade had been ordered to be ready by November, but it was good to go by early October. The solid judgement of the Fusiliers' CO revealed itself when the battalion was about to embark. Foster granted weekend leave, and only two men went AWOL.[51] In October 1950, aboard seven troopships and twenty-four vehicle and store ships, 29th Brigade set sail.[52]

\* \* \*

The Rifles, with elements of 45 Field, were the first battalion to depart, leaving Liverpool aboard the *Empire Pride* on 1 October. There was huge excitement on the quay: the second in command of 45 Field was Major Harry Withers, and his sister came to see him off. When she arrived, 'the entire ship leaned over!' – a natural reaction to a sighting of film star Googie Withers.[53] At the last moment, a deserter, unable to resist seeing the battalion off, was spotted in the crowd. A snatch squad charged down the gangplank and hauled him aboard, where the Provost Sergeant awaited.[54] A raucous crowd on the quay sang 'Ma, Look at the Rifles/Off to the war again' – but as the ship pulled away, families were silent.[55] On 7 October the Glosters left from Southampton on the *Empire Windrush*, an ex-German 'strength through joy' liner. The Fusiliers left from Southampton aboard the *Empire Halladale* on 11 October.

At sea, officers and senior NCOs had cabins; lower ranks slept below the waterline, in hammocks. Training continued. PT and marksmanship

– shooting over the stern at balloons in the water – was enlivened by games, tugs-of-war, lifeboat drills and fire alarms. After hours the men had beer, the officers, duty-free liquor.[56] Rings were set up, and boxing became a key entertainment. On the *Empire Windrush*, one grudge match was so vigorously prosecuted that the referee abandoned the ring as the fight degenerated into an all-out brawl, to the audience's delight.[57] On the *Empire Halladale* John Bayliss, a handy welterweight who had fought all comers in fairgrounds in the UK, found his athletic standing won him popularity; in the cookhouse he was offered the choicest meat. Unarmed combat training was also available. After judo expert Mike Harvey and Sergeant 'Muscles' Strong, the Physical Training Instructor, performed a demonstration, the Glosters' 'local Samson' made his move. 'Right, I'll challenge you, sir!' he told Harvey – and ended up in the scuppers.[58] Harvey also taught some of the more unconventional tricks of the soldier's trade, such as how to construct booby traps.[59] The Glosters RSM, Jack Hobbes, who had been captured near Dunkirk, briefed his men on what to do if made POW. 'He got us together and said, "This is what to do if taken prisoner,"' recalled Mercer. 'We said, "Get away!" We didn't take it in.'

For men who had never been abroad, the trip was exciting. The ships were ventilated by air scoops and motorised fans, but as the temperature climbed many men took to sleeping on deck to escape the crowding and the stink of farts and tobacco down below. In the tropics giant rays, jellyfish, even a whale were spotted.[60] The voyage took in Port Said, Aden, Colombo, Singapore and Hong Kong. Gloster David Green bought a pineapple from a bum boat off Port Said, but spat it out in disgust: having never tried one before, he had gnawed on the skin.[61] In Singapore, many Glosters spent the evening with Chinese 'taxi dancers'. (One officer subsequently observed that their next meeting with Chinese was to be less cordial.[62]) Harvey's arrival had been anticipated: at the Raffles Judo Club, thirty black belts had assembled from Japanese ships, all keen to try their technique on the tall Englishman.[63]

Brodie, with his advance party, arrived at MacArthur's Tokyo Headquarters on 26 October for instructions. The summer crisis was past; the Brigadier received the impression that the war could be over before his men could disembark. He also visited General Walton Walker, commanding 8th Army, who told him his likeliest mission would be counter-guerrilla duties. Brigade officers began preparing for a police action.[64] 'Nobody seemed to think [the war] would last,' recalled Doug Patchett, the medical officer of the 8th Hussars. 'When we got to Singapore there were orders to turn back, as US forces had reached the Yalu.'[65] 'The first thing that dampened us was the rumour that the war would be over by Christmas,' said Nicholls.[66] Lieutenant-Colonel Carson, interviewed by the BBC on departure, had opined that the war was nearing its conclusion.[67]

The ships pressed on. Some nautical ill fortune hit the *Empire Windrush*. A young sapper from 55 Field Squadron – the brigade's Royal Engineers contingent – had been injured in the lower back during a brawl in Port Said. His condition would require an operation. At around the same time, an order came down from the captain of the vessel that there would be no more shooting. A soldier, practising musketry over the stern, had shot a dolphin. Major Tony Younger, CO of 55 Field Engineer Squadron, was informed that killing a dolphin presaged a death aboard. The injured sapper died after his operation.[68] In Korea, Younger would learn to respect premonitions.

Forging further east, the pleasure-cruise elements of the voyage faded. In the South China Sea, the Fusiliers were buffeted by a three-day typhoon that left the ship awash with vomit.[69] As the ships closed in on the war zone, they blacked out at night, and watches were set for mines and submarines.[70] The night before landfall, Korea made its presence felt. 'It was like we had crossed a line – a blast of chill air came down the decks,' remembered Fusilier Wear. The icy shock of the November winds beginning to blow down from Siberia sent many who had been sleeping on deck scurrying below in search of blankets.[71] It was not just the temperature that changed. Offshore winds carried the bouquet of paddy fields through the ventilation and down into the troop decks. For millennia, the fields had been fertilised with human ordure. This was Korea.

* * *

Land hove into sight at last. The Ulsters landed in Pusan on 5 November, the Glosters on the 9th, the Fusiliers eleven days later. Pusan was crowded with merchant ships, their decks piled with equipment and munitions to feed the UN war machine. Catcalls and wisecracks passed back and forth between the British troops and Americans on the ships around them.[72] Curious soldiers crowding the decks could see the docks piled with debris, vehicles and mountains of US stores. Among the bustle wandered Koreans in baggy white peasant garb and military cast-offs, and as the eye rose, Pusan itself could be made out. The city was undamaged by battle, but was swarming with refugees who had fled as far south as possible to escape the communists, and seemed to be constructed largely of rusty corrugated iron; many neighbourhoods were shanties. Beyond Pusan, the brigade's more experienced soldiers noted with apprehension the great grey mountains looming over the city.

A carnival welcome awaited. An African-American US military band, led by a giant drum major, was pirouetting on the docks, alternating martial marches with ragtime hits. The British troops – most of whom had seen nothing like it – looked on, delighted. 'Have you ever seen the antics they were cutting!' said Whybro. 'They'd take three steps forward and backwards, playing all this jazz.'[73] The Rifles, inspired, turned out their pipes and drums on deck and 'returned fire, tune for tune'.[74] Crowds of mobilised Koreans, waving Union Jacks, stood to welcome these strange UN troops.

Disembarkation had its own procedures: booster shots in both arms and will-writing. Live ammunition was issued. 'There was an air of excitement,' thought Nicholls. 'Things were getting under way.' As the men lumbered down the gangplanks, burdened by rifle, webbing and pack, they were each handed a huge apple – a piece of produce for which Korea is famed – by shy schoolgirls. Under banners reading 'Welcome UN Army Apostles of Justice and Liberty' and 'Hurrah, Hurrah for Democracy', the units marched out of the docks towards transport.[75] Further into town one effect that the infusion of tens of thousands of troops had had on an impoverished economy became apparent. Fusilier CO Kingsley Foster noted a sign proclaiming, 'This house no longer dirty brothel, now clean laundry.'[76] However, the rash of rough signboards reading 'Bright Moon Sex Hotel', 'House of Oasis UN' and 'MacArthur Old Style Tea Garden' showed there was more money in sex than soap.[77]

On the ships there had been concerns among 29th Brigade's more warlike souls that they had missed the fun. The Inchon landings had turned the tide. Communist resistance was collapsing; UN units were racing each other to the Yalu River, North Korea's border with China. The divided country was, de facto, unified. Would it all be over before the brigade fired a shot? The day the Rifles disembarked, they were informed that China had entered the war.[78] Those thirsting for action would get it.

# Chapter 3

## CATASTROPHE

*Arise! Arise! Arise!*
*Millions with but one heart*
*Braving the enemy's fire.*
*March on!*

Tian Han, 'March of the Volunteers'
(National Anthem of the People's Republic of China)

FOR THE UN TROOPS storming through North Korea the war had become a pursuit. Pyongyang had fallen. Resistance from the NKPA was negligible. But as his ROK 1st Division dashed ever further north, General Paik Sun-yup, the Japanese Army veteran, could not help noticing how eerily empty the countryside had become. NKPA stragglers and civilians seemed to have disappeared. The thermometer also began its customary winter plunge.[1] Meanwhile, spearheads from the ROK 6th Division had reached the Yalu. The unit dispatched a bottle of its icy waters to President Rhee.[2] It was 25 October 1950. A massive trap was about to be sprung.

For millennia China has kept a close watch on Korea and Vietnam, the nations on its north-east and south-west borders, both of which have been heavily influenced by 'The Middle Kingdom' in their governance, social culture, language, cuisine, literature and religions. In 1950, as a resurgent communist China strengthened itself after over a century of internal strife and foreign humiliation, ideological conflict with the United States became inevitable. In this Asia-wide conflict, both nations on the flanks of the dragon would become battlegrounds.

Red China had reason to fear the United States. After the Japanese surrender in August 1945, when communist and nationalist forces squared off for their final showdown, Washington backed Chiang Kai-shek to the hilt, airlifting his armies to strategic locations and delivering huge amounts of material aid.[3] It was all for nothing. Mao Tse-tung's communists defeated Chiang's nationalists, forcing the Generalissimo to retreat to Taiwan in September 1949. By early 1950 China was assisting Ho Chi Minh's Vietnamese communists with supplies and training, but Peking had even better reasons to support North Korea: Chinese Communist Party (CCP) analysts considered Korea the 'bridgehead' between mainland Asia and Japan.[4] Some 90,000 Koreans had served in Mao's forces, the last of them returning home by 1949.[5] In spring 1950 Peking moved large forces into Manchuria to secure her border as Kim Il-sung prepared his invasion.[6] Once GIs landed and Kim's advance bogged down around Pusan, Mao noted that the crisis 'was being exacerbated on a daily basis'.[7]

The CCP had already decided that if the United States attacked China, it could not defend the country's coasts against overwhelming US naval and air power. Instead, it would lure the enemy deep into the rugged interior, to engage in close-range infantry combat.[8] Chinese military planners believed US troops 'fear being cut off from their communications and retreat lines'. What was required was 'determined and audacious penetration', close-quarter battles and night operations.[9]

Peking's analysis of unfolding events was in-depth and accurate. In August, the People's Liberation Army (PLA), having assessed MacArthur's World War II operations, anticipated an amphibious landing. Mao, comparing Washington to a 'tiger capable of eating human flesh', relayed his concerns to Kim's Peking representative in August.[10] But the NKPA, battering against Pusan, did not respond – even when the Chinese warned them that Inchon was the likeliest site. After the September landings, Premier Chou En-lai dispatched five senior officers to Korea as observers.[11] With his army reeling, Kim wrote to Mao on 1 October, begging for intervention.[12] Mao, having received reports of ROK forces crossing the 38th parallel on the same day, had already made up his mind. On 2 October he informed Stalin of his decision.[13] Chou warned India's ambassador to Peking that if America 'expanded the conflict' by invading the North, China 'would not sit still'.[14]

The test facing PLA troops would be stern. Mao's first choice as commander in Korea, General Lin Biao, refused the appointment, citing ill health.[15] His second choice was Peng Te-huai, a veteran general from the poor inland province of Hunan, who had joined the party in 1928. A big, tough man, he had commanded communist forces in twenty-nine battles, and was at his best when fighting with his back to the wall.[16] A soldier all his life, he was known for his frontal assaults and for capturing enemy materiel.[17] Although renowned for his courage, Peng was so worried the night after being briefed on his mission that he could not sleep, even after moving from his hotel bed to a resting place more appropriate for a guerrilla general: the floor.[18]

The wheels were turning. On 8 October Mao ordered that PLA troops in Manchuria be renamed 'Chinese People's Volunteers' (CPV): a change of name that was no more than a gesture designed to forestall all-out war with the United States.[19] On 18 October Chinese formations removed the red stars from their caps to maintain Mao's fiction and began crossing the Yalu. They marched by night, they had little mechanised transport, and there was no signal traffic. By day they fired scrub and forests, creating vast smoke-screens to hide their presence in Korea's mountains.[20] By the end of October, 18 divisions of 130,000 superbly camouflaged men had infiltrated North Korea's high country, lying in wait as the UN spearheads approached.[21] US intelligence had no indication of their presence.

It was a risky roll of the dice. Mao's People's Republic was just established. After two decades of warfare there were massive economic and agricultural challenges at home; Chiang still threatened from Taiwan. The PLA was underequipped: Mao told Stalin that whereas an American Corps of three divisions had 1,500 artillery pieces, an equivalent Chinese Army had 36.[22] Yet Mao, a man who believed that 'power grows out of the barrel of a gun', had few qualms about using force; in the same month the PLA had marched into Tibet. And China's soldiers had real strengths. They had been fighting since the 1930s, and most were highly experienced veterans of Mao's guerrilla forces or lucky (or opportunistic) survivors of Chiang's defeated army. They were indoctrinated to despise the 'imperialists' who had been plundering China for over a century, and they were immunised to spartan conditions by a tough, peasant existence: all knew how to *cu li*, or 'eat bitter'.* The physical stamina of the soldiers and the porters who supplied them would soon become legendary – one British officer was later astounded to see one man pulling a loaded jeep trailer like a rickshaw, while others pushed.[23] As citizens of a nation that lacked electricity outside the main cities, Chinese troops' night vision was superior to that of Western soldiers. They wore well-padded cotton uniforms appropriate for the coming winter, though on their feet, bound with foot rags, they wore lightweight, baseball-style boots. Carrying rations for five to seven days in sausage-like pouches slung around their torsos, their logistical requirements were minimal. A Chinese soldier needed under ten pounds of supplies a day, compared to sixty for an American.'[24] Their weapons were a hodgepodge: American arms captured from Chiang, Japanese weapons taken in World War II and, increasingly, Russian equipment supplied by Stalin. (The resultant mix of munitions presented logistical difficulties, perhaps explaining why hand grenades were so widely issued.) Unlike the road-bound UN, they could move as the crow flies,

* The origin of the pidgin English term *coolie* for an Asian labourer.
† Obviously, this weight included not just the soldier's own requirements – i.e. food, water, ammunition – but materiel needed by his unit: signalling, medical and repair equipment, transport, petrol/oil/lubricants, etc.

across country. And they were near-invisible: in winter Chinese soldiers carried white sheets that made them indistinguishable from snow; at other seasons they carried what looked like small 'Christmas trees' under which they could lie, giving the appearance of scrub.[25] Air sentries were posted on ridges; as soon as an aircraft was sighted a signal shot would be fired, and the entire unit would freeze in place.* But the greatest Chinese advantage was numbers. Not only was China the world's most populous nation, many troops dispatched to Korea were former nationalists and therefore, to Mao, mere cannon fodder. In what would become a battle of manpower versus firepower, the stage was set for a monumental human tragedy.

* * *

The triumphant 6th ROK Division, the UN's most advanced unit, was dangerously overextended. On 25 October a sudden series of attacks opened down its sixty-mile line of communication. The division disintegrated. Further south, Paik's advance tripped a massive ambush. His men were unable to identify the enemy they were fighting. Paik conducted a fighting withdrawal. The US 1st Cavalry, ordered up to cover him, came under attack from the 'human wave' that UN troops would soon know so well. One of its battalions, the 3rd, was surrounded near Unsan. Unable to break through, three-quarters of the battalion was lost.[26] Chinese troops infiltrated dressed as civilians. Some South Korean troops were killed by panicky Americans.[27] Chaos reigned. Then, at midnight, 5 November, the fighting suddenly faded away. To nothing. After delivering a terrific shock, the Chinese – all 130,000 of them – evaporated.†

Paik's men had captured a prisoner. Paik whisked him to I Corps commander, General Frank Milburn, and, having learned Chinese while serving with the Japanese, translated for Milburn. The prisoner was neither local nor Chinese-Korean, nor even a Manchurian: he came from the 39th Army in China's south. This information was passed up the chain of command.[28] But the High Command – seemingly on the brink of a total victory that would unify the peninsula – seemed blind to the Chinese intervention. 8th Army commander General Walton Walker tried to use American logic to explain the Chinese presence: 'A lot of Mexicans live in Texas'.[29] US intelligence bought Mao's fiction that the men were volunteers, not regulars, and estimates of the number of Chinese were only one-third of the true number.[30] MacArthur, rather than seeing the Chinese

---

* It is movement, rather than shape or colour, that catches the eye at night.
† To this day, it is not clear why the Chinese halted their offensive when they did. Opinions range from their not yet having the logistics in place to support a long-range offensive, to Mao's hope that the Chinese action would force a UN withdrawal from North Korea.

break of contact as a warning, reached the opposite conclusion: the enemy had failed.* Still, the shock ratcheted up the holocaust a notch. At MacArthur's insistence – and to the discomfort of Britain, which feared total war with China – the north-west Korean city of Sinuiju was devastated by 79 B-29 Superfortresses. The Yalu bridges were bombed on 8 November. The same day, history's first jet duel took place, as Chinese MIG-15s went into action against the USAF.[31]

MacArthur wanted an immediate resumption of the UN offensive, but Walker demanded two weeks to consolidate and resupply his shaken forces. Huge amounts of equipment and munitions were moved north – by air, sea, road and train – as winter began to bite. An energetic South Korean entrepreneur – a North Korean refugee who had gained business experience working for US forces in the South – was flown to Pyongyang to see if he could expand the airfield.[†32] To boost morale, Walker ordered that American Thanksgiving on 22 November be cele-brated with the traditional feast. It was: in a remarkable demonstration of logistics, isolated units had turkey dinners, with all the trimmings, airlifted in. Some commanders, convinced that the war was winding down, began crating equipment for the return to the United States. An optimistic MacArthur told journalists that troops would be 'home by Christmas'. But in the front line – in foxholes scratched into the frosty ground and in frozen tank turrets – the mood was ominous. Even senior commanders were fearful. 'This was a new war, a new situation,' said General Paik. On 24 November Walker resumed the offensive that the UN Command hoped would unify Korea and conclude the war.

\* \* \*

By the third week of November the fighting elements of 29th Brigade were travelling north from Pusan, by train and by truck, up the Main Supply Route (MSR) towards the war. The devastation of the summer fighting was ubiquitous. The front had raged across the land twice already: once when the NKPA *blitzkrieg* compressed the UN into the 'Pusan Perimeter' and a second time when the UN armies had thrust north after Inchon. Liberal use had been made of American air- and firepower. Mortarman Bob Nicholls got the impression that every building or tree

---

* Mao, one of the great modern theorists of guerrilla war, is known to have been heavily influenced by the famous Chinese strategist Sun Tzu. One of the latter's most famous dicta relates to intelligence: 'Know yourself and know your enemy, and in a hundred battles, a hundred victories.' The realistic Chinese appraisal of their own weaknesses and American strengths in the weeks and months leading up to the Korean War was a key reason for their early success. UN intelligence had no such base in realism.

† The young businessman never got the chance to upgrade Pyongyang's airfield, but he did build his own empire. He was Chung Ju-young, founder of a company today known worldwide: Hyundai.

was riddled with bullets; around corners and beside roadsides were knocked-out tanks and smashed guns; beside rail tracks lay wrecked carriages, burned out between craters. Most bridges had been destroyed, and US Army pontoons filled the gaps. 'It was very, very poor, very dirty, very backward. We couldn't speak to anybody. The war had rushed to and fro, and the villages got buried,' said Hussar Captain Peter Ormrod. 'Was the country worth fighting for?'[33] Fusilier Roy Rees thought Korea, 'hell on earth; the most devastated place you have ever seen or are ever likely to see'.[34] Conditions were primitive. Roads, including the MSR, were compacted rock and dirt tracks (there were rumoured to be only seventy kilometres of metalled road in the country), and often the only signs of the twentieth century were the telegraph poles that lined the dusty tracks. Due to the atrocious road conditions, some local drivers removed the tyres from their trucks and drove them up railway lines.[35]

With Korea taking on its flinty winter aspect, one officer thought it a 'rather beautiful, but hard country'.[36] In the foreground, dusted with frost, was a landscape of grey and brown terraced paddy fields and foothills, poor villages, war detritus. In the background, blue-grey mountains blurred into the wintry skies. Most of the rocky hills and mountains were treeless. (Korean homes used underfloor, wood-fired heating systems, and by the late nineteenth century, this had caused massive deforestation; Japanese colonists finished the job with industrial-scale logging.) The villages consisted of wattle-walled, thatched-roof cottages, with an occasional walled-in, tile-roofed aristocrat's house in a small copse. Unlike European villages, Korean hamlets had no central feature – no church, no pub, square or war memorial – just a clannish settlement of families scrabbling to farm rice and vegetables. The larger villages, though, had wooden schoolhouses which were frequently used by the troops as accommodation.

Over the paddies – rice fields intersected with raised dikes – hung the stench of human manure used as fertiliser. Among the houses, the pervading smell was of *kimchi*, the condiment of cabbage, garlic and chilli that provided vital vitamins in a rice-based diet, and which was an essential ingredient in every Korean meal: it fermented in huge brown earthenware pots buried in the ground. For Britons who had grown up on starchy meals of potatoes, boiled vegetables and meat, it was a forbiddingly alien ingredient. The inhabitants – largely women, children and old men, as the young men had been press-ganged by one side or the other – were clothed in the baggy white garb that earned Koreans the nickname 'the white people'.

Heading north, the Glosters' train halted for a few hours at a siding. Private David Green and a mate wandered into a village. Hearing noises from an open building, the West Country boys walked in to find two girls pounding grain. To the Koreans' surprise, the Glosters took over. Each time the Englishmen made a mistake with the unfamiliar farming equipment, the girls burst into laughter and playfully punched them in the ribs – to the soldiers' secret delight. When they rejoined their train, the Koreans' 'sad eyes looked up from their bowed heads with shy, gentle smiles'. It was a rare moment of human contact.[37]

Along the MSR the British units began encountering their allies. 'On the train, we saw these Americans with South Korean "dolly birds",' said Morris 'Brassy' Coombes, a young Gloster. 'We wondered if there was a war on!' The more relaxed discipline was not the only difference. The US Army possessed equipment on a scale the British soldiers could only gape at. But His Majesty's troops did have one item denied their allies: Hussar Denis Whybro discovered that the British Army's rum ration – dished out daily from huge glass jars – could be a valuable currency when dealing with the 'dry' American army. When Whybro and his mates came across a supply train in a siding, a swift deal was struck with its American guards: rum was traded for fur-lined parkas. The enterprising soldiers continued their investigations and, discovering a refrigerated wagon, 'liberated' a crate. It turned out to contain Thanksgiving turkeys. The Hussars chopped up a bird with a kukri and feasted. Further north, near Seoul, the Hussars were billeted with a US helicopter unit, and together, they brewed up some hot toddy and held a party. The Americans had a cockerel as a mascot; at the start of the celebration the bird was a private, but by the end it was a major-general.[38]

Brigade units passed through the capital. Whole districts lay heaped in ruins, many buildings were mere shells, empty and blackened. Over the kilometre-wide Han, repairs were under way on the bridges; some were just metal skeletons sagging into the dirty grey water. But the Chinese had disappeared. Again, the question arose: was the war over? 'They told us we'd be home by Christmas. They just didn't tell us which Christmas!' said Gloster Sam Mercer. 'We thought the war was over. We'd just occupy the place,' added Fusilier Lieutenant Malcolm Cubiss. 'It didn't quite work out like that.'

* * *

North of Seoul, the terrain grew more rugged, the hills steeper. And the hills were alive. The NKPA – that force which had been so feared, both for its élan and its cruelty – had evaporated but was not destroyed. Many units, bypassed by road-borne UN forces charging north, had melted into the hills. The UN supply lines, which now extended from Pusan in the far south right up towards the Manchurian border, provided NKPA guerrillas with a wealth of targets. With 8th Army preparing its final offensive, keeping supplies rolling was a priority. On 25 November the Glosters were dispatched to Sibyon-ni, a North Korean hamlet astride a crossroad some fifty-five miles north of Seoul. Guerrilla activity was reported. The battalion dug in on high ground but the night passed without incident. The next day, C Company was ordered to patrol forward; there had been reports of an ambush being laid.

The Glosters spread out in tactical formation across the frosty countryside, accompanied by a pair of troop carriers. Passing through a village, Private Green saw his first battle casualty: in a pool of blood, his thigh shattered by a bullet, lay a dying Korean. He had been shot earlier, after being spotted planting a mine near the bridge across a shallow river. A carrier – which had prudently decided not to cross the bridge for fear of mines – had been destroyed by a mine on the river ford. The patrol continued. Green's platoon was ordered to clear a hill on the left of the road. Green and his sergeant, Jock McKay, led the ascent. Cresting the rise, they were astonished to see around thirty guerrillas huddling around a fire some twenty yards away. The North Korean rifles, with long, sword-like bayonets, were piled in a heap. Both groups spotted each other at the same instant. Both were equally startled. But it was the British, with their weapons at the ready, who reacted first. McKay let rip with his Sten; Green fired and caught a glimpse of the man he had shot – staring, hands in pockets, tunic running blood – as the Gloster dived for a better firing position. The ground gave way underneath him, and Green slid part-way down the hillside, until halted by a straggly bush. Above him, the rest of the platoon made contact. Firing crackled across the hill. Simultaneously, the neighbouring Gloster platoon, in the open across the road, had come under fire from high ground. Green heard a man screaming that his leg had been blown off. The guerrillas on the hilltop ran, dragging their wounded. Green's platoon were ordered to support the pinned-down platoon below. Green, lying in cover, was impressed by his young platoon commander as he calmly gave fire orders. Incoming fire grew sporadic, ceased. The guerrillas fled. A wounded Gloster was lying in the road, his trousers soaked in blood, his leg shattered. A medic sent Green off to find a splint. A sergeant had been hit in the head and killed in the skirmish. The Glosters discovered from a prisoner that they had forced a 200-strong guerrilla band into retreat. Green was pleased at his first taste of combat: he now felt himself a seasoned fighter.[39] Sweeps continued the following day, but found nothing. The North Koreans, familiar with the terrain and its inhabitants, had vanished.[40]

On 29 November, the Glosters were ordered to continue north. They were relieved in their positions by the Fusiliers, the last battalion to disembark in Pusan. Before he departed, the Gloster CO gave the Fusilier CO a warning. While intelligence described the opposition as guerrillas or bandits, Carne told Foster he believed they were, in fact, fully trained soldiers.[41]

Two companies of Fusiliers, with four of 45 Field's 25-pounders in support, deployed. The main terrain feature was a horseshoe-shaped ridge, some six hundred yards long, which overlooked the crossroads and Sibyon-ni itself. X and Y companies dug in on this feature. The highest point on the ridge was 'Gibraltar Hill', occupied by 4 Platoon, X Company. The artillery was placed between curves of the 'horseshoe'. At the open end of the horseshoe, covering the guns, was a small hill. The sun sank behind the hills. It was a chilly, moonless night.

Carne's contention – that the enemy were soldiers, not guerrillas – was proved at 03:15 in the early hours of 30 November. A sudden series of crumps and flashes heralded a mortar barrage landing among the Fusilier trenches as tracers from machine-guns streaked overhead. The North Koreans attacked from three directions at once – east, south and west. This was a professional, co-ordinated assault.[42] Fusilier Vick Wear, in X Company, saw 'shadowy figures' advancing; the enemy seemed to know the British positions exactly. Flares went up. 'Everyone was firing,' Wear said. 'You would catch a fleeting glimpse, you were not taking deliberate aim, everything was happening.' Training took over. 'You do things automatically. It is self-preservation.' The attack was 'ferocious' but didn't last long and was driven off, though several Fusilier NCOs were hit.[43]

Deadlier combat was taking place on 'Gibraltar Hill'. Dug in on its summit were Lieutenant Malcolm Cubiss and his platoon. If they went under, the Fusiliers' entire position would be compromised. As firing broke out, Cubiss – the reservist who had been bored with his bank job – felt 'a ghastly sick feeling' deep in his stomach but was determined to stand fast. 'I was intent on holding what I'd got. If I'd lost it, there would have been serious trouble!' Cubiss's Fusiliers would not see their attackers until the last moment: while their hilltop position granted excellent long-range views, the men could only see fifteen to twenty yards in front of them, due to the short horizons and the fact that the slope of the hill was convex. Suddenly, dark figures appeared over the crest: the North Koreans were upon them.

As the enemy stormed towards him in the blackness, Cubiss stood in his trench and hurled a phosphorus grenade to illuminate the battle space. So close were the enemy – around five yards away – that Cubiss's grenade hit a charging soldier at its moment of detonation. The man flared up like a human candle. Both sides opened up furiously in the grisly light. Mercifully the blazing man was hit in the hail of bullets, but continued to burn, marking the position. 'You couldn't see beyond the flame,' said Cubiss – night vision is temporarily ruined by bright light – 'though that works both ways.' For the first time, the Fusiliers heard the ripping 'brrrrppp' of the fast-firing (900 rounds per minute) Russian PPSh-41 submachine-gun, the 'burp gun'. In the darkness beyond the circle of light, the Fusiliers snap-shot at twinkling orange muzzle flashes. The North Koreans and Fusiliers were pouring fire into each other at distances of fifteen yards: point blank. The first attack was repulsed. 4 Platoon reloaded, and strained to see ahead of them in the lull. A second wave charged in. Fighting flared up again. In all, five assaults hit Cubiss's platoon. All were beaten off.

At dawn, Corporal Joe Thompson, further down the ridge, saw a rare sight. Given the firepower brought to bear in modern warfare, it is unusual for soldiers to glimpse more than a few enemy troops for more than a second or two. Yet down in the paddies, Thompson could see scores, perhaps hundreds, of enemy crawling under the cover of rice stalks. Thompson spotted a one-eyed Royal Artillery officer already known as a crack shot with 25-pounders: it was Captain O'Flaherty, the ex-commando. 'Sir, they're coming!' he yelled. O'Flaherty warned Thompson to keep his head down and gave fire orders. At a range of 300 yards, a barrage of direct-fire shells blasted into the North Korean ranks, hurling up geysers of frozen earth and clouds of black smoke. The enemy ran, pursued across the frozen paddies by the explosive puffs of the Fusiliers' 3-inch mortars.[44] The battle of Sibyon-ni was over.

In the quiet light of dawn, Cubiss was exhilarated. 'We'd done it! We'd held!' Like many officers directing a close-range action, he had felt no fear. 'You have quite a lot to think about – you don't worry about your feelings, you do your job. If it goes well? Fine! If not? Tough! If you can't take a joke, you shouldn't have joined!' Down in the village the Fusiliers learned that their two companies, plus artillery, had repulsed elements of a North Korean regiment some 1,200 strong. Reports from the villagers indicated that the enemy had lost over 100 men, almost certainly with many more wounded, but had removed most of their dead – only 50 bodies were found by the Fusiliers.[45] On 'Gibraltar Hill' seven enemy corpses were found within metres of Cubiss's positions, including the charred body of the man hit by the phosphorus; 4 Platoon might have accounted for as many as fifty.[46] The enemy were well equipped; local money, rice and fowl were found on their bodies. The Fusiliers lost five killed – two from Cubiss's platoon – plus three wounded and three missing.[47] Thompson went over to the regiment's blanket-covered dead. Among them he was shocked to see Doug Thirkettle, his best mate: nineteen years old and newly married. Thompson also ran into an old friend. In 1948, as mess steward in Darlington, he used to serve Kingsley Foster his pre-lunch pink gin. At Sibyon-ni the colonel spotted the corporal. 'Hello, Thompson!' Foster called. 'Keep your head down!'

The retreating North Koreans had assured their compatriots in the village that they would wreak vengeance on the British. In view of this threat Foster ordered Z Company up from the city of Kaesong to reinforce him. There would be more fighting on the subsequent two nights, but nothing on the scale of the first attack.[48] Cubiss's defence of 'Gibraltar Hill' earned him a Military Cross – the Fusiliers' first in Korea. Called upon to receive it later from his CO, Cubiss had a vintage Kingsley Foster moment. '"Hello, little lad," he said to me – Colonel Foster always called me "little lad" as I was fairly small – "You've just won the MC, but it was the men in your platoon who earned it. Don't forget it!"'[49]

On 2 December, the Fusiliers were ordered to hand over their positions to an ROK regiment and move to Pyongyang.* Counter-guerrilla operations were suddenly of minimal priority. Calamitous events were unfolding in the north where UN forces were on the brink of disaster.

* * *

MacArthur's big offensive had kicked off on 24 November. The northern part of Korea, where it joins the Asian continent, is the widest part of the peninsula, meaning UN forces were more dispersed than at any stage of the fighting. Intelligence estimated that there were 40,000–80,000 Chinese troops in Korea; in fact, there were over 300,000.[50] And the 'volunteers' had not been cowed by the American bombing on their border. As the mercury plunged, the Yalu froze, and foot and vehicle traffic crossed at night, undetected by air reconnaissance. While UN troops advanced up the roads, the reinforced Chinese lay in the mountains overlooking the columns. This was the opportunity PLA planners had dreamed of. Their enemy had been lured deep into broken country that favoured their style of fighting.

The UN advance drove headlong into the enemy mass. The CPVA tactics were simple. The 'volunteers' would assault frontally, at the same time infiltrating past their enemy's flanks to establish roadblocks in his rear. With the roadblocks in place, they would launch attacks along the length of the road to annihilate the strung-out UN units. Attacks went in

---

* In fact, the main body of the battalion would not make it to Pyongyang, being ordered south instead.

after dark, when superior Chinese night vision and tactics gave maximum advantage and American air- and firepower was least effective. Lacking radios, the Chinese, like a Napoleonic army, used bugles* to signal their attacks at company level; whistles were used for platoons. Sounding out of the darkness, the bugle's discordant wail – similar to the opening keen of a bagpipe – made a terrifying psychological impact on the UN soldiers.

On 8th Army's right, ROK II Corps, three divisions strong, was smashed, tearing a gaping hole in Walker's line. The leading elements of the US 2nd and 25th Infantry Divisions were overrun. The Turkish Brigade deployed to counter-attack. It, too, was driven back.[51] Brigadier Basil Coad, commanding the Commonwealth 27th Brigade, found an atmosphere of hysteria at higher headquarters: situation maps were marked with red arrows and the words '2 MILLION?'[52] Within three days it was clear that the UN offensive was irreversibly stalled. Even that perennial optimist Douglas MacArthur was shaken. Contacting the US Joint Chiefs of Staff, he requested nationalist Chinese troops from Taiwan; they could be in Korea within fourteen days, he said.[53] However, the key task now was not to resume the attack, but to ensure the survival of UN forces. On 28 November Walker ordered 8th Army to fall back.[54] Thus began the longest retreat in the history of the US Army.

Welcome support came from the United States Air Force. Combat was cold-blooded. Ground-attack pilot Robert Moxley came upon a column of enemy crossing the Yalu. 'I went up that stream of human beings with my guns, did a lot of damage. Did I have adverse feelings? No! I knew what they'd do if they got hold of me, and I don't blame 'em. It was a bare-knuckle fight.' Atmospheric conditions and the Chinese employment of smoke-screens made flying conditions hazardous. Pilot Officer Carl Schneider led a mission to rescue an American unit trapped in a valley. Low cloud greatly restricted visibility, but Schneider knew of a power line that ran through a gap in the mountains. Flying just metres above ground, he led his flight thundering along the power line, through the gap – 'as high as a hotel' – and into the valley. The jets spread out, attacked the Chinese, then climbed out through the murk.[†] However, the Chinese proved as ingenious at ambushing aircraft as they did infantry. Steel cables

---

* Mention of bugles – used to manoeuvre troops since Caesar's time – sounds archaic, but they were reliable. Airborne troops of 2nd Battalion, the Parachute Regiment found bugles more useful than unpredictable radio sets in the streets of Arnhem, and UN forces in the hills of Korea often found radio reception poor or non-existent, making bugles perhaps a more reliable signalling instrument for tactical movement.

† Later, in Japan, Schneider met a survivor of the unit he had supported: the man could not buy him enough drinks. 'Ground support was satisfying,' he said. 'We were helping the troops.' Even so, it was a far more dangerous mission than the more glamorous jet-versus-jet duels of the interceptor pilots. While some 80 fighters were lost in the war, 700 bombers/fighter bombers were destroyed.

were stretched across valleys, shredding aircraft flying down them. Entire CPVA units lying down, armed with automatic weapons pointed skyward, could put up a barrage of lead. On low-level attack runs down valleys, some pilots were shot at from above.[55]

Air attacks could only keep enemy heads down for so long. At the Kunu-ri pass the US 2nd Infantry Division found itself fighting its way down a seven-mile track at the bottom of a valley under the eyes of two Chinese regiments deploying mortars and approximately forty machine-guns. Equipment was hurled off trucks. Tanks bulldozed stalled vehicles off the road. Air strikes were so close that some vehicles were ignited by napalm running down the hillsides. Some GIs returned fire, others were paralysed. The divisional commander left his vehicle and, rifle in hand, fought his way through on foot. Two soldiers from the Middlesex Regiment, holding open the southern end of the pass, were killed by fire from panicked US soldiers. The 2nd Division suffered 4,500 casualties, lost 64 artillery pieces and hundreds of vehicles. Its commander was relieved and the division withdrawn from the line.[56] On the east of the peninsula US and Royal Marines, in terrible winter conditions, were fighting from the Chosin Reservoir to the sea. Marshal Peng was well pleased. 'The enemy had never experienced this kind of battle before,' he wrote. 'Surprise is the combat tactic that guaranteed our victory.'[57] As UN forces crumbled, 29th Brigade was ordered to hold critical points in the disintegrating line.

\* \* \*

Under iron-grey skies, down gloomy valleys and along icy, precipitous tracks carved into mountainsides, tens of thousands of Korean and American soldiers sought desperately to escape. Chaotic jumbles of tanks, half-tracks, trucks and jeeps jammed routes leading south. Vehicles that broke down or ran out of fuel were abandoned, often being simply shoved off the road, into ditches or over precipices. The Chinese had not just defeated the UN forces, they had triggered a rout.

On 30 November, the Glosters and the Rifles, supported by tanks of the Hussars, took up covering positions north of Pyongyang.[58] Marching north, Private David Green watched dejected Turkish troops heading south, and passed a smashed truck, its injured passengers trying to revive a dead body. Americans on passing vehicles shouted down at the British soldiers that they were heading the wrong way. Green, leaning into the vicious Siberian wind as he marched, recalled newsreels of the Russian Front.[59]

The Glosters were ordered to dig in on either side of the road. From scratch positions, they witnessed America's greatest retreat pass through.

Frank Carter, a Gloster Bren gunner, described how 'the whole American Army – it was like Piccadilly Circus at night, nose to tail, tanks, troops, everything – was coming back'. For two days, the column passed. Spread thinly over the frozen hills, the Glosters were dubious of their mission: 'We'll never stop them if this lot can't!' The columns thinned. A jeep sputtered to a halt near Carter's position. American occupants leapt out, told the Glosters, 'It's hell up there!', threw a grenade into the jeep, and jumped aboard a passing truck. On 1 December snow fell. The Glosters could not see the road in the valley they were supposed to be defending. Through the swirling blizzard, they were ordered to retire on the city.[60]

Pyongyang was an apocalyptic sight. General Walker had ordered a scorched-earth policy: thousands of tons of food, clothing, equipment and munitions, intended to supply the 'Home-by-Christmas' offensive, were being fired to prevent their capture.[61] Explosions rumbled, tracers from exploding ammunition dumps arced over the city, and a manic glee seemed to possess defeated UN troops as they looted or destroyed. Huge fires at the railway yards and at the airfield cast flames forty feet into the air. A train containing ammunition for the Hussars' Centurions was one of the victims of the explosive spree that had taken grip.[62] Eighteen American tanks on flat cars at the station were blown up – they had crossed the Pacific to Korea, to be destroyed without firing a shot.[63] Civilians ran into conflagrations, attempting to rescue clothing or supplies at the risk of their lives.[64] Desperate refugees, unable to use the bridges, which were reserved for military traffic, forded the bitter waters of the Taedong; hundreds died.[65] The winter skies reflected the fiery glow. The river was running red 'as if with blood', thought Gloster Lieutenant Mike Harvey.[66]

29th Brigade, under command of General Frank Milburn's US I Corps, was given the most perilous task in any retreat: rearguard, covering the withdrawal through the dying city. The Rifles dug in on hills just outside Pyongyang, while the Glosters held the Taedong bridges' northern thresholds and southern exits as 'close bridge garrison'. Lieutenant-Colonel Carne was authorised to blow the bridges when all units had passed through.[67]

The Rifles were on the perimeter but, with the capital so close, it was impossible to resist the desire to loot, to save something from the destruction. Captain Robin Charley jumped into a jeep, drove to an American supply dump and loaded a 'borrowed' trailer with supplies for a hundred men. An American quartermaster thrust a chit at him. Charley signed it 'Mickey Mouse' and raced off.* Gleeful Riflemen

---

* Subsequently, whenever US military police were spotted in the Rifles' area, fellow officers would tease Charley that they were hunting for 'Mickey Mouse'.

filled their battalion water bowser at Pyongyang's brewery.[68] Gloster Second Lieutenant Guy Temple equipped his men with paint and brushes so that they could overpaint their unit insignia on American vehicles.[69] Fusilier intelligence officer Tony Perrins had been ordered to carry a report of the Sibyon-ni action up to Brigadier Brodie in Pyongyang. After delivering it, he halted at a huge warehouse. 'It was like a huge discount store – and the discount was 100 per cent!' His men chucked the mine-protection sandbags from the floor of their jeep, replacing them with as many sacks of sugar, bacon, cigarettes and biscuits as would fit. Loaded down with booty, they sped south.

The last units were pulling through Pyongyang. A Hussar officer on horseback – like so much military equipment at the time, the animal had been 'commandeered' – directed foot traffic across one of the Taedong bridges.[70] The well-blooded Commonwealth 27th Brigade passed through the Rifles' holding position on 4 December. An officer, listening to the colourful vocabulary flying back and forth, thought, 'Dr Livingstone would have been badly shaken!'[71] Rifleman Henry O'Kane was proud to see the Commonwealth troops. Their morale was high, and he admired their discipline after what he considered the rout of US and ROK units.[72] Along with good-natured insults, the Rifles threw booty to the 27th Brigade men as they motored through.

At thirty-five minutes past midnight on 4 December, the Rifles withdrew over the bridges. In the smoke clouds hanging over Pyongyang, something was buzzing. Mindful of UN air superiority, the Chinese had adopted aerial guerrilla tactics: at night the pilots of ancient biplanes, dubbed 'Bed-check Charlie', would cut their engines, then, gliding invisibly over UN positions, drop bombs out of the cockpit.* One of these silent shadows swooped over the Taedong and dropped his explosives onto the vehicles on the bridge below. One Riflemen was wounded by shrapnel in the battalion's first experience of enemy fire in Korea.[73] But the evacuation was not delayed. The Rifles were across by 02:40. The American liaison officer who was supposed to confirm that all US units were over the river did not appear, so, acting on his own initiative, the Glosters' CO ordered US engineers to blow the bridges.[74] Explosions rumbled. The bridges collapsed into the Taedong, but as the smoke cleared, it was seen that there were still men north of the river: a truck with a pair of MPs on it was stranded. The men abandoned their vehicle and clambered south over the wreckage.[75] The blazing city was left to the Chinese. The communist world scored a major propaganda coup by circulating photos of the ruins to international media.[76]

---

* In fact, the tactic had been pioneered by Russian pilots on the Eastern front during World War II.

The Taedong River – a natural line of defence – was not held. The retreat continued, with British units bringing up the rear. On 5 December, the day after the abandonment of Pyongyang, the Hussars lost their first tank. It was not to enemy action: a Centurion shed a track, and spares were unavailable. With the vehicle on the 'top secret' list, Brodie himself ordered its destruction. Lieutenant Walter Clode packed its turret and engine compartment with explosive shells, then cut the fuel lines, flooding the tank's interior with a hundred gallons of petrol. A camouflage net, soaked in petrol, was dragged for 50 yards; a lit match was dropped,[77] and £38,000 worth of armoured fighting vehicle erupted in a ball of fire.

The pullback continued. Gloster Lieutenant Mike Harvey's 12 Platoon was dug in on a ridge when burp guns sounded from the flank. The platoon stood to and fired illuminating rounds from their 2-inch mortar. To their frustration, half failed to go off (the duds were marked with red paint, meaning that they had been rejected by ordnance officers and should never have been issued). Harvey was informed that there had been an envelopment in his rear: the platoon had to get out in fifteen minutes. Their FOO Captain Michael Newcombe arrived as the Glosters prepared to evacuate. Movement was made out seven hundred yards away: Chinese troops establishing a mortar line. It was the Glosters' first sight of this formidable enemy who had thrown the entire UN force into a rout. Harvey's tense sergeant asked the artillery officer why he was not firing. Newcombe replied that he was waiting until all the mortars were set up. The Glosters watched, until Newcombe radioed an order back. Seconds later, a barrage shrieked overhead and detonated among the enemy. The entire mortar line was knocked out, its exploding ammunition adding to the pyrotechnics. An urgent order – 'Move now!' – came over the radio. The platoon ran off the hillside and into waiting transport. Behind them, they heard detonations. The Glosters had left a parting gift for the enemy: armed hand grenades in bedrolls. As soon as the blankets were moved, the grenades would go off. The explosions marked both the proximity of the enemy and the effectiveness of the booby traps.[78]

But this was just one tiny clash in what was now the headlong, two-hundred-mile retreat of an army. Harvey dubbed the UN concept 'vacuum tactics' – i.e. putting as much space between its forces and the less mobile enemy as possible. But how far behind them were the Chinese, the Gloster officer wondered. Days? Hours?[79] 'It is somewhat alarming to have truckloads rushing past you saying, "They are right behind us!" and you are on your feet,' thought Fusilier Lieutenant Sam Phillips. Never in its history had the peninsula seen such traffic. Perrins watched American colonels directing movement at road junctions. 'You'd never see that in the British Army; a military policeman would do it better,' he thought. 'It was disorganised chaos,' said Cubiss, who watched what looked like 'a hundred miles of solid traffic, with everyone driving too fast'. Cornet John Preston-Bell was amazed. 'One US driver said, "We couldn't have stayed there – we'd have been killed!" I should have said, "That's your fucking job!"'[80] Road discipline was non-existent. Lieutenant-Colonel Sir Guy Lowther pulled his tank broadside across the road to get information about who was passing through. A truck slid to a halt in front of the Centurion, but when Lowther, in his turret, demanded to know the driver's unit and commanding officer, the GI replied that he was a 'refugee'.[81]

Few British soldiers had seen anything like 'The Big Bug-out'. Like the French Army in 1940, or the British Army in Malaya in 1942, the US 8th Army seemed to be disintegrating. Even with the vehicleless CPVA – now being referred to by British correspondents as 'Mao's Ghost Army' – well to the rear, there was no let-up in the pace of retreat. A report in the *Manchester Guardian* noted: 'British staff officers frankly confess they are puzzled by the way United Nations withdrawal has been conducted. They believe with well-trained, stubborn troops available, a firm line might have been established around Pyongyang.'[82] There was a growing feeling among the brigade that the Americans – a more mobile army than the British – were overreacting. 'That's the Americans: firepower and moving forward,' Cubiss said. 'They didn't have any idea of holding a position.'[83] Most worrying was the lack of co-ordination with flanking units. 'No sooner had our unit stopped than a unit on its flank pulled away,' said Hussar Captain Peter Ormrod. 'Communications with the Americans were not very good.'[84] The constant succession of movement, order and counter-order infuriated the soldiers. 'We'd get into an area, de-bus, and the cooks would cook up, then an NCO would say, "Right; get rid of the food. Let's get going!"' recalled Gloster Private Sam Mercer.

On 14 December a UN resolution sought a ceasefire. On the 15th, 8th Army's last units pulled south of the 38th parallel, the pre-war border between the two Koreas. It had taken the Chinese – armed with nothing heavier than mortars – just twenty days to sweep their enemies from North Korea. On 16 December in Washington President Truman declared a state of emergency.

\* \* \*

Intensifying the stress of the retreat was the climate. The Korean winter had arrived in all its stark glory, but this was no ordinary cold season; it turned into the most severe in years. Off the west coast the Yellow Sea froze over. At night the mercury plummeted, and Perrins, the Fusiliers intelligence officer, found the temperatures the UN soldiers endured (−38.9°C) were colder than those Napoleon's troops had suffered in their legendary retreat from Moscow in 1812 (−30°C).[85] Korea would be the coldest campaign fought by British soldiers since the Crimea. The weather alternated from sleet, to snow, to the occasional clear but freezing day. The wind tore through clothing, searing nostrils, stabbing into lungs and whipping up the ever-present yellow-grey dust. On waking, men discovered their eyelashes were iced shut; noses and moustaches froze solid, and Fusilier Corporal Joe Thompson found it impossible to speak for twenty minutes after waking. If anyone put down a hot drink, a film of ice formed on its surface almost immediately, and tea froze before a man could return to his slit trench; lips froze to metal mess tins and liquor flasks.[86]

Survival became the primary concern. 'As anyone who has done any serious camping will know, an immense percentage of your time is spent simply existing,' said Perrins. 'The mere act of getting up, of thawing out your boots, of starting a fire . . . God!' If soldiers removed boots at night, the leather would freeze solid.[87] Frostbite was an ever-present danger. Among the more severe cases were two Fusiliers who slept in the cab of a broken-down truck. One lost all his toes; the other, both feet.[88] A Gloster went into a coma after a forced march: the sweat on his body froze, and he was covered in a sheet of ice. He was medically evacuated and never returned to the unit.[89]

Soldiers raged at their equipment. Winter clothing consisted of string vest, long johns, battledress, woollen pullover, oiled socks and winter boots, plus a camouflage, hooded windproof suit.[90] Lucky men had greatcoats. The windproof suit proved not to be waterproof, and the winter boots were a disaster. The 'Boots, FP' (Finnish Pattern) had been made for a 1940 campaign to help Finland against the Soviet Union that never actually took place; since then, they had been sitting in a warehouse.* 'Finnish snow was evidently not the same as Korean snow, because the uppers tended to come away from the soles, and one saw scenes reminiscent of the Crimean War,' wrote Hussar Lieutenant Ted Paul.[91] 'If you got the boots wet, the stitching burst and the soles fell off,' said Cubiss, who suffered a frost-bitten toe.† Some men were forced to loot corpses: Fusilier David Strachan and his mates stripped clothing from dead Puerto Rican troops to clothe themselves.[92] 'This is typical of the way the War Office kitted out its soldiers,' said Preston-Bell. 'I think if you went back to the Napoleonic Wars, they'd say, "Tell

---

* That the boots were made for Finland was the conventional wisdom. They may have been even older. Perrins claims they were actually manufactured around 1918 for the British expeditions to support Tsarist Russian forces fighting the Bolsheviks. He notes acidly, 'Somebody no doubt received a medal for having found a use for them after thirty-two years in storage.' See Perrins, p. 34.

† He amused himself by sticking a knife into the affected toe: there was no sensation.

me about it!'"[93] There was only one solution to the cold. 'We wore everything we could get hold of,' he said. 'But I was colder than I had ever been in my life.' Fellow Hussar, Captain Peter Ormrod, did not remove his string vest and socks for four and a half months.[94]

Fortunately, the Americans proved generous. Ormrod was in his open jeep in driving rain without a coat when a passing US colonel removed his waterproof and handed it to the British officer.[95] 'My signature lies on several dockets in the Pentagon archives for waterproof boots and tent heaters,' Paul wrote.[96] British liquid rations continued to serve as currency: Scotch was traded by 55 Field Squadron's Major Tony Younger for 360 of the prized American kapok sleeping bags – one for each member of his squadron[97] – and whisky bought Guy Temple a signals truck.

Soldiering became extraordinarily difficult. Vehicle engines had to be run every twenty minutes. Compasses and gunsights lost their accuracy.[98] Weapons seized up. The men learned not to oil small arms. 'We dry cleaned 'em,' said Fusilier Vick Wear. 'They worked better with nothing on 'em.' Some Glosters slept hugging their weapons to their bodies to keep them in working condition.[99] The artillery's 25-pounders stuck to the ground. 'The gun platform would freeze into the ground at night, absolutely solid,' said Lieutenant George Truell. The gunners had to melt the ice with petrol burners.[100] At an 8th Hussars overnight leaguer, Lieutenant David Boyall and Captain Gavin Murray were discussing the possibility of a Chinese attack. Murray had just spoken to a sentry with a Bren; the grease on it had frozen up, and the man thought that even urinating on the weapon would do no good. (Theory had it that warm urine would temporarily unfreeze the mechanism.) Murray, a giant man, raised a pickaxe handle. 'If they come tonight, we'll just have to beat them to death,' he told Boyall.[101]

Home was usually a hole in the snow or earth. 'You'd lean against the side of your foxhole, and you'd freeze to it, you couldn't pull away,' said Gunner Bob Nicholls of 170 Mortar. The men learned to line trenches with rice straw, then covered themselves with groundsheets and blankets,[102] sometimes draping a tent or tarpaulin over the top. In their holes, they huddled together for warmth: One night Thompson, half asleep, reached out and touched a shaven skull. Thinking it was a Chinese, he lashed out with his fists: his panicked companion, who had cut his hair that day, shouted, 'Tommo, it's me!'[103] Elaborate methods were used to make the holes comfortable. Harvey built a fireplace in the side of his dugout using a mortar bomb container as a chimney. For a lamp, he punched his bayonet into a tin of butter, then used a piece of rifle cleaning cloth as a wick; the 'candle' lasted a week.[104]

The deeper the hole, the warmer it would be, but even this had perils. The Glosters' mortar platoon dug so deep they uncovered a nest of poisonous snakes in hibernation. The mortar men were seen leaping around in their pit, evading the bites of the desperate reptiles, before the vipers expired from the cold.[105] It may have been that incident, or simply a highly strung personality, that sparked the panic of a signaller in the Rifles. Captain Robin Charley was at HQ when he heard screaming. Radio batteries were tied together with signal cable, and a length of this cable had become wrapped around a signaller's calf. The man galloped into the darkness, convinced a snake was coiling up his leg.[106]

The problems of the cold were worse for the Hussars: skin stuck to the frozen steel of their tanks. Even with straw insulation on their decks – an innovation which delighted their CO, who thought it 'just like bedding down the horses' – the vehicles were freezing.[107] On a fifteen-hour road march from Pyongyang to Simak, eighty miles south, the Centurions were obliged to keep their hatches open. For the first three hours, the tank engines did not even reach running temperatures.[108] The troopers sat, fully clothed, inside sleeping bags in their tanks. After a 'sorry lesson', when the Centurions leaguered at night on marshy ground and their metal tracks froze solid for three hours, the Hussars learnt to put grass, thatch or branches under the treads.[109] At halts the Hussars would sit in holes covered with bivouac tents, with the Centurion's gun depressed into the hole. The gun's breech would be opened, and the radio microphone placed in it so that the crew, in their bivvy, could listen to radio messages or music.[110] The Hussars also created heaters from 20-pounder shell cases filled with petrol-soaked sand: they burned for hours.[111] The infantry would block off a monsoon ditch, fill it with petrol, then throw a match in to keep warm.[112] Some units received an object that resembled a barrel with a chimney: diesel-fuelled, drip-fed 'space heaters'. Set up in bivvies and dugouts, these American machines proved morale boosters.

Sub-zero ablutions demanded speedy movement. Hussar Captain Gavin Murray amused his comrades with one 'friendly fire' misadventure. He was wearing a one-piece, hooded tank suit, when nature called. He took a shovel, and squatted in the snow to carry out his business, but when he stood up and shrugged the hood on, he found his aim had been awry. He had defecated into the hood, and then unloaded the steaming contents over his head.[113]

Food was cooked over individual solid-fuel stoves, and consisted of a mixture of British and American rations. The British compo rations came in a huge box, and fed ten men for a day. The main ingredients were such classics as bully beef, steak-and-kidney pudding and plum pudding, fleshed out with the ever-present hard-tack biscuits. The diet was monotonous: Hussar Major Henry Huth spiced his with curry powder he routinely carried in a tobacco tin.[114] Adding variety were American C rations: individual ration packs issued to one man per day, containing eight cans of such items as hamburger, pork and beans, peaches and jam, as well as sachets of coffee and sugar. The US rations were particularly prized for the Zippo petrol lighters they contained. Fusilier Lieutenant Sam Phillips witnessed one occasion when rations provided Kingsley Foster with one of those opportunities which so endeared him to his command. The CO was walking among his men, enquiring about food. One Fusilier was about to say the rations were improving, but behind the colonel, the man's section commander was making signs, thrusting his thumb downward. The colonel appeared not to have noticed, but later that night, a tin of 'not very nice' lima beans arrived from HQ for the corporal with a note reading, 'Compliments of the colonel.' Foster had not missed the man's gestures.[115]

Inevitably, this diet was supplemented with local produce. John Bayliss and three men from the Fusiliers' mortar platoon set out in search of fresh food in an Oxford troop-carrier. They drove into a village, where they could hear a pig squealing. The Fusiliers leapt out of the vehicle, grabbed the animal and slung it in the rear. Spotting an old woman, the men thrust a fistful of local currency at her and took off. With rations procured, came the issue of preparation. Their commander ('who'd had a couple of gins') attempted to dispatch the pig with his revolver. He only succeeded, however, in shooting the animal through its snout. Another officer intervened and shot the pig in the head. The on-the-hoof ration was skinned, gutted, roasted and consumed by the mortar men: 'I think the whole battalion had their noses in the air,' said Bayliss.

Soon after, he came across meat of a different kind. American trucks pulled up and appeared to be unloading sacks from the butchery. 'Look at the meat in those wagons,' a hungry Fusilier said. Then one of the bags burst, and its bloodied contents tumbled out. The stunned British soldiers were looking at the bodies of Americans who had been bayoneted in their sleeping bags; the trucks were from a graves registration unit. Wells were another source of dead bodies,* adding to difficulties in water supply.[116] In these conditions of cold, horror and occasional humour, alcohol proved even more welcome than usual. One group of eager Fusiliers, stationed near the brewery in Yongdungpo, south of Seoul, filled their mess tins from the beer vats. The following day, corpses were discovered floating in the tanks.[117]

---

* The bodies are unlikely to have got into village wells by accident. Poisoning wells with corpses is a time-honoured guerrilla – and anti-guerrilla – tactic.

The Chinese 'Second Offensive' had made it obvious to every UN soldier that nobody would be going home by Christmas. Late December found 29th Brigade deployed north of Seoul. In these positions, the units prepared to make things as festive as they could. One Rifleman granted himself a special seasonal treat: he went AWOL. When he returned to his unit, the soldier, a prisoner of the Japanese during World War II, told his commander that he had spotted a former camp guard in Seoul, and had stopped by 'to pay his respects'.[118]

Second Lieutenant Mervyn McCord was fortunate in that he had mobility. The Rifles realised that, with enemy armoured forces having been destroyed, there was no need for their own 17-pounder anti-tank guns, which were sent to the rear. However, the guns' prime-movers, Oxford carriers, were useful. These small armoured personnel carriers, resembling tin cans on tracks, were powered by a ninety-horsepower Cadillac engine and could carry ten soldiers. McCord's anti-tank platoon was amalgamated with the Assault Pioneers to form a 'Battle Patrol' of some eighty men under Captain Geoff Cocksedge, mounted in the Oxfords, and the Rifles 'acquired' American Browning machine-guns to mount on them. The new sub-unit was tasked with long-range patrolling and formed the battalion's mobile reserve. In December the unit's task was reconnaissance around the city and its environs. The Rifles soon discovered that Seoul's top hotel, the Chosun – still standing among the ruins – had been converted into an officers' club, and its co-ordinates were duly marked on maps. 'We made sure our reccces ended there,' McCord said. 'It was a great find.'

Some units received food from the Red Cross and the Women's Institute. For Harvey and his platoon, these were the first rations they had had to supplement World War II-era compo since the campaign began. The Glosters roared with laughter when they spotted the marking on a Dundee Cake: 'store in a cold place'.[119] Some soldiers were supplied with Japanese Asahi beer, but the bottles froze. When placed next to the fire to thaw out, they exploded, causing a momentary panic as the soldiers thought that they were under attack.[120]

The Fusiliers' CO was presented with a special Christmas gift. In a reflection of his men's respect for Foster, the Assault Pioneers converted a Russian truck the battalion had captured at Sibyon-ni into a command caravan for him.[121]

* * *

On 23 December 27th Brigade was paraded for a visit from General Walker, the 8th Army commander, who was to present the British unit with a citation from South Korean President Rhee Syngman. The men waited. 'Bulldog' Walker did not appear.* A truck had driven into his jeep; Walker died in hospital.[122]

His death brought the crisis in the UN command to a head. The direction of the war was uncertain. To many US and ROK units, the Chinese seemed unbeatable. North Korea was lost. Headquarters was drafting orders for the evacuation of South Korea. From Tokyo, MacArthur requested one of America's finest fighting men to lead the UN's frozen, defeated and demoralised forces.

Lieutenant-General Matthew Bunker Ridgway, 55, had grown up in a military family. In World War II, he won renown commanding the crack 82nd Airborne Division during its parachute assaults on Sicily and Normandy. In late 1944 he took command of the XVIII Airborne Corps and led it against the German Ardennes counter-offensive, winning a reputation as one of the very best American commanders. Late on Christmas night Ridgway arrived in Tokyo and met MacArthur the following morning.[123] MacArthur made clear to Ridgway that 8th Army was his to do with as he wished. Landing in Korea on 27 December, Ridgway proved a dynamo. He was shocked by the American troops he met. 'Every command post I visited gave the same sense of lost confidence and lack of spirit,' he wrote. 'The leaders, from sergeant on up, seemed unresponsive . . . I could not help contrasting their attitudes to that of a young British subaltern . . . knowing that the British Brigade had hardly more than a handful of men to cover a wide sector of the front line with a new Chinese offensive expected almost hourly, I asked how he found the situation. "Quite all right sir," he said quickly, then added with a pleasant smile, "It *is* a bit draughty up here".' Draughty was the word for it, with gaps in the line wide enough to march an army though.[124]

Ridgway immediately impressed 29th Brigade. He demanded no more retreats without fights; the UN would hold Seoul. He solicited troops' gripes and promised them better food, better equipment, better medical facilities. When he met officers, he demanded that American units start paying attention to terrain, to break their road-bound mentality.[125] His leadership rejuvenated the UN war machine. A Fusilier officer thought it 'uncanny' the way the atmosphere changed, even down to the smallest levels, within a week of Ridgway's assumption of command.[126]

* General Walker is commemorated in Seoul – in an unusual manner for a soldier. In 1963, South Korean President Park Chung-hee was concerned that so many US soldiers stationed in Korea went overseas for vacations (thus losing the country valuable foreign currency), and so ordered an R&R centre to be set up outside Seoul for their use. Named after Walker, the centre was subsequently developed into an international hotel. Today, a 5-star complex, complete with swimming pools, deluxe restaurants and a casino, sits on Seoul's eastern boundary: the Sheraton Walker Hill Hotel.

At the dedication of the UN Cemetery in Pusan, Bugler Tony Eagles, a keen young Gloster volunteer, was dispatched to play the 'echo' to the Last Post. The brass was in full attendance. While most senior officers at the event were 'shipshape', in their finest uniforms, 8th Army's commander turned up in his usual fatigues – complete with explosive accessories. Ridgway, like Nelson with his bemedalled coat, Custer with his buckskins and Patton with his pearl-handled pistols, understood the impact a commander's appearance makes. His personal trademark was a hand grenade attached to the suspenders of his webbing at chest height, which accompanied him wherever he went. His martial accessory led the British troops to christen Ridgway 'Tin Tits'.[127] With Marshal Peng plotting his next move, the UN's new commander in Korea would soon be tested.

# Chapter 4

# AT WAR IN WINTER

*And I looked, and beheld a pale horse:*
*and his name that sat on him was Death,*
*and Hell followed with him.*

Revelation

NEW YEAR'S EVE 1950. In the northern outskirts of ruined Seoul the Glosters' Support Company prepared to celebrate. Having been on alert over Christmas, the unit had delayed its party until 31 December, when their commander Major Digby Grist ordered that the season be celebrated in Dickensian fashion.

Over the previous weeks, the company had unofficially adopted a band of abandoned children living among the ruins. They were led by a 'thin, hungry, ragged girl of about twelve' nicknamed 'Washy-Washy', as she did the men's laundry. Support Company's celebration would be a party for these orphans. A patrol was dispatched to the Seoul arboretum to liberate a Christmas tree. The Assault Pioneers built a chimney, using bricks from ruined houses. An NCO, wearing a beard of medical cotton wool, played Father Christmas and hid in the chimney with a sack of gifts – mainly ration pack chocolate bars. A bonfire was built to warm and illuminate the scene. In the early evening the tiny Korean children – many shoeless, most clad in sacking against the chill – were led into the circle of light. The fire crackled. As was so often the case in Korea, the orphans – uncertain what was to happen, unable to speak English, traumatised by their experiences – stood silently. Santa appeared from his chimney. The soldiers burst into laughter, and after a few seconds the children caught on. Each received a present – Washy-Washy got two, one for herself, one for a baby she was carrying on her back – and a meal. The cooks had prepared Australian steaks and tinned plum puddings. After the children's party, the men ate and drank: the rum ration had been saved up, and the unit had been supplied with beer. The members of the Support Company were sitting with their feet in a shallow trench dug around the blazing bonfire, toasting the New Year with mugs of rum, when thunder rumbled from the north. Artillery. The Glosters' party spirit evaporated. The fire was doused, the engines of the vehicles coaxed into life.[1]

Marshal Peng had caught up with the UN forces. Above the 38th parallel 237,000 bayonets stood poised – twenty-four Chinese and four North Korean divisions. On 31 December Peng launched them south on his 'Third Offensive'. The attack fell upon UN forces ranged along the Imjin River, just south of the 38th parallel, with a secondary line running over hills and mountains some miles north of Seoul. The Chinese stormed across the frozen Imjin, the main concentration against the ROK divisions, the UN units weakest in support weapons; the South Korean 3rd, 8th and 9th divisions collapsed.[2]

29th Brigade, in reserve, had been tasked with preparing secondary positions north of Seoul for the best ROK division, General Paik Sunyup's 1st, should it be forced back in the expected offensive. It was. The Chinese first infiltrated civilian refugees crossing the ice. Then the attack went in. The Chinese focused on the boundary between Paik's men and the neighbouring 6th ROK Division, for dividing lines between units are traditionally the weakest links in defence. The situation deteriorated. Paik sent his reserve regiment up; many men refused to fight. A scratch battalion of engineers and rear echelon troops was sent in, and this measure also failed: the troops regarded the Chinese with 'unreasoning terror'. 1st ROK fell back. Paik, suffering from malaria, was devastated at the collapse of his previously reliable division.[3]

The crumbling of the Imjin front left the route to Seoul open. At 05:45 on New Year's Day, 29th Brigade was ordered by I Corps to move north and counter-attack into the flank of Peng's thrust. Brigadier Brodie drove immediately to the headquarters of I Corps commander, General Frank Milburn, while elements of the brigade embussed and headed north. But Ridgway, looking at the confusion of southward-pointing arrows on his maps, ordered 29th Brigade back.[4] Before midday the brigade's motorised elements, en route north, were ordered to turn round and occupy the defensive positions they had dug for the 1st ROK Division.[5] The positions were a mile east of the town of Koyang – itself about ten miles north-west of Seoul. Koyang was held by the 25th US Infantry Division. The brigade's vehicles turned off into the snow-covered rice paddies, and the soldiers slogged up to the icy ridges. The British troops would be occupying a position dug for a force three times their size, but there was no choice. Milburn told General Kean, commanding the US 25th Division, and Brigadier Brodie to hold 'at all costs', but Ridgway countermanded this, stating that such an order – which could result in the destruction of complete units – was his prerogative alone.[6]

The British positions were on hilltops and along sharp, frosted ridges. The Rifles took the western portion of the brigade's line, adjacent to the

US 25th Division. To their east, and slightly further north, were the Fusiliers, minus W Company (which was holding the bridges across Seoul's Han River). The Rifles were accompanied by the tanks of Captain Donald Astley-Cooper of the 8th Hussars. The powerful Centurions were too heavy for the bridges and tracks in the area, so 'Cooperforce' was composed of the regiment's four nimble reconnaissance Cromwells, as well as a troop of six Cromwells used as mobile observation posts by 45 Field.[7] A troop of Churchills from the Royal Tank Regiment were also in the area. Behind the Rifles and Fusiliers, the Glosters dug in as brigade reserve. 29th Brigade's deployment was not a continuous line, but a series of company strongpoints. There was a mile-wide gap between the Rifles and the Americans, and two miles separating the Rifles from the Fusiliers.

It was the first time in Korea that 29th Brigade deployed in full strength to meet the onrushing enemy. The panicky retreats of the previous weeks had first shocked, then puzzled, then frustrated the British soldiers. On New Year's Day Brigadier Brodie dashed off his first command message of 1951, to be read to all ranks. It was a communiqué appropriate for a British force dug into a defensive position, typical of the aggressive officer who penned it and no doubt reflecting his command's frustration at the long retreat from Pyongyang.

ORDER OF THE DAY

At last after weeks of frustration we have nothing between us and the Chinese. I have no intention that this Brigade Group will retire before the enemy unless ordered by higher authority in order to conform with general movement. If you meet him, you are to knock hell out of him with everything you have got. You are only to give ground on my orders.

T. Brodie
Brigadier[8]

For the men in the slit trenches, the freezing night passed quietly. So did the following day. Elements of 1st ROK Division started passing through the lines; it no longer appeared to be a 'coherent fighting formation'.[9] The Chinese could not be far behind. Brodie was concerned about the width of his front, and asked for battalions of the broken 1st ROK as reinforcements. Two were sent up; the shaken South Koreans were stationed in villages to the brigade's rear.[10] Then, in the early hours of 3 January 1951, on their rocky, snow-covered hills, the soldiers of 29th Infantry Brigade put their commander's order into effect.

\* \* \*

Corporal Joe Farrell, the tough Belfast boxer, was deep in the freezing darkness of no man's land. After midnight on the 2nd his patrol had been ordered to make contact with the American unit approximately a mile to the battalion's west. As planned, the Riflemen rendezvoused with a patrol of African-Americans, and the two patrols were 'standing about yarning' in the darkness when gunfire barked out about half a mile away. The Americans decided to return immediately to their regiment.* The Ulstermen made the same decision. As his three-man patrol moved back, Farrell became aware of enemy close by. Although he could not see them in the darkness, he could hear them: 'They were chattering like a barrel of bloody monkeys!' Chinese camouflage was masterly, noise discipline less so. The tension ratcheted up. The soldiers continued, warily. 'We didn't even look back,' said Farrell. 'If they knew that we knew they were there, they would have opened fire.'

Farrell's patrol made it back through B Company's positions without incident, where they immediately reported to Lieutenant Robin Bruford-Davies, telling him that they thought the enemy were on their start lines. Above Bruford-Davies, on B Company's highest position – a knoll marked on maps as Point 194 – was Lieutenant John Mole. He had spent an icy night alternating stags with his sergeant. Sitting up in the darkness, Mole would have agreed with Farrell: Although he could see no enemy, he had an ominous sense of imminent peril. 'We knew the enemy were advancing, we knew the ROKs had fallen,' he recalled. 'I was shit scared.'

At 05:00 on 3 January indistinct figures were spotted in front of A Company's positions. The Riflemen opened up, and the firing spread across to B Company. Then it died away. Captain Robin Charley, B Company's second in command, was climbing the hill with the company sergeant major, discussing dispositions. Bruford-Davies hissed at the two to be quiet – not a good idea with a senior officer. Charley and Bruford-Davies had 'a bit of a row'.[11]

A grey dawn was breaking over the snow-covered hills and paddy fields. What was the situation to the front? At 06:45, two more patrols – one under Bruford-Davies, one under Mole – were sent out to discover what was happening in the valley in front of B Company. Mole was warned by his company commander 'not to stick his neck out'. He went warily down with a corporal for about four hundred yards and returned, convinced that enemy were present. The other patrol, six men under Bruford-Davies, reached dead ground – terrain that dipped,

---

* Corporal Michael O'Leary, who was also on that patrol, does not recall rendezvousing with the Americans.

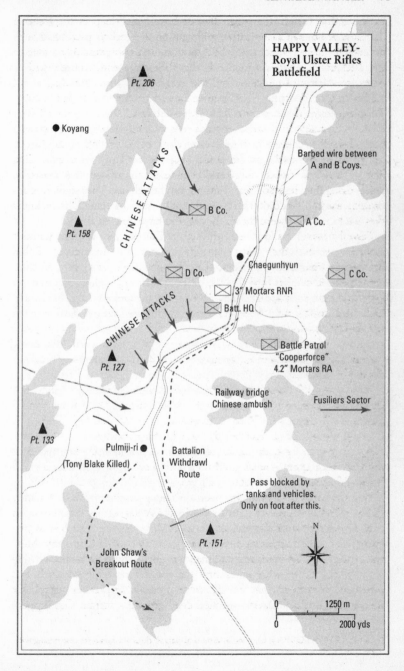

HAPPY VALLEY-
Royal Ulster Rifles
Battlefield

Pt. 206

● Koyang

Barbed wire between
A and B Coys.

CHINESE ATTACKS

B Co.

A Co.

Pt. 158

D Co.

● Chaegunhyun

C Co.

3" Mortars RNR

Batt. HQ

CHINESE ATTACKS

Battle Patrol
"Cooperforce"
4.2" Mortars RA

Pt. 127

Railway bridge
Chinese ambush

Fusiliers Sector

Pt. 133

Pulmiji-ri ●

Battalion
Withdrawl
Route

(Tony Blake Killed)

Pass blocked by
tanks and vehicles.
Only on foot after this.

N

Pt. 151

John Shaw's
Breakout Route

0        1250 m

0              2000 yds

and so was invisible to the watchers above – and disappeared. Silence. The Riflemen up in their slit trenches suddenly heard a grenade go off, followed by a staccato Sten burst. Silence again. The radio returned only static.[12] The patrol had disappeared. Given the nature of his last interaction with Bruford-Davies, Charley felt 'a bit peculiar'.*

The Riflemen in their forward positions had little time to feel apprehensive. Incidents accelerated. A group of men waving white flags, shouting, in English, 'South Koreans – we surrender!' appeared in front of B Company's highest point.[13] Stragglers from 1st ROK Division? Refugees? Mole went forward to investigate; the lieutenant could not tell if they were Chinese, North Korean or South Korean. He was within 'handshake range' of the lead man as they both started talking at once, in different languages: 'It was a ridiculous argument: he wanted me to surrender, I wanted him to surrender,' said Mole. The approach had been a ruse; the men were enemy. The British officer and the Chinese soldier opened fire at the same instant – both missed – then 'all hell was let loose'. A furious, close-range scrimmage swarmed over the hilltop. One of Mole's men was wounded – Mole dived on top of him to protect him as he returned fire – then he found himself in a slit trench below the peak, firing a Bren upward. He was wearing a steel helmet which was hit by a bullet, and the impact somehow knocked him out of the trench – 'an extraordinary experience!'† A corporal attempted to regroup the sections and launch a bayonet charge to retake the crest, but the Riflemen had not prepared their hand grenades and found they could not pull the pins. After minutes of close-range combat, Mole and his platoon tumbled down the hill. The men grouping on the peak were the lead element of the CPV 116 Division.

Bugles wailed. The attack surged in; Chinese assault parties, who had crawled up the hillsides undetected, stormed forward, shouting and shooting. Close fighting engulfed the Rifles' front. One reservist, a communist, shouted to his attackers, 'I am a friend – don't shoot!' When firing continued, he yelled, 'If you are not going to listen, I will fucking join in!' He did.[14] Captain Charley had one of those strange experiences men sometimes encounter in moments of great peril, when brain activity accelerates. 'There were Chinese milling around very close, it was a mêlée, they were looking at you, they fired these burp guns – they

---

* Bruford-Davies would not be seen for another three years. He and his patrol had been surrounded by a superior Chinese force and captured.
† Mole's steel helmet had a hole running round the rim, and the eight layers of clothing on his back were shredded, but he was miraculously unharmed: 'Someone was looking out for me,' he said fifty-six years later. He subsequently swapped the torn helmet with an American for a pair of US boots, a transaction he now regrets: 'It would have been a good exhibit for the regimental museum!'

were not terribly good shots – and you just stepped out of the way. Somehow, you weren't scared at all, you were looking at things from outside, things seemed to move in slow motion.'[15] As well as Mole's 4 Platoon, B Company, 11 Platoon, D Company, were overwhelmed and forced off their feature. Breaking the skyline on Mole's former position, a Chinese bugler in a dogskin cap put his instrument to his lips to summon reinforcements to consolidate the captured knoll. A machine-gun burst cut him down.[16]

The Rifles' CO, Colonel Hank Carson, was on sick leave in Japan. The second in command and acting CO, Major Tony Blake, the Arnhem veteran, reacted immediately. If the enemy consolidated, they would be impossible to dislodge. His counter-attack would orchestrate all forces at his disposal. Those platoons of B and D companies that had not been overrun were ordered to hold at all costs, while the full firepower available to the Rifles was brought to bear on the captured positions. 45 Field, 170 Mortar Battery, the tanks of 'Cooperforce' and the Rifles' own 3-inch mortars rained explosive on the lost positions, which disappeared under clouds of black smoke and flying earth. The Rifles' quick reaction force, the Battle Patrol – already on alert for a deep patrol forward – had its mission changed. It was ordered to exploit forward, securing a jumping-off line for a counter-attack by A Company.[17]

Due to the steepness of the hillsides, the Battle Patrol could not use its Oxford armoured carriers. Moving crouched behind the barrage, the dismounted men clambered upward, then rounds from above started cracking over their heads. 'As we got to the top of the ridge, people started shooting and we could recognise that they were using Brens,' said Second Lieutenant Mervyn McCord, the Battle Patrol's second in command. The patrol thought those shooting must be friendlies and shouted at them to cease fire. The fusillade continued. 'Eventually we shouted, "You silly buggers, we're coming up!",' said McCord. Grenades were hurled, then the patrol crested the ridge. It was occupied by dead Chinese sprawled among the rocks. They were armed with a hodgepodge of weapons, including several Bren guns stamped 'Lend Lease to the Chinese Republic' – captured from Chiang Kai-shek's nationalists, these were identical to the British guns.* With eyes on the forward slope of the ridge, the Battle Patrol called in an air strike. The men had barely laid out their orange fluorescent marker panel when four American Shooting Star jets screamed over their heads. McCord was buffeted by their slipstream as containers tumbled from their bellies: napalm. The 100-lb,

---

* The use of American-donated weapons by enemy forces in the Korean War was an early case of what is today termed 'blowback'.

grey plastic canisters dropped just thirty yards in front of the Riflemen crouching among the frosted rocks. A sheet of bright flame from the jellied petroleum flashed across the mountainside. A hot wind blew over the awed McCord as the napalm flared up. 'As the hills were so steep, they protected us,' he said. 'We were one side of the ridge; the napalm fell on the other.' Stinking of hot petrol, clouds of oily black smoke writhed into the air. The jets streaked away. A glance over the ridge showed that A Company's counter-attack would be redundant. The liquid fire – which poured into trenches, and gaps in the rocks in a hellish torrent burning at 1200°C – plus the massed firepower from the Rifles' support weapons, had done the job. The smouldering, blackened hillside was almost devoid of enemy. The Battle Patrol summoned snipers to pick off the few remaining live Chinese in the vicinity, then stood around, congratulating each other. They had been ordered to secure a start line for a company attack. Instead, they had retaken the position themselves, without suffering a single casualty. 'We were very pleased with ourselves,' said an elated McCord. 'This was our first real battle!' But, as the Chinese had discovered, the most dangerous moment after a successful assault is holding the position against counter-attack. A Company's commander Major Joe Ryan stormed up. 'What the hell do you think you are doing?' he roared at the celebrating Riflemen. 'This is not a funfair!'[18]

Meanwhile, B Company's assault sections were forming up to retake its lost platoon position, Point 195. It is axiomatic that in war nothing ever goes according to plan, but B Company's attack that day did – aided by a tactic to raise the blood of the fighting Irish. 'We gave a rum ration to the counter-attack platoon before they went in,' said Captain Charley. 'We lined them up. There was flanking fire from Brens, and Riflemen in the middle. That attack went in exactly by the book, just like at the School of Infantry!'[19] The position was retaken at 13:10. Mole and his men returned to their knoll. An experienced corporal quietly told Mole that he thought the young officer seemed a bit shaken at first, but had performed well in the mêlée. 4 Platoon dug in again. Its two dead were buried in their slits, which were marked for later retrieval.[20]

With the fighting apparently over, Farrell, in reserve, was sent on another patrol: this time, down onto the forward slopes with a Bren gun team, to see if there were any Chinese still alive. There were – and for the first time, Farrell saw the fearsome effect of a .303 round up close. 'We brought two back – a small fellow and a giant. The big man had a hole in his chest I could have put my hand into.' The Chinese soldier had been hit in the back, and the tumbling bullet had blown a chunk out of his breast. 'How that fellow walked back I can't understand.' The prisoner died the same day.

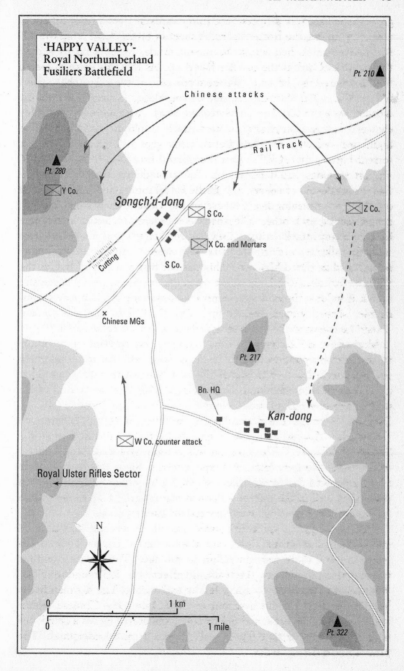

In the valley to their front, enemy were milling around. Captain James Majury, commanding the mortars, the FOO from 45 Field and other officers stood on the ridge with field glasses. 'It was against all rules to break the skyline, but the bottom of the valley was a long way off,' said Charley. The group, joined by an American Forward Air Liaison officer, had a grandstand view of Chinese squads manoeuvring on the valley floor. 'It was like a day at the races: now you see them, now you don't!' Charley said. 'We'd see a group go into a wood, and we'd call in a stonk; we'd see a Chinaman, and we'd drop a mortar onto him!'[21]

Some thirty enemy dead were counted around the forward positions, and the battalion also had the two prisoners taken by Farrell. The Rifles had suffered four men killed,[22] plus the six lost from the Bruford-Davies patrol. They had lost two platoon positions, but immediately regained them. The Ulstermen were delighted at the success of their first engagement in Korea, repelling the feared horde that had propelled their allies into headlong retreat. 'Morale was sky-high,' thought Rifleman Henry O'Kane.[23] The high spirits would not last. After dark, events would take a grimmer turn.

* * *

The Fusiliers were two miles to the east of Rifles, and two miles west of the American 24th Division. Their company positions were on rugged hills, reminding some veterans of the Italian terrain they had fought over in World War II. The hills commanded a T-junction on which stood the village of Songchu-dong. The village consisted of the usual peasant cottages, a schoolhouse and school yard.

The battalion was deployed roughly in a line. Y Company occupied the key hill feature, Point 280 (its height in metres), north-west of the village/junction, X Company a low hill some fifty feet high just south-east of the village, and Z Company another hill to the east. Support Company were in the village in front of X Company. Captain Dick Blenkinsop, the mortar commander, ordered his men to dig in with X Company, rather than at the village.[24] It would prove an astute decision. Battalion HQ was some 1,200 yards south of X and Z Companies, at the foot of the southern slope of a hill, Point 217, overlooking the hamlet of Kan-dong. While the hills dominated the ground, there were considerable gaps between the company positions – this was an area that should have been held by a brigade. 'The Staff College and School of Infantry would view this defensive position with horror,' was the comment of one Fusilier officer. Further weakening Lieutenant-Colonel Kingsley Foster's defence was his lack of W Company, guarding Seoul's Han River bridges.[25]

Like the Rifles, the Fusiliers spent 2 January improving their positions. Despite patrolling, the men had no intelligence of the enemy's location or intentions. At 05:15 on the 3rd, the Chinese answered these questions. Their movement and camouflage was superb – the attack came from nowhere. Surprise was total. X Company and the village of Songchu-dong were hit simultaneously. Sergeant Ben Ambury of Support Company was in his sleeping bag in one of the village houses when a corporal woke him: 'Some bastard's shooting out there!' Ambury, expecting to find a nervous sentry, told his men to stay calm as he laced on his boots. Opening the door, he found himself in the midst of a grenade battle. He dived into a slit trench. Support Company's commander, Major Colin Milward, joined him and asked him for a situation report. Then Milward drew his revolver and ordered Ambury to escape to X Company.[26]

Support Company was overrun. Some men died in their sleeping bags; the signallers manning the telephone exchange were killed. Y Company's echelon in the valley was also overrun, though the company itself held onto its hilltop. Chinese machine-guns were emplaced to dominate the track junction. Snipers began to shoot into X Company's positions.[27] Fusilier John Bayliss, with the mortars at X Company, had dug a trench between two mortar carriers and was asleep in the straw when firing broke out. His mate Ben Wragg shot a Chinese just ten yards away and kicked Bayliss awake. Bayliss jumped out of his trench into a mortar pit and started 'blasting away at them; they wanted the mortars'. The men used small arms to defend themselves: the attackers were inside minimum mortar range.

With the telephone exchange lost, Battalion HQ had little clear information about what was happening up-valley in the village. A party of medics in a jeep and an ambulance headed up to succour the wounded. Almost immediately, they were halted by fire from the machine-guns and from Chinese infantry in the village school yard. The men baled out of their vehicles and crawled up a frozen ditch to X Company's position.[28] Bullets were landing among the Fusiliers' mortar pits, kicking up torrents of earth, and cracking overhead. 'We could hardly move; we were being shot at by snipers,' said Bayliss. 'It was havoc.'[29] Bill Beattie saw three men sniped: all hit in the head.[30]

With the low ground taken, more Chinese attacked the companies on the hills. These proved a tougher nut to crack. Dug in with Z Company, Fusilier David Strachan's first indication of an attack was when a Chinese soldier appeared directly in front of his slit trench. Strachan fired. The enemy was so close he collapsed on top of the Fusilier, but he was not dead. In most actions, those shot die neither immediately nor cleanly, but lie wounded, moaning or screaming, exacerbating the stress of those fighting nearby. 'We were told not to finish him off – he might have intelligence,' said Strachan. The enemy soldier took about four hours to die. The man, most likely on reconnaissance, had no weapon. Those who followed did.

'They came at first light,' said Lieutenant Malcolm Cubiss at X Company. 'That was a mistake.' The Chinese were visible two or three hundred yards away, 'a mass of people in sand-coloured uniforms'. Cubiss's platoon sergeant, a marksman, had a field day knocking down enemy advancing between hillside grave mounds. 'I wish I was at Bisley,' he told Cubiss. 'I'd win the Army Rifle Meeting!' The Geordies opened rapid fire into the onrushing waves. Z Company OC Major John Winn, who had fought throughout World War II, was astonished: he had 'never seen so many enemy'. Winn's entrenched men 'shot them to bits'.[31] Strachan could see Chinese bodies heaped up after attacks. Not only was the enemy crowded into dense formations, like soldiers everywhere, they bunched up under fire. Many of the wounded were moving, leaving crimson trails in the snow as they crawled or were dragged away.

'The Chinese walked right into it. We really pounded them, stopped them dead in their tracks,' said Gunner Bob Nicholls of 170 Mortar, set up on a ridge overlooking the action. He was amazed at their numbers. 'It was like a [crowd in a] football game turning out!' He watched a group of enemy run into a gap in the railway embankment. A mortar bomb landed on top of them. But it was not just the British who had mortars: the enemy assaults were accompanied by crumps, puffs of black smoke and showers of earth, as Chinese bombs impacted among the Fusilier positions. Not every man proved staunch in battle. A Fusilier in the trench next to Stan Tomenson – a National Serviceman and Korea volunteer, nicknamed 'Chico' because he was only nineteen – started 'screaming his head off' in panic. Tomenson's corporal ordered him to go over and shut the man up. As Tomenson crawled across open ground, he felt a sharp blow – 'like someone had kicked me in the arse'. Reservists in nearby trenches congratulated him: 'That's a Blighty wound!' They had seen the blood: a round had ridden up Tomenson's leg and lodged in his pelvis. He awaited evacuation with no pain: 'The adrenalin filled me up.'

The day wore on. The situation remained the same. The British held the heights, the Chinese, from the CPV 149 Division, the village and valley floor. Support was summoned. Intelligence officer Tony Perrins, on the hill above Battalion HQ, found himself looking *down* on a jet flashing along the valley on its attack run to take out a Chinese mortar position identified by Y Company.[32] The company commanders on their hills were assuring Lieutenant-Colonel Kingsley Foster by radio that they could hold – but what of the men captured by the Chinese in the village below? And how could the Fusiliers on the hilltops break out through the Chinese on the valley floor?

Decisive action was essential. Foster radioed brigade to ask for Major Charles Mitchell's W Company to be released from its garrison duties at the Seoul bridges. His request was granted. Mitchell hurriedly briefed his men, telling them their battalion was surrounded. To break them out, W Company would have to fight in at the point of the bayonet. To Corporal Joe Thompson, the mission sounded desperate. The tense men were issued bandoliers of extra ammunition, then trucked into the snowy hills. On the way up they passed the Glosters in reserve. 'I don't know why the full Gloster battalion did not go in,' said Thompson. 'I think it was a prestige thing: regiments look after their own boys!'

Once Mitchell's men reached the mouth of the valley Foster hurried over to them, ignoring his intelligence officer, who implored him to stay at headquarters and direct the battle. 'Stop treating me like my mother!' he snarled at Perrins. 'There was a bit of a boy scout' in Foster, who had spent much of World War II on the staff, rather than with a combat unit, Perrins thought. The worried lieutenant took the role of temporary battalion commander, fielding radio calls from the companies on the hills, while Foster jumped onto the rear deck of a tank to join the assault.[33]

On a low ridge at the valley mouth officers and NCOs chivvied W Company into an extended line. A full devil's symphony preceded the Fusiliers' counter-attack up-valley. With the Rifles' battle temporarily over in the west, 45 Field fired a full barrage, as did 170 Mortar with its 4.2-inch mortars. Four Churchills of the Royal Tank Regiment would support the charge from the flanks. Waiting on their start line, the men of W Company could see mortar bombs and artillery shells exploding four hundred yards up the track in geysers of earth and billowing clouds of smoke. Tension mounted. At 14:15 came the ultimate infantry order: 'Fix bayonets!' The soldiers knelt, drew the weapons and clicked them onto their muzzles. Now was the moment. Major Mitchell – wearing a knitted hat and smoking a large cigar[34] – blew his whistle and gave the command: 'Charge!' Roaring and yelling, the line of Fusiliers swept down into the valley.

Nobody who saw the charge go in that day would ever forget it. Sergeant Beattie, with the mortars dug in near X Company, had been crouched under sniper fire since dawn. He spotted a sudden twinkling: winter sunlight catching the blades. Over the rim of his mortar pit Fusilier Bayliss glimpsed movement, risked a glance over his parapet – and was transfixed. 'There was this long line of men with bayonets, and bullets spurting up,' he said. 'What a sight!' The mortar pits erupted in cheers.

'We shouted, "Go on lads! Good old British pride and guts!" recalled the D-Day veteran. 'I had seen nothing like this in World War II!'

W Company were firing as they advanced at the jog. Some men were shooting on the move, others halting, kneeling and taking snap shots. Tank fire obliterated the Chinese machine-guns covering the track junction and the houses in the village. Corporal Thompson shouted to his section to keep spread out and not to fire from behind him. His apprehension had evaporated. In the midst of this wild charge he felt no fear; instead, intent upon controlling his men, he had a sensation of total awareness. He watched incredulously as a signaller, Bottomley, was bracketed by four mortar explosions. Intent upon speaking into his radio, the man continued running, unscathed. Thompson's platoon commander went down, his foot shredded by mortar shrapnel. 'Go on, get our lads back!' he shouted as he was stretchered off. Thompson suddenly found himself lying flat. He had been knocked unconscious by clods of earth and ice from an explosion; most men were not wearing steel helmets, but berets or cap comforters. He was only out for seconds, but when he came to he was surrounded by dead and wounded Chinese on the frozen paddy. The Fusiliers' line had broken up once they hit the village. In pairs and sections, the soldiers were clearing the buildings. The battle was now a scatter of close-range combats.[35]

The history of weapons development is the history of killing from ever greater distances: from knife to sword, from spear to arrow; from firearm to cannon; from artillery piece to ballistic missile. Firing a rocket, even pulling a trigger, can be impersonal. Bayonet combat cannot. Duelling at close range demands steel-trap nerves; thrusting a sharp object into the guts of another man, twisting it, then watching his agonised reaction from inches away – this makes bayonet fighting intensely traumatic. The battle in the valley was now hand-to-hand, point-to-point. Despite the atavistic fear most men have of such combat, several Chinese[36] and one Geordie were killed with cold steel. The Fusilier was engaged in a bayonet duel with a Chinese between a group of vehicles. The range was so close, the movement so fast, that the Fusilier's comrades could not fire to save him.[37]

In the chaos, Thompson and his mate Ted Shorthouse encountered a bearded Chinese soldier who seemed stupefied – 'perhaps his nerve went; the tank fire might have done it'. Shorthouse kicked him to get him moving. The Fusiliers were in close contact; it was impossible to take prisoners. They motioned him with their muzzles to head back towards Battalion HQ. The pair advanced into the village. Three gunners dashed out of a house; they had been held prisoner by the Chinese the two Fusiliers had just captured. It was later discovered that the bearded enemy had been killed on his way rearwards.[38]

Mortar Sergeant Beattie noted with approval Mitchell's demeanour as he calmly directed the attack.* The W Company commander stood out in the havoc, giving fire orders to one of the tanks via the telephone on the rear of the turret.[39] Even fellow officers were impressed by his *sangfroid*. With firing still crackling around him, the major called a snap 'O' Group. A Fusilier was sniped yards away; a medic rushed up, and the officers 'started to gape at this chap'. 'I will have your attention, please!' Mitchell snapped.[40] He got it, then issued orders to secure the village.

The charge had done its work. By 16:00 the valley was largely clear. Over two hundred dead CPVA troops were strewn over the hillsides and the village.[41] The 'Fighting Fifth' had lost eighteen killed, forty-five wounded and three missing.[42] Major Milward's body was found in the village, surrounded by five dead Chinese.[43] Prisoners were being rounded up, and Perrins was struck by the fact that the Geordies guarding them seemed to display no hostility towards the enemy they had been trying to kill just minutes earlier.

There had been desperate moments, but with a combination of firepower and aggression, both the Fusiliers and Rifles had held their ground. Elsewhere, though, Peng's pressure had proved too great: the UN line north of Seoul was disintegrating. Ridgway had planned to hold the capital, but in the late evening of the 2nd, acknowledging reality, and with the ROK forces to the east having collapsed, he reversed his decision. On the afternoon of 3 January a general withdrawal south of the Han River was ordered.[44] 29th Brigade, the rearguard, would have to move out fast.

The Fusiliers received movement orders at 17:20. The wounded were helped or stretchered down the hills; Tomenson was evacuated to a Norwegian MASH unit. Then the companies pulled back. On the way out, Chinese sniping resumed from among burial mounds in the foothills. 'These Chinese were old soldiers, well trained, good fighters,' Thompson thought as his section walked out of the valley backwards. They were passing a pile of Chinese dead when Shorthouse suddenly shouted, 'Look out!' One of the 'dead' had raised a burp gun. 'He was going to plug me in the back,' said Thompson, who spun and killed him with a close-range Sten burst. 'We got rid of him!' It seemed fitting revenge for his young friend Doug Thirkettle, killed at Sibyon-ni.[45]

Abandoning the hills and valley they had fought for, the battalion, which could see Chinese taking over their positions as they abandoned

* Mitchell received the Distinguished Service Order for his action that day, but his commanding officer received more publicity – to Mitchell's displeasure. In a letter to his sister in July, Mitchell wrote: 'I'm afraid I get a little angry over the part about the CO personally leading the counter attack. I personally planned and executed and led the thing which resulted in about 80 Chinese being killed, 25–30 being captured and all the Bn. transport and a number of our own soldiers being liberated. The CO merely followed in a tank. However, it looked good in the press.' Letter reproduced in Perrins, p. 158.

them, headed south. The Fusiliers leapfrogged the Glosters, who had not been in action. The last to depart were Z Company. By now the Chinese had cut the track; Z walked out, cross-country, in a nerve-racking rearguard march. 'There is always fear that you are going to be cut off,' said Strachan. 'But we weren't.' The company embussed at 01:00.[46] Once the Fusiliers were through, the Glosters pulled back, blowing up three carriers that had broken down.[47]

Pyongyang was a smouldering ruin. Now, as UN forces retreated yet further, it was Seoul's turn. The city was ablaze. In the flickering darkness, trucks packed with exhausted Fusiliers rumbled through the glow. 'Seoul was in the process of being blown up,' said Lieutenant Sam Phillips. 'We crossed a pontoon bridge. We were only too happy to be heading south.'

\* \* \*

Two miles west, the Rifles had not received their movement orders until 18:30,[48] over an hour after the Fusiliers, and two and a half hours after the US 25th Infantry had started moving at 16:00 (the Americans had received their orders at 15:00).[49] The division, which had lost contact with some of its own sub-units, was 'moving to its own timetable'.[50] With the Fusiliers and the Glosters furthest from the MSR, the Rifles would be the last battalion to move out in the step-by-step pull-back.\* Their line of withdrawal was a valley overlooked by low hills and cliffs that ran to the MSR, where trucks were waiting. A railway line, complete with bridges and tunnels, wound through the valley; the hamlet of Pulmiji-ri stood at its southern end. Much of the valley floor was covered by a stream, now a sheet of ice. Totally devoid of cover, the valley was a two-mile enfilade.

Withdrawal while in contact with the enemy is the most perilous operation of war.[†] This night, speed and stealth would be critical. If the

---

\* Several Rifles veterans of the action expressed bitterness that the Americans had pulled out first, leaving their flank exposed, but a retreat does not take place in a single line moving back at the same time: it is a step-by-step action. Battle patrol commander Geoff Cocksedge, in a 2009 letter to Mervyn McCord, opined that the fast American pull-out, leaving behind unnecessary stores, showed that they were more 'street-wise' than the British, who determined to leave nothing for the enemy. However, in terms of timing and positioning, communications between the US 25th Infantry Division and 29th Brigade could have been clearer. The 25th's blocking force, the US 27th 'Wolfhounds' Infantry Regiment, while in place by 19:00, was in no position to assist the Rifles when their situation became grave – though, as we shall see, this did not prevent its commander from volunteering his men for a counter-attack.

† That a retreating unit in the open is less able to defend itself than one in a defensive position or posture is a timeless truism of war, but in the Korean War, it was proved statistically. For the first time in the history of military medicine, all wounded had information related to their actions recorded on punch cards, which were sent to Washington for computer collation and analysis. It was found that average casualties per division per day were 67 when in attack against a main force, 77 when in defence against a main force and 119 during a withdrawal. See Jack McCallum, 'Military Medicine', in Tucker, p. 448.

Chinese on the high ground spotted the Riflemen, the valley would become a death trap; the prospect of withdrawing under enemy observation was 'absolutely horrifying', thought McCord. The Rifles' flanks were already in the air. The Fusiliers were moving; the Americans gone. 'They had gone like the hammers of hell,' McCord said. 'When the Americans bug out, they go hell for leather!'[51]

Captain Donald Astley-Cooper, the Hussar commanding 'Cooperforce', asked permission to lead the way out with his tanks, which were difficult to operate in darkness; moreover, the icy track through the valley was as hard and slippery as polished iron. His request was refused, as the sound of the tank engines echoing around the valley could alert the Chinese to the battalion's movement.[52] Astley-Cooper confided deep concern about his orders to Lieutenant Bernard Dowling, the Hussar leading the tank's supply column, which would move with the infantry companies.

B Company would lead the way on foot, followed by HQ, the vehicles – mainly jeeps and trucks loaded with rations and ammunition – then C, D, A and Support Companies; the latter was largely mounted in carriers. Cooperforce, with a close-support infantry platoon, would provide a mobile rearguard. Behind the rearguard, the Battle Patrol had the riskiest mission. McCord was tasked with establishing a standing patrol north of the village of Chaegunghyon. With a section of 3-inch mortars, and mounted in machine-gun-armed Oxford carriers, the Battle Patrol would cover the battalion out, firing off as much ammunition as they could to keep the attention of the Chinese diverted, before joining the rearguard's withdrawal at 23:20.[53]

It was a freezing, moonless night. A chill wind blew down the valley. Having disengaged without incident from their hill, B Company, the battalion's point, silently entered the black valley at 21:00. Then came the vehicles, slithering across the icy track at walking pace. Beside them, lines of nervous soldiers, maintaining maximum noise discipline, rifles at the ready, crunched through the snow. In their rear were reassuring crumps and flashes as mortars with the Battle Patrol fired onto suspected enemy concentration areas, maintaining the fiction of the withdrawing battalion's continued presence. Lance-Corporal Farrell, the last man in D Company, passed his mate, MP Martin Vance, who was guiding movement into the valley mouth. He whispered at Vance to join him. Vance declined, saying he had to do his duty.*

With flanking units absent and the Rifles' own companies disengaging, there was nothing to stop the Chinese exploiting forward to positions

* Vance was captured soon after this.

where they could overlook the force withdrawing down the valley. Remarkably, though, the enemy appeared not to have noticed the pull-back; all was going according to plan. The column proceeded unmolested. The tense minutes ticked by. B Company exited the valley without incident and linked up with the African-American transport company 'Wag's Truckers', who would convey them down the MSR to Seoul. The black Americans had formed a close relationship with the Ulstermen; each group was relieved to see the other. Captain Charley was amused when a GI, unfamiliar with British insignia, spotted his captain's pips and asked, 'Say, are you a three-star general?'

As this cheerful conversation was taking place, disaster struck the column moving through the valley. At around 21:30, American aircraft – probably supporting bomber sorties on advancing Chinese nearby – dropped a line of flares directly over the lines of Riflemen and vehicles. The flares dangled, burning white in the black sky. Snow and ice reflected their fizzing glare. With the entire landscape illuminated, the retreating soldiers and vehicles were harshly silhouetted against their white surroundings. A gasp went up from the soldiers around McCord. Officers moving with the tactical command post whispered urgently into radios demanding a halt to the flaring. Their pleas were ineffectual; the drizzle of flares continued.[54] But still, for several minutes, there was no enemy reaction. The column continued urgently onwards.

On the ridges overlooking the valley, the Chinese had spotted the retreating force. The pause was the time it took for them to range machine-guns and mortars onto the illuminated column below. Within minutes, firing broke out. Mortars flashed, lines of green tracers streaked over and into the valley. The Rifles were in a shooting gallery. Then came a terrifying cacophony: bugles sounding the charge. Crowds of shadowy figures pelted down the hillsides to engage at close range.

When the flares dropped, Farrell 'had done a wee bit of cursing'. As firing broke out, he became separated from the rest of D Company. He was lying flat, taking cover, when a Chinese unit charging from the hills ran over him – one man literally running over his back. The enemy passed. 'The Chinaman did not stop to kill you,' said Farrell. 'He ran on, you had to fight through him again!' He heard moaning nearby and spotted Sergeant 'Hooky' Walker, weaponless and wounded in the head. Farrell helped him to his feet and the two moved on. An engineers' truck came by, picked them up and carried them through.[55] Quarter Master Sergeant Tommy Sturgeon was driving a four-ton truck. The battalion, he thought, was 'caught with its trousers down': he could see men going down around him, some hit, some lying prone, returning fire. Bullets clattered into his truck's bodywork. Driving without headlights, he tried to ignore the shooting – he had fought in Italy but was shocked by the volume of automatic fire – and concentrate on the icy track ahead. He, too, made it out.[56]

When the firing erupted, men had leapt from Cooperforce's fuel and ammunition trucks. Dowling, leading the Hussar echelon through the valley with the infantry, insisted his men remount and keep driving through the bursting mortars and streaking tracers. Two Bedfords broke down; the Hussars hurriedly sabotaged them by tearing out sump plugs while running the engines. Dowling, fearful about the tanks at the rear of the column, got onto the radio and contacted the Hussar leader. Astley-Cooper was terse: 'It's bloody rough!' Then static. Minutes later, Dowling heard foreign voices over the frequency.

Among the tanks, the Chinese were using pole charges – explosives on sticks that were rammed into suspensions – to disable tracks. Others reached up and physically dragged Riflemen from trucks.[57] Cooperforce's leading tank, commanded by Lieutenant Alexander, slid and clattered along the frozen stream bed, negotiating burning vehicles and replying to Chinese mortars and machine-guns with its 75mm main armament and machine-gun. Enemy soldiers were firing piles of straw to further silhouette the scene. The Cromwell made it to Pulmiji-ri, the hamlet at the southern mouth of the valley; it was on fire but the tank burst through before lurching off the track and shuddering to a halt. As Alexander put his head out of the hatch again to see what was happening, another mortar landed on his turret ring. A crewman dragged him inside but he was already dead. The survivors hurled open hatches, baled out and ran into the dark hills. Behind Alexander, Astley-Cooper's tank lost a track; his men abandoned the vehicle. To their front were some twenty enemy infantry. The tank crew separated, Astley-Cooper and his sergeant, Farmer, running down a ditch. They were never seen again.[58] Gunner Christopher, an artilleryman in Cooperforce, was called out of his tank by an officer. As he clambered down, the officer was mortally wounded by close-range fire, collapsing to his knees, murmuring, 'Oh dear, oh dear.' Chinese infantry were only twenty metres away. An automatic burst ripped into Christopher's thigh. The tank squeaked off. Christopher returned fire, emptying his pistol, then grabbed hold of the wire ration boxes on the hull of a passing Cromwell. He was dragged along until a grenade went off, peppering his face and legs. He rolled into a ditch. Chinese passed, shouting 'Don't shoot, we're friends' and other English phrases. He heard two nearby Riflemen surrender, then gunfire, then Chinese laughter. More enemy passed. He crawled past abandoned scout cars and carriers surrounded by dead Riflemen. He found a Bren, but no ammunition. He heard Chinese starting up an abandoned tank, then was wounded yet again, by burp gun fire in the arm. He played dead.[59]

Burning vehicles blocked the way past Pulmiji-ri. Captain James Majury's carrier was halted outside the village by a brewed-up truck. He and his mortar men dismounted and fought off close-range attacks until they ran out of ammunition. Then they were captured.* The Chinese had taken the village at the bottom of the valley.

Over the command net grim staff officers were listening in on the struggle. Sometime after 01:00 on 4 January Brigadier Brodie arrived at the CP of Colonel John Michaelis, a tough ex-paratrooper who had fought in the Battle of the Bulge and who now commanded the US 27th Infantry Regiment, 'The Wolfhounds', in blocking positions behind 29th Brigade. Michaelis volunteered two of his battalions to counter-attack north and cut the Rifles out. But Brodie, aware that extra men in the confined area would increase confusion and give the Chinese more targets, turned down the offer. The surviving Rifles, he said, 'would have to knock it out for themselves'.[60]

The valley was now a witch's cauldron. In such confused fighting 'blue-on-blues' were inevitable. At the rear of the column, McCord's standing patrol returned to the leaguer held by the rearguard when a tank fired into a group of his men. With the air full of flying metal, he crawled urgently over to the Cromwell and shouted into the telephone on the back. Kaput. Clambering onto the hull, he hammered on the turret, bawling – 'in some pretty soldierly language' – for the gunner to cease fire. The tank complied, but hideous carnage had already been inflicted. As he helped load butchered bodies onto carriers for the per-ilous run through the valley, an officer, demanding that 'nothing be left behind', told McCord, 'You've forgotten something.' McCord looked down. The body he was loading was headless.[†]

The rearguard set off, their carriers and trucks skidding and sliding along the iced track. The nightmare continued to be illuminated by the

* Reports of Majury's capture are conflicting. Charley heard that Majury, a huge man, laid out a number of Chinese with his rifle butt before being taken; McCord, who spoke to Majury about the incident years later, said that he ordered his men to lay down their weapons when their ammunition ran out. The loss of this impressive officer held a silver lining for one of his comrades: with Majury removed from the battalion payroll, Charley, who had volunteered for Korea and taken a pay cut due to the lack of a vacancy for a man of his rank at the time, was bumped up from a lieutenant's salary to a captain's. Majury would prove to be a tower of strength in the POW camps.

† In recent years, 'friendly fire' incidents have surfaced as major issues in the British press. In the chaos of battle such situations are not rare. I found it telling that none of my interviewees who witnessed – or indeed were victims of – such events in Korea bore any animosity towards the perpetrators. Korean War-era soldiers were accustomed to more intense combat experiences and a higher rate of casualties than are current-generation reporters.

flares raining down from the aircraft droning in the darkness above. The going was too slow. The Riflemen abandoned vehicles to break through on foot. Their escape turned into individual games of Cowboys and Indians: small groups fighting muzzle-to-muzzle in the ghostly white light. McCord was pitched into a firefight when he and Lieutenant Arthur McCallum, machine-gun platoon commander, found themselves on one side of a burning truck, Chinese soldiers on the other. McCallum was wounded by grenade shrapnel; McCord, squeezed into cover behind a tire, was unscathed. Like many Ulstermen that night, McCord found the Chinese, at close range, strangely slow-moving, as if drugged. Time and again, Riflemen got the drop on their enemies, shooting first.*

Even so, the favoured Chinese tactic – attack from the flank, while inserting a blocking position in the rear – had been employed. Further down the valley, under a railway bridge, the Chinese had sited an ambush, a machine-gun behind a boulder. Like a plug in a drain, this obstacle blocked all forward movement by the Rifles. A backlog of desperate men built up. Speed and violence were the only solutions. McCord and Sergeant Campbell, arriving at the hold-up, conferred briefly, and moved forward. The two volleyed hand grenades; as they exploded, the tall McCord, who had 'acquired a light machine-gun from somewhere', ran forward, into and through the enemy position, firing the Bren from the hip. The machine-gun was knocked out.† The action took only seconds, but it cleared the escape route for those behind, and the Riflemen moved on again. Another obstacle loomed. Men bunched together in front of Pulmiji-ri. Fighting was raging among the cottages, many of which were afire, their thatch blazing. Tracers were crisscrossing and ricocheting near the group, so McCord, who thought he might have to return up-valley to extricate stragglers, took advantage of the momentary halt to light his pipe. His seemingly innocent act – 'there were bullets flying around, there were tracers, so I thought my pipe . . .' – triggered his second rocket of the battle. Support Company commander Major John Shaw rushed up, roaring at McCord to extinguish the pipe.

Much of the combat in the valley had been leaderless. Shaw, the no-nonsense professional who had fought alongside Yugoslav partisans in World War II, now got a grip. Taking command of the scratch group –

---

* No evidence has ever surfaced that the Chinese were drugged, but every interviewee from the Rifles who fought in the battle mentioned the phenomenon. Perhaps they were suffering from battle shock – they had been under heavy air and artillery bombardment during their approach. Perhaps they were suffering from malnutrition or typhus (both of which did infect the CPVA), or possibly they had taken medications or alcohol from overrun UN dumps – but this is speculation. The matter will be discussed further in the final chapter.
† McCord won a Military Cross for the action, Campbell a Military Medal.

some 60–80 men – and Cooperforce's last tank, he led an assault through Pulmiji-ri.* Covered by fire from the Cromwell, and firing as they went, the charging men broke into the blazing village, stormed through the Chinese – who were still engaged in close combat with men led by acting CO Tony Blake – and into the paddies beyond. There was no pause for breath. Shaw drew on his special forces experience: instead of heading through the pass to the MSR, where he expected another ambush, he led the group up into the hills.[61]

To the south, there were chaotic scenes at the crossing points over the Han. Tense engineers were waiting to blow the bridges, but Dowling, who had got through the valley with his Hussar echelon, insisted they wait for the tanks. An American MP cleared a path for Dowling's column, kicking columns of refugees aside as he sped past in a jeep. Dowling parked his vehicles in line to refuel the tanks. None would arrive. Cooperforce had been annihilated.

Shaw's breakout group, carrying their wounded with them, trekked through the freezing hills. In the distance, they could see the glow of burning Seoul; the dying city made a useful directional marker. Dawn was breaking. Almost as soon as the group reached the MSR a machine-gun barked. Guessing it was American, Sergeant Campbell went forward and persuaded the gunners to cease fire. His guess was spot on. It was a small American rearguard, who 'very excitedly' waved the Rifles onto two trucks. The trucks drove the men down through Seoul, across the Han bridges, dumped them on the south bank, then turned and raced back to retrieve the Americans. The Rifles watched dully from the south bank as 55 Field Squadron prepared to blow the bridges.[62]

Earlier, Engineer Major Tony Younger had driven through the silent, devastated streets of Seoul. His driver had been unnerved by the eerie city, emptied of inhabitants. Now, on the Han's south bank, the experienced engineer noticed the strain of combat on Shaw's face as they conferred briefly. It was daylight. Air strikes – strafing and napalm bombing – were pummelling Seoul and the north bank. With all units south of the river, Younger set about the destruction of the bridges. The last to be blown was the giant iron railway bridge, set on concrete pylons. Three thousand pounds of high explosive was packed around it, but crawling along the tracks just south of the bridge was the last train from Seoul, its carriages and roofs crawling with refugees. The locomotive's fire was low; it could not accelerate. Younger fretted that flying debris

---

* The regimental history calls this a 'bayonet charge', but McCord, who took part in it, does not recall any Rifleman with a bayonet fixed. Regardless, it was certainly a desperate attack which plunged right through the Chinese in the village.

from the explosion would kill or injure the passengers, but his entreaties to the Koreans to abandon the train during the demolition were ignored: nobody dared give up their place. There was no choice but to blow the bridge with the train nearby. The plunger was pressed. A great boom reverberated. The bridge was obscured as a massive cloud of brick dust spread up and over the frozen river; chunks of masonry rained down onto the river banks. The smoke cleared. The bridge was no more. There was silence from the hundreds of refugees packed into and onto the train – all of whom, remarkably, had escaped injury. Suddenly, people streamed from the carriages and charged towards Younger, who feared they were about to lynch him for destroying a national treasure. Instead, the crowd wanted to shake his hand: The British major had severed the Chinese pursuit route.[63]

The battle was over, but for a handful of survivors trapped north of the river, the ordeal continued. Christopher, the Cooperforce gunner who had been thrice wounded, played dead among the wreckage of vehicles while enemy soldiers searched him and other corpses for valuables. They found none, so kicked him in the ribs and moved on. After they departed, Christopher hobbled into the hills, leaning on a stick. He was joined by several wounded Riflemen; the Chinese battlefield clearance had been inefficient. An American observation aircraft spotted them and dropped directional instructions. Christopher and a companion staggered for about half a mile, then an American helicopter, defying sniper fire, landed and picked up the two bloodied soldiers. They indicated to the pilot where a party of three more wounded lay. A second rescue helicopter buzzed in, set down, and lifted them to safety.[64] The Han's north bank was now enemy territory. For the second time in the war, Seoul had fallen to the communists.

Reunited with their battalion, Shaw's men were greeted like ghosts: They had been assumed lost in the valley.* The Rifles' baptism of fire in Korea had been searing. A roll call found 208 missing, though losses were revised downward to 157 as stragglers drifted in and wounded were tracked down in hospitals.[65] For a battalion of some 750 men, this was a grave toll. Among those killed was acting CO Tony Blake.† 'Cooperforce' was wiped out. All its tanks were lost, as were twenty-three Hussars and twenty Royal Artillerymen.[66]

---

* John Shaw's leadership and tactical skills in the breakout won him a Distinguished Service Order.
† An account on the Blake family website alleges that the major was killed not in battle but after capture: a Chinese officer asked who had commanded the battalion. When Blake and his batman stepped forward, both were executed. However, other Rifles officers, including Robin Bruford-Davies (who was also captured at Happy Valley) and Mervyn McCord, in correspondence with the author on this subject, questioned the veracity of the account. Interested readers can consult the website and draw their own conclusions (http://www.turtlebunbury.com/history/history_family/hist_family_blake.html).

War correspondents arrived to talk to the survivors. Second Lieutenant Huston Shaw-Steward was asked what it had been like. Shaw-Steward – 'a man of great *bon mots*' – thought for a moment before passing judgement: 'It was very noisy,' he said, 'and there were a lot of unpleasant peasants.'[67] In describing the Chinese, the officer had coined one of the immortal phrases of the Korean War.

Ridgway had learned of the Rifles' plight at around 06:30 on the 4th. He met with I Corps Commander General Frank Milburn and 25th Division commander General William Kean – under whose command Michaelis's 27th Infantry fell – to demand that everything be done to break the trapped men out. He added that it would be a disgrace if US forces left British behind. (Ridgway was perhaps unaware that the 27th Infantry had held its rearguard position, through which the last survivors of Shaw's group passed, until 05:00; the last group of survivors cleared the valley at around 03:50.) At 07:00, a second conference was held, but no plan for a rescue operation was proposed. By this time, it was too late.[68] The fact that Ridgway himself took a personal interest in the fate of the Rifles – and that such high-ranking officers spent precious time conferring as UN forces were pulling below the Han in a touch-and-go retreat – illustrates the gravity of 29th Brigade's predicament. But with the decision to abandon the capital already made, the question must be asked: was the battle on the 3rd necessary? Certainly the Fusiliers had to fight to extricate themselves, but, if ever there was time for a 'bug-out', this was it. Yet the Rifles, having received their movement orders last, carried them out faithfully.

The nightmarish winter battle fought to hold off the Chinese as UN forces abandoned Seoul has acquired various names; the Fusiliers' regimental history dubs it the battle of Kan-dong, after the village where their HQ was located, while the Rifles called it the battle of Chaegunhyan. But the name by which it has become known to posterity is a product not of Korean geography, but of British irony: 'Happy Valley'.*

\* \* \*

* The Royal Ulster Rifles erected a monument to their lost in the valley in summer 1951. With urban development taking place on the battlefield as Seoul expanded in 1962, the monument was moved to the Rifles' regimental depot in Ballymena, Northern Ireland. In early 2008, with the depot closing, the monument was allocated space outside Belfast City Hall. One of the heroes of the battle – retired Brigadier Mervyn McCord, then the subaltern who took out the machine-gun position blocking the Rifles' escape route – headed efforts to fund the removal, which was enabled with donations from Samsung, the Korean Embassy in London, and veterans. The first service at the new location took place on 4 January 2009; among the attenders were Joe Farrell and Robin Charley. The monument, of Korean granite, bears a quote from Isaiah: 'The people that walked in darkness have seen the brightest light.' Since it was USAF flares that gave away the Rifles' position to the Chinese on that moonless night, the quote has a grim poignancy beyond spiritual metaphor.

Frustration and anger affected the Rifles' morale in the days following the battle. The Hussars' Centurion crews first heard about the disaster when Sir Guy Lowther returned from the front, where he had learnt that Cooperforce had been 'wiped off the map'. The usually cheerful CO was uncharacteristically quiet for days.[69] But, for most soldiers of 29th Brigade, their own misfortunes would prove less emotionally scarring than the tragedy that unfolded before them. Their best efforts had been insufficient to halt the communist drive; now, as the long winter retreat continued, they came face-to-face with the resultant misery. Even for battle-tested soldiers, having to be impotent spectators of the plight of the Korean refugees was wrenching, and would form many veterans' most traumatic memories of the war.

After the blowing of the Seoul bridges Ridgway rescinded Walker's scorched-earth policy, under which all livestock and food was to be burnt, all houses destroyed. There would be no more destruction for destruction's sake. But Walker's policy had already swelled the desperate ranks of refugees – all freezing, many sick and starving – escaping the North. The sub-zero retreat was bad enough for the troops, who at least had transport, rations and medical support. Most refugees had nothing. Perhaps a million Koreans – overwhelmingly women and children – fled their homes and trudged down the frozen tracks of the devastated peninsula in that Arctic winter.[70]

Lee Chun-hee, the ten-year-old who had been woken by artillery as the North Koreans descended upon Seoul in June, had been fortunate. When news of the disaster in the north filtered through to the capital, she had been sent by her parents to stand near the city gate and watch the columns of refugees crowding through for members of her extended family in the north. 'I saw a group of what looked like forty beggars. One woman asked me if I knew a little girl named Chun-hee who lived near here. I said, "Yes! It's me!" She said, "I'm your auntie!"' The family reunion was joyful, but tempered by an awareness of the danger closing in. 'Father had thought it would be a short war,' Chun-hee said. 'Then the UN and the Chinese came in, he thought this could be World War III, that Seoul could become permanently communist.' They made the decision to flee while they could. For rations on the journey, Chun-hee's father cooked grains over a fire in the courtyard of his house, then bought train tickets for Pusan for the whole family. In bullet-scarred Seoul Station, they took their seats inside the train. Outside, hundreds of refugees clambered onto the carriage roofs, where wind chill exacerbated already sub-zero temperatures. The trip through the ravaged countryside took a week. At stops, vast crowds milled around the train, looking for relatives and selling rice balls, pickled eggs and tea, reminding

Chun-hee of a fair. When she arrived in Pusan, she wondered, 'How can so many people live here?'[71]

Those on trains were the lucky ones. The majority of refugees were on foot. Dressed in traditional white garb with black coats and felt boots (or just straw slippers) on their feet, carrying possessions and children on their heads or backs, they stumbled through the snowy landscape in columns, family groups, or sometimes, alone. Some soldiers were impressed at the Koreans' stoicism. One refugee passing a troop from 170 Mortar Battery was about to deliver a child. The soldiers lifted her onto their medical truck. 'She gave birth squatting down, the medics cleaned the baby off, and she set off down the road, with the baby on her back!' said Bob Nicholls. 'I saw it happen! A Western woman would not have survived.'

But the overall impression was not so much of admiration as of horror. Fusilier Preston Little was moved by the pathetic grin of a little boy who had had his hand blown off when Little offered him a bar of chocolate, but he was shocked at the sight of hundreds of bodies, 'frozen stiff in every conceivable posture' on the ice under a blown-up Seoul bridge.[72]

High Command's reaction to the refugee problem was one of harsh necessity. In a letter dated 26 July 1950, US Ambassador to Korea John Muccio had given instructions on the issue. 'The refugee problem has developed aspects of a serious and even critical military nature, aside from the welfare aspects. The enemy has used refugees to his advantage . . . forcing them south and so clogging the roads as to interfere with military movements; by using them as a channel for infiltration of agents; and most dangerous of all by disguising their own troops as refugees, who after passing through our lines proceed, after dark, to produce hidden weapons, and then attack our units from the rear.' If refugees refused to halt, Muccio wrote, warning shots would be fired, but 'if they persist in advancing, they will be shot'. All civilian movement would end at sunset; Korean police would establish checkpoints before nightfall.[73]

Some men were permanently affected by the implementation of this policy. The Fusiliers' Y Company were ordered to keep refugees outside their perimeter as night fell. The men could hear crying and moaning as the temperature dropped and the Koreans began freezing to death. One Fusilier, a former prisoner of the Japanese, broke in the night, going into a raving fit. 'It was getting to us all, but he never recovered – he remained in a mental institution for the rest of his life,' said Lieutenant Phillips. 'I was more affected by the refugees than by anything else.' Troops were ordered to prevent refugees crossing the river. 'There was one case where refugees were crossing the frozen Han, and the Americans went in and said "Stop!"' remembered John Preston-Bell.* 'Adults and children were separated. Who took care of those children?' Fusilier David Strachan and his platoon were ordered to halt refugees lining up to cross a bridge. 'There was this little lad with half his leg shot off, he had no parents, he was stood there crying,' he recalled. 'We had to be tough. That was the worst thing I saw over there.'†

Some refugee columns were fired upon by soldiers or aircraft. Major Tony Younger was reconnoitring a road in a scout car when, passing through a derelict hamlet, he and his driver were struck dumb by the harrowing spectacle ahead. In and out of ditches along the road, and sprawled across it, were hundreds of bodies – almost all women. The scout car slowed to a crawl to avoid the corpses. Younger tried to blank out the carnage in the foreground and focus on distant hills, but did not entirely succeed: his eye was caught by a young mother with a dead baby on her exposed breasts. Twice, he had to climb out of the vehicle to shift a stiff body so that the vehicle could continue. Once through the village, they accelerated away. During World War II Younger had seen refugees strafed by Stukas, but only at Belsen had he seen an atrocity comparable to what he witnessed on that two-mile drive.[74]

While Koreans have powerful family bonds, they also have a strongly pragmatic streak. Lineage continues through the male line, and among sons the first-born is the most prized. For this reason many families in the retreat abandoned their oldest, youngest, weakest and female members to give strong males the best chance. The contrast between this attitude and the Anglo-Saxon 'women and children first' philosophy led many soldiers to an ever-greater detestation of the barren land. Gloster David Green saw the doll-like corpse of a tiny baby abandoned under river ice after refugees had passed. Green's father was deeply religious, but Green himself wondered how God could permit such tragedies.[75]

Abandoned children – silent or crying uncontrollably, often with even smaller children strapped to their backs – were everywhere. Hovering on the fringes of UN units and bases in Korea were tens of thousands of starving orphans. Some worked, doing odd jobs such as cleaning and laundry; others begged, stole or scavenged among the dumps. In November the mortar men of 170 Battery had been given an American Thanksgiving dinner. The cooks prepared the turkey in an abandoned building, then doled it into the men's mess tins. There was no room

---

* Preston-Bell was haunted for decades by the thought of the children separated from their parents on the river ice, before achieving an emotional closure during a veterans' visit to Korea in 2001.

† Fifty-seven years after the event, Strachan still choked on the memory.

inside, so the artillerymen squatted outside to eat. From nowhere, a group of thirty or so children appeared, and stood silently watching the eating men: 'You can't eat in front of them, they watch every bite you take,' said Nicholls. The men shared their meal with the children.[76] Some orphans were fortunate enough to be temporarily adopted by units and sub-units, who clothed them in miniature uniforms. One freezing day, a tiny boy 'two feet high' walked down the road towards the Glosters' B Company, crying his eyes out. 'We picked him up and changed his clothes,' said Gloster Frank Carter. 'We made him an army suit and a beret.' The little soldier, Kim, proved honest and hardworking.*[77] Little remembered watching the Fusiliers' Z Company leaving a position in file, 'with their complement of waifs, in descending heights, in their too-large articles of uniform which they still wore with pride, and at the rear end, the little piglet on a leash led by the smallest member'.[78]

After Seoul fell Gloster Major Digby Grist was relieved to see that his men had managed to smuggle 'Washy-Washy' with them. The girl, with other orphans, was handed to the Red Cross, now getting organised in the south.[79] Grist was less happy when he sent a patrol to the frozen Han. They encountered refugees, too weak or frozen to climb the steep river banks. Forming a human chain, the Glosters heaved them up. One said, 'Thank you very much,' and stumbled on. Grist, astounded to hear fluent English, ran after her. The woman was an English professor. When Grist asked her how his men could help the refugees, she replied wearily, 'Just go away and leave us what's left of our country.'[80] The conversation was a stark reminder of something that escaped many soldiers who had come to Korea believing they were defending the South against communist invasion: for the majority of civilians, the war, regardless of its rights and wrongs, had become a holocaust that was consuming their land, their families and their communities.

Amid the breakdown of society, thousands of women were separated from their menfolk. In desperate straits, many were forced into selling the only asset they possessed: their bodies. They flocked to the UN base areas and camp towns. 'There were swarms of these women after the guys,' said Nicholls. 'We had a church service, and the padre had an umbrella, and he said, "I wouldn't put this umbrella where you lot put

* Thirty years later Carter was staying at the 5-star Lotte Hotel in downtown Seoul on a veterans' visit. A bellboy came up with a message: a Korean outside had asked to see any members of the Glosters' B Company, but felt himself too humble to enter the hotel. Carter told the bellboy to show him up. Immediately he opened the door, Carter recognised the man's face: it was Kim, the little orphan. He had married, had two children and was planning to emigrate to the United States. He wanted a reference to state that he had served honourably in the British Army – as he had. Carter put him in contact with the Gloster Regimental Association to obtain the appropriate documentation.

your dicks!" We all laughed, but he got his point over.'[81] Dire warnings were issued against amorous activities with local businesswomen: officers warned their men, 'Blobby knob stops demob.'[82] *

On occasion, inhabitants were forced from homes. In January Fusilier Lieutenant Tony Perrins requisitioned a house occupied by an old woman. Her relatives argued that she should be left alone. Perrins, too busy to deal with the protest himself, ordered a Fusilier to 'sort it out'. When he returned to the cottage he found his bedding made up in the old woman's room and thought nothing more of it. The following day, he watched a funeral procession winding through the village: the woman had died, and he realised that he had played a part in her death. He would be haunted by the memory for fifty years.[83]

That cruel winter remains seared into Korean memory. Some tales are warm, such as that of the villagers who fled south but left supplies of rice for the refugees following behind. But most are tragic. One story every Korean knows is that of the heavily pregnant woman struggling south, abandoned and alone. In labour, she retreated under a bridge to give birth to a baby boy. The weather was freezing, so the young woman removed some of her own clothes to warm the baby. Snow continued to fall. During the night, the new mother froze to death. The baby was discovered alive and taken to a foreign aid organisation. Some years later, the child asked the missionary who ran his orphanage about his mother. Gently, the man told him of her sacrifice. It was a winter evening. The boy ran to the bridge under which he had been born and laid his own clothes on the freezing ground. 'Mother,' he cried. 'Are you warm now?'

\* \* \*

During the retreat from Pyongyang, the Centurion of Lieutenant Randle Cooke of the Hussars had run over an ROK soldier: the 50-ton monster crushed the man's leg. Cooke immediately halted the tank and jumped down to help him. Cooke was thrust aside by an ROK officer, who drew Cooke's revolver and shot the man dead.[84] It was a harsh lesson in a harsh land: life was cheap.

But that incident was, at least, a mercy killing in the midst of a retreat. The British fighting men would be affected far worse by massacres of

---

\* Soldier-speak for 'Blistered penis will delay demobilisation.' The solution used to treat venereal diseases – a bane of armies since time immemorial – caused blistering of the affected organ. Nevertheless, painful treatment and stern warnings did not prevent soldiers visiting brothels, either in Korea or while on leave in Japan. According to Royal Northumberland Fusiliers medical records (in Perrins, p. 384), over a 69-day period in Korea, 60 of the battalion's 876 men were infected with Cupid's Arrows. In singling out the Fusiliers, I am not insinuating that the Fighting Fifth were any more amorous than the Rifles or the Glosters, but theirs are the only data on this issue I have tracked down.

civilians. They had come to defend the South from communism, and atrocities by the North Koreans had been well documented. American prisoners taken in the fighting in the early months were found murdered, shot with hands tied behind their backs. After Taejeon was retaken after the UN advance from the Pusan Perimeter, some 5,000 bodies were discovered.* And when Seoul was recaptured after the Inchon landing, US Marines came across a trench filled with hundreds of dead men, women and children. From June to September, an estimated 26,000 civilians were killed by the North Koreans.[85] Such incidents might have reassured British troops that they were fighting on the side of the righteous. However, the draconian policies of the Japanese colonial regime that governed Korea for thirty-five years (thirty years longer than the Nazis dominated continental Europe) had brutalised not only those who struggled against that regime, such as the communists, but, equally, those in the police force, who worked for it. Many police in the south remained in their posts after Japan's fall. Furthermore, some Northerners who escaped from Kim Il-sung's republic formed fanatically anti-communist paramilitary units, and such outfits carried out atrocities that matched those of the communists for cruelty. It would be a shock for British troops to find that the South was far from democratic, and that some of their allies were as pitiless as their enemies.

At 07:40 on 15 December men of the Fusiliers' B Echelon had heard shots from a low hill behind their position north of Seoul. When NCOs investigated they found ROK police digging a long, shallow trench. Nearby, a line of prisoners, bound together by wire, were kneeling beside a truck. The thirty-four prisoners were then marched to the trench and forced to kneel in front of it; among them were two women and four children (one boy appeared to be no more than eight).[86] Before the eyes of British and American soldiers, the Korean troops, wearing dust masks over their faces, walked behind the prisoners. There were cries of 'omoni, aboji',† then carbines cracked. The prisoners were shot in the back of the head. Those who twitched were shot again.[87] The British soldiers were told that the men were deserters, and the women had harboured them. When he heard about it, a furious Lieutenant-Colonel Kingsley Foster reported it to the UN Organisation; Brigadier Brodie protested to 8th Army Headquarters. More direct action was taken. On 17 December, on Brodie's orders, men from Major John Winn's Z Company were dispatched, fully armed, to the execution site. 'It was horrible,' said Fusilier

* At the time, the atrocity was blamed on the communists, but recent research indicates one mass killing was executed by retreating South Korean security forces; a second was carried out by retreating North Koreans when the tide of the war turned. The Seoul-based Truth and Reconciliation Commission believes that as many as 100,000 southern civilians were killed by ROK forces, mostly in the early stages of the war.
† Mother, father.

David Strachan. 'They were shooting and leaving them there.' The officer commanding the detachment told the ROK police chief 'in no uncertain terms' to halt proceedings immediately. The man responded by pointing his weapon at the British officer. There was a tense standoff. The Fusiliers began fixing bayonets; the policemen backed down. 'That was one of my greatest achievements over there,' said Strachan, who took part. The Fusiliers ringed the spot with infantry to halt subsequent executions.[88]

Other officers took their own initiatives. Following the retreat from Seoul, Glosters posted near a checkpoint in the Pyongtaek area watched as ROK military police, searching the crowd of refugees waiting to cross the bridge for weapons, relieved helpless civilians of their valuables. A British officer, livid, ran over and ordered the MPs to stop it. They laughed at him. The officer stormed off. Minutes later a 25-pounder shell whooshed low over the heads of the MP detachment. They had not noticed the officer's shoulder flashes: he was a gunner. The stealing ceased.[89] In the same area, the Glosters were running anti-guerrilla night patrols. One patrol, led by Lieutenant Mike Harvey, came across a lost, white-haired grandmother in her eighties, alone in the snow. The patrol gave her a hot drink and dropped her off at a nearby police post, expecting the constables to send the woman to the appropriate care organisation. Just after they left, they were shocked to hear a burst of submachine-gun fire. Dashing back, they found a policeman had the woman tied to a table, and was about to fire another burst next to her head. The enraged soldiers disarmed the man, hurled his weapon into a cesspit, and took the woman to the brigade collecting point.[90]

* The incident sparked a diplomatic storm. A telegram dated 19 December sent from the US Embassy, Tokyo, to the US Secretary of State noted: 'These executions reported having a demoralizing effect on British forces, in whose areas many of killings have taken place.. British troops reported on one occasion to have disarmed firing squad before execution could take place . . . It is feared these excesses may serve to cast discredit on entire UN effort.' A telegram from the State Department back to the Embassy on the 19th quotes recent press accounts of the incident. 'British 29th Brigade Commander tells his officers he is not prepared to tolerate further executions this area . . . . US military reluctant interfere since executions imposed by Korean courts . . . Americans and British horrified see truckloads old men, women, several youths, children lined before open graves and shot down . . . British infantry company took positions around execution hill today to prevent more South Koreans shooting more their prisoners . . . President Rhee defended executions saying "We have to take measures . . . If you resent that, I don't know why" . . . Rhee said he would review all death sentences passed by military or civilians authorities.' Following a report from the Korean Minister of Justice that the executions had been undertaken with all due procedures, another telegram, to the Secretary of State from the US Embassy, Seoul, on 21 December, noted that British troops had halted yet more executions. 'Commanding officer 29th Brigade has issued order prohibiting further executions this area, British troops will stop them and bring responsible person before them by force if necessary to be dealt with. He informed British Charge [d'Affaires] "I am less interested in the type of justice than in the effect on my troops."' The telegram stated that the South Korean lieutenant in charge of the latest execution faced court martial. The author is grateful to Dr Steven Kim of the Truth and Reconciliation Commission, Seoul, for bringing these telegrams to his attention.

Such incidents affected morale. 'They would say, with an old soldier's cynicism, "Why are we saving Rhee Syngman's life? Or are we bailing out the Yanks?"' recalled Ted Paul. For the young Hussar officer, these were difficult questions to answer.

* * *

Despite their success in seizing Pyongyang and Seoul, their native toughness and their formidable reputation, the Chinese, with minimal equipment and lengthening supply lines, were suffering from the weather even more than the UN soldiers. Entire units were afflicted with frostbite. Typhus broke out. Supplies were short. Lacking the means to pursue UN forces further, their offensive fizzled. By February, gaps of as much as twenty miles separated UN and communist forces. 29th Brigade, having acted as rearguard in the retreats from both Pyongyang and Seoul, and following the severe fighting in 'Happy Valley', now entered a period of low-intensity operations.

In the absence of intelligence about enemy intentions, Fusilier Lieutenant Malcolm Cubiss was ordered to carry out a prisoner snatch in a wood where enemy were believed to be hidden. Moving warily, his patrol entered the trees. In the gloom, Cubiss spotted a squat enemy soldier standing in front of him. 'He's the chap for me!' the officer thought. 'I'll have him!' He sprinted ahead of his men and tackled his quarry around the waist, wrestling-style. As Cubiss dived in, the Chinese climbed out of the trench he had been standing in up to his knees – he was a giant – threw the little British officer off with one hand and shot him in the chest. A Fusilier dashed up and killed the Chinese, and Cubiss was amazed to find himself unharmed: a liquor flask in his chest pocket had stopped the bullet. Some of Cubiss's comrades had better luck. Several Fusilier officers had brought their shotguns to Korea and, when not operational, amused themselves by shooting in the countryside. In February Major Charles Mitchell and some fellow officers, having first sent out a covering patrol, had a pheasant drive in front of their positions. It produced sixteen pheasants and two prisoners.[91]

The Fusiliers' shoot, however, did not quite match the (reputed*) feat of the Hussars' CO, Sir Guy Lowther. Spotting enemy from his tank turret, he

---

* John Preston-Bell, who recounted the story, made clear to me that, while he had heard the tale, he had not witnessed it, and so could not vouch for its accuracy. Brigadier Dick Webster, a subsequent commander of the 8th Hussars, who knew Lowther well, thought it nonsensical, on the grounds that 'only a bloody fool, untrained in normal sporting gun disciplines – and Lowther was neither of these – would keep his shotgun loaded inside a tank turret'. While the story has the whiff of legend, it is worth noting that the Hussars lacked hatch-mounted machine-guns, and Chinese often did pop up at close range. The anecdote is reproduced here to exemplify the kind of war story that circulates around charismatic individuals in combat units. The reader must make up his own mind about its veracity.

produced his twelve-bore, fired and bagged two Chinese soldiers: one with the right barrel, one with the left. The Hussar CO was a social as well as a sporting man and impressed a group of American officers at dinner in his makeshift mess when he told them that the candlesticks on the table had been captured by the Hussars at Balaclava. The Americans looked on in wonder at these souvenirs of that legendary charge. In fact, as Lieutenant Ted Paul knew (but did not say), the candlesticks had been looted from a ruined house.[92] Lowther's hereditary baronetcy also made waves. Lieutenant David Boyall was amused to see an American lieutenant-general standing to attention and addressing Lowther, a lieutenant-colonel, as 'Sir'.[93]

On occasion, even the brigade's aggressive brigadier would show his humorous side. Flying over the Rifles in a helicopter, he reprimanded a company commander, from the sky, for being improperly dressed: the man was wearing a sheepskin coat. When Brodie landed, he was wearing an identical coat.[94]

Operations continued. For five weeks C Squadron was the only Hussar squadron in the country. In the strategic indecision following the loss of North Korea and the death of General Walton Walker – and due to official sensitivities about the top-secret Centurions being captured – A and B Squadrons had been shipped to Japan, leaving C Squadron the only regimental unit on operations.[95] Subsequent official policy to safeguard the precious Centurions would be to have only one squadron north of the Han at any time.

The experience of Major Henry Huth, the commander of the Hussars' C Squadron, became manifest for Boyall when the Australian lieutenant was leading his Centurions on a probe to discover Chinese dispositions. He came to a narrow cutting between hills. All seemed peaceful. Suddenly, Huth's voice crackled over the radio, telling him to turn round. Boyall suggested continuing through the cutting before returning. Huth sharply ordered him back. Boyall returned, to find the major sitting atop a scout car with a Bren gun across his knees, looking worried – 'a most unusual posture and expression for him'. It later transpired that there were, in fact, several hundred enemy troops dug into the hillside, and a brigade-sized force was subsequently required to clear the cutting Boyall had been about to enter so blithely. Huth's battle sense had almost certainly saved the lives of Boyall and his troop.[96] The squadron's most junior officer, Cornet John Preston-Bell was finding that the reservists in his tank, veterans of World War II, were teaching him his job. Notable among them was his driver, Trooper Teale, who was proving to have a sharp eye for mines. 'I owed my life to him on several occasions. I'd say things like "Driver! Left!" and he'd say, "I'm not sure that's a very good idea . . . Sir!" So I'd say, "OK . . . Driver! Right!"'

The Centurions were proving their worth. In first gear they moved at slower than walking pace and, with their steel tracks, could crawl up the hills.* This made them one of the few pieces of equipment where the British had an edge over the Americans. US tanks were faster, but they had automatic gearboxes, so could not climb; 'They would charge at the hills at top speed but, with the rubber pads on their tracks, would downshift automatically and come down sideways or backwards!' according to Boyall. The Hussars were also learning to negotiate paddy fields: to avoid bogging down it was vital not to drive in the track-marks of the vehicle in front.[97]

On 11 February, the Hussars gained some revenge for the loss of Cooperforce. Captain George Strachan was sitting in his Centurion, 'Caughoo', covering a road junction at Yongdungpo, a township on the south of the Han, when a tank was spotted sticking its nose out of a tunnel north of the river. This is what the Hussars had been hoping for: an armoured duel! Firing from 3,000 yards, Strachan knocked out the enemy vehicle with his second shot. History was made: it was the first time a Centurion had destroyed another tank, and at an unheard-of range. The victim, however, was no T-34. It proved to be a British Cromwell, captured by the Chinese at Happy Valley.[98]

The infantry were learning the tricks of active service. 'We never wore our badges of rank,' said Gloster Second Lieutenant Guy Temple. 'And tin pots were unfashionable: all they do is give you a headache.' Even on operations, the men preferred American winter caps, berets or the knitted cap comforters popularised by the World War II commandos.[99] The men now had a realistic appreciation of their weapons' capabilities. 'Most people carried two, but I always carried at least eight grenades,' said Rifles Lance-Corporal Farrell. 'I found 'em more effective in action.' The heavy, high-velocity .303 round fired by the rifles and Brens had a massive effect: 'I saw one man come up the hill, he was hit with one round and he somersaulted down the hill, twelve, eighteen times,' said Farrell. 'And with the rifle and the Bren, you very rarely got stoppages.'[100] However, the Bren, for all its reliability and stopping power, was not an ideal area weapon. 'It was almost too accurate. You had to give it a swivel to give it a bit of a spray,' said Rifles Corporal Norman Sweetlove.[101]

Even during this period of relatively low-intensity operations, the horrors of war were unavoidable. Nicholls was with the Fusiliers when they were ordered to occupy a hill recently held by a Chinese unit that had been wiped out by airbursts. 'You could not walk for dead Chinese – some

---

* Later in the war, Chinese POWs would express their astonishment at seeing Centurions on hilltops.

of them had shrapnel sticking out of their heads,' he said. 'We did not dig in, and nobody slept that night; it was too ghostly.'[102] Corporal Joe Thompson remembered one Chinese whose skull had been split as if with an axe. On another occasion, Thompson drank from a small watercourse. Later, he discovered a Chinese corpse rotting upstream.[103] Fusilier Preston Little encountered a pile of napalm victims: 'headless, limbless, bloated carcasses, with that horrible smell reminiscent of roast pork'.[104]

But not all was horror. By now, the brigade had fully functioning welfare sections, including an entertainment detachment from the Royal Army Service Corps, with a mobile stage mounted on a four-ton truck – painted bright blue. When American entertainer Danny Kaye visited Korea the detachment was his support act in Inchon. Corporal John Coleman-Wood, a member of the troupe and his oppo Colin Thackery did a double act dressed as tramps. Their routine included a song:

> Hurry on down to the front line Brodie,
> There's nobody here but us Yanks!
> Hurry on down to the front line Brodie,
> And for God's sake bring us your tanks!
> Jump in your jeep!
> Bring the brigade!
> And when it's all over,
> We'll have a parade!

The reactions of Kaye and Brodie are unrecorded.

In this strange Far Eastern land there were moments of humour and of wonder. Fusilier Little was defecating in what he thought was a suitably secluded countryside spot when an entire Korean family, led by its grandfather, trooped past him on its constitutional; each member gravely bowed to him. Little, squatting down, nodded back with as much dignity as he could muster. One day, patrolling through the wild countryside, he and his mates came across the spoor of a leopard. And on another occasion, in a mountainside Buddhist temple, the soldiers found the resident monks particularly friendly and curious: they had never seen Europeans before.[105]

* * *

By February 1951 Marshal Peng's Third Offensive had run out of steam. In a cautious counteroffensive, Ridgway pushed north. 29th Brigade, under command of I Corps, was tasked to clear a range of mountains some fifteen miles south-east of Seoul. This fastness formed part of the Chinese bridgehead south of the Han, and commanded the two main roads in the sector, both vital for the capital's recapture. The mountains were occupied by a Chinese division, which had been ordered to hold the area while Marshal Peng prepared his 'Fourth Offensive'.[106]

In convoys of trucks, the brigade moved into its operational area. Passing through the burning hamlet of Kumnyangjang-ni, the men received a grisly welcome: in the smouldering police station stood the charred mummy of a prisoner, its blackened claws of hands grasping the bars through which it had tried to escape.[107] The battalions climbed into the mountains.

The setting was magnificent. The air was clean, the views distant, the mountain snows sparkling in winter sunshine. From the infantry's positions near the summits, the tanks, trucks and jeeps below looked like miniatures. For a tourist, such alpine scenery is breathtaking. For a soldier, it is exhausting. The winding goat paths up the rocky hillsides were treacherous; leg muscles knotted on ascents or descents; chill air seared heaving lungs. The equipment each man carried, even on the lightest scale, was a considerable burden. Over winter clothing, each soldier carried, in a small pack, spare socks, pullover, mess tin, shaving kit, a lightweight blanket and poncho – sleeping bags were too bulky – and a 24-hour ration pack. Given enemy numbers, the ammunition carried, in webbing pouches and in cloth bandoliers slung across the chest, had risen from the 50 rounds the manuals called for to at least 150, plus as many hand grenades as feasible. Men also carried spare magazines for their section's Bren gun, and a couple of bombs for their platoon's 2-inch mortar.

On these vertical battlefields, a company of Korean porters was attached to each battalion.[108] These peasants, with their A-frame 'Everest' carrying racks, proved invaluable. Lieutenant-Colonel Kingsley Foster characteristically welcomed the porters to his battalion, telling them, through an interpreter, of the traditions of the Fusiliers and of his expectations of them. They responded positively. Subsequently, a delegation of porters approached him and urged him to stand for the presidency of Korea. If he did so, they said, he would have their vote.[109] One of the Korean interpreters was a nineteen-year-old student, Lee Kyungsik. 'I had a good measure of talent in English, I was well ahead at school, and I think it paid off,' he said. With interpreters so hard to come by, he was well treated when he joined the Rifles: 'One would not think that they thought of the Koreans as they would their own people, but I have no complaints.' Although British pay was not as high as the American, it was 'incomparably higher than the ROKs'', and the Rifles to whom he was assigned – 'and in fact all the British soldiers' – were, he thought, 'good fighters'. His jobs in the battalion included prisoner interrogation and liaising with the porters. The contrasts of a high-tech war in a primitive land were not lost on the brigade commander. In a letter to a fellow general, Brodie wrote, 'We have been using 100 porters per battalion to supply and carry loads . . . and striking right across country into the blue! It is an amazing war – jets, napalm, porters and load-carrying bullocks all in a Brigade area at the same time!'[110]

To replace Major Tony Blake, killed in January, a tough new second in command had joined the Rifles: Major Gerald Rickord. Due to his florid complexion, quiet voice and laid-back smile, he was nicknamed 'Farmer's Boy' by the troops – who greatly respected his toughness.[111] 'He went round all the companies with a map telling everybody, in their slit trenches, where they were and what they were doing,' said Captain Robin Charley. 'The battalion had a lot of confidence in him.' Rickord's military apprenticeship had been served among the crags and ravines of India's Northwest Frontier – a perfect, if often fatal, officers' training ground – and he had subsequently led an airborne battalion in World War II. Having operated around the Khyber Pass, he knew all about mountain warfare, and had a jeep track – an extension of an existing footpath – cut through to the top of the Rifles' mountain, 300 metres up. With a dizzying precipice to one side, jeeps managed the climb in bottom gear; but CQMS Tommy Sturgeon of Support Company thought the way down was terrifying. Jeep occupants had to be 'ready to bale out in a flash if necessary'. Mechanical brakes were useless, so human anchors took up the slack. If a jeep reached a certain velocity, Sturgeon and his Korean porters clung to it and dug their heels into the ground. For the relief it granted from humping ammunition, food, water and equipment up the mountain, the risk was worthwhile, though.

The Glosters and Fusiliers probed forward as they awaited the advance of their flank unit, the US 1st Cavalry Division. On the night of 12 February the Glosters' A Company, in prepared positions, came under attack. 'It was very cold, but my shivering was not only to do with the cold: It was the first time I had been under fire,' said Private Sam Mercer. 'It was a mixture of fright and excitement, but this was why I had joined the Army – for adventure.' The soldiers held their fire until the Chinese were ten yards away, then opened up. In the killing zone, there was no cover, no possibility of retreat. Eleven Chinese were killed and two captured. Several were found dead in front of the Bren gun of Private Allen, who had earlier told a visiting general that 'he had no quarrel with the Chinese'.[112] 3 Platoon's commander was wounded in the action. The following day, his replacement was observing artillery fire from a ridge, when a low shell shattered the top of a tree, bringing branches crashing down onto him; he, too, was evacuated wounded. (The two officers subsequently met in hospital in Japan, each identifying himself to the other as 3 Platoon's commander.[113]) The ill-starred platoon had lost two lieutenants in less than twenty-four hours.

Amid the silence of the mountains, aggressive patrolling was carried out to dominate the ground. On a moonless night Lieutenant Mike Harvey led a six-man Gloster reconnaissance patrol along a tree-covered ridge. They halted in the snow every few yards, listening intently, but this night it would not be sound that gave their enemy away. After about a mile the whiff of garlic or *kimchi* alerted the Glosters to enemy presence. Harvey deployed his men into firing positions and whispered, 'Rapid, await my order!' They lay silently in the snow. There was a clink of metal. Ahead of them, a line of shadows advanced cautiously towards them. As so often in this war, the action would take place at close range. When the enemy patrol was less than six yards away, Harvey shouted 'Fire!' His men opened up. The enemy reacted immediately. A furious five-second fire-fight raged, before the guerrillas turned and ran. The Glosters followed their trails in the snow, to discover three dead. Harvey would never forget the sight and sound of one enemy: he had been shot in the head, and his dripping blood made a faint sizzling sound as it melted the snow.[114]

A big operation was in the works. The Glosters were ordered to take Hill 327, a massive feature with a flat top that was the key to the next succession of peaks. The Fusiliers and Rifles had been blooded at Happy Valley; now Hill 327 would be the Glosters' first major action against the Chinese. On 13 February Lieutenant-Colonel Carne moved his battalion forward to the crossroads in front of the objective. The Glosters dug in on low hills and ridges below the feature. Enemy were in evidence. Mercer was leaning against a Hussar Centurion when a Chinese machine-gunner opened fire, 'signing his own death warrant'. The tank's turret swivelled, then stopped. Its 20-pounder cracked; almost simultaneously, an eruption of smoke, earth and foliage signalled that the machine-gun post had been wiped out. Mercer, crouching beside the tank, was deafened for fifteen minutes.

That night, the Chinese launched a spoiling attack against the Glosters' right flanking unit, the 1st Cavalry. On a low hill adjacent to the Americans, Gloster David Green heard bugles and gunfire in the darkness, then the panicky calls of GIs. An eerie 'ha ha ha' drifted across the valley. C Company commander Major Charles Walwyn radioed the Americans, asking if they needed assistance. They declined but pulled back, leaving the Glosters exposed. After a tense night, the British soldiers spotted a figure crawling towards the abandoned American positions. Several men opened up. The crawling figure was hit. He appeared to be alone. Green and a small patrol moved forward to investigate. Cautiously, they approached the body, which had been shot through the head: it was an American private. Two Americans arrived and glumly told the Glosters that the GI had been trying to retrieve photos he had left in his foxhole the previous night.[115]

I Corps Commander General Frank Milburn now drove up Route 13 collecting American stragglers. The Gloster attack was not to be stalled. On 16 February Carne's men were ordered to take 327. 29th Brigade was to take the hills, clear the ground to the west of Route 13, and advance north to the Han. American units would make a diversionary flank attack, while the Glosters assaulted up the slopes ahead.[116] Carne's plan was for C Company to launch a direct attack up the slopes from the south-east, while D Company would assault up the west flank.

Ridgway had realised that his inferiority in numbers could be overcome by superiority in firepower, hence the application of 'meat-grinder' tactics. As Captain Charley put it, 'The policy was, if you saw even one chap, you'd blow the top of his hilltop off!' For Hill 327 a devastating firepower package had been assembled. 45 Field's twenty-four 25-pounders, and 170 Mortar's eighteen 4.3-inch mortars, plus the twelve 3-inch mortars of the Glosters and Fusiliers and direct fire from seventeen Hussar Centurions, would support the attack up the slopes.[117] An air strike shrieked in against tunnelled positions on the front face of the feature, then the barrage began rumbling up the hillside. Bits of tree and scrub cartwheeled into the air, blasted skyward by the black clouds of smoke and volcanoes of dirt that First World War German soldiers christened the *scheisssturm* ('shit storm'). Watching the barrage and the American diversion, C Company's men gripped their weapons, teeth clenched, waiting for the off. Major Walwyn broke the tension, ordering his men forward with 'Righto, chaps – in we go!'[118] His three platoons spread out, waded the icy stream in front of the hill, and began their ascent. The slope was almost vertical in places; the attackers scrambled up on hands and knees.

The bombardment had churned over the heads of the Chinese burrowed into the hillside. From bunker slits and tunnels, they watched C Company approach. Watchers below suddenly saw 'torrents' of stick grenades whirling through the air towards the advancing Glosters.[119] Automatic fire ripped through the low scrub. Men spun down. David Green's sergeant, Jock McKay, slid down the hill on his backside, a bullet through his leg and a huge smile on his face: the wound would send him home. Basic drills took over: Dash! Down! Crawl! Observe! Fire! The attackers hugged the frozen soil, peering ahead. Green's mate reassured him – 'Don't worry, we'll get the bastards!' – as the pinned-down sections scanned for enemy. A Bren gunner beside Green raised himself to fire. Almost immediately, he jerked backward – gut-shot, vomiting blood, he choked to death. But Green's section had spotted the bunker opening. Hurling grenades they stormed up, killing the two occupants with close-range fire. All around were expertly camouflaged positions. The assault wave broke up as C Company attempted to clear the hillside against dug-in Chinese. One man was hit by a fellow Gloster; his trousers rapidly soaked with blood.[120] The attackers passed a signaller who had been killed kneeling upright, staring up the hillside, the radio on his back still squawking.[121]

D Company was held up by bunkers. Lieutenant Harvey was called up with a 3.2-inch rocket launcher. Spotting an opening, he raised the bazooka, and fired. Miss! In reply, a handful of grenades bounced down the slope, followed by the tearing brrrrppp of submachine-guns. Harvey was hit in the lip by shrapnel, but when the incoming firing halted – probably as the Chinese reloaded – he rose and fired again. The fizzing rocket went through the black slit, exploding with a flash. Thick smoke poured out of the bunker mouth. Glosters rose and charged past Harvey, hurling grenades.[122]

Hussar Captain Peter Ormrod was with C Company, directing fire by radio for the tanks below. The attacking ranks were thinning: 'Each time somebody was wounded, there were four very ready volunteers to carry him down.' Soon, Ormrod's forward observation party was ahead of the infantry. The Hussar used a fluorescent orange air recognition panel to direct tank fire, adjusting shots by radio, calling left, right or upslope of the panel. The high-velocity Centurion shells exploded within twenty yards of the infantry battling their way upward.[123] Far below, Lieutenant-Colonel Lowther and Major Huth watched the assault through tank periscopes while breakfasting on bacon and eggs.[124] In his Centurion, Trooper Dennis Whybro was delighted as his crew nailed a bunker. 'Our gun was spot on: it put a 20-pound shell in the hole before it exploded. Straw and everything else flew out. We really thrashed it with shells.'[125]

Up with C Company, in the midst of the gutter-fighting for the bunkers, Green was inspired by Major Walwyn, who was issuing calm orders and imprecations to his men not to be afraid. Then Walwyn was down, his arm almost shot off. He struggled furiously with the medics who forcibly evacuated him.[126] At the foot of the hill, C Company's second in command, Captain Reg 'Mad' Mardell, had been longing to get into it. With Walwyn out of action, Mardell charged up in such a hurry that he forgot to take a weapon: he was carrying only a pistol and a clipboard. Watchers below could see him waving the clipboard as he directed assaults.[127] Carne was following behind the assault troops with his Tactical CP. Bugler Tony Eagles, engaged in the dangerous and exhausting task of stretchering casualties down the hillside, learned why his commander was nicknamed 'Cool Carne'. An enemy popped up from the scrub and hurled a grenade at the colonel. The bomb bounced off his shoulder – a dud. Eagles watched as Carne drew his revolver, took careful aim, and shot the man dead.

C Company had now fought their way to just below the summit. Green thought one of the NCOs, Sergeant Eames, looked 'like a conquering gladiator' as, framed against the sky, he went over the top. Bayonet fixed, enraged at the loss of comrades, Green roared at the Chinese to come out and fight as he too crested the rise. D Company appeared from the flank. The top of the massif was devastated by artillery; the trees were skeletons. The plateau was criss-crossed with a series of trenches linking stoutly roofed bunkers. A bare-headed Chinese soldier appeared from one, hands up. One Gloster loosed a Sten burst at him, missing. Another cursing soldier threw a grenade into his trench; it was a dud. Green's fury deserted him. 'What's the matter with you bastards? Leave him alone,' Green shouted. Taking the frightened man's hand, he pointed him down the hill.[128]

Firing died down. B Company ascended to mop up and exploit forward. The men sprayed inside tunnels and bunkers with captured burp guns; others used hand grenades and flame-throwers. Bren gunner Frank Carter discovered a cache of booby-trapped bazookas. The Chinese had dented the pipe-like weapons – if a rocket was fired through them, they would explode.[129] On the summit, 'Mad' Mardell was amusing himself with a dud grenade, throwing it up and down like a tennis ball. His men kept well away. Tiring of the game, the officer hurled it away – at which point it exploded, to the men's amusement and Mardell's shock. The Glosters spread out and explored the bunkers. They were well constructed, with entries just large enough to crawl through. Green took over one, with a pistol holster still dangling from the roof.[130]

By 13:00, resistance had ceased. Brodie was delighted, radioing (in breach of signal protocol) 'Well done, Fred!' to Carne.[131] He had reason to be pleased. An American general, surrounded by MPs in shining chrome helmets, had dropped in by helicopter to watch the attack, as had a camera crew.[132] The Glosters, for the loss of ten killed and twenty-nine wounded – plus one artilleryman killed and three wounded – had taken two prisoners and killed fifty-seven Chinese, seizing the feature from a light enemy battalion.[133] In tactical manuals odds of 3:1 are considered necessary for an attack but two Gloster companies had prevailed against superior enemy numbers, fortified on a near-perfect defensive position.* Night fell over Hill 327. On the moonlit summit, Green was unnerved by the glazed stare of a dead Chinese officer lying outside his captured bunker. Extending a booted foot, he kicked the corpse down the cratered slope.[134]

* * *

* Carne won a DSO for his battalion's performance.

The British soldiers had now had the chance to weigh up their foe. 'We didn't call 'em "Gooks" we called 'em "Chinks" or "Tiddlywinks",' said Farrell. 'You never knew when he was going to hit you, but you could hear him coming: "the pitter patter of little feet". And could they move! They were fast; they must have been marathon runners! He was a good soldier – he knew no fear.'[135] Some of 29th Brigade's men came up with theories for the enemy's gallantry. 'I think they were fired up with indoctrination,' said Mercer. 'When you want to get a message across – when Mao captured a lot of his opponent's troops – how do you do it? If they can't read and write, how do you communicate? You sit them down in ranks and harangue them. I think they were pumped up to the eyeballs with how good they were and how evil we were.'

The communist system of information dissemination had an inbuilt weakness. In what would prove a surprising bonus for UN intelligence, it was discovered that even the most junior Chinese soldiers had a good understanding of operational and even strategic objectives. Due to their lack of communications equipment, which made it difficult for Chinese commanders to control units once an offensive had been launched, it was imperative for even the smallest units to know timings and targets. The result was that junior Chinese troops usually had a broader view of the 'big picture' than their UN equivalents, who operated on a 'need to know' basis.[136]

The Fusiliers' intelligence officer, Lieutenant Tony Perrins, got a closer look at the Chinese than most. 'They carried a cotton satchel over the shoulder with a spare pair of socks, a spare pair of cotton underwear, a T-shirt, an enamel bowl, an aluminium spoon if they were lucky, chopsticks if they weren't. They would have a photo of their mum or girlfriend and a letter or two. Most were illiterate, but somebody in their village did the writing, and somebody in their unit did the reading. They did not live high on the hog. They were very like good little Geordie soldiers: they did what they were told to and did not spend too much time thinking about it.'

The Rifles, who had had the most severe engagement, were convinced that the Chinese was 'tough and cunning', his fieldcraft and night control 'excellent.' However, he was poorly armed – at Happy Valley, some had no firearms, only grenades – and his reactions in close combat were slow. The Rifles' adjutant concluded the Chinese soldier 'was an enemy to be treated with respect in mobile warfare and at night; but man to man, the Rifleman was his better'.[137]

\* \* \*

The victory on Hill 327 seemed to prove that contention. The action had opened the route north. The Fusiliers and the Rifles advanced along hilltops and ridges, while tanks crawled through the valleys below. It became clear that the enemy had abandoned the mountains. By 22 February Route 13, leading to the south bank of the Han River, was open. The brigade was withdrawn into reserve.[138]

One unit, however, did not have the benefit of rest. 45 Field Regiment was rushed around to various allied commands. On 23 February it was lent to General Paik Sun-yup's 1st ROK Division. The British officers were pleasantly surprised to discover how good the ROK officers were at map reading. Conversation was limited, however; after showing the British officers co-ordinates, few Korean officers had more English than 'boom boom' and 'OK'. However, the system worked.[139] For his part, Paik was pleased to see that the British gunners assigned battery commanders as FOOs, while junior officers stayed with the guns; the same system had been used when he served with the Japanese Army. Paik would later pay the British gunners the highest compliment, calling them the most accurate artillerymen in the war.[140] In March 45 Field's observation posts were deployed along the south bank of the Han, firing at enemy across the river.[141]

Elsewhere, under Ridgway's leadership, UN forces had for the first time mastered a Chinese attack. Peng's First Offensive had been a sharp, sudden shock; his second had driven UN forces from the North, while his third had swept south of the 38th parallel and taken Seoul. But his fourth, launched on 11 February, was crowned with no such success. On 13 February the US 23rd Regimental Combat Team, the French battalion,* and a Ranger company were enveloped at the village of Chipyong-ni. Commanding a crossroad, the village was a communications hub. Previously, this situation would have prompted a 'bug-out'. Ridgway was having none of it. The 23rd was ordered to dig in. The human waves charged. From prepared positions, the battle group fought back with counter-attacks and massed fire support, holding until 15 February, when it was relieved.[142] The Chinese, with their vast manpower pool, had not lost the strategic initiative, but after Chipyong-ni they lost their moral ascendancy. On 21 February Ridgway launched Operation KILLER, an offensive that drove the enemy north of the 38th parallel. For the first time, Peng's vaunted guerrilla army was in retreat.

In March 45 Field was on the Han River as the US 3rd Division advanced. The infantry had priority, but Lieutenant-Colonel Maris

---

* In recent years it has become fashionable in English-speaking countries to mock French military proficiency. In Korea the French battalion was considered an elite unit, and at Chipyong-ri proved particularly energetic in counter-attacks.

Young was determined that his regiment – which had not received movement orders – would cross too. He lined his vehicles and guns up in column alongside the single bridge available. When a break in the traffic came, the regiment started to roll across. A jeep roared up bearing the divisional commander, who was furious that the British guns had jumped the queue. But it was too late to call them back: all batteries of 45 were across the river. By evening the regiment was in Seoul, which had fallen on the 15th.[143] Lieutenant George Truell's battery was set up around the battered National Assembly building – Truell thought it only proper that his command post be in the speaker's chair.

The capital having changed hands three times, entire districts lay in ruins. However, the British Embassy – a red-brick Victorian pile dating back to 1891, complete with colonnaded patio, lawn and rose bushes – was still standing, albeit with bullet and shrapnel damage. The nearby Anglican Cathedral was also substantially unharmed,[144] and the Hussars 'dusted it down' and held a service.* In the bishop's garden one of the troopers clearing up the area spotted something glittering. It proved to be a damaged mother-of-pearl crucifix dated 1641. Informed of the find, the CO vowed to have the cross repaired at the regiment's expense. The brief sojourn among familiar buildings, Captain Peter Ormrod thought, was morale-lifting. Fighting a brutal war in an alien land, the Hussars had at last discovered 'a little bit of England'.[145]

---

* The cathedral still stands in central Seoul. A book of remembrance for British soldiers killed in the Korean War is in a box attached to the wall of the nave.

# Chapter 5

# VALLEY OF THE WATER DRAGON

*All warfare is based on deception . . .*
*when we are near, we must make the enemy believe we are far*

Sun Tzu

CHINESE COMMANDER LI RU-SONG had crossed the Imjin. Soon after his arrival on the war-wracked peninsula, he had been received by the Korean leader, who had praised his 'great army' and expressed hopes that the Chinese would drive the invaders from the south and restore his government.[1] Li's forces had dutifully taken Pyongyang and Kaesong. He knew that there were enemy forces further south but was confident that, with the river barrier behind him, victory lay ahead. Now, his 20,000-man 'Celestial Army' would seize Seoul. Li led his 1,000-man cavalry spearhead through the hills.

His confidence was misplaced. The enemy commander, a proud and wily old general, had retreated far enough. He had told his comrades: 'Now is the time to seek life in the midst of death.' Near the high pass of Pyokje – a way station where envoys to and from China could refresh themselves on the road, a day from Seoul – Li led his vanguard in pursuit of an enemy scouting detachment. In the thick morning fog his horsemen plunged headlong into their enemy's main force. It was around 10:00 on 27 February 1593.[2]

The Japanese defenders, 40,000 strong under samurai general Kobayakawa Takakage, were deployed in three units. All were dismounted. Given the narrow confines of the pass and the poor visibility, they had put aside missile weapons, arming themselves for hand-to-hand combat. As the Chinese cavalry blundered in, swords and spears flashed in the murk, while the air fluttered with banners and flags. Terrified horses shied and skittered; the fighting seethed at such murderously close range that the Chinese and their Korean allies could not use their mounts to advantage. The samurai, wielding their wicked long swords two-handed, slashed through enemy armour, flesh and bone; Japanese foot soldiers used the crossbars on their spears to drag the cavalry from their saddles to the ground, where they could be skewered in the filth. A chill rain and the churning of tens of thousands of feet and hooves transformed the killing zone into a quagmire of mud and blood. For two hours, the panting armies hacked and stabbed at each other. Li, under attack from a samurai commander who wanted his head in its golden helm, desperately parried until one of his bodyguard charged between the general and his attackers. The Chinese warrior was hacked apart, but his sacrifice allowed Li to escape. With their general fleeing, the Chinese and Koreans broke. Li's forces retreated up the track and across the Imjin, leaving a trail of maimed bodies and gutted horses. The Japanese returned to Seoul in triumph, bearing their trophies: 6,000 severed heads.[3]

The battle of Pyokje was the largest land battle of the Hideyoshi invasion of Korea, a devastating war which pitted samurai-led armies against Korea and her Ming Chinese allies. Pyokje had followed an earlier battle in 1592, in which Japanese, striking up from the south, had lured a Korean counter-attack across the Imjin, then smashed it in a massive ambush. Centuries passed. Times changed. Geography did not. The river, its valley and its hills would be as hard fought over in the 1950s as in the 1590s.

\* \* \*

The 159-mile-long Imjin River – it is named after two Chinese characters meaning 'Water Dragon' – carves through the north-centre of the peninsula. It originates in the distant north and heads south, then changes course, turning south-westwards and curving as it broadens, to eventually empty into the Yellow Sea. In its lower reaches the river is 100–200 metres wide in the spring and winds through foothills like a sinuous Oriental dragon. The ancient capital of Kaesong lies twelve miles north of it. Seoul – Korea's capital since 1392 and the 'belly button' of the peninsula – sits some thirty miles to the south. To invaders from the north, the Imjin and its hills present the last major geographical obstacle before the Han Valley and Seoul.

For millennia the main north–south route through Korea has led down the western flank of the peninsula's mountainous spine and across the Imjin. For two thousand years, envoys, traders, travellers and pilgrims have trodden this route. So have warriors. Mongolian hordes forded the Imjin. Likewise, the Ming Chinese, the Japanese and the Manchurians. By the 1950s the river's location – it crosses the 38th parallel, the border of the divided peninsula – had amplified its geopolitical strategic significance: As it wound through the land, so the Water Dragon wound through the war.[4]

In 1951 the main north–south route was a key highway – Route 33, designated an MSR, or main supply route. Northwards, this was one of two major routes leading to Pyongyang. Southwards, it led through the village of Tongducheon and the town of Uijongbu to Seoul. This road, the

'Uijongbu Corridor', was an artery leading into the heart of the capital. Yet the major obstacles astride it, the Imjin and its tributary the Hantan, are not as formidable as they appear. Like most Korean rivers, the Imjin is shallow. Its fords are usable by men and vehicles. Twice already in the Korean War the Imjin had been breached. A key prong of Kim Il-sung's June *blitzkrieg* had smashed through the ROK 7th Division holding the Uijongbu corridor, entering Seoul's outskirts late on the 27th.[5] Marshal Peng's Chinese had taken the same route on 31 December, breaking through the 1st ROK Division by the end of New Year's Day. In the next phase of the Korean War, the Imjin's banks would be held, for the first time in their bloody history, by European soldiers.

* * *

By April 1951 Matthew Ridgway was on the offensive. After the early disasters in North Korea the paratroop general had ditched the UN's narrow, fast-moving thrusts in favour of a more cautious, broad-front advance. His objective was 'Line Kansas', a line on the map, just below the 38th parallel, that was a phase line from which further advances could be undertaken. What was unclear was when the advance from Line Kansas would resume, how far it would drive north – and what would happen if the Chinese attacked first.

There was indecision well beyond the battle front. On 12 April MacArthur was replaced as the commander-in-chief of the UN forces. MacArthur, at least, had had an aim: total victory. If that meant allying with Chiang Kai-shek, blockading China's ports and attacking airbases across the borders, then, in his view, so be it. But this approach alarmed MacArthur's political masters, who fretted that he might ignite World War III. It had been too much not just for allies like Britain and the Commonwealth, but also for President Harry Truman. MacArthur – who had served in the Pacific throughout World War II, who had saved South Korea and reversed the tide at Inchon, only to preside over the disaster of Chinese intervention and the winter retreat – was given his last marching orders. Ridgway took over in Tokyo and was replaced as 8th Army commander in Korea by General James Van Fleet. A big, tough-looking man, Van Fleet had extensive combat and command experience. He had fought through Normandy, finished World War II as a Corps Commander and gone on to work with the Greek Army on defeating its communist insurgency in 1947. But what was the overall UN plan in Korea? UN forces were pioneering a hazy new strategy: 'limited war'. Asked by a reporter on 22 April what his goals were on the peninsula, Van Fleet replied: 'I don't know. That answer must come from higher authority.'[6] Higher authority was silent.

By late March the snows had melted. On the last day of the month 29th Brigade was ordered to take up position along Line Kansas, just south of the Imjin. The units mounted truck convoys that motored through the silent, scarred streets of Seoul, still largely deserted after its recent recapture. Fusilier John Bayliss was shocked at the destruction: Seoul reminded him of bombed-out Düsseldorf in World War II. The weather was changing. It was chill, but no longer freezing. Snow had been replaced by rain, which was turning the dusty tracks to mud. On the way through burned-out Uijongbu, formerly a light industrial centre, a piece of black humour welcoming passers-by alluded to the fierce fighting that had taken place: on the road sign reading 'This is Uijongbu' some wag had replaced 'is' with 'was'.* The brigade continued. As it approached the Imjin the country rose along both sides of Route 33.

On arrival the brigade relieved the Puerto Rican 65th Infantry Regiment, freeing it to rejoin its parent, the US 3rd Division. There was no fighting as the British troops deployed along the southern banks of the river. The enemy was out of contact.[7] Brigadier Brodie's orders from General Robert Soule's 3rd Division, under whose command he fell, were simple: he was to organise, secure and defend Line Kansas in his sector.[8]

Route 33 was a designated MSR for General Frank Milburn's I Corps, commanding the left, or western sector of the Korean battlefront. Holding the right, or eastern, side of the road was the US 3rd Division. 29th Brigade spread out along the river to the west, or left, of the MSR, to the south of the river. As in January, the brigade's frontage was more suitable for a division. As the crow flies, the brigade was holding almost nine miles, but, taking into consideration the broad curves of the Imjin, it amounted to over fourteen.[9] A front of this length was described by one officer as 'ludicrous'.[10] It made little sense to Fusilier Lieutenant Malcolm Cubiss either. 'A battalion used to hold 1,500 yards, but our front was at least three times that,' he said. 'And it was mountainous country. Mountains eat men.'†

The infantry COs strung their battalions out in company-sized hilltop strongpoints, mostly overlooking the river. There was minimal visual contact between the scattered units. The bulk of the brigade was on the right/eastern side of its sector, close to the MSR. The Fusiliers were deployed over hills on the south bank of the river on the right end of the line. On 10 April the Rifles, accompanied by Hussar Centurions,

---

* The sign is visible in a number of contemporary photographs. Uijongbu, incidentally, was the location of the fictional American unit in the film and TV series MASH.

† Later in the war, the Commonwealth Division – i.e. three full brigades – would hold a nine-mile front north of the Imjin.

mounted an assault crossing of the river to take Hill 194 to its north. The attack hit thin air. There were no enemy. The Rifles dug in on the hill – dubbed 'Fort Nixon' after A Company's commander, Sir Christopher Nixon – to watch 'Operation Dauntless', an American offensive to the east, as it moved north the following day.[11] Hill 194 sits inside the 'hinge' of the Imjin, where it changes course, and its tributary, the Hantan, continues eastward. The guns of 45 Field and a squadron of Hussars were behind the hilltop position of Z Company of the Fusiliers to the south-east. Brigade echelon units were in Uijongbu, fifteen miles south. On the left/western edge of the brigade were the Glosters. To the left of the Glosters – but out of contact – was the ROK 1st Division.

Due to shortage of men, the sector's dominant feature – the 675-metre-high, Snowdon-sized mountain Kamak-san – was unmanned. This left a two-mile-wide hole in the front, between the left-hand company of the Fusiliers, X, and the right-hand company of the Glosters, B. While artillery, mortars and even Vickers could – in theory – cover the empty zone, against an enemy who was a master of camouflage, night movement and infiltration it was a perilous gap to leave. 'If they had had one, the Chinese could have driven an armoured division between us and the Fusiliers,' said Private Sam Mercer. It was no exaggeration.*

There were two key lines of communication in the British sector. The major one was Route 11, a track running north–south along a valley parallel to the MSR. About ten miles south of the river, this route turned south-east to link up with the MSR. Branching west off Route 11 was a very narrow track, Route 57, known as 5Y, or 'Five Yankee'. It led through a narrow defile in the hills to the Glosters' positions from the rear, through the township of Choksong and across the Imjin – via a ford – and then north.

For the soldiers settling into this 'line' it was not just evidence of previous fighting – Chinese corpses on Kamak-san and abandoned fighting positions throughout the sector – that communicated the strategic significance of their location; there were echoes of even older battles. The Glosters' A Company occupied a hill that was marked on maps as 'castle site'; nothing remained of the stronghold, but this had been a defensive position since the Shilla Dynasty. The ford it overlooked was dubbed 'Gloster Crossing', and maps showed another castle site to the north-west. On the brigade's eastern flank the Rifles would soon discover a hill with extant medieval fortifications. Rumour had it that Genghis Khan's hordes had once crossed the Imjin.†

* The US Army Official History of the Korean War agreed, calling the brigade's position 'a gaping front'. See Mossman, p. 373.
† In fact Genghis Khan's hordes had not marched through the peninsula – but Kublai Khan's had.

For all that, though, with the Chinese out of contact, the mission was vague. Most soldiers assumed they would soon resume their northward push. 'I can only describe it as a temporary position: It wasn't a fully prepared defensive position,' thought one. 'It was the kind of position from which [we would continue] to advance further north.'[12] 'Though, as far as we knew, no further plans were cooking, we were still mentally in forward gear,' wrote Lieutenant-Colonel Maris Young, 45 Field Regiment's commander.[13] The widely dispersed companies sited themselves for all-round defence on their scrubby brown hills. In January at Pyongtaek, south of Seoul, the battalions had fortified themselves; the Glosters had dug communication trenches and underground sleeping accommodation.[14] On the Imjin most infantry positions were the kind that would be dug in a single day. 'Previously, we had dug in more,' said Gunner Bob Nicholls of 170 Mortar, whose three-man FOO team was with the Fusiliers. No mines were laid, though some units set up trip flares and armed grenades in tins – 'if someone kicked it, it would go off'[15] – as booby traps. The soldiers dug one- or two-man slit trenches. Some were only knee-deep, as in certain areas spades struck sandstone or granite a couple of feet down. There were no sandbags, so parapets of compacted earth or rocks were raised. There were few bunkers and little wire: just a few rolls strung here and there, covering obvious approaches at ankle height.[16] The men erected their bivvy tents behind, next to, or over their slits.

\* \* \*

The April days passed. The enemy did not attack. The brigade did not advance. Days stretched into weeks. It was very different to those first, intense months of nomadic war. 'It is impossible to prevent the men getting complacent,' Major Pat Angier, an airborne veteran of World War II commanding the Glosters' A Company, wrote to his wife. 'It is very strange and quite unlike a normal war.'[17] Fusilier Stan Tomenson's wound at Happy Valley had defied the reservists' predictions. It had not returned him to 'Blighty', and after a clean recovery, he rejoined Z Company on its hill overlooking the river. He was surprised by the peacefulness. The main event most days was the arrival of the NAAFI wagon behind the company position. 'You'd go down to the bottom of the hill, get your chocolates, sweets, tea, your bits and pieces – then go up again. It was lazy days.'

There was still some soldiering to be done, such as taking two-man listening patrols down to the river after dark. 'We had to go down into the valley and sit in the reeds on the riverside; we were not allowed to talk,' said Tomenson. 'So you sat there with the field telephone – with your hand perched on it, as when it rang it would echo across the whole valley, it would frighten you to death! And then someone on the end of the phone would say: "Is anything happening?" In the early hours of 14 April the Rifles, on their hill across the river, were probed by a Chinese company. After a night of grenade exchanges three enemy wounded were taken and one body was found; the Rifles suffered one man wounded.[18] Compared to the earlier battles, this was a minor skirmish.

The ennui continued. The brigade was enjoying the most restful period it had had since the troopships. Men argued over rations (the favourites were steak and kidney pudding, stewed steak and bully beef in the British rations, tinned fruit and chocolate in the American packs). Cooking was done at platoon and company level; the men arrived with their mess tins, ate, then returned to their trenches to clean their eating utensils with earth. Duty was two hours on, two hours off.[19] Beer and cigarettes were stockpiled among the weapons, ammunition, webbing and packs on the positions.[20] One night in the Glosters' C Company someone began playing a mouth organ. Voices joined in, until a sergeant roared: 'Oi, where in the fucking hell do you lot think you are? This is the front line!'[21] Given the absence of enemy, that was easy to overlook. The relaxed attitude extended to reconnaissance of the ground the brigade was holding. 'We didn't really know where the [river] fords were,' said Cubiss. 'We knew about one, we didn't know about the others.'

The Engineers of 55 Field Squadron were given a task to enliven their days. In the spring rains, many battalion vehicles had bogged down in paddy mud, and Brigadier Brodie promised a week's leave in Japan to anyone who could solve the problem. Squadron commander Major Tony Younger gave the job of collecting suggestions and selecting a winner to Lieutenant Keith Eastgate, a former heavyweight boxer at Sandhurst who had the 'right combination of reliability and humour'. Entries, marked 'Muddy Paddy', poured in. One proposed welding a spade-shaped extension to the exhaust pipes of all vehicles, which could then be reversed onto the paddies to dry them out. Another recommended a maypole, equipped with ropes with buckets on the end, should be erected in the centre of a paddy by the sappers, who could then run in ever decreasing circles – to the accompaniment of the Band of the Royal Engineers – filling and emptying the buckets.[22] The competition amused Eastgate, but by mid-April, as the weather improved, the paddies dried up of their own accord.

In a schoolhouse behind the brigade, the war correspondents were frustrated. There was no news. The copy filed to their Tokyo bureaus via the unreliable, ancient green telephone in their quarters consisted of such 'human-interest' items as a feature on a pair of soldiers who were sponsored on a trip to the UK to watch their home team play in the FA Cup.[23]

It wasn't just lack of action. In April the climate itself engendered relaxation, for in Korea spring is a fine season. The terrible winter was over, and the rains had passed. The skies turned from grey to blue, clear and impossibly high. The nights remained chilly, but the days were cool and invigorating, with bright sunshine. The austere brown countryside – the river banks, plains, paddies and hills – was awakening from its long hibernation. 'Spring was absolutely beautiful,' thought Fusilier Lieutenant Sam Phillips. 'The hillsides were covered in azaleas.' Magpies called from trees or straggly bushes. White cranes pranced, stiff-legged, beside the river. There was magic in the evenings. 'The fireflies played havoc with us,' said Sweetlove. 'If you went out on patrol, you would shoot at them; they looked like someone flashing a flashlight.'

The hilltop positions granted dramatic views. With no incoming fire, the soldiers did not have to occupy their slit trenches: they could sit on the parapets, gazing out over the curves of the blue Imjin, glinting in the sunlight. In the cool breeze, above the dust, men could watch and think. During the bright days the white-clothed inhabitants of the thatched villages that dotted the brigade area stood out in sharp relief amongst the paddies. Soldiers handed out ration-pack sweets to children in the villages on their patrol routes. At the foot of the Glosters' headquarters position, Hill 235, next to the ruined hamlet of Solma-ri, ran a gurgling stream where men could wash. The war seemed distant, unreal. Waking in their sleeping bags in the mornings, the British soldiers would often be treated to a dreamlike spectacle as they looked over the rims of their hilltop trenches. Below them the countryside – the villages, the patchwork paddies, the valley floors, the river – lay invisible under an opaque white mist through which hilltops protruded like rocks in a sea – an effect Koreans call 'Sea of Clouds'. 'You would hear the voices of the people of the village, and you would see where they had lit fires: the smoke would come up straight in a line,' remembered Gloster Frank Carter. 'It was beautiful. I'll never forget that countryside.'[24]

* * *

On 9 April 29th Brigade was reinforced with a fourth infantry battalion: the Belgian contribution to the UN force. While that country has not in recent decades enjoyed a particularly martial reputation, the battalion Brussels dispatched to the Far East (which included a platoon from Luxembourg) proved one of the finest units in Korea. Every man was a volunteer with at least one year's service – 'They wanted boys, not babies!' – with a hard core of twenty-five or thirty veterans with experience in World War II.[25] Out of 2,000 applicants, only 700 were chosen.[26]

The battalion used the same weapons as the British troops and wore British-pattern uniforms topped off with distinctive brown berets.

Twenty-year-old Sergeant Armand Philips came from a family of patriots. His father had spent four years in a German POW camp, and his uncle had been killed by the Gestapo. 'When the war was over I wanted to do something for the country and I wanted vengeance – though it was the wrong enemy!' He entered an Army school at sixteen, then volunteered for commando and parachute training. Then he was instructing recruits. As soon as he heard of Belgium's participation in the UN forces, he signed up: 'I thought it was better for me, as a young soldier, to get experience. Then the recruits would listen to me.'[27] A young NCO, Sergeant Lucien Senterre, and a twenty-one-year-old reserve officer, Henri Wolfs, were similarly motivated. 'Being posted to Germany as a platoon leader, I soon realised that in tactical situations I often had to lean upon my NCOs,' recalled Wolfs. 'So when the Ministry of Defence asked for volunteers to go to Korea, I jumped.'[28] At least one politician shared the soldiers' convictions: former Defence Minister Moreau de Melen appeared in a recruiting station and volunteered as a reserve major in the new battalion.[29] Another sergeant, André VanDamme, thinking that Korea might escalate into World War III, volunteered immediately. He was proud to join a unit where men 'from all walks of life' had come together: 'The spirit was firmly present.'[30]

Fellow Belgians were not all so gung-ho about the UN mission in Korea. The battalion travelled to Antwerp to board their troopship by rail, and as their train passed through stations en route, *gendarmes* cordoned off the platforms for fear that communists would attempt sabotage before the men had even left Europe. 'This was the Cold War,' mused Philips.[31]

The battalion landed in Pusan on 31 January. Some men wanted to get straight into battle, but higher command insisted that they first acclimatise. Early operations were counter-guerrilla missions in the hills. On one occasion Philips was leading a reconnaissance patrol through a village. The Chinese had pulled back, but North Koreans were believed to be active in the area, and his patrol was briefed to be alert. Spies could be identified, the Belgians were told, as they carried coins: gold for officers, silver for NCOs, and copper for ordinary troops. The patrol encountered a young man – 'the North Koreans, the South Koreans and the Chinese all had the same face' – and searched him. He was unarmed but was carrying a notepad and gold coins. The patrol passed him over to another group of men and continued onward. Later, Philips learned that the men he had handed the suspected spy over to – 'They were not in the war, they were still in Belgium!' – had released him. The suspected spy was subsequently recaptured by another patrol. The young sergeant seethed. 'We had been promised eight days' leave if we caught a prisoner, and a man in B Company got it!'

But that they were in a real war became gruesomely clear once the battalion moved up to the Han. The Belgians were crossing ground in company with American tanks when a Belgian officer stepped on a wooden anti-personnel mine. He shouted a warning when several metres behind him, the ground erupted, killing and wounding a group of Belgians and Americans, including ex-commando officer Lieutenant Beauprez. 'He was scattered over about twenty metres,' said Philips. 'We had to bury the bits as best we could.' American mine-clearance tanks were equipped with chain flails on their bows, so the Chinese had linked the wooden anti-personnel mine – which would be detonated by the mine-clearer – to a heavier anti-tank mine several metres behind. The second mine was packed with two kilos of TNT.[32]

On the Imjin, the British soldiers soon got to know their new comrades. 'They had a fantastic CO,' said Rifles Captain Robin Charley of Colonel Albert Crahay, the Belgian commander. 'He had come down in rank to command his battalion. He wore a silk scarf and had tremendous charisma.'[33] Lieutenant George Truell of 45 Field thought Crahay 'a strong, tough chap . . . a very good soldier'. (Truell, perhaps, felt an affinity: Crahay was a gunner not a foot soldier, although his key subordinate officers had solid infantry or commando backgrounds.) 'He was a fine and sober man,' said Sergeant VanDamme. 'Always open to his soldiers.' Second Lieutenant Wolfs thought Crahay had the 'quiet personality and matter-of-fact confidence so typical of a real gentleman'.[34] Crahay was not the only impressive Belgian officer. 'There were some very interesting chaps,' added Truell. 'Albert Guerrisse had won a George Cross and a DSO for work with SOE* during the war. They were a very, very good battalion.'

The Belgians cultivated a devil-may-care, swashbuckling attitude. Moving north by train in cattle cars – 'like the Germans used to send people to Auschwitz in' – the soldiers lit a fire in the straw covering the floor. The straw fire ignited the wagon, forcing the train to halt while the blaze was extinguished.[35] Truell was at a party at Divisional HQ with a Belgian officer when they encountered a British rear echelon officer – a species despised by many combat troops. 'I was with Major Jean Militis, a Belgian company commander. He was pretty drunk, I think, and he had been talking to a British officer from the legal department who was there for some reason. Jean pulled out his pistol and said, "You are a base wallah! You have never heard the sound of a bullet!" So he fired two shots – one

---

* SOE – Special Operations Executive – was the covert, London-controlled sabotage and espionage network that operated across the Nazi-occupied continent during World War II. Its role, according to Churchill, was to 'set Europe ablaze'.

past each ear! – which went through the tent without hitting anyone, for-tunately.'*[36] Even the Belgian chaplain, Vander Goten, was nonconformist. 'He succeeded in making many men believers,' wrote Wolfs. 'At every operation, he would give the men blessings, and full absolution without confession – at the time strictly forbidden by the Vatican.'[37]

The Rifles held a party behind Hill 194 to which the Belgians were invited. A social gathering of hard-drinking Ulstermen and Belgians – heirs to Europe's finest brewing tradition – could only end in fireworks. It did. After the party died down, the Rifles were climbing – unsteadily, in some cases – up the rear slopes of 'Fort Nixon' when mortars began bursting around them: The Belgians, in jest, were bombarding them with smoke shells. 'It was pretty entertaining,' Rifles Lieutenant John Mole conceded. 'The Belgians were as mad as hatters!'[38]

While there had been serious concerns in the brigade about the steadiness of their US and ROK allies, there was no such issue with the Belgians. Brodie demonstrated his confidence in the new battalion when he deployed it on arguably his most exposed position: on Friday 20 April the Belgians replaced the Rifles on Hill 194, on the northern river bank, at the confluence of the Imjin and Hantan.†[39] This freed the Rifles to move into brigade reserve. The Rifles had transformed Hill 194 into a fortress (unlike other positions on the Imjin). Henri Wolf's platoon were pleased at the barbed wire, 'which had never been a common sight until then'.[40] But the Rifles were a full-strength British battalion, with four full rifle companies to the Belgians' three. Philips's platoon found itself taking over positions designed for a company. In a characteristi-cally Irish gesture, the Riflemen left the Belgians of C Company all their spare ammunition, so that, instead of each man having 150 rounds to hand, he would have 300. As the Ulstermen pointed out vantage points, cover and likely attack routes, a Rifleman warned Sergeant Philips: 'This is the hinge: If you open this door, it's the finish for the rest,' Philips recalled. 'Soldiers' talk!'[41]

* * *

If kept on static outpost duty for too long, troops go stale. To remedy this – and to discover enemy dispositions across the river – 29th Brigade instituted an extensive patrolling programme over the Imjin. On 9 April Sergeant Philips and his platoon went across the river with two tanks of

* Militis had fought in the resistance and been wounded in the Ardennes. He later became a member of the Belgian Parliament.
† The across-the-river position was more exposed to enemy attack, but, as events would soon prove, the Glosters' position was more isolated from the bulk of the brigade, due to its line of communication: Five Yankee ran through a steep defile.

N

**VALLEY OF THE WATER DRAGON:**
Imjin Front, April 1951.

Kyeho-dong

Imjin River

Sanjom-ni
Pukch'ang

Yongjong-ni    Chingp'a-ri    Kyonmo-ri    Yonch'on

Unmaurhan

Tanggogae

Sokchangsang-ni

To Pyongyang
Manch'on

Taraktae

Hantan River

Ch'arumul

P.194
BEL

Tagamp'o

Chon'gong-ni    U.S. 3rd
Division

Tunjan

Imjin River

Line Kansas

RNF    P.257
45 FR

P.398    Sop'yonch'an

Choksong
Glos.

Route 11

Mau-san

1st ROK
Division

Solma-ri
P.235

P.675
Kamak San

Hwangbang-ni    RUR

Sangbi-ri    Tongduch'on-ni

Kwangsuwon

"Five Yankee"

Route 33/ MSR

To Uijongbu/Seoul

0        3 km
0        3 Miles

Tokchong

the Hussars. The Centurions forded the river, while the infantry went in boats manned by engineers. Once across, the Belgians mounted the tanks and headed north. 'We rode, spoke, ate, drank – a vacation. It was warm, the sun was up, all OK.' The only things the patrol saw were burning hillsides where American jets were dropping napalm, far to the north. They returned before dark. The following day, Philips went out again with the Rifles and the Hussars. Again they saw nothing. On 14 April another sweep. This time there was a brief firefight. The Belgians, suffering no casualties, killed two enemy and took a prisoner. 'He was a boy – no hair on his chest! – in big pyjamas, the battledress of the Chinese,' Philips said. Brodie, delighted, personally congratulated the Belgians. On 15 April Philips's men provided an infantry detachment for a troop of Hussars stationed over the river. No contact. And so it went. 'It was not dangerous, it was not hard, there was no enemy in sight,' said Philips. 'It was a promenade!'

Some 'promenades' took on an almost festive atmosphere. The Glosters were riding Centurions on a sweep over the river when a deer broke cover. The men blazed away, and venison replaced bully beef for dinner.[42] During this period, the 'Field Postal Service' began to work. 'Out on patrol, you'd find a wooden box full of leaflets, set in no man's land,' said Sweetlove. 'There would be notes saying, "Surrender! You'll be home by Christmas!"' Few, if any, members of the brigade were impressed by such crude propaganda, but a channel of communications had been opened with the enemy. It would later pay dividends.

The inhabitants of the Imjin Valley had become inured to war. The few civilians the patrols encountered had developed survival mechanisms, as a newly arrived Gloster officer, the tall, gangling Second Lieutenant Denys Whatmore, found in one village. 'They hoisted a banner with, written on it in English, "Welcome UN soldiers."* I wondered whether they had another one in their huts that they could hoist when the Chinese came down. They were in a wretched position.'[43] Another new arrival was Lieutenant Peter Whitamore, who had volunteered for Korea and the Rifles from the Loyal Lancashires. 'I was sent up to the Imjin two days after I'd joined in late March,' he said. His first job was a patrol. 'We advanced to contact – mile after bloody mile. I felt pretty green.' There was no contact.

New men were arriving from reinforcement units in Japan as casualty replacements. One, Lieutenant P.J. Kavanagh, joined the Rifles. He was immediately impressed by the veteran appearance of the men who had

---

* In the Korean War Memorial at Yongsan, Seoul, there is a photograph of laughing ROK troops with a confused-looking old peasant who is holding both North and South Korean flags.

survived the winter fighting. The skins of their faces and hands were burnt by frost and wind, their uniforms and assorted headgear had been bleached by the dust, but fitted each man like a skin. 'They've become warriors,' he thought.[44] By now, the troops had worked out the optimal personal equipment scales. Gone were the bulky winter outfits. Most men now wore battledress or camouflage smocks, with berets or cap comforters. The bulky pouches of the 44 Pattern webbing equipment, which fitted on the chest, proved unpopular – they prevented a soldier hugging the ground when lying prone. Most men, instead, carried their ammunition in canvas bandoliers, or down the front of jackets.

Some new arrivals wanted to get into the thick of it. Few were keener than a big, bluff northerner named Derek Kinne. He had completed National Service, but had not taken to the discipline and had been told, 'You'll never make a soldier!' In eighteen months, he had done 158 days' punishment. 'I was an obnoxious bastard,' he admitted. After demob, he was working in a hotel in Darlington when he heard that his brother, Raymond, had been killed in Korea with the Argyll and Sutherland Highlanders. Kinne was stunned: the two brothers had made a pact that if one went missing, the other would find him. That afternoon, Kinne decided to go to Korea, find Raymond's grave and kill as many enemy as he could. He signed up as a 'K Volunteer' and joined the Fusiliers on the Imjin. He was disappointed by the lack of action, but patrolling provided an outlet. 'The front line fascinated me – I was one of those nuts who loved it,' he said. 'I was a walking arsenal: if a bullet had hit me I'd have blown up! I volunteered for every patrol: I used to go out on night patrol, and they'd save me a spot on day patrol.' On 13 April, across the Imjin, Kinne got his first whiff of cordite. The Fusiliers were clearing a hillside. Captain De Quidt, X Company's second in command, directed the operation. Kinne, ordered up the hill, climbed up a trench that led to the top. At the summit he peered over the parapet. Just feet away, a Chinese soldier looked up at the same moment. Contact! Kinne hurled a hand grenade and took cover. 'I counted 4-5-6 . . . nothing happened!' he said; he had forgotten to pull the pin. He clicked off his safety catch, put butt to shoulder and popped his head up; the Chinese had had the same idea. Kinne squeezed the trigger. Hit! It was his first kill. He was ordered to pick up ID from the dead Chinese,* so asked if he should retrieve his undetonated grenade. De Quidt walked off, shaking his head, muttering, 'Oh, God, God! He forgot to pull the pin!' But Kinne had been bitten by the bug. The garrison bad boy had discovered a talent for real soldiering.

---

* British soldiers were trained to pick up the IDs of dead enemy. These were then passed to the Red Cross, who would then inform the Chinese government, who would, it was hoped, inform the families of those killed.

The cross-river patrols became more ambitious. Hussar CO Sir Guy Lowther took a 'small army' dubbed 'Lowtherforce' across the river on an 'armoured swan' eighteen miles deep on 20 April. It consisted of a squadron and a half of Centurions – around twenty-five vehicles – plus the gunner Cromwells, and two companies of Glosters.[45] Fusilier CO Kingsley Foster led an even deeper patrol. These big recces raised huge dust clouds. When enemy were spotted or suspected on the hills, the tanks fired while infantry cleared the (usually abandoned) positions. Sam Mercer thought the Centurions moving cross country were 'quite a sight', but mused: 'There was no Chindit-type fieldcraft by us.' Major Pat Angier of the Glosters considered the recce 'a very cavalry occasion . . . just like the hunting field, tanks roaring, galloping, jumping and bogging down everywhere'. A keen water-colourist, Angier spent the day enjoying the pink azaleas.[46] The patrols suffered minor damage to vehicles and a trickle of casualties from mines.[47]

However, the intelligence gathered was minimal. On 20 April the Fusiliers' Intelligence Officer Tony Perrins flew in a two-seat observation aircraft. Peering out, he tried to spot signs of the enemy. 'Intelligence indicated that they were massing north of the river,' he said. 'We must have flown about twenty-five miles.' Suddenly, a bullet winged past the aircraft. 'Other than that, we saw no indication that there was anyone down there.' On the bucking rear of a tank, Gloster Frank Carter spoke to an eighteen-year-old prisoner via an interpreter. The boy said he had been an army cadet in his village, and his unit was asked to volunteer for Korea. To refuse would have meant losing face, so he did. When Carter asked where the Chinese main force was, the boy's reply was ominous. 'The rest are a few miles back.'[48]

* * *

The daytime 'promenades' were one thing. Being across the Imjin after dark was a different proposition. Captain Peter Ormrod's tank threw a track on the wrong side of the river. The sun went down. REME fitters arrived to work on the vehicle with shaded torches. Ormrod was uneasy. 'Somehow I had the feeling that we were being watched – a sort of sinister feeling. I am not a smoker, but on that occasion, I smoked a cigarette.' The engineers fixed the track, and after half an hour, the Hussars returned to the south bank.[49] When neither reconnaissance in strength on the ground nor aerial reconnaissance succeeded in locating the Chinese mass, more circumspect tactics were tried. 'When we came back across the river at night, we left a platoon in hiding to watch over the village, to see if anyone came,' said Lieutenant Sam Phillips. 'I was left [over the river] and spent a very uncomfortable night; one was too terrified to say anything.' Nothing happened. 'There was damn-all there, apart from locals.'

The most dangerous activity was fighting patrols. The Glosters spent a leisurely afternoon watching American aircraft dive-bombing hills over the river. Days later, B Company was informed that the aircraft had been doing photographic reconnaissance under cover of the attacks, and the photographs showed an entrenched hill. A patrol was to go in on a prisoner snatch. At last light the patrol moved down to the river and was ferried across in aluminium boats. On the north bank the engineers had laid a white tape that marked a mine-free zone, but it only stretched for a hundred yards. Beyond the cleared zone the patrol adopted a diamond formation and moved, warily, deeper into the countryside. Visibility was provided by 'artificial moonlight': huge American searchlights that bounced light off low cloud, bathing the area in a dull glow. The patrol reached the target hill and began climbing. Halfway up, Bren gunner Frank Carter looked down and saw two armed figures in a village, pointing at the climbing Glosters. Carter slapped the boot of the man ahead of him and hissed at him to pass on that they had been spotted. The word came back: 'Continue climbing.' The patrol had just reached the trench that ran around the hilltop when the artificial moonlight went out. In the sudden blackness, the leading men in the patrol tumbled into the trench: 'You have never heard so much noise in your life!' said Carter. 'Everyone was swearing and trying to keep quiet.' The patrol split, with half going one way, the other half walking the other way around the trench. The trench proved empty, but Carter had an edgy, sixth-sense feeling. The patrol commander decided to descend to the village and grab the two enemy Carter had spotted earlier.

The patrol began moving back down the hillside. When they were around twenty yards from the top 'all hell broke loose'. Tracers streaked down from the 'empty' trench, while rifles and automatics opened up from the village below. The patrol froze in the crossfire, as their officer, shot through the jaw, fell unconscious. Sergeant Ted Shaw took command and immediately dropped the idea of grabbing a prisoner. The priority was to get out. Carter raked the hilltop with long Bren bursts; the rest of the section poured rapid fire onto the village below. They scrambled down the hill and ran. Rounds cracked overhead as they dragged their casualty in a groundsheet. The charge for the river was 'like a herd of elephants', Carter thought. At the bank, the engineers issued a challenge. The breathless Glosters shouted the password. As they tumbled into the boats, the engineers told them that with all the shooting, they thought the patrol had been wiped out. Back at their position, the exhausted men were told they would have to go back the following night. From the anonymous darkness, a reservist ejaculated, 'You're not bloody getting me!' In the event, the second patrol did not take place.[50]

While 29th Brigade attempted to gain a picture of enemy dispositions, the stealthier Chinese were doing the same thing. The CPVA assigned 'deep reconnaissance' units of 200–300 men to army groups to undertake intelligence and sabotage missions. These special forces included experienced North Korean officers who knew the land, the people and the language.[51] One detachment inserted a team onto Kamak-san, the highest summit in the brigade area, which offered views over the entire defensive layout.[52] The British battalion commanders, so keen on patrolling across the river, had not seen fit to place a standing patrol on this critical feature. A key issue was the classic guerrilla warfare problem: how to tell enemy troops from civilians? 'We had not been able to establish a no-go zone for civilians, who wandered around,' said Mercer. Most companies had set trip flares around their perimeters, and these were often set off by civilians – or apparent civilians. 'The peasants had a habit of tripping the flares,' remembered Carter. 'We fired on 'em and drove 'em off – they were just trying to find our positioning.'[53] By the third week of April rumours of an enemy offensive were mounting. Civilians were not straying far from their villages. Doors were being bolted at night.[54]

On the night of 21 April there could no longer be any question that the enemy was probing. Bugler Tony Eagles was with a three-man listening patrol under Corporal George Cook on 'Gloster Crossing'. At 22:00 Eagles – his eyesight apparently appropriate to his name – whispered, 'I see movement.' Straining to see, the patrol made out fourteen enemy on the north bank. The Chinese, unaware they were being watched, waded stealthily into the river. The Glosters urgently reported back to the adjutant by field telephone. 'We thought a listening patrol just listened, but Farrar-Hockley said, "Don't let them come close,"' Eagles recalled. The adjutant ordered flares shot up to illuminate the river. When the Chinese were halfway across, Eagles and Private 'Scouse' Hunter opened fire with their rifles: their shooting was so rapid that men to their rear thought it was a Bren. The Chinese retired. Three bodies were spotted floating downstream, and the patrol could see four wounded being dragged up the far bank. For the rest of the night, the Glosters were 'on a knife edge', awaiting retaliation. Nothing happened.[55] At dawn there was no sign of enemy. Like ghosts or vampires, the Chinese disappeared in daylight.

* * *

While 29th Brigade sat on the Imjin, to their east other units of General Frank Milburn's I Corps had been advancing northward as 'Operation Dauntless' was launched across the Hantan. This limited offensive was designed to shove a twenty-five-mile-wide bulge ten miles northwards of Line Kansas towards the city of Chorwon. Once this line, Line Utah, was established, it was to be a springboard for an advance onto the next major phase line, Line Wyoming, twenty miles north of Line Kansas. On 11 April the US 3rd, 24th and 25th Divisions crossed the river against light opposition. Progress was steady. By 21 April they had gained Line Utah.[56] The enemy main force had vanished. But there were sinister signs.

Since mid-April 'Dauntless' troops gazing to their front could see massive billows of smoke, some of it in banks ten miles long. Air observers reported enemy troops, some in company strength, igniting belts of grass and bush. Smoke generators were reported. Even when rain showers extinguished them, the smoke-screens blossomed up again, mixing with cloud and fog to create a dense, smoggy haze that blanketed the north. These were the very tactics the CPVA had adopted to conceal their first infiltration of North Korea's mountains.[57]

Marshal Peng had not been idle. Acknowledging the failure of his Fourth Offensive, he had withdrawn, conserving his manpower, rolling with Ridgway's punches. His forces were massively reinforced with new men from China and re-equipped with Russian weapons. By April three fresh Army Groups – the 3rd, 9th and 19th – had arrived from China to spearhead his next attack.[58] He could now prepare his next move. For this attack he had massed 270,000 Chinese; a North Korean corps of 35,000 men would also join the offensive.[59] Never before in this war had so many troops been marshalled for a single operation. Peng planned his attack for May but – concerned that Operation Dauntless would put UN mechanised forces into the open country around Chorwon (the 'Iron Triangle', a site of major communist dumps and bases) and worried about possible amphibious landings in his rear – he advanced his timetable. The 19th Army Group would strike southwards to the west of the Imjin's northward turn, while the 3rd and 9th Army Groups would strike southward to the east of it.[60] Speed was critical: Peng promised Mao Seoul as a May Day gift.[61]

Peng's 'Fifth Offensive' was designed not just to seize the capital; it would also annihilate three American and two ROK divisions, along with the Turkish and British brigades. In his orders Peng wrote that the attack would 'wipe out . . . the American 3rd Division . . . the British 29th Brigade and the 1st Division of the Puppet Army* . . . after this we can wipe out the American 24th Division and 25th Division'.[62] Such a loss would be decisive; the UN had only fourteen divisions in Korea (seven US and seven ROK, plus smaller brigade- and battalion-sized contingents).[63] If he overcame the UN units in the west, Peng could then cut off and roll up, in turn, the US 3rd, 24th and 25th Divisions from the flank. To achieve

* 'Puppet Army': the ROK Army.

this, the key sector was between the ROK 1st Division and the US 3rd Division, where the Imjin and the Hantan converged, and where Routes 11 and 33 ran – the ground 29th Brigade held. The north–south line of the Imjin channelled any attack onto this very axis. Thus 29th Brigade was holding the historical passageway to South Korea's capital, but, given the dispositions of UN forces in April 1951, its position was doubly critical. In nineteenth-century parlance, it was occupying 'The Post of Honour'.

The man tasked with attacking this vital sector was General Yang Teh-chih, commander of 19th Army Group. His force comprised two armies: the 63rd and 64th. Their officers, communists who had beaten American-equipped troops in the Chinese civil war, were confident in their numerical and spiritual superiority.[64] The 64th Army would hit ROK 1st Division, while Yang would launch his 63rd Army against 29th Brigade. Each army comprised three full divisions;* each division contained three regiments; each regiment, three battalions. The 63rd's divisions were the 187th, 188th, and 189th – 27,000 men grouped into twenty-seven infantry battalions.[65] 29th Brigade's four foot battalions would be facing paper odds of almost 7:1 against; in reality, with the attacker (who always holds the initiative) massing against strongpoints, the odds would be greater.†

In the hazy north, the communist armies stepped up preparations. From army down to division, regiment, battalion and company, communist troops mustered for briefings on objectives and timetables. Ammunition and

---

* A Chinese army, of three divisions, was the equivalent of a UN corps, albeit I Corps was an unusually strong corps.

† The appearance of these divisions, in-theatre, was known to both the UN Command in Tokyo and the general staff in London. Their arrival had been noted by UN intelligence, and reports on their presence north of 29th Brigade sent to Whitehall. Air Vice Marshall Cecil Bourchier, the British liaison officer at Supreme Command Headquarters in Tokyo, had noted in a secret cipher telegram to the Chiefs of Staff on 11 April: 'The Chinese are bringing their 18th and 19th Army Groups to the Western flank of the line. He is thinning out his forces in the centre. Thus when the enemy is able to build up his supplies we may expect the main weight of his counter offensive to be launched in the west down towards Seoul and the Han River valley. I estimate the beginning of May as the earliest date the enemy can be in a position to launch an all out offensive.' This was good intelligence, and good analysis: Bourchier was prescient (albeit a week late in his forecast). But on 18 April, he cabled, again to the chiefs of staff: 'Capability of enemy to resume offensive. In recent telegram I have indicated a definite shift of main bulk of Chinese forces from central area to the extreme west flank. Since then, American headquarters here has fully accepted fresh Chinese 19th Army Group consisting of 63rd, 4th, and 65th Corps . . . *One division of leading Chinese 63rd Corps of this Army Group has been positively identified due west of Chorwon on west bank of Imjin River where this river sweeps sharply to the north with 2 other divisions of this corps immediately in the rear*. In other words [unclear] to British 29th Brigade . . . *It is confidently felt here however that the enemy is not at all in a position to launch and maintain an all out offensive at this time*' (author's italics). This is excellent intelligence but woeful analysis: here is the senior British military officer in the Far East noting the presence of *three enemy divisions* north of 29th Brigade, in echelon (which, as it turned out, is exactly how they would attack), but not raising the alarm, recommending action, or anticipating any offensive 'in the near future'. DEFE 11 210: Situation in Korea from 3 4 1951 to 18 4 1951. Document held in National Archive, Kew.

rations were handed out and stashed in packs, belts and bandoliers. Peng set his attack for the night of 22 April. The axe was poised. What would one day be dubbed 'The Armageddon North of Seoul' had been set in motion.[66]

* * *

Sunday 22 April would be a busy day for Gloster Padre Sam Davies. In addition to ministering to his own regiment, he had been invited by Lieutenant-Colonel Kingsley Foster to preach to the Fusiliers in advance of their regimental celebration, St George's Day, on the 23rd. The spot chosen was behind Z Company's position; the altar would be prepared by the battalion's Intelligence Section. That section had adopted an orphaned boy. 'They hid him from me as long as they could,' said Lieutenant Tony Perrins – who, as it turned out, had no complaints about the pint-sized addition to his command. 'Inevitably, he was called Kim, and he was an absolutely wonderful boy. He helped my soldier servant take care of me, he did the laundry; he probably did the same thing for all the boys in the section.' In preparation for the sermon, Perrins sent Kim up the hillside to pick azaleas for the field altar. The little Fusilier fulfilled his mission – and more. He planted azaleas in food cans dug in around the altar, and placed sprigs of evergreen upon it. 'He did a better job than you will see at most parish services,' Perrins remembered.[67]

Vague rumours of impending battle increased Davies's congregation.[68] Mortar Sergeant Bill Beattie, whose wife had just given birth to a son, had a long chat with the padre; Beattie had not yet decided on a name for his boy. At the service, the men's hymns carried up through the clear morning air. Foster concluded the event by reading out the Fusiliers' awards for gallantry conferred by the King for the battalion's winter actions. Then he invited Davies back to his tent for a sherry.[69] The Fusiliers returned to their positions. 'It was another beautiful spring day,' said Lieutenant Malcolm Cubiss. 'It was perfectly quiet.'

Other members of Foster's battalion were preparing for their customary regimental feast the next day, St George's Day. The men received the red and white roses of England to place in their berets, behind their cap badges.* Beer had been stockpiled – two bottles per man – for the celebration. David Strachan and his mates from Z Company were taken to a trestle loaded with turkey and photographed. After the photographer departed, the bird was removed by the cooks in preparation for the following day.[70] A mobile cinema unit set up, and the Rifles' pipes and drums prepared to 'Beat Retreat' in the evening.[71]

---

* The flowers obtained for the Fusiliers in Japan were made of a kind of fabric; 45 Field managed to get hold of fresh roses.

Davies did not tarry long with Foster. At midday, he had to tend to his own flock. He took a jeep and set his field altar and communion chalice out in the hall of a deserted Buddhist temple that lay behind the most forward Gloster position, A Company's 'Castle Site'. On this Korean holy ground, he ministered. After the service, the soldiers stood and chatted in the courtyard, when word came that a Gloster patrol across the river was in contact. There was no apparent concern.[72] A photograph was taken of two of A Company's officers at this time. The two – the tall, dashing-looking Lieutenant Phil Curtis, the shorter, shy-looking Second Lieutenant Terry Waters – are standing casually, hands in pockets, smiling at the camera; behind them, jeeps are parked outside the temple gates. There is a haunting quality to the shot. Both men had received Communion from Davies. As the padre was later to write, it would prove to be their viaticum. (In both Catholic and Anglican traditions, the viaticum – 'provisions for a journey' – is the Eucharist given to a dying man.)

But nobody, as yet, could know what was to come, or the manner in which these two young men would discharge their duties. Davies climbed back into his jeep and made the bumpy, ten-minute journey to the battalion headquarters area at the foot of Hill 235, where he delivered yet another service beside the stream. A photograph was also taken there. Of the 23 Glosters in the shot, eight were to die in the coming days.

* * *

Fusilier Lieutenant Sam Phillips was spending a less restful Sunday morning – on cross-river reconnaissance. 'I don't remember anyone saying, "Look, the balloon's going to go up tonight,"' he said, but north of the Imjin, he noticed something he had never seen before: telephone cables leading down to the river. He had the lines cut. Soon after, his patrol noticed movement on a ridge to their front. An enemy sentry was running along the skyline, apparently rousing soldiers lying in cover. Phillips's patrol had been spotted. There were sharp cracks as the Fusiliers started taking fire from an estimated forty enemy. Phillips's mission was recce, not combat. He called in artillery and, over the radio, was ordered to withdraw. 'I was very pleased about that,' he said. 'One had the feeling something was going to happen.' As shells devastated the hilltop behind them, the Fusiliers took boats back to the south bank. At Battalion HQ, Perrins was pleased when Phillips, one of his best friends, arrived. 'Sam didn't smoke, so he suffered from intense hunger and always took the opportunity to come back to report,' said Perrins. 'But he was coming for the food!' When Phillips briefed him and Foster on what he had discovered it was Perrins's first intimation that 'something was happening'. Phillips, fed, returned to his company. Perrins was preparing for a nap when the nearby 25-pounders started firing. He remained unconcerned: like many soldiers, he had learned to live with the thunder of bombardments. The intelligence officer turned in.

Meanwhile, reports of Chinese movement were multiplying across the front. Air recce was reporting enemy groups – some numbering in their hundreds – and gun batteries heading south. The Turkish Brigade, to the east of 3rd Division, had seized prisoners; members of a lost artillery survey party. The presence of artillery indicated the imminence of a large-scale attack. The prisoners confirmed that the offensive would kick off after nightfall. Higher headquarters was unperturbed; I Corps was prepared for battle. A massive dump with two days' supply of ammunition stood ready in Seoul; a petrol tanker and an ammunition supply ship were moored in Inchon harbour; most non-combat heavy equipment had been moved south of the Han.[73] It was believed that the enemy's main force was still fifteen or twenty miles north of the Imjin. Any advances on the night of the 22nd were thus expected to be probes, rather than full-scale attacks.[74]

Afternoon. Lieutenant-Colonel James Carne was at the river bank, lying on his stomach above 'Gloster Crossing' with a pair of binoculars, a radio and a map, directing mortar fire at enemy patrols moving to the north. As the bombs exploded far across the river, the Gloster officers and NCOs with Carne could see winks of light and puffs of black smoke that dispersed quickly in the spring breeze. 'That ought to tickle them a bit,' commented an officer.[75] Lieutenant George Truell of 45 Field's 70 Battery, supporting the Glosters, was beginning to get busy. 'There were various odd reports: people seeing movement here and there,' he said. 'The flaps grew steadily.' At 14:00 Truell was firing on targets across the river. He felt a vague uneasiness; no cross-river patrols on previous days had reported any significant Chinese movement.

Information was by now filtering through to the forward units – usually, the last men to hear anything. In the Gloster D Company positions Second-Lieutenant Denys Whatmore was told that Chinese, in strength, had been sighted heading south. Extra ammunition was distributed. The men oiled and cleaned weapons and made last-minute improvements to their slits.[76] On Hill 235 the trenches of the Gloster machine-gunners – yard after yard after yard – were filled with coiled ammunition belts. When machine-gunner Byron Murphy questioned such quantities, RSM Jack Hobbs confirmed their necessity.[77] Similar preparations were under way across the brigade.

Buzzing high above the front, Sapper Major Tony Younger was on a recce flight in a US artillery observation aircraft. Spotting what looked like an overturned cart – a common transport device among the enemy – he asked the pilot to descend and circle. Suddenly, bullets whined past. The plane was hit; the pilot cursed, but landed safely with a dozen holes in his fuselage. Returning to HQ, Younger was pleasantly surprised to find Major Pat Angier, the thoughtful and experienced commander of the Glosters' A Company, with whom he had struck up a friendship on the *Empire Windrush*. The two had a drink, and Younger told him about his flight. Angier was disturbed; the cart was directly opposite his position. Declining Younger's offer of another round, he told the engineer that he had 'a funny feeling about tonight. I think we may have some problems ahead of us.' He hurried back to his command.[78]

Evening was approaching. Forward observer Bob Nicholls of 170 Mortar Battery, with the Fusiliers' X Company, was at a listening post on the river. An excited Korean child appeared. He pointed across the Imjin, exclaiming, 'Many, many Chinese!'* Nicholls gave the boy some rations in thanks; the child took off. Nicholls reported the warning up the chain of command, then returned to his hilltop. 'We liked to get back up the hill before it got too dark.'

At 19:30 Brigade HQ received reports from the US 24th Division, to the north-east, of the approach of 'huge forces'. Brodie ordered his reserve, the Rifles, to prepare for action. The Rifles' quick reaction force – the Battle Patrol – was alerted to move at thirty minutes' notice. The forward battalions were placed on 50 per cent stand-to. Behind the hills, gunners and signallers, staff officers and NCOs sat in trenches, vehicles and tents, listening in on radio nets and standing by field telephones.[79] In dressing stations, orderlies and surgeons laid out instruments.

As night fell Brodie joined the press at their camp for dinner. One reporter asked when the enemy might launch his long-awaited offensive. Casually, the brigadier replied, 'Might be tonight.' The journalists, who had been filing human-interest stories for weeks for want of any significant action, scoffed. One offered Brodie a bet, 'for anything you like' that no attack would come. He declined.[80]

* * *

Twilight, 22 April. The sun dipped behind the Imjin hills. From their hilltop outposts, the British and Belgian soldiers, bathed in the orange glow, watched the light fade, the sky darken and the shadows creep across the valleys and ravines. Despite the 50 per cent stand-to, there was still no indication of anything untoward. Crouched over rifles, Brens

---

* After the battle, Nicholls would return to the location. He found long tunnels penetrating the hillside in which hundreds of Chinese could have sheltered. They were exactly where the boy had been pointing.

and Vickers, men whispered quietly to one another. A short chuckle here; a cough there. In the background, radio sets crackled and hissed.

Let us take one last look at dispositions. Even on staff maps, 29th Brigade was barely a 'thin red line', more a series of isolated dots denoting company strongpoints perched atop hills and ridges.

At the forefront, on the brigade's right (eastern) flank, were the Belgians, holding Hill 194 to the north of the confluence of the Imjin and Hantan. Behind them, holding the Imjin's southern bank were the Fusiliers. The easternmost company was Z, on a dominant hilltop; next along to the west was Y, in the wide loop of the river; X was on another hilltop, the furthest left of the Fusiliers' positions. W was further back from the river in reserve. Behind Z Company, at the north-eastern end of Route 11 (the brigade's main line of communications), the twenty-four guns of 45 Field stood, barrels elevated, ready to shoot onto pre-planned DF targets. 170 Mortar Battery was dispersed: one troop with each of the forward battalions. Some five miles behind the Fusiliers, down Route 11, the Rifles waited in reserve. Also on Route 11 squatted the Centurions of the Hussars' C Squadron.* The great tanks were silent, closed down, arranged in their customary circle for the night, their guns turned outward; the leaguer bristled like a great, armoured hedgehog. Brigade HQ – an encampment of supply trucks, radio trucks, scout cars, jeeps, caravans, tents and radio aerials – was two miles south of the Fusiliers on Route 11. Continuing west along the river bank, to the left of the Fusiliers there was a two-mile gap before the Glosters' B Company, the easternmost company of the battalion. Next to the west was D, on a hill to one side of Choksong; on the other side of the village, on its hill south of the river and 'Gloster Crossing', was A, the brigade's westernmost unit . Out of contact on their left was the 1st ROK Division. Behind the forward Gloster companies, C was in reserve, overlooking the Gloster HQ and Support Companies. The men of the latter units inhabited a little village of trenches, tents and parked vehicles next to the shallow stream trickling over its pebble bed behind the rocky mass of Hill 235 – soon to gain a new name that would be splashed over newspaper headlines across the free world.

Here Second Lieutenant Guy Temple received his orders. The engines of two troop carriers barked into life, reverberating around the valley. Filing down from C Company's hill, the men of Temple's 7 Platoon, faces blacked out and heavily burdened with ammunition, climbed aboard the vehicles. In a cloud of dust and exhaust fumes, the Oxfords rumbled through the gloom, down to the river bank.

---

* Due to the closed-in terrain of the Imjin Valley, the Hussars' A and B Squadrons were deployed further south. They would play no part in the battle.

By 19:07 the sun had sunk into the distant Yellow Sea. Night settled over the landscape. Not a single light winked in the countryside across the river. Everything to the brigade's front was a blur of blacks and greys. A full yellow moon rose and hung over the Valley of the Water Dragon.

To the north – across the silent river, beyond the flood plains and paddy fields, down dusty paths and tracks, through silent villages and dark foothills – a mighty mass was moving through the blackness. In platoons and companies, battalions and regiments, divisions and armies, enemy soldiers were marching and jogging, advancing steadily to contact. Rugged, fit, some would cover twenty miles that night. This was no probing force. The lead element of almost a third of a million communist troops – 305,000 men – was in motion. Across a forty-mile front the human wave rolled south. The greatest offensive of the Korean War had been unleashed.*

Many of the men who watched the sun sink behind the Imjin hills would not see the dawn.

* Not only was the 'Fifth Offensive' the largest attack of the Korean War, even by the standards of World War II, the numbers the Chinese and North Koreans employed were notable. The German Sixth Army which seized Stalingrad in 'Operation Blue' in 1942 deployed around 200,000 troops. At the second battle of El Alamein, also in 1942, Montgomery attacked with approximately 200,000 men. And the Allied forces which hit the Normandy beaches on D-Day 1944 numbered around 156,000. For a modern comparison, at time of writing the entire British Army numbers around 100,000 men – less than a third of the size of the colossal force Peng ordered south on the evening of 22 April 1951.

# Chapter 6

## ONSLAUGHT: 22 APRIL.

*Lord, . . . Come close to those . . .*
*Who in this hour go up the steep ascent*
*To Heaven's Gate, o'ercrowded on this day of battle.*

'Dying' Prayer, Royal Ulster Rifles

SERGEANT ARMAND PHILIPS was waiting for a telephone call. On the western slopes of the Belgian position on Hill 194 north of the river, he sat in his slit trench among B Platoon, C Company. Next to him sat a field telephone. Its line ran approximately 1,500 yards to a listening post, established following a patrol contact in the afternoon. The LP was on level ground in front of the hill; due to the angle of the hillside, men higher up the slopes could not see what was happening at ground level.

Darkness had fallen. The night was silent. Suddenly, the telephone jangled. Philips answered immediately. 'A Chinese section of ten to fifteen men – half armed, half carrying ammunition – is walking past my position, heading for the river!' Sergeant Leiding, manning the LP, hissed. Philips acknowledged the message and passed it to Company HQ, from where it was passed up to Battalion HQ. Minutes later, the phone rang again. Leiding whispered, 'Now, there are fifty of them!' Philips passed the message along once more. Tense minutes passed. Then – again – the phone. 'There are so many I can't count!' the sergeant whispered urgently. Filled with foreboding, Philips passed the message up.[*]

It was now 22:20.[1] Fireworks burst over Philips's head: star shells. The sector was bathed in sizzling white light. 'It was very beautiful to see – they lit the whole landscape.' As his eyes adjusted to the glare, he saw an astonishing sight. 'There were Chinese everywhere – like mushrooms!' The riverside plain was swarming with men, while the river itself was 'black with Chinese' – some wading, some crossing on rafts. This was the human wave.

---

[*] Leiding stayed in position all night, beating off a number of attacks, before fighting his way to the battalion at dawn with his detachment. He was awarded the War Cross with Palm for his leadership.

The spectacle disintegrated into flashes and a thunderous crump-crump-crump: after the illumination, high explosive. A drumfire DF barrage detonated among the Chinese. Philips had no leisure to observe the effect of the fire: the eerie, discordant sound of bugles rose up through the darkness. 'Now,' Philips said, 'it was time to defend ourselves!' The Belgians clicked off safety catches and squinted over their sights at their assigned frontages. Philips caught a snap-shot glimpse of the first enemy onto his position: leading the attack was a Chinese officer mounted on a pony. The Belgian sergeant did not witness the fate of this apparition – 'he was probably shot' – as firing erupted all around him. Havoc swept the platoon. Chinese were running up the slopes, jinking from side to side, attacking in groups of around a hundred, Philips estimated.

At the rear of the hill, C Company's CQMS Sergeant André Van Damme[2] had spent the day in the field kitchen baking cakes for his men. As soon as he heard firing break out, he began ferrying boxes of ammunition up. Already C Company was taking casualties: he helped evacuate five wounded men down the hill to the RAP while automatic fire zipped above and around him.* But Philips and his men received none of VanDamme's ammunition: the platoon was out of contact with the rest of the company – 'I don't know what happened to the radio operator' – as the waves continued to break on his positions. Only the extra ammunition left by the Rifles permitted the Belgian soldiers to maintain the rate of fire necessary to prevent the Chinese overrunning them.

The noise of bugles on all sides was unnerving; Philips found it 'very difficult to get the soldiers to concentrate'. Ahead of the platoon, the Chinese emplaced a machine-gun in a trench on an apron of ground that the Belgians had been unable to occupy due to their low numbers. It was obliterated with a bazooka. In the lulls between rushes, Philips could see red and green tracers criss-crossing and ricocheting up off the hills into the darkness across the river. Ten minutes after the Chinese stormed his position, Guy Temple's patrol had come into contact. Combat was flaring all along 29th Brigade's front.

Philips's platoon leader, Lieutenant Benoit Verhaegen, was badly wounded. Philips assumed command. A Bren gunner shouted that he had a stoppage. To lose the firepower of an LMG would be critical, and Philips knew that the gun could be easily fixed: 'With the Bren, you just have to change the gas,' he said. 'I ran up to kick him in the arse!' Out of his trench, Philips glimpsed movement to his rear and a flash. Just metres away, a Chinese soldier who had run right through the platoon squeezed off a burp gun burst. Philips was slammed to the ground,

---

* Sergeant VanDamme was to receive the Bronze Star for his heroism that night.

unconscious: A round had torn through his left cheek, carried away a couple of teeth and exited under his right ear.

Seconds later, he came to in a lull. Dazed, he sat up. A corporal ran over, and jabbed him with morphine. There was no pain; Philips remained rational and found he could still talk. The situation was critical. From slit trenches all around, men cried out for ammunition. A quick inventory showed they had forty-six rounds, one fragmentation grenade and two phosphorus grenades for the whole platoon. The rest of C Company were fifty metres behind them, further up the slope. 'I said, "We will rejoin the company!"' The platoon dashed back, and were helped through the wire by their comrades. However, in the confusion of battle, it was not clear that all of B Platoon's men had made it; a counter-attack was launched from C Company positions with bayonet and grenade to recover any stragglers.[3] Remarkably, all thirty-six members of the platoon made it.

Meanwhile, the entire battalion was coming into action.* At B Company, Sergeant Lucien Senterre had been roughly shaken awake to find flares dangling above and bugles blaring. He was bewildered, until someone told him they were under attack: this was his first experience of battle. A Bren hammered, sending streaks of red light zipping into the darkness: a probe was being repelled. But the tracers had marked the Belgians. Sudden flashes and showers of dirt engulfed Senterre's position: mortars. One man was killed. Senterre scraped his trench deeper. Lieutenant Paul Walsh, 45 Field Regiment's FOO with the Belgians, was bringing fire onto the enemy within 'a stone's throw' of his OP.[4] Wounded, he continued adjusting fire.†

Lieutenant-Colonel Albert Crahay was concerned about his rear. He had not been appraised of an attempt by the Rifles to secure the bridges (see below), but the firefight had been observed. Before dawn, he sent a fighting patrol, consisting of Lieutenant Hosdain's platoon from A Company and members of the machine-gun platoon under Captain Poswick, to secure his rear. Behind their position, they found a wrecked British jeep and a raincoat full of blood, plus abandoned enemy foxholes.[5] The patrol ventured down to the river bank. There, they came across the tracks of hundreds of Chinese, but met no enemy. The patrol cautiously crossed the bridge – and walked into an ambush on the south bank. Under heavy fire, they retired, having lost six men.[6]

Second Lieutenant Henri Wolfs had been sleeping – soldiers learn to sleep through extraordinary noise – at Battalion HQ when he was woken at around 06:00 on the 23rd. Immediately, he realised 'the atmosphere

---

* In a measure of the ferocity of the fighting, 167 dead Chinese were later counted in front of C Company's position, according to Philips.
† Walsh won an MC for his night's work.

had changed'. After a 'nice breakfast' – the mess was still operating – he and two jeep loads of men were ordered towards C Company's position to watch for enemy infiltration and to make contact with the embattled company. Wolfs proceeded carefully, 'not seeing a living soul', but as he crept up the slope towards the company there was a burst of shooting to his front. Wolfs and his squad dropped to the ground and returned fire. One of Wolf's machine-gunners rose to throw a grenade. He was cut down by a volley of burp gun fire that stitched across his chest, but his grenade went off; incoming fire ceased. At the same moment, Wolfs saw men he recognised – 'all more or less wounded' – running back through a hail of bursting grenades: 'If they had been Mills bombs, they would all have been killed,' Wolfs thought. The retreating men were C Company. Wolfs roared at his squad to hold their fire as their comrades passed back through; to his 'utter surprise' no Chinese pursued them. The firing died down. Wolf crawled forward to get the weapon and ID from his dead machine-gunner, when he felt himself being dragged back by his ankles; at the same moment a burst of automatic fire ploughed up the earth just in front of his face. 'You must be a little more careful in this kind of game, lieutenant!' warned the ex-Foreign Legionnaire who had pulled him back. With C Company having withdrawn successfully, Wolfs and his men fell back.

Sergeant Philips, with a hole through his face, had been ordered to the aid post at the rear of the hill, where the medical officer and the padre were tending to the injured and dying. The doctor told Philips how lucky he was to have been shot with a submachine-gun: a high-velocity round would have tumbled and removed his head. As he waited for helicopter evacuation to a MASH, Philips could have no idea what the personal ramifications of the last order he had given would be. Still, the Belgians had held out. But they were now cut off on the wrong side of the river.

* * *

At 19:40 on 22 April the Rifles, in brigade reserve down Route 11, had been ordered to stand by. The Battle Patrol – in their armoured Oxford carriers, the battalion's most mobile unit – were put on half an hour's notice as a quick reaction force. Its fifty-odd men were resting by their vehicles, waiting for the order that would pitch them into combat, when other members of the battalion became dramatically aware of battle's imminence: the screen of the mobile cinema visiting the brigade* (showing *Tea for Two* with Doris Day and Gordon Macrae) was shredded by a burst of gunfire.[7]

---

* Some of the enemy may have been as disappointed at the film's sudden ending as the Rifles: Gloster Tony Eagles later learned that Chinese recce parties hidden in the hills overlooking the brigade positions had also been watching.

The battalion's officers had been celebrating news of recent gallantry awards – including a DSO for Major John Shaw, who had led the rearguard out of 'Happy Valley' – and singing Irish songs when, one minute before midnight, the duty officer entered the tent, with news that the offensive had begun: The Battle Patrol was to move up immediately.[8] Its mission was to secure the bridges leading to the Belgians at Ulster Crossing. If pressed, the 50-odd men were to fight their way over the bridges and reinforce the Belgians.[9] A group from 55 Field Squadron, including the huge Lieutenant Keith Eastman, joined them as they mounted up.[10]

The Battle Patrol's second in command was the recently arrived subaltern, P.J. Kavanagh. After serving as PR officer on arriving in Korea, he had asked Lieutenant-Colonel Hank Carson for a combat command and was given a job with the mobile sub-unit. When one of his journalist wards heard Kavanagh had volunteered for the front line, he was incredulous: 'What do you want to go and put your head in a noose for?' Kavanagh, like innumerable young men through the ages, wanted to know what combat was like. His first experience of action had been inauspicious. Sharing a slit trench with a highly experienced sergeant, he had been fast asleep under a looted eiderdown when the company was probed. The older NCO, his front-line instincts honed, woke immediately and armed himself. The dozy Kavanagh, confused, could not locate his weapons under the quilt. The sergeant thrust a Luger at him, but Kavanagh did not know how to cock it; silently, the NCO crawled over and did it. Fortunately, he was not called upon to use it that night. Now, Kavanagh found himself rumbling towards contact in the darkness without his mentor – the experienced NCO had left on leave a few hours earlier.

The vehicles halted on the south side of 'Ulster Crossing', engines idling. All was dark across the river. The patrol's two officers stood beside the forward Oxford, striving to see ahead. It looked 'fishy', but there was no choice. They pressed on. The men peered warily over the armoured sides of the leading vehicles as they clattered across the pontoon. They were trundling up the flood plain on the far bank when the blackness exploded around them. One carrier flared up with a whoosh, hit by a rocket. Then another. The patrol had driven into the kill zone of an ambush. The Riflemen vaulted out of the vehicles, which were drawing fire. In the chaos one carrier reversed, crushing the pelvis of a Rifleman lying behind it. More shooting broke out in the rear, by the bridges. The patrol was surrounded.[11]

In the killing zone green lines of tracer streaked past and over the Riflemen. Kavanagh tried to deploy his men and organise return fire. A Bren jammed. The survivors dashed for cover in a copse in the riverside meadow. The patrol commander, Lieutenant Headley Craig, told Kavanagh to retreat across the river on foot with about twenty men while he covered the movement with a small group. Realising Craig was condemning himself to death, Kavanagh tried to argue; Craig repeated the order. Kavanagh led his group out of the copse. A Chinese with a burp gun was waiting. Kavanagh dived to the ground, and an SMG duel began. The British officer fired with his Sten but was hit in the shoulder. He called for help. A Rifleman moved forward, and with one round shot the enemy dead. Kavanagh was given a quick shot of morphine then led his twenty men down to the river, seemingly watched by scores of enemy all around them, who made no attempt to bar their way. The Riflemen crossed the river and took up covering positions on the south bank. Nobody would be following. On the north bank, they heard the clatter of weapons and the 'banshee yell' of a Chinese attack. Then silence. Craig's rearguard had been overrun.[12]

Eastman, the Sapper lieutenant, had been separated in the confusion, and was retreating across the bridge with a small group on foot when the Chinese opened up on the running men. A Rifleman ahead of him was hit and knocked into the river. The powerful Eastman dived into the water to rescue him. Both swirled downriver in the darkness.[13]

As the shocked survivors of Kavanagh's party headed back south down the pale track, lit by moonlight, they became aware of dark masses moving over the hillsides around them. Having infiltrated around the Belgians, the Chinese shock force had crossed the river and was pressing south. Fighting was spreading to other hilltop positions. The patrol came to a British HQ. Kavanagh noticed a lieutenant-colonel in tears at the end of a broken field telephone; the commander was reacting to casualties among his men, each of whom he knew personally.* The wounded Kavanagh stopped at a forward aid post, while the remnants of the patrol continued back to battalion down Route 11. Fighting was getting closer to the aid post. Bullets tore through the tent canvas and, despite the morphine, Kavanagh's nerves were stretched. Would the Chinese capture the post? To his relief, a field ambulance pulled up, already full of groaning men. He crawled in, but had to hold his head at an angle: blood was dripping from a casualty in the stretcher above. The ambulance sped off south, bumping down the track. After a while, the dripping stopped. The soldier had died.[14]

At 02:15 a single Oxford pulled up to the Rifles' Battalion HQ bearing news of the patrol's fate.[15] Of its fifty-odd members and about a dozen sappers, only twenty-seven made it back – ten of those wounded.[16] The Battle Patrol had been wiped out.

* * *

---

* Kavanagh misidentifies the man as Lieutenant-Colonel Carne of the Glosters – who was miles down the river to the west. It must have been Lieutenant-Colonel Kingsley Foster, whose headquarters was set up behind the Fusiliers' Z Company, just south-west of 'Ulster Crossing'.

Lieutenant Malcolm Cubiss's first indication of imminent combat was a group of Fusiliers tumbling through his position, shouting over their shoulders, 'They're just behind us!' They were. Cubiss's 4 Platoon was part of X Company, the Fusiliers' left-flank unit, dug in on a long, low hill overlooking the river. In anticipation of enemy patrol activity, the company had planted an LP on the river bank. At 22:40 the LP men came belting through 4 Platoon.* 'The patrol were coming like the clappers,' said Cubiss, 'and they were followed by people coming like the clappers.' The shadowy figures of Chinese chased the retreating patrol right into Cubiss's position. There was no warning from bugles or whistles – just the sudden thump of hand grenades landing among the slit trenches: 'You can't see them because it's dark; you only see them when they go off.' The grenades exploded. Shooting broke out. Cubiss's men killed three enemy within three yards of their trenches. Then, as suddenly as it had started, it was over. There was a pause for about ten minutes.

At the centre of the hilltop, over a ridge from Cubiss's position, Bob Nicholls – whose forward observation team from 170 Mortar Battery was emplaced with X Company's CP – had been finding the evening 'quite peaceful'. Earlier, some Asahi beer had been sent up, and Nicholls, a non-smoker, had exchanged his cigarette rations for the lager. When Cubiss was attacked Nicholls heard a trip flare go off. 'They had already got onto the hill – how they got on the hill I don't know, but they were driven off in no time.' The forward platoons had broken the probe. Fusilier Derek Kinne was in the rear of the company position. His platoon commander had called for volunteers to resupply the forward platoons with ammunition. He immediately volunteered, but being a Bren gunner, was ordered to sit tight. The firing died out. Frustrated at missing the action, Kinne cracked open the rum ration he had been saving for St George's Day and knocked it back. Then he and Curry, his number two on the Bren, discussed looking over the neighbouring platoon position and collecting souvenirs from Chinese dead at dawn. X Company's OC, Major Reggie Pratt, came round and congratulated the men – though neither Kinne nor Curry had yet fired a round.[17]

In one of those strange incidents of battle, a pair of Chinese wandered into the centre of the company position and stood in the moonlight. The Fusiliers and mortar men could see them clearly, down to the details of their brown uniforms. 'We were shouting *Iri wa*! ["Come here!"],' said Nicholls. The enemy stayed rooted to the spot. 'We just kept an eye on them,' he said. 'Nobody shot them.' Kinne was furious: his Bren foresight

---

* Why the patrol did not call down fire on the Chinese crossing the river is unclear. The fact that this listening patrol did not have the firepower to fight a delaying action on the river bank shows Guy Temple's sagacity in equipping his 'small patrol' with as much weaponry as it could possibly carry.

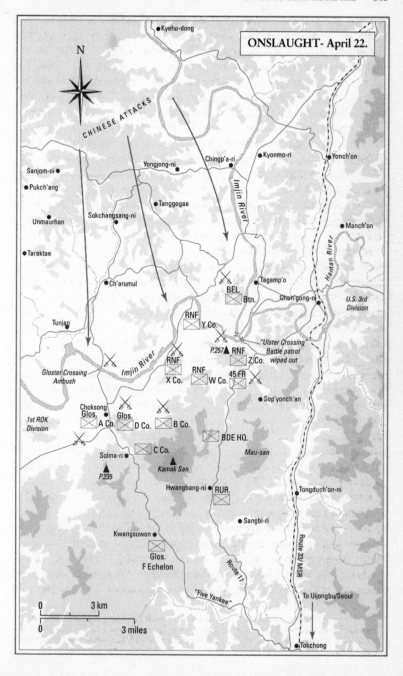

ONSLAUGHT- April 22.

covered one of them, 'I was putting a bead on him, I was going to blow him away' – but Captain De Quidt ordered the men to hold their fire.[18]

The lull did not last. The probe had been beaten off but the shooting in the darkness had revealed the Fusiliers' positions to Chinese officers. To the right of X, Y Company was not under attack, but from his hilltop eyrie Lieutenant Sam Phillips had a fine vantage point as X Company's struggle resumed. Chinese machine-gunners opened up with dense streams of tracer, guiding attackers onto their targets. The main force was going in.

Nicholls could hear bugles (signalling company-level attacks) and whistles (for platoon assaults) sounding from below. He crouched in his slit with his Sten. No enemy was visible. Then, to his front, Fusiliers shouted, 'Here they come!' In the dazzle of flares and star shells, Nicholls saw what looked like shadowy crowds pounding towards him. Fire poured from the trenches. 'When you are under mass attack, you are supposed to pick a man out and fire at him out, but you shoot into the middle,' Nicholls recalled. 'If you miss one, you will get the one behind!' Around him Fusiliers were timing their grenade throws so that they detonated in mid-air above the attackers, for maximum effect. Nicholls fired his Sten while calling down mortar fire on the radio to stonk Chinese forming-up points at the base of the hill. Two charges were repulsed. Nicholls saw dead and wounded enemy sprawled within feet of his position. Firing over the forward platoon was Kinne. 'There were hundreds of them,' he said. 'I just unloaded the Bren gun, I was sweeping away with it, and screaming at Curry to give me spare magazines.' The Fusilier could see the effect of his fire from the tracers he had loaded – one in every five rounds – hitting his targets. 'I could see some of them getting hit around the shoulder and chest – they were bent double as they climbed up, so I aimed low. Later, I learned it is better to wound 'em than to kill 'em – then it takes three or four men to carry them away. But I saved 'em the trouble!' Mowing down attackers, Kinne felt a surge of savage exhilaration: this was why he had come to Korea.

Over a ridge that separated them from the rest of the company, Cubiss's 4 Platoon was locked in combat. Chinese tactics were simple. 'When they get close and haven't decided what to do, they stop about twenty yards away and dig themselves shell scrapes – you can hear them but you can't see them, because of the slope.' Then, the assault. 'There was a lot of tracer fire: their tracer was green, ours was red – and lots of burp guns.' The first attack was on the little ridge, aiming to cut 4 Platoon off from the rest of their company. Three of Cubiss's men were killed and an LMG position destroyed, but the attack was held. Next, two men on the ridge were lost: one killed, one wounded. Between rushes, there were lulls. 'Each time you stop them, there is a pause while they think about what to do next; you can see vague shapes and you fire into the vague shapes. Another attack came though about fifteen minutes later. I lost three more wounded.' The platoon was being whittled down; each man lost meant a reduction in firepower, lessening the odds against holding off the next rush. Mortars landed – 'which was surprising because they were so close'. Phosphorus ignited the scrub, lighting up the platoon's position. Taking a massive risk – he was fully illuminated – Cubiss leapt out of his trench and into the open, attempting to stamp out the fires, while encouraging his men to stand fast. 'I didn't need to say much – just "Hold your ground!"' Another attack. Two more wounded. Cubiss felt, 'something like a slap'. He had been hit by grenade shrapnel that had torn into his arm and head, bursting an eardrum. He staggered over the ridge to the aid post: 'I suppose I told my men something, I can't remember.' At the aid post, fifty metres from his platoon position, a medical orderly 'clagged a shell dressing' onto his wounds, then Cubiss headed back to his platoon. When he arrived, he was dumbstruck: The position was deserted. 'The remnants of the platoon decided they'd had enough and had buggered off, which surprised me. We had lost fourteen out of twenty-six in two or three hours. Most people don't want to let their pals down – that is why you have slit trenches with two men and Bren trenches with three men. But once you start losing people, it changes the character. Chaps think, "Christ, he's gone – I could be next."' Cubiss knew why they had broken. 'If I had been there they would have stayed, they would not have left me.'

Devastated, the officer 'wandered around the hill' until he found De Quidt, who told him that 4 Platoon's survivors had gone to Battalion HQ. Cubiss followed. At the base of the hill, Cubiss climbed into one of 170 Mortar Battery's vehicles. The troop had been set up behind the hill but, with the company teetering, had been ordered to move out.[19] The wounded officer reported to Battalion HQ, where Foster told him to establish a delaying position next to the 25-pounders of 45 Field to block further infiltration. Foster's HQ was pulling back. Cubiss deployed the jittery remnants of his platoon. The scale, fury and persistence of the attack had shaken the men; one was evacuated with battle shock. 'I think they were disappointed in themselves for not staying. We'd lost half of the platoon.'

On the hill Kinne, with his Bren, was ordered to assist the forward platoons. As he and Curry moved up to the ridge a mortar barrage landed all round them. Curry said that mortar bombs never land in the same place twice, so suggested taking cover in a crater. They were moving towards it when another bomb landed directly in it. Neither man said a word. Just before they reached the crest shouts summoned them back.[20] The Chinese had emplaced a machine-gun team on the ridge – as the battle developed, the British would discover that the enemy machine-gun teams were the deadliest elements of the attacking force. The hill was compromised.[21]

Two miles to the west, Gloster Frank Carter, on B Company's hill, watched grimly as X Company was overrun. In the blackness, flashes and explosions crept up the hillside, then a white flare went up. 'We knew the Northumberlands had had it, because when the Chinese had got on the top of a hill and taken the position, they'd fire a white Verey light up.'[22]

At 02:45, X Company began its retreat.[23] 'The order was shouted, "Every man for himself!"' Nicholls recalled. 'Our position had become hopeless.' He was impressed at the lack of panic. 'The soldiers just went one way or the other.' As the Fusiliers moved off, Nicholls, out of ammunition for his Sten, grabbed up his maps and radio and began descending the hill with his mate, McAffery. Chinese were in their rear. The pair ran 'smack bang' into three enemy soldiers. It was a case of who would fire first. It was McAffery. He raked the three with a long burst from his Sten, sending them tumbling, 'They were hit, they went down all over the place.' Fusiliers were coming down, closely pursued in the dark; the last man off the position dropped a Chinese with his fists.[24] The two gunners reached the bottom of the hill and walked east down the Line of Communication – a track widened by engineers – and met another group of stragglers. They all continued south-east, towards Battalion HQ. A flare burst. In the illumination, Nicholls was shocked to see hundreds of Chinese massed in the paddy next to the track, rifles stacked. The British froze. 'They were not fifty feet away, I swear to God, this paddy was full of them! They had broken through in strength, and were waiting for orders or something. Nobody said a word, nobody said, "Look at those gooks!" It was eerie.' The Fusiliers and gunners walked past, virtually on tiptoes: 'Our hearts were in our mouths.' The Chinese did not react. Just as the British had not spotted the Chinese crossing the dark plains lining the river, the Chinese could not see the retreating British with the black mass of hill behind them. Further along the track, the group passed a burning aid post, then stumbled upon a scratch group of soldiers, with an officer preparing a holding position.* Nicholls was co-opted into their defence.

Dawn broke. To the relief of Cubiss's improvised unit, the Chinese seemed to have gone to ground: no charge was launched down the track. Once it became clear that no holding action was required, Cubiss went to the RAP to get his wounds properly dressed. 'I knew I was not badly wounded so I asked the doc if he would take [the shrapnel] out, but he

---

* This was Malcolm Cubiss; the burning aid post was likely where Kavanagh was treated.

had a bit to do at the time, said "no" and sent me back.' As he moved down Route 11 Cubiss passed a long column of Riflemen marching up. Brodie, his line smashed in, was committing his reserve. As the long snake of men began slogging up a hill to the right of the track, Nicholls's mortar fire-control team was ordered to join them on the new strongpoint.

* * *

The Fusiliers' Z Company were positioned on the brigade's right, on Hill 257 – a steep-fronted hill with a flat saddle at the top – overlooking the river. Naturally dominant, it was also critical. Not only did it cover the northern end of Route 11 and have line of sight to the Belgians on Hill 194 across the river, the Fusiliers' HQ and the guns of 45 Field Regiment were set up behind it. Unlike the all-out assaults on the Belgians and on X Company, the Chinese opted to take Hill 257 by taking full advantage of their troops' strengths: fast night movement, ability to cross difficult ground, skill at infiltration and shock action. It would be a surprise attack.*

As the Belgians, and then X Company were engaged, Fusilier David Strachan could hear the reassuring thunder of artillery firing behind him: Hill 257 trembled with the barrage. Z Company remained inviolate, secure on their fastness. Then, at 03:05, the company's right-hand platoon, set on a pinnacle at the top of the position, came under fire: a Chinese machine-gun had somehow infiltrated the high ground.[25] The attack rolled down. Fusilier Stan Tomenson was shocked by the sheer speed of the attacking Chinese. 'They had no packs on, they were free running at us. You saw them, shadows in the flares – we had wire out with grenades on, some of them touched the wire and they went off.' The men in the slit trenches called to each other, shouting out to check to see who had been hit. Tomenson noted the contrasts in behaviour that combat demanded, a balance of self-preservation and aggression: he was trying to keep his head down, while at the same time firing. Few soldiers seemed to be shirking; everyone was shooting. And for the first time

---

* The Fusiliers' official history notes: 'It must in truth be said that it had never occurred to anyone that this position would be attacked without warning. Apart from the precipitous approaches, it was more than 1,000 yards behind Y Company's position, in front of which there was no ford. How the enemy achieved this is still unknown; but one can assume that they infiltrated between the Belgians and Y Company's right flank, and must either have overrun the Belgians' bridge or have found a ford unknown to us' (Perrins, p. 116.) In fact the bridges, some half a mile to the north-east of the company, had been lost some time after midnight. It seems odd that the Fusiliers were unaware of this, as one carrier had made it back to the Rifles and reported the loss of the remainder of the patrol and the bridges at 02:15, and the Z Company position was not hit, according to the Fusiliers' War Diary, until 03:05. Moreover, on the way back from the deadly ambush of the Rifles' Battle Patrol, Kavanagh's group had noted Chinese infiltrating in the darkness.

Tomenson killed. 'It is a funny feeling, firing at someone across your front and getting an awful feeling: "What have I done?"' There was no time for remorse: the enemy were through. The Chinese were skirting the British trenches, bypassing them. 'I think they attacked in battalion strength: they wanted to get through us, and the first lot went right up the valley.' Tomenson's platoon was ordered to pull back.

Fusilier David Strachan had not seen a single Chinese soldier, so was surprised when his platoon got the order to move out – fast. To his annoyance he had to abandon his pack, stuffed with souvenirs, shirts and cigarettes. As he moved down the slope he looked back and realised how close the enemy were: a Chinese soldier was rifling through the pack. Once the Fusiliers reached level ground, blasts erupted among them: enemy mortars had the range. 'One landed by me – I dived automatically, we all dived. One of the reservists said, "That were a close one, keep moving,"' Strachan recalled. 'We were trying to get out quick and bunching up, and NCOs were shouting "Spread out, spread out!" The Chinese were wonderful with mortars.'

Not everyone got the pullback order. For those left, alone in the darkness, on a hilltop overrun with enemy trying to find and kill them, it was a terrifying night. Fusilier Roy Rees was in a deep slit trench across a track that ran over the saddle at the top of the hill with a young soldier. The two were out of sight of the remainder of their platoon. 'It's very steep, and how the Chinese were up that bloody hill, I don't know,' recalled Rees. To his disquiet he could hear Chinese voices nearby, but could see nothing. Suddenly, his trench-mate broke and ran. Rees was alone. Chinese voices passed him. He was cut off. He leapt out of his slit, over the path – and right into an enemy soldier. 'He was about to fire but I beat him to it!' said Rees. 'I fired and he clutched his chest. I threw myself over this bloody hill.' Rees was astonished to find himself alone on the position. 'All the men I was with had disappeared. I thought, "Do I go down the hill or what?" I thought, "I can't, it's bloody desertion!" Where our officer had gone, I don't know. Nobody had come and told us we were pulling out.'[26]

As Rees worked his way down, danger threatened a key arm of the brigade. With the Fusiliers pushed off Hill 257,* 45 Field Regiment was exposed. Behind Z Company, Lieutenant George Truell was with his 25-pounders, supporting the Glosters. Since being ordered to fire support for Guy Temple's patrol at 22:40 he had realised that 'this was definitely more

---

* There is understandable confusion at the exact time of Z Company's withdrawal. The Fusiliers' War Diary notes that the company's right-hand platoon was dislodged at 04:45. The Brigade War Diary reports the same at 06:10. Either way, the Fusiliers' Regimental History notes that shortly after first light, the hill was in enemy hands. However, Truell's artillery versus infantry duel took place in darkness. Obviously, some stragglers, like Rees, were still pulling off the hill before dawn broke.

than a skirmish'. His ammunition expenditure was prodigious: at 01:20 he had to get 300 shells from another battery. Concerned about enemy infantry, Truell placed Bren guns on the flanks of his battery for close security. At 02:40, when the mortars crews were retreating from X Company, he noted with disquiet that, despite the moonlight, he could not tell 'who the hell they were'. He sent two subalterns, one to each of the LMG positions, to tell them to open fire, but not to shoot up the friendly troops coming through as Z Company pulled back: 'They had to use their nerves!'

The gunners soon had to contend with something more urgent. With the Chinese surging over and around Z Company, there was nothing between the enemy assault forces and the guns except for two Brens. As Truell was supporting the Glosters, miles to his west, he was not paying much attention to his immediate front until his gunners, straining as they served their pieces, started coming under small-arms fire from Z Company's position. 'Tracers were firing around us, some were wounded; we could see Chinese moving about.' Truell looked ahead through his field glasses. Enemy were massing at the bottom of Hill 257. If the Chinese – estimated at around 200 – got to within charging range, the gunners could not hope to fight them off. The guns would be lost. Not only would that be the height of dishonour for any artilleryman, it would leave the brigade without fire support. The existence of 45 Field Regiment, Royal Artillery, hung by a thread.

Truell opted to repel the gathering attack with a tactic more familiar on Napoleonic battlefields than in the Korean War. While the rest of his battery continued their fire missions for the Glosters, Truell directed a single gun crew – that of Sergeant Reg Kitchener – to lower its barrel to minimum elevation and traverse onto the enemy who were swarming down a re-entrant at the bottom of the hill. Standing amid a pile of empty brass shell cases, a Sten at his feet, Truell pointed out the target and gave Kitchener's crew their orders: Direct fire! High explosive! Open sights! Range: 150 yards!

A foot-long flame stabbed from the 25-pounder's muzzle. The barrel recoiled. There was a near-simultaneous flash and thunderous crump as the shell detonated on the hillside among the Chinese. 'It caused a fair old bang!' Truell recalled. The shot was repeated, Kitchener's crew urgently reloading at maximum speed. The Chinese infantry scattered under the point-blank fire. 'The firing stopped and the Chinese took themselves off,' Truell said. The action had taken about twenty minutes.*

---

* A painting of Truell's repulse of the Chinese was commissioned, and today hangs in the Royal Artillery mess at Larkhill; a copy hangs in Truell's study. Truell vouches for its accuracy, except for one key detail: it depicts the action in broad daylight, when in fact, it took place in the dark just before dawn. The painting, by Terence Cuneo, was chosen to illustrate the boxed-set edition of Farrar-Hockley's official British history of the Korean War.

Rees was frantically crawling down the hill as Truell's shells crashed in. 'The shells kept landing, and you just wormed your way down the hill,' he said. 'When I got to the bottom of the hill, there was an officer there, directing fire.' Rees continued past the gunners, and made his way to Battalion HQ, where he bumped into Dennis Prout – a friend in the Intelligence Section. 'Christ, I thought you were dead!' Prout exclaimed.[27]

Truell's point-blank shoot had halted the Chinese in their tracks, preserving the artillery. In the aftermath he sent a patrol to clear the front of 70 Battery's position. It returned with a prisoner. The enemy soldier was laden with grenades and, in the sausage-like cloth bandolier slung around his torso, was carrying enough rice for seven days. The ration proved Peng's intention. This was no raid. The Chinese were provisioned to sustain their offensive for a full week before resupply.

* * *

Far out on the left, or western, flank of the Brigade the low mass of 'Castle Site' squatted a mile back from the river. The hill was occupied by Gloster Major Pat Angier's A Company. On the rear of the hill, overlooking the little temple where Padre Davies had held a church service earlier on Sunday, Private Sam Mercer sat in his slit trench. All the brigade's companies were sited in 'hedgehog' positions providing all-round defence. The rearmost platoon was not tasked simply to cover the company rear, though; it was also earmarked for counter-attacks if the enemy overran forward positions. Soon after 22:00, firing broke out on the river: Temple's patrol at the ford was in contact. The men on the forward slopes could see flashes in the darkness; the men in the rear could hear the cacophony. First came the ripping crackle of gunfire as the Glosters engaged with rifle and Bren, then the crump-crump-crump of artillery. 'We could hear it and realised it was only a matter of time before they got to us,' Mercer said. Minutes passed. Then Mercer heard 'a very comforting sound': the steady tock-tock-tock of a Vickers firing on fixed lines. The machine-guns on A and D Companies' hills had been sited to support each other. Things were going according to plan.

At first, firing was intermittent. As the night wore on, it became ever more intense, the crackling non-stop. Mercer was not yet in contact, but already his imagination was at work: 'I imagine 2 and 3 Platoons were eyeball to eyeball. In a sense we were spectators (though, of course, we could not see – they were right up on the ridge, we were behind it on the reverse slope).' His first sight of enemy was when a flare went up and from his right, a single Chinese soldier raced behind the two forward platoons. By the time Mercer got his rifle into his shoulder the runner had disappeared; there was considerable cover, scrub and low bushes around the area. The enemy soldier had broken right into the centre of the company position. Mercer found the realisation unsettling. The forward platoons were obviously fully embroiled; it could now be only a matter of time before the battle reached the rear platoon. Mercer strained to see in the darkness, waiting for orders, waiting for something to happen.

One man with a grandstand view of A Company's fight was Second Lieutenant Denys Whatmore of D Company.[28] Earlier in the day, he had tried to contact a friend in A, Lieutenant Phil Curtis, on the radio' – unsuccessfully. He had then taken an early-evening nap but was shaken awake by his platoon sergeant. As soon as he awoke he realised that battle had commenced: Temple was fighting at the crossing. What Whatmore did not know was that D Company's riverside LP, under Second Lieutenant David Holdsworth, had not enjoyed the same success as Temple: on the flood plain, the patrol had found itself in the midst of massive enemy forces. Where and how they had crossed the river was unknown. The patrol hid in a ditch among a 'sea of Chinese', close enough to smell the wetness of their uniforms from the river crossing, before sneaking back to their company.[29]

Now Whatmore and his platoon could see flashes advancing up A Company's hill. Behind him, a pair of Vickers were firing in support. Whatmore thought the 'the long, slow arcs of their fire beautiful in the night sky', the bright tracers floating almost lazily through the darkness.* His aesthetic delight was interrupted when the machine-gun position began to attract return fire. Behind Whatmore, D Company commander Captain Mike Harvey† was pleased at the 200-yard killing zone the machine-guns cut, but was momentarily disturbed when he realised their effect: carrying clearly through the night air came the screaming of wounded Chinese.[30]

Then Whatmore heard bugles and whistles. Enemy were advancing up the lower slopes below his position. Soon he heard rustling in the scrub. He ordered up flares from his 2-inch mortar. Chinese, bathed white in the magnesium glare, were visible about forty yards away; Whatmore could clearly see young faces, baggy uniforms, burp guns,

---

* In machine-guns, only one bullet in five, six, seven or eight is a tracer. Tracer ammunition allows gunners to see their fall of shot and allows commanders to guide fire onto a target. But while it looks deceptively attractive at long range, between each visible tracer is a stream of invisible – and deadly – bullets. Machine-guns can also be loaded with solid tracer. When fired, these shoot, literally, a luminous line from the gun like a laser, and are used to guide units into the attack. However, excessive use of tracer burns out barrels and pinpoints the location of the guns.

† Harvey had been promoted from lieutenant, and in the absence of Company Commander 'Lakri' Wood, led D Company throughout the battle.

stick grenades. The platoon opened fire. Enemy began falling. The first probe had fixed the Glosters' position. There was a lull, then what seemed like hundreds of Chinese rose from dead ground and stormed forward. Whatmore called for mortar fire from the battalion's 3-inch mortars – which had previously been ranged around his position. The first two bombs landed right on Whatmore's platoon, wounding one man; the corporal controlling the mortar fire cursed, and called in corrections. The next rounds fell among the attackers. D Company's medical orderly ran over to the platoon and dropped into the wounded man's trench. As the Chinese attack swept in, the corporal had no choice but to remain with the platoon.

Soon Whatmore's mortar was out of flares. He called for assistance from the platoon behind. In his excitement he breached radio discipline and was rebuked by a private on the other end, but the flares went up. His men were taking casualties. Bursts of automatic fire raked one of his sections – three, four men were cut down. A Chinese machine-gun had found the range. Whatmore saw its muzzle flashes and shouted out the location to his 2-inch mortarman – his sections were deployed no more than ten metres away. The soldier, a disgruntled, often troublesome reservist, dropped a high-explosive bomb down his tube; seconds later, it detonated exactly where Whatmore had indicated. Incoming fire ceased. Whatmore roared his approbation. Minutes later, the mortar man was wounded and evacuated rearward. The sky lightened but Whatmore was so closely engaged it did not register, until he realised he could now see the Chinese stick grenades as they whirled end over end towards him. To his front he glimpsed a Chinese throwing – the grenade landed on the lip of his slit – there was a bang – stones and dust from the parapet blasted into his trench – no injury – Whatmore hurled back a phosphorus grenade – it caught the enemy soldier in the face. Another Chinese machine-gun was raking the platoon from the flank. The mortar radio was smashed. Next to Whatmore in the slit trench Private Binman raised his rifle, then jerked back, shot through the eye. The medical corporal shook his head; Binman was dead. Everyone left was shooting. Whatmore's Sten seized up. There was no time to clear it. He grabbed Binman's rifle and resumed firing. A corporal in a nearby trench called for more ammunition. Whatmore threw him some – even this was risky, given the fusillade sweeping the platoon, kicking up sprays of dust. The platoon's radio was knocked out, its telephone line cut. There were now no communications to Company HQ. The men fought on. 'It felt as if the entire Chinese Army were marching over my platoon,' Whatmore thought.

Harvey ran over. From behind the platoon, he noticed with approval the accuracy of Whatmore's musketry: he was 'knocking down Chinese like snap targets on a range'. The young officer's rate of fire was so high, Harvey saw, that his rifle was smoking hot; grease was seeping through the wooden forestock. Having witnessed the casualties among the defenders, Harvey determined to draw his perimeter in. Back with his radio operators, he called Battalion HQ for mortar fire support to cover this manoeuvre, but was told that the tubes were down to 90 rounds, and those were being held back for a crisis.[31]

Whatmore ran out of rifle ammunition. He pulled out his pistol and used that – the Chinese were almost at hand-to-hand range. Empty. Desperate, he fired his Verey flare pistol at a shocked burp gunner. The rest of his men were clicking on empty chambers. Having fought to the last round, there was no point fighting to the last man. Whatmore shouted orders. The survivors of the platoon would fall back when he threw his last grenade. There could be no possibility of recovering the dead; they would lie in their slits. Whatmore threw – the grenade exploded – the men took off. Running, the officer snatched a glimpse over his shoulder – the Chinese were not chasing. The crew of one of the medium machine-guns on the ridge behind the platoon ceased fire to let them through. The second gun lay on its side. Whatmore reported to Harvey at Company HQ, who redeployed his survivors in reserve. Whatmore caught his breath and counted heads: 11 Platoon, hours earlier thirty-six strong, had thirteen men left.

* * *

On Hill 148, 'Castle Site', A Company's battle continued. The weight of the attack was falling on 2 and 3 Platoons on the forward slopes. Fire support was unable to keep up. 'I've got targets for you!' the FOO called over the radio. 'You've got more targets than I've got guns!' came the reply.[32] On the rear slope Mercer was listening to the cacophony – firing, explosions, bugles, shouted orders – but had still not seen any combat. Then word came back: 'The Chinese had got into a bunker. There seemed to be a prospect of action.'

Sometime after midnight,* A Company commander Major Angier (who had earlier declined Major Tony Younger's offer of a drink in order to return to his command) took advantage of a lull as the Chinese regrouped: with telephone lines cut, and radio reception spotty, he called a conference of platoon commanders. Crisis. A Chinese machine-gun had infiltrated and occupied a bunker on the summit of Castle Hill, Angier told his officers. The bunker was an earthen construction built

---

* The timings for the Glosters' actions in the battle are less certain than those of other brigade units, because its key record did not survive the battle. As one officer put it, the battalion's War Diary is 'probably mouldering somewhere on a hill on the Imjin'.

by US engineers weeks before, so General Ridgway could view the river. It lay outside the platoon perimeters. The machine-gun made movement – for casualty evacuation parties or ammunition resupply for the two forward platoons – exceedingly hazardous. Moreover, if the two forward platoons had to withdraw, they would be mown down. The bunker had to be neutralised. The attack would be mounted by Lieutenant Phil Curtis's 1 Platoon, the company reserve, at first light. The meeting dispersed. The battle was already heating up again. Lieutenant Maycock was killed on his way back to 2 Platoon.[33]

The moment came. The men of 1 Platoon climbed out of their slits and were formed into sections by Lieutenant Curtis. 'They called us,' said Mercer. 'I found myself moving forward to form a "winkle group".' This was the most dangerous job in any assault. While other sections fired cover, the group had to move in close and 'winkle out' the enemy, prising them from their position like a mussel from a shell. It was a task that called for close, violent action.

In tactical formation 1 Platoon moved warily up to the crest. Day was breaking. They reached the summit just as the enemy were grouping to charge the survivors of 2 Platoon, where Angier was directing the defence following Maycock's death. Below, 1 Platoon saw what looked like hundreds of Chinese standing up, removing camouflage as they prepared to assault. It was a perfect target. The Glosters opened fire and volleyed hand grenades down the hillside. Mortar and artillery, directed by Angier, added to the carnage. The attack broke up.[34]

Ahead of the five-man winkle group the objective loomed. As they stalked forward, Mercer heard a thump. Out of the corner of his eye he registered a Chinese grenade fizzing on the ground just yards away. He dropped – 'You couldn't have got a piece of paper between me and the ground!' – and the grenade exploded in a shower of sparks and shrapnel. Mercer was unwounded. Like many other men, he was saved by the fact that the Chinese grenades, while resembling the German 'potato masher', were less deadly. But the enemy in the bunker had spotted the British attackers. It was close quarters. Automatic fire. The Glosters crawled for cover. They could see the slit opening. With surprise lost, any attempt to storm the bunker would be cut down by the machine-gun. Curtis's counter-attack – so vital to ensure the survival of the remnants of A Company, on the forward slopes – was stillborn.

The 24-year-old Curtis was a popular figure among fellow officers, such as Whatmore, who had got to know him in Kure Battle Training camp in Japan. He had joined the Glosters from another West Country regiment, the Duke of Cornwall's Light Infantry. In photos he is a good-looking, even dashing figure, holding a casual stance while grinning at the camera.

But his wife had died while giving birth, and Curtis, in despair, left his surviving daughter with his mother and volunteered for Korea. Some soldiers, living alongside him in the intimate conditions of the front line, sensed a tragic side to Curtis. 'Something he said to me once – I had done something, I can't remember what it was – still comes back to me: "Mercer, you will be the death of me." Some of us had a feeling we would lose him in the first action.' Pinned down, the winkle group waited for orders – 'We were expecting Curtis to say, "Come on lads, in we go!"' Mercer said – but no command was issued. The next act in A Company's drama remains branded on the memories of the stunned witnesses.

Wordlessly, Curtis leaped to his feet. He had no rifle, only a revolver. He charged forward alone, silhouetted against the dawn sky. There was the flicker of a muzzle flash and a ripping crackle as the machine-gunner in the bunker squeezed his trigger. Curtis, hit twice, was jolted to the ground – he had barely got a couple of metres. His men crawled forward and dragged him back through a few coils of barbed wire. The medical orderly was summoned. 'We said, "Don't worry sir, we'll get Corporal Papworth to take care of you,"' said Mercer. 'He pushed us aside.' Curtis regained his feet. His men, thinking perhaps he was dazed by his wounds, tried to tug him into cover. He broke away. 'We must take Castle Site!'[35]

The wounded officer staggered forward a few yards. For some reason, the Chinese reaction was not so fast this time. Perhaps the machine-gunners, crouched over their smoking weapon, were as astonished as the Glosters. Their hesitation did not last. Again, the machine-gun barked. A long burst of fire riddled Curtis. He fell, dead. But he had thrown a grenade at the very moment he was cut down. The bomb flew through the bunker entrance, and exploded. The bunker shook; smoke billowed out. Just seconds after his death, Curtis's grenade had wiped out his executioners and blasted their machine-gun to scrap. Single-handed, 1 Platoon's commander had cleared Castle Site.*

The men of the winkle group – whose lives were almost certainly spared by Curtis's solo action – froze. 'I often wonder, "Why didn't I dive into the bunker?"' wondered Mercer. 'I don't know – I can't explain it. Then we were ordered to withdraw.' The men moved back to their positions in silence. 'I think we were all taken aback by Curtis going ahead and doing his own thing,' Mercer said. The speed and fury of the counter-attack – it had taken mere minutes – appeared to have shocked the Chinese. They made no attempt to retake the bunker.

* * *

* Curtis was awarded a posthumous Victoria Cross for his action.

Dawn broke. Fighting continued. A mile to the rear of Castle Site, at an observation post on C Company's hill, the Gloster CO, with a group of officers, signallers and fire controllers, was watching the struggle of the forward companies in characteristic silence. In the valley behind, the mortars were thunking away furiously. 'There were competitions between the different mortars – how many could you have in the air at the same time before they exploded?' said Lance-Bombardier Tom Clough of 170 Mortar Battery. Vickers from Hill 235 were hammering away. The Gloster adjutant, Captain Anthony Farrar-Hockley, was called to the radio. He raised the headset. It was Angier. The A Company commander requested reinforcements as 'my numbers are getting very low'. Farrar-Hockley told him to wait out, and summoned his CO. 'I'll talk to him myself,' Carne said. Farrar-Hockley did not catch the full conversation, only its termination. 'You will stay there at all costs and until further notice,' Carne ordered.[36] A withdrawal of the forward companies would have exposed the ROKs to the left and the Fusiliers to the right.[37] The colonel, returning to his binoculars, stopped to light his pipe. Farrar-Hockley noticed that his famously cool commander was pale; his hand shook as he raised the match.[38]

Farrar-Hockley got back on the radio to Angier, telling him that ammunition resupply was heading for his position in Oxford carriers. Angier concluded with, 'Don't worry about us, we'll be all right.' Fifteen minutes later, he was dead.[39] Soon after, a last radio call came in from A Company's HQ signaller. 'We are overrun. We've had it. Cheerio.' Then static.[40]

The remains of A Company continued fighting. Medical orderly George Newhouse, the Burma veteran, had been down to the foot of the hill's rear, helping walking wounded down to the track for carrier evacuation; he and Corporal Cyril Papworth had been tending wounded and shuttling them back to the RAP, an action that would save many. By the time he got back up, both Angier and Curtis were dead.[41] The survivors of the two forward platoons pulled back to join 1 Platoon on the rear slopes for a last stand. Papworth and Newhouse argued briefly over what to do with Angier's body: it was standard practice to leave the dead *in situ*.[42] In the event, the OC's body was removed, his orderly following in tears. The company was leaderless, all its officers dead or wounded. CSM Gallagher took command.[43] At 07:50 air recce informed Carne that there were around a thousand Chinese swarming around A and D Companies, and thousands more moving south.[44] The ROKs had held off assaults, and the Fusiliers X Company had pulled back; now, unless withdrawn, A and D companies would be annihilated. Orders were radioed.

A Company had almost a mile to cover before reaching the shelter of Hill 235. As the men moved down the track and past the little temple a Chinese broke the skyline behind them. 'I fired, and a Bren gunner fired at the same time,' said Mercer. 'The target went down.' Ahead, the line of retreat, a dirt track, offered no cover. 'The adrenalin was flowing,' Mercer said. 'It was a horrible muddle, we had lost our officers, and all the platoons were mixed up as we came off the hill.' The wounded – and Angier's body – were shoved into Oxford carriers at the bottom of the hill, which then revved up and roared off for Battalion HQ.[45] The rest walked. Covering artillery fire rained down on the lost position; an air strike screamed in. 'Castle Site' disappeared under a maelstrom of smoke and dust. Yet Chinese mortars began pounding down among the retreating Glosters, and bullets whipped overhead; closer rounds cracked. Men dropped, then dashed on. 'When Old Nick is in charge, you move rapidly!' said Mercer. 'There was a fair bit of metal in the air that morning; they were throwing everything they had at us.'

Men from Support Company moved forward from Hill 235 to cover A Company's survivors with fire from small arms. They straggled in amid bursting puffs of mortar fire. Once round the curve of Hill 235, they were out of Chinese sight. The exhausted men, their uniforms filthy, their skin black with powder, their eyes staring and faces gaunt, sank to the ground. Papworth and a section of Field Ambulance men moved among the casualties. A number were suffering from battle shock. 'They got tearful and afraid of bangs – they'd had enough,' Papworth recalled. 'You evacuate them. Some you treat a little bit firmly. It's a question of getting over the initial shock.'[46] Once casualties and shock cases were sorted out, a roll call was taken of A Company. Of the approximately 120 men who had started the battle, there were fifty-four effectives left.[47]

As A Company left Castle Site, D Company was ordered back. As they moved off, Whatmore spotted a Chinese machine-gun team setting up 600 yards off. Despite the extreme range, he directed his men to bring it under fire. The Chinese took cover, then replied. Dust kicked up at Whatmore's feet. Although not hit, he was astounded at their marksmanship.[48] As they arrived at Battalion HQ, RSM Hobbs came round distributing ammunition, but Whatmore found the hot water and hard-boiled eggs that were passed around more welcome. Then came the order to move up onto Hill 235. The weary survivors of A and D Companies clambered up the rocky slopes. Most had lost entrenching tools, so used bayonets, mess tins and bare hands to dig slits and build sangars.[49]

* * *

On, around and below the positions they had won, the Chinese went to ground. In slit trenches, holes and tunnels, they dragged shrubbery over their heads as top camouflage. At night, their strength in numbers was to their advantage. In daylight, their mass was vulnerable to UN air attack. A throbbing buzz sounded above. Had they peered up – carefully, for a group of pale faces looking up in unison is a dead giveaway to a ground-attack pilot – the Chinese soldiers would have seen giant metallic insects circling in the blue. Daylight brought the American casualty evacuation helicopters. From their vibrating Perspex bubbles, looking down past their boots and their helicopters' skids, through the tendrils of dark smoke drifting over the lost British strongpoints, what would the pilots have seen?

Around the rocky, dust-coloured hills, among smouldering scrub, the dark brown slit trenches were still carved in their defensive symmetries. Most were empty; some were still occupied by dead British soldiers, the bodies in their khaki battledress and camouflage windproofs already stiffening in the brisk morning air. On the parapets stood empty metal ammunition crates and, glittering in the early sunlight, innumerable spent brass cartridge cases. Around the fighting positions was scattered the detritus of battle: scraps of webbing, equipment, broken weapons, lumps of jagged shrapnel. Here, a bloody field dressing fluttered in the breeze; there, a black and white photograph of a wife and child blew in the dirt. Around and among the trenches, sprawled like Xs, lay the corpses of the attackers. Most were shaven-headed, in mustard-coloured uniforms, many stained dark with blood. Winding parallel tracks marked the paths of Chinese casualties – pulled away by comrades, their heels dragging in the dust. And the topography of the hills had changed. The surfaces of the deathscapes were now pitted with hundreds of scorched circular craters, gouged into the soil by mortar bomb and artillery shell.

It was another fine April day.

# Chapter 7

......................

# ST GEORGE'S DAY: 23 APRIL.

*Hard pounding this, gentlemen.*
*We shall see who can pound the longest.*

Wellington

**C**APTAIN ROBIN CHARLEY, second in command, B Company, Royal Ulster Rifles, was having a pleasant morning. On waking, he was troubled by neither frost nor dust. There was no dawn stand-to, no shouted commands – certainly no rumble of artillery, no crackle of gunfire. He had woken in a soft bed, between clean sheets, after a most remarkable day.

Charley was one of several 29th Brigade officers who had been detached to battle camp in Japan to prepare reinforcements for what awaited them in Korea. His twenty-sixth birthday fell on 25 April, so he had arranged to take his R&R – officially, 'Rest and Recreation', more colloquially 'Rack and Ruin' – in Tokyo a few days before. On arriving, the young officer had been contacted by the British Embassy, who informed him that a family acquaintance had been in touch and wished to meet him. The meeting was the idea of Charley's cousin who chaired a charity, the Florence Nightingale Trust, and had contacted the trust's president, a resident of Tokyo, to see if she could greet him. As a result, to his utter astonishment, Charley found himself being conducted into a chamber in the Imperial Palace for tea with Princess Chichibu.

Charley's appearance was inappropriate for palace duties – 'my uniform was in shit order!' – but he was received with exquisite Japanese decorum. The two sat on cushions, the khaki-clad British officer opposite the kimono-clad Japanese princess, sipping minute cups of tea. 'She was tiny, absolutely extraordinary – and spoke perfect English, just like she had been at Roedean,' a charmed Charley thought as he struggled to make polite conversation. After this encounter, he was conveyed back to reality: his R&R billet at Tokyo's Marunouchi Hotel.

Now it was the morning of St George's Day 1951. From his bed, Charley drowsily reached over and switched on the bedside radio. The news: a massive enemy offensive had hit the UN line in Korea. Charley snapped awake. Reaching for the telephone, he told the receptionist to put him through to a Korean switchboard, where he requested connection to 'Newmarket Blue Two' (29th Brigade, Royal Ulster Rifles, B Company). 'I didn't expect to get through,' he recalled; seconds passed, then he was speaking directly to the battlefield: 'It was amazing!' From his hotel bed, Charley spoke to his company commander, Dickie Miller, on the Imjin. Charley enquired whether he should return. 'There are thousands of them!' Miller snarled. 'For Christ's sake, stay where you are!' End of conversation. Bemused, Charley put the receiver down and settled back into bed.

Charley was not the only 29th Brigade officer absent that morning. It was an indication of the brigade's relaxed attitude towards its sojourn on Line Kansas that the Rifles' CO, Lieutenant-Colonel Hank Carson, was on leave.* Also absent was Major Henry Huth, commander of the Hussars' C Squadron. Likewise Major 'Lakri' Wood, commanding the Glosters' D Company, and Brigade Major Ken Trevor, Brodie's key assistant. Some of these men would rejoin their embattled units. Others would not.

* * *

Another Rifles officer, Second Lieutenant Mervyn McCord, was experiencing a rather different morning. Having returned to regular infantry duties after his heroics with the Battle Patrol at Happy Valley, he was leading a foot patrol to make contact with the Glosters, far out on the left flank. His route led around Kamak-san, the great mountain that dominated the brigade's sector.

As he and his men probed cautiously onto the foothills, signs of enemy presence multiplied: the landscape was overrun with Chinese. 'There were hundreds of them – thousands of them – walking around like little Michelin Men.' He called in artillery, but realized that his mission was hopeless. 'There was no way I was going to get to the Glosters.' He returned to headquarters and reported his findings. 'I think they took it with a pinch of salt,' he said. 'Everyone thought I was exaggerating.' Events were to prove he was not.

At Battalion HQ – headed, in Carson's absence, by the tough ex-airborne soldier Major Gerald Rickord – McCord was reassigned as signals officer. When he protested that he knew little about signalling, he was assured that that was unimportant. What was needed was someone adept at patrolling, McCord's forte. It was imperative to keep the telephone lines open. It would prove a dangerous job; the Chinese were lying up in scrub all around the hillsides, cutting every wire they saw, and McCord's new task pitched him into dozens of small actions. 'We were attacked fifty-something times,' he recollected. 'It was almost non-stop; there was a lot of shit flying around.'

---

* 'Every time he left us, we got hit!' one Rifleman told the author: Carson had also been absent from 'Happy Valley'.

Meanwhile, in headquarters across the peninsula and in Tokyo, staff officers were assessing the results of the first night's fighting. The entire I Corps front had been hit. The Turkish Brigade, part of the US 25th Division, had fallen back from Line Utah, as had another of the division's units, the 24th Regiment. To the east of the 25th Division, the US 24th Division had been hard hit and was in retreat. Still further east calamity had struck. The ROK 6th Division had collapsed. The Commonwealth 27th Brigade was being rushed up from reserve to plug the gap at Kapyong. The brigade's ability to stem the Chinese tide flowing through this hole in the line would be critical to the continued survival of I Corps on its left and the US 1st Marine Division on its right.

It was time to roll with the punch. The situation was serious enough to merit a general pullback. By the morning of the 23rd, all UN divisions still north of it were retreating to Line Kansas.[1] However, units on Kansas, like 29th Brigade, were not at liberty to withdraw. Despite the intensity of the combat, higher headquarters were still unsure whether the brigade had withstood a major attack or simply a probe. Captain Michael 'Recce' Newcombe, the Glosters' FOO, was certain it was the former; listening in on the net, he was deeply concerned to hear contrary views being expressed.[2]

Brigadier Tom Brodie had been forward to assess the situation. Soon after dawn Fusilier Sergeant David Sharp was clearing up behind Hill 257 as Lieutenant-Colonel Kingsley Foster moved his headquarters south. Sharpe had just set two phosphorus grenades in two boxes of ammunitions and was taking off 'at a rate of knots' down Route 11, when the brigadier rolled up in a staff car. Sharpe, who had known Brodie while working in the brigade's intelligence section, warned him that there was about to be 'one hell of a bang'. The ammunition exploded. The brigadier ordered Sharpe to 'get the hell out' and drove off. Sharp rejoined the Fusiliers HQ.[3]

At Brigade HQ, staff officers updated situation maps. The Americans to their north-east were pulling back, bringing them level with the brigade. To their left, ROK 1st Division had stood firm. But the brigade's own line was ragged. The Fusiliers' X and Z Companies had been pushed off their hills. W, positioned further back, had also been hit – from three directions at once – but had held. On the Glosters' front, A and D Companies had been withdrawn; B Company, which had only been probed, was being pulled in by Carne. The brigade had lost the river bank. Moreover, two units were in mortal peril: the Belgians and the Fusiliers' Y Company. The former were holding out in the hinge of the Imjin and the Hantan. The latter, in its outpost in the bend of the Imjin, was exposed by the withdrawal of X and Z Companies. It was critical to extricate these units before nightfall.

From the Chinese perspective the assault by 187th Division appeared successful. The CPV had forced the river and seized its southern bank, while elements of the division had gone to ground well past the front screen of the brigade in the Kamak-san area. Breakthrough had been achieved. However, in contrast to what had followed previous communist offensives across the Imjin, the defending unit had not broken or retreated. Although muscled back from the river, the brigade was holding the roadhead of Route 11, so maintaining the security of the western side of Route 33, I Corps's critical MSR. On the left, the Glosters still dominated the Choksong track at the head of Route Five Yankee. And the assaulting division was shredded. Its breakthrough had come at terrible cost. The British and Belgian hill positions, which on calmer mornings had loomed out of the river mist, had broken up the Chinese attacks like rocks in a human sea. Under relentless fire the 187th had forced its way through a meat grinder. It was in no position to cut behind UN lines further east.

Before dawn, Brodie had ordered his reserve up. Woken at 04:00, Lieutenant Gordon Potts of the Rifles' A Company immediately regretted the whisky drunk the previous night, and awaited orders with dread: if ordered to counter-attack, he was sure his platoon would take heavy casualties in hand-to-hand fighting.[4] It was not to be. The Rifles arrived behind Z Company's Hill 257 to find 45 Field Regiment shooting over open sights. Major Rickord went forward on a personal reconnaissance. He returned twenty minutes later, pursued by the puffs of mortar explosions. He was not strong enough to take the lost hill, but some 1,500 yards south-east of Hill 257, on the right side of Route 11, stood Hill 398. Rickord ordered A and D Companies up: from this position, the Rifles could dominate Route 11 from the north-east.[5] Brigade ordered B Company to hold a 'backstop' position on a saddle or hump where Route 11 rose, some four miles south of the river, near the hamlet of Hwabang-ni. C Company was readied for an operation to re-establish contact with the Glosters.*

While the Rifles' mortars and HQ set up at the foot of the hill, A and D Companies, with a section of Vickers machine-guns and Rickord's tactical CP, slogged up 398, sweating under eighty-pound loads. There was no opposition. At the summit, the Riflemen found the position had been prepared for defence long before their arrival: an ancient keep crowned the hilltop, its walls, some ten to fifteen feet high, encircling the crest. The medieval fortification provided proof of the strategic significance of

---

* This operation – for which McCord's reconnaissance towards Kamak-san was a prelude – was never launched.

the brigade sector, if any were needed. Three spurs – one to the north-east, one to the north, and one to the north-west – ran down to the paddy fields from the summit. A Company skirmished forward, driving off a Chinese patrol. Then the Riflemen dug in, incorporating the stone walls into their defences.[6]

In its armoured leaguer C Squadron, 8th King's Royal Irish Hussars, had spent the night listening in on the death struggle further up the valley. Even the squadron's veteran second in command had spent an anxious night. 'We were unnerved. We couldn't see anything,' said Captain Peter Ormrod, commanding in the absence of Huth. 'Practically every hill seemed to have a contact.' While organising defences, Ormrod noted cooks sitting inside the leaguer with saucepans over their heads, and a mess sergeant taking cover in the back of a truck, rather than on the ground. At dawn, he sent away his non-combatants. The Hussars climbed into their Centurions.[7] The squadron had been given its first task: three troops under the giant captain, Gavin Murray, would extricate the Fusiliers' Y Company.[8] Engines roared into life. Spreading out, the tanks headed up-valley.

* * *

In the bend of the Imjin, Lieutenant Sam Phillips had watched the battle the previous night but had not joined it: while other companies were assaulted, Y Company lay low. 'We were not making ourselves obstreperous. We were not attacked.' By morning Y Company was isolated two miles north of the remainder of the battalion. And there were Chinese, in platoon or company strength, on a hill to the left of the company. That position threatened any extraction; it had to be neutralised. Calls were made. High above in the blue, the Fusiliers could see silver flashes – then the jet fighter-bombers screamed in on their attack run. 'You could see the plane circling, then the canister come down, and you could see the sheet of liquid flame spreading,' said Phillips. 'They hit it fair and square.' After the wind of heat from the napalm came that shocking smell, reminiscent of roast pork. 'Perhaps it was your imagination, but you could smell people burning. It was unpleasant.'

The jets pulled up and away. The cavalry closed in. But as the Centurions approached the Fusiliers' position, there occurred one of those accidents of war. A tank gunner, mistaking the Fusiliers for enemy, opened fire. One platoon commander, Ben Smith, was immediately hit; Sam Phillips watched another officer, Terry McNamara, who was laying out recognition panels, blown into the air by blast. The company had no radio contact with the armour. Major Robbie Leith-MacGregor moved downhill to guide the tanks in. As the OC left, the dry scrub caught light from the tank fire. The hillside began burning. Fortunately, Leith-MacGregor reached the Hussars. Firing ceased.

Shouldering weapons, equipment and ammunition boxes, the Fusiliers climbed out of their slit trenches and down the hillside. The tanks waited, engines idling. Two Centurions were used to carry wounded; the remainder were delivering covering fire on the surrounding hills. Phillips had just finished loading one tank – 'it was covered with our troops'* – and gave a wave to the commander. As the tank jerked off, a short burst of machine-gun fire was loosed from its Besa. In a neighbouring tank, Cornet John Preston-Bell saw exactly what happened. 'One officer jumped up on the front of the tank and the gunner saw him, pressed the pedal and shot him in the leg. When the officer climbed on the front of the tank, we said, "Stupid man! He should know better!" But how would he have known?' Phillips collapsed. 'Something hit me hard and knocked me sideways. I felt the pain and said something fairly rude.' Two rounds had torn completely through his right leg just below the knee. 'I was no longer able to walk,' he recalled. 'My radio operator, a miner, tried to stick a syringe in me, which frightened me even more.' Phillips was placed on the Centurion, then the column moved south. The tanks shepherded Y Company, with the marching troops spaced in tactical formation, back to Battalion HQ. Phillips was left at the RAP. 'The shock probably removes some of the pain; you don't say, "Ah, this is unbearable,"' he recalled, but as he was prepared for evacuation from the battlefield, a different shock hit. 'I was sorry to leave the others: one's reaction is that you are leaving your people, leaving them behind.'†

Y Company redeployed along a ridge to the north-west of Route 11, but 'friendly fire' had taken three lieutenants out of the battle. Leith-MacGregor's platoons were now officerless.

It was St George's Day, the regimental day of the 'Fighting Fifth'. The irony of dragon-slaying was probably lost on the men in the slit trenches, and the day 'did not turn out to be that riot of fun that is customary in the regiment', Z Company commander John Winn wrote.[9] Only one Fusilier unit enjoyed the traditional dinner: mortar commander Captain Dick Blenkinsop dished out turkey while his men fired just yards away.[10] However, another regimental tradition was maintained. A reporter visiting the front that morning was astonished to see a

---

* According to Korean War veteran John Rickson of the Royal Tank Regiment, the 8th Hussars set an army record for the number of troops carried on a single tank during the Imjin battle: 58. I would guess that it was during the extraction of the Fusiliers' Y Company that this record was set. The Hussars would have more troops to ferry to safety in this battle, but the next time they did so, it is highly unlikely anyone had time to make a head count.
† Phillips bears no ill will towards the Hussars for the incident. 'This was the fog of war. It was in no way their fault.'

Fusilier patrol moving forward with each man wearing a red and a white rose in his beret. At 45 Field's CP, where he was handed a mug of 'Gunfire' (rum-laced tea), he noticed gunners also wearing red roses, flown in from Japan, in their head-dress. Seeing 'the rose of old England' worn in battle – some of those wearing them would be killed later that same day – he felt deeply humbled.[11]

Lieutenant-Colonel Kingsley Foster was not enjoying the celebratory day. Engineer Major Tony Younger visited the Fusilier HQ to co-ordinate the handover of a knoll his sappers had held the previous night. After the arrangements had been made, Foster asked Younger to follow him out of earshot of his men; he had something private he wished to disclose. Outside, the colonel quietly confided that he had had a premonition of his own death. The two men talked for a while in the sunlight. Younger tried to reassure Foster that nobody could foretell the future, but was helpless to ameliorate his anxiety. There was nothing more to say. Foster returned to his headquarters. Young left for his own unit, which was moving its heavy equipment south of the Han.[12]

* * *

With Y Company safe, Foster moved to retake Z Company's lost position: Hill 257. Not only did it dominate the northern end of Route 11, it had line of sight across the river to the Belgians. If they were to be exfiltrated, the enemy on Hill 257 had to be dealt with. Immediate counter-attacks have the best chance of success, but by now, the enemy had had hours to consolidate. Still, reinforced with a platoon of W Company, Z formed up at the base of the hill to assault. It was midday.

As the Fusiliers prepared to go in, Lieutenant George Truell was pulling out. It had been a good night's work: not only had his men fired all night in support of the Glosters, they had halted the Chinese attempting to exploit forward. As the gunners prepared to withdraw, a mortar barrage landed among them. Three artillerymen – Camp, Cruickshank and Hewitt – were killed. 'If we had gone ten minutes earlier, it would not have happened,' said Truell. 'A lot of people were in vehicles, and the vehicles were going to move off, but you always keep some guns firing – two batteries ready to fire, one moving: two legs, one on the ground, one moving. I was trying to keep the guns moving, trying to keep things our end going.' Towed by their trucks, the guns moved down Route 11 to new positions.[13]

An air strike seared Hill 257 while a troop of Centurions elevated their guns. At 12:45, under cover of their bombardment, the Fusilier lines began slogging up. By 13:00 the advance sections were nearing the summit. One minute later the enemy reacted: a volley of hand grenades came whirling over the crest, bouncing down and exploding among the attackers.[14] Fusilier Roy Rees, climbing back up the hillside he had escaped down hours earlier, felt sudden agony: from buttock to calf he had been riddled with shrapnel. Someone jabbed him with morphine. He was carried down to a field ambulance that had been waiting, a grim sentinel, at the foot of the hill.[15] The attack continued. Lieutenant Bill Cooper of W Company was shocked to hear the 'thwack' of Chinese rounds striking his men. He saw a signaller go down, the radio on his back disintegrating as a high-velocity bullet exited through it. But the leading wave had reached the top, and as it crested the rise, enemy soldiers leapt from their positions and ran for their lives. The attack was home! Then, beyond the first line of Chinese, a second line of enemy rose from the ground and stormed towards the panting British soldiers.[16]

The nineteenth-century French battle analyst Ardant du Picq wrote: 'Each nation in Europe says: "No one stands his ground before a bayonet charge made by us." And all are right.'[17] It is rare in modern war for two charging lines of men to actually clash; inevitably, the nerve of one side breaks before impact. At the top of Hill 257, the Chinese were fresh, the Fusiliers breathless. Moreover, the sudden appearance of the Chinese counter-attackers from the ground was a shock – unexpected, unplanned for. As the Chinese charged, the British attack disintegrated. The men turned and scrambled down the hill, rounds whining over their heads.

The Fusilier counter-attack had started at 12:45. By 13:20, it was over. That key position, overlooking both the head of Route 11 and across the river to the Belgians, remained firmly in enemy hands.

\* \* \*

On the brigade's left flank redeployments were under way. Major Denis Harding's B Company, on the Glosters' right, had been probed on the night of the 22nd, but had not suffered the mass attacks that had nearly destroyed A Company and whittled down D. In daylight, fifteen Chinese dead were counted in front of one platoon position, and about thirty in front of another. B Company had not suffered a casualty. 'The night's operations were very satisfactory,' Harding would later report.[18] But although it had lost no ground, the company's position, like that of the Fusiliers' Y Company, was compromised by the exposure of its flanks. It was ordered to withdraw 1,500 yards south-west to Hill 316, to the east of the ridge held by C Company.

A recent addition to B Company, who had joined just a few days before the Chinese offensive began, was six-foot-six Private Lofty Large, a self-described 'country bumpkin' from the Cotswolds. He had already served five years in the Wiltshire Regiment, but, fed up with parade grounds, had volunteered for Korea. He was so fresh from training camp in Japan that when battle commenced he was wearing a tie with his battledress.[19] During the night of the 22nd he had fired briefly at shadowy Chinese grenading his position; in the morning a patrol had found tracks where casualties had been dragged away. Now, he looked on with interest as the old hands – men who had served in North Africa, Sicily, Italy, Normandy, Burma – booby-trapped the position they were about to abandon.[20]

B Company moved down from its hill, platoons well spaced. The countryside basked in spring sunshine. A fighter-bomber circled in the sky like a silver hawk; the Glosters hurriedly unrolled coloured air recognition panels. Then the jet swooped down to ground level to strafe a group of civilians fleeing south: it was so low and close as it thundered over the Glosters that the soldiers could see the concentration on the pilot's face. It was a massacre. The jet vanished into the blue. The sudden silence after the strike was interrupted by a baby's screams. Nobody halted. Large fumed, but a veteran told him the enemy commonly infiltrated wearing civilian clothes.* The Glosters continued towards their destination through low scrub, ashes and oaks. Suddenly, firing broke out in front of Large. The leading men came running back through his platoon. The enemy had reached the hill before B Company. An attack would be needed to clear the feature.[21]

A sergeant bellowed at the confused Large, who was carrying a tired man's Bren, to get level with the assault line. The platoon commander, Second Lieutenant Arthur Peal, quickly briefed his men. Once the Chinese grenades came over, they were to charge forward under them and 'get in among the bastards'. Then he ordered 'Fix bayonets'. There was a sinister clatter as the soldiers attached the 'pig-stickers', and Large was energised by a sudden burst of adrenalin. At the order to advance, the platoon stood up and in extended line proceeded through the trees and up the slope. About twenty-five yards from the top, a shower of hand grenades came over – the line of Glosters broke into a charge – the grenades exploded behind them. Large, running, broke over the crest. A Chinese soldier was there, 'close enough to shake hands with'. Firing on the run, Large gunned him down – glimpsing the dying man's face as he

---

* In fact, Chinese and/or North Korean units in civilian clothing had been spotted in the area, according to B Company's after action report. As we shall see, civilians or disguised enemy led the enemy towards B Company, and enemy disguised as civilians were instrumental in the taking of the Glosters' F Echelon. By 25 April, the risk was so great that I Corps issued an order regarding civilians in the area of operations: 'To all units. Enemy is reported to be fighting in civilian clothes. Be cautious. Shoot first and ask questions later.' (See 3rd Infantry Division Command Report, in 'Reports of US Formations in Connection with the Battle of the Imjin 22–25 April 1951 (29th Independent Inf, Bde Group)'.)

dashed by – then reached down the front of his battledress for another magazine to slap into the Bren's breach. Automatic fire clattered from his front. He returned it. Chinese were running through the trees. Moving forward, he fired bursts into anything suspicious – patches of undergrowth, abandoned packs. Ten yards ahead, a Chinese with a Tommy gun appeared. Both men fired long bursts at each other at near-point-blank range; both missed. The Chinese turned and jumped over the edge of a small cliff. Large reloaded, peered over the edge and saw the enemy running through the shale some thirty feet below. He roared at him to halt. There was no response. Large fired a long burst; the man dropped. The skirmish was over. Gunsmoke drifted through the trees.

As he drew breath, Large realised how lucky he had been: His cap comforter, rolled under his shoulder strap, had been shredded by a bullet. He was relieved to be unhurt, impressed at the Glosters' decisiveness and pleased at his own reaction to combat. He was less happy when ordered to search dead Chinese. Among the bleeding corpses, he discovered black and white photographs of wives, children, parents.[22]

Hill 316 was in B Company's hands at 10:45. A foothill of Kamak-san, the mountain dividing the Glosters from the rest of the brigade, it was the highest point of a rocky ridge that ran east–west. Unlike most of the battlefield, it was covered in trees – which would have unpleasant implications for its defenders. The lower, western part of the feature was held by C Company, some eight hundred yards away. Entrenching proved difficult in the rocky ground. The sections dug shell scrapes, then raised stone and earth parapets. B Company was still digging in when a Chinese platoon was seen approaching their previous position, led by a Korean dressed in white.[23] A mortar fire controller spoke into a radio mike. Seconds later, puffs of smoke marked the bombs' explosions in the valley. The Chinese were scattered, their guide killed.

The company's second in command, Captain Morris, arrived with rations and ammunition.* Morris then left for F (Forward) Echelon, but found the road cut. He returned to B Company to share its fate.[24] Also joining Harding's company was Royal Artillery FOO Newcombe, who, anticipating a 'big fight', arrived in the early afternoon. Enemy activity increased. At 15:30 a group of some three hundred Chinese came into view moving across a valley in front of B Company, heading towards Kamak-san. Newcombe requested a 'Mike Target'. He was given fifteen rounds per gun. The first shells hurtled in, and Newcombe walked the

---

* Although this rule is not always observed, a unit second in command is customarily not with his command – be it battalion or company – in action, so as not to become a casualty in the same place as the commanders. The battalion's second in command, Major Digby Grist, was also not based with Carne at the battalion command post, but at the echelon position.

barrage down the column. The Chinese dashed for cover, leaving a handful of corpses scattered over the ground. Newcombe spent the remaining time before darkness ranging rounds on expected avenues of approach: the killing grounds.[25]

The day wore on. On the highest point, Large was given binoculars and ordered to watch for an American relief force.* None appeared, so he spent his time watching Chinese, now some two miles to the north, crossing the river under murderous UN artillery fire and air strikes. Jets dived down, dropping napalm: as the explosions of jellied petrol blossomed and ran along the ground, Large watched in horrified fascination as men flared up, ran in circles, then fell in heaps, leaving little human bonfires. The aircraft shrieked in lower, strafing with rockets and cannon. Dense clouds of smoke and dust were hanging over the river, blurring the picture, but in the murk Large could still see the tiny figures of Chinese, in their hundreds, swarming south.[26] Contrary to usual Chinese practice, the mass of men was moving in daylight: General Yang was pushing his forces over the Imjin at maximum speed.† Two more divisions – the 188th and 189th – were joining the 187th on the south bank.[27]

Both sides were sniping. Large and his section spotted a Chinese squad some 350 yards away. The men were given permission to open fire – though no automatic weapons were to be used, to prevent their positions being given away. The Glosters set the brass-backed wooden butts of their Lee-Enfields against their shoulders, placed their cheeks next to the rear sights, squinted down the barrels, released their breaths to steady their torsos, and began squeezing off shots. Nobody registered a hit. The enemy party continued walking, unperturbed. The last man, before reaching cover, turned and loosed a submachine burst in the Glosters' general direction, as if in insult. A Gloster old sweat nearby, who had been watching his shooting, told Large his marksmanship had deteriorated as he kept missing. It was not only the Chinese who demonstrated coolness. A Gloster was digging in when he came under fire. In a show of bravado he indicated the sniper's fall of shot – left, right – with his spade. Like Large, the Chinese sniper was put off by his continued inaccuracy.[28]

* * *

* What expedition this was is unclear. No relief force was ready to be dispatched to the Glosters until the following day.
† For his Fifth Offensive, Marshal Peng, understanding that his troops could not sustain an offensive for more than a week due to their primitive logistics system, wanted to maximise speed and shock, so decreed that all units must be prepared to fight in daytime (see Zhang, p. 147). While most commanders continued to mount attacks in darkness, exposure to UN firepower in daylight caused tremendous casualties.

After the extraction of the Fusiliers' Y Company and the support for Z Company's failed counter-attack, Captain Ormrod received a telephone call. It was Captain Anthony Farrar-Hockley, the Glosters' adjutant. 'He said could we send a troop of tanks around the front of the brigade along the river to help the defence of the Gloster position?' Ormrod recalled. 'I didn't like the idea at all. They would have gone for two or three miles without any contact or support.' Moreover, the hilltops along the river were now held by enemy. With the Centurions engaged in fire-support tasks, Ormrod sent the squadron's reconnaissance troop. They came under severe fire; two tanks were damaged. The vehicles were dragged back.[29] The Glosters remained without support.

That morning, in the shadows of the headquarters area at the foot of Hill 235, the Gloster medical officer had been tending to stretchers of wounded from A and D Company. His hands were covered in blood; his RAP staff, triaging casualties, handed him dressings, drugs, instruments. American helicopters clattered in, squatting on the ground as stretchers of seriously wounded – those who would not survive the bumpy ambulance ride south – were fastened to their skids.[30] At the side of the track leading from A Company's lost hill lay Major Pat Angier. Three officers stood to attention next to his body as Padre Sam Davies intoned a short service. When Davies finished, each man saluted and walked off to his duties.[31] Angier was laid next to the stream, under a boat left by the engineers.[32]

In the early afternoon, Major Digby Grist, formerly Support Company OC, now the Glosters' second in command, arrived from F Echelon, established at the end of the Route 5Y defile, with supplies. At Hill 235 he encountered the aftermath of combat: groups of dirty men, wearing the shock of recent battle on their faces, tiredly digging in. The mortars in their pits were firing over the hill. Grist was impressed to see Farrar-Hockley, lying curled up on the grass. A true professional, he was grabbing what rest he could. Soon sleep would be a precious commodity. Grist spoke briefly to Carne, who ordered him back to F Echelon.[33] The CO was busy. Lance-Corporal Charles Sharpling was with the signallers when a radio call came from brigade. 'Good,' Carne said, and hurried over to speak to Brodie, telling him that his men were tired, his ammunition low, and the Chinese were crossing the Imjin *en masse*. 'What? You must have spots before your eyes, man!' the brigadier retorted.* Carne, disgusted, walked away in his customary silence.[34]

---

* Sharpling was unsure of the exact timing of this discussion, but stated it was before the forthcoming Filipino counter-attack. This corresponds with Newcombe's concern that higher HQ was underestimating the seriousness of the attack on the sector, and Large's observations of the Chinese crossing. There is also a note in the Gloster regimental archive from Farrar-Hockley noting that the brigade was more concerned with events on its eastern flank. Given the dangers faced by the Belgians and the Fusiliers X Company, this seems particularly true on 23 April.

Major Grist climbed into his jeep next to his driver George Bainbridge – a veteran who had fought in World War II and subsequently driven buses in Nottingham before being called up for Korea.[35] The two set off, passing the various sub-units of Support and Headquarters Companies. A hundred yards or so along the valley bottom the track turned south. The jeep entered the narrow defile. Also in the valley was the anti-tank platoon. It had been having a quiet battle – until sniper rounds from a hillside hide began cracking over the mortar crews. A sergeant bawled orders. Private Ben Whitchurch was ordered to take a 17-pounder further down the valley road to take out the sniper. Whitchurch was shocked by the order; there was no cover on the track where the carriers were sitting. The sniper appeared to be in a little cutting up the valley. Whitchurch would have to run, in plain view, to the Oxford carrier, then drive it to the gun so the crew could hook it up. He sprinted over to the tracked metal box and dived into the cab. He was not hit. 'I sat in the cockpit, steering, thinking, "Christ, I was lucky to get out of that!"' he recalled. Under the cover provided by the vehicle the gun crew attached their weapon and rumbled to a firing position. They unhitched. The anti-tank gunners loaded armour-piercing and let fly. Rock splinters blasted into the air. 'There was a big old bang at the first shell, and everyone looked round – "What was that?"' The gun was reloaded with high explosive and fired again. The 17-pound shell detonated on the hillside in a blast of smoke, dust and scrub. 'We used AP to open the gap and HE to blow him up,' said Whitchurch. 'There was no more sniper fire after that!' It was the first time the Glosters had fired their anti-tank guns in Korea.

Grist and Bainbridge motored down Five Yankee. With the riverside hills overlooking the track south of the river in enemy hands, this winding defile was now the Glosters' only line of communications. On both sides sheer rock cliffs loomed over the track. As they approached the southern entrance to the tunnel-like stretch of road there was a stutter of machine-gun fire. Gravel kicked up around the wheels. Ambush! Grist recognized the position the bullets were coming from: he had sited a machine-gun there himself for defence against enemy from the north. 'Keep driving!' he ordered Bainbridge. The jeep accelerated, bullets shattered the windscreen and a round drilled through Grist's wrist. Grist could clearly see the machine-gunner ranging in, just thirty yards away. Another Chinese soldier was standing next to him. Grist, unable to do anything but sit tight, watched the standing soldier reach over and slap the machine-gunner on the head, presumably for poor aim. At point-blank range, the slap saved the Glosters' lives. Momentarily distracted, the gunner fired – the burst zinged overhead – the jeep shot past. Next, they raced past a wrecked British ambulance on its side, a body hanging upside down from its door. A group from Grist's F Echelon command flashed by in a blur; the dejected men were standing beside the track, prisoners. One would later tell Grist that the major looked like Toad of Toad Hall as he zoomed past in the jeep. Chinese were still shooting. The jeep hit a bump in the road – it took momentary flight – Grist's customized sleeping bag, complete with arms, flared up as it bounced out of the back – there was a cheer from watching enemy – then the vehicle was shielded by a break in the ground. They were through. The gunfire ceased. The two continued out of the pass and along the track over the paddies. Tires shredded, the jeep was rattling on its wheel rims when it pulled up at Brigade HQ. Grist dashed in to report. Bainbridge went in search of a camera, to snap a picture of the pepper-potted jeep for his mantel shelf.[36]

The two had escaped by the skin of their teeth, but F Echelon was lost. A handful of escapees from the position later related how the Chinese had taken it. Korean peasants had approached the British position, then, at the last moment, cast aside their white clothing and produced burp guns. They were Chinese infiltrators. One man, Private Morgan, was cornered by four attackers. He raised his hands, holding aloft his Sten gun. With his captors at point blank, Morgan squeezed the trigger; the burst, fired from above his head, dispatched all four, and Morgan escaped.[37] But he was the exception. The loss of the rear position had critical implications. The Chinese had penetrated miles into the Glosters' rear, and, positioned astride Five Yankee, had plugged their bolt hole. Events were spiralling out of control. The battalion was cut off.*

* * *

So were the Belgians. The massive weight of the Chinese offensive on the first night had pushed the entire UN line back. To the north-east of 29th Brigade, covered by air and artillery strikes, the US 3rd Division had withdrawn across the Hantan by mid-afternoon. The Belgians had stood fast, but, with US forces heading south, their hinge position was now redundant. The question was how to extricate them. Brigadier Brodie conferred with his superior, 3rd Division's commander General

---

* In fact, Grist and Bainbridge were not the last Glosters to return from F Echelon. Before they headed down-valley, two ammunition trucks, under Second Lieutenant Tony Preston, had set off up-valley – perhaps in response to Carne's comment to Brodie that his ammunition was low – even though they had heard that there was an ambush in the defile. They were captured, and held on a hill near Kamak-san. The hill came under air attack with napalm. In the confusion Corporal Wateridge escaped, later meeting up with Private Pickard of B Company. The two arrived at Brigade Headquarters on the evening of the 24th bearing the news – and confirming Mervyn McCord's report – that the Kamak-san hills and valleys were swarming with enemy. See Harding (2000), pp. 22–3.

Robert Soule, by telephone. Brodie suggested the Belgians destroy their vehicles and break across the river on foot. Soule, however, decided on a two-pronged operation. His 1st Battalion, 7th Infantry, would launch a diversionary attack on Hill 257, Z Company's former hill, while a covering force on the Hantan, provided by two tank platoons and an infantry company, would shoot the Belgians across the river.[38] The American infantry assaulted Hill 257 at 18:00.[39]

Ormrod watched. 'They were going to clear up the position – "We were all being a bit soft, they'd do it,"' he recalled. The Hussar officer pointed out enemy dispositions to the Americans. 'They advanced up a hill and never came down again. I later found out that they had advanced up one hill and then went down the other side and returned to their own lines. They weren't much cop.' Ormrod was unaware that the attack was not designed to take the position, but to divert the attention of the Chinese on the hill from what was happening over the river.[40]

The Belgians were preparing to fight their way out. At 10:00, Major Moreau de Melen, the former Belgian defence minister and his battalion's liaison officer at 3rd Division, had accompanied an American tank platoon to the area of the bridges.[41] Once the main American covering units arrived in the early evening, the operation began. On the north bank Second Lieutenant Henri Wolfs had been given an unenviable mission: his squad, with two armed jeeps, was to hold a blocking position in the Belgian rear, close to Ulster Crossing, and 'close the door' once the main force was across. 'Ours not to reason why,' he thought. He took up position then 'started to wonder what was going on'; like most soldiers, he had little idea of what was happening beyond his immediate horizon. A little later, he was 'put in the picture': The Americans were going to use tank fire and an air strike to cover the Belgians' retreat over the river. The men on foot would wade; the vehicles would dash across the bridge. The Chinese ambushers near the bridges had disappeared.

Even for the daredevil Belgians, this would be a perilous operation. They would have to break contact, pull down from their positions and cross the river under the noses of the enemy while the Americans provided covering fire. One group of vehicles was cut off by a low knoll, some ten metres high, along the river. Due to enemy observation they could not drive around it. Assault Pioneers were summoned. They packed the knoll with a mass of explosives, and blasted a gap.[42] The vehicles flowed through.

Wolfs was offered extra ammunition, but refused – he had a full load – however, he gratefully accepted two extra men. The two 'didn't seem very enthusiastic when they heard our mission'. A nearby truck ditched hundreds of C rations in order to carry more essential equipment. Wolfs assured the sergeant responsible that he would destroy the food; the sergeant seemed only too pleased to pass the responsibility along. After he disappeared, Wolfs's men got the chance to 'do a little pilfering'.

Meanwhile, American tanks and artillery opened fire. Shells whistled over the men's heads, then exploded with a crash. Clouds of dust and smoke rose over Hill 194. The Belgians pulled back in two segments: the vehicles raced across the meadow behind their hill, where helicopters had evacuated their casualties earlier in the day, rattled across the pontoon bridge over the river, then drove through the cutting in the southern bank and onto the MSR under the protective guns of the American force. As the vehicles crossed the river, the infantry, in long company files, holding their weapons over their heads, waded in. Such was the weight of covering fire, only desultory Chinese mortaring hindered the crossing. Sergeant Lucien Senterre was apprehensive, but not due to the enemy fire: he was only five feet five inches tall. Gingerly he entered the flow, but his fears proved unfounded: as the Chinese had discovered, the river was fordable. His soaked company reached the other side and scrambled out, up the shingle beach, and headed for American transport. Sergeant André VanDamme, driving a jeep over the bridge, snatched a glance over his shoulder and saw movement: the Chinese were advancing over the Belgians' abandoned positions, but there was no panic among his men: 'It is important to stay cool in such situations.'

On the north bank, watching the battalion pull back, Wolfs with his rearguard felt a sense 'more of bewilderment than fear'. He ordered a Browning machine-gunner on his jeep to shoot a full belt into the hilltop, then to hold his fire unless he saw clear targets. The machine-gunner let rip. He did not have to shoot again. The Chinese, taken by surprise by the fast withdrawal and under heavy fire themselves as the Americans churned up the hilltop, kept down. Napalm strikes were screaming onto the abandoned position. Sergeant Cor Feyt looked back and saw distant Chinese soldiers writhing in the inferno.[43] At last it was Wolfs's turn. By now it was dark, but the young officer noticed neither damaged vehicles nor casualties as his two jeeps rattled across the pontoons to the south bank and safety. While helping a doctor salvage a broken-down ambulance Wolfs ordered a pot of coffee to be brewed during the repairs and refused to let his men move until they had finished it; the repairs were speedily undertaken and the coffee guzzled at a record rate.* He and his squad then bedded down with an American artillery unit. Even the cotton wool the grateful medic had given him to plug his ears did not diminish the thunder of the guns.

---

* Years later, some of Wolfs's men would recall the race to drink the coffee as the most memorable incident of the battle.

ST GEORGE'S DAY:
Battle of the Imjin River, April 23.

The river crossing could have been a disaster, but in terms of speed and co-ordination, had been a near-textbook operation. The battalion was clear by 20:00.[44] 'We had quite some luck,' thought VanDamme; he estimated the crossing had taken about 45 minutes.* The steadfastness of the Belgians in holding the critical hinge between the Imjin and Hantan on the night of the 22nd would win them a US Presidential Unit Citation. However, as the Belgians regrouped down the MSR, the luck of another brigade unit was fast running out.

* * *

St George's Day 1951 was coming to an end. A bright moon rose. Yang's offensive could recommence. An entire division, the 189th, was aligned against the Glosters.[45]

B Company's commander, Major Harding, sent a listening patrol to the foot of his hill soon after dusk. The men moved down in silence, then sank into cover at the bottom. After a while, they picked up a strange swishing sound. They had to listen intently to recognise what it was: the sound of the rubber-soled boots of men – hundreds of men – moving through the grass parallel to the company position. The patrol returned, silently, to their hilltop and reported what they had seen and heard to the artillery FOO. Commands were whispered across the airwaves. Minutes later, shells came whistling over the treetops, impacting with flashes and crumps in the valley.[46] But still there was no attack; the Chinese, moving diagonally across their front, appear not to have pinpointed the Glosters' position.† This luck could not last. A full regiment, 189th Division's 559th,[47] would be employed against Harding's men, outnumbering them by about 18:1. At around 23:00 B Company's death struggle began.

Corporal Albert Perkins could not see his attackers but could hear talking, spitting and chattering. 'As soon as you heard a noise, you opened fire,' he said. That was the probes. Then came the eerie, tinny bugles summoning company-level attacks, and the Glosters could see shadowy crowds pounding towards them. 'They were running and firing,' Perkins said. 'They could not see us.' (At ground level, the Glosters were invisible to the Chinese.) Shells hurtled in. As the rounds struck, with their sudden white flashes, earth was hurled up and rained down. The ground inside Perkins's sangar vibrated.

* Two sources for this section, Wolfs and VanDamme, do not recall seeing any vehicles lost or destroyed during the withdrawal. However, the US 3rd Division Command Report states seven were lost. For an operation fraught with such peril, this seems a tiny price to pay.
† It is not clear whether the Chinese moving across the front of B Company's position were under orders to bypass it, and head south, or were looking for the company in the dark hills in order to pinpoint it and to destroy it.

Bren gunner Frank Carter was behind a parapet of rocks in a shallow three-man trench in a forward position on the right-hand slope. During the day scrub had been cleared, creating a beaten zone for twenty yards to their front. Before the attack, things had been quiet. Lance Corporal 'Spud' Taylor, beside Carter in the trench, was smoking his pipe, with one hand over the pot, when Carter noticed a circle of Chinese, in section strength, had arrived at the edge of the cleared area. A leader seemed to be pointing out positions. The British soldiers froze momentarily – then Taylor ordered Carter to open fire. Carter unloosed a full thirty-round magazine. When he ceased, a pile of prone bodies lay where the Chinese had been; one figure was staggering down the hill. Then mortar bombs exploded all round; then the human wave. 'There were thousands,' Carter recalled. 'It was like they were coming out of an ants' nest!' Yet the Bren team, covering a twenty-yard front, held them off. Another lull. The Glosters could see Chinese heaped in front of their trench. Some enemy casualties remained alive, writhing and groaning. By now the Bren team was down to eight magazines; during the break in the action they reloaded, feverishly pressing .303 rounds down onto the springs. As they did so Carter's head bobbed above the parapet. He was stunned by a sudden flash in his face. He came to seconds later, looking up to see his mate, Cornish, bandaging his face with a field dressing. A bullet had entered Carter's left eye and exited near his ear. He was sure the sniper was lying among the bodies just yards ahead. Through a gap in the parapet, with his good eye, he spotted a rifle barrel about six yards ahead, moving among the dead and wounded. Warning Cornish to stay low, he fired a long burst. The bodies shook as the rounds hit. Carter was sure he had silenced the sniper, when another bullet ricocheted overhead. Cornish, looking through a gap in the parapet, burst out, 'There he is, Frank!' – then his head jolted back: the sniper had hit him between the eyes. 'He fell into the back of the trench. I thought, "Christ, what am I going to do?" It came out the back of his head. I bandaged him – he was still breathing. I got on the little radio and said, "Send blokes with a stretcher!"' Carter looked to Taylor for help – the corporal lay motionless at the bottom of the trench. The neighbouring slit was silent. Alone, half-blind, Carter reloaded magazines and called urgently into the radio. Chinese advanced past him in the darkness. Carter's section was overrun; he could not understand why they were ignoring him. Behind him, he could hear close-range fighting as the enemy collided with the next positions. Then the enemy came streaming back down, repulsed. In a long, hammering burst, Carter emptied a magazine into the running figures. Still, they seemed not to have noticed him. Another lull. Cornish, unconscious, was breathing with difficulty. Again, Carter radioed for help. Nobody came.[48]

Large was in the thick of the action. Panting Chinese were scrambling up the slope to his front, firing burp guns. Visually, battle was an intense, confusing mosaic: the attackers were sometimes visible in the moonlight; sometimes they appeared as shadows upon shadows as flares fizzed up or went out, and grenades exploded. Otherwise, it was a case of shooting at flickering orange muzzles. An experienced soldier next to Large told him to shoot at 'the moving lights' as he readied a phosphorus grenade. He threw. It burst. Screaming enemy soldiers, spattered in droplets of liquid flame – 'moving lights' – scrambled to their feet. Without cover, they were mown down; Large was sickened by the stench of cooking flesh. He was reloading at the bottom of his shell scrape when a shadow loomed over his parapet. With his magazine empty, he reacted instinctively and thrust up with his bayoneted rifle, skewering the soldier. The Chinese did not defend himself: Large wondered whether he had already been shot. In lulls men refilled magazines, primed grenades, and dripped oil onto the working parts of their smoking weapons. All the men had faces blackened by powder; all were bleeding on their exposed skin from cuts inflicted by the tiny rock fragments blasted across their position every time a grenade or mortar bomb burst. Large's shoulder ached from the continual kick of his rifle, his head rang with the cacophony. Wounded screamed in the darkness all around. Large stuffed moss into his ears and with bleeding fingers tried to claw deeper into the soil. 'Stand fast, Glosters!' an officer yelled. 'Remember the back badge!' 'Fuck the back badge,' someone shouted. 'I want out!' Laughter swept the besieged platoon. Large's emotions veered between terror, excitement and exultation – and a determination not to be beaten.[49]

At the CP, Newcombe was adjusting artillery by sight: he could see by the flash where his shots fell. He varied between shooting into the waves attacking the platoons and engaging enemy support weapons; the Chinese mortars were visible by their flash, machine-guns by their tracer. He was irritated when the battery requested a rest, and switched to interval fire. The 25-pounders were close to overheating.[50]

Chinese mortar shells were going off in the treetops. Showers of shrapnel and wooden splinters, like airbursts, drenched the defenders; branches crashed down. But it was the machine-guns that proved deadliest. Large's slit was raked by an automatic from somewhere to his front. When mortaring ceased and machine-gun fire lifted, an assault surged in. Large rose to shoot, and felt 'a sledge hammer with a knife on it' tear into his left arm. His rifle, smashed, spun away. A machine-gun burst had caught him. There was another lull; artillery had broken up the attack. The man next to him in his trench, who had been fighting hard all night, looked at Large, saw his wound, and went to pieces, hiding, shaking,

under a poncho in the corner of the slit trench. Large's platoon commander, Second Lieutenant Peal, arriving with extra ammunition, immediately recognised the situation. The young officer levelled his Sten,
cocked it and ordered the cowering soldier up. The man surfaced with a
startled look, faced front and resumed firing. Large, amazed, could not
understand why Peal was not hit by the machine-gun ranged onto his
trench. Another assault was coming in. Wounded, Large lay low. His
trench-mate, who seconds before had been useless, heaved an entire box
of primed grenades over the parapet and ducked down. A blast of dust
and smoke engulfed the trench: Yet another attack had been beaten off. A
medical orderly ran over and bandaged Large with a shell dressing. He
was helped out of his position, and found he could walk. He was taken up
to the aid post and left leaning against a tree. Bodies lay scattered around.
In front of him, he dully noticed a severed arm.[51]

The sky was lightening. On C Company's position, some eight hundred yards west of B Company and just across the valley from Hill 235,
Second Lieutenant Guy Temple had heard firing throughout the night
over at B Company, but now it was quiet. More disturbingly, he could
not see a single sign of any other battalion units. 'It was most eerie, so
very, very quiet. I looked around and I could not see a single soul. I
wondered what the hell was going on.' Disturbed, he took out a map,
then passed it to his signaller while he got his binoculars out. The man
jerked back as the crack of a rifle shot sounded: the signaller had been
sniped. Temple and those around him took cover; there was nothing
they could do for the casualty. 'I felt a bit guilty,' Temple said. 'It was
meant for me'; the sniper had aimed for the white map. C Company
Sergeant Major Riddlington arrived from Company HQ to inform
Temple that the company commander had vanished. Temple, his anxiety
increasing, attempted to contact Battalion HQ on a 31 Set. All it
returned was static.* Temple wondered what had happened to the rest
of the battalion. 'I thought, "Here we are – C Company's been left on
their own. Everybody's bugged out!" I was a bit bothered.' Riddlington
presumably had similar misgivings. 'You're in charge!' he told Temple.
The two could see Chinese moving on distant hills. Looking across to
Hill 235 – slightly above their own position – they spotted movement. 'I
thought we'd better get up there,' said Temple. C Company seemed
largely complete: Temple issued orders. Messengers went to the other
platoons. A runner arrived at the position held by Private Morris
'Brassy' Coombes and told him that the company was heading out.
Temple led his men down and across the valley previously occupied by

* Presumably, the hills were causing interference, as commonly happened in Korea.

Support and Headquarters Companies. Carne had ordered those companies up Hill 235, following skirmishes with Chinese moving through during the night. C Company moved down into the valley. Vehicles – carriers, trucks, jeeps – stood abandoned. Temple spotted a signals truck he had acquired from Americans for a bottle of Scotch during the retreat from Pyongyang; it was burning. 'Oh, well,' he thought. A lone Chinese soldier looting the vehicles was shot. The company began climbing Hill 235. Snipers ranged in. As he crossed the stream, Coombes fell over and lost his glasses, but clung to his rifle. Ascending the slope, his trench-mate was sniped; at the top, another man was shot in the stomach. 'He kept saying, "I'm cold, I'm cold,"' recalled Coombes. 'I don't know his name; he died.' At the top, they were ordered to dig in, covering the southern slopes of the hill.*

---

* The above contradicts other accounts of C Company's action – notably Harding's *The Imjin Roll* and Farrar-Hockley's two works on the battle (*The Edge of the Sword* and volume II of the official British history of the war). Their accounts state that a 'strong' or 'rolling' attack was made upon C Company at 03:30 hours, and Carne ordered Support, Headquarters and C Company back. During this movement, C Company's Commander, Major Jack Mitchell, went missing as he crossed the valley 'to find out what the situation was'. This is odd. If, as Harding states, C Company had suffered 'two platoons overrun' and 'the whole of their position . . . was threatened', why would Mitchell depart? The above accounts are somewhat corroborated by C Company's David Green, who in *Captured at the Imjin River* tells how his platoon came under fire from higher ground, was forced back towards Company HQ, then moved down into the valley with Mitchell, who disappeared in the confusion. All accounts indicate that the units in the valley *did* come under light attack before/while moving up to Hill 235 in the dark. However, neither Farrar-Hockley nor Harding were with C Company, and I wonder whether their accounts have covered up an inglorious episode. Temple and Coombes, both C Company survivors, separately stated to me that C suffered *no major attack* on the night of the 24th. Michael Newcombe, B Company's FOO, states in his book (pp. 184–5) that he had heard no calls for fire support from C Company over the artillery net and did not believe them to be under heavy attack. Furthermore, Temple makes clear that there was no order from higher command to abandon the hill – he ordered the early-morning movement by the bulk of the company on his own initiative. Temple and Coombes also state that they did not leave the hill at night; they moved in daylight (according to 3rd Division's weather report, sunrise on 24 April was at 05:44). So what happened? It is my opinion that the Support and Headquarters Companies moved up Hill 235 around 03:30, as stated, and that C Company's OC, Major Jack Mitchell – perhaps in receipt of garbled orders by radio, and seeking clarification – headed, with a small party, into the valley to confer with higher command on Hill 235, which is only about a hundred and fifty yards away as the crow flies. There, in a confused skirmish, he was forced off by Chinese infiltrating through the valley. (Along with several members of the mortar and anti-tank platoons, he arrived at Brigade HQ on the 24th, after escaping and evading through the hills.) This left his company leaderless. Newcombe states an (unnamed) C Company platoon commander later told him that, in an information vacuum, he had taken part of his platoon from its position to probe forward, then returned to find his trenches occupied by Chinese, and so departed. Farrar-Hockley (1995) states there were signalling problems at the time; this is confirmed by Temple and by 29th Brigade War Diary – which, noting the Glosters had given up the valley floor at 03:45, reports that this news was received not via battalion radio, but by 45 Field Regiment's net. If Temple, Coombes and Newcombe are to be believed (and there is no reason why they should not be), if there was an attack on C Company, it was a minor one. Then there was confusion and a breakdown in leadership, until Temple took command at daybreak.

As C Company climbed to join the bulk of the battalion, the curtain was falling on B. Just after dawn a platoon counter-attack under Lieutenant Geoffrey Costello had gone in to clear Chinese from the forward positions. Some attacking men, already wounded, were hit a second time. Company numbers were dwindling. Medical orderlies came down the hill to Carter's trench, placed the dying Cornish on a stretcher and told Carter to abandon his Bren and pull back to where the remnants of the company were regrouping higher up. Carter removed the LMG's barrel, hurled it away, picked up Cornish's rifle and walked up the hill to an aid post, where a number of wounded were lying on the reverse slope. Carter, blind in one eye, was placed there to protect them with his rifle.[52] B Company had beaten back five full assaults, calling in artillery to within thirty yards of its position, but their grenades – critical weapons in such close-range fighting – had run out.[53] B Company had been amazed at the volume of Chinese automatic fire. Some felt conned by their earlier briefers.* 'We were told they only had one rifle between three men,' said Perkins. 'They didn't tell us the rest had automatics!' Shooting into the hail of Chinese fire with a Lee-Enfield, Large had felt as if he were spitting against a fire hose.[54]

By daylight, Newcombe could clearly see enemy in C Company's positions, but was having difficulty firing on them: his radio battery was dying. Two men from Costello's greatly depleted platoon fled towards him. Fearing a rout, Newcombe drew his pistol and ordered them back. The shocked men complied. Shortly afterwards Harding withdrew the platoon's survivors. The Company CP was now the front line. Another charge was repelled. A mortar bomb burst on the lip of Newcombe's slit: he was stunned, and a splinter killed the gunner behind him. A World War I joke flashed through his mind: 'The bullet sped safely past me to bury itself harmlessly in the head of my sergeant.' He was immediately ashamed at the thought. Major Harding still issued no orders to retreat; instead, with enemy massing only seventy yards away, he ordered bayonets to be fixed. Newcombe asked the major if he could call fire onto their own position.† Harding assented. As the enemy advanced, the barrage shrieked in. The Glosters ducked into their slits: none were hit, but the enemy, above ground, recoiled as the shells detonated.[55] The seventh and last Chinese assault rolled up the hill at 08:10. By now even small-arms ammunition was running out. Carter, incredulous, watched one officer blazing away with a pistol in each fist.

---

* On other sectors of the battlefield, some Chinese troops behind the first waves were only armed with hand grenades, but the accounts of B Company's survivors make clear their assailants had a high complement of automatics.

† Calling fire onto one's own position is certainly a desperate tactic, but is not as suicidal as it sounds. If the defenders have cover, most will survive, but attackers in the open will be decimated.

B Company had held as long as it could. Harding called his survivors in close and said: 'We are not going to hold this hill for another charge. It's every man for himself. Get back to the battalion hill – if you can.' Carter had noticed a small ravine leading downwards; overgrown with bushes, it offered excellent cover. He followed it down to the valley floor. At the bottom more Chinese soldiers than he had ever seen before were milling about, along with mules pulling artillery. 'They were getting behind us,' Carter said. 'We were left there – the whole battalion.' Carter was joined by eight men who had followed him down the re-entrant. They could not cross the track; if they did, they would be seen. They thought they could hear tanks firing on the other side of a ridge, but as they climbed up, were spotted by a Chinese patrol, which fired warning shots over their heads. It was over. The Chinese smiled. 'They came down, shook our hands,' recalled Carter. '"Good fight," they said in broken English.'[56]

On the hilltop, Large, with bullets in his side and arm, followed a pair of men to the same cliff from which he had killed a Chinese the previous day. It was twenty or thirty feet high, with loose shale at the bottom. There was only one way down. Terrified, Large jumped, landed safely and, running down the scree, scrambled into a thicket. Ahead of him was a Chinese face. Nothing happened. It took several seconds for Large to realise that he was dead, killed by blast. On the valley floor, he spotted a line of Glosters. He was following them when a machine-gun hammered from the hill above: B Company had fallen. Around Large, retreating Glosters spun to the ground. With his good arm Large helped another wounded man stagger along, but suddenly, the man shuddered and fell, hit by a burst – Large had been saved by the human shield. Then he was over a ridge and out of the fire. There were eight men there, but only two unwounded. The latter were both armed, though with only three bullets between them. Fire from Chinese submachine-gunners behind them raked them. They ducked into cover. Ahead was a valley swarming with Chinese troops digging in. The Glosters debated what to do. An enemy soldier, carrying a rifle and a piece of paper – a messenger – approached them, unsuspectingly, from out of the valley. The corporal in charge, George Baker, handed his rifle to someone and told him that if the messenger shot him, the man was to kill the Chinese. Then Baker stepped out in front of the messenger. The startled man levelled his rifle at the British soldier. The other Glosters stepped out of cover. The burp gunners who had been pursuing them suddenly appeared, yelling. The Chinese with the rifle pointed it at the submachine-gunners and marched the eight Glosters – his prisoners! – hands on heads, into the valley.[57]

More groups and individuals were trying to break through the ring of Chinese around the hill. Corporal Perkins, unwounded, had moved down into the valley, when a 'flock' of Chinese poured over the hill. A Gloster sergeant harshly ordered, 'Destroy your weapons!' Then they were captured. Captain Newcombe ran towards the enemy firing his pistol – he leaped over a cliff – his cap flew off – he hit a patch of scree running – Chinese fired down at him. He retrieved his cap, waved it at the enemy, shouted an insult and headed for cover. He was still stunned by the mortar. He passed a group of bodies flattened by blast – or were they abandoned uniforms? Then he, too, was taken.[58]

The last group to leave the hill, commanded by Major Harding, were from Company HQ; perhaps twenty men. Chinese were sniping from only thirty yards away. At a shouted signal, the Glosters broke cover, charged down the slope, right through a line of stunned Chinese – who could not react fast enough to open concentrated fire – and into the cover of pines at the bottom of the hill.[59]

On Hill 235 the Glosters had been listening all night to B Company's battle. Only at dawn could they do anything: the Vickers started firing over the abandoned C Company position into Chinese silhouettes. Farrar-Hockley was on the radio to brigade. There was cheering news: a task force comprising a Filipino infantry battalion and Hussar Centurions was going to punch through to reinforce the Glosters later that day, Tuesday. On Wednesday the battalion would be relieved and pulled out of the line to refit. Farrar-Hockley signed off cheerfully, looking forward to a drink on Thursday night. Then he heard excited shouting from the soldiers around the radio position. B Company was coming in.[60]

On the slope, Bugler Tony Eagles and his mate Jones had been 'having some fun': they would sound their bugles and, when a Chinese head popped up, open fire. 'I don't know if we got any, but they scurried away,' Eagles said. Farrar-Hockley ordered them to cease fire: he didn't want Harding's men confused. The adjutant crawled to the edge of the hill with his binoculars, joining other watchers. There was tension in the air. Below, a small group of men had appeared around a bend in the track. Some had fair hair: they were British! But as they got closer to Hill 235 and safety, a group of Chinese appeared round the side of a ridge to head them off. Burp guns sounded. On the hilltop, heads craned forward, watching the drama below. Carne arrived. Would the survivors be mown down under the eyes of the battalion? Then came the sudden hammering of a Bren. Without orders, Corporal Walker of C Company was halfway down the rear slope of Hill 235, single-handedly counter-attacking, firing an LMG from the hip. Faced by this berserker, the Chinese squad retreated around a rock face. Harding's remnants straggled up to the main position, where they were combined with C Company, holding the southern slopes of Hill 235.[61]

Their numbers were pitiful. After a night of relentless combat, the company, approximately 120 men strong, had been decimated: only twenty soldiers under Harding made it to Hill 235. Although he later wrote two separate, clinical accounts of the action,* the major never put his personal feelings about the events of the night of April 23rd/24th on paper. The inner devastation must have been overwhelming. His command – B Company, 1st Battalion, the Gloucestershire Regiment – had effectively ceased to exist.

* The official B Company after-action report (unpublished; in the Soldiers of Gloucestershire Museum archive), and a record of the Glosters' battle, *The Imjin Roll* (Northamptonshire, 1976; third edition, 2000). In an interview with academic Hugh Driver in 1983, Harding described the night only as 'a very testing time'. (Interview transcript in Soldiers of Gloucestershire Museum archive)

## Chapter 8

# CRESCENDO: 24 APRIL.

*As well the soldier dieth who standeth still*
*as he that gives the bravest onset.*

Sir Philip Sidney

**D**AWN, 24 APRIL. At the Royal Ulster Rifles' Tactical Command Post on Hill 398 there was a lull in the firing. Lieutenant John Mole, the man whose helmet had been holed at Happy Valley, and who was now operating as Mortar Fire Controller, was catching his breath. He had spent the night beside Major Gerald Rickord as the acting CO orchestrated responses to attacks. Major John Shaw, Mole's company commander, had just arrived at the Tactical CP from his position with the mortars further south down Route 11 to confer with Rickord. Mole liked and respected Shaw, who had led the rearguard out of Happy Valley, but found him something of a martinet. The major proved true to form. Noting Mole's dishevelled appearance, Shaw snapped: 'John, I expect my officers to shave. Why have you not shaved?' 'I've been a bit busy,' Mole replied. 'I don't care,' Shaw retorted. 'See to it!' Although put out to receive such an order in the midst of battle, Mole had little choice but to comply.

He had reason to look dishevelled; it had been a long night. While the Glosters' B Company was being decimated in the west, the Chinese waves had rolled into the Rifles in the east. On their fortified hilltop covering the east of Route 11, A Company came under attack at 02:15 hours. In the light of the dangling flares, machine-guns and hand grenades took their toll as the bugles urged the attackers on. When Chinese squads took cover among rocks to their front, the Riflemen blasted the boulders with a bazooka. The rockets, at close range, were devastating: Lance-Corporal Joe Farrell could see bodies 'flying all over the place'.

Rickord asked Brigade to release B Company from its backstop position at the saddle. The request was denied. Instead, Rickord moved C Company to a ridge 800 yards south-east of Hill 398 to cover his right; enemy movement had been noted to the east but, curiously, the Chinese made no flanking attack on the hill. With daylight, air strikes screamed in over the low ground where Chinese were forming up ahead of the battalion; the jets came at such low level that the battalion had to halt mortar fire.[1] But after the napalm had burnt out, machine-guns resumed firing from the smouldering ground. Throughout the morning, attacks on the Rifles continued. All were beaten off.[2]

The Fusiliers had also been hit. W Company held, but Y, holding the north-west position on Route 11 came under attack at 03:15. By 03:45, the company – all its platoons leaderless after the friendly fire incident with the Hussars – was pulling back.* At 03:50 W Company sent a patrol up to cover the gap. Y was successfully extracted for the second time in the battle, but by 05:15 its abandoned position was 'teeming' with enemy. At 07:00 Centurions rumbled up to bolster the Fusiliers with fire support, while a patrol from X Company took up sniping positions. With full daylight, the attacks on the Fusiliers petered out, allowing Lieutenant-Colonel Kingsley Foster to redeploy his battered command.[3]

After a second night of defiance 29th Brigade was still holding the northern end of Route 11. With the situation at the roadhead apparently stable, a critical operation could get under way.

* * *

A mile and a half behind the saddle on Route 11, 29th Brigade HQ was a hive of activity. Tanks revved their engines and turned on their axes; officers and NCOs shouted orders; men prepared weapons, adjusted equipment and sorted themselves into companies and platoons. The battle group that would punch through to reinforce the surrounded Glosters was mustering.

The ad hoc force consisted of the infantry of the Filipino 10th Battalion Combat Team and a troop of the 8th Hussars. The Filipinos had fought a successful action on the night of 22 April with 3rd Division, and had arrived in the headquarters area at 20:00 on the 23rd, after Brodie, with all his infantry deployed, had requested reinforcements from I Corps. The Filipinos, the main muscle of the task force, would clear the high ground along Five Yankee. A mixed armoured force, consisting of four Filipino M-24 light tanks and six Centurions† would be the mailed fist in the defile. Bringing up the rear would come a 'rag tag and bobtail' of Glosters: some had been in the rear at Uijongbu when battle commenced; others had returned from R&R.[4] They had been gathered by the battalion's second in command, Major Digby Grist. Grist was sporting a bandaged wrist after his escape from the ambush along 5Y – the route the battle group was to force open – the previous day.

---

* Exactly what happened to Y Company that night, with all three of its platoons officerless, remains unclear. The company's commander, Robbie Leith-MacGregor, declined to discuss it with the author in 2008, other than saying that his men were exhausted, not having slept for forty-eight hours: 'The lack of sleep was such that a good man was no longer a good man.' Indeed – and the stress of battle adds to exhaustion. The Fusiliers' official history, when discussing the company's counter-attack in the early morning of the 25th, alludes obliquely to its action on the 23rd being unsatisfactory.

† There are different accounts of the number of armoured vehicles that took part in the operation that day. I have elected to use Ted Paul's recollection: as Paul was in the leading Centurion behind the Filipino tanks, he was in a good position to see the column.

There was cheering news for the Hussars. The previous night their premier warrior, C Squadron commander Major Henry Huth, had reached the battlefield from R&R in Japan. He would command the armoured column. However, the terrain along the track through the Kamak-san foothills was an unknown. 'I don't think anyone had used it, as it was a very narrow road, in a defile, all the way,' said Hussar Lieutenant Ted Paul. 'I think the Glosters had been supplied round the front, but by then it was necessary to go round the back!'* With C Squadron having replaced B Squadron just before battle commenced, nobody from C had driven up 5Y, and it was not known whether the bulky Centurions would fit up the track – which wound through the defile with rock outcrops on each side – or whether the track would support the fifty-ton vehicles. Given these uncertainties, the Filipino light tanks would lead.

On 23 April UN forces on Line Utah had withdrawn south, more or less intact, to Kansas. Now, on the 24th, General James Van Fleet, determined not to let his phased withdrawal turn into yet another bug-out, had made the decision to go firm. He would fight a holding action on Line Kansas, using his firepower to grind up as many enemy as possible. The Glosters' position – between ROK 1st Division and the rest of 29th Brigade, and at the head of 5Y, where it winds through Choksong and across the Imjin – remained vital. The relief force, therefore, was not to break the Glosters out, but to break in and reinforce them *in situ*.† At 07:00 Lieutenant-Colonel Carne had spoken to Brigadier Brodie about the operation. Carne suggested that the force was not strong enough to carry out its intended task and requested permission to break out. On the orders of General Robert Soule, 3rd Division commander, Carne's request was refused.[5]

---

* In fact Digby Grist's F Echelon troops had been supplying the Glosters through the defile, but using jeeps and trucks, not Centurions.

† A number of accounts state, incorrectly, that the task force was designed to free the Glosters. But Farrar-Hockley (1995) notes that at 09:00 the brigade's earlier orders to stay put were reversed, and Carne was given permission to break out; he decided to remain in place as, if he tried to fight south to join the force, he would have had to abandon his wounded. However, the Soldiers of Gloucestershire Museum archive has a document typed by Lieutenant-Colonel Carne, commenting on early accounts of the battle. Carne states clearly that the purpose of the force on the 24th was not to relieve – 'I was NOT given the option to fight our way out on the 24th' – but to reinforce the Glosters; if it broke through, it was to remain under his (Carne's) leadership and help him hold the position. Presumably Carne, who had already stated that he did not believe the relief force strong enough to break through, was unwilling to risk his men in a fighting retreat through three to four miles of broken country dominated by enemy when the column was moving in his direction and making (perhaps to his surprise) progress. Whether he had forgotten that he had been given permission to break out – this permission appears in the Brigade War Diary – or was attempting to justify his action in retrospect (an action out of character for Carne) is unclear. Even with hindsight, I agree with Carne's decision to stay put on the day. He was familiar with the battle of Chipyong-ri in February – when a surrounded UN force *had* been relieved. Moreover, we will see the near-disaster that occurred when the Fusiliers and Rifles had to fight their way out – in considerably more open country, and with strong tank support – on the 25th.

At 08:00 engines whined, tracks squeaked, gravel crunched. The force was under way. Driving through the paddies, the first part of the operation proceeded according to plan. The Gloster F Echelon was reached: it had been abandoned by the enemy. Grist's men recovered vehicles and equipment, and the major salvaged a singed and tattered copy of T.H. White's journal of rural life, *England Have My Bones*.[6]

But now, ahead of the column, the track wound into the hills. The enemy was invisible. The infantry slogged up to the ridges. The armour clattered into the shadowed gorge. As the road column had to match the speed of the Filipino soldiers clearing the high ground, the tanks crawled at walking pace. Even so, the operation progressed. At 09:00 this was reported to Carne – as was a new order: permission to break out. But to fight south would require abandoning his wounded. The Gloster CO elected to remain in position and await the column which was making progress towards him.[7]

Paul, in the lead Centurion behind the Filipino tanks, was travelling 'open', his head out of his turret, guiding his driver via intercom. The further the column advanced up the defile, the narrower the track became. Rock walls closed in oppressively on either side, but Paul, from his turret, could see no Chinese – or, for that matter, Filipino – infantry above him: the crags were too steep to see on top.

Mortar and small-arms fire began to fall around the tanks, the noise amplified by the close walls of the gorge. Reluctantly – the move greatly restricted his vision – Paul retreated inside his turret and slammed the lid shut. The only views outside now were through the periscopes and the reinforced-glass vision blocks set around the turret hatch. Still the column, with bullets and shrapnel pinging off armour, was grinding towards the Glosters. Encouraging radio messages were sent. At 12:40 Huth reported that he had advanced one mile through the gorge. By 14:15 another mile had been covered.[8]

About halfway along the defile, to the right and several metres below the track, is a patch of open ground: a couple of acres of paddy with a thatched hamlet in the middle. As the column approached this – the only open terrain in the gorge – an explosion sounded at the front. It was around 15:00.* The leading Filipino tank slewed across the track and

---

* Various times are given for the halting of the relief column: 15:30 by Mossman, 15:00 by Henry Huth in a post-battle interview with the Appleman (Appleman, p. 475.) Oddly, Appleman also says the squadron second in command (Ormrod) had done a reconnaissance of the route the previous day (the 23rd) and told Huth the defile was too narrow for Centurions. This is certainly incorrect (Ormrod was operating on the eastern flank of the brigade for the whole day on the 23rd, and no Hussars were anywhere near the Glosters' position); Huth may have been referring to Ormrod's abortive attempt to reach the Glosters along the track running south of the river. Had it been known Centurions would not fit up the track, why would they have been part of the operation?

jerked to a halt, oily black smoke pouring from its rear, fuel blazing. Paul could see the damage, but was unsure of the cause. 'I think it was more likely a mine, but it was on fire. That is why I thought perhaps it was a mortar setting the fuel alight; a mine breaks the track, but does not normally cause a fire.' Either way, the M-24 was blocking the route. Behind the stalled vehicle, the column ground to a halt. Attempts by the following tank to ram it off the track were unsuccessful.[9] Firing continued.*

Several tanks back, Major Huth, determined to see what the hold-up was, levered himself out of his turret. Thirty metres above, the Chinese on the ridges had a perfect view of the unprotected Hussar below them. They rained automatic fire onto the target at their feet. Despite the firepower the armoured column had available, not a single tank could cover Huth: none had turret-mounted machine-guns, and it was impossible to elevate either their main guns or their coaxial machine-guns high enough to put suppressive fire onto the ridges. Rounds drummed off armour and churned up gravel. There was only one way to move forward without getting hit. Huth dived under the hull of the Centurion ahead and crawled through the protective steel tunnel formed by the stationary tanks' bellies. Reaching the head of the column, it was clear that there was nothing to be done: the knocked-out M-24 was blocking 5Y. Huth returned to his Centurion the way he had come.[10] He could see Chinese infantry, including tank-killer parties – squads with pole charges and sticky bombs – closing in.[11] In the defile, unable to manoeuvre, the tanks were helpless at close range.

* Discussing with the author a photograph taken after the battle of the knocked-out Filipino tank (the photo is in the Soldiers of Gloucestershire Museum), some Hussars expressed doubts about its accuracy: The photo clearly shows open ground beyond the vehicle, and all accounts emphasise the narrowness of the gorge. I had similar doubts about the veracity of the photo until, in April 2008, together with British Military Attaché to Seoul Brigadier Matt O'Hanlon, I drove the full length of what used to be called 5Y, now a country road set with small restaurants catering for hikers. Using maps and looking at the photograph, it was a simple piece of deduction to find the exact spot where the tank was hit, the geography being virtually unchanged over fifty-six years. However, the Hussars' confusion is understandable. To anyone further back in the column, it would have been impossible to see the open ground (particularly if looking through turret blocks, or snatching a glimpse from a hastily opened hatch), as the track curves and rises just before it is reached. Moreover, from the photograph, it appears as if there is adequate space on the track to pass it on the left. However, according to Second Lieutenant Denys Whatmore – who visited the area in late May – the tank was rammed off the track after the battle (Whatmore, p. 93). Given that the rest of the route does, indeed, run through a claustrophobic defile, one has to wonder if the Chinese deliberately set an ambush with either mines and/or mortars just before this piece of terrain: the only place where armoured vehicles could feasibly deploy (albeit only for about 200 metres) and elevate their guns to engage enemy on the ridges. One must admire the Chinese eye for ground in halting the column at this point: it would be hard to find a piece of terrain so ideally suited to infantry ambush and so ill-suited to armoured thrust. Not only were the tanks unable to elevate or turn their guns, they could not manoeuvre in the bottom of the gorge – or even turn round. By this standard, even the exposed road across the Dutch dikes, over which the British armoured column attempted to relieve the airborne forces at Arnhem in 1944, is a better route.

Paul heard his squadron commander's order crackle over the intercom: Withdraw! The Centurions, unable to turn due to the narrowness of the gorge, clattered back in reverse. The Filipino infantry, in contact with an estimated enemy battalion, leapfrogged back;[12] five Filipino soldiers died in the operation.[13] 'It was pretty forlorn,' said Paul. 'I think we needed a much more substantial force.' The breakthrough had failed. The Chinese around Kamak-san had split the Glosters from the rest of the Brigade.

* * *

Those Hussars not on the relief operation were spread around the eastern hills, assisting the Fusiliers and Rifles as mobile artillery platforms. The Hussars would spot movement through their turret binoculars; their 20-pounders would crack. They would see the almost simultaneous puff of smoke as their high-velocity round impacted, but had little indication of whether their fire was effective. It was just another day for the crews cramped inside the Centurions. 'One heard artillery quite a lot; if it's not local, one tends to ignore it,' said Cornet John Preston-Bell. 'I wasn't aware of a battle going on; we did not know the seriousness of the situation.' The heavy fighting took place at night; most enemy went to ground during the day. But they were close. Trooper Denis Whybro was in his turret with an American M-1 carbine 'doing a bit of shooting practice'. He fired on a nearby feature to check the range – and somebody shot back. 'That stopped that!' he said.[14]

The gunners, on constant call, were finding the battle a grind; so were the units supplying them. Ammunition for the 25-pounders was flown in from Japan, then loaded onto RASC three-ton trucks and driven some forty-five miles to the brigade. A truck could take 180 rounds, each weighing well over 25lb.* After the truck was unloaded and the rounds piled next to the guns, the artillerymen would give the truckers a meal and send them off for the next load.[15]

But the uneasiest men were the infantry. In the spring sunshine there were continual signs of enemy movement and reinforcement. Companies contacted Brigade HQ to enquire whether the movements they spotted all around were friendly or otherwise. Sizeable enemy units were now visible even in daylight. At 10:15 the Fusiliers requested an air strike on a dug-in battalion. At 13:50 large numbers of enemy were reported moving around the abandoned Belgian position.[16] Nine captured Glosters of B Company, who subsequently escaped from Kamak-san during an air strike, arrived at Brigade HQ. They reported that the mountain was occupied by enemy *en masse*.[17]

---

* The brass shell case and explosive charge weighed several pounds.

Men spent the day sniping, piling ammunition and grenades around their positions or setting out trip flares. Many improved their slit trenches; by regulation, six feet long, two feet wide and five feet deep, they made convenient coffins. Some men heated tinned rations over fuel burners at the bottom of their slits; if they were lucky, a nearby Centurion might pass out a mess tin of hot, sweet tea brewed on the onboard stove. Many pulled nervously at cigarettes.

Below the Rifles' A Company positions, the Chinese ignited ground scrub. Flames flickered up the slope. Lieutenant Gordon Potts of 1 Platoon ordered his men to crouch in their slits and let the fire burn over their heads, then face front immediately. As the fire swept over his head, Potts leapt up, and ordered his Brens to fire: parties of enemy were forming up to attack below. They scattered. There was a lull, then a Vickers section spotted an enemy O Group a thousand yards away. Potts ordered the machine-gunners to hold their fire until they had 'settled themselves down'. Watching through field glasses as around twenty enemy with maps huddled for the briefing, he could barely believe his luck. Two Vickers fired long bursts. The Chinese were bowled over; survivors dashed for cover; the wounded crawled. Through his binoculars, Potts counted eight bodies.[18]

The increasing daylight enemy movement was frightening. Watches ticked; mouths dried; teeth were ground. Once the sun went down, it was obvious that the Chinese would close in again. For troops who had already endured two nights of relentless fighting, the strain mounted. Many soldiers are curious about how they will behave in action; few of 29th Brigade's men now harboured any illusions. In battle the natural fear of darkness was intensified by the visual and aural confusion and exacerbated by the alien wail of the Chinese bugles. Another childhood fear – of thunder and lightning – was replicated by the sound and flash of bombardments, though artillery and mortars, spraying razor-sharp metal fragments, were far deadlier than any electrical storm. Then there was the shocking sight of wounded men, parts of their faces or bodies resembling something seen in a butcher's shop through the bloody rags of shredded uniforms. More intimately, there was the loss of friends and the question, echoing deep inside: 'Who's next?' Some soldiers were now openly asking their officers when they would get out. A Fusilier was evacuated for court martial when he insisted Jesus had forbidden him to continue fighting.[19]

Sinister sights on the battlefield wound the tension tighter. Between skirmishes with Chinese infiltrators, Second Lieutenant Mervyn McCord's signals party, fighting to keep the Rifles' communications open, had spotted an eerie apparition in the night fighting: a Chinese with long, black hair, who appeared to be wearing a flowing cloak as he

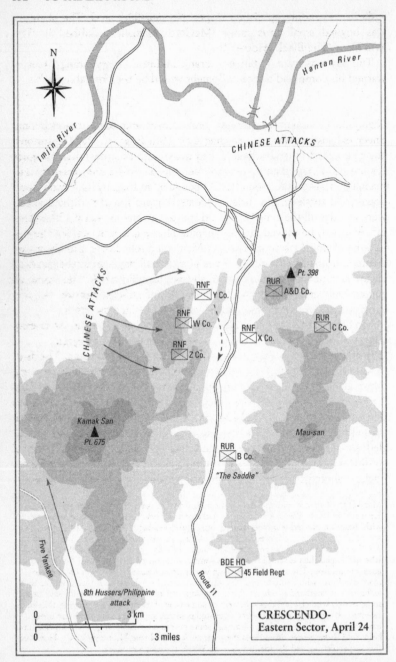

N

Hantan River

Imjin River

CHINESE ATTACKS

CHINESE ATTACKS

RNF Y Co.

RUR A&D Co.

▲ Pt. 398

RNF W Co.

RNF X Co.

RUR C Co.

RNF Z Co.

Kamak San
▲ Pt. 675

Mau-san

RUR B Co.

"The Saddle"

Five Yankee

BDE HQ
45 Field Regt

8th Hussers/Philippine
attack

Route 11

0                3 km
0                3 miles

CRESCENDO-
Eastern Sector, April 24

– she? – led enemy up distant slopes. No signallers fired: The phantom was beyond small-arms range. McCord's signallers dubbed it 'The Witch', or 'The Black Widow'.*

The day was waning. General Frank Milburn, commanding I Corps, warned his command to brace. Tonight would be the critical night.[20]

* * *

Nightfall. Thousands of Chinese broke cover and began manoeuvring. Sheer exhaustion was now settling over 29th Brigade. The Centurions, having bombed up and refuelled, had drawn into their customary leaguer for the night. The men were at 50 per cent stand-to; half sleeping, half manning Brens on the ground or 20-pounders in the turrets. Those stood down tried to sleep, but Trooper Denis Whybro found it difficult: 'You were on edge all the time.'[21] Ormrod spotted an enemy patrol 150 metres off. Alarmed, he moved among sleeping Hussars, quietly waking them – 'It's the enemy, look to your front!' Many men rolled over. Simply sitting cramped in the smoky, oily confines of a tank all day – amid the throb of engine and auxiliary generator, the squawk of radio traffic, the whine of gun-control equipment and the clatter of tracks outside – was exhausting.[22] The patrol disappeared without attacking the tanks.[23]

For the infantry on the hills, there could be no reprieve. As enemy crept up their slopes, the demonic cabaret started up once again.

Just after midnight, the Chinese move on the Rifles began. The first probe against Potts's platoon was 'the old Japanese ruse'. There were shouts from below, supposedly from a wounded man. The Riflemen didn't move.[24] Then, at 01:30, the attack went in. Shells whooshed overhead. Barrages of artillery and mortar fire burst with drumfire crumps and irregular series of white flashes, like sheet lightning. Spitting flares dangled above, illuminating the ground through dense clouds of reeking cordite and dust billowing up into the black sky from the artillery blasts. Bugles sounded from left and right as attacking companies co-ordinated.

* Many of the Chinese soldiers who fought in Korea were veterans of the war against the Japanese. In World War II, the Japanese had employed psychological tactics originating with their samurai and ninja forefathers, such as the wearing of demon masks in attack, and of black uniforms that blended into the landscape like shadows. Could 'The Witch' have been a Chinese soldier influenced by such methods – or even a captured Japanese who had joined their erstwhile enemy, as some are rumoured to have done? An alternative guess comes from Taiwan-based American writer Brian Kennedy, an expert on Chinese martial culture, who wrote to me: 'The only comment I would make is that Chinese, then and now, educated and uneducated, are very superstitious. This creature could have been some person who claimed magic powers or some type of medium or Daoist priest. Even in twenty-first-century Taiwan, college-educated politicians, police and the military often have in their employ or in their entourage some person who claims to provide supernatural help. And these people often dress the part; i.e. long wild hair, black robes, etc.' However, this is speculation, and the identity of 'The Witch' remains a mystery.

Gunfire rippled across platoon frontages. Bren gunners risked burns as they changed red-hot barrels. Tracers hit rocks and ricocheted upwards in luminous blobs of light. Visible in the on-again, off-again flashes of shellfire and the fizzing flare light, shadowy crowds rose from cover and charged forward to the accompaniment of tearing bursts of burp-gun fire. British officers and NCOs shouted orders over the din. Wounded men screamed. Field telephones jangled with requests for fire support, ammunition, casualty evacuation.

Gunner Bob Nicholls of 170 Mortar Battery was on 398 with the Rifles, who, crouched in their slit trenches and behind the walls of the ancient keep, repulsed attack after attack. 'The Ulsters knocked hell out of them,' he said. 'They had an abundance of grenades – it is a good night-time weapon – and they were throwing them all over the place.' Working his Vickers section, Sergeant 'Doc' Holliday swept cones of bullets over the attacking lines. Many Chinese, he noted, had no small arms, only grenades; the second wave picked up the weapons of the fallen. 'If they wanted to commit *hara-kiri*, that was fine with us,' he said. 'But I discovered then that there is a God: I called on him often enough.' There were few atheists in the Imjin trenches, and in battle, where courage is as infectious as cowardice, inspirational leadership strengthens morale. Defying incoming fire, Major Rickord toured his forward sections. 'He was a rough man, a hard man,' said Farrell with D Company. 'He came walking along – how the hell he wasn't hit, I'll never know. He paraded up and down, giving us a wee bit of encouragement. We thought he was a great man.' Farrell was finding it more effective to listen for 'the pitter-patter of little feet' than to watch for the enemy in the visual confusion. With Chinese jumping up from cover and rushing forward ('You'd see them running at you – and they could run!'), the shooting was 'pop-up style'. A and D Companies bore the brunt. Then the attack spread to C Company.

Lieutenant Peter Whitamore, who had felt so green on his first patrol across the Imjin days previously, was apprehensive, but his men seemed excited at the prospect of action. Above, flares – British parachute flares and Chinese flares with revolving fins – hung in the air. 'They were running at us, they rushed in groups,' said Whitamore. 'We killed many within twenty yards. I don't know how they got so close. They simply appeared; there was quite a lot of scrub.' Amid the mayhem, the officer led his platoon. When adrenalin levels are high even well-trained soldiers may shoot wildly, shoot high – or simply retreat into their trenches and hope nobody notices them. It is critical for officers or NCOs to ensure that their men are firing effectively, making the job of junior leaders exceptionally hazardous. To see what is happening, to pinpoint the enemy, to command, they must expose themselves. 'I don't recall firing my own weapon,' he said. 'I was in my slit trench shouting fire-control orders to my sections – mainly "Fire for effect!"' The Chinese were driven off; the combat lasted forty minutes. 'It was terrifying at the time,' Whitamore recalled. 'Exhilarating afterwards!'

The Rifles Battalion HQ, in a re-entrant on the valley floor, was spotted. Mortar fire rained down, pulverising the position. 'You could hear it whistling in – then boom! You took cover,' said Corporal Norman Sweetlove. 'There would be a flash of light, splinters and shrapnel. You don't see it, you feel it!' Blast sucked his breath away; dust, dirt and scrub pelted down. Everybody was scrabbling, digging in deeper. Sweetlove's mate Kelly told him, 'Don't dig down – dig in!' so the two tunnelled into an earthen bank for overhead cover; McCord revetted his slit with wood from mortar ammunition crates. The bombardment lasted half an hour. When the smoke cleared, wrecked equipment and shredded tents were strewn over the cratered ground.

The Rifles on 398 would repulse a total of sixteen enemy attacks. At dawn, Potts's position, carpeted with brass cartridge cases, looked like 'the firing point on the ranges'.[25] A Company's second in command, Captain John Lane, counted some ninety dead enemy to the front;[26] nine dead and three wounded lay in front of D Company, and one prisoner was taken;[27] many more enemy casualties were dragged away. The battalion gave up not an inch of ground and had lost just one man killed. But as the Ulstermen stood off wave after wave, the closest combat of the battle, was taking place on the western side of Route 11.

\* \* \*

Having being been pushed off Hill 257 in the early hours of 23 April, and having failed in their counter-attack, the Fusiliers' exhausted Z Company had been ordered to hold a 600-foot-high knife-edge ridge on the eastern side of the valley overlooking Route 11. 'Odds and sods' from Fusiliers sub-units were ordered up to reinforce them.[28] The mission was critical. This ridge was the Fusiliers' southernmost outpost; if it went under, then the rest of Kingsley Foster's battalion, stationed on hills a mile and a half north, as well as the Rifles on Hill 398 to the north-east, would be cut off from the south. There could be no lost ground. This fight would be to the death.

The ridge was so rocky that in many places it was impossible to dig down. Major John Winn sited his defences as best he could. Soldiers, ignorant of strategy, appreciate learning their part in the bigger picture, and at twilight, Winn toured his sections, briefing his men on the importance of their position. Winn was 'a great bloke' thought the young Fusilier Stan

Tomenson: 'He was an old-style major; he didn't have that brusqueness. He usually walked around with a crook – didn't even have a weapon. He was very quiet.'

The Chinese, observing the brigade's dispositions from Kamak-san, could see that Z Company's ridge was key if they were to annihilate the companies further up the valley. Lines of enemy began closing on Winn's men soon after dark. At Battalion HQ, the reports came in. At 20:15 movement was spotted; at 20:20 the enemy was probing the ridge. By 20:55 the probes had been driven off – but the Chinese now knew the layout of the defences. At 21:20 stronger attacks went in, supported by mortars and machine-guns. At 01:00 one of the two pinnacles flanking the ridge was lost; then a counter-attack by Lieutenant Sheppard's 10 Platoon regained it. At 02:20 the tempo intensified. Most battles are a series of combats and lulls – attackers take a position and consolidate before advancing further, or are beaten off and regroup – but on Z Company's front there would be no break in the action from 02:20 till dawn.[29]

On the eyrie, Tomenson was employed as company runner by the CSM, Edward Radcliffe, distributing ammunition. 'It was scary. If he wanted a message delivered, I had to scoot off,' he said. 'You were running around, getting down, sometimes men were firing overhead.' His mobile role gave him the opportunity to see the two men whose actions that night would become legendary. One of them was Winn. The other was Fusilier Ronald Crooks. Crooks had already won a Military Medal in bayonet action in Italy in World War II, but Tomenson thought him unsuited to peacetime soldiering: 'He didn't like being shouted at; he was a soldier-of-fortune type.' A former Durham Light Infantryman, Crooks refused to answer to 'Fusilier', insisting on being addressed as 'Private', and was one of the company's worst disciplinary cases.[30] On this jagged rock ridge, the major and the Fusilier would find their moment in a battle where ranges were measured in feet, rather than yards.[31] By the light of the flares Winn and Crooks were visible dashing to wherever the perimeter was threatened, Crooks firing a Bren, Winn throwing grenades – he would personally hurl sixty that night.[32] A key position was a large rock pinnacle. 'Crooks was running up and down to the pinnacle changing magazines; him and the company commander were working together – it was unbelievable!' said Tomenson. 'They were these two tall guys, running up and down this little ridge, really giving it to them!'*

Even experienced soldiers were staggered at the ferocity of the assault. D-Day veteran and mortar man John Bayliss was in the rocks on the ridge

---

* Winn won the Distinguished Service Order that night; he had hoped that Fusilier Crooks would get a Victoria Cross; instead, he received a Distinguished Conduct Medal. Many Fusiliers believed Winn should have won a VC.

with an American carbine to his shoulder, squinting down the barrel as crowds of attackers surged up the lower slopes. 'I had never seen anything like it,' he said. 'In World War II you used to see Germans from a distance, but out here, it was close up!' The density of numbers astonished him. 'They'd come in with a platoon; if that didn't work, they'd come back with a company,'* he said. 'They were like bees – they were coming at us like ants!' Bayliss and everybody around him was rapid-firing as the range closed. Men furiously worked bolts; streams of cartridge cases poured from the smoking breeches of the Brens. Bayliss's carbine overheated and jammed. More enemy. Grenades ran out – but there were substitutes to hand. As the Chinese stormed up, the Fusiliers stood among the rocks and volleyed ration cans into the attacking wave. Tins of bully beef and fruit pudding thudded into the enemy ranks. 'They thought they were grenades,' said Bayliss. 'It gave us a bit of respite.' The Chinese ducked into cover from the unexpected barrage – then charged again. Suddenly, they were among the Fusiliers. Bayliss's position was overrun. A furious hand-to-hand mêlée seethed among the rocks. Grunting, straining men lashed out at each another with rifle butts, spades, boots – in fighting this close, firearms were as dangerous to friend as to foe. Bayliss struck out with his fists. 'As they were coming through, you'd bang 'em, though if you have room to shoot, you shoot,' he said. 'The boxing training was useful; if you hit 'em, they stayed down. It was desperate: You had no time to think, or you were dead!' The fighting surged back and forth for minutes – then the position was clear.

Behind Bayliss, Fusilier David Strachan was covering the rear slope. Over the ridge, he could hear bugles wailing and wounded men screaming. 'You just had to take it, you didn't know what was happening.' He had been ordered to hand ammunition over to those holding the front slope; now, he was down to three magazines and four grenades as Chinese broke through, running to the rear. One was cut down nearby: 'That was the first time I had seen a brain – his head was split open.' Another was hit by a phosphorus grenade, lighting the scene: Strachan discovered that a human corpse drenched in white phosphorus burns for hours. Sergeant Nobby Clarke – a friend of Strachan's who had been 'over the moon' when he discovered, just before the battle, that his wife had given birth to a baby girl – was killed. Bullets cracked in from all angles. 'They were running from front to rear,' said Strachan. 'I was throwing hand grenades, they were running fast – I was trying to shoot, I was a first-class shot, but only wounded one. I fired everything.'

* Most probably a description of the probes that would fix British positions, followed by mass attack.

The battle was devouring munitions. At 03:50 the 25-pounders were running out of star shells; aircraft were dropping their last flares. And the company was surrounded. At 05:15 mortars were firing to the rear of Z Company, onto Chinese behind them in the valley.[33] Other troops grimly watched the combat. Leading an assault up a cliff, a frightening figure could be made out in the flashes: 'The Witch'. Men watched in awe: despite the prodigious firepower being expended, the black-clad figure bore a charmed life. 'She was invulnerable!' thought McCord.

Yet amid the murderous struggle along the ridge, morale never flagged. 'British squaddies shout at each other to get each other going, and everybody was shouting: "There's somebody on the right, can you see?" "What are you doing in that trench: sleeping or fighting?"' said Tomenson. 'There was all kinds of banter!' But nobody could play a leading role in such intense combat and remain unscathed. Z Company's leadership was decimated. Apart from Winn, only CSM Radcliffe and a wounded sergeant remained in action.[34] The major was hit again and again – in the head, the arm, the backside* – but continued fighting. 'Christ, I've been hit in the arse!' a Fusilier yelled. 'I've got one in the arse too,' Winn roared back. 'Keep cracking!'[35] The 'big man', Crooks, standing without cover on the ridge, firing a Bren from the hip, was shot through the chest. He somersaulted off the ridge and into a tree; another Fusilier killed the sniper. Crooks was patched up and resumed firing from a prone position.[36] Bloodied Fusiliers piled up along the ridge. At 03:45 Z Company reported twenty-five stretcher cases – about a quarter of strength. Winn requested relief at first light.[37]

* * *

At Battalion HQ, Kingsley Foster summoned Robbie Leith-MacGregor. 'The position was extremely grave,' Y Company's major was told; he was to fight through to Z at dawn. The plan: Y would attack along the valley floor, while a platoon of W Company assaulted southward along the ridge. In preparation, Y Company, officerless apart from its OC, was reinforced with officers from other sub-units. One was Second Lieutenant David Rudge, who had just completed his National Service and was with the echelon, awaiting transport home. Hearing of the crisis, he volunteered to lead a platoon.[38] Dawn was breaking. The Fusiliers formed up in half-light. A milky Imjin mist covered the valley floor. The company was 'feeling sore as a result of being dislodged from their positions the previous night.'[39] Leith-MacGregor deployed two platoons forward, one back, and advanced towards the sound of the guns. Following a stream of Vickers

---

* In letters home, this particular wound of Winn's was politely referred to as being in 'the thigh'. Winn was no stranger to wounds: he had been hit in North Africa and Italy.

tracer being fired to guide the attack onto its objective through the mist, Y Company ran smack into the opposition.

'We found the Chinese lined up,' said Leith-MacGregor. 'They were disregarding a lot of the rules; they did not cover their rear.' Forming up to assault the rear of Z Company, the enemy presented the counter-attacking force with the perfect opportunity. 'We charged them, we rushed through them,' Leith-MacGregor said. 'I did not give the order to fix bayonets, but bayonets were being used.' The enemy line collapsed, the Chinese scattered, ran, were pursued, shot down. Y Company's charge had taken just minutes. Z Company was relieved.

It had been quite a fight. Twenty-seven stretcher cases and five dead were carried from the smoking ridge to two Hussar half-tracks and a group of ambulances and carriers waiting on Route 11. Walking wounded were helped down the rocky slope. The tall, tattered figure of John Winn, bundled in bloody bandages, was the last to leave the position. Refusing a stretcher, he staggered down the hill like a geriatric.[40] At the bottom, the Fusiliers' second in command, Major Miles Speer, greeted him: 'Good morning, John. You are looking extremely untidy!'[41]

Fusilier Derek Kinne of X Company had volunteered to help evacuate Z's wounded. The ridge was a gruesome tableau. Heaps of enemy bodies, like broken dolls, lay scattered on either side of the sharp rock. His eye was caught by the enemy who had had the top of his head shot off.[42] Strachan – who had earlier noticed the man, whose mess of brains was spilling over the rocks – was in shock and out of ammunition; he left his rifle as he scrambled, dazed, down the rear slope he had defended. Snatching one last look over his shoulder, he thought, simply, 'God . . .' Tomenson, looking at the survivors around him, wondered what had happened to his comrades: they all had the same glazed, staring eyes.

As Z Company – shocked, exhausted, filthy, unshaven – evacuated their wounded down Route 11, orders had been dispatched up the valley. The previous evening, I Corps had planned to hold firm throughout the 25th.[43] However, the night's pressure had proved too much. At 05:00 orders had been issued to all subordinate units for 'Plan Golden', I Corps's general withdrawal from Kansas to the next phase line south, Line Delta.[44] Movement would commence at 08:00.[45]

Reeling, 29th Brigade could at last pull back. The British and Belgian soldiers had carried out their orders. For three nights, they had held the shock phase of the Chinese offensive and maintained the western security of the MSR. Yet for the men preparing to withdraw down the mist-shrouded valley, the sternest trial was still to come. And for one battalion 'Plan Golden' came too late. Three and a half miles to the west, the Glosters were going down fighting.

# Chapter 9

# FORTRESS IN THE CLOUDS: THE GLOSTERS' LAST STAND

*By our deeds we are known*
Motto, The Gloucestershire Regiment

THE COUNTRYSIDE OF GLOUCESTERSHIRE is, perhaps, England's most beautiful. It is a gentle shire of grey stone villages hidden among rolling green hills; of shaded lanes winding through patchworks of fields and woods; of quiet country pubs serving ale and cider. For the surviving Glosters, sitting in their trenches and sangars in the Korean sunshine on Hill 235 on 24 April 1951, home might as well have been on another planet.

Their surroundings, sunlit though they were, were deeply forbidding. Among the austere brown hills and grey rock ridges, flickers of movement could be seen all around, as their besiegers adjusted their positions, tightening the noose on the trapped battalion. Only to the north was open ground. 'There was nowhere you could look and say, "There are no Chinese there",' said Private Sam Mercer.

Many were pessimistic about the relief force; others clung to hopes that the Filipino/8th Hussars column would, somehow, break through. The mortar men of C Troop, 170 Mortar had heaved their heavy barrels up Hill 235, rather than destroying them, in the expectation that they could resume operations once relief arrived.[1] The prospect of another night battle was daunting. Of the previous day, Padre Sam Davies wrote: 'It was simply a matter of hours before darkness fell, and the lonely battalion would be assaulted on all sides in the nightmarish moonlight. I longed to be able to say "Stop" to the rushing minutes; to prolong this quiet, sunny afternoon indefinitely.'[2]

Yet the Glosters still held the pass through the hills – a pass the Chinese needed. 'We could see Chinks pulling up a heavy gun or something – they had mules – and someone said to the artillery officer, "Take that out!"' said Charles Sharpling, who was with the signals section. 'The second shell got them; you could see mules being blown into the air.' And they still packed the punch to undertake limited initiatives. Below, in the valley, lay the abandoned Battalion HQ, with its dugouts, tents, vehicles and dumps. It was deserted, but for the scattered bodies of several Chinese who had tried to loot – unwisely, since the area was overlooked by the Gloster guns on Hill 235. Under the command of the RSM, Jack Hobbes, a party of Glosters, Gunners and Korean porters prepared to sortie down to obtain ammunition, radio batteries and rations.* On the hilltop, machine-guns were positioned to cover both ends of the valley. Five miles to the east, the guns of 45 Field were elevated, on standby to fire a smoke-screen onto the enemy-held ridges.

White phosphorus shells tore overhead and burst on the surrounding hills. Thick, brilliant white smoke billowed up. The salvage parties scrambled down. On the valley floor, the men split up – all had been briefed to recover specific items. A section of Chinese appeared; they were cut down by fire from one of Guy Temple's Brens. Minutes later, the party was clambering back up through the brush and rocks on the slopes of Hill 235. The men were loaded down, the Korean porters' A-frames stacked with equipment.† With the foragers clear, the artillery pounding the ridges switched from smoke to high explosive. The raid had been a success. Captain Anthony Farrar-Hockley was delighted: 'almost as good as Christmas', he thought as he looked at the little dumps spread on the ground. Most critical was the ammunition. All companies were resupplied.[3]

Brigadier Tom Brodie had attended a forenoon command conference with General Robert Soule, 3rd Infantry Division's commanding general. Soule ordered Brodie to 'push' the joint Filipino/Hussar relief force through to the Glosters, adding that he was planning a major counter-attack to restore 29th Brigade's main line of resistance – through which the Chinese had carved a three-mile gap – at dawn on the 25th. The force would be as strong as Brodie's entire brigade: two battalions of the Puerto Rican 65th Infantry (the 1st and 3rd), supported by the Filipino battalion, the 64th Tank Battalion and the 10th Field Artillery Battalion. When Soule asked

---

* The supply recovery raid was launched by the Glosters on their own initiative before hearing of the failure of the Filipino/Hussar relief force – which, had it managed to fight through, would have ensured security of all the supplies in the valley. This suggests that Carne had little faith in a breakthrough, so sent the sorties into the valley to get hold of enough ammunition for the battalion to hold out for another night. Indeed, speaking to Brodie, Carne had already expressed his doubts that the operation could succeed. An entry in the 29th Brigade War Diary from the Glosters at 07:00 on 24 April reads: 'CO [i.e. Carne] doubts possibility of success of any attempt to reach them. Enemy build-up is considerable and thinks relieving force would become heavily engaged.' Having watched the massive forces crossing the Imjin on the 23rd, the Glosters had a clearer idea of enemy strengths in the Kamak-san foothills than did higher command.

† The fate of the Korean porters on the last night is a mystery. A party of around twenty escaped during the confused move of Support Company and elements of C Company up to Hill 235 on the night of 23/24 April, but there was still certainly a contingent with the battalion during the daylight on the 24th. No interviewees recall them being on the hill during the fighting or during the breakout on the 25th. Queries in Korea have drawn a blank. It seems likely that the remaining porters slipped away in the early hours of darkness before attacks began.

Brodie if the timing was satisfactory, the British commander replied affirma-tively. At 15:15 Soule's assistant divisional commander visited 29th Brigade HQ. He asked Brodie about the progress of the Filipino/Hussar relief force, and reminded him that there was plenty of divisional artillery on call.[4] Soule also spoke to Brodie, to ask him about the position of the Glosters.* The British commander – a man of the stiff upper lip, who believed in main-taining a cool head and was accustomed to reporting in low-key style – replied with a turn of phrase that has become legendary.[†] 'It's a bit sticky,' he told Soule. 'Things are pretty sticky down there.'[5] By mid-afternoon, the peril facing the Glosters had the attention of the highest level of the UN command. In a conference at 3rd Division's airstrip, Soule briefed General Frank Milburn, I Corps commander, General James Van Fleet, 8th Army Commander, and Supreme Commander General Matthew Ridgway, on his planned attack with the 65th Infantry. When the senior commanders asked Soule why he was not expediting it sooner, Soule replied that the 65th could not complete their concentration in 29th Brigade's sector before 17:30, so could not attack in the last hours of daylight. He added that he believed the Glosters could hang on for another night.[6]

The situation worsened dramatically when the leading Filipino tank was knocked out, and Major Henry Huth decided to withdraw his Centurions.[7] At about the same time Brodie called 3rd Division and spoke to the chief-of-staff, requesting permission to withdraw the Filipinos. Soule came on the line, directing Brodie to leave the Filipino troops *in situ*,** repeating that a major attack by the 65th would be mounted the

---

* Farrar-Hockley (1995) states on p. 127 that the famous discussion between Soule and Brodie took place 'shortly after 3 o'clock that afternoon'. US records (see Headquarters, 3rd Infantry Division, 'Operations of 29th BIB, from 22–25 April 1951') indicate that Brodie and Soule spoke twice that day: In the 'forenoon' commanders' conference and later, by telephone, at around 17:30. Roy Appleman (who interviewed Huth after the battle) states that the column was halted at around 15:00. The 29th Brigade War Diary states that at 15:15 command orders came down that the Glosters and Filipinos were to hold in their position; it also notes that Brigade passed orders to the road column to pull back at 17:35. The decision to pull the Filipino infantry back was the subject of some debate later, but in the opinion of Farrar-Hockley (1995) had no bearing on the Glosters' fate; I agree.

† Writers and military professionals on both sides of the Atlantic have used this choice of phrase to suggest that, had Brodie used a more robust expression to describe the Glosters' plight, Soule would have grasped the imminence of the tragedy, acted decisively and rescued them. My belief is that Brodie's preference for understatement had no bearing on the outcome of the battle. This will be discussed in the final chapter.

** It is unclear who made the decision for the Filipinos to withdraw: Huth had received orders from Brodie, and the Filipinos' CO, Lieutenant-Colonel Dionisio Ojeda, may have decided to withdraw his infantry with the armour. One account of Ojeda ('Heroes of the Korean War: Lieutenant Colonel Dionisio Ojeda' posted at http://rokdrop.com) states that it was, indeed, his decision to pull back. Regardless of who gave the order, in my opinion, it was the right decision. If the small (three-company) battalion had dug in among the Chinese-dominated hills for the night, with no line of communication back to brigade or to open ground, they would almost certainly have faced annihilation.

next morning.[8] However, it seems likely that the relief force was by then already pulling back.

Brodie himself radioed Lieutenant Colonel James Carne to deliver the news about the failure of the relief column and tell him that the Glosters would have to hang on for another night.* Carne, for once, overcame his customary inarticulacy. Farrar-Hockley was beside his CO as he spoke into the handset. 'I understand the position quite clearly,' Carne said. 'What I must make clear to you is that my command is no longer an effective fighting force. If it is required that we shall stay here, in spite of this, we shall continue to hold. But I wish to make known the nature of my position.'[9]

At the time of the two commanders' discussion the Glosters' strength – which included C Troop, 170 Mortar Battery – had been whittled down to 400–450 effectives. The only weapons it had beyond small arms and the toy-like 2-inch platoon mortars, were the Vickers. LMGs were in short supply: in the centre of the hill RSM Hobbs had dismantled several damaged Brens and was trying to assemble working weapons from the different components. Ammunition was only sufficient for one night's fighting. There was little food and – critically – very little water on the hilltop.[†] And there was no freedom of manoeuvre. Cut off from the rest of the brigade by over three miles of rugged hills swarming with a Chinese army, if the Glosters lost any section of their perimeter, they would be overrun.

News of the failed breakthrough operation spread. Second Lieutenant Denys Whatmore was not particularly affected. The men, he thought, were feeling 'jaded and worn down . . . a bit more bad news really didn't make any difference to our morale'.[10] Second Lieutenant Guy Temple had no reaction; he had never expected the force to make it. The relief's failure had tragic consequences for one group of men on the hill: the wounded. An RAP was just the first in a line of casualty clearing stations that stretched back to a MASH, with its 'meatball surgery' facilities, then a hospital train, ship or aircraft, and finally a clean, quiet, safe hospital in Japan. Although he had drips, plasma, transfusion equipment and field surgical tools, the Glosters' medical officer Captain Bob Hickey was limited in the care he could administer to the dying men sprawled in his dusty hollow on 235. The most plaintive record of the Glosters' last day is in the Brigade War Diary. At 09:05 the

---

* Farrar-Hockley (1995) says this discussion took place at 15:10. However, according to the timings mentioning the halting of the road column in other reports (29th Brigade War diary gives 17:35, the US official history says sometime after 15:45) the discussion must have taken place later. The loss of the Glosters' War Diary means that the timings of incidents and conversations on Hill 235 are hazy.

† Humans can last for weeks without food, but only days without liquid. A number of the Glosters on the hill who received rations on the last night were so dehydrated that they did not eat them. Many would regret this later.

Glosters radioed for the urgent helicopter evacuation of four seriously wounded. At 13:00 the brigade liaison officer at I Corps reported that a helicopter would be unable to land on the battalion position. At 14:05 a message reads simply, 'Please expedite helicopter.'[11] None came.

At Brigade HQ the battalion's second in command Major Digby Grist had gathered about fifty Glosters. With the crisis mounting to their north-west, these men sought a role. Given that the artillery was providing the best aid to the trapped battalion, Grist offered his troops to Lieutenant-Colonel Maris Young as close support for 45 Field Regiment, while he and a group of engineer officers improvised a supply drop of ammunition, Brens and radio batteries from two American L-5 spotter planes. Grist overheard one soldier saying that he had never flown before but volunteering to act as a dropper, hurling (no parachutes were available) equipment out of the tiny aircraft. Six loads were wrapped in blankets to soften the impact. The aircraft took off, circled over Hill 235, then swooped low, but the Glosters' perimeter was so constricted that most items tumbled down the slopes. On their return, those who had taken part in the abortive drop told how the Chinese had drawn an 'iron ring' around the battalion. A parachute drop, using 'Flying Boxcars', was scheduled for the following morning.[12]

Relentlessly, the hours passed. The radio batteries, Hill 235's last link with the outside world, were fading. Hope, too, dwindled. Padre Sam Davies reread then tore up a bundle of letters from home 'with an awesome finality'.[13] Yet nobody recalls any sense of self-pity as the end approached. Some remained defiant: a member of Support Company told Carne, 'We shall be all right, sir. 'Twill be like the rock of Gibraltar up here.'[14] A fatalistic calm settled. 'Like it or lump it, we put two and two together,' said Mercer. 'We realised we weren't going to walk away from this one.'

\* \* \*

As the sun sank on 24 April the Glosters' padre watched the western sky turning crimson. The darkening landscape made an apocalyptic spectacle. 'A thousand conflagrations' glowed like bonfires on the surrounding hills, for miles into the distance: scrub set alight by napalm and artillery.[15] Chinese units were still crossing the river, illuminated by American air flares. Bombs and guns hit targets in the water. Among their victims was a light artillery battery,\* smashed on 'Gloster Crossing'.[16]

---

\* The destruction of artillery and cyclist (see below) units, the presence of the horse-drawn artillery, and the dead mules found in the Glosters' vicinity after the battle indicate that, for all that the light CPVA was far better at moving cross-country than the road-bound UN forces, even in a guerrilla army some units needed roads or tracks. Hence the importance of Gloster Crossing and Five Yankee, winding south through the hills, its steep sides providing some protection from air attack.

Under cover of darkness, Carne made his last redeployment, pulling his soldiers back into the tightest possible perimeter along the ridge running along the summit of Hill 235.[17] This was tactically sound. The Glosters had been under enemy observation from Kamak-san all day. If they stayed put, the enemy would know exactly which positions to hit. Moreover, the pullback shortened Carne's line. For the first time in the battle, the Glosters – those left – would be fighting as a battalion, rather than in company-sized outposts that the enemy could destroy in detail. Passing around the few entrenching tools available, the soldiers fortified their positions as best they could. Some managed to dig slits or shell scrapes; others raised sangars. Some sheltered among rocks; others took what cover they could behind piled packs and pouches.

Hill 235 – its height in metres – was a typical Korean hill. Spurs and slopes ran down to paddies at its front (northern) edges and down to the valley floor at its rear (southern) end. Some of its faces were granite cliffs; in other areas, the slopes were covered in scree. A rough path ran across the ridge at the top. Scrawny copses crowned the skyline; rock outcrops broke through the topsoil. The battered D Company, under Captain Mike Harvey, was covering the north-eastern spur. In the centre of the position was Carne's CP and the RAP; this area was held by Support Company, under Major Sam Weller, as well as the mortar men of C Troop, now operating as infantry. Covering the south were the merged B and C Companies, under Major Denis Harding. And on the north-west spur were the survivors of A Company, commanded by Captain 'Jumbo' Wilson. The north-western and south-eastern slopes were the most vulnerable to attack.

The Glosters were fortunate to have a fuller than usual component of FOOs. On the 23rd, 45 Field Regiment's bulky counter-mortar radars 'Rancid' and 'Ringworm', which had been stationed with the Glosters – and proved 'not only useless, but an embarrassment in the battalion area', as 45 Field's commander put it[18] – had been sent down Five Yankee. Their officer, Captain Carl Dain – perhaps to make up for his radars' failure – elected to remain behind as FOO. This gave artillery major Guy Ward two captains – Dain and Ronnie Washbrook – to call in fire. Every survivor on the hill would speak of the excellent support they received from the Royal Regiment in their final battle.

After digging in off the centre of the ridge, the men at the CP drew lots for the rations brought up earlier from the RSM's raid into the valley: a tin of bully beef, some pound cake, a chunk of chocolate, perhaps, half a loaf of bread? But with no spring on the hilltop, it was water that most men craved, making milk and peaches the most prized cans. Many put the food away for later. Lit cigarettes were passed from hand to shaded hand. Near the CP was the RAP; already, several of its brown-stained stretchers were empty, their occupants dead.[19] Soon, this area would be crowded. Once battle resumed, stretchers would run out and casualties would be dragged back in blankets.[20] Surrounded and outnumbered in the dark,* the Glosters waited. In an echo of Alexandria and the badge many men were wearing on the rear of their berets, the regiment would, once again, be fighting back-to-back.

\* \* \*

At 22:00 bugles sounded. In dead ground around the foot of the hill, assault parties marshalled and climbed. Their aim: to eliminate this stubborn battalion for good. Carne moved forward to tour the fighting positions, while Farrar-Hockley, speaking to brigade, discussed an air strike for first light. Radio batteries were running low: it was decided to keep just one call sign, the artillery FOOs', operating on 45 Field's net. Returning from the perimeter, Carne confided to Farrar-Hockley his concerns about A Company. The previous night the colonel had personally repelled attackers with rifle and grenades ('just shooing away some Chinese', he commented); now he remarked to his adjutant: 'It seems we are going to find a job for ourselves as riflemen before long.' The two of them emptied a haversack of grenades, laying out eighteen along the parapet of their slit trench.[21]

Enemy assault waves were ascending. Glosters listened intently for the clink of metal, the sound of scrambling feet or enemy chatter; as always, Chinese noise discipline was poor. Crowds of shadows broke the skyline. Gunfire crackled. There were no tactical formations apparent; just masses, charging upward, firing burp guns, throwing stick grenades.† 'That was when the shit really hit the fan, when the balloon went up,' said Mercer. 'If I hadn't known I was at war before, I knew it then.' If a single position went under, it would compromise the integrity of platoon, company, battalion. If anyone shirked, the Chinese would gain a foothold. Every Gloster with a Chinese in his foresight had to shoot. 'It was part training, part survival,' said Private Tony Eagles, with Drums Platoon. 'They were targets; I suppose I was frightened – but it didn't

---

* It is impossible to say how many Chinese troops were now surrounding the Glosters, though most accounts and analyses believe they were the focus of an entire division on the Imjin. Some accounts say Hill 235 was surrounded by two regiments on the night of the 24th/25th. The weight of incoming mortar and heavy machine-gun fire suggest it was at least one regiment, more likely two.

† Captain Mike Harvey, who drew a series of sketches of the action and terrain soon after the battle, captioned one of his efforts, of a crowd of Chinese charging forward, 'Final attacks made in mad rushes. No formations – only mass!' The sketches are reproduced in Harvey's book At War in Korea.

NKPA troops and T-34 tanks roll into Seoul on 28 June 1951, just three days after their shock offensive jumped off. Kim Il-sung's invasion ignited a war that would suck in soldiers from across the globe, devastate the peninsula and litter it with the corpses of millions. *Courtesy National War Memorial of Korea*

Children scrabble through the ruins of Seoul. In the first nine months of the war, the capital changed hands four times, tearing apart society and families. *Courtesy National War Memorial of Korea*

**Left:** In this photograph of a daytime Chinese attack, taken in November 1951, the 'human wave' is more dispersed than those encountered by 29th Brigades' troops, who could usually only make out crowds of men looming up out of the darkness, with no apparent tactical formation.
*Courtesy National War Memorial of Korea*

**Above:** A Chinese soldier, in close combat, hurls a stick grenade. These were less effective than British grenades but were liberally used, and 29th Brigade was amazed at the near-suicidal courage of the Chinese attackers.
*Courtesy National War Memorial of Korea*

**Left:** Bren gunners of the Ulster Rifles in a typical hilltop slit trench. Although they have good views over the distant pass, the 'dead ground' on the slopes below would allow the enemy to approach unseen before launching a final assault from a distance of only twenty or thirty yards.
*Courtesy Mervyn McCord*

**Above:** China's intervention triggered a mass exodus from North Korea: an estimated million refugees struggled south through sub-zero temperatures. Many veterans recall the suffering of the refugees as their most traumatic memory of Korea. *Courtesy National War Memorial of Korea*

**Left:** Ulster Riflemen with a tiny addition to their unit. In the first months of war, when NGOs such as the Red Cross were not yet fully effective, all units adopted orphans. The American 'space heater' in the foreground was a greatly appreciated piece of kit in the coldest campaign fought by the British Army since the Crimea. *Courtesy Royal Ulster Rifles Museum*

A brigade vehicle on the icy track through 'Happy Valley', Ulster Rifles sector. A ferocious rearguard battle was fought by the Northumberland Fusiliers, 8th Hussars and Ulster Rifles in this frozen landscape. *Courtesy 8th King's Royal Irish Hussars*

Stunned Glosters of C and D Companies regroup on the pulverized summit of Hill 327 after storming it and seizing it from a dug-in Chinese battalion during the UN counter-offensive south-east of Seoul in February 1951. *Courtesy Soldiers of Gloucestershire Museum*

**Right:** The commander of 29th Brigade, Brigadier Tom Brodie. The Chindit veteran was considered 'a soldier's soldier' by his men.
*Courtesy Cheshire Military Museum*

**Left:** Lieutenant-Colonel James 'Fred' Carne, DSO, VC, sometimes known as 'Cool' Carne because of his habitual taciturnity. He is facing Hill 235; behind him are the stream, the vehicles of Battalion HQ, and C Company's position.
*Courtesy Soldiers of Gloucestershire Museum*

**Right:** Lieutenant-Colonel Kingsley Foster, who turned down promotion to lead his Fusiliers in battle, photographed just before the brigade's departure from the UK.
*Courtesy Royal Northumberland Fusiliers Museum*

Major Henry Huth (left), the Hussars' C Squadron commander, and Lieutenant-Colonel Albert Crahay (right). This photograph was taken on the last morning of the battle: hours later, Crahay was terribly wounded. Despite the brigade's extreme peril – it was about to fight its way out of a closing trap – Huth, one of those rare warriors who actually enjoyed battle, appears to be having the time of his life. (Note the 29th Brigade patch – 'the frozen arsehole' – on Huth's sleeve.)
*Courtesy 8th King's Royal Irish Hussars*

Major Gerald Rickord, acting CO of the Rifles, was greatly respected by his Ulstermen for his professionalism and quiet toughness. To his right is Second Lieutenant Mervyn McCord, one of the heroes of 'Happy Valley'. The photo was taken on a trip out to the cruiser HMS *Belfast*, patrolling in the Yellow Sea, after the battle.
*Courtesy of Mervyn McCord*

A haunting photograph taken just hours before battle commenced on the Imjin, after a church service in the abandoned temple behind the Glosters' A Company position. On the left is Lieutenant Philip Curtis, VC; on the right, Second Lieutenant Terry Waters, GC. Neither would live to collect his award.
*Courtesy of Soldiers of Gloucestershire Museum*

**A Hussar Centurion loaded with Fusiliers returns over the Imjin. The extensive patrols the brigade conducted across the river garnered virtually no actionable intelligence about the massive force poised to surge south on the night of April 22.** *Courtesy 8th King's Royal Irish Hussars*

A beautiful shot of Korea at war, taken from a typical hilltop position. Smoke rises (possibly from an artillery ranging shot), a thatched village squats in the paddies at the foot of the hill, and the river winds through its valley in the background. *By William May/Courtesy Royal Ulster Rifles Museum*

This picture, taken from the Belgian position, shows the sight that greeted 29th Brigade's soldiers in the mornings: the Imjin mists shrouding the valley floors. The strongpoint peaks, floating in the mists like islands, would soon be bulwarks against the 'human waves'.
*By Vander Goten, Courtesy Jan Dillen*

This photo was taken in the 1970s from the backstop position in the saddle on Route 11, held by the Ulster Rifles' B Company, looking north. It was down this valley that the bulk of 29th Brigade would retreat on 25 April. The large hill in the centre was the Rifles' bastion, Hill 398; the hills on the left were held by the Northumberland Fusiliers. *Courtesy Royal Ulster Rifles Museum*

**Below:** When this Filipino light tank was knocked out on the only open ground up Five Yankee it doomed the attempt by the Filipino Battalion and the Hussars to punch through to relieve the Glosters. The photo was taken after the battle, when the tank had been bulldozed off the track. *Courtesy Soldiers of Gloucestershire Museum*

**Above:** Route Five Yankee was the constricted defile through the Imjin hills that served as the Glosters' 'back door'. *Courtesy Royal Ulster Rifles Museum*

**Above:** Covered by American artillery and tank fire, the Belgians pull back over the Imjin under the noses (and mortars) of the Chinese. A remarkable photograph taken by the battalion's unorthodox padre, Vander Goten. *By Vander Goten/Courtesy of Jan Dillen*

**Right:** American ground-attack jets strike a Chinese-held hill. One has dropped its ordnance (off camera); a second (right) is making its attack run. Photograph taken by Hussar Cornet John Preston-Bell from his Centurion turret during the operation to extricate the Northumberland Fusiliers' Y Company on 23 April. *Courtesy John Preston-Bell*

**Below:** Shepherded by Centurions of the 8th Hussars, tactically spaced Northumberland Fusiliers of Y Company pull back from the bend of the Imjin, past a burning hamlet. Korean thatch was easily ignited by tracer and tank fire. *Courtesy John Preston-Bell*

Lieutenant George Truell directs Sergeant Reg Kitchener's gun as it fires point-blank into the Chinese who have just overrun Hill 257, held by the Fusiliers' Z Company. Note the St George's Day rose in Truell's cap. The painting (a print hangs in Truell's study) is accurate, except that the action took place in the near-darkness before dawn on 23 April. *By Terence Cuneo/Courtesy Royal Artillery Institute*

Mortars near the Ulster Rifles' Battalion HQ shoot into the Kamak-san foothills on 25 April; stacks of empty ammunition crates make clear the intensity of the firing. Note the slit trench in the foreground, revetted with empty ammunition crates. *Courtesy Mervyn McCord*

**Left:** 8th Hussar Lieutenant Ted Paul, his Centurion a blazing wreck, opens fire on advancing enemy with a carbine picked up from the battlefield. This shot was taken in the closing stages of the action at the bottom of Route 11; the photographer, prudently, is staying low. *Courtesy 8th King's Royal Irish Hussars*

**Right:** As the breakout was about to begin, Ulster Rifles Major John Shaw asked Second Lieutenant Mervyn McCord to take his photograph and give it to his wife, Marion. Shaw had had a premonition, and he was killed thirty minutes later. Note the closeness of the hills down which the Chinese would swarm to cut off the brigade's retreat. *Courtesy Mervyn McCord*

**Below:** David Rowlands' *Crash Action* shows the Ulster Rifles' half-section of mortars firing to cover the retreat. While the landscape is over-large, and one veteran called the painting 'too tidy', details are accurate: Oxford carriers stand waiting, the Riflemen wear caubeens and cap comforters, Chinese dot the valley and Centurions fire with their guns traversed backwards. *Courtesy David Rowlands*

A view looking south down Route 11, taken from the western side of the valley, shows wrecked Hussar armour in front of the copse where the Chinese placed their ambush on 29th Brigade's line of retreat. The tracks on the right are where Hussar Captain Peter Ormrod's tanks swerved around the roadblock. Some infantry escaped by traversing the hills beyond. *Courtesy John Preston-Bell*

Smashed Centurions line Route 11. Like the photograph above, this shot was taken one month after the battle, when the brigade retuned to the Imjin to bury its dead. *Courtesy John Preston-Bell*.

Chinese light artillery, shattered by gunfire and air strikes, lies in the Imjin after the battle. Guy Temple's ambush site on the riverbank is out of sight on the left. *By Vander Goten/Courtesy Jan Dillen*

A Gloster signal section in action on unidentified high ground. The men are wearing the popular camouflage windproofs over their battledress. *Courtesy Soldiers of Gloucestershire Museum*

**Above:** Part of the ridge running along the top of Hill 235, site of the Glosters' last stand, photographed after the battle. The ridge was under constant fire during the battle. Chinese tracer and mortar fire was so heavy that survivors compared the pyrotechnics to Blackpool Illuminations and Guy Fawkes Night.
*Courtesy Soldiers of Gloucestershire Museum*

**Right:** The iconic moment of the battle. Just before dawn on the 25th, Gloster Drum Major Buss stands and answers Chinese buglers with a full rendition. Glosters cheer him; soon after they will curse him, as the heaviest hail of fire yet sweeps the trapped battalion.
*Painting by Ken Howard.*
*Courtesy Soldiers of Gloucestershire Museum*

Riflemen pray at the dedication of their battle monument at 'Happy Valley' in summer, 1951. Lieutenant John Mole kneels in foreground, while Father Joe Ryan leads the service. In 2008 the monument was relocated to Belfast City Hall. *Courtesy Royal Ulster Rifles Museum*

**Left:** A self-confessed 'obnoxious bastard', Fusilier Derek Kinne was captured at the Imjin and fought a private war in the prison camps, where, despite horrific treatment from his captors, he proved utterly unbreakable. He is seen here outside Buckingham Palace after receiving the George Cross. *Courtesy Derek Kinne, GC*

**Below:** ROK Colonel Kim Yu-seok, Gloster survivor George Newhouse and his granddaughter Jennifer stand in the British memorial park in April 2008. Today Kim's men hold the ground once occupied by the Glosters. The park is the old HQ area; in the background loom the southern slopes of Hill 235, the site of the doomed battalion's last stand. *Photo by the Author*

occur. None of us wanted to get our heads blown off. The discipline of soldiers was there. You obeyed orders.' Grenades were the weapon of choice. With such short horizons on the hilltop, the Chinese, hidden from direct fire by the slope, massed close to the British line, then rose from cover and charged. The Glosters pulled pins and rolled grenades down the hillside into enemy below the contour.[22] The Chinese tried to hurl their grenades over the British slits, so that they hit the slopes above, then rolled down and detonated inside the trenches.[23]

45 Field was delivering its thunder. The FOOs on the hilltop were adjusting fire to within twenty-five metres of the perimeter. The tell-tale, shrieking whoosh sounded overhead, followed by a flashing series of drum-fire crumps that burst like giant flashbulbs, illuminating the landscape for a split second, ploughing the slopes and shredding assault parties clambering up. 'When I saw those 25-pounders going in, I was proud to be an artilleryman!' said mortar man Tom Clough, crouched in his shell scrape. Even compared to previous nights, the volume of pyrotechnics unleashed around, over and onto the fire-ringed hill was awesome: Lance-Corporal Charles Sharpling was reminded of the Blackpool Illuminations. 'It was like fireworks night, tracers here, there, everywhere – Christ Almighty!' said Private Morris Coombes. 'It was keep your head down or get it blown off!' A hurricane of fire and flying earth whirled around the battalion.

Chinese mortars joined the battle. Men desperately scratched into earth to improve their cover. 'All we could do was scrape with a bayonet and not make too much noise,' said Mercer. 'They could pinpoint the sound, and send over a mortar bomb. The Chinese were probably within a couple of hundred yards all round. The pincers had really closed.' With mortars detonating around him, Mercer decided that his own trench was not good enough, so asked to join Colour Sergeant Buxcey – ' a real crack shot, a pre-World War II regular' – in the trench behind him. 'Find your own fucking trench!' the NCO replied. By an odds-against chance, a bomb landed directly in Buxcey's trench, killing him instantly. When the mortars landed, men hugged the earth; shockwaves passed over, and the soil trembled with the impact. 'The earth wasn't all that was shaking,' said anti-tank gunner Ben Whitchurch. 'You had to change your trousers!' Such symptoms of fear as freezing motionless and excreting may once have been instinctive survival mechanisms. Scientists speculate that in the prehistoric past, when stalked by a predator, man would freeze, for it is movement that catches the eye. If that tactic failed, he would urinate or defecate, to dissuade the predator with his unsavoury scent. The many terror-inducing incidents taking place that night may, indeed, have triggered the atavistic self-defence response of self-soiling among the British and Chinese soldiers battling for Hill 235.

The battalion's key defensive weapons were the medium machine-guns. They had started the battle with trenches full of coiled ammunition; now riflemen around the perimeter were ordered to empty bandoliers and pass cartridges along to the Vickers crews, who inserted them into links, fed them into guns, and fired them off into the Chinese. Eagles was in a trench below a Vickers position. The section had set three ranging points – 'Conservative', 'Labour' and 'Liberal'. When, in the flare light, they saw bushes moving at the appropriate range, they let fly. 'They had a crossfire with four Vickers – a cone – but they kept coming,' said Eagles. 'Later I saw the Chinese stacking bodies ten feet high.' Enemy machine-gunners on the surrounding hills had had all day to fix their targets. From a distance, their tracers appeared to arc over slowly, then suddenly accelerate, zipping over the Glosters' slit trenches. Padre Davies crouched in the RAP as rapid fire scythed through brush just above his head.[24] With only one radio set in operation on the Gloster position, the company commanders had to dispatch runners to the CP with fire requests. Major Harding sent Temple, who, crouching, dashed along the ridge of Hill 235 – 'it was as wide as a kitchen table' – to deliver his message. Sprinting back, he dropped into his shell scrape as a machine-gun volley kicked up dust from the parapet inches from his nose. 'It was from far, far away – it must have been a Maxim or something, it was really impressive.' Not everyone was so lucky: Temple saw one officer shot through the forehead on the ridgeline. Remarkably, he continued talking for thirty seconds before dying.

The Chinese machine-gunners loaded their belts heavily with tracers; while the Vickers fired lines of red blobs, the Chinese shot laser-like streaks of green light. It was an error. The Glosters could trace the fire directly to the enemy muzzles, giving Vickers and artillery the target coordinates to knock them out.[25] The Chinese duelled the Vickers with medium mortars. 'They tried to get Murphy with mortars, but they never did!' said Eagles. 'Some mortar bombs were hitting the walls of the cliff, some were hitting alongside us. You didn't hear them coming – just shouts of, "Keep your bloody head down!"'

The overworked guns needed more than .303 rounds to keep them running. The Vickers is a water-cooled weapon – water circulates in a metal jacket enclosing the barrel – but with the extreme rate of fire, coolant was evaporating. There was no spring on Hill 235. The battalion's meagre water supply was at the RAP: wounded men, losing pints of blood, need hydration to live. An old infantry expedient was called upon. Defying the fire lashing the hilltop, a crouching sergeant ran from position to position, ordering men to urinate into a container; the liquid gathered would be used to cool the guns. For many soldiers – who had been without water for two days – the task proved impossible. 'He was saying, "Pee in this, pee in this. Come on, come on!"' Whitchurch said. 'And we were going, "I can't, I can't!"' The sergeant was killed as he made his rounds. Somehow, the guns kept firing. Belts of cartridges tore through the hands of operators, ejected cases spun from smoking breeches and orange flames spat from muzzles as the MMG men traversed their hammering weapons across crowds of attackers. The vibrating barrels glowed in the darkness.

\* \* \*

Throughout the history of battle there have occurred incidents that would stretch credibility were they fiction, but which, when they happen, pass into military legend, not because they are decisive, but because they epitomise dash, panache, defiance. Nelson refusing to read withdrawal signals by raising his telescope to his blind eye; Lord Lovat's bagpiper leading his commandos inland on D-Day; General McAuliffe's one-word reply to the German surrender demand at Bastogne – 'Nuts!'; all fall into this category. For fighting men, such incidents, however short-lived, inject a potent shot of morale. At the Battle of the Imjin River, the iconic moment would come on Hill 235 just before daybreak on 25 April.

For the Glosters, the incessant enemy bugling was both unnerving – the Chinese instruments had a haunting, eerie quality – and demoralising: every man on the hill knew that the calls were summoning yet another assault from the darkness. With the enemy's musician-signallers chiselling away at morale, Carne, in his CP with Farrar-Hockley, suggested the Glosters return fire. Farrar-Hockley yelled down the hillside to the Drums Platoon, positioned just below the CP. Did anyone have a bugle? The senior bugler, Drum Major Buss, did not. He called to Eagles. 'Have you got your bugle?' he asked. Grasping what was about to happen, Eagles rummaged in his haversack and produced his – 'I never needed an excuse to play!' – but the warrant officer told him, 'No, I'll do it. Stay here with your grenades.' With first light approaching, Farrar-Hockley shouted to Buss to play 'Reveille'. Then, warming to the idea, he ordered him to play every call in the book – everything except 'Retreat'.

In the pre-dawn darkness, amid the cacophony of battle, the tall Drum Major climbed to his feet. Defying incoming fire, standing to attention next to his slit trench in the centre of the embattled hilltop, he placed the bugle to his lips.

Whatmore was in his trench with D Company when he heard a bugle blare out from over the rise behind him. A Chinese! So close! He spun, rifle in shoulder, finger on trigger – then recognised the tune. It was the 'Long Reveille'.[26] The strident notes carried across the hilltop, echoing off the rock walls across the valley. Buss's first tune was followed by the calls every British soldier knew so well: 'Cookhouse', 'Officers Dress for Dinner', 'Fire Call', 'Last Post' and the rest. 'He always played a bugle well,' wrote Farrar-Hockley, 'and that day he was not below form.'[27] As a piece of leadership, Carne's order was inspired; as a gesture of bravado, Buss's rendition was inspiring. A hoarse cheer rippled around the embattled perimeter. 'All of us knew it was an answer to the Chinese bugles,' said Temple, a hundred metres away. 'It lifted the spirits.' The last notes echoed away. Buss put down his instrument.

Silence.

The Chinese bugle calls had died. It is not clear if the end of Buss's performance coincided with a lull in the action, or whether the enemy surrounding the Glosters were straining their ears to identify this strange new noise, no doubt as alien to Chinese ears as their own bugles were to British. Either way, there came a pause in the aural assault.

It could not last. Soon after – perhaps it was only seconds, maybe it stretched to minutes (accounts differ) – the Glosters cowered behind any cover they could as the most intense hail of fire yet flailed the hilltop. 'We cheered him when he stood up and played, but we cursed him after that,' said Medical Orderly George Newhouse. 'The Chinese opened up with everything they had!' 'The Battle of the Bugles' had ended. The battle for Hill 235 continued.

* * *

On 25 April the sun rose at 05:43. Dawn cast its light on a battle tableau. In a ragged line around the battered brown hilltop, from under khaki cap comforters and dark blue berets, red-rimmed eyes stared out of blackened faces. Men licked cracked lips, but were unable to moisten throats – dry due to lack of liquid, the dust blasted up by guns and mortars, and the ever-present fear. And yet, from behind rocks, sangars, trench parapets and piles of pouches, the ragged line bristled with Vickers, Brens, rifles and Stens. All still spat fire. The battalion remained unbroken. The perimeter held.

On the pulverised, dusty slopes, in their mustard-coloured uniforms, flapped caps and plimsoll-style boots, lay dead and dying Chinese. Some – infiltrators – had died a lonely death. Others – assault squads – lay in bloody heaps where they had been caught by automatic fire or artillery blast. Littering the slopes and gullies were gruesome chunks of human detritus, hurled this way and that by high explosive. Scattered around were abandoned weapons: burp guns, Simonov rifles, the ever-present bundles of stick grenades. Patches of brushwood, ignited by tracer or phosphorus, smouldered. The Glosters' last stand was taking place on a granite-and-earth fortress that appeared to be floating in the sky, for the lower slopes and the valley floor were obscured by the 'Sea of Clouds' – the Imjin mist. Haunting notes echoed up from the fog. Bugles. Another attack was forming up. 'Come on you bastards!' shouted a Gloucestershire voice. 'Come and get your breakfast!'[28]

Black mortar smoke shrouded A Company. Shocked, wounded men, their dull uniforms leaking bright blood, reeled down the ridge to the RAP. Some were carried unconscious, among them, the young subaltern Terry Waters, wounded in the leg on the 22nd, now hit in the head. All night, Chinese attacks had probed different sectors of the Gloster perimeter. Now the enemy concentrated on A Company. The crisis of the battle was at hand.[29]

During the dark hours, in the centre of the position, the Glosters' adjutant had been raising spirits, moving from position to position, roaring orders, advice, encouragement. 'Farrar-Hockley kept us going,' said Newhouse. 'He was walking back and forward, saying, "We're not leaving, we're staying. We've nowhere left to go!"' Some Glosters found the demandingly professional captain a terror in barracks; some members of the brigade found 'Horror-Fuckley' aggressive and over-opinionated. Yet none denied that this pugnacious, pipe-smoking professional was a formidable fighting man. An adjutant's job is to assist his colonel with administration, organisation and operations. An adjutant had no job in this battle. Farrar-Hockley armed himself, climbed out of his slit, and headed up the ridge to join A Company.[30]

The company, its numbers already halved in the battle for 'Castle Site', had been fighting all night. Mercer was in a trench with two other soldiers, scrabbling around on his knees for any spare rounds at the bottom. Not only was ammunition in short supply; exhaustion was also taking its toll. 'At dawn, all of us had been awake for seventy-two hours, and forty-eight without food,' Mercer said. A Gloster left his trench to get a better view then jerked back, shot. Mercer squinted down his sights. A shape in the scrub! Three rounds rapid. Mercer was certain he was hitting the target, but to no effect. Realisation: he was shooting chips off a rock. Noise. Mercer's world spun. Confusion. A bright splash of blood. Comprehension: he had been caught in a mortar explosion. Lying upside down, the river to his back, he found himself looking up the spur. He could see a pair of legs in Finnish pattern boots sticking out of a trench. The owner of the legs seemed unconcerned by incoming fire. 'It was Farrar-Hockley, calmly directing fire,' said Mercer. 'He was standing up in full view of the enemy.' Mercer unsteadily regained his feet. The adjutant took one look and ordered him down the ridge. The private staggered back, crawling into a bivouac tent near the RAP inhabited by another man who had been wounded by British artillery. He produced field dressings, slapping one over Mercer's eye and another over his leg. Mercer had been concussed by blast, a fragment of jagged steel had torn into his left eye and other pieces had peppered his right calf. 'I know it sounds damned silly, but it didn't hurt at all,' he said. As soon as his head touched ground, he sank into a coma-like sleep. For Sam Mercer, the battle was over.

For A Company, it was not. A key knoll – Point 235, the highest position on the hill – had been lost. If the Chinese charged down, they could sweep the entire ridge clear of Glosters. The only option was immediate counter-attack. In such situations, a single man, armed with fortitude, leadership and the ability to inspire, can make a difference. The adjutant arrived at a small group of men clinging on below the peak. Some had been hit, but had not abandoned their positions. Other, experienced soldiers, sensing the critical situation, arrived without orders. Looking round, Farrar-Hockley saw 'a good lot of faces to be in a tight corner with; reliable faces; the faces of old friends'. The captain smiled; the men smiled back. Then they charged.[31]

The knoll was thirty yards off. Red-brown earth flew beneath their feet as the handful of Glosters sprinted forward, firing on the run. They were in among the Chinese on the knoll before they had time to react. A breathless mêlée, then the enemy broke, scattering down the rear slopes into a clutch of pines and dwarf oaks. Success! Farrar-Hockley deployed his few men into defensive positions, then lit his pipe. He did not rest for long. Seven counter-attacks piled into A Company within an hour. So desperate was the fighting that the Glosters declined an air-drop, which would have required the halting of artillery fire.* As Chinese waves surged up the north-west spur to attack A Company, D Company, on the north-east spur, poured rapid enfilade into them. Through the smoke, Harvey could see enemy soldiers slipping on rocks: they were slick with blood.[32]

Below Point 235 squatted a mound from which an entrenched automatic was supporting the Chinese assaults. Washbrook, the FOO, dashed forward in response to requests for fire support. Would Farrar-Hockley risk 'unders'? Absolutely: this was no time for artillery-school niceties. An express train shrieked over the heads of the crouching Glosters. Earth geysered up. Choking black smoke swirled, then cleared. Enemy fire had ceased. The feature was a mass of craters. Moments passed. Grenades thumped down among the forward Glosters. Chinese were concealed among felled trees fifteen yards to their front. Farrar-Hockley

* The entry is in the Brigade War Diary at 06:45. Lieutenant-Colonel Maris Young, 45 Field's CO, thought the Glosters' request to keep firing was 'the finest compliment we could ever have had'.

and two men pulled pins on their own grenades, counted down, bowled over-arm. The bombs detonated behind the timber. A Chinese, the back of his tunic bloody, broke cover, staggered, fell. Another ran. Automatic fire stuttered. The running man spun, killed by a Sten burst.[33]

The valley mist was now clearing. A grimly amusing incident both cheered those who saw it and underlined the risks run by the Chinese, who lacked radio communications and so were not updated on dispositions.* A unit of enemy troops appeared up the track from the river crossing, mounted on a novel form of military transport. Gaping Glosters could tell from the way they turned their heads that they were talking casually. A Vickers crew traversed their weapon, adjusted sights and squeezed their trigger. The enemy bicycles clattered to the ground like a line of dominoes; a few confused Chinese were seen getting up and running. The Glosters around Private David Green erupted in hysterics.[34] Despite the loss of company strongpoints; despite the many dead and dying; despite reaching a final terminus on this smoking hilltop; the Glosters were still dominating the route from the river.

* * *

With the sun up and the enemy in close contact, the battalion at last received air support, their first since the 23rd, when Castle Site had been abandoned. Far above Hill 235, F-80 Shooting Stars wheeled in the blue. With the enemy so close, their attack would have to be perfectly delivered or the jets would kill the men they had come to save. It had happened before. The previous summer the USAF had bombed the Argyll and Sutherland Highlanders with the most diabolical weapon in the UN arsenal: napalm. That same munition would be used to clear the ground around the Glosters.†

Around a hundred Chinese were assembling in the trees in front of A Company – by now, the company, with less than forty men, was at

* As we have seen, due to the difficulty of maintaining command and control over troops once operations began, Chinese officers made sure that even their lowest-ranking soldiers were well briefed about tactical, operational and even strategic objectives. The bicycle-borne unit probably expected to be passing through an area that had been cleared of enemy two nights before. By now General Yang's offensive on the Imjin was well behind time, hampered by 29th Brigade's refusal to give up ground.
† In 2001, at the 50th anniversary battlefield tour, Farrar-Hockley recalled being asked by a woman if he had had any moral qualms about using such a weapon. 'Madam, I did not!' was his reply. It is a fair point. A high-velocity bullet can splinter bone and rupture organs; a machine-gun burst can cut a man in half, sever limbs or decapitate. The jagged metal fragments blasted around the battlefield by high-explosive mortar and artillery fire can leave a human body looking as if it has been mangled by a shark. Napalm and white phosphorus are nasty munitions; but whether their effect on human flesh is any worse than that of other modern weapons is questionable.

platoon strength. The marker for the air strike would be smoke, but the battalion had only one marker grenade left. Farrar-Hockley gripped it. The flight leader swooped down on his attack run over the hill. The Gloster captain threw the grenade as hard and as high as he could into the trees to his front. It burst. Violet smoke billowed up.[35] The fighter-bomber screamed over the Glosters' heads. Canisters were released. Clough, crouching terrified, watched the bombs tumbling over his position: 'They dropped it towards us, we could see the canisters turning over in the air, we thought, "My God, this is it, it's another Argyll incident, we've had it!"'

The shadow of the leading jet streaked off the hill, over the low ground beyond, leaving behind the displaced air of its passage and the bombs in its slipstream. Momentary silence. The canisters landed right among the massing Chinese. Bright orange flame bloomed up. The strike was dead on target. At D Company, Whatmore felt a 'whoosh' as if a blast-furnace door had been opened; an enemy machine-gun to his front was engulfed in the inferno.[36] The remaining jets dived in and dropped their loads.

The napalm was not completely efficacious. Harvey watched, astonished, as Chinese rolled into craters and depressions, pulling groundsheets over themselves. The liquid fire surged over them; they jumped up again, apparently unharmed.* But elsewhere, the air-dropped blaze lived up to its fearsome reputation. Jellied petroleum, like white phosphorus, sticks to uniforms or skin, searing through clothing and tissue, burning off ears, noses, lips, transforming arms and legs into fleshless sticks, turning bone itself to white ash. Some Glosters were unnerved to hear the screams of burning Chinese.[37] Eagles, watching enemy soldiers flaring up in the valley, felt exultation, mutating into human empathy: 'We all shouted, "Go on, get 'em!" But afterwards I thought, "That poor bastard's just like me."'

The fighter-bombers made seven runs. Having unloaded their fire canisters, the aircraft howled over the position, strafing the slopes. Soil sprayed up. Then the F-80s pulled up and away until they were just distant silver twinkles in the spring sky. Then, nothing.

Again, the Glosters were on their own, but the USAF air strike, brilliantly executed, had broken the back of the enemy assaults. Fearful of further bolts from the blue, the Chinese went to ground. Quiet, broken

---

* Harvey described this to me in 2001. Perhaps the Chinese groundsheets were coated with some form of heat-resistant material. Newcombe, p 180, recounts Gloster Lieutenant Tony Preston, captured at F Echelon, experiencing the same thing during an air strike on Kamak-san. A Chinese soldier had passed him a spare rain cape, and, although it was splashed with napalm, Preston was unharmed.

only by the crackling of burning brush, settled over the smoking hill. A Company was stabilised. Farrar-Hockley was summoned to Carne's CP. He dashed back along the ridge under machine-gun fire. When he arrived, Carne was sitting in his slit trench studying a map. The colonel appeared so calm that the captain could not guess the information he was about to impart.

* * *

While Farrar-Hockley had been fighting with A Company, a series of radio conversations had taken place between Grist, at Brigade HQ, and his commanding officer. Grist was in the back of a three-ton truck, the radio post of Lieutenant George Truell, whose battery was supporting the Glosters.

The rest of the brigade was in a critical situation. Chinese, infiltrating around both flanks of the Glosters, had moved south-east of Kamaksan. 29th Brigade had held its ground; the human wave, unable to break the unit, had washed around and beyond it. The bulk of the brigade – the Fusiliers, the Rifles, the Hussars and the Belgians (moved into position the previous day) – were now threatened with encirclement, for across the entire front a massive retrograde movement was under way. I Corps was pulling back to Line Delta, some four miles south of Kansas. For three nights Carne's battalion had carried out its orders. It had held its section of the line, dominating the Imjin ford and the track south. Now Kansas was being abandoned. The Glosters' duty was done – but there were no troops available to break them out.

The force Soule had massed to restore the front in the brigade's sector was being redeployed. The battle group, stationed to the west of 29th Brigade HQ, and south-west of the Fusiliers and Rifles, was placed to attack after dawn, but it had come under small-arms and mortar fire at daybreak, as had Brigade HQ and the nearby Belgians. The right-hand regiment of ROK 1st Division had been forced back four miles, and units of 189th Division were flooding south.[38] This was what the Chinese had planned for. I Corps was no longer master of its own destiny. Soule tasked his infantry battalions with an urgent new operation: wipe out the enemy in the rear and defend the MSR, his escape route to the south.[39] In the brutal triage of command decisions, the Glosters, to whom senior commanders had paid such attention the previous day, had dropped off 8th Army's priority list. The decision had the backing of Britain's high command. On the evening of the 24th, the senior officer in the Far East, Australian Lieutenant-General Sir Horace Robertson, Commander-in-Chief, Commonwealth Occupation Force Japan, touring Korea, had contacted Milburn's staff. Anticipating the battalion's fate, he told Milburn not to endanger his corps to extricate the Glosters.[40]

At 29th Brigade HQ, in the morning mist, in the back of Truell's 3-ton truck with the 25-pounders firing all around, the gravity of the situation – the electric tension as this information was conveyed to the Glosters – may be imagined. Grist was on the set to Carne. Brigadier Tom Brodie and Lieutenant-Colonel Maris Young, the Gunners' CO, came in and out.[41] The entries in 29th Brigade's War Diary tell a terse story of their discussions.

06:05: Command Memo: Glosters given permission to break out.*

06:10: Glosters: Very hard pressed, asking for air support.

06:20: Glosters: Surrounded, impossible to withdraw.

06:45: 45 Field Tac: Report air drop not going in as Glosters have asked for continuous artillery fire.

07:55. Glosters: Only another 30 minutes of [radio] battery left.†

It was obvious to everyone in the back of the truck that the final curtain was falling. At 07.55, sensing the emotion of the moment Brodie scribbled on a signals pad, 'NO ONE BUT GLOSTERS COULD HAVE DONE IT.' Grist, wearing the headset, read the brigadier's message out to his colonel. There was nothing more to say. Grist switched off the radio and broke down in tears.[42] The Glosters were doomed.

* * *

At the CP in the centre of Hill 235 Farrar-Hockley stood before his CO. Carne and Grist had concluded their discussions. 'You know that armoured/infantry relief force that's coming from 3rd Div to relieve us?' said Carne. 'Well, it isn't coming.' 'Right, sir,' was all Farrar-Hockley could say.[43]

Some time before 10:00 the remaining company officers were summoned by their commander for a last O Group. Farrar-Hockley; Mike Harvey from D Company; Bob Hickey, the medical officer; Guy Temple, representing the combined B/C Company; Sam Weller of Support Company – all were there as Carne gave instructions for the breakout. 'It was a most peculiar order: "Every man to make his own way back,"' Farrar-Hockley mused. 'It was an order I had never heard before, and hope never to hear again.'[44] The surviving Glosters would be

---

* Fifty-six years later, George Truell, recalling the exact time (06:05) that the breakout order was given, wondered to me why the Glosters had delayed their withdrawal for several hours (i.e. until just after 10:00). There are two possibilities: one is that Carne, exhausted and under massive stress, was not thinking clearly. The second is that the battalion was too closely engaged to consider any such manoeuvre. There are no accurate timings of the final fighting, but only after A Company's position had been stabilised, the last air and artillery strikes had gone in, the Chinese taken cover and the mist had lifted (around 10:00) did the remnants of the Glosters break for freedom.

† This entry proved inaccurate. At 09:25 the Glosters reported enemy vehicles to Brigade, and Farrar-Hockley (1954) and Truell (author interview) both mention that the last radio contacts with the Glosters were as late as 10:00 or 10:30.

easily spotted and destroyed if they moved as a unit. Instead, the men would break out south-westwards in small groups, in the hope of linking up with the ROK 1st Division and their American tank support, four miles away. No artillery could support the move: 45 Field Regiment, under attack itself, was in the process of moving back. And not everyone was to leave. Carne ordered his wounded – lying in bloody heaps in the RAP – to be abandoned to the enemy.*

The officers returned to their companies and issued orders. Things were quiet. There seemed to be no dismay or defeatism among the exhausted men; Temple recalled some of his soldiers discussing the quality of ale in the town of Stroud. (Considering how thirsty most men were by this stage, beer was an appropriate topic.) For some, the realisation that battle was over was a relief. 'There was a numbness, a feeling that this was the end,' said Coombes. 'A feeling of relief, to a point, that there was no more gunfire, but also a feeling of "What will happen next?"'

The Glosters had fought virtually to the last round. A Company had three rounds per rifle, a magazine and a half for the Brens, and half a magazine for the Stens, plus seven fragmentation and four white phosphorus grenades.[45] Many men, such as Coombes, had nothing at all, so pulled out their rifle bolts, smashed the firing pins and broke the butts on rocks. Signallers and Vickers gunners set about destroying their equipment. Eagles did not think Buss would appreciate it if the Chinese seized his bugle as a trophy. Taking his last phosphorus grenade, he pulled the pin, shoved it down the bell of the instrument, and threw it into his slit trench. Without waiting for the detonation, he set off down the hill. Lines of men were now scrambling down into the valley. The last radio call from the trapped battalion was from Washbrook to fellow gunner Truell. 'I am shutting down the wireless,' he signalled at around 10:20. 'We are trying to break out!'

As Farrar-Hockley was departing, he noticed that Hickey, the doctor, seemed unprepared to move. The adjutant advised him to hurry. Matter-of-factly, Hickey told him that he had decided to remain with the wounded.† Farrar-Hockley was momentarily stunned: that meant certain capture. Too moved to speak, he clapped Hickey on the shoulder and

---

* The total number of Gloster wounded is given, in a British Embassy handout on the battle, as 180, but this includes those from the separate A, B and D Company battles. It seems likely that the number on Hill 235 would have been around 100.

† A number of early accounts of the battle state that Carne elected to remain with the wounded. This was false, and would, indeed, have been against King's Regulations. However, the CO was one of the last men off the position. He evaded initial capture, but was taken on the evening of 26 April. Some soldiers, however, *were* ordered to remain behind. According to George Newhouse, Captain Hickey ordered two unmarried medical orderlies to remain with the wounded, while the married orderlies – Newhouse included – were told to leave. Newhouse was taken at the bottom of the hill.

began climbing down the slope himself.[46] Padre Davies watched the men leaving. Earlier, he had given absolution to the seriously wounded. Among them was Sergeant Eames, who had so impressed Green as he had stormed over the crest of Hill 327 in February. Among the blackened scrub of Hill 235, Eames had prayed with Davies and asked the padre to write to his young wife and mother. He died quietly. Now, as the Glosters pulled out, Davies noted to RAMC Sergeant Brisland, 'This looks like a holiday in Peking for some of us!' In fact, Davies's own capture was certain; he, too, had elected to remain with the wounded. So had Brisland, who prepared a Red Cross flag as they awaited the enemy. Drum-Major Buss, passing by on his way down to the valley, spotted the flash of white cloth and thought Brisland was planning to surrender. Cursing, Buss brandished his rifle and ordered the sergeant to drop the flag.* Davies hastily intervened, telling Buss to save himself. Buss took off down the slope.[47]

Below the crest of Hill 235 gruesome signs of the fighting were everywhere. Farrar-Hockley carefully counted 216 Chinese dead on just one slope.[48] Eagles noticed enemy bodies down-slope from his trench, victims of the grenades he had rolled down during the night. Whitchurch found just how close the enemy had got to his position by the corpses lying there, and Temple came across a pile of smouldering napalm victims: 'Have you ever cooked sausages without making a hole in them with a fork? They looked like that.' The engineers' boats, left at the bottom of the hill, had also been incinerated. The body of A Company's Major Pat Angier, cremated beneath them, had a cleaner end than would most of the Gloster dead left on the battlefield.

In small, wary groups, the soldiers advanced, in bright sunshine, down the valley and into the ravine. There were no live enemy on the valley floor, but they were watching, under camouflage, from hilltops and in re-entrants. They could not fail to spot the breakout.

Clough came to a stream churned up by the boots of men in front. Despite the mud, everyone in his group dropped to drink, then continued. Suddenly, a Chinese machine-gunner popped up in front of him. 'I fired instinctively – and got him between the eyes,' said Clough, who had only two rounds. 'Pure luck! Then we were surrounded. There was this dead Chink with a bullet through his head, and our sergeant major said, "Very good!" I said, "No, no, it wasn't me!"' Then they were prisoners. A Chinese officer walked up to Clough and said, in English: 'For you, the war is over!' Clough could barely believe what he was hearing.

---

* The incident is telling. Clearly, after three nights of ferocious battle, some men – most particularly, perhaps, Buss, who had been specifically ordered not to play 'Retreat' – were determined that whatever happened to the Glosters as individuals, no formal surrender of the battalion must take place.

'I thought, "How many times have I heard that in films?" But I suppose that is where he learned it – from an American war film.'

Other men were being taken all around the hill. Eagles, who had smashed his rifle, walked down the defile and into a squad of Chinese. He was fascinated to note their equipment up close: one man had a machine-gun with a drum magazine strapped to his back; when it was in action he crouched down on all fours while his mate fired and another man changed magazines. At the bottom of the hill, Green fell face down beside the stream, plunged his face in and drank deeply. Sated, he stood to see a crowd of Asians in tan uniforms laughing and shaking hands with the Glosters. For a moment he thought that they had been relieved by South Koreans. Then he realised they were Chinese.[49] Temple moved out with B Company's OC, Major Denis Harding. The two headed west. Harding had a pistol, Temple an empty Sten. 'I don't know why I was carrying it,' he said. 'I had been hallucinating due to lack of sleep or lack of water.' Suddenly, a Chinese sentry rose in front of them. Harding shot at him with his pistol and missed. 'Then it seemed as if the whole valley stood up,' said Temple. Fighting was not feasible; the two officers had stumbled into a camouflaged battalion position. The Chinese proved friendly: all found the shooting incident amusing, except the man Harding had fired on, 'who had a sense of humour failure'. The Chinese soldier detailed to guard Temple offered him his own foxhole and greatcoat to sleep on, and gave the British officer a self-rolled cigarette. 'It is not the front-line soldiers who do the hating,' Temple discovered. Farrar-Hockley was leading men up a ravine. Above him, a US observation aircraft was monitoring events. The pilot radioed that a group of British soldiers, acting 'as if they are lost' had walked to the end of a track, reached a dead end, returned to their positions and sat down.[50] He had, in fact, witnessed the end of Farrar-Hockley's attempt. Machine-guns had fired from a ridge above, and the Glosters had dashed on. More bursts – much lower. Realising these were warning shots, that there was no way to fight back, and that the next bullets would be fatal, Farrar-Hockley ordered his men to lay down their weapons. They were ordered to sit down. 'After all we had done, after all the effort we had exerted in fulfilling our task, this was the end,' he wrote. 'Surrender to the enemy!'[51]

* * *

Not every Gloster broke south. Mike Harvey's D Company, covering Hill 235's north-east spur, was the last to move. After the O Group with Carne, Harvey's mind wandered to the Judo HQ in Tokyo, where a calligraphy scroll on the wall read, 'Deliberate in Council – Prompt in Action!'[52] Judo encourages its practitioners to avoid using force against

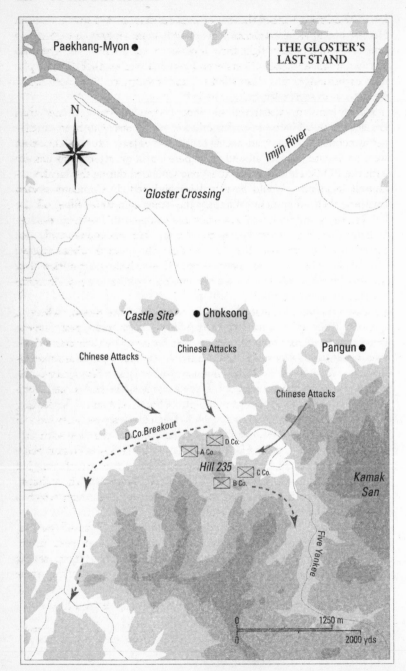

Paekhang-Myon ●

THE GLOSTER'S
LAST STAND

N

*Imjin River*

'Gloster Crossing'

'Castle Site'   ● Choksong

Pangun ●

Chinese Attacks

Chinese Attacks

Chinese Attacks

D Co.Breakout

D Co.

A Co.

*Hill 235*    C Co.

B Co.

*Kamak
San*

*Five Yankee*

0
1250 m
0
2000 yds

force, prioritising instead the line of least resistance. Perhaps this was on Harvey's mind as he summoned his platoon commanders and CSM. He offered them a choice: fight their way out or surrender.* There was no discussion; none of the officers even looked at one another. 'All the platoon commanders said, "Let's fight,"' said Whatmore. 'It simply didn't occur to us to surrender, quite frankly.'[53]

Harvey now demonstrated his independent thinking. Rather than heading south with the rest of the battalion, he opted to head north – the direction the enemy, advancing south, would least expect – then turn west and south, boxing around their position in an attempt to link up with the ROKs. He ordered that anyone wounded during the breakout – himself included – would have to be abandoned. D Company started smashing their equipment. Watching the other companies filing off the hill, Harvey stood with 'a heavy heart as I watched this pathetic disintegration of the finest battalion in the Army'.† He was momentarily disturbed as his eye ran over the huddled mass of wounded, whose capture was certain. His own men were paired off, the little ammunition they had was distributed – Harvey led the breakout with an empty .45 pistol – and D Company set off.[54]

They scrambled down the scree below their position, where a number of men's boots were carved up by the sharp rocks, past Chinese corpses – already divested of weapons and footwear by their comrades – then formed into a loose file and headed north. Harvey ensured that his vanguard, the best shots in the company, had at least a few rounds. The eighty-one men moved through the quiet countryside, and turned westward. Five surprised Chinese appeared in front of them. The leading Glosters fired from the hip; the enemy was mown down. They proved to have no firearms, only grenades. The column pressed westward into the hills. There was a buzzing from above. A US T-6 observation plane had spotted the men; the Glosters waved berets. The aircraft waggled its wings in acknowledgement, and continued flying over the column. They turned south, channelled into a narrow defile through which a stream ran. Their luck seemed to be holding.[55]

Machine-guns barked from the ridges above. At the head of the line, some men broke into a desperate run; others, exhausted, past caring, sank down. Long bursts traversed over rocks, sending sharp shards spraying over the escapees. The Chinese gunners were walking their

---

* Whatmore mentions this in both his book and his IWM recording; Harvey, in his own book, does not mention giving his officers any choice.
† It is one of the tribal features of the British Army that every soldier believes his regiment is the finest in the service. Just as every Gloster would automatically agree with Harvey's opinion, no soldier in any other regiment would.

bursts towards roving targets on the valley floor; if they had created a beaten zone of fire, it would have completely halted the Glosters' forward progress. Some men were firing back; others, in small groups, were getting up, running, diving into cover, dashing forward again. Harvey felt like a target in a shooting gallery.[56]

Further back, Whatmore could see men 'dropping like flies'. He dived into a mud-filled ditch, about a foot deep. It provided minimal cover; some soldiers were shot in it. Crawling through the clinging muck, the exhausted officer had one of those existential moments some men experience in combat. A round cracked past his face, and buried itself into the side of the ditch. It was a tracer. Whatmore paused for long seconds, mesmerised by the bright glow as it slowly burned itself out in the mud. His reverie was interrupted by panicked shouts from behind: 'They are coming down the rear of us with knives!' Whatmore crawled frantically, before being halted by a terrifying sight. Ahead of him stood a tank. The vehicle rocked back as its main armament fired. A squad of Glosters collapsed. Its machine-gun opened up, spraying fire all round. Transfixed, Whatmore saw the steel fortress turn, place a track over the ditch and trundle forward, aiming to churn its way over the helpless soldiers crawling up the ditch.[57]

Colonel Kim Chum-kon, the China veteran and former guerrilla fighter commanding the 12th Regiment of the ROK 1st Division on the Glosters' left flank, had fought a flexible defence for three days. In close contact, he had withdrawn earlier that morning. It had been a tricky operation; he had ordered his driver to destroy his radio jeep with a hand grenade, and in the mêlée a Chinese soldier had grabbed him by the shoulder. But he and most of his men made it to a fallback position. Kim then sent forward a combined infantry/armour patrol when he heard radio reports of unidentified soldiers approaching from the northeast. From the description, they sounded like Soviet troops.* Without binoculars, Kim strained to see into the distance ('I had excellent eyesight') and could just make out a group of men with sleeves rolled up – 'British style!' Guessing who the soldiers were, he got on the radio.

Harvey, lying flat near the head of the column, was certain the tank was friendly. Frantically, he jammed his beret on a stick as identification, raised it and waved it. A burst tore it away. The observation plane dived over the tank, wagging its wings. On his second pass the pilot dropped a note attached to a streamer from his cockpit.[58] Meanwhile, Kim, on the radio, was ordering the tanks to cease fire. The American crews, realising

* Early in the war, British battledress and British troops' practice of wearing knitted cap comforters had caused some retreating NKPA soldiers to mistake a group of Argyll and Sutherland Highlanders for Russians – with fatal consequences.

their error, traversed their weapons onto the ridges. Immediately, incoming enemy fire slackened.

The surviving Glosters ran forward and, using the tanks as shields, pulled back as they reversed, with bullets bouncing off their armour 'like kettle drums'.[59] With the tanks were retreating ROK infantry. The tanks were from the US 73rd Tank Battalion, the foot soldiers from Kim's 12th Regiment.* Once out of Chinese small-arms range, the exhausted British soldiers climbed aboard the tanks. It was 12:30.[60]

The American tankers were appalled at their mistake, repeatedly asking how many Glosters had been hit by their fire. Harvey, grateful for the salvation of the remnants of his command, refused to tell them that six men had been cut down. He made a gift of his binoculars to the lieutenant commanding the tank platoon – himself wounded in the action to extricate the Glosters – and regretted never learning the name of the pilot who had shepherded them.[61] When they reached his sector, Kim was amazed at the condition of the Glosters – almost all were weaponless, they looked starved and parched. He was also surprised that so many were barefoot.† 'The US Army had supplied us with really good socks, and all my men had two pairs,' he said. 'They didn't want to hand them over, but I ordered them to!'

Of the eighty-one members of Harvey's breakout group, only forty-one got out – sixteen of them wounded. Six members of Lieutenant Bob Martin's machine-gun platoon, who had joined D Company but were separated when the Chinese opened fire in the valley, also reached the ROKs.** The exhausted Glosters did not yet know it, but they would be the only defenders of Hill 235 to escape. Just 9 per cent of the battalion got out: effectively, the Glosters had been annihilated.[62] Yet while they had been attempting to escape, an equally desperate crisis was flaring three miles east. Along Route 11 the rest of 29th Brigade was fighting through a valley of fire.

---

* Farrar-Hockley (1995) states the ROKs and tanks had been ordered to attack and make contact with the Glosters: Kim, however, says the attack was made on his own initiative, and had not been ordered by higher command.

† Kim was so surprised at the barefoot soldiers – several men lost their boots on the scree of Hill 235, while Whatmore lost his in the mud of the ditch – that he asked me if it was British custom to go barefoot. When told about the 'Finnish pattern' boots, Kim laughed. 'They were too proud to ask the Americans! The Americans would have given them good boots!'

** There is some dispute about the numbers of Glosters who were in Harvey's group. The figures above are those reproduced in Harding's *The Imjin Roll* (p. 26). Whatmore, in *One Road the Imjin* (p. 86) has the same figure, of 41 escapees. Harvey's *The War in Korea: The Battle Decides All* (p. 133) puts the original number in the breakout party at 104, with 46 escaping. All told, sixty-three men – mainly Harvey's group, plus a handful from B, C and Support Companies – escaped the battle area on Hill 235. See Harding, p. 87.

# Chapter 10

......................

# Death Ride: Breakout Down Route 11

*Nous sommes dans un pot de chambre, et nous y serons emmerdé!* *
General Ducrot, Sedan

I
N THE EARLY HOURS of 25 April, Lieutenant Tony Perrins, the
Royal Northumberland Fusiliers' Intelligence Officer, freshly show-
ered, was luxuriating in his first decent sleep since battle had begun.
He had been relieved at Battalion HQ, and was now well in the rear, at
B Echelon, where the Fusiliers maintained a billet that the infantry on
the hills probably would not have believed existed. 'It was a heated
house with plumbing,' said Perrins. 'It was a thing of beauty, it would
have won the Turner Prize!' His rest was not to last. At around 04:00 he
was shaken awake, and ordered to report to Brigade. At 04:30 he
jumped into a jeep and set off.[†] On arrival, he took a seat at the back of
Brigadier Tom Brodie's command caravan. It was already filling up with
officers. Maps were pinned up, awaiting the brigadier.

Brodie arrived at around 06:00. 'He was calm and brilliant as always,'
recalled Perrins. 'He said "Good morning, Tony, sorry to have woken you
up!"'[**] It was the first time the brigadier had addressed Perrins by his
Christian name. 'He said, "The situation is this," and proceeded to tap
with his pointer at the positions of the Chinese,' Perrins recalled. 'He was
tapping his map five, ten miles behind us. It was the first time I had
realised.' Chinese had infiltrated in force: the entire brigade was in imminent danger of being cut off from the south. Perrins was handed orders to

* *We are in a chamber pot, and we are about to be buried in shit!* The French general made
  his piquant observation while marking staff maps on the morning before the Battle of
  Sedan in the Franco-Prussian War in 1870. Prussian forces were positioned on the high
  ground overlooking the French.
† Perrins was lucky to make it north to the brigade. According to the Hussars' War Diary
  their CO, Sir Guy Lowther – who was with the Hussars' A and B Squadrons, which
  played no role in the battle (the Imjin terrain was too constricted for more than one
  squadron) – attempted to reach Brigade HQ from the south that morning but found the
  MSR cut. It was this threat to his rear that compelled 3rd Infantry Division Commander
  Robert Soule to reassign the force that was preparing to strike north-west to relieve the
  Glosters to protect his line of communication.
** At this point Brodie was fully aware of the plight and likely fate of the Glosters; indeed, he
  would soon be in George Truell's radio truck, speaking to Carne for the last time. Given
  this, the calm that so reassured Perrins was a masterly display of self-control and leadership.

pass to his CO, Kingsley Foster, with the battalion up-valley. 'Plan Golden', the withdrawal to Line Delta, was to be executed. The brigade would withdraw to Tokchong, at the bottom of Route 11, where it joined the MSR: a distance of some six miles.[1] 'I didn't have any sense of panic,' said Perrins. 'I assumed, as I had faith in Tom Brodie and the brigade, that there was no point in me worrying about the bigger picture.'

Other officers were less sanguine. Major Tony Younger of 55 Field Squadron and Major Henry Huth of the Hussars' C Squadron had arrived before both Perrins and Brodie. A young staff officer came in and said he could not wake Brodie; the brigadier, massively stressed, had taken sleeping pills. As a unit commander, Younger could sympathise but, sensing the critical importance of the meeting, ordered the staff officer to wake Brodie – even if it meant emptying a bucket of water over his head. While they awaited the brigadier, the majors discussed how to extract the infantry battalions from their positions up the valley.[*] Huth decided that the best use of his tanks would be to drive up Route 11 to cover the infantry as they pulled back, but they would need bayonets to help keep the valley open during the withdrawal. Younger offered Huth a troop of his engineers to operate as riflemen. Huth accepted. After the O Group, Younger set off for I Corps for a meeting with the chief engineer officer, who had ordered him – again – to prepare Seoul's Han bridges for demolition. As Younger departed, he noticed that elements of Brigade HQ were already departing.[2]

Perrins drove up Route 11 towards the Fusiliers' HQ. A thick mist blanketed the valley, masking the hills along the side of the road. Major John Shaw of the Royal Ulster Rifles, who had also attended the O Group, was in another jeep heading for Major Gerald Rickord's Tactical CP on Hill 398. The bastion remained intact: the Riflemen had held off everything the enemy could throw at them. Lieutenant John Mole was with Rickord when Shaw arrived. This time, anticipating a visit, he had found time to shave; Shaw had not. Mole considered saying something, but decided against it. The two men's eyes met. No words were spoken, but Shaw gave Mole 'a gentle smile, with a funny little twist to it'. Shaw briefed Rickord on the withdrawal, then left for Battalion HQ on the valley floor.

How far would the infantry have to retreat? The northernmost companies – the Rifles' A and D, the Fusiliers' W and X – had around six miles to go as the crow flies to the bottom of Route 11, where it joined Route 33, the MSR, at a junction at the village of Tokchong. The backstop position, held by the Rifles' B Company at the saddle in the road,

---

[*] Although Brodie had not yet given the orders for withdrawal, which the Brigade War Diary says took place at 06:05, Younger's account indicates he and Huth had anticipated what was to happen.

was approximately three miles down Route 11. For most of its length, this route is overlooked by high ground – the foothills of Kamak-san. These hills petered out into paddy fields above Brigade HQ and 45 Field Regiment's gun line, both approximately two miles behind the saddle. South-west of the British battalions, and about a mile and a half west of Brigade HQ, were the Belgians; they had arrived on the 24th after their cross-river breakout the day before. They were dug in on a long ridge covering the western approach to Brigade HQ.

This stretch of back country south of the Imjin is pretty but unspectacular. Thatched hamlets stand at the foot of hills, and the landscape is broken up by occasional copses. Route 11 winds through the paddies. The four miles between the northernmost companies and Brigade HQ would be the most critical.

\* \* \*

With Brodie at Brigade HQ – Americans had arrived with plans to rescue the Glosters – Foster was appointed to command the Fusiliers'/ Rifles' breakout. The two battalions both had their HQs on the valley floor, but the Rifles' acting CO, Rickord, was not at his; he was at his CP on Hill 398. The two COs' discussion thus took place not face-to-face but by field telephone. And there was contention. While the breakout would require the tactical equivalent of precision engineering, the two officers disagreed over the manner of withdrawal.

'Kingsley told Rickord that when the time came to withdraw, turn 180° and get the hell out. The Ulster Rifles were *not* to do it by the book – i.e. covering fire, blah, blah, blah,' recalled Perrins. 'The reason that order was given is that in Korea, most of the time, you had Americans or South Koreans on your left or right. You could faithfully assume that, if the order was to withdraw at 12:00, chances were that the Americans had left the day before, and the South Koreans were the same; what you found was that you were still sitting there at 11:59 with your flanks totally unprotected.'*

In other words, the pullback was to be a 'bug-out' with speed taking precedence over tactical doctrine. The infantry would abandon the high ground and move, fast, down the track in the valley, past Brigade HQ, on to the MSR and safety.

To Rickord, the tough, quiet Northwest Frontier veteran, this plan was anathema. 'The situation was deteriorating,' Rickord said. 'It did

* Foster may have been concerned about a repetition of the Rifles' disaster at Happy Valley, when the Americans had left their flank exposed. In fact, Ridgway's leadership had worked. Bar the collapse of the ROK 6th Division, most US and ROK units, while making tactical withdrawals, did not 'bug out' during Peng's Fifth Offensive; the US 7th Infantry Regiment, 3rd Infantry Division, was still holding its ground to the east of 29th Brigade at this point.

occur to me that if we ever had to [withdraw], there was one place we did not want to do it' – the valley floor. When he heard the orders, Rickord was 'horrified'. He asked Shaw to query Brigade: could he select an alternative route, departing via the high ground east of Route 11? The request was refused. 'It was pretty evident' that enemy strength had been underestimated, Rickord thought.[3]

The Hussars had risen at first light, been briefed and moved up the valley. Huth set his tanks two major tasks. Lieutenant Ted Paul's 2 Troop (four tanks) was dispatched to support the Belgians, deployed to the west of Brigade HQ and south of Kamak-san. Captain Peter Ormrod was to move up the valley with Centurions, half-tracks, Oxford carriers and the artillery's Cromwell tank to support the Fusiliers and Rifles. The armour would drop Younger's sappers off at the blocking position, then cover the infantry as they moved off their hills. Huth, with two roving tanks, elected to remain at the southern entrance to the valley – between Brigade HQ, the battalions up Route 11 and the Belgians – from where he could control squadron operations.

The Hussars' mission – covering infantry as they retreated – was an unusual one for tanks. In fact, withdrawal itself was not a subject British officers studied in depth. 'The British Army teaches a lot about attack, a little bit about defence, but it practically never teaches anybody anything about withdrawal,' said Ormrod. 'I was trying to pass the Staff College exam, and I had just finished the chapter on withdrawals, otherwise I'd have known absolutely nothing. It said you must keep one foot on the ground at all times and put the other foot behind you before you lift the next one. If you move both at once, you can't step. The main thing was to keep firm bases, and I planned a number of firm bases.'[4] One was manned by the troop led by Australian Lieutenant David Boyall, dropped off as a covering force near the saddle held by the Rifles' B Company. The Centurions took positions where they dominated the ground. Boyall positioned his tank on an eminence; Cornet John Preston and his crew were ordered to 'tuck ourselves into a re-entrant off the road and keep an eye on the hills'. With no action under way nearby, the crew climbed out to tighten a loose track.

Ormrod, advancing up-valley towards the Fusiliers' Battalion HQ with the remainder of his force (which included carriers loaded with extra ammunition for the infantry), was now drawing enemy mortar fire. The tank commanders closed down, limiting their vision. In the thick mist, periscopes fogged. Two tanks careered off Route 11 and into paddies, and one threw both tracks. Without supporting infantry, the crippled tanks were vulnerable. Chinese tank-killer parties with pole charges and sticky bombs crept forward along the valley floor. However, the immobile tanks still had working turrets. Closed down, they machine-gunned each other, hosing off Chinese attempting to climb onto their hulls. The other tanks continued north. A sticky bomb on Lieutenant Radford's tank blasted a hole through his armoured skirt plate, but left his suspension undamaged; he continued. Ormrod stalked Chinese through the mist. An enemy section took cover in a house, which he obliterated with his 20-pounder. By now, Fusiliers, surprised at the action on the road, were arriving; the Chinese infantry fled. Captain Gavin Murray remained behind with an Armoured Recovery Vehicle to salvage the immobilised tanks as Ormrod continued north. His path was barred by a Chinese wielding a sticky bomb. Valour could not compete with fifty tons of armour: the enemy soldier died under the thrashing tracks. Time was ticking, though. Arriving at Foster's HQ, Ormrod briefed the colonel on the dicey situation to his south.[5] At 10:00 the Hussars informed the Fusiliers that the route was cleared of automatics, but 'there might be a few snipers left'.[6]

Following the counter-attack that had relieved Major John Winn's decimated Z Company, Fusilier wounded were evacuated at 09:25. Down the valley, Hussar medical officer Doug Patchett had been preparing an early lunch of American C rations when Major Miles Speer, the Fusiliers' second in command, approached and asked if he could take care of some wounded. Patchett, who 'didn't really have much option', acceded. Speer advised him to raise his half-track's armoured visor. Patchett did so, and 'chugged up and down three or four times', ferrying wounded to field ambulances at Brigade HQ.[7] The first Fusilier company to move, Major Robbie Leith-MacGregor's Y, was already heading down the valley by 09:55. The Fusiliers' order of march was Y Company, Z Company, Battalion Headquarters, W Company and X Company.[8] The Rifles' was C Company, Tactical CP, Main HQ, A and D Companies, and finally B Company and the engineers holding the saddle.

How long the dispute between Foster and Rickord delayed the withdrawal is unclear, but at 10:45 a note of frustration appears in the Fusiliers' War Diary: the Rifles 'had still not passed through'. 'Kingsley knew the Chinese were coming, and knew we had to get out fast,' said Perrins. In fact, the Rifles – whose hill was longer and higher than the Fusiliers' and whose withdrawal was delayed when covering artillery killed and wounded several members of C Company – were not assembled to move until 12:00 – two hours after the first Fusiliers had departed.[9] Foster was livid with Rickord. 'I'll court-martial that bastard!' he fumed to Perrins.*

---

* In an indication of the seriousness of the situation, Perrins noted that Kingsley Foster very rarely swore.

Still, movement was under way. Orders had gone to the companies on the hills. Picquet platoons would remain in position to cover those pulling out. Officers briefed men. Packs were stuffed, gear heaved on, webbing tightened. In the mist, wounded men were loaded onto ambulances; equipment was slung onto trucks, jeeps and carriers idling on Route 11. For most men – having held off the enemy for yet another night and unaware, at this stage, of the Glosters' fate, there was no especial fear. But time was passing and the mist was clearing.

Fusilier Derek Kinne, after assisting the evacuation of Z Company's wounded, returned to his platoon at X Company to find them assembling by the road for withdrawal. He had left his pack – with a St George's Day turkey sandwich and a photograph of his dead brother Raymond in it – at his platoon's abandoned sector. He doubled over to get it, ignoring cries of 'There are Chinese over there!' Grabbing the pack he sprinted back to the platoon, where his officer told Kinne he ought to be court-martialled. There was no heavy fire – yet – but rounds were whining in from the western hills.[10]

Among mounds of discarded ammunition crates, the combined mortars of the Fusiliers, Rifles and 170 Mortar Battery had been firing furiously. A decent mortar man can have twelve bombs in the air at once – the first one bursting on the target as the last one is dropped down the tube – and they had been ordered to fire off all ammunition,* before piling onto vehicles and getting out. Fusilier John Bayliss, having survived Z Company's hill battle, joined them as they headed down valley. Fusilier Vick Wear drove up past Z Company as they were departing. He had been sent to the rear the previous night; in the morning, he was dispatched up-valley in an Oxford carrier loaded with ammunition, escorted by Ormrod's Centurions. The carriers came under fire on the way, but Wear was more worried about being crushed by bouncing ammunition boxes than about the enemy rounds. The thunk-thunk-thunk of three mortars firing could be heard as the other tubes packed up and drove south: it was a half-section of Mole's. Wear, passing, noticed the half-section had a couple of Chinese prisoners loading bombs while Riflemen adjusted the sights: the barrels were at maximum elevation, minimum range. The mortars, with two Oxfords, had been ordered to remain as a rearguard, dropping a barrage as close as possible to the Rifles' positions on 398 to cover the pullback and maintain morale, for despite the Rifles' successful defence, the enemy was in close contact. At first light A

* No mortar ammunition could be left. Chinese forces had an advantage over the UN forces, in that their mortar bores were slightly larger, which meant that they could fire captured UN bombs from their tubes, whereas the reverse was not possible. See William B. Harrington, 'Mortars', in Tucker, p. 460.

Company's second in command, Captain John Lane, had moved just outside his perimeter to defecate. Chinese opened fire on the round white target, and Lane dashed back into cover with his trousers round his ankles, to the cheers of the company.[11]

Lance-Corporal Joe Farrell, on Hill 398, had been 'a wee bit annoyed' to receive withdrawal orders. 'Retreat? We'd kicked the shit out of 'em!' he said. 'We couldn't finish the job.' His platoon NCO, Sergeant Steward, had been wounded; blood was pouring down his legs. 'I wanted to hurt him for all the punishment he had given me, so I got a hold. You should've heard the squeals when I grabbed his legs! But he was a good old fella.' At the foot of the hill, Steward was loaded into an ambulance.* It would be the last one. Then the men on foot headed down the valley. Other soldiers on Hill 398 were much happier to move than Farrell – among them Mole, who knew of the Glosters' predicament. 'There was a feeling of "Bloody hell!"' he said. 'Some were saying they were disappointed to be pulled out – well, I bloody wasn't!' Gunner Bob Nicholls, with his observation team from 170 Mortar Battery, was with the Riflemen when the orders came. 'Men were swearing. We knew we were in trouble, but there was no panic,' he said. At the bottom of 398, 'there were dead Chinese lying everywhere. One Chinese guy had the cap off the bottom of a grenade, the fragmentation, buried in his thigh, and torn pants – I don't know if he had torn them himself,' Nicholls recalled. 'He wanted help, he was still alive. I felt sorry for him, but there was nothing we could do.' On the valley floor, rounds started coming over. 'They could see us from the other side of the valley,' Nicholls said. 'A ricochet hit a boulder in front of me – it pinged off in the other direction.' He joined men forming up by the track.

Lieutenant Peter Whitamore, with the Rifles' C Company, had successfully held off enemy probes throughout the night. There had been resentment among his men at having to withdraw. As they prepared to move off, artillery fire whooshed in to mask their pullback. One round landed short: two men were killed and more wounded, causing a delay. Lieutenant Max Nicholls and a medical orderly volunteered to remain behind and await an ambulance.[12]

Most of the infantry would have to walk three to four miles before they reached the comparative security of the open ground near Brigade HQ. Normally this would be about one hour's march, but this was not a normal time. The men were exhausted and shocked after three nights of sleepless combat. Yet this was the moment when their leaders and reactions had to be at their sharpest, for withdrawal while in contact with

---

* Farrell later met 'Stewardy' – whose wounds had healed – in Hong Kong. 'He wouldn't let anyone buy him a drink,' Farrell said. 'He was buying for us!'

the enemy is a desperately perilous enterprise. If a withdrawal breaks down, it can become a rout; a rout can turn into a massacre.

Even if they could not see the activity taking place in the valley through the layer of mist, the Chinese could hear movement. On the Imjin they had pushed 29th Brigade back, but had been unable to break its resistance. Now, with the British in the open, the Chinese opportunity had arrived. No longer in defensive posture, their enemy was vulnerable. 'The quality of decision is like the well-timed swoop of a falcon which enables it to strike and destroy its victim,' noted the great strategist Sun Tzu, a strong influence on guerrilla guru Mao. The 'Great Helmsman' himself advised concentrating superior force to destroy isolated enemy in detail, and to wipe out the enemy when he is moving.[13] Even a puppy has a chase instinct that compels it to pursue fleeing prey. As the British companies filed off their positions, the Chinese filled the vacuum. Surreptitiously, employing all their skill at camouflage and tactical movement, Chinese began massing on the western hills overlooking Route 11.

Along the valley floor – 100–300 metres wide – carriers, trucks, jeeps and ambulances bumped south down the winding track, carrying equipment and wounded. On foot, lines of weary infantrymen trudged beside Route 11. The men were spaced out; already bullets were cracking overhead. Puffs of smoke among the scrub and rocks on the hillsides marked the positions of snipers; spurts of dust on the track and in the paddies marked their fall of shot. Centurions squatted in defiles and perched on knolls, their commanders in their turrets scanning the ground for enemy firing points through binoculars.

It was now after 10:00.* On the valley floor, in the re-entrant holding the Rifles' Battalion HQ Second Lieutenant Mervyn McCord was preparing to move, waiting for the forward companies – A, C and D – to pass through. 'It was calm and orderly,' he said. 'There were battle drills for such things; we knew what to do.' Having returned from his meeting with Rickord, Shaw stopped to speak to McCord. Like many UN soldiers, the signals officer had a camera, obtained on R&R in Japan. The major asked McCord to snap his picture and send it to Marion, his wife. McCord was mystified at the request. Perhaps Shaw was concerned about the peril the battalion was in (this, after all, was the man who led the rearguard out of Happy Valley) – or perhaps – as McCord believed – he had a premonition. McCord took the picture. It shows the stocky officer standing grim-faced next to his jeep, in combat uniform, wearing a baggy caubeen and

---

* For reasons which will become plain, the events of 25 April on Route 11 are highly confused; unless otherwise stated, timings given here are approximate. Likewise, the exact locations of some events down Route 11 are uncertain.

leaning on a walking stick. There are ammunition boxes on the bonnet of the jeep; around him stand armed Riflemen. In the background, the mist is clearing. The narrow valley floor was becoming dangerous. Shaw warned passing men to stay away from the tanks – for tanks draw fire.

In the night battles, the Fusiliers and Riflemen had been fighting to hold ground, to win the battle. On this increasingly clear April morning the soldiers, in a four-mile enfilade, would be fighting for their lives. The bloodiest stage of the Battle of the Imjin River was about to begin. Half an hour after McCord snapped his picture, Major John Shaw would lie dead on the valley floor.

\* \* \*

For the Chinese, the key to keeping the British bottled up was the back-stop position on the saddle, held by the Riflemen of B Company and the Royal Engineers of 55 Squadron. Fighting broke out in this sector, while the troops struggling south towards it came under increasingly accurate gunfire. Roving tanks, shepherding the column and firing into the hills, could keep enemy heads down temporarily, but then shooting would resume somewhere else.

Fusiliers were posted as close support for one of the Centurions damaged earlier Kinne, who was one of them, settled into a covering position and debated what to eat. Deciding that his turkey sandwich would be more enjoyable if he ate it later, out of action, he cracked a C ration can. Meat noodles. Disgusted, Kinne hurled them into a paddy. The tank, repaired, roared into life. The Fusiliers were ordered to follow it south. By now, the fire coming in from the western hills was such that the men had to shout to communicate. For the first time, Kinne noticed Riflemen around. The retreat was becoming general.[14]

Farrell's platoon reached C Company. As they passed through C's positions, one of Farrell's mates, 'Big' Davy Crawford ran over and said, 'Joe, if I don't get out, go to my girl and tell her I love her!' Farrell reassured his friend that he would do so – though in fact he had no idea who Crawford's girlfriend was.\* By now skirmishes were erupting along the track between the retreating infantry and squads of infiltrators. 'We were fighting our way out,' said Farrell. 'They came running at us; we had a wee bit of a dig at them.' Still, there was no panic. 'I don't remember being sort of frightened that way – we were quite capable of taking them on. Every time we'd met 'em, we'd hammered 'em.'

C Company was moving when firing increased. 'It was calm and quiet, then it started to go wrong: we came under heavy fire from the hillside to

* Crawford was captured.

the west,' said Whitamore. 'It was mortar, machine-gun, small-arms fire – everything was being thrown at us. It was distinctly unpleasant.'

The situation was deteriorating. Kinne, moving south in short rushes, thought the increasing chaos was 'like a film running too fast, images on the screen passing too quickly for comprehension'. He took cover in a ditch next to a Rifles officer. The two recognised each other: the officer had given Kinne punishment duty on the ship on the way to Korea. The man grinned, wished Kinne luck, and ran on.[15]

Foster's plan – retreat down the valley floor at maximum speed – was coming unstuck. Captain Andrew Scott, second in command of the Fusiliers' W Company, was leading two platoons and Company HQ down the track while Major Charles Mitchell, the hero of Happy Valley, commanded the rearguard. From further down the valley, Scott radioed that he would wait for Mitchell and the picquet platoon. Mitchell told him 'unceremoniously to bugger off'! With the valley floor swept by fire, and with fighting under way around the saddle position ahead of them, Scott ditched the orders to move down the track and led his men up into the hills on the eastern side of the valley.[16]

Other groups were taking the same route. McCord, with the Rifles' Battalion HQ, was moving down the valley in fighting formation. 'We were dodging behind rocks and dodging Chinese. It took a long time to go a short distance.' McCord found himself behind a rock with the adjutant, Captain Hugh Hamill. 'The Chinese were using us as a shooting gallery from the other side of the valley. Someone had us in his sights, clipping the top off the rock. The adjutant said, "I'm senior officer here, you'd better fuck off!" So the next time there was a pause, I left. He was stuck there for some time afterwards.'* As groups approached the backstop position, it became apparent that continuing down Route 11 was suicide. 'In front of the saddle it was chaos, absolute confusion,' said McCord. 'I don't remember anyone giving orders – I think it was instinct or good soldiering – we took to the hills.' Signals Corporal Norman Sweetlove was with the same group, pinned down in a paddy. He too got up and ran. Hamill arrived at where the panting men were regrouping in a gully. 'The adjutant gave the order: "From now on, it's every man for himself!"' Sweetlove and the men around him ran off the road and began clambering up the scrub on the eastern hills. Rickord, with his CP, decided to move up too. 'I could see no point in slavishly sticking to the road . . . and ordered my company commanders to make use of whatever cover they could find in the hills on their left.'[17]

---

* The fact that so many officers – Foster, Mitchell, Hamill and others – opted to remain behind covering their subordinates' retreat reflects highly on their leadership at this desperate stage of the battle.

Whitamore was marching south, fast, with C Company, accompanied by clanking Centurions firing in support. 'A platoon of A Company commanded by Gordon Potts came past us marching very, very fast. They said to us, the faster we went the faster we would be out of it! We were running: I looked back and saw the rest of the battalion heading up the hills: as soon as I saw them, in a snake heading up into the hillsides, I thought, "God, we are on our own!" '*

Fusiliers Mortar Sergeant Bill Beattie was crouching in the back of an Oxford as it surged down the track; the carrier had armoured sides, but bullets were whining over its open top. He could see Chinese alongside the road, some with sticky bombs. Armed with a rifle, he could not shoot from the bucking vehicle, though men with automatics – Brens, Stens and carbines – were returning fire. Any vehicles that stalled were shoved off the roads by their tank escorts.[18] Many men were saved by the inaccuracy of Chinese fire. Nicholls, crouching in the cover of trucks, noticed that their canvas covers had been shot to pieces, but the drivers, and men hugging the wooden slats of the 3-tonners, keeping as low as possible, were not hit. Interpreter Lee Kyung-sik, moving back with the Rifles' porters, had lost all his personal equipment. The Chinese bullets, he thought, were 'pelting down in the paddies like raindrops'. Yet he got out – those behind were not so lucky.

The commander of the withdrawal was at the saddle held by the Rifles' B Company and sappers of 55 Field, supervising the loading of his last wounded onto vehicles. As Kinne's group came through, Foster reassured the Fusiliers, 'Just another mile, then you are home.'[19] Perrins, who a few hours previously had been snug in the rear, was now in the thick of it: he was asked to go up-valley by Foster – 'he didn't order me; the Fusiliers were a gentlemanly operation' – to find out how many Fusiliers remained north of the saddle. He did so, then returned to find that Foster had departed. 'When I got back I said, "Where is the colonel?" Two privates said, "He left in a jeep." I said, "Damn!"' Moments later, a pair of Centurions, heavily loaded with infantry piled on their hulls, rumbled up. Among them was Major Mitchell, in fine form – Fusilier Preston Little, with Perrins' intelligence section, had earlier seen him 'grinning and standing up as though on a Sunday School outing'.[20] Perched on the front of one of the tanks, Mitchell spotted Perrins and his men. 'He shouted, "Get on!"' Perrins said. 'So I jumped on and we hightailed it.'

---

* Rickord had got his way: Believing that this was no time to 'slavishly' stick to orders, he led his CP up along the ridges. Although he had earlier queried Foster's withdrawal plan, the reader should not assume that his action was insubordination. In the British Army, while orders are to be obeyed, officers and senior NCOs are also expected to exercise initiative and flexibility with respect to a changing situation. On the valley floor, the situation was rapidly going downhill.

Ormrod had earlier asked Foster if he would like to join him in his turret.[21] Foster had declined. At the saddle, he climbed into an artillery jeep. Major Dickie Miller, OC the Rifles' B Company, warned Foster that firing had broken out in the rear; and a jeep might not be the safest form of transport. 'Balls!' said Foster. 'You're a windy bugger. Get out of my way!'[22] Getting behind the wheel of the jeep alongside a pair of artillerymen, he gunned the engine.

What was on the mind of the Fusiliers' CO as he motored south? Probably matters tactical: his battalion, heavily outnumbered, had held a mass attack for three nights, losing just 2,000 yards of ground. Possibly matters personal: in a series of letters to his wife, Audrey, he had discussed the possibility of hiring one of his older reservists as a worker on the Foster estate. It was a kindness typical of Foster – but one that would never come to fruition. Crossing a small stream that cut across the track, his jeep's engine sputtered. Foster got out. A machine-gun crackled from the hillside. The Fusilier's CO – the paternal commander who had refused promotion to lead his battalion in battle – spun down, hit in head and chest.* The gunners in the jeep escaped on foot, under fire. Kingsley Foster lay face down in the water trickling across Route 11.[23]

\* \* \*

Preston-Bell and his Centurion crew, in position near the saddle, had finished adjusting the links on their track. The young Hussar was scanning the western hillsides when he was transfixed by a heart-stopping sight. 'In England in those days, you'd go shooting in the morning, and you'd go over the brow of a hill, and that whole hill would be moving with rabbits,' he said. 'It was just like that: suddenly, the whole hillside was moving!'

Watching the British withdrawal from the high ground, the Chinese had been sniping, machine-gunning, mortaring, infiltrating. Seeing their prey slipping through their grasp, their commanders made a bold decision. If they could get close enough to 'grab the enemy by his belt' his air and artillery support would be rendered useless, while their own

---

* One 29th Brigade officer considered Foster 'an ass' to die as he did. Others differ. 'I think in the case of [Lieutenant-Colonel H.] Jones in the Falklands, it is no business of a CO being a platoon commander,' said Malcolm Cubiss. 'But Kingsley Foster had fought a reasonably successful action and was seeing out the remnants of his battalion. He was in the rearguard – that is where he should have been! His job was to lead the battalion and inspire his soldiers, and they needed inspiring because it was a pretty peculiar affair.' In a letter to Foster's father – himself a former Fusilier colonel, who had seen his son off at the Southampton docks – Miles Speer, the battalion's second in command, wrote: 'I feel, writing as one soldier to another . . . that, if Kingsley had to be taken, to be killed in action commanding a battalion of the 5th Fusiliers is the way he would have liked it.' (Speer's letter is reprinted in St George's Gazette, 31 May 1951, p. 91.)

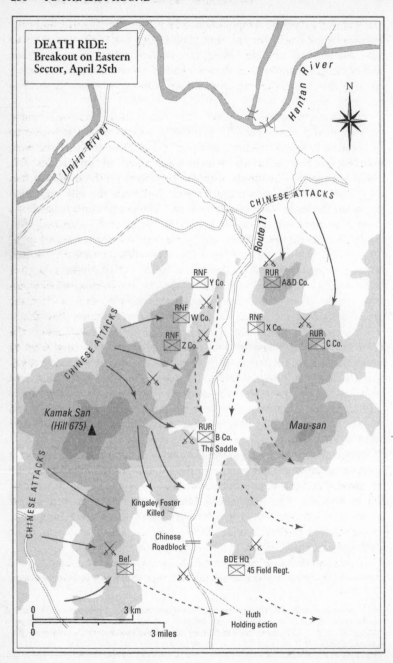

DEATH RIDE:
Breakout on Eastern
Sector, April 25th

short-range, automatic weapons would be maximally effective, and their numbers would tell. For the first time in this battle the enemy mass revealed itself in daylight. Along the western ridges, first tens, then scores, then hundreds, then thousands of Chinese soldiers broke cover. Dotting the slopes, they stood poised *en masse*, then surged down onto the valley floor.*

Whitamore, doubling along the valley floor with his platoon, thought he had left the enemy behind when the hills came to life. 'It happened in seconds: it was absolutely terrifying – the realisation that we were doomed,' he recalled as the human wave rolled on top of him. 'We could see enemy – hundreds of them! They were on the road, just feet away. I thought the tanks might leave us, so I made the silly suggestion to get on the tanks – we just jumped on.' The cross-country speed of a Centurion is fifteen miles per hour – far faster than exhausted, desperate men could run. Infantrymen scrabbled onto the armoured hulls. Wounded were manhandled onto rear decks and frantically secured with rifle slings or webbing to any protuberance. With soldiers dangling from their turrets like bunches of khaki grapes, the fighting vehicles barrelled down the track. But with infantry clinging to their hulls many would be unable to use their weapons effectively. And tanks draw fire.

Those men who had not found space on board ran alongside the Centurions, using them for what cover they offered as they tried to break through the swarming Chinese, who were now also running alongside the tanks, at ranges of from thirty metres to a few feet, firing burp guns and hurling grenades. 'We were in close proximity – shoulder to shoulder with the Chinese,' said Whitamore, perched on a tank and seeing the enemy clearly for the first time. 'I was amazed that they were wearing helmets; we were wearing caubeens.'

Patchett, in his ambulance half-track, was driving close behind a Centurion.† As the tank slewed round a bend, its tracks flung up a spray of gravel; Patchett, whose field of vision was restricted to the narrow slit in his visor, was momentarily blinded. His half-track swerved off Route 11, and clunked to a halt in a ditch.[24] Over their intercoms, Hussars heard Patchett's voice crackle over the net. 'I am about to be captured,' he reported. Then: 'I have been captured!'[25]

Where Patchett was taken, Route 11 curved around an S-bend, with a copse overhanging the track; a bank, ditches and trees provided cover.

---

* It is not known how many Chinese attacked down into the valley, but it was clearly a co-ordinated action. Farrar-Hockley (1995) estimates their numbers at a regiment (i.e. three battalions: 1,800–2,200 men); the 8th Hussars' regimental history puts the numbers at around 2,000.

† Patchett won the Military Cross for his succour of wounded men under fire.

Vehicles coming down this section of road had to decelerate to negotiate the sharp curve. Chinese commanders, past masters at placing ambushes on lines of communication, had seen the area's tactical potential, and troops with close-range anti-tank weapons had been fed down to this choke point. After three nights of bloody breakthrough attempts, the Chinese could now fight a battle of annihilation. The door on 29th Brigade's escape corridor was slammed shut.

Kinne, reaching the sector, watched a carrier try to move past a stalled tank. The track was too narrow, and the carrier teetered on the brink; another tank nudged it into the monsoon ditch. Bobbing among the copse, in ditches and behind banks, were seemingly hundreds of Chinese helmets. Kinne realised what he was looking at – a roadblock. Hearing the clatter of a Centurion behind him, he decided to run through in its wake. Jogging along in the exhaust fumes, he threw a grenade. Chinese returned fire. The tank accelerated – leaving the Fusilier exposed in the dust whirling over the track. He dived for a ditch and crawled past Patchett's half-track, hoping against hope that the enemy would miss one man in the mêlée. He rounded a bend. A Chinese squatted there, pointing a burp gun. Wordlessly, he motioned Kinne back towards the half-track, where prisoners were milling.[26]

Perrins, with W Company's rearguard and his intelligence section, was perched precariously behind a Centurion's turret. Reaching the bend in the track, the tank braked. Perrins was jammed against a young Fusilier; suddenly, his shoulder felt as if it had been hit with a hammer. The man had been shot, and his body had transmitted the kinetic energy to Perrins. The banks along the sides of the track, and the copse overhanging it, were alive with enemy. 'It was obviously an unhealthy place to be,' Perrins said; he jumped off the slow-moving tank and into the cover of Patchett's half-track. Dust fountained up around his feet. 'My mind went into slow motion. I remember thinking "What the bloody hell is this?" It eventually dawned on me that it was some bloody Chinaman shooting at me. So I walked around the back of the half-track in slow motion. Your brain switches off; it gets rid of the extraneous when you are under great stress, though I didn't realise it. Well, on the far side of the ditch were half a dozen Chinese firing burp guns. The stream between was full of Fusiliers, unarmed – some wounded, some not. I thought, "Do I fire back with my .45?" But the odds were insurmountable. I threw my pistol down.' Perrins was placed beside the track. Little had also abandoned the tank as it nego-tiated the curve. He ran. Burp guns sounded around him, grenades burst around his ankles. Lurching on, he realised that he had had it; it was time to give up. But at that moment another tank passed and he was somehow dragged aboard.[27]

The retreat was disintegrating. Whitamore, horrified, saw men shot off the tanks, and ground under the tracks of the Centurions behind. As his tank entered the roadblock's kill zone, a Chinese soldier hurled a phosphorus grenade. At that range – a few metres – he could hardly miss, but his timing was perfect: the explosive detonated on the rear deck. Liquid flame was sucked into the engine's air intakes. The vehicle brewed up. The crew threw open hatches and tumbled out. The men riding on the hull were hurled to the ground as the smoking tank shuddered to a halt.* 'It set my battledress ablaze and I was thrown into a ditch,' said Whitamore. 'I tugged off my blouse; I had phosphorus burns on my fingers and my back was bloody sore. Running, I came face to face with a Chinaman who aimed his rifle at me. I hadn't got one, so thought, "Enough is enough!" It was the worst moment, being captured: complete desolation. I had read all about the ill treatment of the Japanese; I was terrified of being taken prisoner by Orientals.'

\* \* \*

To the north, the Riflemen of B Company, who had been holding the saddle, were heading into the hills; the engineers were also moving out. Sapper Sergeant Reg Orton had organised the men riding on the hull of his tank to shoot back at Chinese lining both sides of Route 11. As the tank charged down-valley, a Molotov cocktail burst on the front armour; the vehicle barrelled off the track. Orton was thrown to the ground. As he staggered to his feet a Chinese with a burp gun appeared and ordered him, in English, to surrender. Orton, unarmed, stepped in close and knocked the man unconscious with a flurry of punches. Then he ran over to the tank, stripped off his jacket and doused the fire – saving the driver, in his front hatch, from having his face burned off. The tank commander was wounded. Orton scrambled up into the turret, and gave rapid orders. The gunner traversed and fired into the Chinese surrounding them, then the tank restarted and accelerated away – saved by the engineer's action.†

Captain Peter Ormrod had been fighting north of the saddle when he heard Patchett's last radio call in his intercom. 'This alerted me to the fact that something pretty disastrous was going on in the rear,' he said. With innumerable enemy dotting the hillsides, Chinese formations were

---

\* The Centurion did not burn for long. Perrins, lying with a group of captured, noted that once the fire burned out, the tank looked only as if its paintwork had been scalded.

† Orton won the Distinguished Conduct Medal for this action. He was subsequently invited to the United States with other decorated veterans of UN units, where he was granted the freedom of New York and met President Truman. This information, and the account of Orton's action, comes from Tony Younger's obituary of Orton (undated fragment) passed to me by Brigadier Dick Webster, 8th Hussars.

heading for his Centurions. 'With the tank gun we would just mow them down. They were everywhere! They were coming on and on, we couldn't hold them,' Ormrod recalled. 'They were coming along the valley, along the sides of the hills.'[28] In the chaos several drivers closed down. Peering through periscopes and vision blocks in close combat against infantry, the crews had little time to react to changes in the ground. Sergeant Holberton's Centurion careered over a paddy bank at speed, and speared its gun deep into the paddy. His vehicle was immediately immobilised.[29]

With the last of the Fusiliers and Rifles now behind him, climbing up into the eastern hills, or clambering onto tanks, and with Chinese all around, Ormrod realised that his tanks, lacking infantry protection, were in danger of being cut off. Of the Centurions disabled in the morning, one had been recovered; the other was destroyed by Murray. Ordering the half-squadron to move south, Ormrod set off down-valley, at the head of his seven remaining runners.[30] Preston-Bell, watching the general move south, decided to join.* 'I thought we should go, too; it seemed the obvious thing to do,' he said. With his gun traversed backward, the cornet took aboard as many infantry as he could.

Ormrod's Centurions thundered over the now-abandoned saddle and down the other side. Ahead was the roadblock. 'I could see the doctor's half-track, and two of my tanks on fire as well, and a swarm of Chinese – fifty or so – crowding around, and the doctor standing with his hands up and I knew that a pretty awful ambush had occurred,' Ormrod recalled. Among the trees lurked Chinese anti-tank teams with incendiaries, pole charges and sticky bombs. As his racing Centurion bore down upon the roadblock, Ormrod's instincts – honed by the cavalry officer's favourite pastime – took over. 'I, personally, am a horse-racing man: many of us rode to hounds, galloping across country,' he said. 'That certainly helps when you are commanding a tank across country, so I called on everyone to take off and follow!' The captain led his tanks off Route 11: bumping and banging across the open paddies in a cloud of dust, they hurtled around the ambush before rejoining the track two hundred metres further south.[31] Preston-Bell caught a snapshot glimpse of Patchett, surrounded by enemy, next to his wrecked half-track. 'He was standing there, smiling, waving at us as we went by.'

Trooper Denis Whybro was astounded by the enemy's sudden proximity. 'There were Chinese all around us, on either side, getting under the tracks,' he said. And his tank had engine problems. 'We were backfiring all the way, blowing the exhaust manifold – it was scary. I was

---

* Boyall says he ordered the rest of his troop back while he held the rear. In the confusion, orders may have been misheard or misunderstood.

halfway out of the turret and I had all my Mills bombs, ready to bale out.' His tank did not follow Ormrod, but plunged into the ambush. A smoking Centurion was blocking the track. 'We came to the roadblock – it was a terrific fire, they'd set something alight.* I said [to the driver], "Go on Dickie boy, go on, right through it!" He stuck the old tank in and we climbed right up over the top.'[32] A wounded Fusilier lying captured at the roadblock, Sergeant David Sharp, watched in amazement as Whybro's Centurion rammed the blazing tank out of its path and rumbled through.[33] Whybro looked helplessly down at the prisoners from his turret. 'I was looking over the side and all the Chinese were running round all the prisoners – we couldn't do nothing.' But not every Chinese was running. Whybro spotted a group carrying sticky bombs. So did the Centurion following him. It fired without stopping. Twenty pounds of high explosive blew the tank-killing group, and a hut behind them, to pieces.[34]

With armour thundering past and through the ambush, the prisoners around the roadblock were in as much danger as the Chinese. 'The one moment in the whole experience when I knew I was dead was when I found myself staring up the barrel of a Centurion's 20-pounder,' said Perrins. 'The gunner saw us, he saw the Chinese around us, and as he roared past, his turret moved.' The big gun did not go off, but its machine-gun squeezed off a single round. At such close range, the high-velocity bullet was devastating. 'It tore parts off of John De Quidt, took a shilling piece out of the shinbone of Peter Whitamore, and what was left of the bullet landed in my leg and broke it,' said Perrins. 'It was like being hit by a sledgehammer,' said Whitamore. 'It was bloody painful.' Whitamore, 'white as paper', asked Perrins if he had any morphine. Perrins fiddled around inside his camouflage smock, produced a dusty pack of syrettes, gave him a shot, and then 'said "Would you mind giving me one?" and Whitamore said, "What the fuck for?" I said, "I've got a broken leg!" He turned deep puce and gave me a shot. Boy, it was wonderful stuff.'

Past the ambush, Ormrod led the charge. His tanks were spaced out, enemy scattering to their front. A deep ditch appeared ahead of him – too late to brake – his Centurion ran in and stuck fast. Ormrod could hear bullets pinging off his armour, but stuck his head out to instruct his driver. The driver engaged reverse – the tracks thrashed – the tank began climbing out backwards. As it did so, a Chinese clambered onto the rear deck. Ormrod drew his pistol, fired, missed. The urgent voice of the tank commander following crackled over his intercom – 'Get your head down, I'll blow them off!' Ormrod ducked into his turret, as the Centurion

---

* Obviously, the tank brewed up by the phosphorus grenade.

behind sprayed his hull with a long burst of Besa fire, killing the attacker. Ormrod's tank exited the ditch. A nearby group of British infantry, seizing their chance, jumped aboard.[35]

The one-eyed Hussar's ride recommenced, but his luck ran out further down the track. His head was out of his turret when there was a flash. Grenade shrapnel ricocheted from his tank's armour; Ormrod felt as if a 'heavyweight boxer had given me a blow on the side of the head'. Ormrod put his hand up; it came away bloody. Concussed, his skull cracked, the captain wavered in and out of consciousness as his pitching tank continued down the valley.[36]

Sergeant Cadman's crew were driving closed down when they heard a hammering on their hatch: an enemy soldier on their turret. If he could fix a magnetic mine to the thin top armour, they were dead men. Cadman ordered his driver to aim for a cottage beside the road and accelerate. The engine rose to a roaring whine; the speeding tank struck the building, which disintegrated in an explosion of thatch and wattle as the Centurion burst through; the unwelcome rider didn't stand a chance. Coming out the other side, trailing bits of house, the tank was confronted by a machine-gun in the paddy; Cadman ploughed the gun and its crew under his tracks. An enemy company rose from cover. Geysers of earth and dust blasted up among their ranks as the charging tanks opened fire.[37]

The breakout was almost surreal for some. Despite the intense fire – Chinese were lining the track shooting, some barely six feet from his tank – Preston-Bell was unaware of noise. 'The brain said, "There are more important things to do than listen."' Scenes flashed by. 'Too much was happening to be frightened. It seemed like a game, a daydream.' Standing in his turret with his hatch up 'like a saucepan' for rear protection, the cornet shot into the enemy crowds with a carbine. 'Whether I hit anything, I don't know, but I was a good shot. Then I heard a "ping!" as a bullet went off the turret rim in front of me. My immediate reaction was to raise two fingers and shout "You've missed" – until I began to think what would happen if any of the enemy alongside threw a grenade in.'

That thought did not last, as Preston-Bell spotted the most extraordinary sight of the Imjin battlefield. A dozen Chinese piled out of a ditch, pursuing the tank as it pounded past them round a curve in the track. As the Centurion took the bend, the turret traversed, the 20-pounder swung over them and the squad dropped. One remained standing. 'Their leader – I saw him for a fraction of a second – turned his back to us to shout at his troops. He seemed to be wearing a Napoleonic hat and was carrying a scimitar! I thought: If they are attacking us with swords . . . !'* The thought of fighting with bladed weapons planted 'a worm of fear' inside the Hussar. Then another peril on the road in front seized his attention.

The Chinese were using everything in their arsenal to kill the tanks. Over the intercom, Preston-Bell's driver alerted him that a string of box mines – wooden boxes packed with explosive, designed to blow off tracks – had been dragged across the road. Route 11 at this point was a bund, raised some four feet above the paddies. At the speed they were moving, a fall would be disastrous. To avoid the mines, the driver swerved off the road exactly where an abandoned jeep lay burning alongside the track. The right-hand tread of the Centurion spun over the jeep, and a piece of the crumpled vehicle was whipped up into the moving track. Metal, caught between track and sprocket, causes a tank to stall; once it restarts, the track rolls off the sprocket; the tank is disabled. 'This had happened twice in training,' said Preston-Bell. 'So I knew this was the end of us.' The tank juddered to a halt, and the engine stalled as the metal caught in the sprocket. Time slowed. Cramped inside their steel shell, the crew held their breaths. Long seconds passed. The engine roared back to life. The driver engaged gear. The track – miraculously – sprang back on. The adjustment the crew had made earlier had saved them. The dash south recommenced.

The final tank down the valley was David Boyall's. The Australian lieutenant had been fighting off enemy with the last members of the sapper detachment who had been holding the saddle, commanded by Captain Desmond Holmes. Wounded were shoved onto Boyall's rear deck, then sappers climbed aboard. 'There were Chinese all around,' said Boyall. 'It was obvious that they were behind us, they were down at the road and I could see others coming down the hillside.' Holmes stood in the turret next to Boyall, firing his rifle, as they set off south. The last Centurion was now the sole focus for hundreds of Chinese. Bullets thwacked into the bundles of men clustered round its turret,

---

* Again, I am indebted to Brian Kennedy for a possible explanation. 'My first guess is that this was some idiosyncratic thing with the specific officer – like Patton walking around with his riding crop, which was neither standard issue nor particularly necessary to goad a tank along, or like some of the photos you see of US troops deploying to Iraq and wearing the old, Indian War-type US Army Cavalry hats. What I am driving at is, it may well have been some CPVA officer who thought wearing a Ching dynasty helmet and carrying a sabre into combat a good way to rouse Chinese *esprit de corps* or to somehow spook the other side. My other guess is this was some officer from northern China, and he decided to outfit himself in a way that would have been fairly normal about a decade earlier. "Big knife" [scimitar] units fought along the Great Wall during the early part of World War II and, because of their poverty, were often self-outfitted with older rattan-style helmets/conical hats and double-handed sabres.' Perhaps the apparition was not that bizarre after all: one wonders what Chinese soldiers would have made of seeing the Hussars' commander, Sir Guy Lowther, hurling a lance into the soil while celebrating affiliation with the Royal Australian Regiment.

explosions rang against its armour, and bursts cracked overhead. 'It was a dreadful business!' said Boyall. Revving their whining engine at maximum pitch, churning up great clouds of dust behind them, the last crew of Hussars thundered south through the funnel of fire.

\* \* \*

After covering the Belgian breakout across the river on the 23rd, and having spent the night with an American artillery unit, Second Lieutenant Henri Wolfs had been listed as missing. When he and his armed jeeps returned to his battalion on the 24th – to the surprise of all – Lieutenant-Colonel Albert Crahay reappointed him a platoon commander in C Company, which, having taken the weight of the attack on the first night of battle, was short of officers. Wolfs had made himself immediately popular with his new command by distributing a haversack of cigarettes and coffee obtained from the Americans. After repositioning one of the platoon's two Brens, he dozed off. He awoke in sunshine to find his grinning men standing over him: he had slept the entire night. One told him that they had been poking him without success, as they 'were worried his snoring would alert the entire Chinese Army'. He was handed a scalding mug of coffee. It was the morning of the 25th.

Having regrouped after their pullback over the river, the Belgians were dug in on a long, low ridge, covering the western side of the valley in which lay Brigade HQ. They had no visual contact with the Fusiliers and Rifles to their north-east. Supported by Hussar Lieutenant Ted Paul's four Centurions, they sat in their positions. At mid-morning Wolfs was informed that the Puerto Ricans* had pulled back, and large numbers of Chinese were advancing. A and C Companies were ordered to fall back to the east, to set up blocking positions at the bottom of Route 11. Their orders: hold open the route for the Rifles and the Fusiliers as they fought south. Wolfs's platoon position would be on the battalion's extreme right. This would mean he would be the last to come into contact with Chinese advancing from the north or west, but also the last to leave during a pullback to the east or the south. His platoon took up new positions in front of the low hills, and waited. Watching from his tank, Paul became aware of enemy contact when firing started crackling. He could see enemy movement on the high ground through his binoculars. The firing grew more intense; the Belgians were under attack from two directions -- the south-west and the north-west.

---

* These were the Puerto Ricans of the 65th Infantry Regiment. The two battalions, plus a Filipino Battalion Combat Team, were the force that 3rd Division commander General Robert Soule had massed for the breakthrough to the Glosters. But, with reports of Chinese to the south, the relief force was given a new mission: it was ordered to protect the MSR.

RASC vehicles had been ordered up to load the Belgians' heavy equipment in preparation for their withdrawal. Corporal John Coleman-Wood, by now well known among 29th Brigade for his comedy act, arrived in a convoy of jeeps and trucks. Incongruous amid the tactically painted vehicles was Coleman-Wood's bright blue entertainment truck – 'It stuck out like a sore thumb!' It was his first time at the front line. The vehicles pulled into a paddy where Belgian soldiers hurled gear aboard. Over a rise some 400–500 metres away, Coleman-Wood could see advancing Chinese. 'I yelled at the Old Man, "I think it's time we left!"' The convoy took off, but to return to the track, they first had to drive towards the enemy. Coleman-Wood jumped into the jeep next to his commander, Major Allan Andrews – 'and the bloody thing wouldn't start!' The ignition kicked in on the fourth try. The jeep bumped up the track towards the Chinese, who were now so close Coleman-Wood could see them smiling. The entertainer groped for his rifle, then realised he had left it at base. The jeep sped past the Chinese to catch up with the rest of the RASC column.

The Belgians' orders were to stand fast until the Rifles had cleared the valley to their north-east, but Rickord had taken his CP into the eastern hills, and radio contact was lost. Strong enemy forces were now closing in from two sides, threatening to cut off the Belgians. Crahay and his French-speaking liaison officer, Hussar Captain the Honourable Roland Winn,* were in tense radio contact with Brigade. With minutes to spare before the pincers closed, Major Huth, in open ground at the bottom of Route 11, reported that he could see Ormrod's tanks approaching down the track, and lines of infantry heading south down the eastern hills. Permission was given to pull out.

A fighting withdrawal began, with the Centurions, their guns traversed to their rear, shooting behind them. One of the tanks' transmissions jammed in reverse gear, meaning it could move at less than walking pace. Huth radioed Paul to destroy it, but Crahay, moving alongside the tank with his tactical CP, refused, saying, 'No, no, we must keep it as long as we can!'[38] With enemy pressing into close contact, the tank's firepower – its Besa and 20-pounder were both firing into the advancing Chinese, and the Belgian executive officer, Major Viverio, was firing a machine-gun from the turret[39] – made it too valuable to give up, however slow.[40] Shooting over their shoulders, the Belgian troops kept pace with the crippled Centurion. 'They were splendid!' said Paul.

---

* Winn had served with SOE in World War II and left the Hussars, his original regiment. When he heard the Hussars were deploying for Korea, he turned up at the last moment and was taken on board – though, with no paperwork, he was not officially on strength for months.

246 · TO THE LAST ROUND

Wolfs's platoon was holding its blocking position near the bottom of Route 11. At around 13:00 word came down that most British were clear of the valley, that Chinese had taken their former company position and were advancing in his platoon's direction. At this point, the platoon radio 'went permanently onto no-sound channel', so Wolfs sent the signaller off to see if he could do anything; he never saw him again. A Chinese platoon was advancing towards Wolfs and his men. At 300 metres Wolfs's platoon opened fire; they were also pleased to see explosions bursting among the enemy ranks from tank fire. But fountains of dust were spurting across his position. The Chinese had their range. A Bren gunner was killed, the loader wounded. The platoon only had two LMGs, and their firepower was critical to stave off assaults, so Wolfs dived behind the smoking weapon, and took over, firing bursts at enemy closing in from his front and flank. Concentrating totally, he was locked into what fighter pilots call 'target fascination' and was totally unaware of what was happening to his rear. Snatching a glance backwards, he 'nearly had a fit'. He had not realised that the rest of the battalion, and the tank rearguard, had passed behind him. His platoon was now the focus of the entire attacking force. Deciding 'to call it a day', he ordered his men to abandon the Brens – weighing twenty-two pounds, they would be an encumbrance – and escape. With his platoon fleeing, Wolfs threw the Bren he had been firing on top of the abandoned one and hurled a grenade at the pile. Then he ran too. He seemed to be outside his own body – 'it was as if I were playing in someone else's show' – as he sprinted for the tanks. There came a sudden 'searing pain' in his right buttock – 'but it didn't interfere with my running!' A second round tore into him. Again it was in the backside; again it was a flesh wound. He collapsed safe behind the Centurions. For the second time in the battle Wolfs had been the last man off the Belgian position.*

Paul was attempting to tow the lame Centurion, and his tank had its turret traversed back to shoot behind it. By extraordinary bad luck – a million to one chance – a Chinese bullet ignited one of the phosphorus grenades in its launcher on Paul's turret. Burning liquid seethed into the engine intakes. As the Centurion brewed up, the crew jumped clear; Crahay, standing next to the tank, was severely burned on the arm. But the Belgians had made it to the bottom of the valley, to the cover of a small copse. Huth rolled forward, and from fifty metres, fired armour-piercing rounds into the damaged Centurions. Paul, tankless, picked up a carbine lying on the battlefield.

* * *

* Wolfs was awarded the American Silver Star for his actions. The citation states that he refused an order to abandon the position, which he denies, but his rearguard action was critical.

It is a Hollywood tradition that the cavalry will arrive just in time to save the situation, but during three days of relentless combat, 29th Brigade had enjoyed no such luck. By midday on 25 April its continued existence looked doubtful. Contact with the Glosters was lost, and up Route 11 the western hills had been abandoned; the only British troops still up the valley were desperate pockets of men, vehicles and tanks fighting their way south or retreating on foot along the hills and ridges to the east. One man now stood between the advancing enemy and Brigade HQ and the British line of retreat: Henry Huth.

A photograph was taken of the major on the morning of the 25th, before the battle commenced. He is perched on his turret hatch. Around him are Belgian officers and his loader. These are experienced soldiers, hard men tested in battle. There is a grimness to their expressions. All know the risks they will have to run this day. Having discussed the tactical difficulties of the withdrawal with Younger, Huth was fully aware of the perils facing the brigade. Yet this soft-spoken veteran, this highly experienced Hussar 'who enjoyed the challenge of battle', has a great grin on his face; he appears to be having the time of his life.

With the last Belgians moving behind him through the copse, Huth's tank stood for three minutes, holding off the enemy at a range of around seventy metres. His turret swivelled back and forth, his chattering machine-gun stitched the ground, blasted bark off trees, forcing the enemy into cover as the Belgians retreated. Then he stationed his own tank and that commanded by Lieutenant John Lidsey at the mouth of the valley.[41] Bravery is only one qualification for a professional soldier. Tactical judgement, a sense of timing and appreciation of terrain are equally critical. At the bottom of the valley, where Route 11 emerges from between the low hills tumbling down into paddy, Huth had chosen a piece of open, flat ground where he could optimise his tanks' firepower and manoeuvrability to delay the on-rushing Chinese.

Ormrod, leading his tanks south, appeared at the bottom of the valley. Blood pouring from his head, he slewed his Centurion to a halt in front of Huth's to report. Reeling in his turret, half conscious, he blurted, 'I'm sorry, I've lost half your squadron!' Huth's response was terse: 'For God's sake, get out of the way!' Ormrod's tank was in his line of fire.[42] Whybro, following, noticed Paul, standing behind Huth's turret, legs apart, firing his carbine:* 'He looked like he was shooting pheasants!'[43]

---

* A dramatic photograph was taken of Paul, taking aim, in the last hour of battle. While the Hussar officer says the enemy was around 200 metres away and incoming fire was not heavy, the menace of the situation may be surmised from the photographer's position: the shot is taken from behind Paul, at a low angle. Paul did not remain shooting long, however. With no extra ammunition for the carbine he had picked up, he only had the rounds in the magazine.

With Chinese close behind the retreating British, Huth and Lidsey opened fire. The leading Chinese pulled back at the sight of the two vehicles. The tanks advanced, taking ground, firing again. Cramped inside the vibrating Centurions, amid the fumes blasted back from the breeches, the crews communicated in snatches of conversation over the intercom, instinctively reacting to the orders of their commanders – 'Driver, advance 100 yards!' 'Gunner, fire front!' Tugging the heavy shells up from lockers in the deck as the tanks lurched unexpectedly this way and that, banged against the metal protuberances inside the turrets, the crews fired and reloaded. The whine of the engines and the squeaking of tracks mixed with the buzz of radio sets, the crack of the 20-pounders and the hammer of the Besas. Both commanders, defying bullets buzzing around their ears, stayed in their turrets. Visibility was critical. In contact this close, if a tank went over a paddy dike, or missed a tank-killing team as it crawled forward, its crew would not have a chance.

Everyone who saw those two Centurions, operating almost instinctively, agreed that their command of the battle was exceptional. At times they were firing at right angles to the line of withdrawal, as Chinese tried to get past. Observers could clearly see the safety zone the tanks created shifting back and forth as they manoeuvred in response to enemy movements. The holding action bought critical time and space for those escaping.

The last knots of infantry were straggling in. Sweetlove was in a group of some twenty-five Riflemen who had gone over the hills. As they descended the slope, above them, enemy shouted, 'Stop! You are fighting America's war!' 'They had to bend over to see us,' Sweetlove said. 'We had to run for it. They were shooting down on us – we couldn't shoot up there. Luckily, none of us were hit.' The men came to a natural pool and dropped flat to drink. Chinese bullets kicked up fountains ahead of them – 'contaminating the water'! The Riflemen splashed through, and ran on to the MSR. Sweetlove jumped onto the mudguard of an American ambulance, which carried him south.

With enemy forty or fifty metres behind, McCord, traversing the western slopes of the eastern hills, strove to keep a grip on his men as they moved by leaps and bounds, firing back to cover the next group. One man broke and ran. This was no time for niceties. McCord smashed him with his rifle butt, and got him back in line.* A group of enemy prisoners escaped in the confusion; pursuing Chinese fired on them. Below, the valley was a maelstrom. 'We could see the fighting down there, it was a death trap, a mêlée,' said McCord. 'You could see a tank running through a house, you could see tanks shooting Chinese off

* After the battle, the man who had panicked thanked McCord for saving his life.

each other . . . it is etched in one's mind, like a film.' After three days of patrol actions, he was drained. 'I was on autopilot, but the training keeps you going. You fight your way down; you make for the place you are going to.' Reaching the end of the ridge, McCord plunged down the hill, dragging an artillery FOO who had lost his glasses and was clinging to McCord's webbing.* Running across the paddies under fire, he approached a tank firing at Chinese 200 metres away. McCord recognised Huth in his turret, 'looking as calm as if he were on exercise'! Dashing behind the Centurion, McCord called, 'Thanks, Henry!' 'For fuck's sake get out of it, I can't hold much longer!' Huth roared back.

One of the last Riflemen out of the trap was Farrell; he had become separated from his unit. 'I don't know how. After a couple of hundred yards, I'd lost the company!' He followed D Company along the hillside, when he heard something behind him. He turned to see a giant Chinese – 'He looked to be 6 feet 5!' – twenty yards away, in pursuit. 'I fired and I could see the front of his jacket plucking; it was the last round in the Sten. He turned and fell down the hill, but I had no faith in a Sten at that distance, so I gave him a couple of grenades.' Hurling away the empty SMG, Farrell ran on. Ahead was a body, with a rifle and eighty rounds in a bandolier. Farrell grabbed it – 'I was happy again' – and jogged on. Reaching the southern slope of the hill, he slid down and headed south across the paddies. A squad of Chinese broke cover and gave chase. The Rifleman dropped flat, picked a target and started firing when he heard a voice behind yelling 'Hubba, hubba!' Farrell 'nearly fell through the floor' – like Wolfs, he had tunnel vision, and had not heard a Centurion pull up right behind him. Fire from the tank swept his pursuers: 'It must have got them all.' Farrell scrambled onto the tank's piping-hot engine deck and was carried off. 'I was knackered, finished up,' he said. 'That was my war over for the day.'

* * *

At 08:00 American officers had gathered at Brigade HQ to discuss the Glosters' rescue with Brodie. Colonel William Harris of the Puerto Rican 65th Infantry Regiment, part of General Robert Soule's US 3rd Infantry Division, was invited to join the Brigadier for tea in his mess tent. He was astonished at the scene. 'What I saw and heard scared the hell out of me. Their CP tent was actually being hit by rifle bullets and the entire area was being bombarded with heavy mortars.' Harris's force had been stripped of its infantry, who were heading south to hold the MSR; all he had left were tanks. Although Brodie had given Carne

* McCord, a keen middle-distance runner, was one of the brigade's fittest officers.

permission to break out at 06:05, Soule's deputy, Brigadier Armistead Meade, also visiting, demanded a relief operation go in. Harris, aware that tanks would be vulnerable, decided to risk the smallest possible force: the attack that was to have been mounted with a battalion of tanks, three battalions of infantry and heavy artillery was launched with a single platoon of four light tanks that left without an FOO. The tanks fired off all their ammunition, then retired. Harris sent out another platoon, but Huth, familiar with Route Five Yankee's unsuitability for armour, intervened. The platoon was recalled.[44]

Alongside Brigade HQ was the gun line of 45 Field Regiment. Lieutenant George Truell, working his guns, came under machine-gun fire from enemy infiltrators on a ridge 400 metres to his front at around 10:15. The gunners had an appropriate reply. There had been no use for anti-aircraft fire in 29th Brigade's war so far, but now its AA element – 11 'Sphinx' Light Anti-Aircraft Battery – found a role. With high rates of fire and muzzle velocity, their Bofors guns replied with 40mm rounds. As Truell put it, 'a 40mm could be used like a very heavy machine-gun', and each round caused a grenade-like impact. Major Digby Grist's scratch group of Glosters, deployed to provide close support for the pitching, crashing 25-pounders, added small-arms fire, holding the Chinese off. But Truell had little leisure to watch the duel under way to his front. 'A hell of a lot of things were going on. We had a couple of soldiers wounded, I was busy trying to co-ordinate our eight guns, and infantry arrived at our position, completely worn out.'

Moreover, the artillery were pulling out. The guns' withdrawal got under way soon after the Fusiliers had started their move down the valley. At 10:30 the first battery moved back three miles. At 11:30 the second battery limbered up and drove off. At 14:00 Truell – who had been firing his battery at ranges of just 1,500 yards to support the retreating infantry coming south – was visited by Brodie. 'He said, "I think you had better go, or we will have the guns overrun."' Truell hitched up his pieces, loaded his vehicles, took aboard as many infantry as he could and headed south.

Most members of 29th Brigade fought desperately to get out, but one man – Fusilier Lieutenant Malcolm Cubiss, evacuated wounded after the first night – made his way back to the battlefield. Conveyed through dressing stations and MASH units where he was patched up and then sent along to the next, he had discharged himself from a Seoul hospital and hitched a lift up the MSR. Arriving at Brigade HQ he was shocked. The Bofors were firing with barrels depressed at milling Chinese he could see further up the valley. 'It looked like the retreat from Moscow. It was bloody chaos.' He found his way to Battalion HQ. The RSM was breaking open ammunition crates and sending the rounds up about 300 yards where a holding action was under way. Foster was dead, Cubiss was told. 'It was pretty hairy,' he said. 'The soldiers looked knackered; they had had no sleep for three days.' He found his platoon. Of twenty-six men who had entered the battle, eight remained.

The scarred, battered tanks were arriving from up-valley, dropping bloody heaps of wounded at a casualty collection point. 'We'd got a lot of blokes on the tank, some wounded and some of them dead,' said Whybro. 'I don't know if they were dead when they got on. They were when they got off.' He and his crew unloaded the infantry next to a waiting ambulance. One man was unable to move; with a bullet in his back, he was helped down. Then, the dead. One casualty had 'a little cut in his abdomen, there was no blood, but he was as dead as a doornail. The other bloke . . . it was colossal.'[45] The head-shot Ormrod, half-conscious, was lifted out of his turret; his radio operator tried to reassure him by telling him that he would write to his mother if the captain didn't make it. His crew wiped him down and bandaged him up, then left him at an American dressing station on the MSR. He was pumped full of morphine and laid among a group of casualties lying on stretchers. He could hear enemy fire approaching. Spotting a British ambulance 'covered with blood' he asked for a lift. The ambulance halted, the Hussar was pitched into the back among a jumble of wounded, and the driver took off. 'I reckon the people on the stretchers never got away,' he said.[46] Preston-Bell's tank pulled up at Brigade HQ, where the infantry 'climbed off, fell off, were taken off'. A fortunate few had not been hit; they had been lying under others. Most were in shock. 'There was none of this "Oh my God, you have saved my life!" It was just "Thanks, mate."' The hulls and turrets of the Centurions that had ferried infantry were streaked with crimson. Others, having ground enemy – and, in some cases, friendly – troops under their tracks, had human debris hanging from their treads and suspensions. McCord took one look at the tanks: 'God, they were covered in blood and gore!'

Preston-Bell realised his own nervous reaction when, after sitting down on a petrol drum, he tried to stand: 'I was so shit scared, I could not make my legs work,' he said. Exhaustion was also taking its toll. Having led his company out, Fusilier Major Robbie Leith-MacGregor sat for a smoke. He was suddenly jerked up by a hot sensation in his fingers: he had nodded off, and the cigarette had burned down to the stub. Cubiss noted that his platoon survivors were so punch drunk it took them a minute and a half to light a cigarette. Younger watched a line of shattered infantry straggling in; despite their imminent peril, they seemed to be moving in slow motion.[47]

The wreckage of Brodie's command – zombie-like groups of infantry, bullet-holed vehicles, tanks heaped with bloody wounded – was falling

back around him. HQ was packing up and racing south to the next position. The Brigadier appeared devastated. 'He thought he had lost the
brigade,' said Cubiss, who passed him as he led the survivors of his platoon south. 'He thought he had lost the Glosters completely; he wasn't
sure about the Ulsters and the Fusiliers. The whole thing was collapsing.' Boyall, in the last Centurion, caught a glimpse of Brodie as he
drove through with his cargo of wounded: it was the only time the lieutenant had ever seen him without his red-banded brigadier's cap on.

Everyone left was getting out. The Belgians of B Company had earlier
been detached from their battalion to cover Brigade HQ's withdrawal. From
their position Sergeant Lucien Senterre could see the Chinese up-valley 'like
ants'. Firing was getting closer. An NCO commanding a machine-gun crew
cracked under the strain, sobbing, 'We've had it, we've had it!' Things were
getting 'quite awkward', Senterre thought. Then came the order: Pull out.
Senterre's platoon commander, Second Lieutenant Marcel Fichefet, a
former Foreign Legionnaire, ordered his men to set a smoke-screen by firing
the grass. Solid-fuel cooking blocks were lit and rolled in the grass; the dry
scrub obligingly flared up. The Belgians headed for the MSR, leaving the
now-deserted Brigade HQ area wreathed in smoke.

After dropping off the riders on his tank, almost all of whom were
wounded or dead, Boyall glanced over his vehicle: he counted fifty-nine
bullet holes in the equipment bins, plus a hole from a sticky bomb and two
from shaped charges in his skirt plates. But the Centurion was still running.
Remounting, Boyall rattled back to join Huth and Lidsey's crews holding
the valley mouth.* By the time he arrived they too were disengaging.

Nobody else would be coming south. Up Route 11, the hills, Line
Kansas, the river – all had been abandoned to the enemy. Groups of
Chinese picked over the ground, and weary, ragged prisoners, many
wounded, were being formed into columns and slowly marched into the
hills. Most of the habitations lining the valley floor had been destroyed
during the breakout. Little was left of the cottage that Cadman's tank
had burst through; others were smoking heaps, their thatched roofs
ignited by tracer, phosphorus or tank fire. Columns of oily smoke curled
up from wrecked vehicles – jeeps, carriers, tanks – smouldering in
ditches and slewed along the track. Heaped, here and there, were dead
and wounded: British soldiers sprawled around smashed vehicles;
Chinese lying in groups where they had been caught by tank fire in the
paddies. But the frantic noise, movement and chaos had passed. The
valley appeared almost at peace. The Battle of the Imjin River was over.

---

* The following day, Belgian and Fusilier officers visited Huth to thank him for his
squadron's actions, and Brodie lunched with the Hussars. Gerald Rickord considered Huth
'the man of the match'; many thought he should have won a VC.

# Chapter 11

●●●●●●●●●●●●●●●●

# FLAGS AND BODY BAGS

*In England, they will remember for a little while . . .*

Glosters' Battle Memorial Service

**9** MAY 1951, 29th Infantry Brigade Headquarters, Sosa. The sun shone on the parade ground. Flags – American, Belgian, British, Luxembourg – fluttered in the breeze. On the reviewing stand, in starched fatigues, a pearl-handled .45 in the holster on his belt, stood General James Van Fleet, Commander, US 8th Army, Korea. By his side, in pressed battle-dress, his ever-present swagger stick tucked under his arm, was Brigadier Tom Brodie. Detachments from every unit of 29th Infantry Brigade, as well as representatives from ROK 1st Division,* were formed up in a hollow square, but the man commanding the parade was Major Digby Grist – the Glosters' new CO. Film cameras whirred on the perimeters of the parade. The survivors were about to receive a US Presidential Unit Citation on behalf of the Glosters and C Troop, 170 Mortar Battery, Royal Artillery. As the pipes and drums of the Royal Ulster Rifles played, artillery rumbled in the distance.[1]

Van Fleet spoke. 'By fighting beyond the call of duty, they saved their area of the front,' he said. The battle for Hill 235, he continued, was 'one of the most gallant of modern times'. Commander-in-Chief, UN Forces Korea, General Matthew Ridgway, also sent remarks. 'All members of the United Nations Forces fought with distinction during that particular action, but the indomitable spirit of the 1st Battalion the Gloucestershire Regiment was outstanding,' he wrote. 'Their refusal [sic] to withdraw prevented an early penetration of our lines and provided critically needed time for other units to regroup. It is with great pride that I join all the freedom-loving peoples of the world in expressing admiration of their gallant stand.'[2]

The deeply purple prose of the unit citation was even more gushing (and even less accurate): 'These indomitable, resolute and tenacious soldiers fought back with unsurpassed fortitude and courage. As ammunition

---

* Colonel Kim Chum-kon, the 12th Regiment CO, was sick at the time, so sent his deputy in his place. 'He couldn't speak any English beyond "yes",' Kim said, 'but he was proud to be there.'

ran low and the advancing hordes moved closer and closer, these splendid
soldiers fought back viciously . . . time and again efforts were made to
reach the battalion, but the enemy strength blocked each effort . . . every
yard of ground they surrendered was covered with enemy dead until the
last gallant soldier of the fighting battalion was overpowered by a final
surge [sic] of the enemy masses.' [3]

The regimental quick march, 'Kinnegad Slashers', was played. The
citation was presented. All members of the Glosters and 170 Mortar
were now entitled to wear the blue shoulder flashes signifying the award
of the unit citation. 'I feel deeply the loss of so many fine soldiers,' Van
Fleet said. 'It was unfortunate for them, but it was fortunate for us that
members of this gallant band were in the right place at the right time.'[4]
Cameras clicked as Van Fleet walked into the ranks and personally
shook Captain Mike Harvey's hand, 'for a job well done'.[5]

It was the culmination of an uncertain few weeks for the decimated battalion. The survivors had gathered for a roll call in a muddy yard in
Yongdungpo, south of Seoul, on 26 April. Out of a paper strength of 850
men, 129 answered their names. Numbers increased when Harvey arrived
with the unwounded members of his 41-man breakout group, but still the
force was little stronger than a company. Grist, fretting that the Glosters
might be disbanded, was determined to keep his battalion alive. He sent
men to Kimpo Airfield in trucks, with instructions to grab any man arriving
from the reinforcement holding unit in Japan, give him a hot meal, and
convince him to volunteer for the Glosters. He was also determined to
keep them in Korea, where the fate of their lost comrades was unknown.
Hearing a rumour that the Glosters were to be sent to replace the Royal
Marine detachment in the distant Falkland Islands, Grist stormed into
Brodie's headquarters and demanded a mission. The brigadier concurred:
the Glosters were tasked with guarding the Han bridges. Ten days after
their annihilation on Hill 235, Grist wired the Duke of Gloucester, the
regiment's Colonel-in-Chief: 'We are operational again.'[6]

Three Glosters returned from enemy territory. On 12 May a pair of
ragged figures arrived at UN lines. Private Fox, of D Company, had been
captured at the tail end of Harvey's breakout. Private Graham, of the
Assault Pioneer platoon, had managed to escape south, but had been
picked up in the hills. The two had later been joined by Captain Anthony
Farrar-Hockley, who had slipped away while crossing the Imjin with a
POW column, but had also been picked up by North Koreans. On their
seventh night after capture, during an artillery strike on the North Korean
unit, the three Glosters broke away. For two days they were hidden in a
hillside monastery by an old woman, the gate-keeper. The third morning
four NKPA soldiers walked in, and immediately discovered Farrar-

Hockley. The captain and the woman were beaten, but Farrar-Hockley insisted that he was alone. The two privates had hidden in a cellar; after the enemy departed with their adjutant, they ran off. The following afternoon, they were, again, recaptured. Given the NKPA's reputation for brutality, they were taken aback to be well fed, shaved, and placed in front of a colonel. He told them it was too much trouble to send them north to join the other prisoners and, after a verbal interrogation, had his men escort them towards UN lines. They were released.[7]

On 20 May soldiers of the Greek Battalion, probing north towards the Imjin, heard of a British soldier in the village of Kawol-ri. There they found the grievously wounded Private Essex. He had been shot in both legs while attempting to escape from B Company's disintegrating position on the morning of 24 April. Unable to walk, he was discovered; the Chinese beat him when he refused to reveal anything beyond his name, rank and number, then threw a grenade in his direction and departed. The Chinese grenade proved typically unlethal: though it wounded him in the eye, it did not kill him. He crawled into a trench near the village of Paegun; Gloster patrols had visited it before the battle and given sweets to the children. Villagers brought him food and water. A week later Chinese spotted him in his trench. He moved. Shortly afterwards, the trench was mortared. Villagers carried him over twenty miles to another village, where he was discovered by the Greeks. Medically evacuated to the UK, he read the introduction to the King's Speech on Christmas Day 1951.[8]

Essex's reappearance came at an appropriate moment, because the Glosters were suddenly the most fêted regiment in the British Army. Given the scale of the Chinese offensive – the greatest clash of arms of the entire war – the press was looking for drama, for heroes. The battle for Hill 235 provided both, and as the story circulated the doomed battalion's stand seized the imagination of the world. Surviving Glosters were inundated with requests for interviews. Grist shoved Harvey – tough, articulate, the hero of the breakout* – to the fore. The best early account of the battle, 'Only the Glosters' by E.J. Kahn, Jr, in the *New Yorker*'s 26 May edition (which became the basis for several subsequent accounts in the British press), was based heavily on an interview with Harvey. Countless others followed.

In the UK audiences stood and cheered when newsreels of the citation parade played in cinemas. General Lord Ismay, in a national radio broadcast in July entitled simply 'The Gloucestershire Regiment', asked his listeners: 'Can we doubt that when they crossed over, the heroes of old, the

---

* Harvey received a Military Cross for leading D Company out.

men who held the pass at Thermopylae, the men of the Light Brigade who charged at Balaclava, their own forefathers who fought the world over, rose up and saluted them as worthy comrades?'

Admiration for the battalion's stand spread beyond British shores. A cartoon in the *Toronto Telegram* showed John Bull and Uncle Sam, the former asking, 'Why ask me for more? Other nations have troops.' and the latter replying, 'Not that kind!' as a column of Glosters march past. The *Boston Daily Globe* devoted a full page to the Glosters, headlined 'Only 5 Officers And 34 Men Left Out Of Battalion Of 622. A Gripping, Factual Account of the Stand Made by Famous British Outfit which Allowed US Units to Escape from Chinese Trap.' In Paris, *Le Figaro* wrote: 'L'histoire de ce siège est en passe de devenir légendaire parmi les combatants des Nations Unies. Le courage et l'obstination des Britanniques comme l'étendue de leurs pertes font qu'on en parle ici seulement a voix basse, avec un mélange d'admiration et d'une sorte d'honneur sacrée.'*

In Spain, the Toledo Infantry Academy's Director of Military Training, General José Ungría, had the story of the stand read to all cadets, citing its 'tactical value and its singular importance from a moral standpoint'. Ungría wrote: 'The Toledo Infantry Academy . . . has studied the unsurpassable action of The Gloucestershire Regiment and has rendered proper homage to its men, with whom it feels the same spiritual solidarity . . . that existed between Great Britain and Spain in the War of Independence against Napoleonic invasion.'

US Secretary of State Dean Acheson said on 2 June, 'It was a superb thing . . . they held up the entire advance of the Chinese in the western sector until the rest of the troops could get themselves into position.' At a dinner held for General Eisenhower in London in July, a message from President Harry Truman was read out. 'In recent months, Britain and the US have stood shoulder to shoulder on the battlefields in Korea. There, too, our men died, but none more heroically than the gallant Glosters.'[9]

The regiment found itself rebranded 'The Glorious Glosters'; Hill 235 was dubbed 'Gloster Hill'.† Some soldiers decided to live up to the hype. At a press conference Second Lieutenant Denys Whatmore listened, amazed, as one of his men spun an eager reporter a tale of how his mate had floored hordes of Chinese, swinging his rifle butt and

---

* 'The story of this siege is becoming legendary among the fighters of the United Nations. The courage and obstinacy of the British, together with the extent of their losses, compels one to speak of them only in hushed voices, with a mixture of admiration and a kind of sacred reverence.'
† To the Glosters who were captured, and so unaware of their sudden fame, it was known simply as 'The Last Hill'.

roaring, 'Banzai you bastards!' Whatmore, who knew of no such event, glared at the soldier, who gave him a broad wink.*

The Belgians were also honoured with a US Presidential Unit Citation – for their gallantry and professionalism in holding the 'hinge', for inflicting 'thirtyfold losses' and for holding open the valley mouth that allowed the Rifles and Fusiliers to break free[10] – but, having escaped the trap, failed to win the recognition accorded the Glosters. Other units of 29th Brigade, left in the shadows by the flashbulbs illuminating the West Countrymen, were less than delighted.

'They read out the Presidential Citation, the general came up – it was a load of bullshit, really,' said Hussar Denis Whybro of the citation cere-mony. 'I don't belittle the Glosters, but when you see what the Northumberland Fusiliers and the Ulster Rifles went through; they were every bit as brave. It brings tears to your eyes to think about it.'[11] 'We thought we had done well [in the battle],' said Fusilier Major Robbie Leith-MacGregor. 'We didn't think the Glosters had.' Some Riflemen muttered that the Americans had granted the Glosters the Presidential Citation to cover up their failure to relieve the trapped battalion on the 25th.[12]

The rest of the brigade might have been happier with a 3 May edit-orial in *The Times*. 'The Gloucesters, for what they have now done . . . deserve to be singled out for honourable mention, but they did not stand alone. The Northumberland Fusiliers, the Royal Ulster Rifles and other Commonwealth units, each with a past to live up to, shared with the Gloucesters in this most testing of all hazards of the battlefield – attack by overwhelming numbers of enemy.'[13]

* * *

By mid-afternoon on the 25th, the remnants of the brigade that had escaped from the Chinese up Route 11 walked or were driven to the MSR, through American roadblocks, to their next defensive position on Line Delta: Tokchong crossroads. Some wanted to get right back into action. 'A few of our boys were with the American unit on the road,' said Lance-Corporal Joe Farrell. 'Big Paddy Hennessy and a couple of others jumped off – they wanted to stay – but the RSM ordered them back on.'

* Whatmore (p. 88) writes that the tall tale did not make it into print, but I have come across three accounts that read suspiciously like it: one in a US magazine article, one in a British newspaper report, and one in an account of the battle published in a respected American work on the Korean War. The tall stories did not stop there. In a taped interview by a Gloster veteran I also came across an account of Captain Mike Harvey taking out a Chinese machine-gun position using nothing but his martial arts skills; Gloster survivor Ben Whitchurch had heard a similar tale – of Harvey chopping his way through enemy ranks with bare hands. When I met Harvey in 2001 he was still keen enough to demonstrate various locks and holds on me (in the lobby of Seoul's Sofitel Ambassador Hotel) but made no mention of any hand-to-hand exploits at the Imjin.

But most men, even fire-eaters like Second Lieutenant Mervyn McCord, were dismayed that they would have to fight again. 'We got on trucks, and we were told to get off and dig in again. I remember thinking, "Not again! Aren't we going to get something to eat?"' Lieutenant Malcolm Cubiss, with his platoon reduced to section strength, was ordered onto Line Delta. 'By that time it was pretty obvious that the brigade was knackered. The Glosters were gone, the Ulsters had lost a lot, the companies were at about half strength. We went to new positions – a bare hill – and dug in again.'

Hussar Cornet John Preston-Bell pulled his Centurion up near 45 Field and curled up on the rear deck as the guns fired over his head. 'It was like being lulled to sleep, like a lullaby – the most comforting sound in the world, like being in bed, hearing the rain pattering on the roof.' Whybro's tank had been backfiring all day. Opening the engine flaps, the crew found a chunk missing from the exhaust manifold 'which had burned through the fan belt . . . only a foot off the petrol tanks. And we'd run that all the way out!' The crew pulled into a river bed alongside the MSR and fell asleep until the next morning. 'I said, "Well, we'll have a good wash, have a good breakfast and take our time." We walked up the road and saw a Yank officer. I said to him, "Where are the Chinese now?" and he said, "You see that tree over there? My men are in contact!" That was 200–300 yards from where we had spent the night! We cancelled breakfast and washing and hitched up.'[14]

The brigade would not defend Delta. Brodie had protested the order to hold the crossroads, but was overruled.* The orders were only rescinded after the brigade's liaison officer with I Corps, Fusilier Captain 'Sir William' Ellery personally approached I Corps Commander, General Frank Milburn, and made the case that the brigade was at breaking point.[15] It was pulled into reserve. Other units, retreating methodically through a series of phase lines, ground up the ongoing enemy advance. 29th Brigade had played a crucial role in halting the opening phase of the offensive and preventing the enemy from fulfilling his objectives. But the biggest battle of the war was not over.

* * *

Peng's 'Fifth Offensive' did not go as planned. On 22 April his army groups had attacked on a forty-mile front down the western half of Korea – the peninsula is about sixty miles wide at this point – against I Corps. His 64th and 63rd Armies had attacked, respectively, the 1st ROK

---

* The fact that the battered brigade was assigned further defensive positions after three days of intense combat that had almost destroyed it indicates the poor communications between it and higher command. This will be discussed in Chapter 13.

Division (with the US 73rd Heavy Tank Battalion under command) and 29th Brigade. The Chinese 15th and 12th Armies had assaulted the US 3rd Infantry Division, with the Turkish Brigade and the Filipino Battalion Group under command, and parts of the US 25th Division. The 27th and 20th Armies had attacked elements of the US 25th Infantry Division and the US 24th Infantry Division. The two key lines of attack towards Seoul from the north were along the Munsan MSR (held by 1st ROK) and the Route 33/Uijongbu MSR (held by US 3rd Division, flanked by 29th Brigade). To the east of I Corps was IX Corps, with the 6th ROK Division, flanked by the 1st US Marine Division.

The night's first attack fell on the Turks and the US 25th Division. By morning they had withdrawn to Line Kansas; US 24th Division, hard hit and giving ground, also fell back. 29th Brigade and the US 3rd Division held for the night, but the 3rd, its right exposed, moved back to Kansas on the 23rd. On I Corp's eastern flank 6th ROK Division collapsed. The Commonwealth 27th Brigade was rushed north to hold the line and dug in around Kapyong. The Canadian Princess Patricia's Light Infantry and the 3rd Battalion, Royal Australian Regiment held off all attacks for two days in a masterly defensive action that won both battalions US Presidential Unit Citations. Their stand prevented Peng from moving behind I Corps from the east and cutting it off from the rear, while 29th Brigade held its western flank. On the extreme left the ROK 1st Division lost four miles of ground, but was backed up with the US 15th Infantry Regiment, and fought with such success that I Corps Commander General Frank Milburn thought it had done as well as any US division.* The division made sterling use of the eleven battalions of artillery to its rear, and also benefited from carrier-borne naval air support.

Given that a division comprises three brigades (or regiments in the case of the US army), the heaviest odds in the offensive were faced by 29th Brigade. Van Fleet noted that the main battle 'has been a I Corps fight',[16] and 3rd Division, holding the MSR north of Seoul, was covering the Corps' key sector. 3rd Division's command report noted that the 'heaviest attack' in its sector fell on the British sector, and a subsequent intelligence report on the CPVA surmised that the 63rd Army, a shock formation, was the offensive's key spearhead.[17] The three divisions of 63rd Army attacked in such strength that they had to assault in echelon, with the 187th, 188th and 189th Divisions going in one after the other. Chinese commanders later stated that they were handicapped by the narrow terrain of the Imjin valley and suffered heavily from enemy firepower – a

* ROK 1st Division's outspoken 12 Regiment Commander, Colonel Kim Chum-kon was unimpressed by Milburn's praise: he thought his unit customarily fought harder than the Americans.

testament to the defensive efforts of 29th Brigade and the ROK 1st Division.[18] 63rd Army was not withdrawn from Korea* but was severely ground up by 29th Brigade and was passed through by 65th Army on the 25th. Its casualties may have exceeded 7,000.† On 26 April – the day after 29th Brigade withdrew – Peng admitted, in a telegram to Mao, that he had failed to achieve his objectives: after three days and nights of fighting, he had neither taken Uijongbu nor cut the UN line of retreat.[19]

Yet the offensive did not halt after 29th Brigade withdrew. As I Corps pulled back from Line Kansas, 24th Division was forced to fight down a narrow road overlooked by enemy. Eleven howitzers were lost; seven tanks destroyed. The 25th Infantry Division also had to clear roadblocks in its rear. Two men of the 7th Infantry Regiment (the 3rd-Division unit on 29th Brigade's right flank) won the Medal of Honor. The ROK 1st Division, formerly on 29th Brigade's left flank, held its positions until late in the afternoon.** The fighting on Line Kansas had bought critical time to finish work on, and man, a new defensive line just north of Seoul: Line Golden. By 25 April, in the 25th Division's sector alone, this line was fortified with 786 crew-served weapons positions protected by 510,000 sandbags and 74,000 yards of wire.

---

\* Many British accounts incorrectly state that 63rd Army was so decimated after the Imjin battle in April that it was withdrawn from theatre. In Peng's 'Sixth Offensive' in May (the last major Chinese offensive of the war, before it settled into its 'Sitzkrieg', or static phase) the ROK 6th Division, which had fled in April, found itself facing 63rd Army. Some 6th-Division officers swore an oath to wipe out the April disgrace, and at Yongmun-san on the central front they fought 63rd Army to a standstill. This is the subject of a huge display in the Korean National War Memorial in Yongsan, Seoul. It is ironic that two of the most celebrated defensive actions of the war – 29th Brigade's stand in April, and ROK 6th Division's in May, both legendary in the home countries of the units involved – involved the same enemy army.

† The official number for enemy casualties incurred by the brigade, 10,000, is given in various accounts, but is obviously a very broad-brush figure. My estimate of 6,000–7,000 (i.e. a quarter of front-line strength; coincidentally, the same percentage of casualties suffered by 29th Brigade) was reached as follows. If we look at actual body counts noted beyond some of the company positions – 90 dead outside the Rifles' A Company perimeter, 167 dead outside the Belgians' C Company position and 216 counted on one slope of Hill 235 (probably below A Company), the mean average is 157. If we then multiply that by the major company-level actions fought throughout the battle – 14 – we get a total of 2,207. If we assume, again, that there are three wounded for every man killed, the enemy casualties in the fighting for the hilltop strongpoints are 6,621. Of course, many more were casualties of artillery, and tank fire; if we put those numbers as high as another 1,000, the figure for total enemy killed and wounded is 7,621. (Only a handful of prisoners were taken from 63rd Army.) However, notwithstanding all this grisly (and highly speculative) mathematics, the decisive factor in battle is not the body count, but the achievement of objectives. In that respect the Chinese Fifth Offensive failed.

\*\* A number of British accounts, and even letters home from survivors, say the ROKs broke, so exposing the Glosters. This is unfair. The ROKs did make tactical withdrawals, which opened a gap on the Glosters' left flank, but the Glosters and the ROKs were not in contact even before the battle began. Moreover, the same thing happened on the Glosters' right, after Carne and Foster pulled in their respective right (Gloster B) and left (Fusilier X) flanking companies.

On the 26th the US 24th and 25th Divisions pulled back. The Filipino Battalion and the 3rd Battalion, US 65th Infantry, were cut off: a prompt armoured counter-attack the same day carved them out. Late on the 26th a withdrawal was ordered from Line Delta, which had been held for only one day. On the 27th the CPVA took Uijongbu. The same day the US 7th Infantry massacred an NKPA battalion marching south in parade-ground formation; the unit had been informed by the Chinese that there were no UN troops left north of the Han. On the 28th UN forces were on Line Golden. With the Han River five miles behind them, Van Fleet ordered his forces to stand fast. Huge parks of artillery in central Seoul maximised firepower.[20]

Fighting continued. One company of the ROK 1st Division was cut off – it was relieved by a tank/infantry force on the next morning.* A POW captured on the 29th said his unit, the CPVA 179th Division, had tried envelopments three times; each time they had hit air, as I Corps withdrew. Intelligence indicated that enemy forces were disappearing on the night of 29/30 April, and enemy units evaporated as the Chinese pulled back north. The Fifth Offensive had reached its high-water mark just five miles north of South Korea's battered capital. As indicated by the ration bandolier carried by 45 Field Regiment's prisoner, taken on the morning of the 23rd, it had lasted one week.[21]

* * *

UN forces suffered heavily in the greatest Chinese assault of the war. In April 1951 the United States lost 607 men killed in action (KIA) and 891 missing in action (MIA); ROK forces lost 518 KIA and 7,465 MIA. 'Other UN forces' lost 217 KIA and 924 MIA.[22] But Peng's offensive had been a colossal failure. Chinese casualties had been tremendous, perhaps as many as 70,000.† And not only had the Chinese failed to take Seoul, they had also destroyed only one UN unit: the Glosters. It was a far cry from the destruction of I Corps that Peng had planned. If he had succeeded in destroying the three US divisions of the corps, he could well have won the war. By wiping out the Glosters, all he did was strengthen the resolve of the British public.

* * *

* The prompt counter-attacks to relieve surrounded units on the 25th and 28th indicate that the UN Command was not risking a replay of the Gloster tragedy.
† The actual casualty figures for communist forces in the Fifth Offensive are, at best, guesstimates. Farrar-Hockley (1995) puts them at 13,349 killed, with 246 POWs, and those killed and died of wounds at 24,000. American estimates are higher. Daniel Beirne ('The Chinese Fifth Offensive', in Tucker) uses the widely quoted figure of 70,000 casualties – the figure used by Van Fleet.

Behind the front, 29th Brigade licked its wounds. Material losses had been significant. All the forward vehicles and equipment of the Glosters had been lost; the remaining infantry battalions had lost trucks, jeeps and carriers. The Hussars had lost six of their precious Centurions and one Cromwell.

The butcher's bill made grim reading. On the Imjin 29th Infantry Brigade suffered 1,091 killed, wounded or captured,[23] including 141 KIA.[24] Of the killed, the Glosters lost 56, the Rifles 36, the Fusiliers 30, the Artillery 10, the Royal Engineers 6, the 8th Hussars two and the Royal Army Medical Corps, one.[25] Some men had suffered appalling bad luck: Fusilier Lieutenant David Rudge, the National Service officer due for his discharge who had volunteered to lead a platoon in Y Company's last attack to relieve Z, was among the killed. Men mourned the fallen in their own ways. Fusilier Sergeant Bill Beattie, who on the morning battle began had spoken with Gloster Padre Sam Davies about his new-born child, learned that his mate, Provost Sergeant McDonald, was among the lost. He named his son Robert Andrew after his dead friend.

There was no information on the missing. Affected families in the UK did not know whether their men were dead or in captivity somewhere in communist Asia. This created a dilemma for commanding officers, traditionally those who write letters home to the families of casualties. 45 Field Regiment CO Maris Young wrote to the family of FOO Captain Michael Newcombe saying he had been killed with the Glosters; this information would prove inaccurate. Many believed killed had, in fact, been captured, which created considerable emotional turmoil for the families of those reported dead when the news of their loved ones' captivity eventually arrived.*

The dead lay where they had fallen. On the last day of May the brigade returned to the Imjin. The front was quiet; the enemy were, again, out of contact. The weather was magnificent: the skies cloudless, the hills and valleys green. Birds sang from bushes and scrub. None of this made the gruesome task of identification and burial any more pleasant.

Lieutenant-Colonel Kingsley Foster was found exactly where he had fallen,† but other bodies proved more difficult to locate and identify. 'The Chinese had just covered the dead with this thin skin of earth,' said Preston-Bell. 'We had to dig them up. I was wearing gauntlets and it was terribly hot and muggy. There were cuckoos everywhere. Over and over again – it drives you mad – the whole day.' As bodies were exhumed, the cornet wiped sweat off his forehead. As he did so, fluid – his sweat, mixed with pieces of decaying corpse – trickled down his face

---

* In 1961 Newcombe presented his regiment with a silver salt shaker engraved 'To Commemorate the Tenth Anniversary of My Death' (author interview with George Truell).
† Today he lies in the UN War Cemetery in Pusan, next to Rifles Major John Shaw.

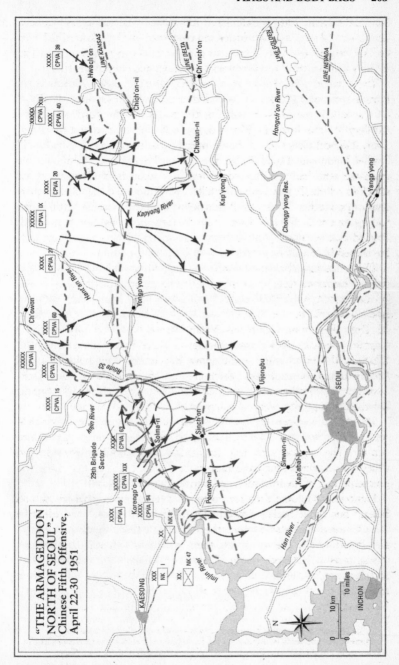

"THE ARMAGEDDON
NORTH OF SEOUL"-
Chinese Fifth Offensive,
April 22-30 1951

and into his mouth. 'That taste of corruption – of dead soldier in my mouth – was very, very horrible for a moment.'

Whybro volunteered to excavate a grave near the wrecked tank of his friend, Bill Holden. Maggots crawled everywhere. The stink was appalling. He and his burial party also found bodies complete with tourniquets and splints lying near a wrecked ambulance.* The Hussars laid the remains out next to a set of body bags. A Rifles officer came by, looking for a fellow officer. Whybro pointed out one of his men; the officer said, 'He's only an infantryman.' Whybro was infuriated – 'I could have killed him!' He told the man to bugger off.[26]

Examining the wrecked Centurions, the Hussars were surprised to find that the Chinese had removed none of the top-secret gun-stabilisation gear. Lieutenant David Boyall, inspecting one tank, discovered the only thing taken was its set of adjustable spanners; others had lost the pin-ups inside their turrets.[27] All but one were recovered.[28]

The recovery of his dead would be the most traumatic experience of the war for Fusilier Lieutenant Malcolm Cubiss. 'I went back to bury my men. I was told not to by the company commander, but I said, "They stayed with me, I'll bury them." So I went back. They were still in their trenches, exactly where they fell. When I went to bury them, their heads came off and their feet came off, and they were people I had known . . . If it was someone you didn't know, it wouldn't matter, but if it was someone you have known for eight or nine months, and his head came off in your hand . . .'†

When it came to their own men, the Chinese battlefield clearance had been more effective. In his escape attempt a day after capture Captain Anthony Farrar-Hockley had been amazed at the numbers of dead enemy and pack mules, all churned up in a wrack of broken equipment, littering the battlefield.[29] Yet by the time the brigade returned to the river, most enemy had disappeared.

In the Glosters' sector Second Lieutenant Denis Whatmore tramped the hills. Among the C and B Company positions, he was told that the Greek Battalion, which were now occupying the area, had buried a number of men in their trenches. The sickly stench of death hung over the area, but there was life swarming inside the corpses. One headless body had wasps nesting in its skull, and when Whatmore searched for a pay book in the pockets of another, a mass of worms writhed out of its

---

* A number of accounts noted that in the chaos of the last day the Chinese had attacked ambulances.

† Even fifty-six years later, Cubiss – an extremely tough officer who could describe his own horrific wounding (see below) with detached black humour – was visibly moved to recollect the experience of disinterring his dead soldiers. 'The company commander was quite right. I shouldn't have done it.'

chest cavity. In his platoon positions on the first night of battle, ten men – including Private Binman, shot next to Whatmore – lay where they had fallen. They were buried in their slits, their positions marked for the War Graves Commission (WGC). Whatmore and his detail continued up to Hill 235. Only a few bodies were found. Along the ridge Whatmore came across an unexploded grenade; he carefully removed it and threw it down the slope, where it exploded, panicking the battalion's new chaplain. Whatmore ignored his furious complaints.[30]

Gloster Captain Mike Harvey, with WGC representatives, traced his breakout route. He recovered the beret he had raised to signal to the American tanks – it was riddled with seven bullet holes. In the ditch lay broken skeletons in rotting uniforms. ID tags, photographs and pay books were scattered around. One NCO was identified by the remains of a prominent tattoo, stretched 'like a fragmented jigsaw' across his breastbone.[31]

55 Field Squadron CO Major Tony Younger went in search of Lieutenant Keith Eastman, lost during the ambush of the Rifles' Battle Patrol on the first night of battle. Younger had received a letter from a wounded Riflemen who had survived that action, saying that Eastman had been captured and held with a group of Rifles and Belgians when an air attack had hurtled in. The Chinese officer in charge of the POWs yelled orders; the guards turned their weapons on the prisoners and mowed them down. In the chaos the Rifleman escaped. He sent a grid reference of the site. Younger and his engineers were unsure whether to believe the story, but went to the area. There was a mass of remains. One corpse seemed bigger than the others. Searching through its rotting battledress, they found paper inside a pocket. The writing was legible. It was marked MUDDY PADDY – the competition Eastman had been chosen to judge in mid-April.[32]

Younger was summoned to Gloster Crossing to clear the ford for traffic. On the way he noticed Chinese corpses lying toe to toe for miles: they had been buried in ditches, but rain had washed away the soil covering. At the river he and four sappers waded carefully in, probing around for mines laid underwater by the retreating enemy. There were several. Younger had removed one when he was called to the radio truck, and left the rest of the detail to finish the job. That evening a subordinate showed him a four-inch metal tube. It was a release mechanism. The Chinese had placed mines beneath the mines – when the top mine was cleared, the one below would blow up and wipe out the clearance party. By some quirk, the mechanism had failed when Younger lifted the top mine.[33]

* * *

With the experiences of the Imjin fresh, the British battalions took greater care in co-ordinating with flanking units. Colonel Kim Chum-kon was impressed with the 29th Brigade Liaison Officer dispatched to his regiment. 'He was very responsible. Our war room in Paju leaked when it rained. There was a dry area where the American liaison officers were, but he never went over there.* When we had coffee breaks, he would join the American officers, but we said to him, "Don't you like tea?" So sometimes, he joined us.' The key lesson from the battle was the need to institute defensive solutions against mass attack. The Hussars acquired ('for a couple of cases of whisky') American .30 calibre Browning medium machine-guns, which, welded to the turret hatches, enabled the tanks to fire in two directions at once.[34] The infantry constructed defensive works more diligently than before. The Rifles' adjutant noted that 'for the first time in Korea the battalion began in earnest to lay mines, to put up barbed wire and to dig shell- and bomb-proof bunkers'.[35] The Glosters, taking over a position from the Belgians, were greatly impressed: the sector was so fiendishly well defended, with mines and explosives, that the Glosters decided it was safer to blow the defences up completely and start again.[36]

The battle still had a few shoulders to tap; one of them was Malcolm Cubiss's. The Fusiliers had been having problems with mines exploding prematurely, so Cubiss, taking on the task instead of his men, was lying down rather than standing as he laid a minefield. He pulled the pin on a mine. It exploded in his face. 'There was a flash, the earth came up, and it blew my hand off. I thought, "Christ, I am blind and I have lost both hands!" I opened one eye – I could see the moon; that's one eye alright. I looked at my left hand: I could move the fingers. The right was just a stump dripping blood.' He staggered up the hill. His soldiers, hearing the explosion, dashed to the scene but couldn't find him. Following blood trails, they discovered Cubiss curled up in his sleeping bag. One asked, 'Do you know you have lost your hand?' Cubiss, in shock, replied, 'Of course, but it'll grow back by morning.' He was dispatched to a US hospital in Japan. After a few days, War Office accountants struck. The hospital was too expensive ('£34 a day!'), so Cubiss, with one arm missing, and skin grafts on his flash burns, was ordered to relocate to the British hospital in Kure. 'I said, "I don't feel frightfully well, can I stay?"' No. He was told not to worry; two Australian nurses would meet him on the platform to escort him. He arrived at Tokyo Station, Platform 11, with a pair of orderlies, too late: his train – 'with two rather worried looking nurses aboard' – was pulling away. The orderlies told him that there would be another train in an hour, and left him on the

---

* A key leadership lesson for British Army officers is 'If your men are wet, you should be wetter!'

platform. He was wearing a dressing gown with a label around his neck; he had one arm missing, a splint, a wire cage covering his grafts and 'not much skin . . . I looked like a penguin!' On the next train, two drunken American sailors treated him with medicine of their own making: bourbon and coke. He arrived at Kure. The mutilated officer waited on the platform, to the amusement of locals, until a rail-transport officer eventually arrived and told him he had been expected the previous day.

Worse was to come. Cubiss embarked for home on a Danish hospital ship, where he was locked in the hold with a Turk, a Greek and an Ethiopian – all had lost their minds with battle shock. Only two British officers were on the ship. The other Briton was a psychiatric case, but his and Cubiss's papers had been mixed up. 'I knocked on the door and said, "All the people in here are mad!" There was a pause for a few minutes, then these two "plug-uglies" came in, jabbed me and said, "Don't worry, you'll be home soon!" It made me wonder how many perfectly sane people are locked up in asylums.' Cubiss's saviour proved to be the British officer whose place he had taken. After he had emptied a bucket of sand over the ship's captain, the administrative error was discovered. Cubiss was belatedly released and 'kept in Carlsberg for the rest of the trip'. Despite his wounds, he was determined not to return to banking. He wrote to the Chief of the General Staff, the legendary fighting general Bill Slim. Slim offered him a regular commission, but warned him that, disabled as he was, he was unlikely to advance beyond major. Cubiss accepted.

In Korea the lightly wounded returned to their units. Hussar Captain Peter Ormrod had been evacuated to a hospital ship with a note attached: 'Right eye blown out.' In fact he had removed his glass eye and placed it in the pocket of his uniform, which was cut off in a Seoul dressing station. Aboard ship Ormrod was asked if there was anything he wanted. He asked for his eye back. The nurse said she would see what she could do. A week later, she returned with the orb: 'A miracle'! Ormrod had been 'peppered from nose to ear, and had two indents in his skull' but within four weeks, shaven-headed and covered in scars, the one-eyed Hussar was back with his regiment.[37] Lieutenant Sam Phillips, hit by Hussar fire on the 23rd, was fortunate: his bone had been chipped, not shattered by the machine-gun fire. When he returned to the Fusiliers after two months, 'It was very different. There had been a lot of casualties. It was not a particularly joyful atmosphere.' Those who had survived 'the big battle' had a superior air towards reinforcements. 'The ones who had been through the Imjin had a "you don't know what you are talking about, Sonny Jim" attitude,' he said.

* * *

Battle fatigue was creeping in. The Glosters went from 'The Glosters' to 'The Glorious Glosters' to 'The Gloomy Glosters' in the space of several weeks; the Fusiliers were dubbed 'The Northumblebums'.[38] Younger noticed that two of his key officers were drinking heavily and seemed less cheerful. The major found himself unable to sleep without alcohol or sleeping pills.[39]

Armistice negotiations had opened on 10 July, but the war continued to smoulder, sputter and flare. On 28 July, 29th Brigade was merged into the 1st Commonwealth Division, a move widely welcomed. Under divisional command the brigade units engaged in further operations. That fighting falls outside the scope of this work. In October and November 1951, 29th Infantry Brigade's tour of duty came to its end. The sub-units embarked on a succession of ships and left Korea.

But not all the brigade's men were on the vessels cutting through the China Sea, recuperating in hospitals in Japan, or lying buried on the Imjin hills or in the UN Cemetery in Pusan. For those taken prisoner, home was further away than ever.

## Chapter 12

# In Enemy Hands: The Camps

*He that is taken and put into prison or chains is not conquered,*
*though overcome, for he is still an enemy*

Thomas Hobbes

**T**HE CACOPHONY OF BATTLE had died away; the smoke had cleared. On Hill 235, all was silent. The wounded Private Sam Mercer woke in the tiny tent near the RAP. It was the morning of 25 April. 'I could hear murmurs, there were people wounded, the MO was there, the padre was there.' Mercer poked his head out; someone handed him a tin of peaches. 'Everyone suddenly swung their heads around – there were two Chinese soldiers coming up the hill from the river. One had a PPSH,* one an American Garand rifle. We sat in a group and put our hands up. The Chinese motioned to us and said, "Hubba, hubba."'

The walking wounded were ushered down the slope. With an eye lost, and his leg punctured by shrapnel, Mercer was not moving fast enough for his captor. A shot rang out from behind. 'A Garand has a muzzle velocity of 2,700 feet per second, and it went clean through my left leg. It just missed the kneecap and spun me right round. I collapsed onto the ground. I was looking at the business end of his rifle. We eyeballed each other for a few seconds, while I dispersed some barrack room invective. I realised I had two options. It was difficult to stand or to walk. If I stayed on that hill, I would be at the mercy of marauding Chinamen – of which there were many. A moment later, one with a Thompson submachinegun pulled my wrist so I took off my watch and gave it to him. I went down the hill on my bum – I lost consciousness a couple of times – but there was no pain in my wounds.'† Numbed, Mercer arrived at Battalion HQ, where the Chinese were indulging in some destruction among the abandoned vehicles. 'I saw a Wasp flamethrower carrier blown up – that was quite a pyrotechnic display!' One Chinese fell victim to a secret British weapon. 'His eyes lit up when he saw the cook's three-tonner. He

---

* A 'burp gun'.
† When humans are severely traumatised, if danger persists, the nervous system floods the body with chemical painkillers – endorphins. (Survivors of many accidents recall that there was no pain until they were rescued.) Later, when they are safe, endorphin production shuts down, and the nervous system reverts to normal, producing sudden agony. In the early days of his captivity, Mercer was not out of peril by a long chalk.

opened a tin of mustard powder, dug his spoon in and shoved it in his mouth. There was a pregnant pause, then he dropped the spoon, dropped the tin and ran for his life. That made my day!'

The wounded were gathered into groups. The seriously injured, Mercer included, were placed in a barn for the night. Mercer's four-man group was given a tin of C-ration jam; each had a couple of licks. After dark an ambulance drove them down into the river and over Gloster Crossing. It was a grisly ride. Scores, perhaps hundreds of enemy had been slaughtered by Temple's ambush; other units, including a light artillery column, had been smashed there on succeeding days. 'I had the feeling we were driving over dead men and horses,' said Mercer.

Other Glosters were facing up to new realities. 'The first meal was a dirty tin of oatmeal, all mixed up,' said Private Ben Whitchurch. 'We looked and thought, "No thanks," but one chap put his hand in. I said, "How can you eat that?" and he said, "When you are a POW, you can eat anything."' The man had been a prisoner in World War II. Artillery spotter planes wheeled overhead. The Chinese ordered captured Glosters to expose themselves. 'We thought the planes were going to attack, but they turned away from us, up over the hill,' Bugler Tony Eagles said. The British had been recognised. There was a poignant moment as the aircraft departed. 'As they flew off, they waggled their wings,' said Eagles. 'We like to think they were saluting.'

Fellow Gloster Frank Carter, taken with B Company, was in a valley full of hundreds of camouflaged Chinese. An air strike thundered in. 'I had never been so terrified. The planes were so low I could see their machine-gun bullets coming up the hill.' A burst went between Carter's fingers. Of his group of eight prisoners, one escaped during the strike; another was killed. The aircraft departed. The POWs were moved towards the Imjin. Carter was surprised to note that some houses on the battlefield were still occupied by old Korean peasants, including one he had been talking to before the fighting began.

As the prisoners headed for the river through the mist, shells shrieked overhead. UN artillery was firing airbursts over the Imjin. The Chinese urged their captives into a run. Carter's head wound reopened and began pouring blood. The POWs were halted short of the river. The guards had watches out, counting the seconds between shell bursts. 'Suddenly the Chinese were up, screaming, "Run, run!" The river was a hundred yards wide; it came up to my waist. You could see the panic in their eyes. We had to get across before the next airburst. I have never run so fast. We heard the whistling of shells again. We all got down. We could hear the splash. But we were out of the downward spiral of shrapnel.' On the north bank were clusters of bullock carts crammed with Chinese dead. The Chinese had used the POWs to see if it was feasible to cross under the barrage.[1]

On the eastern flank, amid the wreckage alongside Route 11, other prisoners were also coming under 'friendly fire'. Rifles Lieutenant Peter Whitamore spent the night of the 25th lying beside the ambush site; during the night, he had heard the cries of someone trapped under a wrecked tank calling for his mother. The Centurion was still on the top secret list, and on the 26th F-80s streaked in to destroy it. The strike was on target. Whitamore – already scorched by phosphorus on his back and shot through the leg – had his eyebrows seared off and his forehead burnt. The prisoners were ushered up a more protected gully. As they passed, a Chinese soldier grenaded them. 'We ducked,' said Whitamore. 'It was sheer devilment, I suppose.'

Rifleman Henry O'Kane had come to, lying half out of a stream after being blown off a Centurion. A comrade bandaged his head and removed his blood-soaked camouflage smock. The Chinese gathered POWs together and gave each a large, leafy branch from a conifer. As they were marched up to the hills, they were told to carry the branch over their shoulder, and to drop to a knee if aircraft were spotted. 'So this was how the Chinese did it,' O'Kane realised. His group were marched into the blackened Kamak-san foothills, past hundreds of dead Chinese and battle-shocked enemy who gazed at the POWs without comprehension.[2]

In groups and columns, the prisoners, whole and wounded, were shepherded off the battlefield into the mysterious north. For the captured men the end of the battle marked the conclusion of one story, the beginning of another. Three days of fighting would be followed by two and a half years of captivity.

* * *

For the first three weeks, the men marched by night, covering between eight and eighteen miles, going to ground during the day to avoid UN aircraft. Their fitness was severely tested. 'We had to march or die: I don't know if they shot the wounded, but we thought they might,' said Whitamore, who was with a group of walking wounded. 'They said, "Can you walk eight miles?" That was the first night.'

Soldiers in combat have narrow views. On the march, mingling with men from other units, the prisoners got a picture of the larger battle that had engulfed the brigade. Gloster Private Lofty Large, in pain from bullets in his arm and side, heard of the Fusilier cook who had chased a Chinese submachine-gunner around his field kitchen with a cleaver and of the cheer that had gone up when a NAAFI van had been hit by artillery, sending the money fluttering into the air.[3]

As the POWs trudged north, columns of Chinese troops, trucks and mule trains passed them, making for the inferno in the south.* The trucks had their headlights on, for the Chinese had effective anti-aircraft drills: relays of sentries with rifles along the high ground. Once a plane was heard or seen, rifle reports warned the column to douse lights and take cover. There was no animosity. O'Kane was moved by a young Chinese nurse standing beside the road calling 'God bless you,' in her sing-song voice to every passing POW.[4] Padre Sam Davies, exhausted, collapsed. Passing Chinese soldiers splashed cool water on his face, helped him up, gave him sugar and carried him for miles, before placing him on a truck which caught up with the POW column.[5] Relationships formed between prisoners and captors. Carter's group tried to outmarch the Chinese, and volunteered to carry their packs.[6]

Medical treatment was minimal or non-existent. O'Kane requested treatment for his shrapnel wounds. His captors took him to an aid post where his wounds were smothered with a gooey black ointment that reminded him of a horse treatment back home. He immediately grew pessimistic about the medical situation.[7] Large was examined: two bullets were still inside him, and two ribs appeared to be broken. There was no question of an operation; Large walked on. Other men suffered more. Large heard the screams of one man as friends tried to extract a lump of shrapnel from his skull with pliers.[8] Captain Anthony Farrar-Hockley, having lost his boots in an escape attempt, suffered agonies after his feet became infected. Held down by other men, he was operated on by Doug Patchett, the Hussars' doctor, with a safety razor. Before the operation, Lieutenant-Colonel James Carne removed himself from the scene so Farrar-Hockley could swear as loudly as he liked. The adjutant was carried for days afterwards by other men, including Fusilier Derek Kinne.[9] MOs advised men on their wounds. 'My wounds were tolerable, but only just,' said Whitamore. 'It was extremely painful.' The burns on his back, head and hands healed, but his gun-shot shin worsened. 'I took the field dressing off and put in on again quickly: I had maggots in my shin that ate all the bad stuff. I thought it was horrible.' Mercer's wounds, though serious, were not life-threatening. 'I was blind in one eye – but I could see, talk, hear. I was alive,' said the Gloster. 'Eventually, most bits and pieces healed. I knew that, once I got off that hill, I was going to survive.' A Chinese medical team arrived to help the worst of the wounded. Large had a tube of iodine squirted into one of his bullet holes; it squirted out of the other.[10] Care was little better for the enemy. Mercer was appalled to

---

* Few, by now, had any illusions about the war in Korea: Chinese troops dubbed the Yalu crossings 'the gates of hell'.

see one enemy napalm victim: his flayed body was entirely covered in Vaseline gauze. 'He was a zombie,' said Mercer. 'I hope he didn't survive.'

The Glosters kept their morale up on the night marches, singing songs they had learned in Jamaica, like 'Brown Skin Girl' and 'Blue Tail Fly'. When – as frequently happened – the Chinese got lost, a wag would sing out, 'We are poor little lambs who have lost our way,' and the entire column would chime in with 'Baaaaaa!' And once, as Large's column marched up a track, he saw his CO standing by the side of it, encouraging and greeting every man by name as he passed. Large, a new arrival to the battalion, was uplifted that Carne remembered his name.[11]

The march north led up tracks, over hills and mountains, across rivers, through forests. The best place to be in the column was near the front, where the pace was even. Those at the back were constantly having to wait as they caught up with the leaders, or running to catch up as the marching column concertinaed. North Korea was devastated. Many towns lay smashed by air raids, leaving only chimneys standing; the populace lived in hovels and dugouts. Davies was saddened to see burned-out churches.[12] At some stops, the men were ushered into air-defence bunkers. Since they were often just a couple of feet high, time spent in these tunnels was claustrophobic and uncomfortable.[13] Bridges were crossed at the run, for fear of air attack. During rest halts, guards were posted. If any prisoner moved away from the area, warning shots were fired.[14]

The front receded, but danger persisted. Mercer was sleeping in a Korean cottage when he was gripped by a nightmare: something terrible was bearing down on him, from which he was trying desperately to escape. Still asleep, he slid down the wall he was leaning against, into a foetal position. There was a flash and thunderous crash; a bomb exploded, obliterating a nearby outhouse, showering the area with excreta and wounding an American POW. Mercer's nightmare was real: his subconscious had picked up the menacing drone overhead. O'Kane's group encountered a wrecked column of Chinese trucks and dying mules strewn across the track, the screams of the animals mingling with the cries of the men. The POWs were doubled past.[15] For a lucky few, air attack proved a boon. Rations – mixtures of millet, sorghum, corn, ground soybeans – were dubbed 'bug dust', but in a way station, Kinne and Farrar-Hockley were given an unusually nutritious ration: a bowl of beef stew from an ox killed the previous day by an F-80.[16] Once past the 'bomb line', north of the Taedong Valley, the prisoners marched by day and slept at night.

The deeper they penetrated into North Korea the more the prisoners realised that, if they should escape, their biggest threat would be the locals. Having been taught that it was South Korea which had started the war, and watching the USAF lay waste their country, their hatred was at boiling point. 'We were taken through the ruins of Pyongyang,' recalled Mercer. 'We had a Chinese driver and a soldier with a rifle. Word spread that there were British and Americans around. The locals became belligerent, waving their fists and shouting. I never thought I would be grateful for the presence of a Chinese soldier, but he fixed his bayonet and stood his ground. We felt very threatened.' Gloster Private David Green passed through a bombed town where casualties were being dragged from the ruins. Korean troops wanted to execute every POW and argued fiercely with the Chinese guards. They did not relent until the Chinese cocked their weapons and levelled them at their allies.[17]

Even so, there were surprising moments of kindness. 'In a compound north of Pyongyang, there was an old *mama-san*,' said Mercer. 'One night, on several occasions, she crept along the balcony and gave us corn on the cob and other things. If she'd been found out . . . She was risking her life for us, her enemies.' Green lacked a critical item: a food container. (When the Chinese handed the POWs their boiled, watery grains it was in a large pot, and it was up to the prisoners to serve themselves with mess tins, mugs, gourds or whatever they had.) Green was resting by a roadside near a group of locals – who, it turned out, spoke English. They started conversing. The Koreans offered Green some sugar cane they were preparing in a two-pound tin. Green asked if he could keep the tin. 'OK, you keep!' they replied.[18]

With poor food, foul water and exhaustion taking their toll during the 'death march', health deteriorated. Lice began to infest the men, raising fears of typhus. Dysentery set in: a common sight would be a man staggering to the side of the track, tugging down his trousers, and expelling his bloody bowels into the paddy. Many boots disintegrated; men marched on bare, blistered feet. After eight to twelve weeks, the groups arrived at their destinations: a string of POW camps run by the North Koreans around Pyongyang, and Chinese-run camps just south of the Manchurian border.

The camps bore no relationship to the POW compounds of World War II. These were simple villages with no barbed wire fences, no searchlights, no watch towers. Race was a much greater deterrent to would-be escapers, for, deep in communist Asia, Caucasians had little chance of passing unnoticed through the countryside. Most British were placed in Choksong,* Pinchon-ni and Pyoktong. Choksong was typical. It consisted of a village in a valley, flanked by a tributary of the Yalu. A track passed through the camp. In the mornings the prisoners mustered on a parade square. In some ways, set amidst the alpine scenery, it was a beautiful location. But what the British troops found on arrival shocked them.

* * *

* Variously spelled, in different accounts, Chongsong, Chongsung and Chiangsong.

GIs, captured early in the war, were dying in droves. Many were sick and starving; some were insane. A Chinese guard with an arriving British column was so unnerved by the sight of a mad American POW approaching that he shot him dead.[19] 'The American soldiers seemed to have no resistance to hardship,' said Carter. 'They were literally lying down and dying. We were saying to the Chinese, "Can we go across and help them?" Eventually we were allowed to.' Many were walking skeletons. 'There were one or two fit ones. One or two had probably had a hard life, but others were brought up in cities and didn't know how to look after themselves,' Carter said. 'We went across, and some you had to kick, get them on the move. The place smelt terrible. The strongest ones got food, the weakest were left to die.'[20] Comradeship and unit spirit seemed absent. One giant prisoner had collected a huge wad of US dollars from his fellows.[21] 'The Americans had this disease called "give-up-itis",' said Second Lieutenant Guy Temple. 'One said "I hope I wake up dead tomorrow" – and he did, though not before I'd checked out the size of his boots (they didn't fit). You had to be a bit callous.' A Rifleman captured at 'Happy Valley' was found blind, deaf, crippled. He was taken into care by his newly arrived comrades, who supplied him with their own minuscule sugar ration. Soon his eyesight and hearing were restored; later he learned to walk again.[22]

Within a couple of months, fewer bodies were being carried up to 'Boot Hill', Choksong's hillside cemetery. But not every American suffered 'give-up-itis'. Marines were found to be real stoics. Gloster officers had been accompanied on the march north by a Marine pilot with appalling fuel burns over his face and arms: he did not utter a word of complaint.[23] The Turks, too, were admired for their toughness and discipline. Filipino and Puerto Rican POWs, familiar with a rural diet, primitive conditions and herbal soups and medicines, bore up better than many Europeans and Americans.

In 1951 both China and North Korea were young communist states, imbued with ideology. Neither was party to the Geneva Convention. Both held the view that anyone who fought against them was a criminal who should repent. The communists' task in the camps was thus to convert captives to their creed and to wring propaganda out of them. For the POWs the shooting war had finished. Now, an ideological war began. The Chinese approach was 'The Lenient Policy'. Based on the methods used by Mao's communists to rehabilitate Chiang Kai-shek's captured nationalists, it included heavy doses of 're-education'.[24] 'Progressives' who absorbed the teachings of their socialist brothers were redeemed and guaranteed security of life, retention of personal belongings, freedom from ill treatment and medical care.[25] Those who defied communist contentions – that UN soldiers were dupes of their capitalist rulers and that their war in Korea was a crime – were dubbed 'reactionaries'. For these, the lenient policy did not apply. A Chinese officer warned inmates in Pyoktong that, if they did not become 'progressive', 'We will keep you here ten, twenty, thirty or even forty years if necessary, until you learn the truth, and if you still don't learn it, we will bury you so deep you won't even stink!'[26]

The men settled in. The prisoners were divided into companies and squads – usually those occupying the same billet. A 'monitor' among the prisoners was placed in charge of each billet. In late 1951 officers and senior NCOs were separated from the other ranks and taken to separate camps. The daily routine in the Chinese-run camps was 'education' sessions, delivered through interpreters, on the thoughts of Marx, Engels, Lenin, Stalin and Mao. Many sessions – with titles such as 'The Democratic Reformation and Democratic Structure in North Korea and the Peaceful Reunification Policy of the North Korean Government' and 'The Inhumanity of the American Forces'[27] – were harangues. Reactions varied. A minority of POWs had been left-wingers at home, and listened with interest. Many decided to take the easy way out, and play along. Lectures could last for hours, and some men would nod off. 'Every morning at 06:00 we had to parade on the square and be harangued by a pseudo-Chinese American on the wonders of communism,' said Eagles. 'We were there for about four hours. Then we had to go back to our huts and discuss what we had been told. Then they would come around and ask about the discussions. We said, "Of course, you are right" – we didn't want to argue. But they would say, "Why are we right?"' Some men spent discussion sessions endlessly arguing over football teams and the results of long-forgotten matches – causing problems for the monitors who had to report the discussions. Others argued at length. 'The lectures were awful: "The Twilight of World Capitalism" was read to us,' said Whitamore. 'I thought it a waste of time arguing, but Farrar-Hockley was a real resister. I admired him as a very brave officer, and very knowledgeable.'

Some interrogators tried to get military data. Farrar-Hockley was asked about the qualities of Brigadier Tom Brodie by a Chinese interrogator; after he refused to answer, the interrogator chummily assured him that he would keep their conversation confidential. When a group of 'apprentice commissars' were led in to watch the master at work, the discussion moved on to the 'slavery' abounding throughout the Commonwealth. Farrar-Hockley lost control. The 'model session' ended in a yelling match.[28]

Re-education did not last. 'The Chinese thought we were uneducated, illiterate and stupid,' said Mercer. 'When they discovered we were not, lectures tailed off.' Compulsory sessions evaporated in late 1951; those who attended voluntarily were communists, those who hoped for better treatment if they showed willing, and those who simply had nothing better to do. In the afternoons work details went into hills to cut wood – fuel for camp stoves and heating systems. To maintain fitness, the men arranged daily PT sessions for themselves; the PTIs also offered physical therapy for the wounded.

Medical facilities were largely non-existent for the first year. The 'hospital' in Choksong, a temple on the side of the valley, gained a reputation as a 'death house'. 'They only had iodine,' said Lance-Bombardier Tom Clough of 170 Mortar. 'If you went up with a headache, they put iodine on your head!' One of O'Kane's mates went with a splinter in his finger. He returned without the finger.[29] Due to the poor diet, some men developed night blindness. Toothache was particularly dreaded. One man in camp had a rusty pair of pliers, and would undertake agonising extractions while a group held the sufferer down. Carter asked one patient how he felt afterward: 'Not too good, but a damned sight better than with toothache,' he said. Some were infested from drinking paddy water. Carter was sitting on the wooden bar suspended over an open pit that formed the communal latrine when the man beside him started choking violently. The Gloster watched in horror as his neighbour coughed up a six-inch-long pink worm. 'I thought, "Christ, we don't have those inside our bodies, do we?"'[30] The men were also swarming with lice and fleas. 'They were very itchy,' said Mercer. 'You'd wake up in the morning and see the little buggers standing on their noses drinking, having breakfast! We picked 'em out, but the way to get rid of them was to run a lighted match down the seams.'

Amoebic dysentery was a particularly unpleasant affliction, given the disgusting state of the latrines. Some men made so many trips to evacuate their bloody bowels that their lower intestines hung below their rectums. 'Everybody in the camp had it, but the Chinese systems were used to it; ours weren't,' Mercer said. 'Sometimes it was a close-run thing: only once did I fail to get my trousers down. There was nothing you could do about it. If they brought us propaganda paper, it was useful.' Droppings were found around the camp from a man (or men) who had not made it to the latrine: he was dubbed 'the Phantom Arsehole'.[31] In the winter the excrement and urine froze into blocks; latrine emptying duty entailed hours of chipping, but was better than the stink and flies of summer.[32] Due to their poor nutrition, men's lower limbs puffed up painfully with beriberi. Jaundice set in. Some ended up with the full deck. 'People died from disease, wounds, malnutrition, "give-up-itis",' said Temple. 'I had gangrene, beriberi, jaundice and dysentery all mixed up, which didn't make you a wonderful physical specimen!' As medical facilities slowly improved, charcoal tablets were issued to treat the dysentery, vitamin pills cured the night blindness, and medicine killed the worms.

Water was drawn from wells. In the early days, the staple foods were millet, sorghum, rice or bean powder,* sometimes with a side dish of turnip or cabbage. Once a week, there was a pork ration – half a pig for 300–500 men. Some World War II POWs thought the diet had been better under the Japanese.[33] Only the sugar ration made it bearable. Once peace talks got under way ovens were provided, and baking began. The men also learned to pickle vegetables like the Koreans to provide winter vitamins. 'We'd dig a trench, put cabbages in and earth it over,' said Mercer. 'By the end of the winter, there would be considerable deterioration in the cabbage, but that is what we had, and would eat it.' By the second year, there were potatoes and beans.

Billets were traditional Korean cottages, with straw roofs and an *ondol*, or under-floor flue heating system. The men slept in rooms around twelve feet square, on woven mats or on the hard-packed earthen floor. O'Kane found the *ondol* so effective that even when the inner walls of the houses and the blankets (one per two men) were coated in frost, the sleepers remained toasty.[34] *Ondols*, though, had an innate problem: whenever cooking was carried out, it heated the entire house, making the billets unbearable in summer. Fire was always a risk. 'The previous occupants had made a second channel so we thought, "Fine, we'll build a fire in each," ' said Mercer. A Chinese guard came in, said "too hot!" and poured water on the floor. The water hissed up as steam. There were wisps of smoke, then flames began licking around the building. Guards attempted to beat out the blazing thatch. 'We were laughing like drains!' said Mercer. An ancient fire pump arrived with twenty Koreans aboard, but the Chinese ordered them to leave. 'They didn't like each other,' said Mercer.

The dreary months passed. Using sugar the Chinese gave them to put in their soya milk, some men secretly collected fruit from the hillsides to make wine. Floors in the huts were dug up, the materials were thrown into cans and tubs and a couple of spoonfuls of sugar thrown on. But when a couple of men staggered around the camp merrily drunk, the Chinese discovered the tubs and poured the contents away.[35] At Easter 1952 the Chinese served sake to the officers and senior NCOs. Weakened by their poor diet, and with no resistance to alcohol, many

---

* Bean powder remains a staple in North Korea today. Defectors escaping from 'Kim's Kingdom' to China mention their astonishment at seeing this foodstuff fed to pigs.

became roaring drunk. The camp commandant was horrified when they started a conga across the parade square: he thought it might lead to a riot.[36] Americans from rural states knew of another intoxicant: marijuana grew wild on the Korean hillsides. Some prisoners learned of it from locals. Carter was sitting on the mountainside when an old peasant came down the hill, leading an ox. They smiled and bowed at one another. Carter offered him tobacco; in return, the Korean passed the British soldier his pipe. Carter rolled the contents in a leaf from his Bible and inhaled. 'Marijuana was mixed with it, and all of a sudden my head started to go around,' he said. 'I was as high as a kite!' The cheery old Korean rose, smiled, bowed and departed.[37] The presence of the weed proved a boon for the wounded, who had no other painkiller.

Some prisoners established a barber's shop, leading to a craze for bizarre haircuts: mohicans, pigtails, Friar Tucks, even patterns in the shapes of diamonds, hearts, clubs and spades.[38] During the long winter months, when it was too cold to go outside, men sat in billets and played endless card games, to the point where they called out plays in their sleep – to be answered by other sleepers.[39] Camp bands, using paper and combs, were formed; later the Chinese donated instruments. In the clement months, prisoners gathered for singalongs and open-air concerts; everything from British favourites such as 'Land of Hope and Glory' to tunes learned from the Americans, such as 'Shotgun Boogie'. Local Korean peasants would sometimes sit on the hillsides, listening.[40] The river near Choksong Camp could be swum in during the summer and offered other diversions. Once, when it was in a roaring spate, Green and his mate Tom Clough leapt in for fun, riding the torrent down to the American sector of the camp.[41]

Relations were forged with locals. In Carter's camp it was clear that many infections originated in the stinking latrine. The prisoners asked to build another one; the Chinese assented. The saw-man in a nearby village cut flat planks for use as seats (with holes cut in them) over the pit. The prisoners were surprised to find they had a tradable currency: their excreta. Koreans asked if they could empty the camp latrines for fertiliser. The POWs were only too happy to have the locals clean out their pits in return for turnips and cabbages. Locals also waited downriver from the camp: when the prisoners slaughtered their livestock ration and threw the entrails in the river, the Koreans would collect them.*[42]

The guards came in a range of characters, some congenial, some cruel. Some were known by surnames – Chen, Ding, Cheng. Others gained (usually unflattering) nicknames: 'Pig-face', 'Snake-eyes', 'Hedgehog'.

---

* In Korean cuisine, entrails are both barbequed and used in soups.

Two female guards were dubbed 'Myrtle' and 'Pudding-face'. The guards' English amused the prisoners. One interpreter, Zee, would murder American English: 'Say you guys, the company commander, he say, you gotta get outta your goddam beds, OK?'[43] Another, 'Goggles' (so named due to the eyewear he habitually wore) was keen on using his bayonet. He had a change of attitude after he stuck it into a telegraph pole that had fallen into electric power cables; a massive shock rendered him unconscious. Two Riflemen revived him. From then on, 'Goggles' took his duties less seriously, and often left his rifle leaning against a hut when he went inside to play cards with his captives.[44] One interpreter, 'Maggot' supplied Green with tobacco in return for lessons in English slang that he carefully noted down. Green, who invented much of the material, felt guilty and taught him some real phrases.[45]

Christian faith became a support for many. Rifles Major James Majury, captured at Happy Valley, organised services; prayers were written on rice paper.* Once he arrived, Gloster Padre Sam Davies considered his camp a 'parish behind barbed wire' and was at constant war with the Chinese, who were deeply suspicious of Christianity. Davies wrote baptismal certificates on cigarette paper; over forty hymnals were written on the same material. Each service finished with the hymn 'Faith of our fathers, living still/In spite of dungeon, fire and sword.'[46] The Chinese were usually obstructive towards religion, but occasionally not. The officers and senior NCOs were astonished to be turned out on Easter Morning 1953 and sent up-valley: camp authorities had arranged an Easter Egg Hunt, complete with rewards.[47]

There was a morale boost for Glosters when, later in the war, prisoners familiar with the story of their stand trickled into the camps. A US infantryman was introduced to Mercer. When he discovered Mercer's regiment, he was bowled over. 'He said, "The Glorious Glosters? Goddam!"' The Glosters were nonplussed, Mercer recalled. 'We said, "So what? We had a job and we did it." But he just said, "Wow!"' Their battle, the Glosters realised, had not only not been a disaster; it had attained legendary status.

Air activity signalled to the POWs that the war continued. With 'MiG Alley' – a strip of airspace along the Manchurian border that was the key hunting ground for the aggressive US F-86 Sabre pilots – above the camps, vapour trails frequently bisected the skies. 'One Chinese was telling this American, "Your Air Force does not dare come up here" – and at that exact moment an F-86 shot by close enough for us to see what

---

* Majury's prayer book was eventually smuggled out through Panmunjon when he was repatriated. It is now kept at the Rifles' regimental chapel, St Anne's Cathedral, Belfast.

kind of toothpaste the pilot had used,' Mercer said. 'Morale went up for a couple of hours.' When a squadron of Fleet Air Arm planes passed overhead, the men defied the guards and ran onto the square to wave. The aircraft wagged their wings in recognition. For O'Kane, the realisation that his own side knew where he was provided a huge boost.[48]

The identities of the POWs were slow to leak out. In summer 1951, in no man's land far to the south, a British officer came across a note in one of the 'field post boxes'. It contained a propaganda message from the Chinese and a list of captured officers. He passed it up the chain of command. For many families, this was the first indication they had that sons, brothers, husbands or fathers were alive.[49] Confirmation was slow to reach many families, and official channels were not always the fastest. Dorothy Newhouse, who had received a telegram stating that her husband was MIA, was working in her local co-op when a customer arrived with a sheet of newspaper. 'The customer said, "Look at the photo here – and your husband's name!"' she recalled. 'When I got home there was a letter saying he was all right. It was a relief.'*

After the early months some prisoners were allowed to write. 'In the camp we could write letters, so amongst ourselves agreed to say we were being well treated, just to get letters through,' said Clough. 'One of my letters, and one from Major Denis Harding, got through and were reported in the *News of the World*.' Lofty Large received some three hundred letters from Ann, his future wife – some addressed simply to Lofty Large, Glosters, POW Camp, Korea, c/o Peking – but another four hundred she wrote were never delivered.[50] Although the Chinese blamed US bombing for mail dislocations, troublesome POWs were punished by having their letters withheld; one man saw a bonfire of mail.[51] One of the most recalcitrant prisoners, Farrar-Hockley, would discover that his wife had sent over three hundred letters before he received the first one.[52] Eagles joined a musical group to celebrate Christmas; their performance was recorded by the Chinese. 'It was a bit of propaganda by them, and they sent this thing with the names of the people.' The Army, armed with the information, contacted Eagles's family in the UK, 'saying I was alive and being well treated – a load of rubbish!'

In late 1952 the Chinese arranged an inter-camp 'Olympics' at Pyoktong Camp. This included football, basketball, precision drilling, boxing and gymnastics. Green was a member of his company's boxing and gymnastics teams. Losing to a Rifleman, he was glad not to have to face a

---

* The newspaper was probably the communist *Daily Worker*. The Chinese disseminated considerable information, such as photos of prisoners, exclusively through the communist press. However, the activities of the paper's journalists in the camps would cause considerable controversy.

handy Mexican-American in the final. But after the training, the build-up and the excitement of the week-long Olympics passed, depression settled in. Green, his nerves stretched by the continuing uncertainty of captivity, began to fear for his sanity.[53]

Seeing men dying due to lack of bare necessities, some POWs decided to become 'progressive' and play along with the Chinese in 'Peace Fighter' camps, where they took part in propaganda activities, including penning articles praising the clemency of their captors or fuming against the war. Some were published in the communist newspaper *The Daily Worker*. Only one British serviceman refused repatriation at the war's end: Royal Marine Commando Andrew Condron.* 'I was lectured to by him on "The Advantages of Communism",' said Whitamore. 'He was a bum. The reaction was disgust; we took it as we saw it. He circulated freely. He was ignored; that is probably the best word. If anything, we felt sorry for him.' Other men remained defiant.

* * *

Resistance took many forms. While the Chinese lectured on the evils of capitalism and tried to convince their prisoners that the only reason they had been sent to South Korea was to rape local maidens and steal Korea's famed apples, Farrar-Hockley organised pre-Staff College lectures for fellow officers.† Bizarrely, education proved a two-way street. In the brutally surreal atmosphere of the North-Korean-run camp 'Pak's Palace', Temple was ordered to teach Korean sergeants English. 'If they brought food or cigarettes, I gave them good marks,' said the Gloster officer – who found that he had the power to punish his captors. 'If not, I gave them bad marks, and this stupid sergeant was put in a hole in the ground, just like I had been, on my recommendation!'

The Chinese indulged in regular self-criticism sessions and expected the same of POWs. Miscreants were paraded before other prisoners and ordered to confess. Such self-criticisms often began with 'I have been a very naughty boy . . .', greeted by cheers and whistles. At the first session he watched, O'Kane was impressed by two Gloster NCOs who had attempted to escape. Among comments for the benefit of the Chinese – 'If it wasn't for the goodness of the "peace-loving" Korean and Chinese volunteers, we would not be here now . . .' (cheers) – the two imparted information for would-be escapees, such as that all bridges were guarded, and to beware of children.[54]

* Fellow commandos in the camps insist that Condron did what he did to help other prisoners. Among Korean War veterans, Condron, now deceased, remains a controversial figure.
† When Farrar-Hockley attended Staff College after being repatriated, he became the first student to lecture the faculty.

But many broke. One American officer, badly beaten and released from solitary, had the decency to tell fellow officers that he had cracked, and warned them not to discuss sensitive issues in his earshot. He died weeks later.[55] The Chinese nurtured informers, bribing them with small gifts – food, tobacco and the like. For 'reactionaries', the 'progressives' were a hateful bunch. 'We hated 'em. We could not stand 'em. We cold-shouldered 'em,' said Clough. 'We didn't do anything physical – though one got thrown in the river.'*

The Chinese had an insatiable appetite for information. Whitamore was asked about the organisation of the British War Office: he told his captors that he had no idea. Temple was told that he must know London well, so was ordered to draw a map of the city's docks, about which he knew little. 'After one or two pieces of "persuasion" – like a revolver to your head – you thought, "Oh, actually I do know!" and you drew a map,' said Temple. 'The snag was, they'd "lose" the map and say "Could you do it again?" If it was not the same, you were in trouble.'

Much resistance had a naughty-schoolboy flavour to it. The lack of women among the prisoners made even the camps' female interpreters objects of lust. Green wore a strip torn from a pair of 'Myrtle's knickers round his neck as a collar – the undergarment had been 'liberated' from a washing line by an enterprising prisoner who became the most popular man in his company overnight.[56] In the officers' camp there was 'crazy week', during which men played games of invisible cards; one man went everywhere on an invisible motorbike, and after morning roll call the men stood around in a circle staring at the ground.[57] In other camps men played sports – table tennis, tennis, football – often with full crowds of supporters – but without any tables, bats, balls, or nets. Others walked invisible dogs. Sometimes, men would stand staring and pointing up into the sky at nothing. A popular song did the rounds:

> *Who flung dung at Mao Tse-tung?*
> *It was Kim Il-sung!*
> *He flung dung at Mao Tse-tung!*[†]

At a concert party on Labour Day 1952 a group parodied the grandiloquent phraseology used by the communists in the Panmunjom truce talks. Uttered in rapid-fire Cockney, this went over the heads of attending Chinese. Gloster Sergeant Bill Sykes then appeared for a song:

---

* Clough heard that one of the 'progressives' later committed suicide.
† Both Mercer and Whitamore recalled the ditty with relish. Subsequent verses are, regrettably, unprintable.

> *They seek him here; they seek him there;*
> *They seek the bastard everywhere!*
> *Should he be shot? Should he be hung?*
> *That damned, elusive Mao Tse-tung!*

As the audience collapsed, the Chinese caught on, called out the guard company and attempted to arrest Sykes. There was an uproar as his comrades rose. It could have been a massacre, but the guards saw sense. 'We came off the parade square and knew they would not open fire,' said Clough. 'The commander was telling them not to shoot.' Sykes remained at large; the prisoners hurriedly dispersed.*
Another riot almost ensued in 1952, when the Chinese attempted to segregate prisoners along racial lines; all African-Americans were marched from Choksong. Among the British POWs was a black Gloster from St Helena. When the Chinese arrived to remove him, several hundred milling prisoners yelled for them to desist. He remained.[58]

A Chinese concert troupe visited Choksong to showcase its production of the tragic revolutionary opera 'The White-Haired Girl' – about a virtuous maiden who undergoes such severe trials at the hands of a villainous landlord that her hair turns white. The POWs watched the six-hour masterpiece on the parade square in midwinter, and, to the irritation of their captors, applauded at all the wrong moments – notably the repeated rapes of the unfortunate lass by the rapacious landlord.[59] The formidable array of personalities among the prisoners in the camps and the strong bonds of comradeship made the unbearable bearable. 'I could not have been in prison with a more congenial bunch of people,' said Whitamore.

There was no reason for the Chinese to treat the majority of the prisoners[†] – whiling away the days, passively resisting or maintaining a low profile – brutally. But the minority who engaged in high-profile acts of resistance would see their captors at their worst. Punishments included various forms of hanging – with arms pulled up high behind backs, by the thumbs – beatings, water torture and binding with handcuffs and telephone wires so tightly that blood flow was cut off and muscles became unusable, resulting in 'drop wrist' (an inability to straighten the hands). In winter, some men were marched to the river

---

* Farrar-Hockley (1995), p. 274, conjectures that the lenience may have been due to the fact that, the same month, the communist side was accusing the UN forces of shooting prisoners, and did not wish to be tarred with the same brush.
† The most famous resister, Derek Kinne said, 'I went to two or three reunions of POWs. Now, they are all reactionaries, but that was not the case: 99 per cent were sitting on the fence.'

and water was poured over their feet so that they froze to the ice. Others were forced to kneel for hours on sharp rocks. Solitary confinement – often for months – was made worse by lack of sanitary facilities. A lenient guard would allow the prisoners out to use latrines several times a day; others would only permit one visit, forcing prisoners to foul their cells. For those with dysentery this was particularly disgusting. In some cases mock executions were held for those who failed to 'confess'.*

In filthy solitary confinement, sometimes for months on end, with no exercise, company or reading material, the days were mind-numbing. When guards were out of earshot men encouraged those in adjoining cells. Davies, in solitary following a brush with camp authorities over religious services, was heartened on a low day when Farrar-Hockley, in the next cell, told him, 'Steady on, Padre. Something will turn up.' The two men looked at each other through a tiny hole in the wall dividing their cells, broke into giggles and whispered prayers.[60]

The prisoners were visited in the camps by several Western leftists – notably Australian journalist Wilfred Burchett, accredited to the French dailies *L'Humanité* and *Ce Soir*, and British communist writers Alan Winnington and Michael Shapiro, both of *The Daily Worker*. One prisoner was disgusted to see a picture of an apparently healthy American POW in *The Daily Worker*: he had known the man, and knew he had died of dysentery.[61] Shapiro, questioning a sick Rifles sergeant, was told by the NCO that he was 'the poorest excuse for an Englishman I have ever seen and if I could get my fingers round your scrawny neck, I'd wring it'. Shapiro told the sergeant (who later died), 'I could have you shot.' Even a communist POW was shocked by Shapiro.[62] The prisoners were infuriated that Commonwealth men and women would work with the enemy. 'It was like Lord Haw Haw in World War II,' seethed Clough. 'Burchett never came to the officers' camp,' said Whitamore. 'He was a bad bastard. He should have been shot!' Even so, the journalist contacted Whitamore's father with news of his son. 'My father knew him – Burchett had been a war correspondent in Burma – and he asked [Burchett] to find out. My father got a letter signed by a Chinaman saying I was alive and being well treated. I was ambivalent, but I had sympathy for my parents.' On occasions, the communist reporters were greeted by prisoners holding miniature nooses. 'One or two of these people were quite amenable, but the general attitude was "Wilfred Burchett wants a noose around his neck,"'

* The Chinese were always determined to get written 'confessions' for prisoners' transgressions. As Kinne put it half a century later: 'You had to prove your innocence. It was a bit like dealing with the taxman!'

said Mercer.* Burchett had the misfortune to run up against the man who was to become the most famous 'reactionary', a soldier whose indomitable spirit would become legendary in the camps.†

Fusilier Derek Kinne had volunteered for Korea to avenge his brother, Raymond, killed in North Korea. 'I did not like the Chinese,' he said. 'My only intention was to kill them, which I did in the front line. I was upset, as I had been happy doing what I was doing.' His first act of resistance came soon after his capture. 'The Chinese who captured us were asking us what the different stuff in [ration] cans were – one was a can of fuel we used to heat our food with,' he recalled. 'I said it was "chop-chop", then disappeared among the crowd; I didn't want to be around when he ate it!'

Kinne had been infuriated to see one of Burchett's articles, in which he had reported that POWs were being held in holiday camps in North Korea and fed chicken and pork. 'We were, but the quantities were minute,' said Kinne, who had seen the bodies of those dead from mal-nutrition dragged up to 'Boot Hill'. Then he got a chance to meet him. Burchett was at a table on the football field, lecturing. The conversation began amiably. Kinne first asked if Burchett would take him to visit his brother's grave. That proved impossible. 'I said "Why do you refer to the Americans as them and the Chinese as us?" He said, "That's the side I correspond for." So I said, "Tell your side that there are men dead of malnutrition."' An argument began. It got heated. Fellow POWs dragged Kinne off; he went to the river to cool off. A guard came down and said, 'You – off to jail!' It would not be Kinne's last brush with

---

* The strength of feeling former POWs have about Burchett has not diminished with time. While some accusations against him – such as helping Chinese authorities interrogate POWs – appear baseless, none of my interviewees had any sympathy with either the man or his activities (and as noted in Whitamore's case, Burchett had the decency to pass details of POWs back to their families in the UK). In recent years there have been attempts to rehabilitate Burchett, mostly by fellow journalists; it is telling that so many POWs testified against him in a 1976 court case. (Burchett sued Australian politician Jack Kane for libel after Kane, using KGB defector Yuri Krotkov's testimony to the US Senate, accused him of being a KGB agent. Burchett lost the case but won an appeal.) While there is much to admire about Burchett – he helped Jewish refugees escape Nazi Germany and was the first Western reporter to travel to Hiroshima and report on radiation sickness – he was ideologically compromised, and some of his activities, such as helping Chinese draft reports on POW activities, are anathema to objective journalists. He was an apologist for Stalinism, endorsed Chinese and North Korean allegations of US germ warfare (since the opening of Soviet archives, these allegations have been discredited) and as an acquaintance of mine put it: 'You didn't hear of any of our lot going into Colditz and interviewing prisoners during World War II.' Whether Burchett was a traitor, as every former POW I have spoken with believes, a 'useful fool' for the Eastern Bloc, or a man of conscience doing what he believed was the right thing, the reader must judge for himself. He died in Bulgaria in 1983.
† It is a measure of the respect in which Derek Kinne was held that many published accounts by British POWs – Farrar-Hockley's, Green's, Large's – contain sections on him.

Burchett, but it would be the start of some of the worst treatment meted out to any POW.

That evening, after chastising him for his attitude towards Burchett, guards ordered him to divulge the names of POWs who shared his views. 'I said, "OK, but I need a smoke." They pulled out tobacco, but I said, "No, I want tailor-made cigarettes!" They brought them out – they were difficult to get – and I smoked like a storm! I wrote thirteen and a half pages of *Goldilocks and the Three Bears*! They got mad, really peeved. The Chinese commander – I think he was a homo; we always used to pat his bum! – got furious. He took a flying leap at me – but I'd been learning boxing, and I nailed him with a left: cold as a cucumber! Then they kicked the shit out of me.' Kinne was tied with a noose around his neck and around one leg pulled up behind his back; if he tried to release the pressure by lowering his leg, he would strangle himself. 'I decided, "If I'm gonna go, I'm gonna go."' He jerked his leg down. Guards, watching through a crack in the wall, rushed in and cut him loose.

But the guards were still determined to get a confession. Kinne was screaming so loudly during a beating that a guard stuffed his mouth with a bundle of kapok; he bit down savagely on the guard's fingers. They skewered the material with a bayonet, and thrust it into the back of his mouth. Kinne was beaten senseless and strung up; when he came round, he hallucinated, thinking he was drinking wine at a wedding. In fact, the bayonet had cut open the back of his throat; the wine was blood. Choking, Kinne panicked. Moonlight was shining on a nail sticking in the wall. He rammed himself backwards against the nail, hoping to drill it into his own skull. Guards ran in and cut him down. The next morning, he was brought a platter of barley. Smuggled in with the barley was a message from another prisoner: 'Greater Truth – And It Shall Prevail'.* 'Everything changed from that moment,' Kinne said. He never again considered suicide.

These experiences were just two of many, many brushes Kinne was to have with punishment. In October 1952 he was ordered to confess to being a reactionary and a 'poor student'. 'There was this particular Chinaman, we called him "Machine-gun" because he talked very rapidly. He said, "You must confess." He took out a piece of paper already written. I signed it really close, so they could not add anything else.' Kinne and four other reactionaries were lined up for an open trial in front of fellow prisoners. 'They started from the end. [The prisoners] all said "Guilty." I thought, "Shit, six months hard labour, twelve months . . . " So

* The sender was Gloster Padre Sam Davies, who had heard of the terrible conditions the non-commissioned reactionaries were being held in. See Davies, p. 144.

when it was my turn, I said, "Not guilty!" They said, "Twelve months" automatically – then had to cancel it as I'd said, "Not guilty!"' The man beside Kinne whispered, 'You oughtn't to have said that.' The Chinese said, 'You slander the CPVA and NKPA!' Kinne replied, 'No,' and turned to the other prisoners and said, 'If their lenient policy is torture and star-vation, I've had my fair share!' The audience applauded. Kinne was sen-tenced to eighteen months solitary. When another man was subsequently sent in to join 'the bad guys', Kinne was pleased to discover that he had been sentenced solo: the show trials had ended. 'I screwed that up for them,' he said. 'I had a habit of doing things like that!'

Kinne also experienced one of those rare moments of human kind-ness. After an escape attempt, he had been in solitary, tightly hand-cuffed for eighty-one days. 'There was this one guard, part-Japanese, who, when he kicked you, the force would not be there, and he would smoke and throw cigarette butts near you. When my handcuffs disap-peared into the flesh, he realised what was going on and he got the key and went to release the cuffs. I fainted under the pressure of him touching me.'

Large once encountered Kinne strolling breezily through the camp. He expressed surprise at seeing him: he thought Kinne was in solitary. 'I am, but they haven't missed me yet!' Large thought Kinne was joking, but later found out that the Fusilier had broken out.[63] The big Gloster was greatly impressed by the Fusilier.* So was Green, who, despite making one escape attempt himself – he was recaptured before he had even left the camp boundary and did a spell in solitary – took a live-and-let-live attitude towards captivity, and wondered where his duty as a soldier and his well-being as a man intersected.[64] Clough, who had attempted to escape with Green, had plenty of leisure to think over his own decision. 'We bumped into a guard who should not have been there,' he said. 'We had been given a route out of the camp by the escape committee. We thought it a strange coincidence that the guard was there – or someone had given the game away.' He was imprisoned for weeks in a latrine – a cubicle with a squat toilet, with a plank over it – tightly handcuffed. 'I lost track of time. I thought back over my life, people I had known. There was a crack in the door, where the sunlight came through, and there used to be this spider. It sat and waited for a fly to land. I used to watch that spider for hours.' Clough was taken out and ordered to name collaborators in the escape plot. He was threatened with being sent to China, that he would never be released. At first he gave false names,

* This was no light praise. Large himself would later become a semi-legendary figure as one of the most experienced NCOs in the SAS, with whom he fought in Malaya, Dhofar and Borneo. ▪

then relented – and gave the names of known 'progressives' in the camp.* Eventually, months later, he was released. As he walked back to the British compound, hands dangling uselessly with 'drop wrist',† the Americans cheered him.

One of the most notorious punishments in the Chinese-run camps was 'The Kennels': wooden boxes five and a half feet long by four feet wide. 'We couldn't stand. They rarely let us out, and we had to piss in the cans we used for food: That place stunk!' said Kinne. 'The guard came round with food, he gave me just the barley water in my can and laughed, so I threw the hot water back at him.' Kinne was taken out and beaten. Then he was returned to his box, and made to stand, bent over. For the six-footer it was torture. 'I thought, "Enough."' Guards dragged Kinne out of his box and rained blows upon him. He fought back. A sergeant appeared with a submachine-gun and started striking Kinne with the butt end – but the spring chambered a round. 'The damned thing went off! I heard a pop.' There was sudden silence. The NCO lay motionless – dead. The Chinese stood around in shock. 'One guard was standing there, with a lit cigarette, so I took it, said, "Thank you very much," sat and smoked it.' Kinne was returned to his box. On a stick, he passed another prisoner his signet ring to give to his mother – 'I figured I was going to get shot.' Instead, he was taken to solitary in a mud-floored hut. Then it was time to confess. 'They told me I was sick, and they were my doctors – they were going to "cure my mind". I wasn't going to sign. I said, "You write it – I'll approve it!"' Kinne was marched out, certain that he was to be executed. 'I asked for a blindfold, because I didn't have the balls to look down the rifle barrels of the firing squad. But they didn't shoot me – all I got was a butt in the belly, then they beat me – with sticks, not guns, because of the guard commander who had shot himself!' He was returned to solitary.

Another punishment was to make prisoners sit in a circle scraped in the dust – sometimes for seventeen hours – motionless. 'One guard drew a circle for me to sit in, but I used to move, and draw another circle on the floor with a twig,' said Kinne. 'When he came round again, I had moved, but he couldn't work out how!' Kinne found it worse than 'The Kennels': 'There you could lean against the wall and rest when the guards passed, you could talk to others.'

The death of King George VI was considered fine news by the Chinese. One guard made the mistake of approaching one of the most formidable

---

* Once he was returned to the general population, Clough made 'discreet enquiries' about what had happened to some of the 'progressives' whose names he had given as fellow plotters. It turned out that they had been quizzed, but nothing more. 'I think the Chinese realised I was having them on, but at the same time, it cast doubts in their minds about them,' he said.
† The condition continued intermittently for nine months.

Rifles NCOs, Ulsterman Andy McNab, with the happy tidings. 'I have news for you,' said the guard. 'Your king is dead!' 'I have news for you,' said McNab – a heavyweight boxer – and punched him unconscious. He was dragged away to solitary.[65] Kinne, typically, insisted on celebrating the Queen's Coronation in June 1953. He and a fellow 'reactionary' wore rosettes in their lapels. The Chinese arrived with bayoneted rifles, to take them. There was a scuffle, then Kinne was strung up in a hut. 'They hung me up in storage with the garlic, salt and pepper. But I was able to get off the hook, tie my ankles together and stuff my trousers with peppers and stuff – so I had all kinds of goodies to put in our food when we came out.'

Rank was no defence against brutality. At Christmas 1951 a party was held for the officers' camp. Communist reporters were in attendance to record the festivities. After the media departed the atmosphere changed. The prisoners had refused to send seasonal greetings to Marshal Peng and were resisting 'education'. Senior officers were to be punished. Major Denis Harding – who had just been treated for pneumonia – was arrested. He was hung from the ceiling, arms behind him, for hours. Then he was taken outside, stripped to the waist in the freezing air. An American colonel was placed in an open hut, with no coat or bedding, in the sub-zero temperatures. Trials were held. The senior officers – an American colonel, Carne, Harding, and three American majors – were sentenced to solitary confinement of between three and six months.[66]

Carne – that coolest, most taciturn of officers – was perhaps better equipped to endure isolation than the vast majority of men. During his nineteen months in solitary, the West Countryman, the senior officer in his camp, occupied mind and body working on a piece of art that was later given to Padre Sam Davies, who used it as the centrepiece of camp services. In darkness and silence, from a ten-inch block of North Korean rock, the Gloster CO carved an austerely beautiful Celtic cross.

\* \* \*

In war, the optimum time to escape is immediately after capture. The further prisoners are moved, the further opportunities recede. Three days north of the Imjin, Temple made his first bid for freedom. Temple, two Glosters and an American discovered a trapdoor in the floor of the schoolhouse where they were being held. Nearby were four sacks of rice chaff. The four arranged for someone to answer their names at roll call, and to place the sacks on top of the trapdoor once they were under it. The ruse worked. The escapees subsequently raised the hatch and started off into the night. With dawn, they took cover in hillside scrub.

In the distance, the four could see a range of mountains. Prospects were good, until an old Korean and her grandson walked over them. It was incredible bad luck. 'We thought, "Do we kill her and her grandson?" We did discuss it, but we weren't that kind of people, so we just let her go.' Before long, shots rang out, and the fugitives were surrounded by armed North Koreans. 'This was awkward, as we had just passed though this village that had been bombed by the Americans,' said Temple. 'We all said, "We are *Yongguk*, not *Miguk*."'* The four were taken by NKPA soldiers to a nearby village. 'We had a meal: it was dried squid and was really very pleasant. There were always surprises when you were a POW.'

Then they were moved to a compound, a schoolhouse in a mining village. Again, they decided to escape; this time, the plan was to reach the west coast, hijack a boat and sail it south to friendly territory. 'Escaping was easy – the guard walked one way, we walked the other,' said Temple. 'Evading was the problem!' Rain came pelting down. One man began suffering from hypothermia. 'We came across this farmhouse with an old woman and her grandson or nephew. She was absolutely terrified: We just said we wanted to lie on the *kang* [a raised, heated floor]. We were stupid: The little boy slipped away and raised the alarm. In three hours, bullets were going through the mud walls. That was that.' The men were returned to the Mining Camp. The commandant had lost face; he moved the would-be escapees into a small house. The men were tied up, but when their captors departed they undid each other. The guards returned and trussed them up again, much tighter. 'I lost all circulation in my arms, and gangrene set in after about eight days,' said Temple. 'My arms were just a sea of yellow pus up to the armpits. There must have been a terrible smell – Koreans passing by outside the newspaper windows were holding their noses and crossing the street. Fortunately, these blue-arsed flies came in and laid eggs, which turned into maggots, and ate all the nasty stuff. Most of them turned yellowish, but some were turning red – they were eating the good stuff! We scooped the red ones out.' When he eventually had his bonds undone, Temple had 'drop wrist' for days.

Other men also tried to get out during the progress north. Several days into the march, Eagles was asked to join an escape with two Americans and a fellow Briton; the Americans had just been recaptured after an earlier attempt. He assented. The four dived into a bush. The column plodded past. The escapees marched for days. One night, they rested up in a house with an old man and an old woman, who treated them kindly, giving them food and drink. Then they were told to get

* British, not Americans.

out: the couple's grandson had seen them and warned the authorities. As they were leaving, shots were fired over their heads. A Chinese soldier appeared with a group of North Korean police. Hands bound with wire, the POWs were led to a nearby town and ordered to crouch against a wall. The senior policeman offered Eagles a cigarette. Would this prove to be one of these acts of human warmth? As Eagles pursed his lips to receive the smoke, the man reversed it, burning his mouth. 'I spat at him, and another one hit me with a rifle butt in the groin'; he was saved from permanent injury by a metal cigarette tin in his pocket, which was bent double by the impact. The four were shoved into a shed. Some time later the door opened, and an old lunatic came in and started furiously beating them with a stick. Eagle kicked at him; eventually the guards removed him. (The escapees later learned that the man's family had been killed in an air attack.) Then the guards returned for the two Americans. 'As they were being led out, they said, "Well, it's been nice knowing you";' it seemed apparent they were going to their deaths. Later Eagles was taken out of the shed. He heard shooting. Looking over, he saw laughing Koreans firing into a covered trench with the two GIs cowering in the corner: they were shooting to frighten, not kill. A Chinese patrol doubled over – 'they must have heard the shooting' – and took charge of the POWs.

They were marched north. At a stop, Eagles was taken out and shoved against a concrete post. The muzzle of a revolver with a single bullet in it was placed against his head. The chamber was spun. 'This guy called "Scarface" – he had been burned by napalm – said, "You are the ringleader,"' Eagles recalled. 'I said, "We have no ringleader!"' The man nodded and the soldier holding the pistol pulled the trigger. 'It went "click" – a very loud click!' said Eagles. 'If you spin a revolver cylinder with a round in it, the weight carries the bullet to the bottom. But I thought, "What if . . . ?"' The process was repeated. 'I was a bit scared, then. He said, "You are the ringleader?" and I said, "All right, yes."' As punishment, Eagles was confined in a covered pit for a week. Those in the hole were subject to infections from the damp, with bronchitis being the mildest. One of the Americans, in the pit for two weeks, died of pneumonia.

Escapees found the North Koreans worse than the Chinese. Kinne, during a period of close confinement, managed to loosen his cuffs and 'bug out over the hills'. He was recaptured by North Koreans – 'real bastards!' He was jammed into a tiny cell with a tiny window high up in the wall. Through a hole in his cell door a stick was shoved into his mouth, and when the guards walked past they would strike it, splitting open the sides of his mouth and sending a shock rattling through his teeth, jaws and spine. When Chinese arrived to return him to the POW camp, Kinne was 'Thrilled to bits; going back was like heaven.'*

Escape was an incredibly long shot, but that did not stop the Glosters' adjutant from trying again and again. Farrar-Hockley made his second attempt almost as soon as he reached the camp north of Pyongyang. With another officer, he slipped out at night. Several days later, they were both recaptured. Again he escaped. Again he was recaptured. Each time, treatment worsened. In one camp a guard slashed his foot; in another he was made to empty the filthy latrine – a huge, buried stone jar served by a leaking bucket. After yet another escape and recapture he fell foul of North Korean police. In Pyongyang jail he underwent interrogation. Asked about other escapees, he declined to answer. He was led to a concrete cell. Ropes dangled from metal rings on the ceiling; a water butt stood against one wall. The walls and floor were discoloured by what looked like bloodstains. The officer realised with a shock that he was looking at a twentieth-century torture chamber. He was stripped to the waist, bound to the chair and kicked to the floor, then a towel was placed over his face and water dribbled over it. He choked, thinking that they might drown him – then realised that was the aim. More questions. More water on the towel. Every time he breathed in, the wet cloth was sucked into his mouth and over his nostrils.† His lungs began to fill. Falling unconscious, he was brought round by cigarette burns. The process was repeated three times, then he was slung, bound, into a dark cell. The treatment continued for days. Each time he told himself he would resist for another day. Each night, he prayed. Then he was told he was to be shot. It seemed a mercy. As he awaited execution that night, a policeman came in, loosened his shackles and offered him a cigarette. The British officer smoked. The two men looked at one another. The North Korean gave the doomed Englishman a sympathetic smile. Farrar-Hockley – the hard man, the professional, the warrior – could not prevent tears rolling down his cheeks. By next morning, he was at peace. The hour came. He was ordered out.

---

* This incident happened before the brutalities Kinne suffered after the 'Comrade Burchett' incident.
† The Korean proclivity for water torture did not end with the Korean War – nor was it restricted to North Korea. During the period of authoritarian government in the South, only ended after the pro-democracy protests of 1987, the practice was used against opponents of the regime. I had occasion to visit the notorious Korean CIA building on Namsan, Central Seoul, soon after it had been turned over to the Seoul Development Institute in the millennium. When I wondered to the female professor who was my guide whether the (vast) basement had been full of torture chambers, she replied that yes, every room had been a bathroom. Indeed, the fire that ignited 1987's people-power demonstrations was the death of Park Jong-chol, a student protester, in police custody in an infamous plain black building – a secret police station near the US Army base in Yongsan – that year. Twenty years later, in 2007, the cell Park drowned in was turned into a permanent shrine. It still contains the fitted bathroom where the twenty-one-year-old was murdered.

294 · To THE LAST ROUND

He marched into the sunlight, past a file of armed troops, quietly intoning the 23rd Psalm. He was joined by another prisoner. Without explanation, they were marched out of the prison, to a jeep, and driven to a POW camp outside the city. It was like a homecoming.[67]

Fusilier Intelligence Sergeant David Sharp teamed up with Second Lieutenant Leo Adams-Acton, a Fusilier officer who had been seconded to partisan forces operating in North Korea.* The two found it easy to escape the camp. 'Adams-Acton obviously knew where partisan teams were working; at one stage we crossed the Yalu into China,' said Sharp. 'We moved by night and laid up during the day above the tree line, and stayed away from all signs of habitation.' One night, moving parallel to a road, they boxed around a hamlet; they could see lights and hear music and conversation. But all Korean villages had a built-in alarm: dogs. Barks rang out. The escapees were spotted and surrounded by a patrol of North Koreans and Chinese. 'There was a row going on between the Chinese and the Koreans, and we knew if the Koreans got us we'd be in very, very serious trouble,' Sharp recalled. The two were returned to the camp, where Sharp was placed in the 'kennels'. [68]

As Clough had found, the dangers would-be escapees faced were not all external. In March 1953 Whitamore and a fellow officer hatched a plan to escape, follow the Yalu to its estuary, steal a boat and sail south. The pair asked escape maestro Farrar-Hockley his advice. 'We were shocked that he was planning to go the same way,' Whitamore said. Even so, the men made their preparations. The night they planned to leave, Whitamore was suddenly grabbed by guards, 'and we were in durance vile'. The two were placed in solitary confinement and questioned; 'the interrogation was a bit physical'. They realised that there was a snitch in the camp. 'Someone saw us blanching soya beans on a fire outside; we cooked them for protein,' said Whitamore. 'We suspected who it was.' After being released from solitary, he asked permission from a senior officer 'to hit this one fellow over the head with a rock. I was told, if I did I'd be up on a charge of murder; it would be no help.'

In North Korea escapees were identifiable simply by the colour of their skin and hair. Unlike in Nazi-occupied Europe, there was no escape network, no sympathetic civilians. Although one POW was rumoured to have made it two hundred miles south before being recaptured, not a single Korean War prisoner escaped the camps.

* * *

* Adams-Acton was to be killed during another escape attempt just a month before the POWs were freed.

'Shit-house rumour' in the camps had always focused on the peace talks, on when the prisoners would be released. Everyone craved information. 'The Chinese only told us what was happening with the peace talks when it suited them,' said Mercer. Armistice negotiations had started on 10 July 1951, and senior officers embargoed escape attempts when it was understood talks were going well, but progress was tortuous. What soon became clear to the Chinese was that POWs were an important bargaining chip – the more alive, the better – but while they claimed to hold 65,000 prisoners, they discovered they actually held only 12,000. Almost half the Americans had died, mostly in North Korean camps in the first terrible year of captivity. At the end of 1951 all POWs in North Korean hands were transferred to Chinese-run camps.[69]

Conditions gradually improved to something approaching those endured by Chinese troops and the local Koreans.[70] Green enjoyed far more freedom than he expected, and found the Chinese 'surprisingly ready to smile and leave us to do our own thing, provided that we played the game by their rules'.[71] Even Padre Davies, a staunch anti-communist, conceded that from late 1951 the Chinese attitude towards the POWs was reasonable – even magnanimous. In the final six months Red Cross parcels were allowed. The men received cigarettes, candies, razors, toilet bags, beer and wine. Bunks were built. [72] In March 1953 a Chinese surgical team arrived in Choksong to replace the filthy and incompetent doctor. In April Large was efficiently operated on: a tracer round was removed from his body and given to him. [73] In the officers' camp, Carne emerged from nineteen months in solitary. Men queued up to shake his hand. [74]

The first prisoner exchange, 'Little Switch' in April 1953, was for the wounded.* Among them was Mercer. The men chosen travelled south in a convoy with air recognition panels spread over their bonnets. 'We were worried because Americans are a bit trigger-happy,' said Mercer. 'I noticed to my horror a battery of AA guns tracking two F-80s circling up there. I

---

* In fact, a large number of 'progressives' were released along with the wounded. Once freed, a number of these men, who included hard-core leftists, made comments that were harshly critical of the war, and voiced pro-Chinese and pro-North Korean sentiments, adding to alarmist rumours of brainwashing sparked by the statements of captured USAF pilots who had, under immense physical and psychological pressure, 'confessed' to germ warfare. However, among the bulk of prisoners released in August and September there was far less pro-communist sentiment; likewise, the USAF personnel later retracted their confessions. In the event, the considerable communist attempt to convert POWs to their cause seems to have been a huge failure. A dozen men were later identified as having been actively engaged in enemy propaganda and in betraying comrades' escape attempts; these prisoners amounted to 0.07 per cent of all POWs. No charges were laid against them in the UK; all left the armed forces. For details, see Farrar-Hockley (1995), pp. 411–12.

prayed, "No! Not now!"' The last staging post before the border crossing was a temple. Mindful of previous disappointments, the twenty members of Mercer's group waited. The atmosphere was electric. 'The Chinese are past masters at psychology,' said Mercer. 'One came in, took out a piece of paper, looked around, folded it up, and walked out.' The POWs waited – then, suddenly, they were released. Senior officers greeted the men as they crossed into UN hands.

But 'Little Switch' only involved a small minority of POWs. In the camps news of the peace talks from Radio Peking was broadcast over tannoys. Rumours multiplied, and stress caused wild mood swings. On days when there was no air activity above, men wondered excitedly if peace had broken out. Their hopes would be dashed when vapour trails reappeared, signalling ongoing hostilities.

Then, on 27 July 1953, it happened. Far to the south of the POW camps a strange silence – one unheard for three years – settled over Korea. Across cratered paddy fields and ruined villages, blackened hills and fortified mountains, the gunfire ceased. A truce had gone into effect. Yet, after three years of war, there was no victor. Despite the death of hundreds of thousands, probably millions, the Korean War had ground to a halt along the 38th parallel, the same border on which it had started.*

In the officers' camp, the commandant called a parade. Optimists were convinced it meant peace; pessimists thought it was to announce that the USSR had entered the war.† The entire camp staff was there. Commandant Ding – 'Snake Eyes' – spoke in Chinese. There was a tense pause as his remarks were translated. An armistice was to take effect. Chinese press hovered to capture the delighted reaction. There was none. The parade broke up, prisoners walking off 'like men in a dream'.[75]

From 5 August to 6 September Operation 'Big Switch' took place. By trains and in trucks, groups of UN prisoners journeyed to the truce village of Panmunjom. For many the lingering near the border – some had to wait for weeks before their names were called – was the most nerve-racking

---

* There are no accurate figures for total deaths in the Korean War. What can be said with reasonable certainty is that 33,667 Americans and 3,960 UN allies (1,078 of them British) died. Beyond that, all figures are conjecture. The ROK Armed Forces suffered between 184,573 and 257,000 dead and missing. ROK civilian deaths have been estimated at around 244,000, about half killed by the NKPA, the remainder dying of starvation, exposure, disease, or being killed by ROK forces in counter-insurgency operations or by UN troops in 'friendly fire' incidents. For the communist side, North Korean death estimates vary from a low of 294,931 to 2.5 million. China admits to 152,400 combat dead, though some Western historians estimate them as high as 1 million. For more on this controversy see Allan R. Millet, 'Casualties', in Tucker, pp. 98–101. Given the discrepancy between these figures, it is difficult to come up even with a reliable guesstimate of total deaths. Most historians think the total is in the millions.

† On the march north, and throughout their captivity, the POWs had seen Caucasians – Eastern-bloc technicians and advisers – and even Soviet anti-aircraft troops in North Korea.

period of captivity. Green fretted that if there was a ceasefire violation, fighting would break out again, and he would be returned to a camp.[76] The days passed. Names were called. Men departed. When Carne's name was called a cheer went up from American officers. Davies found himself one of the last to leave: having arrived at Kaesong on 21 August, he was not released until 5 September. His group included Majury and was largely composed of those who had led religious services.[77]

Freedom engendered different reactions. Temple was amused as his group crossed: 'When we were coming over Freedom Bridge, there was a Redcap [Military Policeman] standing there, and one of the men went up to him, flung his arms around him, kissed him and said, "Now I know we are really home!"' Kinne, crossing the demarcation line, saw communist POWs, arriving in the opposite direction, hurling away American clothing and boots in defiance. 'I stripped off too – naked!' he said. Across the line, he had to borrow a new set of clothes. There was a surprise for Davies. Within half an hour of arrival, the senior British chaplain handed him his field service paten, lost in action. It had been discovered, half buried in a paddy field, by a patrol near the Glosters' position when UN troops had returned to the Imjin after the battle. The patrol had realised immediately that it could only have belonged to the battalion chaplain.[78]

The initial reaction of many on crossing into 'Freedom Village' was confusion at the process: fumigation, hot showers, new uniform issue, debriefings, briefings. Journalists waited, seeking quotes about 'what it had been like'. The prisoners were given anything they wanted to eat or drink, from fresh bread to banana milkshakes. 'They fed us – "Do you want steak? Mashed potatoes? Ice cream?"' Mercer remembered. 'They meant well, but we had been living on rice and turnip soup and weren't equipped for it.' Due to shrunken stomachs, many suffered appalling cramps. 'All I wanted was fresh bread – I ate half a loaf of bread, and four hours later thought I was changing sex!' said Sharp. 'My goodness, it was painful.'[79] The variety, the ability to actually have as much as one wanted, overwhelmed others. 'They said, "What would you like? Tea or coffee?"' recalled Kinne. 'I said, "Tea." An American said, "I want milk." So I said, "Can I have some milk too?" I ended up with coffee, milk, tea, a doughnut, candy, and I remember people laughing, because we were making idiots of ourselves.' Later, when the POWs arrived at the British base in Kure, Japan, the cookhouse was open twenty-four hours. 'We were putting mashed potatoes in our shirts, hiding steaks – we didn't realise you could go back any time and get the stuff,' said Kinne. 'The toilets were overrunning – we made a hell of a mess.'

In hospital in Japan a dream came true for Mercer. 'They said, "The bathroom is over there." The last bath I had had was over two years ago.

I ran the tap until it came up to the overflow, got in and wallowed. That was luxury. That was the best moment.' After a week the badly wounded Gloster was flown home. On the way to the plane the crew insisted he get on a stretcher. 'I had been struggling around for two years, but they said, "Get on that stretcher." That annoyed me.' Other men found that reality did not match dreams: in the camps Whitamore had lusted after canned peaches, but when he was given as many as he wanted he found them anticlimactic.

Despite the improved treatment at the end of their captivity, the POWs had suffered drastic weight loss. Large found that only a few mouthfuls of food filled him. He had gone into battle weighing fifteen stone, eight pounds. When he was weighed upon release, he was nine stone ten.[80] Kinne had lost so much weight he could not sit down comfortably: his tailbone banged against the seat.

In the camps Kinne had promised himself that he would tell everyone he later met about his experiences. When he was in hospital for treatment of his hernia, a nursing captain came and asked him what it had been like. 'I started to tell her. She was listening, then she started looking at this watch. She was not taking it in. So I never told anyone else – I just said, "The food was lousy. It was rough."' But word of Kinne's feats had spread. An officer arrived with a map of the camp. 'He knew where the toilets were and everything,' Kinne recalled. 'He was saying, "You were here, here and here." I said, "You know more than I know!"' The officer debriefed Kinne and left, telling the Fusilier that he might get a medal or mention in dispatches. Kinne thought nothing more of it.

At last, the men embarked on troopships for home. At sea there was plenty of time to recollect. Many former prisoners found that they could not overcome the disrespect for authority that they had nurtured as POWs. Temple, as Duty Officer, was leaning on the rail of the troopship as it docked in Hong Kong with the formidable Ulsterman Andy McNab at his side. The two were watching as men staggered up the gangway from a run ashore, when McNab spotted a mate being hauled along by a pair of MPs. 'McNab said, "That's my mucker!"' Temple recalled. 'He went down the gangplank. Bang! One MP is in the harbour. Bang! He knocks the second one in. Two more redcaps come up the gangplank. He knocks their heads together.' The provost marshal ordered Temple to deal with McNab. Temple said he would do so. Later, the provost marshal asked if he taken appropriate action. Temple nodded. In fact, he had invited McNab to his cabin for drinks. 'We had this spirit of resistance,' he said.

Temple was also put in charge of six former 'progressives'. Rumour had it that other men were plotting their demise. 'I heard that they were planning to drop them overboard near The Needles: "Nice and foggy; nobody will see."' Temple told Farrar-Hockley what he had heard and suggested the six be put ashore. The men were unloaded in Singapore for a separate route home. Repercussions continued for other 'progressives'. Farrar-Hockley was urgently summoned to the stern rail by a warrant officer: a group was attempting to throw several 'progressives' overboard. They were taken into protective custody.[81]

The troopship *Asturias*, with the Glosters aboard, arrived in Southampton to a flotilla of boats and even press helicopters overhead. Men lined the rails and sang 'There'll always be an England'. On the dock David Green was greeted by his family – and by his old company commander. Major Walwyn was immaculate in uniform, with one sleeve empty: The wound he had received on Hill 327 had necessitated amputation. He apologised to his soldiers for not having been with them in their final battle.[82] Then the men embarked on buses for the trip to home towns and villages. Some would continue army careers; for others demobilisation beckoned. And for some there would be the totally unexpected.

Kinne decided not to remain in the army, so was surprised to be summoned to York, where the Fusiliers were garrisoned. He was met by an officer as personal escort. Kinne repeatedly asked him what on earth was going on; the officer was equally mystified. Still, the Fusilier enjoyed the attention. 'I said, "I need a haircut,"' and he was taken for one. When he returned to the barracks the library had been turned into a press room, and a crowd of reporters from national dailies were there, notebooks poised. The CO was waiting. He stated that he would normally deliver the announcement himself, but had decided to hand that privilege over to an officer who, like Kinne, had been in the camps. That officer faced Kinne and intoned, 'It is my honour to inform you, you have been awarded the George Cross!' Kinne's first reaction – in the past, he had been threatened with court-martial and been told he 'would never make a soldier' – was disappointment. 'God, I wish it had been the Military Medal,' he sighed. The officer was dumbfounded. 'Good God man, do you know what you are saying?' he spluttered. Then the penny dropped. Kinne had been fascinated by the 1950 film *Odette* – about SOE agent Odette Sansom, awarded the George Cross for courage after capture and Gestapo torture – and watched it five times. Now, he was walking in his heroine's footsteps. The soldier who had gone to Korea to avenge the death of his brother, Raymond, had not defiled the family name.

But not every POW returned to home, family and freedom. On Sunday 22 April 1951, on the eve of battle, Gloster Lieutenants Terry Waters and Phil Curtis had had their photograph taken in the little temple behind their company position. On the dawn-lit summit of

Castle Site, Curtis had died knocking out the machine-gun bunker that dominated the hill. His friend's lonely sacrifice would take place deep in the blackness of North Korean rock. Waters was the only officer in A Company to survive the first night. Despite a leg wound, he fought again two nights later, during the Glosters' last stand on Hill 235. Again he was hit, in the head. On the march north his group of wounded prisoners was incarcerated in the most notorious of the North Korean-run prison camps, 'The Caves'. North of Pyongyang, The Caves could hardly be dignified with the name of 'camp': they were a series of dank mining tunnels burrowed into the hills. There were North Koreans there, swarming with lice, hair hanging past their shoulders: they were Christians. There was no light, no heat. Subterranean streams ran along the floors. In the disease-riddled, dank darkness, men began to die. Their captors told the wounded British soldiers that they could leave the dungeon and receive decent food and medical treatment if they co-operated and joined a 'Peace Fighters' camp where they would undertake propaganda activities. All refused. But, seeing men dying, Waters reached a decision. Calling his sergeant over, he told him that in the interest of saving the men's lives, he should acquiesce, take the POWs to the 'Peace Fighter' camp and undertake minimal propaganda activities. The NCO asked whether the officer would join them. Waters replied, 'No, not me.' Then he ordered the men to leave. He stayed. Four times the North Koreans tried to tempt Waters out, with offers of rich food and medical treatment for his wounds. His body weakened. His spirit did not. Each time, Waters refused. There could be only one ending. Philip Curtis, 24, was awarded the Victoria Cross; Terry Waters, 22, the George Cross. Both medals were posthumous.[83]

Of the 1,060 British POWs taken in Korea, seventy-one are known to have died; a further eleven are presumed to have died.[84]

# Chapter 13

## IN RETROSPECT

*Quis Seperabit?*[*]

Regimental Motto, Royal Ulster Rifles

**M**ILLENNIAL SEOUL BEARS scant resemblance to the deserted, rubble-strewn wreck that 29th Brigade left behind in spring 1951, as it motored north to the Imjin. A sprawling metropolis of ten million people, today's city is built on a scale that makes London look twee. Gleaming ranks of office buildings line broad boulevards; battalions of identical concrete apartment blocks march towards the hazy horizon; huge markets teem with raucous traders. To European eyes, Seoul is not a beautiful city, but it is hard not to be impressed by its size, its bustle, its sheer dynamism.

The geography is unchanged from the 1950s: the great granite mountains still encircle the city centre, just as the broad Han – now crisscrossed with road and rail bridges – still meanders down to the Yellow Sea. The urban landscape, however, is unrecognisable. Relentless development has bulldozed all but a few hundred of the traditional cottages that once formed the majority of its residences. The great domed Capitol Building in which George Truell sited his artillery CP has been razed as a remnant of Japanese colonial rule. James Van Fleet would have difficulty deploying the hundreds of artillery pieces he sited along the road from the city centre to the Han to halt the final phases of Peng Te-huai's greatest offensive; a constant logjam of traffic dominates it. And George Strachan would not be able to fire his Centurion's 20-pounder from Yongdungpo across Youido Island and the river into targets on the north bank. The island is a high-rise financial district, and all that remains of its old airfield is a concrete plaza in the park at its centre.

The city's last battle scars are stabbed into the masonry of the palaces. Lines of bullet holes stitch across the south-eastern gate of Kyongbuk Palace. Visitors to Toksu Palace, entering under the great gate, may notice the shrapnel and bullet damage in the stonework of the old bridge. The British embassy residence and the Anglican Cathedral still stand. The seventeenth-century silver cross discovered and restored

* 'Who shall separate us?'

302 · TO THE LAST ROUND

by the Hussars after the city's recapture* now lives in a glass case in the bishop's office. Old soldiers might enjoy the hearty Korean War-style *budae jiggae* ('regimental stew') still served in cheap restaurants: a mix of frankfurters and spam with *kimchi* and noodles. Spam, the tinned meat that sustained so many refugees during the war, remains a popular gift for the older generation.

What then of the Imjin battlefield? The site of 29th Brigade's stand is (just) inside South Korean territory, forty minutes from the capital. To get there, it is better to head west, then north, for the 'Uijongbu Corridor' is usually bumper to bumper – moreover, the western route is more scenic. Speeding along the *Chayuro* ('Freedom') expressway beside the Han, river-side apartments whip by in a blur. But just minutes down the motorway is the first sign that this nation is not at peace. What looks like a bridge, covered in advertising, looms over the eight-lane road. It leads nowhere. It is, in fact, a massive slab of concrete set on stanchions, designed to be blown to block the road in the event of another North Korean invasion.

Signs of military activity multiply further west. A razor-wire fence lines one side of the motorway near the Han estuary, a potential infiltration point for North Korean frogmen. Sandbagged bunkers and dug-in troop carriers are stationed at the roadside. About thirty minutes from Seoul, the route turns right off the expressway, past a petrol station and restaurant, to follow a quiet country road set among low, rolling hills. On the left is a river: the Water Dragon.

Little villages (of brick and tile – for wattle and thatch were replaced in the 1970s) and rural restaurants dot the road and hills. But, in the words of writer Michael Breen, this part of South Korea resembles 'a Steven Spielberg movie set'. It is impossible not to notice the giant artillery bunkers, the walled army bases in the valleys, the truck convoys rumbling along the roads, the zig-zag trenches, the knee-high barbed wire entanglements, the bunkers carved into the hills. Nearly sixty years after the Korean War ended with a ceasefire, the Demilitarized Zone carves across the peninsula. The border is just ten kilometres north of the river. Nowadays 29th Brigade's sector is held by the ROK 25th Division, headquartered close to the southern exit of Five Yankee, the Glosters' line of communication. Testimony to the continuing strategic importance of this area is the fact that the last US ground combat unit in Korea – a mechanised brigade of the 2nd Infantry Division – is stationed north of Uijongbu at Tongduchon, a garrison town on the MSR some four kilometres east of the position of 29th Brigade's HQ on the last day of battle.

---

* I am grateful to Brigadier (ret.) Mervyn McCord, Royal Ulster Rifles, and Brigadier (ret.) Dick Webster, 8th Hussars, for bringing the story of the cross to my attention.

The first township on the Imjin's south bank is Choksong, now a gritty main street of low-end restaurants, car-repair shops and a small bus station. A few minutes' drive to the west of the town is Hill 235. The valley is now a memorial park maintained by Paju City; Paju's mayor is a frequent visitor to the annual April services held here by the dwindling band of British veterans. A footbridge crosses the stream at which parched Glosters dropped to drink before attempting to break out. It leads to a glade where a stone memorial carved into the hill's granite base commemorates the stand of the Glosters and C Troop, 170 Mortar Battery; a bilingual plaque tells the story of the battle. Behind the hill an expressway traverses C Company's old positions. Further along the valley, Route Five Yankee winds into the hills.

Even though ROK forces are stationed north of the river, the battlefield is still heavily garrisoned. A watchtower looms over the cutting where Guy Temple's patrol massacred the Chinese spearhead in the river; a base stands behind it. But across the Imjin – you can now drive over a fine bridge, rather than wade 'Gloster Crossing' – the area where the Chinese formed up before entering the waters is a cluster of real estate agents. Despite the proximity of North Korea and the heavy military presence, the pretty countryside is a popular weekend destination; holiday villas are scattered among the farms and bases. Beside the road south of the river stands a tiny temple; here Philip Curtis and Terry Waters were blessed by Sam Davies on the eve of battle. Though renovated, it is otherwise unchanged, and the gatekeeper is happy to unlock the front doors for visiting veterans. A dirt track leads up to 'Castle Site'. The hill is criss-crossed with 25th Division's trenches, bunkers and firing points – all more substantial than A Company's flimsy slits. The summit, where Curtis won his VC, is crowned with concrete vehicle bunkers and a viewing stand overlooking the Imjin, glinting to the north.

Further east on the south bank, along what is today a fine road, is Hill 257, the eminence held by the Fusiliers' Z Company on the first night of battle. On a knoll rising from its forward slope is a tactical helicopter landing zone and, further up, a monument to ROK troops who defended the area earlier in the war. From the LZ there are good views across the river to the Belgian position, Hill 194. Barracks stand at the rear of the hill (the hinge in the Imjin and Hantan remains vital). A dirt track winding around the lower slopes of Hill 257 leads to the top end of Route 11, where George Truell fired his 25-pounder into the advancing Chinese.

The area further south down Route 11 – asphalt has replaced compressed dirt and rock – has more small farmhouses and villages than before, but the landscape – paddy fields, with copses and bushes sprinkled here and there – is largely unchanged. Driving south, on the right are the hills held by the Fusiliers; on the left is the imposing bulk of Hill 398, the Rifles' bastion. There are more bases here, and the saddle, or backstop position, held by the Rifles' B Company, is carved with zigzag trenches. South of this rise, the dogleg in the road where the Chinese sited their ambush on 25 April is now a small reservoir. There are more rough little farms, and more army bases, in the hills down which the Chinese swarmed.

Could – should? – the struggle that took place among these haunted hills have been fought differently? And how critical was 29th Brigade's battle in terms of the overall UN effort in Korea?

\* \* \*

In *Billy Budd*, Hermann Melville wrote: 'Forty years after a battle it is easy for a non-combatant to reason about how it ought to have been fought. It is another thing personally and under fire to direct the fighting while involved in the obscuring smoke of it.' Indeed. But in assessing Britain's bloodiest post-war battle, it is germane to ask what went wrong and what did not.

The unusual combination of troops that fought on the Imjin – jaded reservists and young regulars, sprinkled with National Servicemen, led by NCOs and officers with solid service records from World War II – proved a potent mix. While there were isolated examples of cowardice, most men fought hard. The American battlefield analyst, S.L.A. Marshall,\* found that among US infantrymen in World War II, less than 15 per cent fired their weapons, but none of my interviewees found this true of 29th Brigade in Korea. 'Everyone did their job' was the common reply when the question was asked. The infantry's weapons, however, were ill-suited to repelling close-range mass attack. The *Wehrmacht* on the Russian Front, facing a similar tactical problem, was, by 1945, arming its grenadiers with the *Sturmgewehr* 44 assault rifle (the model for Mikhail Kalashnikov's iconic AK-47), general-purpose machine-guns (the fast-firing MG-42, or 'Hitler Scythe') and hollow-charge, disposable anti-tank/anti-bunker weapons (the *Panzerfaust*). British troops would not adopt a similar weapons mix until the 1980s. As it was, in darkness, at close quarters, the aimed single shot from a Lee-Enfield was not the ideal defensive solution. 'What we could have done with automatics!' said Ben Whitchurch. 'There were ten of you fighting for

---

\* Marshall's findings are respected by many of today's leading military academics – such as John Keegan and David Grossman – but some British officers strongly disagree with his findings and research methodologies. However, Marshall, who also studied the Korean War, noted that the firing rates of US troops increased dramatically in desperate perimeter defence situations – such as 29th Brigade faced on the Imjin.

your bloody lives and there were 150 of them coming at you, and you were trying to pick them off!' The Stens lacked knockdown power and reliability. The Vickers and Brens, while durable, both had relatively low rates of fire – just over a third that of the murderous MG-42, which fired 1,200 rounds per minute. Given these shortcomings, the British were fortunate that their grenades – the Mills bomb, or fragmentation grenade, and the phosphorus grenade – were both effective and lavishly issued. And, critically, they enjoyed effective fire support, from mortars, 45 Field and the 8th Hussars.

Of the four infantry battalions engaged, it seems unwise to praise any above the others. The only one which lost no ground was the Rifles – but the Ulstermen did not face the onslaught on the first night, and on the 23rd and 24th had two companies on Hill 394 (a feature that had pre-built defences) rather than isolated companies spread among outposts that could be overrun individually. The Glosters, once they concentrated on Hill 235, held off all assaults. Bar the Fusiliers' failure to recapture Hill 257 (where the Chinese had consolidated hours before the operation was launched), counter-attacks were successful: Curtis's on the 23rd, Farrar-Hockley's and Leith-MacGregor's on the 25th. Why was the tactic not used more frequently? The answer must be lack of numbers. Some troops who visited Hill 235 in May 1951 criticised the Glosters for leaving ammunition on the battlefield and for their flimsy defences. But the doomed battalion's last positions were scraped into the soil after dark on the 24th, and, with Chinese on the hills all around, the munitions on the valley floor were out of reach.

The brigade's dispositions were the key to the disaster that engulfed it – yet, with his limited numbers, it is difficult to see how Brodie could have better positioned his men. Where he may be faulted is in his failure to defend the river itself. As recently as the Falklands War in 1982 – where the Argentinians had night-vision devices but still failed to spot advancing British from 3 Para until they tripped mines – the lesson was relearned that infantry advancing across broken terrain in darkness are difficult to spot. Yet the one place where the Chinese had to slow down, without cover – the river – was undefended. LPs on the Imjin proved ineffective: the Fusiliers' riverside LP ran for X Company, and the Glosters' D Company patrol narrowly escaped, having achieved nothing. Moreover, despite the April river being at its low spring ebb, not all crossing points were known to the brigade.* Yet Guy Temple, on

* Malcolm Cubiss told me that the river fords had not been well reconnoitred, and the Fusiliers' regimental history, in stating it has no idea where the enemy force that attacked Z Company came from, tacitly admits that there was a crossing point on its front that was unknown. On the Glosters' front, it is clear that the enemy used a ford to the north-west of 'Gloster Crossing'.

his own initiative, fought a denial action, knocking at least a company – possibly a battalion – out of the fight. That showed what could have been achieved if, say, machine-gun bunkers had covered the crossings. While such fieldworks would almost certainly not have halted the enemy, they would have forced him to deploy, bloodied him and delayed him before he hit the MLR – the hilltop positions.

With the exception of Hill 194, minimal attempts were made to fortify the MLR. There were no mines; little wire or other obstacles to fix the enemy, so he could be killed; no bunkers; no communication trenches to enable safe movement by defenders. There were wide gaps between outposts; only a few (such as the Glosters' A and D Company positions) were mutually supporting. Moreover, most were not within small-arms range of the river itself. The result was that the brigade's soldiers were unable to kill the enemy before he came within range of their own slit trenches, and there the British troops were at equal hazard from enemy fire. 'We were not mutually supporting, we were isolated penny packets of battalions guarding too large an area,' summed up Peter Whitamore. 'And we had a lack of defensive stores.' Two geographic features assist defenders: water obstacles and high ground. The brigade did not make use of the first, thus denying itself defence in depth, and inadequately fortified the second. These factors – and the fact that the fiercest action took place at night, when the Hussars were unable to operate – negated the brigade's key advantage, its firepower.

Why 29th Brigade was not in a fully defensive posture remains unclear. Before taking over from MacArthur, Ridgway had stated: 'I wanted it clearly understood in the G-3 Section.* that the basis of our tactical thinking for the immediate future was the retention of the strong ground along the Kansas Line.'[1] The brigade's orders on the Imjin were clear: 'Organise, occupy and defend Line KANSAS.'[2] Moreover, an enemy army group had been identified to its north by intelligence two weeks before the attack. Why was the brigade not dug in?

One clue may be found in 29th Brigade's early encounters. At Sibyonni and at Happy Valley similar defences had proved adequate; the only positions lost to enemy action had been retaken by counter-attack. But at Happy Valley the enemy had not assaulted until dawn and had been repelled in daylight. At the Imjin he took full advantage of darkness and attacked for three nights. Another clue may perhaps be found in the brigade's aggressive commander. 'Brodie used to come up and say, "You are too defensively minded,"' said Whitamore. 'He was a good man, but was offensively minded.' In accordance with his mindset and his orders,

* G3: Operations.

Brodie instituted a series of increasingly ambitious patrols across the river. All came up empty – but motorised patrols hunting a guerrilla enemy skilled in camouflage and concealment would seem to have been a product of flawed thinking.* And then there was the nature of the war hitherto. 'The whole of the time we were in Korea it was very fluid,' said Tony Perrins. 'You never expected to be anywhere long.' Even when massive enemy forces broke cover on the 22nd, there was an assumption that the first night's attacks would be probes, rather than an assault launched off the line of march.† The 29th Brigade after-action report states: 'The most surprising feature of this Chinese offensive was not so much that it came, but the manner of its coming.'[3]

All the above, however, requires context. A post-battle summary by the US 3rd Infantry Division, after laying out the orders the brigade had received, noted: 'These orders were carried out in letter and in spirit.'[4] In other words, if, in hindsight, 29th Brigade appears poorly prepared, its preparations were considered perfectly adequate at the time.

The key controversy of the battle concerns the loss of the Glosters. In command, as in management, the ability to communicate clearly is critical, but the Gloster CO's taciturnity was remarked upon by virtually all who knew him. Some officers considered him old-fashioned, the kind of man who lacked initiative, who stuck to his orders to the letter. Douglas Charlton, a brigade intelligence officer who had served in World War II, was scathing:

> It always irked me that 'Fred' Carne got the VC for losing seven and a half hundred men overnight . . . I came out of the line and I picked up some English newspapers . . . there was this banner headline, 'The Glorious Glosters!' . . . they had been routed through the fault of a man who was still living in the 1914–18 era. He was an old-fashioned, rigid-thinking British colonel. Whenever you hear about courage, the stiff upper lip and all the rest of it, you hear about the charge of the Light Brigade, Dunkirk, Arnhem – and now you hear about the 'Glorious Glosters'. All glorious balls-ups![5]

---

* This point was acknowledged in the 'Lessons Learned' section of the brigade's after-action report, which says of the poor intelligence of enemy locations before battle: 'This situation obtained for the 10 days prior to this action . . . one answer to this would be small foot patrols prepared to op[erate] for a period of 3–4 days following the trails and ridge lines that the enemy uses . . . in the task forces that were sent out the standard of observation was not of a high order . . . better tr[ainin]g on the part of intelligence section and all OP personnel, including cam[ouflage] . . . coupled with a better knowledge of the habits and tactics of the Chinese, would be an improvement.' See '29th Independent Infantry Brigade Group History, September 1949–October 1951', in National Archive, Kew.

† In affairs military, assumptions are dangerous things. As the US Army puts it: 'Assumption is the mother of all fuck-ups!'

Did Carne have the instincts of a battle group commander sniffing his way out of danger? One wonders whether the Glosters' fate might have been different had a more independently minded officer – say, Gerald Rickord – commanded them. A tantalising question hangs over 24 April: if the Glosters had fought south towards the Filipino/Hussar relief force, which advanced to within 2,000 yards of their position, would most have escaped? The hills around were alive with enemy in at least divisional strength, and the Glosters, outside the relative safety of defensive positions, could have been wiped out in the open. But a determined thrust *might* have made the link-up. The answer, of course, can never be known.

Charlton's is a harsh, but defensible, judgement. But it overlooks Carne's key strength. At the head of a surrounded battalion fighting a hopeless action, 'Cool' Carne's leadership inside the trap was never faulted. While he may be criticised for not seeking withdrawal permission, and for not breaking out on the 24th, he kept his battalion fighting – morale never flagged – and personally led bayonet counter-attacks. No Gloster I have spoken to, nor any who has left an account of the battle, has a bad word to say about the man who commanded them as they were overwhelmed by catastrophe. Even the unit's aggressive adjutant – a personality very different to Carne, a man who became a British Army star and who retired as a full general – remained loyal; he attached no blame to his CO in his extensive writings on the battle. While another commander might – just might – have led the Glosters out of the cauldron, it is difficult to think of a man better fitted to leading them effectively once in it.

The Glosters were in an unenviable position. Lacking contact with flanking units, they were open to infiltration, and with Five Yankee vulnerable as a line of communication and hemmed in as an axis for a relief attack, the battalion was in a trap with no bolt hole through which to escape. Considerable ink has been expended, largely by American historians, on Brodie's apparent disobedience of Soule's order to leave the Filipinos *in situ* overnight, either so they could continue their attack in the morning, or act as a launch pad for a counter-attack on the 25th. But why would an attack that failed on the 24th succeed on the 25th? Moreover, *there was no relief force available* the following day – so the launch pad was never used. Any casualties incurred by the Filipinos overnight would thus have been for naught. This points to a wider controversy. The British brigade fell under the American commanders of 3rd Division and I Corps. Did US officers do enough to save the Glosters?

The tragedy of the battle, in my opinion, stemmed from American faith in British defensive abilities and a failure to keep a closer eye on developments in the British sector, combined with British pride in their abilities and a reluctance to request assistance. So far in the war, British units had proved solid; there had been no 'bug-outs'.* In January, 27th Brigade's commander, Brigadier Basil Coad, had been told by US Major-General John Church that he liked British to act as rearguards, as they were a steadying influence on US troops.[6] Lieutenant-Colonel Andrew Man, CO of the Middlesex battalion, was told by American officers that 27th Brigade 'was worth a division to us',[7] and a number of Americans (as well as ROK officers such as General Paik Sun-yup) saw the British as tenacious defensive fighters. Colonel William Harris, commanding the 3rd Division's 65th Infantry Regiment, wrote of 29th Brigade, 'on our left flank we had that reliable, unflappable British brigade'.[8] Before battle commenced, Brigadier Brodie had asked for more men, and was told they were unavailable – but that higher command had faith in his ability to hold.[9] This reputation may explain why 29th Brigade was holding a front as long as that which, later in the war, would be held by the entire Commonwealth Division.

The British had been scathing about earlier American bug-outs and took pride in their reputation as line-holders. Moreover, Ridgway himself had demanded that positions be held as long as feasible – but how long *is* feasible? Farrar-Hockley comments, 'Directives of this kind are entirely justified, but their implementation demands a nice judgement.'[10] On the Imjin, John Johnson, I Corps' Intelligence Officer, considered the British too proud to request help: 'They suffered significant casualties before they would even acknowledge that they were in trouble.'[11] American historian Roy Appleman, who interviewed Brodie after the battle, criticised British communications: 'The British tended to understate the case . . . while the Americans sought a realistic understanding.'[12] This brings us to Brodie's famous comment to 3rd Division's commander, General Robert Soule on the 24th, that the Glosters' situation was 'pretty sticky'. Brodie's phrase has been jumped upon on both sides of the Atlantic. Queried on it, one soldier in the trap, Sam Mercer – not an emotional man – exploded: 'A bit sticky! What he meant to say was, "We are up shit creek without a paddle!"'. On a battlefield tour of Gloster Hill in November 2007 for US Special Forces Command Korea, US 8th Army historian Ron Miller noted: 'This was a case of cultural miscommunication – between two allies who speak the same language!'

I contend, however, that Brodie's choice of phrase was irrelevant. It seems odd for 3rd Division or I Corps officers to state that they were left in the dark regarding the Glosters' plight when the peril *was* recognised

---

* It is important to note that, while many American forces engaged in the first six months of the war proved unreliable, the quality of US troops improved steadily as the fighting progressed.

by Generals Frank Milburn, James Van Fleet and Matthew Ridgway. Although none of these senior commanders was in direct contact with Brodie, at their conference at the 3rd Division airstrip on the afternoon of the 24th they quizzed Soule as to why he was not expediting his counter-attack towards the Glosters. Soule replied that his force was not yet in position, adding that he had been assured by Brodie that the Glosters could hold out until the following morning.[13] Events proved Brodie correct: the Glosters *did* hold off all attacks. What sealed their fate was that Soule's attack was never launched. By the 25th the overall battlefield situation had deteriorated, and Line Kansas was being abandoned; therefore it was no longer essential to restore the line in the Glosters' sector – the aim of Soule's planned attack. Moreover, Chinese units had infiltrated around the flanks of the Glosters and were threatening the MSR. Soule, prudently, redeployed his force to contain that threat. If the 65th had successfully attacked early on the 25th, the Glosters – mauled but intact – would have been saved, regardless of Brodie's penchant for understatement. Or as Mercer put it: '[Brodie's comment] made no difference. We were on a hiding to nothing in those positions.'

The brigade held the opening, shock phase of the offensive with no respite and minimal reinforcement. UN units to its north-east on Line Utah had some freedom of manoeuvre, falling back on the 23rd, and holding on Line Kansas until the morning of the 25th, then withdrawing to Line Delta – and Delta was held only for one day. In the first days of fighting, in 3rd Division's sector, the Turkish Brigade and the 65th Infantry Regiment were temporarily replaced by (respectively) the US 7th Infantry Regiment and the US 35th Infantry, before returning to the front.[14] 29th Brigade, on the other hand, had no replacement, and had to remain in place with no opportunity to move or to catch its breath: it was forced, by the necessities of higher strategy, to hold firm. The force Soule mustered to restore the brigade's MLR emphasises how under-manned the sector was. Two battalions of the 65th Infantry, the 64th Tank Battalion, plus the Filipino Battalion Combat Team, and the 10th Artillery Battalion, would have *doubled* 29th Brigade's strength. The minimal assistance higher command sent to the British is in stark contrast to that dispatched to the 1st ROK Division (itself almost three times larger than 29th Brigade), which was supported by the 73rd Tank Battalion, backstopped by the 15th Infantry Regiment and supported by 11 artillery battalions.[15] The Filipino force sent to support 29th Brigade was too little; Soule's counter-attack force was too late.

Some have criticised 29th Brigade for not 'rolling with the punch'.* This seems myopic. Sub-units did make tactical withdrawals but a full brigade withdrawal would have exposed the right flank of ROK 1st Division, holding the 'Munsan Corridor,' the left flank of 3rd Division, holding the 'Uijongbu Corridor' (Uijongbu was a key Peng objective, astride two key roads to Seoul), not to mention the left flank of I Corps. Unlike the units to their right, who withdrew from Line Utah, Brodie's troops had no freedom of manoeuvre until a general pullback from Line Kansas.

The top US commander acknowledged some American responsibility for the Glosters' tragedy. Ridgway wrote to Van Fleet on 9 May:

> . . . relating to the sacrifice of any unit, particularly of another nationality. The case of the Glouc. Bn. is of course uppermost in my mind. . . . I cannot but feel a certain disquiet that down through the channel of command the full responsibility for realising the danger to which this unit was exposed, then for extricating it when the danger became grave, was not recognised nor implemented. There are times . . . when it is not sufficient to accept the judgment of a subordinate commander that a threatened unit can care for itself or that a threatened situation can be handled locally. The responsibility in each case goes straight up through the command chain . . . each commander should search his soul and, by personal verification, satisfy himself that adequate action has been taken. It may be that such was the case of the Gloucesters. I have the feeling that it was not; that neither the Div. nor the Corps Commander was fully aware by direct personal presence, as near the critical spot as he could have gotten, of what the actual situation was.† Had he known it, I feel sure some vigorous action would have been taken to extricate the unit. I feel in conscience bound to state these views at this time, . . . [16]

American battlefield historian Roy Appleman wrote: 'It is the author's opinion that the British 29th Brigade commander was most remiss of all.'

---

* Max Hastings (1987, p. 219) writes that Farrar-Hockley was always bitter that the Glosters did not pull back to a mined, wired line they had prepared further back. However, I have come across no information on this fallback position, which is not mentioned in any of Farrar-Hockley's own writings on the battle.

† To the best of my knowledge, neither Soule nor Milburn visited 29th Brigade during the battle. In fairness to Soule, he had his own division to command, and by the 25th its units were scattered across the battlefield: the 15th Infantry were supporting the ROKs, the 65th Infantry was holding the MSR, and only the 7th Infantry was holding his front. Likewise, Milburn was commanding I Corps as it took the full weight of the enemy offensive. General Paik Sun-yup made very clear to me that he had always felt Milburn was fair to all the units under his command and did not show favour to American units. While 27th British Brigade commander Basil Coad had a strained relationship with his superior, General John Church, there is no indication that Brodie had such problems with Soule or Milburn.

I disagree: Ridgway's comment above reads far more like a reprimand of senior American commanders than of Brodie; and Brodie, after all, had been assured that Soule's counter-attack would carve the Glosters out on the 25th.

While Soule blamed Brodie for not requesting a stronger break-through force on the 24th[17] (indeed, Carne had warned Brodie that he felt the Filipino/Hussar force was not strong enough), by the 25th, when the peril was even greater, Soule's deputy, Brigadier Armistead Mead (who insisted that the 65th's commander, William Harris, attack only with tanks) showed an even poorer appreciation of enemy numbers and the nature of the terrain. The same criticism could be levelled at Soule for his orders to leave the Filipinos in position up Five Yankee overnight. (American historian Clay Blair suggests that the battlefield crisis was beyond Soule's ability to handle: as well as controlling his own division he also had an allied brigade to oversee.) Brodie, in both cases, took matters into his own hands. He appears to have permitted the Filipino withdrawal, and certainly ordered Carne to break out, *before* the planned operation by Harris's tanks. That operation, I assume, was only mounted as a matter of honour or in acquiescence to orders, most likely with Brodie's full connivance. Harris was sympathetic to Brodie* and asked Mead to leave him and Brodie alone to finish their planning for the attack – indicating that he did not want a senior American officer looking over his shoulder during the conference.[18] It is difficult not to sympathise with Harris, who had been given a 'mission impossible'. According to Blair, he even had his legal section prepare a defence in case he was blamed for failing to rescue the Glosters.[19]

Many 29th Brigade officers still have tremendous respect for Brodie, a man they consider 'a soldier's soldier'. Yet some *do* fault him. In a letter to his mother in June, Fusilier Major Charles Mitchell wrote, regarding the newly formed Commonwealth Division,† 'Div. Comd, a first-class chap who can handle Americans!! Tom Brodie I often felt didn't stand up to them enough – not really surprising as he was usually junior in rank – American generals sometimes have a surprising idea of what can and cannot be done.'[20]

Brodie, a stoic, fought his battle independently. 'Brodie was under orders to stay where he was,' said Tony Perrins. 'An American general in Brodie's position would have just said he couldn't hold: end of story. If

---

* Blair (p. 845) quotes Harris as saying Brodie was furious at the failure to relieve the Glosters, 'and I didn't blame him'.

† Some British accounts state that the Commonwealth Division was formed to ensure that there would be no recurrence of a disaster like the Imjin. In fact, the plan to form a division was already in the works in March.

you are a British soldier, you bloody well stay there! And he did.' However, there is a fine line between a commander's duty to carry out his orders and his responsibility for his men. Brodie's command directive from Whitehall, dated September 1950, reads:

If an order given to you . . . by any American commander . . . under whose command you have been placed, appears, in your opinion, to imperil the safety of United Kingdom troops under your command to a degree exceptional in war, you will inform the Head of the United Nations Unified Command, Korea . . . that you will carry out the order but that you intend to report the circumstances and your reasons for your opinion to the Commander-in-Chief, British Commonwealth Occupation Force, for transmission to His Majesty's Government, and you will take such action.[21]

Although Brodie was holding a critical section of Line Kansas with inadequate forces, I have discovered no indication that he informed London that his mission held especial risk. Even in a war as desperate as Korea, for the brigade commander to come within a hair's breadth of losing the Rifles at Happy Valley, then to lose the Glosters three months later, suggests an excessive appetite for risk, a lack of prudence or plain bad luck. In this light, the judgements of Johnson and Mitchell, quoted above, appear sounder. As it was, Brodie himself accepted fifty per cent of the blame for the loss of the Glosters, and attributed fifty per cent to Soule.[22]

So why were the Glosters wiped out? Farrar-Hockley, in the British official history, states that the battalion was lost 'by oversight'.[23] While it is reasonable to conclude that Brodie was more focused on the eastern flank, where the bulk of his forces were fighting, and that Soule and Milburn had other matters to occupy them, this judgement seems harsh. A relief thrust *was* launched on the 24th; a major counter-attack *was* planned for the 25th. On the 23rd Brodie had no reserves available – the Filipinos arrived in his sector too late to attack that evening – and was concerned with the more immediate peril of the Belgians. Moreover, the brigade-strength counter-attack planned for the 25th had the attention of the UN's highest commanders.

In my opinion, the Glosters were lost due to a combination of factors. The first is their lack of contact with flanking units – itself a consequence of a brigade holding a divisional front – and the hemmed-in nature of their 'back door'. Once the Chinese attacked, they were doomed by a failure of their own and/or higher command to take more decisive action on the 23rd and/or 24th. Finally, it must be remembered that their position covered an important LOC and tied down major enemy forces. Had the Glosters pulled out on the 23rd or 24th, they would have left a gap some four miles wide in Line Kansas, which would have opened the floodgates, especially as Five Yankee was such a well-covered route, ideal for infiltrating vehicles or heavy equipment south. That is the long answer. The short answer is: the fortunes of war.

While Peng's guerrilla *blitzkrieg* bypassed the battalion, he could not simply leave it *in situ*, where its mortars, Vickers and called-in artillery could wreak havoc on his rear. Moreover, its presence set back his timetable by denying his artillery and mule trains the use of the track south of the river and through the hills. Hence the determined attempts to eliminate the Glosters. Yet the battalion's destruction was *not* due to enemy attack – 'If we had had water and ammunition, we would still be up there now!' as one Gloster put it – but to being forced to abandon Hill 235 in a general withdrawal. This is the crux. Van Fleet, in a letter to Ridgway on 11 May, wrote:

> Had he [Carne] not held . . . I believe it would have been a proper decision by higher commanders to order him to hold. . . . I feel that this battalion was not lost in vain – that this is one of those great occasions in combat which call for a determined stand, and the loss of 622 officers and men saved many times that number.[24]

If, as some brigade soldiers believed at the time, the Glosters were awarded the presidential citation not for valour, but for a US failure to rescue them, this belief has not been shared by posterity. Van Fleet later called the Glosters' stand 'the most outstanding example of unit bravery in modern war',[25] and leading US historians – Appleman, Blair, Fehrenbach, Mossman – pay generous tribute to the battalion's gallantry. The US 8th Army in Korea conducts only four regular battlefield tours. Three are American: Chipyong-ri, the Inchon Landings and Taskforce Walker (the last being the first US combat unit committed – disastrously – to the war). The fourth is Gloster Hill. For a non-American battle to be so remembered, from a war in which America lost 36,914 sons,* is an honour. The last stand of the Glosters looks set to remain one of the iconic stories of the Korean War. What is regrettable is that only the Glosters, and not their comrades in the Belgians, Fusiliers, Hussars and Rifles, have gained the recognition of posterity for 29th Brigade's stand.

---

* A figure of 54,000 American dead in the Korean War is frequently cited but is now widely considered incorrect, although it continues to be reproduced. See Allan R. Millett, 'Casualties', in Tucker, p. 99. Even so, for a three-year war, 37,000 is a massive number; compare, for instance, the 58,000 US deaths in Vietnam – a much longer war, spanning the years 1965 to 1972 in terms of the involvement of American ground troops (longer if one counts the various US 'advisors' who played a role from the early 1960s).

What can be said of the Chinese 'volunteers'? First, that they fought with immense bravery and élan. An attacking force always holds the initiative, and the Chinese overcame their weaknesses – poor communications, poor logistics, lack of artillery and air support – by forcing the British to fight the kind of battle that played to their strengths. By moving far, fast and with stealth, they forced close-range night combats where their advantages – numbers and high volumes of fire – were optimised. Moreover, the Chinese took full advantage of a key principle of the 'human wave': its ability to flow around strongpoints and through unit boundaries. Where 63rd Army's troops were weak was in tactics and weapons. Many brigade soldiers were saved by poor enemy marksmanship, ineffective enemy grenades and the fact that some Chinese soldiers in the rear waves did not even have firearms, but picked up those of the dead. On the other hand, Chinese machine-gun and mortar crews were first-rate.

The CPVA must be judged in software as well as hardware terms. To march through the night (in some cases, for twenty miles), to ford a river and to assault, as 63rd Army did on 22 April 1951, is an infantry feat of the highest order, overturning UN assumptions of a 'probing attack'. Even today few Western troops have the fitness required to undertake such a challenging 'march and shoot'. Like their old enemy the Japanese, the CPVA relied heavily on 'spirit' rather than materiel. But Tokyo had launched a war of attrition – in technological/industrial terms, in the Pacific; in manpower terms, in China – against enemies with greater resources. Peking's prospects in Korea were more favourable. Once Washington decided not to go nuclear and to wage a 'limited war', Mao's vast pool of manpower gave him the advantage in attritional battle. 'There is a saying, "Quality is better than quantity," but there is another saying, "Quantity has a quality of its own," ' said Mercer. 'And we had too long an administrative tail. Every one of the Chinese could be put in the front line with a weapon.' Moreover, Chinese officers did not face the public pressures of a democracy: They could be spendthrift with their men's lives. Their tactics – notably, failure to win the firefight, pre-assault – guaranteed heavy losses when faced with stubborn opposition.

Did Chinese infantry, who attacked with such élan, value their own lives less than did their UN enemies? Almost certainly not. Then why did so many UN soldiers considered them drugged or fanatical? There is a telling quote in Zhang's excellent *Mao's Military Romanticism*. An American pilot, watching columns of Chinese advancing while UN artillery tore through their ranks, wrote, 'This is the strangest sight I have ever seen . . . Our shells are landing right in their columns and they keep coming.'[26] If this sounds frightening or culturally alien to Western readers, they might recall their own, not-too-distant military heritage. Just thirty-five years before the Korean War, British soldiers, in assault, would have looked little different from the Chinese of the 1950s: advancing in line, directly into fire, closing ranks as comrades fell. Were the men who attacked in close order at Waterloo, the Alma or the Somme, drugged fanatics? Or simply soldiers fighting as they had been trained? To modern Western troops, whose aim was to cause maximum casualties while incurring minimal losses, the Chinese way of war was alien, but it had parallels in their own military heritage as recently as 1916. Another issue is battle shock. Lofty Large noted how some Glosters, after battle, did not bother to take cover from incoming fire. Exhausted, they were 'bomb-happy' in Large's phrase.[27] Troops who advance under artillery or air attack before entering firefight range may well appear drugged. I have tried to avoid the clichés of Korean War literature, such as 'fanatical communist hordes'. The Chinese soldiers who fought with such courage – and, on the whole, fairness* – deserve better.

The battle echoes down to the present. In the 1991 Gulf War Britain's commander, General Sir Peter de la Billière, a Korean War veteran, had the Imjin in mind when he insisted that Britain deploy a division, not a brigade, citing an 'unhappy incident in the Korean War when a British brigade had fought under American command'.[28] In an email he observed:

> The thing that was of paramount importance to [General Norman] Schwarzkopf and me was the need to avoid casualties . . . in my mind this came from Korea, where there were heavy casualties, and to his mind, from his experience in Vietnam . . . The problem the British often have with the Americans is understanding that they are not expat Brits – you have got to understand them as foreigners. They have significantly different approaches to operations and other military functions and planning, and they were more extreme in Korea than in the Gulf.

In the invasion of Iraq, too, Britain went in with a division. In the current wars that Britain is fighting alongside America in Iraq and Afghanistan, while long-term attrition appears certain, the potential for carnage on the scale of Happy Valley or the Imjin does not, given that the insurgents lack the offensive power and manpower that the CPVA deployed.

The battle of the Imjin was no classic in terms of tactical ploys or sweeping manoeuvres; it was a bloody slogging match as irresistible force ploughed into immovable object. 29th Brigade was undermanned to cover

---

* With notable exceptions – such as the shooting of ambulances on Route 11, and the massacre of prisoners in the Belgian sector.

the ground allotted to it – ground which communist forces had seized on the opening day of two previous offensives. It had no defence in depth and was ill-prepared to fight off prolonged mass attack. The Glosters' vulnerability was unforeseen; their lack of contact with flanking units made it inevitable that they would be surrounded. Communist sources, with justice, consider the Imjin a victory: they won the ground.*

What, then, *is* the battle's strategic significance? The US 3rd Division, deployed over the Uijongbu Corridor/MSR, held the critical route to Seoul. According to the April 1951 Command Report of that division, under whose command Brodie's men fought: 'Heaviest attack in the divisional sector was against the 29th BIB [British Independent Brigade].'[29] Outnumbered 7:1, the overstretched brigade defended the most critical sector of Line Kansas, with minimal support, in the Fifth Offensive's shock phase. Peng's 26 April message to Mao (quoted in Chapter 11), admitting that he had failed to seize Uijongbu, pinpoints 29th Brigade's achievement. The Belgian and British soldiers denied their enemy his objectives. I Corps was not cut off and rolled up from the left, nor was its LOC, the Uijongbu corridor, cut. Seoul did not fall. The remarkable thing is not that the Chinese wave washed over 29th Brigade and seeped through cracks between units, but that it took them so long to do so. In sum, 29th Brigade's stand made a critical contribution to the failure of the enemy's greatest offensive – and, hence, to the outcome of the war as a whole. 'We were sacrificed, certainly as a battalion, possibly as a brigade, for the bigger picture,' said Mercer. 'We got a bloody nose but we did what we were asked to do.' So much for strategy. On the human level, the battle's value is as a study of backs-to-the-wall defiance, of the qualities of the fighting man in the slit trench. That is the story I have tried to tell.

* * *

No veteran of the Imjin is, to my knowledge, a particularly rich man. Most would probably be better off today had they never donned uniform. Yet they have memories civilians cannot match. In their twilight years, many can reflect on the fact that they fought in a battle which has since attained epic status. 'I wouldn't have missed it for the world,' said Malcolm Cubiss. 'It gives you a little spice in life.' Another veteran, who, through no fault of his own, did not fight in the battle, broke down fifty-seven years later during a telephone conversation with me: he was still devastated that he had been unable to take part, with his

---

* Some brigade veterans deny even that. 'The Royal Ulster Rifles are proud that we did not lose even an inch of ground!' said Mervyn McCord. 'I maintain that the honours were more than even,' said Mercer. 'We blunted them. They wanted to celebrate May Day in Seoul. They didn't.'

friends, in the battle. 'You sense that people of our age who were vaguely involved wish they had been there,' said Perrins. 'I am sure Shakespeare was right: I am sure people living, who could have fought at Agincourt and didn't, regretted that they didn't.'

No engagement fought by British forces since World War II compares with the Imjin in terms of losses. In the Suez Invasion of 1956 there were 22 men KIA.[30] In the Falklands War the Royal Navy, Royal Marines, Royal Air Force and the Army – which deployed two brigades and fought six major battles – lost 258 KIA in seventy-four days.[31] Some 137 British soldiers from multiple battle groups died serving in Afghanistan between 2001 and December 2008, and in Iraq 176 servicemen (again from multiple battle groups) were KIA in the invasion and the first five years of counter-insurgency duties.[32]

By comparison, a single brigade on the Imjin suffered 1,091 casualties in three days, including 141 KIA[33] – a figure that does not include those who later died of wounds or in POW camps.* The number is over 10 per cent of total British deaths in the Korean War. (Out of 87,000 who served, 1,078 were killed; 2,674 were WIA.[34]) Moreover, the loss of a battalion (622 Glosters, out of around 750, failed to return from Hill 235) is the single largest unit loss the British Army has suffered since World War II. (The nearest comparison is the capture of the 68 Royal Marines of Major Mike Norman's Naval Landing Party 8901 in the Falklands. The men of that unit were not held as POWs, but immediately returned to London.[†])

Another indication of the battle's intensity is the expenditure of artillery ammunition. 'The regiment fired 23,000 rounds – roughly a thousand rounds a gun,' said George Truell of 45 Field. 'That is as much as we fired [per gun] at the battle of El Alamein in seven or eight days, about fifteen years of training ammunition in Germany in the 1970s, or twice the amount we fired in the entire Falklands War.' Some men found the Korean War more murderous than World War II. 'A lot of reservists who had been in North Africa and Italy said those battles in Korea were worse than the battles against the Germans,' said Bob Nicholls. John Bayliss, who landed on D-Day and fought in Operation Market Garden, is one. 'The battle of the Imjin, I would say that was the worst; there were so many [enemy].'

---

* The KIA figures also do not include those suffered by the Belgian Battalion, nor by the Filipino Battalion during the attack up 5Y. The breakdown of KIA among the three British units engaged is as follows: Glosters: 56; Royal Ulster Rifles: 36; Royal Northumberland Fusiliers: 30; Royal Artillery: 10; Royal Engineers: 6; 8th Hussars: 2; Royal Army Medical Corps: 1. The heaviest death toll occurred during the breakout down Route 11 on the 25th.
† By a curious coincidence, after the battle the rumour mill in 29th Brigade had it that the surviving Glosters were to be removed from Korea to replace the Marines on the Falklands.

Given the intensity of combat and the sheer, odds-against drama, the Anglo-Belgian defence of the Imjin River in 1951, although a smaller battle, must rank with the French epic at Dien Bien Phu in 1954 and the Israeli fight for the Golan Heights in 1973 as among the greatest stands mounted by Western forces since World War II.*

* * *

The Korean War was a stern proving ground for professional soldiers. 'It was ninety per cent boredom, five per cent fright and five percent exhilaration,' said Sam Phillips. 'In thirteen years of army life, that was the one year that I felt that I was doing what I was meant to be doing.' Tom Clough added: 'Nothing matched it in the rest of my army career, and I came out in 1977.' Yet few veterans discuss their experiences with outsiders; only when they gather at unit reunions do they talk. 'When we get together, that's when the bullets fly!' as one put it.

Few memorials to the war stand in the UK. 'It was only in 1987, when Her Majesty unveiled a memorial in the crypt of St Paul's, that we could say, "There you are lads, we haven't forgotten you,"' said Sam Mercer. Of those which do exist, several are connected with 29th Brigade. In Gloucester's tenth-century cathedral the 'Korea Cross', carved by Carne during his solitary confinement, sits in a glass case beside the tomb of Edward the Confessor. Across the aisle from the Glosters' chapel, with the regiment's colours hanging from their pike shafts, the US Presidential Citation hangs in its frame. In the Cotswolds, in Carne's tiny home village of Cranham, a copy of the citation still hangs in the local pub. In 2008 the old RAF barracks at Innsworth outside Gloucester was renamed 'Imjin Barracks'. Visitors to the Royal Northumberland Fusiliers Museum at Alnwick Castle will see the medal collection owned by Kingsley Foster. In St Anne's Cathedral, Belfast, is the prayer book used by Captain James Majury to conduct services in the POW camps. Probably the highest-profile memorial to 29th Brigade is in central Belfast: The granite obelisk the Rifles erected in 'Happy Valley' in 1951 stands outside City Hall. After Koyang urbanised, it was relocated to the Rifles' barracks in Ballymena, then, when St Patrick's barracks closed, it was moved to its present location in 2008, thanks to sponsorship from veterans, Samsung and the South Korean Embassy.

In Korea, Seoul has generously raised memorials to the foreign contingents that fought under the UN banner: the British memorial is carved into the foot of Hill 235, or 'Gloster Hill'. In 2008, as part of the celebrations

---

* At Dien Bien Phu some 16,000 French Colonial troops faced 50,000 Viet Minh, or odds of 3:1 against. On the Golan 180 Israeli tanks faced 1,200 Syrian tanks, or odds of almost 7:1 against. For numbers, see Robert Thompson (ed.), pp. 76–7 and 234–5, respectively.

to mark the sixtieth anniversary of the ROK Armed Forces, the memorial was named an official cultural asset. In Pusan the UN War Cemetery is immaculately maintained. There, British soldiers whose bodies were recovered lie under simple black headstones on the lawns; those whose bodies were not recovered are memorialised in regimental lists on the Commonwealth monument at the centre of the British plot.

Despite being the bloodiest struggle fought by British troops since World War II, the Korean War has faded almost totally from the public memory: it was fought too far from home, and for too opaque a cause, to inspire a populace still getting over the struggle against Hitler. 'We were not welcomed back as heroes,' said Nicholls. 'Everybody was already fed up with World War II.' Returning battalions paraded through their home towns, but there was no mood of victory; that the war ended with a ceasefire on almost the same line as it had started contributed to the lack of interest. 'It was not like the Falklands,' said Perrins. 'Victories get all the publicity. The Korean War is still on.' Several veterans lamented that since Korea – and the Soviet walkout that allowed the free world to take the decisive action it did – the UN has proved a less purposeful organisation than they had hoped.

If few men came home to plaudits, some returned to the opposite. A number of captured officers are convinced that their subsequent army careers were blighted. Peter Whitamore, having been turned down for a posting in 1968, was told that those who had been prisoners of communists could not be granted access to classified material. 'My reaction was horror, disbelief,' he said. 'I went through the Army Act and made an appeal. I got no reply from 10 Downing Street, so appealed to the Queen. I got a response that restored me . . . but made certain jobs unavailable. I didn't think the army could treat me so unfairly.' Perrins was furious at the reception for returning POWs. 'If I am bitter, it is at the treatment the prisoners received when we got back,' he said. 'I have images of those bastards from the War Office, who wrote all kinds of scurrilous stuff.' Another officer said, 'There was this thing that they had been "brainwashed", and it does appear that there was an element of discrimination . . . many officers' careers did not blossom.' Others, however, point to Anthony Farrar-Hockley* and James Majury, both POWs who reached general rank.

Amid talk of brainwashing, spies and double spies, veterans were careful to avoid any suspicions. On returning to England, Guy Temple

* Farrar-Hockley would lecture extensively on communism and his experiences in captivity. The experience of Korean War POWs led to two training films on conduct after captivity, *Captured* and *I Escaped*. Farrar-Hockley and Fusilier Sergeant David Sharp advised on these.

was introduced to George Blake – their mothers were friends. 'It was arranged that we spend Christmas together, and George and I got along famously – it never occurred for one second that he'd gone the other way,' said Temple. 'I always make a point of saying that, in case people ask, "Why did you hide it?"'*

Bitterness lingers over the lopsided recognition accorded the Glosters.† 'I think we, the Ulster Rifles, were very poorly recognised for that one,' said Norman Sweetlove. 'I can't understand it,' added Joe Farrell, also of the Rifles. 'Why is there no publicity? An American general sent a letter to my platoon officer, congratulating us on the work the platoon had done, and the number of Chinese dead in front of our platoon position. That's the way! The Glosters were captured – we fought our way out.' Non-Gloster Imjin veterans who return to the battlefield are deeply disappointed that annual tours do not revisit their old positions. 'The only place we went was back to the Gloster position; I wanted to go to our positions but we were told we could not,' said Bayliss. 'I think the world of my regiment, I think the world of being a Fusilier.' In fact, the publicity given to their stand was almost an embarrassment for some members of the Glosters – a regiment that is, by nature, undemonstrative. 'We got the publicity because of the alliteration, "The Glorious Glosters",' said Temple. 'Tony Farrar-Hockley's father had been editor of the Morning Post, and he knew columnists, so we had an entry to Fleet Street which the other regiments did not.' 'The "Glorious Glosters" was media hype,' added Mercer. 'It was a brigade battle.'

The ranks of the Imjin's last survivors are being whittled down by an enemy more implacable than any Chinese machine-gunner: time. Perrins, in the thoughtful Afterword to his A Pretty Rough Do Altogether: The Fifth Fusiliers in Korea, 1950–51, lamented that the officers he had fought alongside in Korea are a vanished breed in modern Britain. This may be so. While it would be presumptuous of me to claim to have established friendships with any interviewees, I did get a sense of the kind of men they are: proud but understated, patriotic but not nationalistic, tough but without machismo. The officer-and-gentleman and the gentleman-ranker have almost disappeared from popular culture. Even

* Blake was the M16 officer in the British Embassy in Seoul. Captured by the North Koreans when the city fell in June 1950, he converted to Marxism. He was revealed as a communist spy in 1961, and it was found that his betrayal of Western bloc spies had led to their deaths (which he would later claim to regret). He was imprisoned, but escaped from Wormwood Scrubs in 1966 and fled to Moscow, where at the time of writing he was still living.
† Some Rifles and Fusilier veterans, speaking in summer 2007, were particularly incensed about a recent BBC television programme on the battle that had concentrated almost exclusively on the Glosters.

the hard men of the battle bear no relationship to the snarling, testos-terone-fuelled heroes of film and television: Daredevils and man-killers like Malcolm Cubiss, Joe Farrell, Mervyn McCord and Guy Temple are, in person, solicitous, pleasant, polite. All vividly recall intense and some-times horrific experiences, yet all leaven their recollections with humour. Beyond regimental pride, none has a hint of boastfulness. Temple's quote is indicative: 'Here's the thing about being brave: I was never frightened, I just enjoyed battle. And if you are not frightened, you are not brave.' Old soldiers may have a reputation for being crashing bores, but these men, and most other interviewees, proved the oppo-site. They were, in short, terrific company.

In his fine study of battlefield heroes, *Warriors: Portraits from the Battlefield*, Sir Max Hastings writes: 'Ruthlessness of purpose was indis-pensable to them, and many were fired by a measure of anger. Few stars of the battlefield have been popular comrades.' This judgement does not fit the men above. What, then, of the only living survivor of the battle to win his country's highest decoration? The youthful Derek Kinne almost certainly matched Hastings's analysis: one officer burst into laughter at the mention of Kinne's name. 'Kinne!' he roared. 'He just gave the Chinese more of what he had been giving the Northumberland Fusiliers!' By his own account, Kinne had a large chip on his shoulder, but today the fearsome front-line soldier and iron-willed POW is a doting grandfather. Still, some traits endure. His wife Anne says he retains his stubbornness and sense of right and wrong. Many real-life heroes are quiet, understated men, yet Kinne fits the 'larger than life' stereotype.* His courage was dis-played not in the brief drama of combat, but over a period of two and a half years – what force drove him? 'Like everybody, I did what I felt I had to do,' Kinne said. 'Compared to people in Nazi concentration camps I feel very lucky. If I had been with the Japanese, my head would have been knocked off the first week – why it stayed on, I don't know. It's not that I didn't want to be intimidated, it's that I went out [to Korea] for my brother; I didn't want to desecrate his name. I did what I did for him. As you get older, you get philosophical. You can say gallant – you can say stupid. It would have cost me nothing to sit on the fence – it was my stu-pidity that got me what I got. You rationalise what you do – but for others it could be stupid.'

No veteran I interviewed harbours any hatred for the Chinese – who, as John Mole puts it, were 'bloody good soldiers'. 'One must be

---

* A story circulating in Seoul's British expatriate community tells how Kinne, on his last Korean visit, went to the British Embassy and politely asked if anyone could help him arrange a trip to the Imjin. When embassy staffers turned him down, he exploded, declaring that a war veteran and George Cross winner deserved better. He was taken to the battlefield.

like Edith Cavell, the British nurse in Belgium in World War I who was shot by the Germans for helping her fellow countrymen,' said Temple. 'She said, "One must not just forgive. One must have no hatred or bitterness in one's heart for anyone." That's not bad when one is being led out.' 'The Chinese are good fighters and an intelligent race of people,' added Joe Thompson. 'Being brought up Christian, I have never had a hateful feeling. They fought for their cause; we for ours.' I am unaware, though, of any reunions between enemies who fought in Korea, unlike some British and German veterans, who, living on the same continent, have met in peacetime to discuss old battles. 'Most interpreters in the camps were not too bad,' said Clough. 'I don't think I'd have any animosity if I met one now. It'd be quite something!' 'I have no hatred for my interrogators: If I saw one today, I'd buy him a drink,' said David Sharp. 'In my twisted mind, it was a personal war. They thought they were doing right; I thought I was doing right.' Sharp believes that captivity made him a better man. 'I no longer need company to keep me going. The fact that I can sit up and talk, look out of the window and see daylight – I can get up and walk around if I want to – that is of value. Many material things that people strive for today are of less value.'[35]

\* \* \*

An experience as intense as war – and a war as intense as Korea, with its terrible civilian suffering, close-range night battles and desperate breakouts – leaves a psychological legacy. For some veterans, the smell of barbecue charcoal transports them back to Korea's *ondol* heating. John Preston-Bell finds the songs of cuckoos and bush warblers evoke the wartime Korean countryside. He also had an eerier experience. Late one evening he was at his computer, working on the design of the maps for his friend Tony Perrins's 2004 book, when the contours of the hills enclosing Route 11 writhed before his eyes. 'I seemed to see in it the shape of two leaping, hopping, fantastical nightmare creatures,' he said. 'Since they bestrode the road which has been, for centuries, the traditional route for invaders into Korea, they became, in my mind, symbolic of the Chinese, the Mongols, the Japanese and others whose predations have so often threatened the peninsula.' In his album of Korean War photos, Preston-Bell superimposed over the graphic a Korean tiger; a beast that is said, in its dreams, to be pursued by demons.

Their experiences in Korea buried time bombs deep in many soldiers' psyches; bombs which, in some cases, would not explode for years. In an age when post-traumatic stress disorder was little understood, few received treatment for the teeth-grinding nightmares, the flashbacks.

Roy Rees suffered recurring dreams about the massacre of prisoners by masked ROK policemen in December 1950. 'That bloody mass murder,' he recalled. 'We never had no counselling.'[37] Some men prefer to keep quiet about their experiences. 'He won't admit it, but he still has dreams,' Wendy Cubiss said of husband Malcolm. 'I know when he's chasing a Chinaman. He's racing, and his arm is hitting me as he runs.'*
Thompson did not realise what he was suffering from, he just considered himself 'a bit ill-tempered', before being diagnosed and counselled. 'I'd have flashbacks – you have feelings that something is going on that you want to be away from; sometimes you are panic-stricken; at night you hear a bang, and you're back in battle. I've been married twice – I feel sorry for my wife.' Sights or sounds trigger memories of specific incidents. Near a Korean village one night, Ben Whitchurch, on a snatch patrol, disturbed a village dog: its bark froze the Gloster's blood. 'Today, when the Alsatian down the road barks at night, I go cold,' he said.

Even Kinne was affected. He had read about post-battle stress and considered it nonsense – until he, too, was struck. 'In 1966 I banged my head, and that started it,' said Kinne. 'I was in a dark Chinese restaurant, and I thought a rubber tree tried to attack me! They took me to the Funny Farm, and I used to escape – my wife used to bring me back after dinner!' He was given shock treatment (no longer used), and his wife, who was as traumatised as her husband – 'we had two small children, it was terrible' – arranged for him to start a laminating and framing shop as therapy. Over time, Kinne regained his balance: 'Me and my doctor from the Nut House are really close friends now!'

Perhaps the most extreme case was David Strachan's. The Fusilier, then aged twenty, shot the first Chinese soldier to reach his trench at 'Happy Valley' at such close range that the man fell on top of him, then took four hours to expire. After the war Strachan, restless, unable to settle down, joined the Navy. He was mentally sound for years – then it started. Late at night, asleep in his bedroom, his subconscious sensed a presence. He awoke in the darkness. Someone was sitting at the foot of his bed. The silent figure was staring intently at him. Strachan looked back in terror: it was the enemy soldier he had killed on 3 January 1950. The visitations continued for years. Finally, a psychiatrist specialising in PTSD told Strachan that he was the worst case he had ever encountered. He advised that the only way to exorcise the spirit was to revisit Korea.

* * *

* Cubiss's riposte was a classic: 'It's not the Chinese. I am trying to escape *you*, my dear!' he joked.

Many veterans have no interest in seeing Korea again. 'I hated that place,' said Nicholls. 'I have met Koreans (in fact a neighbour across the road – a great guy, a scientist – is Korean), but when I was there, that country . . . well, there is no describing it.' For soldiers who had been told they were fighting aggression and defending democracy, only to witness killings by ROK troops, the shock still lingers. 'I feel bitter: I don't believe in democracy,' said Rees. 'Watching that bloody massacre . . .'[37] 'I don't think we achieved anything,' said Vick Wear. 'Stalemate, peace talks. A lot of men got killed, a lot of civilians got killed – for nothing.'

Yet those who do return discover a brave new South Korea. The price the UN forces paid in blood was subsequently underwritten with American gold and repaid in Korean sweat. Armed with advantageous trade and technology transfer agreements with Washington, and with authoritarian governments in power in Seoul, Korea leveraged its only natural advantage – its people. Huge investments were made in education (Seoul today claims more PhDs per head than any other capital), and diligence was elevated to the premier virtue. From nowhere, industries sprouted. Now South Korea is the world's thirteenth-largest economy, with core industrial strengths in semiconductors, electronic devices, automobiles and ships. Its mobile telephone and Internet networks are best-of-breed. But Korea's achievements are not purely economic. After people-power protests in 1987 – just before the 1988 Summer Olympics – democracy was instituted. The generals who had followed the increasingly despotic Rhee Syngman* into the presidential mansion, delivering economic growth at the cost of political repression, were given the boot. In terms of standard of living and individual freedom, today's South Korea is comparable to a mid-sized European nation.

Veterans are astounded. The cityscapes bear no resemblance to the bombed-out shells of the 1950s. Poverty has been virtually eradicated; the child beggars, base-side garbage dumps and shanty towns have disappeared. Asphalt expressways have supplanted dusty tracks, traffic jams replaced refugee columns. Even the landscape has changed. Returners gape at the verdant hillsides: a vigorous national tree-planting programme has reforested the land, and lent a leafy coating to once scrubby slopes.

---

* Although they fought for him, few British veterans (if any) have a positive view of the late South Korean president. The media furore after the Fusiliers halted killings at 'Execution Hill' put him under considerable pressure, with even the US State Department weighing in. Moreover, Rhee was angry at what he saw as Britain's anti-MacArthur stance. (MacArthur shared his view that the goal of the war should be victory and reunification of the peninsula under Rhee's government.) Soon after the Imjin Battle, Rhee took a petulant revenge. In the first week of May 1951 he told an Australian UN official that British troops were no longer welcome in Korea. (His remarks were subsequently denied by his spokesperson.) A Foreign Office document in the National Archive at Kew details Rhee's comments.

And then there is the population. The cowed, broken people of the war years have been replaced by a fiercely proud, dynamic populace. An Australian veteran at Gloster Valley, surrounded by laughing school-children, was asked the biggest difference between then and now. 'The children,' he answered. 'Now they are noisy, cheerful, happy. In the war they were all silent, all terrified.' He moved off, choked.

Travelling in coaches bedecked with banners reading 'Korean War Veterans', the old soldiers are greeted by the majority of the population with a fervour hard to imagine in any other former theatre of oper-ations. 'I think Korea is the only place in the world where British ser-vicemen can go back and be received with open arms,' Mercer said. 'I remember all these little Korean children came out – they all had a grubby little piece of paper and a pencil, and they thrust it at you for your signature. That is when you get things in perspective. I often hear people say, "Was it worth it?" But among those who go back, I think the answer would be "Yes."'

Perrins, in Korea on business in 1998, decided to visit the War Memorial. 'I got into a cab with a young driver,' he recalled. 'At a red light, looking in the mirror, he asked in English, "First trip to Seoul?" I said, "No." He said, "Were you here during the war?" I said, "Yes." He said, "Thank you." That impressed me.' Phillips returned on the battle's fiftieth anniversary in 2001. 'The general feeling was that something posi-tive had been done as a result of this unpleasant war – I'm damned certain that won't happen in Iraq,' he said. 'When we went to the War Memorial, they had a guard of honour for us. We thought we had turned up on the wrong day; we thought they were waiting for President Bush!'

With increasingly affluent Koreans travelling the world, incidents have occurred in third countries. Temple and his wife Caroline, keen skiers, were dangling over the Valle Blanche in a crowded cable car, when someone, gesturing at a group of Asians, said 'Look at those Japanese.' Temple thought they were Korean and asked their group leader. 'She asked me a few questions, and asked me about the Imjin. Then she harangued her group, there was much clapping, and she said, "Thank you for defending our country." Everyone else in the cable car was mystified, and a little impressed.'

Strachan, the haunted Fusilier, took his doctor's advice. He could barely reconcile the country he disembarked in with the one he had fought over. 'Modern Korea – my God! I couldn't believe it! I had a belt, and the clasp broke. I went into a shop and the man bowed and put a buckle on. I said, "How much?" and he said, "No, you fought for our freedom!" I was very moved – we did some good, they appreciated it.' The Korea trip did its job. The Chinese soldier's ghost never returned.

Other men achieved closure. At the truce village of Panmunjon, inside the DMZ, one of the most thoughtful Imjin veterans, Preston-Bell, fell into discussion with a Korean-American US Army officer, Captain June Cho. 'She asked me what my most memorable experience was, and I talked about the refugees, about those white columns of wrecked humanity,' he recalled. 'She said, "Let me tell you a story. There were two families that managed to get out of Pyongyang – you might even have seen them. They made it out. They had children, and their children got to know each other; the boy and the girl got married. They emigrated to America. Their children grew up, went to school and one of them joined the US Army." She took my hand in her hands and said, "If you hadn't been there then, I wouldn't be here now." It was then that something happened in my mind that hadn't happened for fifty years.'

Some men, such as Joe Thompson, who has written a book on the country, have discovered a new interest in their autumn years: Korea. 'I have tried to spend the last seven years learning about the history, music and literature of Korea and I have met a wonderful Korean family,' Preston-Bell said. In 2004, in the company of that family, the Mins, he drove up Route 11. With the aid of his old photographs, maps, and an eye for ground, he located the stream bed where Kingsley Foster had fallen. While the Mins intoned a Buddhist blessing, the Hussar clambered down to the stream bed to lay flowers. On his way up, he caught his hand on a thorn – making him probably the last British soldier to spill blood on the Imjin battlefield.

Others, sensing the centrality of the Korean War in their life experience, have gone further. In the last decade two British soldiers who fought in the war but who died in the UK asked to leave their ashes on the land they fought for. Their wishes have been granted. The ashes of both have been scattered in commemoration ceremonies on a location emblematic of the sacrifices Britons made in Korea: 'Castle Site', the hill held by the Glosters' A Company on the first night of battle.

If the free world did not win the war – the fighting was halted by an uneasy truce – South Korea, with the strong backing of the United States, won the peace. One only has to look at the stark contrast between the two nations on the peninsula. On the one hand is South Korea. The 'zero-to-hero' rise of the country from the ashes of the 1950s is arguably the greatest national success story of the twentieth century. North Korea, on the other hand, is arguably the world's most isolated, most insulated, most paranoid nation; unlike South Korea, it is still run by the same government as in the war years. Trapped in the past, Pyongyang received a slap in the face when Peking, its Korean War 'blood ally' bowed to *realpolitik* and established diplomatic relations with Seoul in 1992. Two years later its 'Great Leader' Kim Il-sung, the man who had launched the disastrous war, died. His son, 'Dear Leader' Kim Jong-il, took over. The country retreated ever deeper into itself. A famine in the late 1990s killed perhaps two million people, or 10 per cent of its population. Today, it is a land ruled by force and dogma, ravaged by ignorance, poverty and hunger.

'Taking into account the living standards of North and South Korea, [the war] was certainly worthwhile,' wrote Henri Wolfs. 'Freedom has never been free.' In this light, the 'Forgotten War' has, with the hindsight of half a century, proved a just one. Of all the Imjin veterans, John Preston-Bell most eloquently put into words the redemption born from that realisation. Sitting in his sun-dappled sitting room in Kent, in the summer of 2007, he mused: 'What do giving and loving have in common? There is no difference; they are the same. Fifty years ago, I had given a year of my life, and nearly lost it. I hadn't realised what the Koreans had done with that little contribution. When I saw their gratitude – and, more than that, the way they'd created this brand new, wonderful, cheerful, homogeneous, vulgar, prosperous new nation – I wanted to say, "Don't thank *me*: It is *you* who have made *my* life worthwhile . . . it is *you* who have magnified *me*."'

# WHERE ARE THEY NOW?

*The fever of life is over*
*The busy world is ended*
*And our work, done*

Book of Common Prayer

## Formations

### 8TH KING'S ROYAL IRISH HUSSARS

In 1958 the regiment was amalgamated into the Queen's Royal Irish Hussars, which was in turn amalgamated into the Queen's Royal Hussars in 1993.

### 63RD ARMY

The Chinese shock formation that 29th Brigade fought on the Imjin was stationed in Shanxi Province after the war. According to website www.globalsecurity.org, it was deactivated in 2003.

### THE BELGIAN BATTALION

The Belgian United Nations Command battalion was disbanded after the war. Its colours are today carried by the 3rd Parachute Battalion.

### THE GLOSTERS

The Gloucestershire Regiment was amalgamated in 1994 into the Royal Gloucestershire, Berkshire and Wiltshire Regiment. Then, in 2005, the RGBW was merged (amid considerable controversy – its commanding officer was reportedly 'devastated' at the move[1]) into 1st Battalion, The Rifles. The back badge is still worn, however. In 2008 the US Presidential Unit Citation was framed and hung in Gloucester Cathedral, under Carne's 'Korea Cross'.

### ROYAL NORTHUMBERLAND FUSILIERS

The regiment was amalgamated into the Royal Regiment of Fusiliers in 1968.

### THE ROYAL ULSTER RIFLES

The RUR was amalgamated into the Royal Irish Rangers, which has since become the Royal Irish Regiment. One of its reservist units (in Afghanistan at time of writing) is 'Imjin River Company'.

# Individuals

### BAYLISS, JOHN
The boxing Fusilier who fought across Europe in World War II and survived hand-to-hand combat with Z Company still considers the Imjin the fiercest battle he fought in. After leaving the army he joined British Caledonian airlines. Retired, he lives in Suffolk.

### BOYALL, DAVID
The adventurous Australian remained in the British Army ('the British Army went to much more interesting places than the Australian'), serving in Malaya, Suez, Northern Ireland and Libya before retiring as a colonel and returning to his native land. After a 2002 veterans' visit to Korea, the commander of the last Centurion down Route 11 was so impressed by the strides the country had made that today he drives a Hyundai 'out of loyalty!' He lives outside Sydney.

### BRODIE, TOM
29th Infantry Brigade's commander won a DSO for his leadership in Korea. He was promoted to major-general in 1952, and took command of the 1st Infantry Division. He also became the colonel of his regiment, the Cheshires. He died in 1993.[2]

### CARNE, JAMES
After release, the Gloster CO claimed that while in solitary confinement he had been brainwashed with drugs by the Chinese. Having won a DSO for Hill 327, he was awarded a US Distinguished Service Cross (the highest award the American government can give a foreigner) and a VC for his battalion's stand on Hill 235. He was promoted full colonel, and commanded the Young Soldiers Training Centre at Harrogate. The very private individual then retired into obscurity in his home village of Cranham (where a copy of the Glosters' Presidential Unit Citation hangs in the local pub). Some thought he became a recluse after the battle, but one Gloster maintained, 'He didn't become one – he always was one!' He died in 1986.[3]

### CHARLEY, ROBIN
After retiring as a colonel, he commanded Queen's University Belfast Officer Training Corps and became a Justice of the Peace. The easy-going officer retains his considerable charm and stays active as chairman of Belfast's Somme Heritage Centre.

### CLOUGH, TOM
A regular attender at Gloster reunions, the 170 Mortar Battery veteran of Hill 235 is considered an 'honorary infantryman' but remains proud to have served in the artillery: 'People say, "Artillery? Nine-mile

snipers!" and I say, "Oh? How did I get captured, then?"' He still occasionally gets a recurrence of the 'drop wrist' that came from being tightly bound in the camps: 'It can make it difficult to hold a pint!' After spending hours during his solitary confinement watching a spider lie in wait for its prey in the only square of light in his cell, Clough, to this day, remains unable to harm one of the insects.

## COLEMAN-WOOD, JOHN

The RASC concert party member left the army in 1952 and entered the entertainment business before suffering from an ulcer: 'You can't run around the country like that. Better a live coward than a dead hero!' He left the stage and entered accountancy, but still does amateur theatricals: 'I entertain old age pensioners, and I am older than some of 'em!' On a trip to Korea in 2008 he wondered what had happened to an orphan he had taken care of. 'We had twenty-one men in the unit, and twenty-one kids. There was a little girl I used to clothe and feed – she was five – and I often wonder if she is still alive.' He never found out.

## CUBISS, MALCOLM

The one-armed officer opted to remain in the army, where he was wounded yet again. When his eardrum was blown out for a second time in Northern Ireland in 1974 the surgeon asked, 'Have I done you before?' Just as Tom Brodie was alleged to have had difficulties speaking to US officers, Cubiss would suffer a cross-cultural miscommunication while serving as chief-of-staff of NATO's ACE Mobile Force, which included British, Canadian, Italian, German and American battalions. The last two's commanders did not get on. Cubiss was busy in his office when the American called. The German answered the phone. Cubiss casually directed the German to tell the American to 'fuck off' – meaning, delay him, so he (Cubiss) could call back later. The German snapped: 'Fuck off!' – citing Cubiss's order. Cubiss was aghast; an international incident was narrowly avoided. Typically, Cubiss has little fear of the violence that plagues modern Britain – a topic that came up over lunch. Rising from the table, he showed me two customised attachments for his false arm: one a piratical hook, the other a commando dagger. His wife Wendy confided that in a riot that had occurred during his military career, several miscreants were hospitalised with 'sword wounds'. Defying General Bill Slim's warning that he would never rise above major, due to his disability, Cubiss retired a brigadier. He lives outside York.

## EAGLES, TONY

The Gloster bugler left the Army in 1954, being declared medically unfit for infantry service after his captivity – something he is still bitter about. As he says, 'I played rugby until I was fifty!' He worked for Shell and the DSS and earned an MBE for his work as national chairman of the British Korean War Veterans Association. 'I am glad to be married and have children,' he said. 'It's like a dream after all we had been through.'

## FARRAR-HOCKLEY, ANTHONY

The Glosters' formidable adjutant fought at Suez, in the Radfan and Borneo, then went on to command Land Forces, Northern Ireland, and NATO Forces, Northern Europe, as well as being Adjutant-General to the Queen. He retired as a general and escaped IRA assassination in 1990, when a bomb attached to his garden hose was spotted. Farrar-Hockley was as noted an author as a soldier: his account of combat and captivity in Korea, *The Edge of the Sword*, has been translated into Korean, and his two-volume British official history of the war is an indispensable source. One of his sons also ascended to the rank of general. He died in 2006.[4]

## FARRELL, JOE

The tough Ulsterman left the Army in 1953, the year the Korean War ended. He worked on the Belfast docks, then entered the security business. The former light welterweight still has the bounce in his stride that marks the athlete and a handshake like a vice. Most days, he rises at 04:00 to walk his dogs. During an interview, he introduced me to a novel cure for back pain which he swears by: a length of rope tied loosely round the waist under the clothes.

## GREEN, DAVID

Green left the army after completing National Service and emigrated to Australia in 1970. On a trip to China he attempted – unsuccessfully – to enter North Korea to see the site of his POW camp. His autobiographical *Captured at the Imjin River: The Korean War Memoirs of a Gloster* was published in 2003. He died in 2007.[5]

## HARVEY, MIKE

The captain who led the only Glosters to escape the trap commanded the regiment's 5th territorial battalion, before heading to Dhofar and war against Marxist insurgents, where he was seconded to the Sultan of Oman's Northern Frontier Force Regiment. In 1971 he orchestrated a retaliatory cross-border raid into Yemen which proved decisive. By the time he left in 1972 the war had turned in the Sultan's favour. He retired a brigadier, wrote a number of books on judo and self-defence, and created unarmed combat programmes for the Customs and the Armed Forces. He visited Korea for the first time since the war in 2001 and died, at his retirement home in Ecuador, in 2007.[6]

## HUTH, HENRY

The popular and apparently fearless Hussar, who several officers credited with saving the infantry during the breakout on 25 April, retired from the army in 1960 as a lieutenant-colonel to farm in County Waterford, Ireland. There, by all accounts, he was as popular with his tenants as he had been with his troops. He died in 1987, but his name lives on in Holland: a street in Linne, which he liberated during World War II, is named 'Major Huthstraat' in his honour.[7]

## KIM CHUM-KON

The commander of the ROK 12th Regiment that extricated the only Glosters to escape the trap remains in good health. The jeep he lost on the last morning of battle was not, in fact, destroyed. His divisional commander, Paik Sun-yup, spotted its identification number during armistice talks at Panmunjom: it had been captured by the Chinese. After retiring as a major-general, Kim entered academia and became president of Kyunghee University's Institute of Peace Studies. He was saddened when I told him the late Mike Harvey had visited Korea in 2001; he had been unaware of his trip. This widely experienced officer thought British troops were among the best he ever encountered, though 'the Japanese fought the best!' Remembering the dance parties on the eve of North Korea's 1950 attack, he said, 'I can't dance – even now.'

## KINNE, DEREK

Despite winning the George Cross, Kinne decided to leave the army. Some years later he was standing on an underground platform in London when a voice behind roared: 'Kinne!' It was Farrar-Hockley, the officer with injured feet he had carried for days during the march through North Korea: he had recognised Kinne by the back of his head. Kinne subsequently left England for Canada, and later, the US. In 1973 he was flown to Australia as a witness for the defence of the politician Jack Kane, sued by journalist Wilfred Burchett for character defamation. After he had 'let loose for an hour' on the witness stand, Burchett's attorney asked, 'You don't like Mr Burchett do you?' Kinne replied, 'No! He's a bastard and a traitor, and he should be shot!' The following day Kinne attempted to strangle Burchett – 'It was a good job the jury didn't see that!' When the Australian reporter subsequently launched an international appeal for funds, Kinne made a contribution: he defecated in a box and mailed it to Burchett. Kinne and his wife Anne spent their tenth wedding anniversary with fellow GC winner Odette Sansom, Kinne's personal heroine. Though still a larger than life character, Kinne has mellowed: 'With the medal, I've nothing left to prove,' he said. He lives in Arizona.

## LARGE, LOFTY

Despite his arm gunshot wounds (which pained him for the rest of his life), he married his sweetheart Ann and worked his way back to exceptional fitness, joining the SAS, with whom he fought all over the world, notably in Borneo and the Middle East. His autobiography, *Soldier Against the Odds: From Korean War to SAS* was published in 1999. He died in 2006. 'He never forgot the people who were killed alongside him,' said his widow. 'I always knew when he was thinking about them. He was a good man.'

## LEE CHUN-HEE

The little girl who was awoken by artillery as the NKPA bore down upon Seoul returned to the capital after the war. A talented seamstress, she ran a *hanbok* (traditional Korean silk dress) business in central Seoul for decades. After the tribulations of her youth, she lived a peaceful life, but encountered misfortune once again in 1992 – when her daughter, Ji-young, married the author. Now a grandmother, she lives in Seoul.

## LEE KYUNG-SIK

After the Rifles departed, the interpreter served with other British regiments for the duration. In post-war Korea his English abilities were in demand, and he won various translation awards, but was fired from an editorial position at the *Korea Herald* newspaper under the dictatorial Chun Do-hwan regime. He set up his own publishing company, *The Korea Post*, which puts out two e-dailies and a print monthly. 'The Royal Ulster Rifles gave me a job and got me started as a fully qualified interpreter-translator and made me what I am today, of which I am very, very proud,' he said.

## LEITH-MACGREGOR, ROBBIE

After leaving the army as a lieutenant-colonel, the former pilot and commander of the Fusiliers' Y Company worked for Guinness, then retired in London. He died in 2008.[8]

## MCCORD, MERVYN

McCord remained in the army for his full career. Distractions in Hong Kong, his posting after Korea, put paid to an athletic career: 'I discovered wine, women, song and all!' He retired as a brigadier in December 1984 and was appointed Colonel of the Regiment. In that capacity, he organised 'one of the longest parties ever' for the Royal Ulster Rifles' third centenary: it stretched from Northern Ireland, via London, to West Germany. 'Irish regiments enjoy life to the full,' he said, 'whether fighting, drinking, partying – you name it!' He is grateful to have served in Korea as a young officer. 'It gave me a sense of proportion for the rest of my military career. I knew what really mattered – the basic elements of soldiering: morale and *esprit de corps*.' Retired in Sussex, he remains active in regimental affairs: in 2008, he led efforts to relocate the Rifles' Korean War monument to Belfast City Hall.

## MERCER, SAM

After returning from the Korean POW camps to a British hospital, the boy who had joined the Army for 'travel and adventure' was given a false eye to replace the one lost in battle, and was medically discharged in 1954. In 1955 the leg shot through on 25 April was amputated – 'the final solution' as Mercer calls it. But there was a silver lining. A nurse in Queen Mary's hospital, Audrey Evans, felt sorry for the shy veteran – 'He never said much, and didn't have many visitors' – and asked him out to a concert. In 1956 they married. For years, Mercer, mindful of the near-starvation diets in the camps, was unable to tolerate even a bit of food being thrown away. That passed, but, haunted by the sight of the disfigured Chinese napalm victim in North Korea, he still refuses to have a paraffin heater in his home. Retired from a career in insurance, he spends a lot of time in his attic, where he keeps army memorabilia and a military history library: 'He doesn't like TV and is still very "army". He loves it up there,' says Audrey. He won an MBE for services to the British Korean War Veterans Association in 1995. The Mercers' London home is named after the now-vanished hamlet at the foot of Hill 235 where the Glosters made their last stand: 'Solma-ri'.

## MOLE, JOHN

On being stationed in Northern Ireland, the Rifles' Mortar Fire Controller on the Imjin was perturbed to discover that his Catholic religion could be an issue, so rejoined his old CO, Gerald Rickord, then commanding a battalion of the 2nd Gurkha Rifles, and fought in Malaya. He left the army in 1968 and joined Glenfiddich. Now retired in Somerset, he is a keen artist.

## NEWHOUSE, GEORGE

With his wife Dorothy, the Gloster reservist and medical orderly revisited Korea for the first time in 2008 and was surprised to find himself a minor celebrity. At time of writing, his granddaughter Jennifer is on a Samsung/British Legion Scholarship at Seoul's Yonsei University. Newhouse was Gloucester-area chairman of the Burma Star Association, and had been regimental secretary of the Glosters Korea Veterans Association for twenty-five years. He died in November 2008, seven months after his last trip to the battlefield.

## NICHOLLS, BOB

The former mortar observer from 170 Mortar Battery emigrated to Canada, then moved to the US and worked for Chrysler for thirty-six years. Though Americanised, he cannot forget the behaviour of the

Fusiliers and the Rifles during the battle's most desperate moments. 'I won't hear a bad word about the British Army,' he said.

## ORMROD, PETER

The one-eyed Hussar retired from the Army in 1954 to run his Welsh estate, where he became master of the Border Counties Otter Hounds. He worked in countryside affairs – forestry and fishing – and was a devout churchman. He died in 2007.[9] By a curious coincidence, his funeral was attended by my literary agent, a family friend of the Ormrods.

## PAIK SUN-YUP

The ROK 1st Division Commander was posted to command the ROK 1st Corps just before the Fifth Offensive. As successful in that command as he had been in his first, he subsequently represented his government at truce talks in Panmunjom. The most respected of the ROK commanders, Paik is one of the last senior participants of the conflict still living. He maintains an office at the spectacular National War Memorial in Seoul; no Korean War-related event is complete without him.

## PAUL, TED

The officer photographed firing his carbine in the battle's closing stages left the army in 1952 and joined Tate and Lyle as an international sugar trader, but stayed in touch with the Hussars. When he met his regiment's Colonel, Princess Ann, at a social function after the 1988 Olympics (where she competed as an equestrian), she was surprised when he told her that he, too, had been to Korea. Today he lives in London and is active in charity work.

## PENG TE-HUAI

The guerrilla general who commanded the Chinese 'volunteers' in Korea was the only senior member of the communist party with the courage to confront an increasingly irrational Mao with the disastrous results of the so-called 'Great Leap Forward' – a famine that killed as many as thirty million. An angry Mao removed Peng from all official positions in September 1959 and had him paraded in chains and humiliated in front of 40,000 troops of the PLA, the force he had, after its harsh experiences in Korea, wanted to modernise and professionalise. During the Cultural Revolution, Peng was arrested, faced harrowing 'criticism' sessions and was imprisoned and tortured. In 1974 he fell ill, and Mao ordered that he receive no medical treatment. He died that year, aged 76, but his death was kept secret. The old soldier was rehabilitated as a 'great revolutionary fighter' in 1978, two years after Mao's own death.[10]

## PERRINS, TONY

The Fusiliers' intelligence officer retired from the Army in 1955. In 1959 he joined Reynolds Aluminum in the US. On retirement in 1992 he journeyed, on foot, by bicycle and by boat, across America with his eldest son. The following year he crewed a yacht across the Atlantic to Gibraltar, then resettled in his birthplace, London, where he was outraged by treatment of veterans. He required an operation on his nagging bullet wound, but 'couldn't get National Health, so flew to the US, where I had Medicare'. He heard that one of his Fusiliers had been found wandering the streets of Bristol. 'His wife had died and he'd become totally rudderless. He had family in Yorkshire, so I said, "Send him up there; he's got a support system." Well, they put him on the train to Colchester. But there's no point being bitter; this has always happened to British soldiers.' In 2002 he published the excellent *A Pretty Rough Do Altogether: The Fifth Fusiliers in Korea, 1950–51*. In 2008 Perrins returned to the US and settled in Oregon, where he is working on a book about his experiences as a POW in Korea.

## PHILIPS, ARMAND

Philips recovered from his facial wound, but on returning to Belgium was astonished to find himself court-martialled for ordering his platoon's retreat from its position on the first night of battle. His platoon commander was furious at the treatment of his sergeant; Philips was acquitted. He served a full army career, rose to the rank of warrant officer, and frequently trained with British troops: 'I still like British people – and Koreans too,' he said. His last comment to me was: 'I want to thank those men of the Royal Ulster Rifles: their extra ammunition saved us.'

## PHILLIPS, SAM

The Fusilier officer wounded by friendly fire made a full recovery. In 1953 a friend asked him if he wanted to try skiing. 'I thought, "After what I went through in Korea in that winter?"' he recalled. 'Well, I thoroughly enjoyed it and have been every year since.' Now retired from a career in stockbroking, he kindly drove me from Newcastle to the regimental museum of the 5th Fusiliers, in the magnificent castle at Alnwick. There our interview took place in an appropriate setting: in a turret surrounded by the medal collection of Lieutenant-Colonel Kingsley Foster – Phillips's CO, killed in action on the Imjin – given to the regiment by his family.

## PRESTON-BELL, JOHN

The young cornet who joined the Hussars because he liked the headgear left the army after his eighteen months were up. A keen photographer – he took some of the finest shots of the battle from his Centurion turret –

he entered the camera business in Singapore, and in 1957 founded his own advertising agency. He returned to Korea in 2001 and was so impressed with the resurrected nation that he asked the British Embassy to put him in touch with a Korean family. They did; he was introduced to the Mins in 2002 and is in daily email contact with them from his Kent home.

### RICKORD, GERALD

After Korea, the tough airborne officer commanded a battalion of the 2nd Gurkha Rifles in the Malayan Emergency, then became Administrative Commandant of the School of Infantry. After retiring from the army as a lieutenant-colonel, he worked for Guinness. He died in 1990.[11]

### SENTERRE, LUCIEN

Returning to the peacetime Belgian Army, Senterre was unimpressed with senior NCOs, most of whom had spent World War II in POW camps and who envied the younger troops their combat experience. Heading to Africa, he served as a military adviser under Colonel Robert Lamouline (as mentioned in Frederick Forsyth's *Dogs of War*) in the Congo bush fighting. Lamouline had commanded the Belgian Battalion in Korea late in the war, and one mercenary serving alongside Senterre was a former comrade from Korea. Now retired in France, Senterre is in frequent touch with Armand Philips who 'had the good taste' to marry Senterre's cousin.

### STRACHAN, DAVID

When the Fusiliers left Korea, Strachan was reassigned to the Royal Leicestershire Regiment for another year of combat – a move he believes was illegal, and has since been compensated for. He left the army, then served eleven years in the navy, before going into nursing. Today, he lives in Spain; his son is an officer in the Royal Regiment of Fusiliers.

### SWEETLOVE, NORMAN

The Rifles corporal left the army in 1953, but later rejoined and served in The Royal Norfolks ('I had to learn 'em a wee bit!'). After retiring from the army a second time, he became a postman, but remained in the Territorials. He married, has seven children and 'can't count the grandchildren'.

### TEMPLE, GUY

The easy-going but highly competent officer whose river ambush opened the battle served forty-four years in uniform: 'I have known no other employment!' Temple fought in Kenya during the Mau Mau insurgency, then in Cyprus, which was 'a little like Northern Ireland . . . enough to keep it interesting for everybody'. He was subsequently approached to serve in the nascent Dubai Armed Forces. 'I had to think about it for about five seconds,' he said. 'It was an attraction being in something that was growing rather than running down.' When he joined, the Dubai Army had a strength of 100 men; when he retired eighteen years later, it had 24,000. Today he and his wife Caroline are keen skiers and sailors. At the 2001 veterans' return, when Farrar-Hockley introduced personalities during his battlefield lecture, Temple raised the yachting cap he was wearing in preference to a beret. He still carries scars around his upper arms – souvenirs from the Chinese bindings in the camps.

## THOMPSON, JOE

The corporal who charged into 'Happy Valley' fell ill in April 1951 and was medically evacuated just before the Imjin fighting began. He left the army in 1953 and worked for the GPO but, as a reservist, later saw action in Aden. He returned to Korea in 1988, where he was amazed at the country's transformation, and has since written a book on it, *Korea: The Divided Peninsula*. He is also fascinated by modern China. He still attends combat stress therapy twice a year in Scotland.

## TOMENSON, STAN

The Fusilier who was Z Company's runner stayed in the army for twenty-six years, retiring as a sergeant major. He suffered from nightmares and flashbacks, but a 2003 veterans' visit to Korea was 'one of the best trips I had ever had'. He was deeply moved when Korean shopkeepers insisted that he and other veterans only pay half price for gifts.

## TRUELL, GEORGE

45 Field Regiment continued to play a role in the life of the man whose cool thinking and precise firing saved it as the Chinese attacked before dawn on St George's Day. He was at a regimental reunion in Dortmund on 23 April 1960 when 'at 8:00, I was introduced to a wench. By midnight, I said to this wench, "You and I ought to be united in holy matrimony." She said, "No, because you will be embarrassed in the morning at what you have to get out of."' Four months later Mary relented; they have been married forty-seven years. The couple's eldest son is named Edmund Imjin Truell. At a Korean Embassy party to commemorate the end of the Korean War Truell senior told the Korean ambassador: 'I probably have the only child in England called Imjin!' The ambassador rose to the occasion and ordered him a bottle of champagne. Truell retired as a lieutenant-colonel in 1986.

## VANDAMME, ANDRÉ

The decorated staff sergeant served a full term in the Belgian army, revisited Korea four times, and is in almost daily contact with his old comrades. Immensely proud to have served, he said, 'Despite my age of eighty-three . . . my goodness, I would enlist again for any noble cause!'[12]

## WEAR, VICK
The Fusilier returned to Korea in 1960 to command the UK's UN Honour Guard platoon, to find little had changed, beyond tarmac roads and cheap taxis. He left the army in 1972 as a sergeant major. An excellent shot, he suffered occasional flashbacks of an enemy running at him, and being unable to stop him with aimed fire. 'I did Aden. I did Northern Ireland,' he said. 'But nothing like Korea.'

## BEN WHITCHURCH
The Gloster whose anti-tank gun knocked out a sniper behind Hill 235 left the army after release from the POW camps – 'Instead of 18 months National Service, I did four and a half years!' – and went into butchery. Retired in Bristol, he still meets his old comrades at least once a month. 'We developed such a camaraderie, like brothers,' he said. 'When we talk about the battle to ordinary people we don't say much, but when we meet each other, it is fought from beginning to end!'

## WHITAMORE, PETER
The officer who was shot and captured on the last day on the Imjin remains bitter about the disadvantages in promotion and postings that officers captured in Korea were subject to. 'I retired as a lieutenant-colonel, and regard myself as lucky: my pension is adequate to meet my needs without luxury,' he said. 'But I think I should have gone further.' However, he is not bitter in person: to oil the conversation during our interview he poured me the longest, strongest gin and tonic I have ever encountered.

## WOLFS, HENRI
The officer who was the Belgians' rearguard twice during the battle served for twenty-six years, retiring as a lieutenant-colonel, having commanded an armoured battalion on the German border. He married a German, has two children, four grandchildren and one great-grandchild. In a beautifully written letter to me he reflected on the luck he enjoyed in combat: 'Your questions make me realise for the first time that, in fact, the Gods of War must have been with us during the battle,' adding – in a nod to the military heritage of his wife's homeland – 'Gott mit uns.'

# GLOSSARY

**Assault Pioneers** Engineers attached to infantry battalions.

**AWOL** Absent without leave.

**Bivvy** (noun or verb) Short for bivouac. Can refer to a small tent, or simply a basic encampment for the night.

**Blue on Blue** British Army term for friendly troops firing on friendly troops – a not uncommon occurrence in the fog of battle. Colloquially known as 'friendly fire' – a term disliked by most soldiers, who consider all incoming fire unfriendly.

**Bren** Czech-designed light machine-gun used by British forces. Popular for its accuracy and reliability; had a fast barrel-change but a slow (500 rounds per minute) rate of fire and was fed by a 30-round magazine.

**Brew up** (noun or verb) Two distinct meanings, depending upon context: either making a cup of tea, or blowing up/setting fire to a vehicle/armoured vehicle.

**Bomb up** To load a tank with ammunition and fuel.

**Burp gun** Russian-made Shpagin PPSh-41 submachine-gun: rugged, dependable and with a 71-round drum magazine, it was a formidable weapon and superior to its British equivalent, the *Sten*. Its fast rate of fire gave a 'brrrrppp' sound – hence the nickname.

**CCF** Chinese Communist Forces.

**CCP** Chinese Communist Party.

**CO** Commanding officer of a battalion. Usually a lieutenant-colonel.

**CP** Command Post.

**CPV** Chinese People's Volunteer. In actual fact, not a volunteer but a regular soldier of the PLA deployed to fight in Korea.

**CPVA** Chinese People's Volunteer Army.

**Dead ground** Military term for a dip in the ground, or ground behind a hill or ridge, which it is impossible to see into.

**DMZ** Demilitarized Zone. The heavily militarised border which currently divides the Korean peninsula.

**DRPK** Democratic People's Republic of Korea, i.e. North Korea.

**F Echelon** Forward echelon position, closest to the combat unit.

**FOO** Forward Observation Officer (pronounced 'Foo'). Artillery officer, usually a captain, with the forward troops. With a signaller, his job is to call in and to adjust the fire of artillery.

**Fire for Effect** Fire-control order. Once the enemy's position and distance is known, and fall of shot or ranging fire (often with smoke shells) has been noted, infantry or artillery fire can cause actual casualties among the enemy.

**GI** 'General Issue'; slang term for US serviceman.

**Gook** (noun or adjective) Korean War slang for Asian. Fifty years before Korea, the pejorative 'goo-goo' was used to describe the guerrilla enemy during the American war against the 'Moros' in the Philippines, a brutal campaign lasting from 1898 to 1902; it may have derived from 'gobbledygook', which American troops thought the natives spoke. Whether 'gook' was a carryover from this, or whether it arose in Korea independently is unclear. If the latter, its origin was probably innocent. The Korean word for America/American is 'Miguk', and Koreans seeing US soldiers would have used this word to describe them. Americans overhearing this could have misinterpreted it as 'Me, gook' – and so started using it to describe Koreans themselves. The term took on a negative tone, becoming a racial pejorative, and was used in Vietnam.

**Hubba Hubba** GI slang meaning 'Hurry up'.

**IWM** Imperial War Museum.

**KIA** Killed in Action.

**LOC** Line of Communication.

**LMG** Light Machine-gun. A portable machine-gun, usually crewed by two men, though operable by one. In the British Army, this was the much-loved Bren.

**LP** Listening Post.

**MASH** Mobile Army Surgical Hospital.

**MFC** Mortar Fire Controller; essentially, the same job as an artillery FOO, but for mortars.

**MIA** Missing in Action.

**MLR** Main Line of Resistance. The main – rather than the forward, or fallback – line of a defensive position.

**MMG** Medium Machine-gun. In the British Army in Korea this was issued at the battalion level and was the trusty, belt-fed and water-cooled Vickers, a weapon that could fire non-stop for hours.

**MP** Military policeman, or provost.

**MSR** Main Supply Route. A road or track used exclusively for military traffic; civilians were not permitted on it. MSRs were an important target for Chinese infiltrators, who would set up roadblocks to ambush retreating UN troops.

**Mucker** Best friend.

**NCO** Non-Commissioned Officer, such as corporal or sergeant.

**NKPA** North Korean People's Army.

**OC** Officer commanding a company or squadron. Usually a major.

**O Group** Officers' Group, or Orders Group; a briefing for a group of officers.

**OP** Observation post.

**POL** Petrol, oil, lubricants.

**POW** Prisoner of War.

**PLA** People's Liberation Army; i.e. the regular army of communist China.

**PTI** Physical Training Instructor.

**PTSD** Post-Traumatic Stress Disorder.

**R&R** Rest and recreation (sometimes 'rack and ruin'). Short leave, usually spent in Japan.

**RAMC** Royal Army Medical Corps.

**RAP** Regimental Aid Post. A field dressing station, usually set up at Battalion HQ, to stabilise battle casualties before they can be sent rearwards.

**Recce** (noun or verb) British Army shorthand for reconnaissance; pronounced 'recky'.

**ROK** Republic of Korea, i.e. South Korea. Pronounced 'Rock'. During the Korean War, the acronym also referred to the country's army and soldiers ('the ROKs').

**REME** Royal Electrical and Mechanical Engineers.

**Redcap** British military policeman, so named from their red headdress.

**Sangar** A legacy of the British Army's long service on the Indian subcontinent, 'sangar' is a Pushtu word for an embrasure of stones or rocks, raised when it is impossible to dig into ground. On the Imjin, due to the rocky nature of the hills, many defensive positions were a combination of a trench, dug down a couple of feet, and a sangar parapet.

**Sapper**  Military engineer.

**Stag**  Night sentry duty.

**Start line**  The start point from which an attack is launched. Ideally, this is reconnoitred and marked, often with tape. In reality, it is often just a line on the map.

**Sten**  Mass-produced, unreliable and unpopular British SMG.

**SMG**  Submachine-gun, such as the British Sten or the Russian 'burp gun'.

**Stonk** (noun and verb)  British military slang, meaning bombard with mortars or artillery.

**UN**  United Nations. Although US and ROK troops made up its main elements, the forces fighting in defence of South Korea were deployed following UN resolutions.

**UNC**  United Nations Command. The American-led multinational force established, in response to UN Security Council Resolutions of 15 and 27 June and 7 July 1950, to repel the attack on South Korea and to establish 'international peace and security in the area'.

**Unpleasant peasants**  British term for Chinese infantry.

**WGC**  War Graves Commission.

**WIA**  Wounded in Action.

# LIST OF SOURCES

'29th Independent Infantry Brigade Group History, September 1949–October 1951' (WO 308-42). (In National Archives, Kew, Surrey.)

'29th Brigade Order of the Day, Jan 1st, 1951'. (In Soldiers of Gloucestershire Museum Archive, Gloucester.)

'29th Infantry Brigade War Diary'. (In Royal Ulster Rifles Museum, Belfast.)

Appleman, Roy E., *Ridgway Duels for Korea* (College Station, TX, 1990).

Aynsley, Cyril, 'Into Battle – And There Was the Major, Five Dead Chinese Around Him', *Daily Express*, 27 November 1959.

—— 'The Imjin Flows Red', *Daily Express*, 28 November 1959.

*The Back Badge: The Journal of the Gloucestershire Regiment*, vol. 3, no. 10, June 1951.

*The Back Badge: The Journal of the Gloucestershire Regiment*, vol. 3, no. 11, December 1951.

Birt, E. J., transcript of interview with academic Hugh Driver, 1983. (In Soldiers of Gloucestershire Museum Archive, Gloucester.)

Blair, Clay, *The Forgotten War: America in Korea, 1950–1953* (New York, 1987).

Boyall, David, *Here and There* (New South Wales, 2002).

Breen, Michael, *The Koreans: Who They Are, What They Want, Where Their Future Lies* (London, 1998).

British United Press, 'British Troops Silence the Firing Squads', *Yorkshire Post*, 19 December 1950.

Carew, Tim, *Korea: The Commonwealth at War* (London, 1967).

Chang Jung and Jon Halliday, *Mao: The Unknown Story* (London, 2005).

'Command Report, 3rd Infantry Division, April 1951'. (In US National Archive, Washington DC.)

'Command Report, I US Army Corps, 1 April 1951–30 April 1951'. (In US National Archive, Washington DC.)

*The Crossbelts: Journal of the 8th King's Royal Irish Hussars*. (In possession of Brigadier (ret.) Dick Webster, 8th Hussars.)

Cumings, Bruce, *Korea's Place in the Sun* (New York, 1997).

Cutforth, Rene, *Korean Reporter* (London, 1952).

'David Rudge, Obituary', in *St George's Gazette: The Regimental Journal of the Fifth Fusiliers*, 31 May 1951.

Davies, S.J., *In Spite of Dungeons* (London, 1954).

De la Billière, Peter, *Storm Command* (London, 1992).

'Directive to Brigadier T. Brodie CBE, Commander, 29th Infantry Brigade Group' (WO308/68). (In National Archives, Kew, Surrey.)

Dunstan, Simon, *Armour of the Korean War, 1950–1953* (London, 1982).

—— *Tank War Korea* (London, 1985).

—— *Centurion Universal Tank 1943–2003* (Oxford, 2003).

Durney, James, *The Far Side of the World: Irish Servicemen in the Korean War 1950–53* (Naas, Co Kildare, 2005).

Eagles, Tony, letter dated 24 January 1977 to editor of *The Back Badge*, concerning the engagement on the night of 21 April 1950. (In Soldiers of Gloucestershire Museum Archive, Gloucester.)

Eckert, Carter J., Lee Ki-baik, Lew Young Ick, Michael Robinson and Edward W. Wagner, *Korea Old and New: A History* (Harvard, 1990) .

Evans, Michael, 'Historic Regiment Turns to Hoon in Battle for Survival', *The Times*, 17 February 2005.

Farrar-Hockley, Anthony, *The Edge of the Sword* (London, 1954).

—— *The British Part in the Korean War*, vol. I: *A Distant Obligation* (London, 1990).

—— *The British Part in the Korean War*, vol. II: *An Honourable Discharge* (London, 1995).

Fehrenbach, T.R., *This Kind of War: A Study in Unpreparedness* (London, 1963).

Fisher, Peter, and Patrick Lohan, *In Memoriam: Korean War* (Bath, 2006).

Fitzroy, Olivia, *Men of Valour*, vol. III: *History of the 8th King's Royal Irish Hussars, 1927–1958* (Liverpool, 1961).

'Fore and Aft', *The Times*, 3 May 1951.

Green, David, *Captured at the Imjin River: The Korean War Memoirs of a Gloster 1950–1953* (Barnsley, 2003) .

Grist, Digby, *Remembered with Advantage* (Gloucester, 1976).

Grossman, David, *On Killing* (New York, 1995).

Halberstam, David, *The Coldest Winter: America and the Korean War* (New York, 2007).

Hamill, H., *The RUR in Korea* (Belfast, 1953).

Harding, E.D., 'Battle Report, "B" Company, 1st Battalion The Gloucestershire Regiment' (undated). (In Soldiers of Gloucestershire Museum Archive, Gloucester.)

—— *The Imjin Roll* (Northamptonshire 1976, 3rd ed. Northamptonshire, 2000).

—— transcript of interview with academic Hugh Driver, 1983. (In Soldiers of Gloucestershire Museum Archive, Gloucester.)

Harvey, M.G., *The War in Korea: The Battle Decides All* (County Durham, 2002).

Hastings, Max, *The Korean War* (New York, 1987).

—— *Warriors: Portraits from the Battlefield* (London, 2005).

Hawley, Samuel, *The Imjin War: Japan's Sixteenth Century Invasion of Korea and Attempt to Conquer China* (Seoul/Berkeley, 2005).

Hays, J.L., 'RNFs Saved By Hussars Tanks', *Daily Dispatch*. (Undated fragment in the Royal Northumberland Fusiliers Museum Archive).

Headquarters, 3rd Infantry Division, 'Operations of 29th BIB, from 22–25 April 1951' (14 May 1951). (In US National Archive, Washington DC.)

Hickey, Michael, *The Korean War: The West Confronts Communism* (New York, 1999).

'The Hill of Honour', *Soldier*, June 1951.

Hoare, J.E., *The British Embassy, Seoul* (Seoul, 1999).

Huish, Len, letter dated 29 January 2001 describing his role in battle. (Passed to author by Brigadier (ret.) Dick Webster, 8th Hussars.)

Kahn, E.J., Jr, 'Only the Glosters', *New Yorker*, 26 May 1951; reprinted in '29th Independent Infantry Brigade Group History, September 1949–October 1951'.

Kavanagh, P.J., *The Perfect Stranger* (London, 1966).

Kennedy, Brian, and Elizabeth Guo, *Chinese Martial Arts Training Manuals: A Historical Survey* (Berkeley, 2005).

Kinne, Derek, *The Wooden Boxes* (London, 1955).

Korea Institute of Military History, *The Korean War*, vol. II (Seoul, 1998).

Korea Ministry of National Defense, *History of the UN Forces in the Korean War*, vol. VI (Seoul, 1977).

Lankov, Andrei, *The Dawn of Modern Korea* (Seoul, 2007).

Large, Lofty, *Soldier Against the Odds: From Korean War to SAS* (Edinburgh, 1999).

Le Roy, David (trans. Guy Van Attenhoven), 'The Belgian Battalion'. (In possession of Commandant (ret.) Jan Dillen.)

'Lieutenant-Colonel K.O.N. Foster. Obituary', *St George's Gazette*, 31 May, 1951.

Li Xiaobing, Allan R. Millet, and Yu Bin, *Mao's Generals Remember Korea* (Lawrence, KS, 2001).

Littlewood, T.R., 'MMG platoon after-action report'. (In Soldiers of Gloucester Museum Archive, Gloucestershire.)

McCord, Mervyn, 'The Imjin Battle, Korea 22–25 April 1951', Staff College lecture notes. (In possession of Brigadier (ret.) Mervyn McCord, RUR.)

Malkasian, Carter, *A History of Modern Wars of Attrition* (Westport, CT, 2002).

Ministry of Defence, *Treatment of British Prisoners of War in Korea* (London, 1953).

Mossman, Billy C., *The United States Army in the Korean War: Ebb and Flow* (Washington DC, 1990).

Newcombe, Michael, *Guns and the Morning Calm* (Newcastle upon Tyne, 1999).

O'Kane, Henry, *O'Kane's Korea* (Ulster, 1988).

Paik Sun-yup, *From Pusan to Panmunjom* (Washington DC, 1992).

Paul, Ted, 'A Year in Korea 1950/1: Recollections of a Subaltern with the 8th KRI Hussars', in *Vanguard: The Journal of the Inns of Court and City Yeomanry*, November 2006.

Perret, Bryan, *Last Stand: Famous Battles Against the Odds* (London, 1991).

Perrins, Anthony, *A Pretty Rough Do Altogether: The Fifth Fusiliers in Korea, 1950–1951* (Alnwick, 2004).

Potts, Gordon, 'The Battle of the Imjin', unpublished private document. (In possession of Lieutenant-Colonel (ret.) Peter Thomas, Royal Marines.)

'POWs in Korea' (DEFE 13 220). (In National Archives, Kew, Surrey.)

Queen's Royal Hussars Historical Society, *8th King's Royal Irish Hussars in the Korean War, 1950–51*, transcript of seminar held in London, 11 June 2006. (In possession of Brigadier (ret.) Dick Webster, 8th Hussars.)

'Reports of US Formations in Connection with the Battle of the Imjin 22–25 April 1951 (29th Independent Inf, Bde Group)'. (In National Archives, Kew, Surrey.)

Ridgway, Matthew B., *The Korean War* (New York, 1967).

Salisbury, Harrison E., *The Long March: The Untold Story* (New York, 1985).

Salmon, Andrew, *American Business and the Korean Miracle: US Enterprises in Korea, 1866–The Present* (Seoul, 2003).

—— 'Slaughter at Happy Valley', *Belfast Telegraph*, 4 January 2009.

'Signals Log of Battle' (WO 305-21). (In National Archives, Kew, Surrey.)

'Situation in Korea from 3 4 1951 to 18 4 1951' (DEFE 11 210). (In the National Archives, Kew, Surrey.)

Speer, M.C., letter from second in command, 1st Battalion, Royal Northumberland Fusiliers on the death of Colonel Kingsley Foster to his father Lieutenant-Colonel O.B. Foster, part-reprinted in Kingsley Foster's obituary, *St George's Gazette: The Regimental Journal of the Royal Northumberland Fusiliers*, 31 May 1951

*St George's Gazette: The Regimental Journal of the Royal Northumberland Fusiliers*. (Royala Northumberland Fusiliers Museum, Alnwick Castle.)

Stuek, William Whitney, *The Korean War* (Princeton, NJ, 1997).

Thompson, Joe, *Korea: The Divided Peninsula* (Newcastle, 1997).

Thompson, Robert (ed.), *War in Peace: An Analysis of Warfare Since 1945* (London, 1981).

Tucker, Spencer C. (ed.), *Encyclopedia of the Korean War: A Political, Social and Military History* (New York, 2002).

Turnbull, Stephen, *Samurai Invasion: Japan's Korean War 1592–1598* (London, 2002).

'US Forces Korea/8th Army Staff Ride Read Ahead Package, Battle of the Imjin River, 15 June, 1992'. (In Historians' Office, Yongsan Base, US 8th Army, Korea.)

US State Department documents related to ROK troop executions and 29th Brigade reaction (uncategorised/unnumbered). (In Truth and Reconciliation Commission, Seoul.)

Walker, Adrian, *A Barren Place: National Servicemen in Korea, 1950–1953* (London, 1994).

Warner, Denis, 'Gloucesters Win Highest US Military Honour', *Daily Telegraph*, 9 May 1951.

Whatmore, Denys, *One Road to Imjin: A National Service Experience* (Cheltenham, 1993).

Winn, Roland, *The Crossbelts: Journal of the 8th King's Royal Irish Hussars*, Korean Campaign Supplement, 1950/51. (In 8th King's Royal Irish Hussars Archive, Eastbourne.)

'X Company' in *St George's Gazette: The Regimental Journal of the Fifth Fusiliers*, 31 May 1951.

Young, Maris, 'Korean Episode' (unpublished manuscript). (In Soldiers of Gloucestershire Museum Archive, Gloucester.)

Younger, Tony, *Blowing Our Bridges: A Memoir from Dunkirk to Korea via Normandy* (Barnsley, 2004).

Zhang Shu-guang, *Mao's Military Romanticism: China and the Korean War, 1950–1953* (Lawrence, KS, 1995).

## AUDIO RECORDINGS

Carter, Francis Edward. IWM recording 18262.

Charlton, Douglas Johnson. IWM recording 15256.

Lane, John. Taped interview. (In possession of Brigadier (ret.) Mervyn McCord, RUR.)

Man, Andrew. IWM recording 9537.

Murphy, Byron James. IWM recording 15338.

Ormrod, Peter Charles. IWM recording 9387.

Papworth, Cyril James. IWM recording 16618.

Patchett, Douglas Robert. IWM recording 16759.

Pilbeam, G.E. IWM recording 17275.

Rees, Roy. IWM recording 19854.

Rickord, Gerald. Taped interview. (In possession of Brigadier (ret.) Mervyn McCord, RUR.)

Scott, Andrew Montagu Hamilton. IWM recording 16855.

Sharp, David Maurice. IWM recording 17929.

Utting, Roy Frederick. IWM recoding, 17568.

Whatmore, Denys. IWM recording 12663.

Whybro, Denis. IWM recording 20008.

## AUDIO-VISUAL MATERIALS

*The 8th King's Irish Hussars in the Korean War* (DVD publication pending).

*Korea: The Forgotten War* (Belgian Army DVD).

## WEBSITES

www.armchairgeneral.com

http://belgian-volunteercorps-korea.be/

www.globalsecurity.org

www.glosters.org.uk

http://www.medals.be/

www.nationmaster.com

www.qrh.org.uk

http://www.geocities.com/peftok/10thbct3/html?20082

http://rokdrop.com/

http://royalirishrangers.co.uk/rifles.html

www.sogm.org.uk

http://www.turtlebunbury.com/history/history_family/hist_family_blake.html

www.wikipedia.com

# NOTES

For full details of source works, see the List of Sources on page 344.

## PROLOGUE

1. All details of the patrol's activities and actions in this chapter, unless otherwise cited, come from an author interview with Guy Temple.
2. Peter Whitamore, Royal Ulster Rifles (author interview).
3. John Denley, Gloster Regimental Secretary (author interview). As an army cadet, he learned this technique from a Korean War Gloster veteran. Firearms enthusiasts have filmed the technique and posted the result on the video-sharing site YouTube.
4. Sam Mercer (author interview).
5. Brigadier Colin Parr, British Military Attaché to Seoul, on a battlefield tour, 1998.

## CHAPTER 1

1. Good general sources on Korean history include the academic work by Eckert *et al.*, and Bruce Cumings's lively modern history.
2. See Salmon, pp. 14–16. I am grateful to the American historian Thomas Duvernay for much of the information on the fate of the *Sherman*.
3. Details of weaponry and troop numbers from Kim Young-ho, 'Korea, Democratic People's Republic of, Invasion of the Republic of Korea', in Tucker, pp. 341–2.
4. On Kim's co-ordination with Stalin and Mao, see Kim, *op. cit.*

5. Kim Jinwung, Lee Rees, Spencer C. Tucker, 'Timeline for Korean History', in Tucker, pp. 775–6.
6. Lankov, p. 131.
7. Hastings (1987), pp. 59–61.
8. For biographical information on MacArthur, see Duane L. Wesolick, 'MacArthur, Douglas', in Tucker, pp. 399–403.
9. Hickey, pp. 41–2.
10. Eric W. Osborne, 'United Kingdom', in Tucker, p. 671.
11. Hickey, pp. 62–3.
12. Spencer C. Tucker, 'Task Force Smith' and 'The Battle of Osan', in Tucker, pp. 639, 500–1.
13. Farrar-Hockley (1990), pp. 103–4.
14. *Ibid.*, p. 113.
15. *Ibid.*, p. 119.
16. *Ibid.*, p. 126.
17. For troop strengths in the first week of August, see Farrar-Hockley (1990), pp. 137–8.
18. *Ibid.*, p. 135.
19. On potential problems of an Inchon operation, see Spencer C. Tucker, 'Inchon Landings: Operation CHROMITE', in Tucker, pp. 273–8.
20. MacArthur's speech, and naval reply, quoted in Hastings (1987), pp. 101–2.
21. Timings of events surrounding Inchon landing from Tucker, 'Inchon Landings: Operation CHROMITE', in Tucker, pp. 273–8.

## CHAPTER 2

1. Grist, p. 7.
2. Farrar-Hockley (1990), p. 117.

3. *Ibid.*, pp. 115–19.
4. Hickey, p. 95.
5. Mervyn McCord (author interview).
6. Farrar-Hockley (1990), p. 117.
7. *Ibid.*, Appendix N. See also Hickey, pp. 153–4.
8. Farrar-Hockley (1990), footnote, p. 128.
9. I am grateful to David Read of the Soldiers of Gloucestershire Museum for a précis of the Glosters' history.
10. George Truell (author interview).
11. Guy Temple (author interview).
12. George Truell (author interview).
13. Mervyn McCord (author interview).
14. 29th Brigade officer (author interview).
15. George Truell (author interview).
16. Guy Temple (author interview).
17. Green, pp. 1–3.
18. *Ibid.*, p. 11.
19. Guy Temple (author interview).
20. Sam Mercer (author interview).
21. For the Fusiliers' regimental history I have borrowed from Perrins, pp. 15–18.
22. Obituary, Lieutenant-Colonel K.O.N. Foster, *St George's Gazette*, 31 May 1951, p. 90.
23. Malcolm Cubiss (author interview).
24. Joe Thompson (author interview).
25. Sam Phillips (author interview).
26. http://royalirishrangers.co.uk/rifles.html.
27. See the Blake family history website: http://www.turtlebunbury.com/history/history_family/hist_family_blake.html.
28. Peter Whitamore (author interview).
29. O'Kane, p. 5.
30. William Holliday (author interview).
31. O'Kane, p. 10.
32. www.qrh.org.uk/history5a.htm.
33. Bernard Dowling, email to author.
34. Communication to author, Brigadier Richard Webster, 8th Hussars.
35. David Boyall (author interview).
36. Queen's Royal Hussars Historical Society, seminar transcript.
37. Whybro, IWM recording.
38. Dunstan (2003), pp. 5–14.
39. John Preston-Bell (author interview).
40. Dunstan (2003), p. 12.
41. David Boyall (author interview).
42. Dunstan (2003), p. 13.
43. Anthony Perrins (author interview).
44. Whybro, IWM recording.
45. Malcolm Cubiss (author interview).
46. George Truell (author interview).
47. I am indebted to Bob Nicholls, formerly of 170 Mortar Battery, for his insights into the mortars' role.
48. Harvey, pp. 17–18.
49. Farrar-Hockley (1990), p. 119.
50. Green, p. 13.
51. Malcolm Cubiss (author interview).
52. Farrar-Hockley (1990), pp. 320–1.
53. Robin Charley (author interview).
54. Hickey, p. 97.
55. O'Kane, p. 12.
56. Hickey, p. 98.
57. Green, p. 25.
58. Sam Mercer (author interview).
59. Harvey, pp. 21–2.
60. Perrins, p. 13.
61. Green, p. 26.

62. Harvey, p. 23.
63. Ibid., p. 23.
64. Farrar-Hockley (1990), p. 319.
65. Patchett, IWM recording.
66. Bob Nicholls (author interview).
67. Hamill, p. 11.
68. Younger, pp. 137–9.
69. Joe Thompson (author interview).
70. Perrins, p. 18.
71. Vick Wear (author interview).
72. O'Kane, p. 21.
73. Whybro, IWM recording.
74. Mervyn McCord (author interview).
75. O'Kane, pp. 21–2.
76. Perrins, p. 21.
77. O'Kane, pp. 21–2.
78. Ibid., p. 21.

## CHAPTER 3
1. Paik Sun-yup, p. 85.
2. Hastings, p. 130.
3. Zhang , p. 31.
4. Ibid., p. 44.
5. Ibid., p. 45.
6. Ibid., pp. 44–5.
7. Ibid., p. 56.
8. Ibid., p. 47.
9. Ibid., p. 62.
10. Ibid., pp. 74–5.
11. Ibid., p. 74.
12. Ibid., p. 75.
13. Ibid., pp. 77–8.
14. Ibid., p. 78.
15. Ibid., p. 81.
16. Susan M. Puska, 'Peng Dehuai', in Tucker, pp. 516–17.
17. Salisbury, pp. 191–2.
18. Peng Dehuai, 'My Story of the Korean War', in Li Xiaobing et al., p. 31.
19. Arnold R. Isaacs, 'China Enters the Korean War', in Tucker, p. 120.
20. Paik Sun-yup (author interview).
21. Daniel R. Beirne, 'Chinese Military Offensives and Chinese First Offensive', in Tucker, p. 130.
22. Zhang, p. 79.
23. Tony Perrins (author interview).
24. Hastings, p. 138.
25. Tony Perrins (author interview).
26. David Halberstam, p. 41.
27. For a good overview of China's surprise attack, see Beirne, in Tucker, pp. 130–2.
28. For vivid details of Paik's personal experiences in the midst of the Chinese First Offensive, see Paik, pp. 85–103.
29. Hastings, p. 130.
30. Beirne, in Tucker, p. 132.
31. Kim Jin-wung, Rees Lee and Spencer C. Tucker, 'Timeline for Korean History', in Tucker, p. 778.
32. Salmon, p. 86.
33. Ormrod, IWM recording.
34. Rees, IWM recording.
35. Pilbeam, IWM recording.
36. Fusilier Lieutenant Michael Kearney in a letter to his wife, in Perrins, p. 22.
37. Green, p. 33.
38. Whybro, IWM recording.
39. For on-ground details of the Glosters' sharp little action, see Green, pp. 43–4.
40. Farrar-Hockley (1990), p. 343.
41. Ibid., p. 344.
42. For timings, see the regimental history of the battle, reproduced in Perrins, p. 27.
43. Vick Wear (author interview).
44. Joe Thompson (author interview).
45. Letter from Major Charles Mitchell, officer commanding the Fusiliers W Company, to his mother, in Perrins, p. 35.

46. From Cubiss's Military Cross commendation, in Perrins, pp. 366–7.
47. Perrins, p. 28.
48. *Ibid.*, p. 28.
49. Malcolm Cubiss (author interview).
50. Joe Dunn, 'Home-by-Christmas Offensive', in Tucker, p. 260.
51. Daniel R. Beirne, 'Chongchon River, Battle of', in Tucker, pp. 146–7.
52. Hastings, pp. 142–4.
53. Hickey, p. 125.
54. Beirne, 'Chongchon River', in Tucker, pp. 146–7.
55. Author interview with USAF pilots Edwin 'Buzz' Aldrin, Wilbur 'Pete' Carpenter, Charles Cleveland, Harold Fischer, Ralph 'Hoot' Gibson, Robert Moxley and Carl Schneider.
56. Hickey, pp. 124–8.
57. Peng, quoted in Li *et al.*, p. 34.
58. Farrar-Hockley (1990), p. 342.
59. Green, p. 47.
60. Carter, Imperial War Museum recording.
61. *Ibid.*
62. John Preston-Bell (author interview).
63. Paik, p. 110.
64. *Ibid.*, p. 110.
65. *Ibid.*, p. 110.
66. Harvey, p. 44.
67. Farrar-Hockley (1990), p. 342.
68. O'Kane, p. 32.
69. Guy Temple (author interview).
70. Winn, p. 3.
71. Major Shipster of the Middlesex Regiment, quoted in Farrar-Hockley (1990), p. 343.
72. O'Kane, p. 32.
73. O'Kane, p. 32.
74. Farrar-Hockley (1990), p. 344.
75. Carter, IWM recording.
76. Priscilla Roberts and Jinwung Kim, 'Pyongyang', in Tucker, p. 547.
77. Winn, p. 25.
78. Harvey, pp. 48–50.
79. Harvey, p. 44.
80. John Preston-Bell (author interview).
81. Hickey, p. 145.
82. Quoted in US State Department telegram, 14 December 1950, sent to US Embassy, Seoul, and to Supreme Commander, Tokyo. Supplied to me by Dr Steven Kim of South Korea's Truth and Reconciliation Commission.
83. Malcolm Cubiss (author interview).
84. Ormrod, IWM recording.
85. Perrins, p. 62.
86. Utting, IWM recording.
87. Boyall, p. 70.
88. Letter from Colonel Kingsley Foster to his wife, in Perrins, p. 67.
89. Harvey, p. 45.
90. O'Kane, p. 27.
91. Paul, in *Vanguard*, p. 15.
92. David Strachan (author interview).
93. John Preston-Bell (author interview).
94. Ormrod, IWM recording.
95. *Ibid.*
96. Paul, p. 15.
97. Younger, pp. 178–9.
98. Grist, p. 23.
99. Harvey, p. 58.
100. George Truell (author interview).
101. Boyall, p. 71.
102. Vick Wear (author interview).
103. Joe Thompson (author interview).
104. Harvey, p. 52.
105. Grist, p. 32.

106. Robin Charley (author interview).
107. John Preston-Bell (author interview).
108. Hickey, p. 146.
109. David Boyall (author interview).
110. Pilbeam, IWM recording.
111. *Ibid*.
112. John Bayliss (author interview).
113. Boyall, p. 71.
114. Bernard Dawling, email to author.
115. Sam Phillips (author interview).
116. Ormrod, IWM recording.
117. Stan Tomenson (author interview).
118. Mervyn McCord (author interview).
119. Harvey, p. 51.
120. Carter, IWM recording.
121. Kingsley Foster, letter to his wife, in Perrins, p. 68.
122. Farrar-Hockley (1990), p. 383.
123. Joe P. Dunn, 'Ridgway, Matthew Bunker', in Tucker, pp. 565–6.
124. Ridgway, p. 87.
125. Hastings (1987), pp. 189–90.
126. Scott, IWM recording.
127. Tony Eagles (author interview).

## CHAPTER 4

1. Grist, p. 26.
2. Farrar-Hockley (1990), p. 384.
3. Paik, pp. 115–19.
4. Mossman, p. 191.
5. Farrar-Hockley (1990), pp. 385–6.
6. Mossman, p. 194.
7. Farrar-Hockley (1990), p. 386, note.
8. A copy of this order is preserved in the archive of the Soldiers of Gloucestershire Museum.
9. Hamill, p. 24.
10. Farrar-Hockley (1990), p. 387.
11. Robin Charley (author interview).
12. Joe Farrell (author interview).
13. Mervyn McCord (author interview).
14. Mervyn McCord and Joe Farrell (author interviews).
15. Robin Charley (author interview).
16. O'Kane, p. 41.
17. Hamill, p. 28.
18. Mervyn McCord (author interview).
19. Robin Charley (author interview).
20. John Mole (author interview).
21. Robin Charley (author interview).
22. Hamill, p. 28.
23. O'Kane, p. 42.
24. William Beattie (author interview).
25. For details of the Fusiliers' dispositions, see the regiment's official report 'The Battle of Kandong' in Perrins, pp. 48–55. Traditionally, after-action reports are anonymous, but this is believed to have been written by Lieutenant-Colonel Foster.
26. Aynsley, 27 November 1959.
27. Perrins, pp. 48–55.
28. *Ibid*., p. 54.
29. John Bayliss (author interview).
30. William Beattie (author interview).
31. Letter from John Winn to his mother, in Perrins, p. 62.
32. Perrins, p. 64.
33. Tony Perrins (author interview).
34. Perrins, p. 65.
35. Joe Thompson (author interview). See also his book, p. 21.
36. Letter from Charles Mitchell to his mother, in Perrins, p. 63.

37. Joe Thompson (author interview).
38. Unless otherwise noted, all information about the bayonet charge is from Joe Thompson (author interview).
39. William Beattie (author interview).
40. Scott, IWM recording.
41. Farrar-Hockley (1990), p. 390.
42. Perrins, p. 55.
43. Aynsley, 27 November 1959.
44. Appleman, p. 58.
45. Joe Thompson (author interview).
46. Royal Northumberland Fusiliers War Diary, in Perrins, p. 242.
47. Farrar-Hockley (1990), p. 390.
48. Hamill, p. 28.
49. Appleman, p. 66.
50. Farrar-Hockley (1990), p. 390.
51. Mervyn McCord (author interview).
52. Fitzroy, p. 262.
53. Hamill, p. 30.
54. Mervyn McCord (author interview).
55. Joe Farrell (author interview).
56. Tommy Sturgeon (author interview).
57. O'Kane, pp. 43–4.
58. Fitzroy, pp. 262–3.
59. *Ibid.*, pp. 263–6.
60. Appleman, p. 73.
61. Mervyn McCord (author interview).
62. Mervyn McCord (author interview).
63. Younger, pp. 166–7.
64. Fitzroy, pp. 265–6.
65. Farrar-Hockley (1990), p. 391.
66. Fitzroy, p. 263.
67. Mervyn McCord (author interview).
68. Appleman, pp. 72–5.
69. John Preston-Bell (author interview).
70. Tucker, 'Scorched Earth', in Tucker, pp. 582–3.
71. Lee Chun-hee (author interview).
72. Letter from Preston Little to Dennis Prout, in Perrins, p. 215.
73. A copy of this document was given to me by Dr Stephen Kim of Seoul's Truth and Reconciliation Commission.
74. Younger, pp. 181–3.
75. Green, p. 72.
76. Bob Nicholls (author interview).
77. Carter, IWM recording.
78. Little, in Perrins, p. 216.
79. Grist, p. 28.
80. *Ibid.*, p. 30.
81. Bob Nicholls (author interview).
82. Rees, IWM recording; Perrins, p. 384.
83. Perrins, p. 71.
84. Hickey, p. 147.
85. Duane L. Wesolick, 'Atrocities', in Tucker, pp. 56–8.
86. Report by WO2 M. Brown, in Perrins, p. 39.
87. Rees, IWM recording.
88. See British United Press report, in Perrins, p. 42.
89. Harvey, p. 62.
90. *Ibid.*, p. 62.
91. Charles Mitchell, letter to his mother, in Perrins, p. 76.
92. Ted Paul (author interview).
93. David Boyall (author interview).
94. Captain Robin Charley (author interview).
95. Winn, p. 6.
96. Boyall, pp. 69–70.
97. David Boyall, Ted Paul, John Preston-Bell (author interviews).
98. Winn, Korean Campaign Supplement to *The Crossbelts*, p. 8.
99. Guy Temple and Sam Phillips (author interviews).

100. Joe Farrell (author interview).
101. Norman Sweetlove (author interview).
102. Bob Nicholls (author interview).
103. Joe Thompson (author interview).
104. Little, in Perrins, pp. 216–17.
105. *Ibid.*, p. 218.
106. Farrar-Hockley (1995), pp. 46–7.
107. *Ibid.*, p. 47.
108. *Ibid.*, p. 36.
109. Hickey, p. 171.
110. Quoted in *The Back Badge*, June 1951, p. 153.
111. Joe Farrell, Mervyn McCord, Norman Sweetlove (author interviews).
112. *The Back Badge*, June 1951, p. 144.
113. See Harvey, p. 67, and Farrar-Hockley (1995), p. 49.
114. Harvey, pp. 67–9.
115. Green, pp. 75–6.
116. Farrar-Hockley (1995), p. 50.
117. *Ibid.*, p. 50.
118. Green, p. 81.
119. Carter, IWM recording.
120. Green, pp. 83–4.
121. Carter, IWM recording.
122. Harvey, p. 71.
123. Ormrod, IWM recording.
124. Winn, Korean Campaign Supplement to *The Crossbelts*, p. 7.
125. Whybro IWM recording.
126. Green, pp. 83–4.
127. Farrar-Hockley (1995), p. 51.
128. Green, pp. 84–5.
129. Carter, IWM recording.
130. Green, pp. 84–5.
131. Farrar-Hockley (1995), p. 51.
132. Whybro, IWM recording.
133. Farrar-Hockley (1995), p. 51.
134. Green, p. 85.
135. Joe Farrell (author interview).
136. Author's discussion with US 8th Army Command Historian, Dr Lewis Bernstein.
137. Hamill, p. 34.
138. Farrar-Hockley (1995), pp. 51–3.
139. *Ibid.*, p. 74.
140. Paik, p. 145.
141. Farrar-Hockley (1995), p. 35.
142. Sherman D. Pratt, 'Chipyong-ni, Battle of', in Tucker, p. 142.
143. Farrar-Hockley (1995), pp. 75–6.
144. Hoare, pp. 70–72.
145. Ormrod, IWM recording.

## CHAPTER 5

1. Hawley, p. 308.
2. *Ibid.*, p. 319.
3. Turnbull, pp. 144–8.
4. For their comments on the critical strategic importance of the Imjin River, I am indebted to General Paik Sun-yup and Dr Nam Jeong-ok, Senior Researcher, Institute for Military History Compilation, both at the War Memorial of Korea; and also to Lieutenant-Colonel (ret.) Ronney Miller, US 8th Army Historian, at Seoul's Yongsan Garrison.
5. Kim Young-ho, 'Korea, Democratic People's Republic of, Invasion of the Republic of South Korea', in Tucker, pp. 341–2.
6. Hastings (1987), p. 208.
7. Farrar-Hockley (1995), p. 89.
8. Headquarters 3rd Infantry Division, 'Operations of 29th BIB, from 22–25 April 1951'.
9. Calculation of the brigade's frontage was made using maps reproduced in Farrar-Hockley (1995).
10. Scott, IWM recording.

11. Hamill, p. 58.
12. Whatmore, IWM recording.
13. Young, p. 2.
14. *The Back Badge*, June 1951, p. 146.
15. Joe Thompson (author interview).
16. Whatmore, pp. 57–8.
17. Hickey, p. 208.
18. Hamill, p. 61.
19. Sam Mercer (author interview).
20. Carter, IWM recording.
21. Green, p. 97.
22. Younger, pp. 184–5.
23. Kavanagh, pp. 73–5.
24. Carter, IWM recording.
25. Armand Philips (author interview).
26. Henri Wolfs, letter to author and Lucien Senterre, interview. I am grateful to Jan Dillen for the introduction.
27. Armand Philips (author interview).
28. Henri Wolfs, letter to author.
29. George Truell (author interview).
30. André VanDamme (author/Jan Dillen written interview).
31. Armand Philips (author interview).
32. Armand Philips (author interview).
33. Robin Charley (author interview).
34. Henri Wolfs, letter to author.
35. Armand Philips (author interview).
36. George Truell (author interview).
37. Henri Wolfs, letter to author.
38. John Mole (author interview).
39. Farrar-Hockley (1995), p. 111.
40. Henri Wolfs, letter to author.
41. Armand Philips (author interview).
42. Papworth, IWM recording.
43. Whatmore, IWM recording.
44. Kavanagh, p. 92.
45. Winn, Korean Campaign Supplement to *The Crossbelts*, p. 11.
46. Quoted in Hickey, p. 208.
47. Farrar-Hockley (1995), p. 92.
48. Carter, IWM recording.
49. Ormrod, IWM recording.
50. Carter, IWM recording.
51. Farrar-Hockley (1995), p. 109.
52. *Ibid.*, p. 114.
53. Carter, IWM recording.
54. Farrar-Hockley (1995), p. 111.
55. Tony Eagles (author interview). He also wrote to the editor of *The Back Badge* describing the incident. See List of Sources.
56. Elizabeth C. Schafer, 'Operation DAUNTLESS', and Clayton D. Laurie, 'Kansas–Wyoming Line', both in Tucker, pp. 180–1 and 305–6 respectively.
57. Mossman, p. 374.
58. *Ibid.*, p. 380.
59. Korea Institute of Military History, p. 607.
60. *Ibid.*, p. 380.
61. Mossman, p. 380.
62. Farrar-Hockley (1995), pp. 106–9.
63. Zhang, p. 145.
64. *Ibid.*, p. 149.
65. 'CCF and NKPA Spring Offensive (22 April–1 May 1951)' , post-battle intelligence summary in Tab D, 'US Forces Korea/8th Army Staff Ride Read Ahead Package'.
66. Korea Institute of Military History, p. 607.
67. Tony Perrins (author interview).
68. Farrar-Hockley (1995), p. 113.
69. Davies, p. 16.
70. David Strachan (author interview).
71. Hamill, p. 61.

72. Davies, pp. 16–17.
73. Appleman, p. 458.
74. Farrar-Hockley (1995), pp. 113–14.
75. Farrar-Hockley (1954), p. 17.
76. Whatmore, IWM recording.
77. Murphy, IWM recording.
78. Younger, pp. 192–3.
79. Farrar-Hockley (1995), pp. 114–15.
80. Cutforth, p. 184.

## CHAPTER 6

1. 29th Infantry Brigade War Diary.
2. André VanDamme (author/Jan Dillen written interview).
3. Le Roy.
4. Young, p. 4.
5. 29th Infantry Brigade War Diary.
6. Le Roy, and Korea Ministry of National Defense, p. 110.
7. Walker, p. 29; interview with Albert Tyas.
8. Mervyn McCord (author interview). See also Potts.
9. Hamill, p. 64.
10. Younger, pp. 186–7.
11. A vivid account of the Battle Patrol's destruction, from which much of the above account is sourced, is in Kavanagh, pp. 79–91.
12. Kavanagh, pp. 78–8.
13. Younger, p. 187.
14. Kavanagh, pp. 88–91.
15. Hamill, p. 64.
16. Younger, p. 187.
17. Kinne, pp. 16–17.
18. Derek Kinne (author interview). The text here merges Kinne's published account and his recollections in two author interviews.
19. War Diary of 1st Battalion, Royal Northumberland Fusiliers, in Perrins, p. 272.
20. Kinne, pp. 18–19.
21. War Diary of 1st Battalion, Royal Northumberland Fusiliers, in Perrins, p. 272.
22. Carter, IWM recording.
23. War Diary of 1st Battalion, Royal Northumberland Fusiliers, in Perrins, p. 272.
24. 'X Company' report in St George's Gazette, p. 105.
25. War Diary of 1st Battalion, Royal Northumberland Fusiliers, in Perrins, p. 272.
26. Rees, IWM recording.
27. Ibid.
28. Whatmore has left the most vivid accounts available of what it was like to be a platoon commander on the Imjin, in his book, pp. 68–75, and his IWM recording. I have merged both accounts here.
29. Harvey, p. 101.
30. Harvey, p. 102.
31. Harvey, pp. 102–3.
32. George Newhouse (author interview).
33. I have relied heavily on an interview with Sam Mercer for the details of Curtis's charge, but supplemented with the literature where necessary, in this case, Harding, Imjin Roll, pp. 10–12.
34. Ibid., p. 12.
35. Farrar-Hockley (1954), p. 28.
36. Ibid., p. 29.
37. Farrar-Hockley (1990), p. 117.
38. Farrar-Hockley (1954), p. 30.
39. Ibid., pp. 29–30.
40. Fehrenbach, p 451.
41. George Newhouse (author interview); see also Papworth, IWM recording.
42. George Newhouse (author interview).
43. Harding, Imjin Roll, p. 12.
44. Farrar-Hockley (1995) p. 121.

45. Papworth, IWM recording.
46. Ibid.
47. Harding, Imjin Roll, p. 12.
48. Whatmore, pp. 73–4.
49. Ibid., pp. 74–5.

CHAPTER 7

1. Appleman, pp. 458–63.
2. Newcombe, pp. 174–5.
3. Sharp, IWM recording.
4. Potts, 'Battle of the Imjin'.
5. Hamill, p. 65.
6. Ibid., pp. 65–6.
7. Ormrod, IWM recording.
8. Winn, Korean Campaign Supplement to The Crossbelts, p. 12.
9. John Winn, letter to his mother, quoted in Perrins, p. 124.
10. St George's Gazette, 31 May 1951, p. 107.
11. Cited in Young, p. 5. Young quotes the full report but does not identify the reporter or the media.
12. Younger, p. 199.
13. George Truell (author interview).
14. For timings, see War Diary of 1st Battalion, Royal Northumberland Fusiliers, in Perrins, p. 273.
15. Rees, IWM recording.
16. Cooper's account is from Hastings (1987), p. 216.
17. Quoted in Grossman, p. 125.
18. Harding, 'Battle Report', p. 4.
19. Large's autobiography has a superb account of B Company's battle. See Large, pp. 11–22.
20. Ibid., pp. 26–7.
21. Ibid., pp. 26–8.
22. Ibid., pp 28–31.
23. Harding mentions this in his interview with Hugh Driver.
24. Harding, 'Battle Report', p. 6.
25. Newcombe, p. 178.
26. Large, pp. 32–3.
27. Farrar-Hockley (1995), p. 125.

28. Large, pp. 33–4.
29. Ormrod, IWM recording.
30. Farrar-Hockley (1954), pp. 32–4.
31. Ibid., p. 34.
32. George Newhouse (author interview).
33. Grist, p. 42.
34. Charles Sharpling (author interview).
35. Grist, p. 35.
36. Ibid., pp. 42–3.
37. Harvey, p. 122.
38. Mossman, p. 388.
39. Farrar-Hockley (1995), pp. 118–19.
40. Ormrod, IWM recording.
41. Korea Ministry of National Defense, p. 111.
42. André VanDamme (author/Jan Dillen written interview).
43. Jan Dillen interview, email to author.
44. Mossman, p. 396.
45. Farrar-Hockley (1995), p. 125.
46. Albert Perkins (author interview). See also Large, p. 35.
47. Mossman, p. 412.
48. Carter, IWM recording.
49. Large, pp. 35–44.
50. Newcombe, pp. 184–5.
51. Large, pp. 35–44.
52. Carter, IWM recording.
53. Harding, 'Battle Report', pp. 8–9.
54. Large, p. 22.
55. Newcombe, pp. 189–90.
56. Carter, IWM recording.
57. Large, pp. 45–8.
58. Newcombe, pp. 192–5.
59. Farrar-Hockley (1954), pp. 45–6.
60. Ibid., pp. 45–6.
61. Ibid., pp. 45–6.

CHAPTER 8

1. Major Gerald Rickord (taped interview in possession of Mervyn McCord).

2. Hamill, pp. 66–7; also Captain John Lane, second in command, A Company (taped interview in possession of Mervyn McCord).

3. See War Diary of 1st Battalion, Royal Northumberland Fusiliers, in Perrins, p. 274.

4. Grist, p. 44.

5. Farrar-Hockley (1995), p. 126.

6. Grist, p. 44.

7. Farrar-Hockley (1995), pp. 126–7; see also Mossman, p. 413.

8. Farrar-Hockley (1995), pp. 126–7.

9. Fitzroy, p. 278.

10. The account of Huth's crawl under the bellies of the tanks comes from the letter by Trooper Len Huish, who was in Huth's tank, to the archivist of the 8th King's Royal Irish Hussars..

11. Hays, 'RNFs Saved By Hussars Tanks'.

12. *Ibid.*, pp. 475–6.

13. The Philippines in the Korean War: http://www.geocities.com/peftok/10thbct3/html?20082.

14. Whybro, IWM recording.

15. George Truell (author interview).

16. '29th Infantry Brigade War Diary'.

17. Mossman, p. 414.

18. Potts, p. 10.

19. Hastings, p. 220.

20. '29th Infantry Brigade War Diary', signal from UK liaison officer at I Corps HQ, 21:10, 24 April.

21. Whybro, IWM recoding.

22. I am grateful to Brigadier Dick Webster for his description of the atmosphere inside a Centurion on operations.

23. Ormrod, IWM recording.

24. Potts, p. 12.

25. *Ibid.*, p. 13.

26. *Ibid.*

27. Hamill, p. 69.

28. Bill Beattie (author interview).

29. See the official regimental account of the action in Perrins, p. 119, and the Fusiliers' War Diary, also in Perrins, p. 275.

30. Carew, pp. 196–7.

31. See Crooks's medal citation, in Perrins, p. 366.

32. See Winn's DSO citation, in Perrins, pp. 376–7.

33. Fusiliers' War Diary, in Perrins, p. 275.

34. See Winn's DSO citation, in Perrins, pp. 376–7.

35. See Miles Speer's letter to John Winn, 8 May 1951, in Perrins, p. 138.

36. David Strachan (author interview); see also Crooks' citation in Perrins, p. 366.

37. Fusiliers' War Diary, in Perrins, p. 275.

38. 'David Rudge, Obituary', *St George's Gazette*, 31 May 1951, p. 91.

39. According to the regimental history, in Perrins, p. 119.

40. See the regimental history, in Perrins, p. 119; also Kinne, pp. 24–5.

41. Carew, p. 204.

42. Kinne, p. 24.

43. 'Command Report, I US Army Corps, 1 April 1951–30 April 1951', p. 130.

44. Mossman, p. 419.

45. 'Command Report, I US Army Corps, 1 April 1951–30 April 1951', p. 135.

## CHAPTER 9

1. Tom Clough (author interview).

2. Davies, pp. 18–19.

3. Farrar-Hockley (1954), pp. 49–50.

4. Headquarters, 3rd Infantry Division, 'Operations of 29th BIB, from 22–25 April 1951', Annex 14 (submitted to Headquarters, I Corps, 'in accordance with instructions'). ['BIB' = 'British Independent Brigade'.] The annex was written by Brigadier Meade, Soule's assistant divisional commander.
5. Farrar-Hockley (1995), p. 127.
6. Mossman, p. 414.
7. 29th Brigade War Diary.
8. Headquarters, 3rd Infantry Division, 'Operations of 29th BIB, from 22–25 April 1951', Annex 11. The annex was written by Colonel Newman, Soule's chief of staff.
9. *Ibid.*, p. 127.
10. Whatmore, p. 77.
11. 29th Brigade War Diary.
12. For details of the supply drop, see Grist, pp. 44–5, and *The Back Badge*, vol. 3, no. 10, p. 157.
13. Davies, p. 21.
14. *Ibid.*, p. 21.
15. *Ibid.*, p. 22.
16. Farrar-Hockley (1995) p. 129.
17. Harding, *Imjin Roll*, p. 16.
18. Young, p. 7.
19. Farrar-Hockley (1954), p. 51.
20. Davies, p. 25.
21. Farrar-Hockley (1954), pp. 52–5.
22. Tony Eagles (author interview).
23. Mike Harvey (author interview).
24. Davies, p. 23.
25. On this, see Newcombe, p. 182, and Littlewood's 'MMG platoon after-action report', written on the *Empire Orwell* on the trip back to the UK.
26. Whatmore, p. 78.
27. Farrar-Hockley (1954), p. 56.
28. The defiant cry is quoted in Davies, p. 24.
29. Farrar-Hockley (1954), p. 56.
30. *Ibid.*, p. 56.
31. The details of A Company's counter-attack come from *ibid.*, pp. 56–8.
32. Harvey, p. 126.
33. Farrar-Hockley (1954), pp. 57–60.
34. Green, p. 102.
35. Farrar-Hockley (1954), pp. 61–2.
36. Whatmore, p. 79.
37. Birt (interview with Hugh Driver).
38. Mossman, pp. 417–18.
39. 'Command Report, 3rd Infantry Division, April 1951', p. 20.
40. 'Command Report, I US Army Corps, 1 April 1951–30 April 1951', p. 131.
41. George Truell (author interview).
42. Grist, p. 46.
43. Farrar-Hockley (1954), p. 64.
44. Speaking at the fiftieth anniversary of the battle, on a tour of the Glosters' A Company position. I was present.
45. Farrar-Hockley (1954), pp. 64–5.
46. *Ibid.*, p. 66.
47. Davies, pp. 25–6.
48. Farrar-Hockley (1954), p. 73.
49. Green, pp. 104–5.
50. Mossman, p. 429.
51. Farrar-Hockley (1954), p. 67.
52. Harvey, p. 128.
53. Whatmore, IWM recording.
54. Harvey, pp. 129–30.
55. *Ibid.*, pp. 130–1.
56. *Ibid.*, p. 131.
57. Whatmore, IWM recording.
58. Harvey, p. 132.
59. *Ibid.*, p. 132.
60. Harding, *Imjin Roll*, p. 26.
61. Harvey, p. 133.
62. Harding, *Imjin Roll*, p. 27.

**CHAPTER 10**

1. Tony Perrins (author interview). See also the Fusiliers' Regimental History, in Perrins, p. 120.
2. Younger, pp. 200–2.
3. Gerald Rickord (taped interview in the possession of Mervyn McCord). Rickord, tactfully, did not mention Kingsley Foster in the interview.
4. Ormrod, IWM recording.
5. Winn, Korean Campaign Supplement to *The Crossbelts*, pp. 15–17.
6. From the Fusiliers' Regimental History, in Perrins, p. 120.
7. Patchett, IWM recording.
8. According to the Fusiliers' War Diary at 10:45 (in Perrins), the order of march was Z Company, Battalion HQ, X, W and Y, but a previous entry has Y Company already departed (at 09:55). Major Robbie Leith-MacGregor told the author that he (i.e. Y Company) led the way south. Clearly there was considerable confusion on the morning of the 25th.
9. Hamill, p. 70.
10. Kinne, p. 25.
11. Mervyn McCord (author interview).
12. Hamill, p. 70.
13. Zhang, p. 255.
14. Kinne, p. 25.
15. *Ibid.*, pp. 25–6.
16. Scott, IWM recording.
17. Quoted in McCord.
18. Bill Beattie (author interview).
19. Kinne, p. 26.
20. Aynsley, *Daily Express*, 28 November 1959.
21. Ormrod, IWM recording.
22. Mervyn McCord (author interview).
23. Speer, letter reprinted in *St George's Gazette*, 31 May 1951, p. 91, based on eyewitness accounts of Foster's death. A number of men coming up behind, including Derek Kinne, saw Foster's body lying face down in the stream.
24. Patchett, IWM recording.
25. Hickey, p. 229.
26. Kinne, p. 28.
27. Aynsley, 28 November 1959.
28. Ormrod, IWM recording.
29. Dunstan (1982), p. 19.
30. Ormrod, IWM recording.
31. *Ibid.*
32. Whybro, IWM recording.
33. Sharp, IWM recording.
34. Whybro, IWM recording.
35. Ormrod, IWM recording.
36. *Ibid.*
37. Winn, *The Crossbelts*, Korean Campaign Supplement, p. 19.
38. *Ibid.*, pp. 15–17.
39. Korea Ministry of National Defense, p. 111.
40. Winn, *The Crossbelts*, Korean Campaign Supplement, pp. 15–17.
41. *Ibid.*, p. 19.
42. Ormrod, IWM recording.
43. Whybro, IWM recording.
44. Blair, p. 845.
45. Whybro, IWM recording.
46. Ormrod, IWM recording.
47. Younger, p. 204.

**CHAPTER 11**

1. For description of the ceremony, see Warner.
2. Quoted in Harvey, pp. 137–8.
3. The citation is reproduced in Harding, *Imjin Roll*, p. 97.
4. 'The Hill of Honour'.
5. Harvey, p. 138.
6. Grist, pp. 47–51.

7. Harding, *Imjin Roll*, pp. 28–32.
8. *Ibid.*, pp. 27–8.
9. Details of the tributes to the regiment drawn from *The Back Badge*, December 1951, pp. 226–30.
10. The Belgian citation appears in the 'Battle of the Imjin River' entry in the online encyclopedia www.nationmaster.com.
11. Whybro, IWM recording.
12. Mervyn McCord (author interview).
13. 'Fore and Aft', *The Times*, 3 May 1951.
14. Whybro, IWM recording.
15. Letter of 29 April 1951 from Major Miles Speer, the Fusiliers' acting CO, to Majors John Winn and Charles Mitchell (both recovering in hospital in Japan). Reproduced in Perrins, p. 128.
16. Appleman, p. 495.
17. 'CCF and NKPA Spring Offensive (22 April–1 May 1951)', post-battle intelligence summary in Tab D, 'US Forces Korea Staff Ride Read Ahead Package'. See also 'Command Report, 3rd Infantry Division, April 1951'.
18. Zhang, p. 149.
19. *Ibid.*, pp. 149–50.
20. Paik Sun-yup (author interview).
21. For an excellent and detailed overall account of the Fifth Offensive (of which the above is a summary), see Appleman, pp. 449–87.
22. UN Command Report, quoted in Appleman, p. 493.
23. Farrar-Hockley (1995), p. 135.
24. Fisher and Lohan, pp. 39–47. This book, by two veterans, is the most up-to-date and exhaustively researched document on Britain's Korean War KIA.
25. Count from Fisher and Lohan.
26. Whybro, IWM recording.
27. Dunstan, *Tank War Korea*, p. 98.
28. Dick Webster (author interview).
29. Farrar-Hockley (1995), p. 152.
30. Whatmore, pp. 94–6.
31. Harvey, p. 144.
32. Younger, pp. 188–9.
33. *Ibid.*, pp. 196–7.
34. Boyall, p. 77.
35. Hamill, p. 77.
36. Grist, p. 53.
37. Ormrod, IWM recording.
38. Malcolm Cubiss (author interview).
39. Younger, pp. 208–9.

**CHAPTER 12**

1. Carter, IWM recording.
2. O'Kane, pp. 64–8.
3. Large, p. 55.
4. O'Kane, p. 73.
5. Davies, p. 44.
6. Carter, IWM recording.
7. O'Kane, p. 72.
8. Large, p. 58.
9. Farrar-Hockley (1954), pp. 117–18; Derek Kinne (author interview).
10. Large, p. 63.
11. *Ibid.*, pp. 59–60.
12. Davies, p. 51.
13. O'Kane, pp. 70–1.
14. Sharp, IWM recording.
15. O'Kane, p. 74.
16. Farrar-Hockley (1954), p. 109.
17. Green, p. 113.
18. *Ibid.*, p. 113.
19. *Ibid.*, p. 115.
20. Carter, IWM recording.
21. Tom Clough (author interview).
22. Large, pp. 70–1.
23. Farrar-Hockley (1954), p. 116–17.
24. Hickey, p. 338.
25. Farrar-Hockley (1995), p. 267.

26. Ministry of Defence, p. 2.
27. Quoted in Ministry of Defence, p. 5.
28. Farrar-Hockley (1954), pp. 110–11.
29. O'Kane, p. 86.
30. Carter, IWM recording.
31. Large, p. 78.
32. Davies, p. 64.
33. Green, p. 153.
34. O'Kane, p. 93.
35. Carter, IWM recording.
36. Farrar-Hockley (1954), p. 230.
37. Carter, IWM recording.
38. Large, p. 91.
39. Green, p. 145.
40. *Ibid.*, p. 118.
41. *Ibid.*, p. 157.
42. Carter, IWM recording.
43. Farrar-Hockley (1954), p. 211.
44. Large, p. 99.
45. Green, p. 126.
46. Davies, pp. 85–6.
47. *Ibid.*, p. 99.
48. O'Kane, p. 107.
49. Hastings (1987), p. 286.
50. Large, p. 78.
51. Farrar-Hockley (1995), p. 277.
52. *Ibid.*, p. 220.
53. Green, p. 160.
54. O'Kane, pp. 81–2.
55. Ministry of Defence, p. 20.
56. Green, p. 152.
57. Davies, pp. 77–8.
58. Large, p. 99.
59. O'Kane, p. 95.
60. Davies, pp. 120–1.
61. Farrar-Hockley (1954), p. 249.
62. Ministry of Defence, p. 27.
63. Large, p. 96.
64. Green, p. 136.
65. Guy Temple (author interview).
66. Farrar-Hockley (1954), pp. 214–17.
67. *Ibid.*, pp. 181–91.
68. Sharp, IWM recording.
69. Farrar-Hockley (1995), p. 268.
70. Ministry of Defence, p. 2.
71. Green, p. 123.
72. Davies, p. 142.
73. Large, p. 107.
74. Farrar-Hockley (1954), p. 270.
75. Davies, pp. 145–6.
76. Green, p. 178.
77. Davies, pp. 148–9.
78. *Ibid.*, p. 136. The paten was reconsecrated and Davies continued to use it in services at his parish in the UK.
79. Sharp, IWM recording.
80. Large, p. 110.
81. Farrar-Hockley (1995), footnote, p. 412.
82. Green, p. 178.
83. Sam Mercer and Guy Temple (author interviews). See also Waters's George Cross citation in Harding (2000), pp. 93–4.
84. Perrins, p. 361.

## CHAPTER 13

1. Malkasian, p. 130.
2. Headquarters, 3rd Infantry Division, 'Operations of 29th BIB, from 22–25 April 1951'.
3. See Appendix G, 'Review of the Battle of the Imjin', in '29th Independent Infantry Brigade Group History, September 1949–October 1951'.
4. Headquarters, 3rd Infantry Division, 'Operations of 29th BIB, from 22–25 April 1951'.
5. Charlton, IWM recording.
6. Farrar-Hockley (1990), p. 395.
7. Man, IWM recording.
8. Blair, p. 835.
9. Carew, p. 182. Carew's information was based on an interview with Brodie.
10. Farrar-Hockley (1995), p. 136.
11. Blair, p. 845.

12. Appleman, p. 473.
13. Mossman, p. 414.
14. Blair, p. 826.
15. *Ibid.*, p. 835.
16. Appleman, p. 501.
17. Mossman, p. 430.
18. *Ibid.*, p. 423.
19. Blair, p. 846 (footnote).
20. Quoted in Perrins, p. 157.
21. 'Directive to Brigadier T. Brodie' (WO308/68).
22. Blair, p. 848.
23. Farrar-Hockley (1995), p. 136.
24. Quoted in Farrar-Hockley (1995), p. 135.
25. Quotes in Blair, p. 847; also in Stuek, p. 169.
26. Zhang, pp. 260–1.
27. Large, p. 51.
28. De la Billière, p. 81.
29. See '3rd Infantry Division Command Report', in 'Reports of US Formations in Connection with the Battle of the Imjin'.
30. H.P. Wilmott, 'The Suez Fiasco', in Robert Thompson (ed.), p. 99.
31. Figures from the Falklands War Wikipedia entry, based on the Ministry of Defence's Roll of Honour for the conflict.
32. Ministry of Defence, as of 26 March 2008.
33. Different sources provide a variety of figures for the number of KIA at the Imjin. I have used what I believe is the most comprehensive and up-to-date source for British dead in the Korean War: Fisher and Lohan, pp. 39–47. Its collators are both Korean War veterans.
34. Farrar-Hockley (1995), Appendix F, p. 491.
35. Sharp, IWM recording.
36. Rees, IWM recording.
37. *Ibid.*

## APPENDIX

1. Evans.
2. Information supplied by Geoff Crump, researcher at the Cheshire Military Museum.
3. Information supplied by David Read at the Soldiers of Gloucestershire Museum.
4. Obituaries in *The Times* and *Daily Telegraph*, 14 March 2006.
5. Green; also Tom Clough (author interview).
6. Obituary, *The Times*, 7 August 2007.
7. Biographical data in Huth's obituary in *The Crossbelts*, supplied by Brigadier Dick Webster.
8. Obituary, *The Times*, 25 November 2008.
9. Obituary, *Daily Telegraph*, 20 November 2007.
10. Farrar-Hockley (1990), p. 417; see also Chang and Halliday, p. 651.
11. Obituary, *The Blackthorn* (Journal of the Royal Irish Regiment), undated fragment.
12. I am grateful to Jan Dillen for expediting and translating VanDamme's interview.

# INDEX

Page numbers in *italic* refer to maps; (fn) after a page number indicates a footnote.

Acheson, Dean 16, 256
Adams-Acton, Second Lieutenant Leo 294
Aden 339
Admin Box, Battle of the (Burma) 27-8
Afghanistan 316, 318
African-American troops 70, 84, 284
air operations
  bombing 47
  carrier-borne naval air support 259
  Chinese night operations 57
  Happy Valley 84
  Hill 235 213-14
  MIG Alley 280
  napalm drops 123, 163, 169, 214
  reconnaissance 125, 126, 132-3
  support for US Army retreat 54-5
aircraft
  artillery spotter planes 270
  B-29 Superfortress 47
  bombers/fighter bombers 47, 54(fn), 167
  casualty evacuation helicopters 158, 170
  Chinese 47
  F-80 Shooting Star 73, 213, 214, 271, 273, 295

F-86 Sabre 280-1
  interceptor 54(fn)
  losses 54(fn)
  MIG-15 47
  North Korean 15
  T-6 observation plane 221
  Yak fighter-bomber 15
Alexander, Lieutenant 85
Alexandria, Egypt 26
Allen, Private 103
ambulances, attacks on 264(fn), 316(fn)
Ambury, Sergeant Ben 77
ambushes 87, 238, 265
American Civil War 28
Andrew, Prince, Duke of York xi
Andrews, Major Allan 245
Angier, Major Pat 116, 125, 133, 150, 153, 154, 156, 170, 218
anti-aircraft drill, Chinese 54, 55, 272
anti-communist paramilitary units 96
anti-tank teams 240, 241, 243
anti-tank/anti-bunker weapons 171, 304
Appleman, Roy 188(fn), 309, 311-12, 314
Argyll and Sutherland Highlanders 20, 67, 124, 213, 222(fn)
armistice negotiations 268, 295
'artificial moonlight' 126
Assault Pioneers 64, 173, 254

Astley-Cooper, Captain Donald 69, 83, 85
*Asturias* 299
Atrocities xvi, 19, 20, 22, 93, 96, 97
Attlee, Clement 18, 19, 20
Australian forces in Korea 259
awards and decorations
  American Silver Star 246(fn)
  Bronze Star 137(fn)
  Distinguished Conduct Medal 196(fn), 239(fn)
  Distinguished Service Cross (US) 330
  Distinguished Service Order 81(fn), 89(fn), 107(fn), 140, 196(fn), 330
  George Cross xiii, 299, 300
  Medal of Honour 260
  Military Cross 53, 87(fn), 138(fn), 237(fn), 255(fn)
  Military Medal 87(fn)
  US Presidential Unit Citation 176, 253-4, 257, 259
  Victoria Cross xii, 155(fn), 300, 330
  War Cross with Palm 136(fn)

Bainbridge, George 171, 172
Baker, Corporal George 182
Balaclava 32, 99, 256

Bannister, Roger 31
battle fatigue 268
'Battle of the Bugles'
    209, 210
battle shock 87(fn), 145,
    157, 267, 316
battlefield clearance
    262, 264-5
battlefield tours 314,
    321
Bayliss, Fusilier John 29-
    30, 40, 63, 77, 79-80,
    114, 196-7, 229, 318,
    321, 330
bayonets 25, 79, 80,
    88(fn), 167, 178, 181
bazookas 107
bean powder 278
Beattie, Sergeant Bill 30,
    77, 79, 81, 130, 234,
    262
Beauprez, Lieutenant
    120
Bedfordshire Regiment
    25(fn)
Beirne, Daniel 261(fn)
Belfast 319
Belgian Battalion xiii, 6
    fn, 118-21, 123, 134,
    147, 215, 226, 227,
    252, 313, 314,
    318(fn), 337, 338
    breakout 244-6, 247,
    252
    Imjin River, Battle of
    136-9, 161, 172-4,
    176, 313
    post-Korean War 329
    unit citation 176, 257
Belsen 29, 32, 93
beriberi 277
Berlin airlift (1948-49)
    17
Bevin, Ernest 19
Binman, Private 152,
    265

Blair, Clay 312, 314
Blake, George 320-1
Blake, Major Tony 30,
    38, 73, 88, 89, 103
Blenkinsop, Captain
    Dick 76, 164
'blowback' 73(fn)
blue-on-blue see friendly
    fire incidents
booby traps 40, 58, 116,
    167
boots 60, 223(fn)
Boston Daily Globe 256
Bottomley, Signaller 80
Bourchier, Air Vice
    Marshal Cecil 129(fn)
box mines 243
Boyall, Lieutenant David
    34, 61, 99, 100, 227,
    240(fn), 243, 244,
    252, 264, 330
Breen, Michael 302
bridge destruction 88-9
Brisland, Sergeant 218
Britain xv, 18-19, 20
    Anglo-Korean
    contacts 19
    British communists
    285
    Imperial Strategic
    Reserve 20
    response to invasion
    of South Korea 18-
    19, 20
    sends military force to
    Korea 23-4, 39-41
    sends Royal Navy
    units to Korea 19
    'special relationship' 20
British Army
    assault and defence
    tactics 25
    battalions: structure
    and command 24-5
    batteries: structure
    and command 36-7

battledress 124
brigades: structure
    and command 24
casualties 296, 318
companies: structure
    and command 24-5
'K volunteers' 23, 124
National Service
    conscripts 23
platoons: structure
    and command 25
reservists 23-4
rum ration 49, 67, 74
training 28, 38, 39-40
units
    8th King's Royal
    Hussars see 8th
    King's Royal Irish
    Hussars (main
    entry)
    27th Brigade 20, 21,
    24, 64, 309
    29th Brigade (29th
    Infantry Brigade)
    xiii, 6(fn), 7, 20,
    22, 23, 24, 25, 28,
    32, 33, 36, 37, 39,
    42, 47, 55, 56, 64,
    65, 68, 69, 81,
    82(fn), 86, 90, 91,
    98, 101, 105, 114,
    118, 121, 127,
    128, 129, 134,
    137, 159, 160,
    161, 172, 186,
    187, 191, 193,
    199, 201, 202,
    213, 215, 216,
    222, 226(fn), 231,
    238, 247, 250,
    253, 257, 258,
    259, 260, 262,
    268, 301, 302,
    304, 306, 307,
    309, 310-11, 312,
    314, 316, 317,

318(fn), 319, 329, 330
45 Field Regiment 5, 6(fn), 36-8, 51, 69, 76, 79, 105, 109-10, 115, 134, 147, 148-9, 162, 201, 205, 207, 217, 226, 250, 305
55 Field Squadron 41, 88, 117, 140, 232, 234
170 Independent Mortar Battery 37-8, 73, 79, 92, 93-4, 105, 116, 134, 142, 145, 200, 203, 229, 253, 254, 303
Argyll and Sutherland Highlanders 20, 67, 124, 213, 222(fn)
Assault Pioneers 64, 173, 254
Bedfordshire Regiment 25(fn)
Glosters Regiment (Gloucestershire Regiment) see Glosters Regiment (main entry)
Middlesex Regiment 20, 55
Royal Engineers 232, 262
Royal Northumberland Fusiliers see Royal Northumberland Fusiliers (main entry)
Royal Tank Regiment 69, 79
Royal Ulster Rifles

see Royal Ulster Rifles (main entry)
weaponry 25, 304-5
winter clothing 60, 124
Brodie, Brigadier Tom 23, 38, 40, 57, 58, 68, 69, 86, 96, 99, 102-3, 107, 114, 117, 121, 123, 147, 161, 162, 170, 172-3, 186, 201-3, 216, 224, 249-50, 252, 253, 258, 276, 305, 306-7, 308, 309, 310, 312-13, 330, 331
brothels 42, 95(fn)
Broughton, Captain William 19
Bruford-Davies, Lieutenant Robin 70, 72, 89(fn)
bug-outs 20, 59, 187, 226, 309
bugles 54, 73, 209-10
bunkers 107, 266, 273
Burchett, Wilfred 285-6, 333
Burma 23, 26, 27-8
Buss, Drum Major 209-10, 217, 218
Buxcey, Colour Sergeant 207

Cadman, Sergeant 242
Caine, Michael xv
Cairo Conference (1943) 13
camouflage 46, 271
Campbell, Sergeant 87, 88
Canadian troops 259
Carne, Lieutenant-Colonel James 1, 2(fn), 26, 28, 51, 56, 104, 105, 106,

107(fn), 132, 156, 161, 170, 180, 183, 187, 188, 201(fn), 203, 204, 205, 206, 209, 215, 216, 217, 249-50, 260(fn), 272, 273, 290, 295, 297, 307, 308, 312, 319, 330
Carson, Lieutenant-Colonel Hank 30, 41, 73, 140, 160
Carter, Frank 56, 94, 107, 118, 125, 126, 127, 146, 177, 181-2, 270, 275, 277, 279
Castle Site 115, 131, 150, 153, 155, 157, 211, 220, 303, 327
casualties
    American 261, 296, 314(fn)
    British 296, 318
    Chinese 260, 261, 296(fn)
    civilian 96, 296(fn)
    North Korean 296(fn)
    POW deaths 300
    ROK 261, 296(fn)
    UN allies 296(fn)
caubeens 30, 231, 237
cavalry 33, 34, 36
Cavell, Edith 322-3
'Caves, The' 300
Ce Soir 285
Centurion tanks 34, 35-6, 62, 69, 99, 100, 104, 105, 114, 123, 125, 188(fn), 193, 237, 240, 264
Chaegunghyun 71, 83
chaplains 27, 121, 130
    see also Davies, Padre Sam
Charley, Captain Robin 31, 38, 56, 62, 70,

72-3, 74, 76, 84,
86(fn), 90(fn), 103,
105, 120, 159, 330
Charlton, Douglas 307,
308
Ch'arumul *122*, *143*, *175*
Cheju-Do 15
Chiang Kai-shek 43, 45,
113
Chichibu, Princess 159
children, abandoned 93-4
China 9-10, 12, 17-18,
43-5
anti-American policies
43-4
armed forces *see*
Chinese People's
Volunteer Army
(CPVA); People's
Liberation Army
(PLA)
civil war 14, 16, 17-
18, 43, 129
diplomatic relations
with South Korea
327
Great Leap Forward
336
military intervention
(1950) 42, 44-7
nationalists 17-18, 43,
54, 73, 275
pre-war appraisal 43-
4, 47(fn)
support for North
Korea 43-4
Chindits 23, 27
Chinese Communist
Party (CCP) 43, 44
Chinese People's
Volunteer Army
(CPVA) 55, 59, 128,
261
anti-aircraft tactics
54-5
assessment as a

fighting force 314-
16
casualties 260, 261,
296(fn)
deep reconnaissance
units 127
'drugged' appearance
of soldiers 87, 315-
16
Fifth Offensive xvi,
128-30, 135,
226(fn), 258-61,
*263*
*see also* Imjin River,
battle of
First Offensive 44-6,
109
Fourth Offensive 102,
109, 128
infiltration of North
Korea (1950) 44-5
intelligence and
sabotage missions
127
post-Korean War 329
Second Offensive 53-
9, 64, 109
Sixth Offensive
260(fn)
Third Offensive 68-
90, 101, 109
UN soldiers' opinions
of 87, 108, 315-16,
322-3
units
3rd Army 128
9th Army 128
12th Army 259
15th Army 259
19th Army Group
128, 129
20th Army 259
27th Army 259
63rd Army xiii, 129,
259, 260, 315, 329
64th Army 129

65th Army 260
116th Division 72
149th Division 78
179th Division 261
187th Division 129,
162, 169, 259
188th Division 129,
169, 259
189th Division 129,
169, 176, 215, 259
559th Regiment 176
weaponry 108, 315
Chinese People's
Volunteers (CPV)
xvii, 44
*see also* Chinese
People's Volunteer
Army (CPVA)
Ching Dynasty 10
Chingp'a-ri *122*, *143*,
*175*
Chipyong-ni 109, 314
Cho, Captain June 327
Choksong 115, *122*,
134, 162, *175*, 187,
*220*, 274, 303
POW camp 274, 275,
277, 279, 284, 295
Chongjin *11*
Chon'gong-ni *122*, *175*
Chorwon 127, 128
Chosin Reservoir 55
Chosun 9
Chou En-lai 44
Ch'owon *263*
Christmas celebrations 67
Christopher, Gunner 85-
6, 89
Chukfun-ni *263*
Ch'unch'on *263*
Chung Ju-yung 47(fn)
Church, Major-General
John 309, 311(fn)
Churchill, Winston 17,
120(fn)
Churchill tanks 69, 79

City Hall, Belfast,
    Korean War Memorial
    319
civilian disguise, soldiers
    in 92, 167, 172
Clarke, Sergeant Nobby
    197
Clode, Lieutenant
    Walter 58
Clough, Lance-
    Bombardier Tom 156,
    207, 214, 218-19,
    277, 279, 281, 283,
    284, 285, 288-9, 319,
    323, 330-1
Coad, Brigadier Basil 54,
    309, 311(fn)
Cocksedge, Captain
    Geoff 64, 82(fn)
Colchester 38-9
Cold War xi, xvi, 13,
    119
Coleman-Wood,
    Corporal John 101,
    245, 331
Commonwealth 27th
    Brigade 54, 57, 161,
    259
Commonwealth Division
    33, 114(fn), 268,
    309, 312
Condron, Andrew 282
Cook, Corporal George
    127
Cooke, Lieutenant
    Randle 95
Coombes, Private Morris
    49, 179, 180, 207,
    217
Cooper, Lieutenant Bill
    166
Cooperforce 69, 73, 83,
    85, 88, 89, 91, 100
Costello, Lieutenant
    Geoffrey 181
counter-guerilla

operations 53, 119
court martials 191, 337
Crahay, Lieutenant-
    Colonel Albert 120,
    138, 244, 245, 246
Craig, Lieutenant
    Headley 140-1
Cranham 319
Crawford, Davy 232
Crimean War 60
Cromwell tanks 34, 69,
    100, 125
Crooks, Fusilier Ronald
    196, 198
Cubiss, Lieutenant
    Malcolm 29, 38, 49, 51,
    52, 53, 59, 60, 78, 98,
    114, 117, 130, 142,
    144-5, 146-7, 235(fn),
    250-1, 252, 258, 264,
    266-7, 305(fn), 317,
    322, 324, 331
Curtis, Lieutenant Philip
    xii, 131, 151, 154-5,
    299-300, 303, 305
Cyprus 338

D-Day landings 135(fn),
    318
*Daily Worker* 281, 282,
    285
Dain, Captain Carl 205
Dandong *11*
Davies, Padre Sam 27,
    130, 131, 170, 200,
    204, 208, 218, 272,
    273, 280, 285,
    287(fn), 290, 295,
    297, 303
De La Billière, General
    Sir Peter 316
De Quidt, Captain 124,
    144, 145, 241
Dean, General William
    20
dehydration 203(fn)

Demilitarized Zone xi,
    302
Democratic People's
    Republic of Korea
    (DPRK, North Korea)
    xv
  anti-American feeling
    273-4
  invasion of South
    Korea (1950) 8, 15-
    17, 20-2
  isolation 327, 328
  *juche* (self-reliance
    philosophy) 16(fn)
  nationalism 16
  nuclear capability xv
  Soviet occupation of
    13
  *see also* North Korean
    People's Army
DF (Defensive Fire)
    SOS 5
Dien Bien Phu 319
Ding, Commandant 296
Dowling, Lieutenant
    Bernard 83, 85, 88
drop wrist 284, 289,
    291, 331
Dubai Armed Forces
    339
Ducrot, General 224
Dunkirk 26
dysentery 274, 277, 285

Eagles, Bugler Tony 66,
    106, 127, 139(fn),
    183, 206-7, 208, 209,
    214, 218, 219, 270,
    281, 291-2, 331-2
Eames, Sergeant 107, 218
Eastman, Lieutenant Keith
    117, 140, 141, 265
8th Army (UN/US) 19,
    20, 21, 22, 50, 54, 59,
    65, 113, 314
  *see also* US Army

8th King's Royal Irish Hussars xiii, 32-6, 49, 58, 61, 62, 85, 89, 95, 98-100, 105, 110, 114-15, 123, 125, 134, 160, 163, 164, 186, 187, 188(fn), 189(fn), 190, 193, 200, 215, 224(fn), 225, 245(fn), 262, 264, 266, 305, 306, 314, 318(fn), 329
  breakout down Route 11 227-44
  covers US retreat 55
  Happy Valley, battle of 69, 73, 83, 85, 88, 91, 187, 200
  Imjin River, Battle of 134, 163, 164, 183, 186, 188(fn), 189(fn), 190, 193, 306
  post-Korean War 329
  regimental history 32
  units
    A Squadron 34, 99, 134(fn)
    B Squadron 34, 99, 134(fn)
    C Squadron 33, 34, 99, 134, 160, 163, 187
Eisenhower, Dwight 256
El Alamein xiv, 135(fn), 318
Elizabeth II, Queen 319
Ellery, Captain Sir William 258
Empire Halladale 39, 40
Empire Pride 39
Empire Windrush 39, 40, 41, 133
entertainment 101
  POW camps 279, 283-4
equipment carried

British 102
Chinese 108
Essex, Private 255

Falkland Islands 254
Falklands War xiv, 235(fn), 305, 318
Farmer, Sergeant 85
Farrar-Hockley, Captain Anthony 26-7, 38, 127, 156, 170, 180(fn), 183, 201, 202(fn), 203, 206, 209, 210, 211, 212, 213, 214, 215, 216, 217-18, 218, 219, 223(fn), 237(fn), 254-5, 261(fn), 264, 272, 273, 276, 281, 282, 284(fn), 285, 293-4, 299, 305, 309, 311(fn), 313, 320, 321, 332, 333
Farrell, Lance-Corporal Joe 31, 32, 70, 74, 76, 83, 84, 90(fn), 100, 108, 185, 194, 230, 232, 249, 257, 321, 322, 332
Feyt, Sergeant Cor 174
Fichefet, Second Lieutenant Marcel 252
Field Postal Service 123, 281
Fighting Fifth see Royal Northumberland Fusiliers
Filipino Battalion 183, 186, 188, 190, 200, 201, 202, 244(fn), 259, 261, 310, 312, 318(fn)
Filipino POWs 275
Filipino troops 183, 186, 188, 190, 200, 201, 202, 244(fn), 259,

261, 308, 310, 312, 313, 318(fn)
fireflies 118
flashbacks 324, 339, 340
Florence Nightingale Trust 159
food and cooking 62-3, 117
  see also rations
foraging 63
'Fort Nixon' see Hill 194
Forward Observation Officers (FOOs) 37, 76, 109, 138, 153, 161, 205, 207, 249
Foster, Lieutenant-Colonel Kingsley 28-9, 38, 39, 42, 51, 53, 63, 64, 76, 79, 96, 102, 125, 130, 141(fn), 145, 161, 165, 186, 198, 225, 226, 228, 233(fn), 234, 235, 260(fn), 262, 319, 327, 337
Fox, Private 254
foxholes 61-2
Franco-Prussian War 224(fn)
Franks, Sir Oliver 20
French Battalion 109
friendly fire incidents 86, 164, 223
frostbite 60, 98

Gallagher, Sergeant Major 156
Gallipoli 26
gangrene 291
Garrison, Private 184(fn)
General Sherman 10
Geneva Convention 275
George VI, King 289-90
germ warfare 286(fn), 295(fn)

Ghenghis Kahn 115
'Gibraltar Hill' 51, 52
Gloster Crossing 3, 115, 127, 132, 204(fn), 265, 270
Gloster Hill *see* Hill 235
Gloster Regiment (Gloucestershire Regiment) 25, 26-8, 41, 48-9, 50-1, 62, 97, 115, 116, 118, 125, 126, 127, 131, 262, 266, 268, 273, 316
  at Happy Valley 69, 79, 82
  back badge xi-xii, 26, 206, 329
  battle honours 26
  break-out 216-23
  covers US retreat 55, 56, 58
  first major action in Korea 104-7
  'Glorious Glosters' 256, 280, 307, 321
  Hill 327 victory 104-7
  Imjin River, Battle of 1-7, 150-8, 161, 162, 166-72, 176-83, 185, 190, 305, 306, 308, 313-14, 318
  last stand (Hill 235) 200-23
  loss of the battalion 223, 313-14, 317, 318
  memorials 303, 319
  post-Korean War 329
  presidential unit citation 253-4, 314, 319
  public acclaim 255-7, 280, 321
  regimental history 26
  return to England 299
  sent to Korea 39-41
  units
    A Company 103, 115, 116, 131, 133, 134, 150, 156, 157, 161, 166, 170, 205, 206, 211-14, 217, 306, 327
    B Company 94, 107, 115, 126, 134, 138, 146, 161, 166, 167, 168, 172(fn), 176-9, 181-2, 183, 184, 185, 190, 205, 255, 264, 270
    C Company 1, 6, 50, 104, 105-7, 117, 134, 137, 138, 139, 168, 179-81, 184, 205, 303
    D Company 105, 106, 107, 132, 134, 150, 151, 152, 156, 157, 160, 161, 166, 170, 205, 209, 212, 214, 216, 217(fn), 219, 221-3, 254, 255(fn), 305, 306
    Drums Platoon 209
    Support Company 67, 77, 87, 134, 157, 180, 205
  War Diary 153(fn)
  *see also* Imjin River, Battle of; prisoners of war
Gloucester, Duke of 254
Gloucester Cathedral Korean War Memorial 319
Gloucestershire Regiment *see* Gloster Regiment
Golan Heights 319

Goten, Vander 121
Graham, Private 254
Greek Battalion 255, 264
Green, Private David 27, 40, 48-9, 50, 55, 93, 104, 105, 106, 107, 180(fn), 213, 219, 274, 279, 280, 281-2, 288, 295, 297, 299, 332
grenades 25, 100, 154
  booby traps 116
  Mills bomb (fragmentation grenade) 305
  phosphorus grenades 197, 239, 305
Grist, Major Digby 67, 94, 168(fn), 170, 171-2, 186, 188, 204, 215, 216, 250, 253, 254, 255
Grossman, David 304(fn)
guerrilla warfare 50
  aerial tactics 57
  counter-guerrilla operations 53, 119
Guerrisse, Albert 120
Gulf War (1991) 316

Hamill, Captain Hugh 233
Han River 8, 17, 49, 69, 76, 81, 88, 93, 109-10, 120, 261, 263, 301
Han River bridges 17, 254
Hantan River 113, 115, 121, 122, 127, 129, 134, 161, 172, 173, 176, 263, 303
Happy Valley 11, 68-90, 71, 75, 98, 100, 108, 140, 226(fn), 275, 306, 319

Harding, Major Denis 166, 176, 180(fn), 181, 182, 183, 184, 205, 208, 219, 281, 290

Harris, Colonel William 249, 250, 309, 312

Harvey, Lieutenant/Captain Maurice 'Mike' 07, 27, 40, 56, 58, 61, 64, 104, 106, 151, 152-3, 205, 206(fn), 216, 219, 221, 222, 223, 254, 255, 257(fn), 265, 332, 333

Hastings, Max 311(fn), 322

headgear 30, 100, 231, 237

Hennessy, Paddy 257

Hickey, Captain Bob 203, 216, 217-18

Hideyoshi Toyotomi 9

Hill 148 153

Hill 194 115, 121, 134, 136, 174, 306

Hill 235 xi-xii, 118, 131, 132, 134, 156, 157, 170, 176-9, 180, 183-4, 200-1, 204-15, 216-18, 220, 253, 255, 265, 269, 300, 303, 305, 314, 319-20

Hill 257 147-8, 149, 161, 165-6, 173, 303, 305

Hill 316 166-8

Hill 327 11, 104, 105-7, 109, 299

Hill 394 305

Hill 398 162-3, 185, 195, 225, 226, 230, 304

Hiroshima 286(fn)

HMS Jamaica 19

HMS Triumph 19

Ho Chi Minh 43

Hobbs, Sergeant Major Jack 40, 132, 157, 201, 203

Holberton, Sergeant 240

Holden, Bill 264

Holdsworth, Second Lieutenant David 151

Holliday, Sergeant William 31, 194

Holmes, Captain Desmond 243

Hong Kong 24

Hongch'on River 263

Hosdain, Lieutenant 138

Hunter, Private 127

Huth, Major Henry 33, 63, 99, 106, 160, 187, 188(fn), 189, 202, 225, 227, 245, 246, 247, 248, 249, 250, 252(fn), 333

Hwabang-ni 122, 143, 162

Hyundai 47(fn)

IDs, enemy 124(fn)

Imjin River 11, 68, 111, 115, 122, 129
course 112
cross-river patrols 125, 126, 131-2, 307
fords 113, 115, 305(fn)
geopolitical strategic significance 112
Gloster Crossing 3, 115, 127, 132, 204(fn), 265, 270
Ulster Crossing 140, 143, 173
see also Valley of the Water Dragon

Imjin River, Battle of xiii-xiv, 1-7, 130-252, 220
22 April 1-7, 130-58, 143
23 April 159-84, 175
24 April 185-210, 192
25 April 210-33
ammunition, exhaustion of 217
ammunition, expenditure of 318
annual commemoration xi-xiii
battlefield clearance 262, 264-5
battlefield today 302-4
battlefield tours 314, 321
breakout 216-23, 220, 226-52, 236
casualties 262
post-battle analysis 304-17
relief operation, planned 183, 186-90, 200, 201-3, 249-50, 313
strategic significance 317

Inchon 11, 12, 21-2, 44, 132

Inchon Landings 21-2, 42, 314

Indian Mutiny 30

Indian Northwest Frontier 103

Innsworth RAF barracks 319

intelligence
American 1
British 53, 307(fn)
CPVA 127
UN 108, 129(fn)

interpreters 102, 280, 283, 323, 334

Iraq, invasion of (2003) 316, 318
Irish Republican Army (IRA) 332
Irish soldiers 31-2
  *see also* Royal Ulster Rifles
Iron Curtain 17
Iron Triangle 128
Ismay, General Lord 255-6

Jamaica 2, 273
Japan 9, 10, 12, 13, 159
  colonial rule in Korea 13
  Hideyoshi invasion of Korea 111-12
  Meiji Restoration 10
  World War II 12, 13, 18
jaundice 277
jeep tracks 103
Johnson, John 309, 313
Jones, Lieutenant-Colonel H. 235(fn)

'K volunteers' 23, 124
Kaesong 16, 53, 111, 112, *263*, 297
Kahn, E.J. 255
Kamak-san 115, *122*, 127, 160, 162, 168, 172(fn), 190, 196, 205, 226, *236*, 271
Kan-dong *75*, 76, 90
Kane, Jack 286(fn), 333
Kangwha 10
Kap'abal-li *263*
Kap'yong *263*
Kavanagh, Lieutenant P.J. 123, 140-1, 146(fn)
Kawol-ri 255
Kaye, Danny 101
Kean, General William 68, 90

Keegan, John 304(fn)
Kennedy, Brian 193(fn), 243(fn)
'Kennels, The' 289, 294
Kenya 338
Kim Chum-kon, Colonel 12, 15, 16, 222, 223, 253(fn), 259(fn), 266, 333
Kim Il-sung xv, 8, 13, 14, 15, 16, 22, 44, 113, 327-8
Kim Jong-il 328
*kimchi* 48, 104, 302
Kimpo Airfield 254
Kinne, Fusilier Derek 124, 142, 144, 145, 199, 229, 232, 233, 238, 272, 284(fn), 285(fn), 286-8, 289, 290, 292-3, 297, 298, 299, 322, 324, 333
Kinne, Raymond 124, 229
Kitchener, Sergeant Reg 149
Kobayakawa Takakage 111
Koguryo 9
Komun-do 19
Korea
  division of 13
  geography 9
  Hermit Kingdom 10
  history of 9-10, 12-14
  Japanese colonial rule 12, 96
  landscapes 9, 48
  North Korea *see* Democratic People's Republic of Korea
  South Korea *see* Republic of Korea
  strategic importance 9
  winter 1950-51 59-62

Korea Cross 290, 319
*Korea Herald* 334
*The Korea Post* 334
Korean War
  armistice negotiations 268, 295
  assumption of early end 40-1, 47, 49
  civil war xvi, 8
  'conflict'/'police action' designation xv
  first 'hot' war of the Cold War xvi
  first UN war xv
  ideologies, clash of xvi, 8
  movies of xv
  psychological legacy 323-4
  static phase 260(fn)
  truce 296
  UN Security Council resolution 18
Korengp'o-n *263*
Koryo 9
Koyang 68, *71*
Krotkov, Yuri 286(fn)
Kublai Khan 9, 115(fn)
Kumnyangjang-ni 102
Kunu-ri *11*, 55
Kure 266, 267, 297
Kure Battle Training Camp, Japan 154
Kwangsuwon *122*, *143*, *175*
Kyeho-dong *143*
Kyonmo-ri *122*, *143*, *175*

Lamouline, Colonel Robert 338
Lane, Captain John 195, 230
Large, Private Lofty 166-8, 169, 170(fn), 178,

179, 181, 182, 271, 272, 273, 281, 288, 295, 298, 316, 334

Lasalle, General Antoine Charles Louis 32

The Last Hill *see* Hill 235

*Le Figaro* 256

Lee Chun-hee 8, 14-15, 17, 22, 91, 92, 334

Lee Enfield rifles 3-4, 25

Lee Kyung-sik 102, 234, 334

Leiding, Sergeant 136

Leith-MacGregor, Major Robbie 29, 163, 164, 186(fn), 198, 199, 228, 251, 257, 305, 334

*L'Humanité* 285

Li Ru-song 111, 112

lice and flea infestation 274, 277, 300

Lidsey, Lieutenant John 247, 248

'limited war' concept xv, 113, 315

Lin Bao, General 44

Line Delta 199, 215, 225, 257, 258, 261, *263*, 310

Line Golden 260, 261, *263*

Line Kansas 113, 114, *122*, 127, 160, 161, 187, 215, 252, 259, 260, 306, 310, 311, 313, 314, 317

Line Nevada *263*

Line Utah 127-8, 161, 187, 310, 311

Line Wyoming 128

Little, Fusilier Preston 92, 94, 101, 234, 238

Lovat, Lord 209

Lowther, Lieutenant-Colonel Sir Guy 33,

59, 91, 98-9, 106, 125, 224(fn), 243(fn)

Luxembourg 118

M-24 tanks 186

McAffery, Gunner 146

MacArthur, General Douglas 18, 21, 22, 46-7, 54, 65, 113, 325(fn)

McAuliffe, General 209

McCallum, Lieutenant Arthur 87

McCord, Second Lieutenant Mervyn 31, 33, 38, 64, 73, 74, 83, 86, 87, 89(fn), 90(fn), 160, 162(fn), 191-2, 195, 198, 231, 233, 248-9, 251, 258, 302(fn), 317(fn), 322, 334-5

McDonald, Sergeant Robert 262

machine-guns
Bren 3, 25, 100, 137, 246, 305
Browning 64, 266
MG-42 304, 305
Vickers 25, 208, 305

McKay, Sergeant Jock 50, 105

McMichael, Major Scott R. 5(fn)

McNab, Andy 290, 298

McNamara, Terry 163

Main Supply Routes (MSR) 47, 48, 49, 82, 84, 88, 112, 114, 115, 162, 199, 215, 225, 257, 259, 310

Majury, Captain James 76, 86, 280, 297, 319, 320

Man, Lieutenant-Colonel Andrew 309

*Manchester Guardian* 59

Manch'on *143*, *175*

Manchuria 16, 44

Manchus 9-10

Manley, Corporal 3, 6

Mannes, Marya 8

Mao Tse-tung xv, 15-16, 43, 44, 45, 47(fn), 128, 231, 315, 336

Mardell, Captain Reg 106, 107

marijuana 279

Marshall, S.L.A. 304

Martin, Lieutenant Bob 223

MASH units 81, 203, 250

*MASH* (film and TV series) xv, 114(fn)

Mau Mau 338

Mau-san *143*, *175*, *236*

Maycock, Lieutenant 154

Mead, Brigadier Armistead 250, 312

Meadows and Co. 10

'meat-grinder' tactics 105

Melen, Major Moreau de 119, 173

Melville, Hermann 304

memorials
City Hall, Belfast 90(fn), 319
Gloucester Cathedral 319
Happy Valley 90(fn)
Hill 235 303, 319-20
Hill 257 303
Pusan, UN War Cemetery xiii, 320
St Anne's Cathedral, Belfast 319

Mercer, Private Sam xi-xii, 2(fn), 26, 27, 28, 40, 49, 59, 103, 104, 108,

115, 125, 127, 150-1,
153, 154, 155, 157,
200, 204, 206, 207,
211-12, 269, 270, 272-
3, 274, 276-7, 278,
280, 281, 283(fn), 286,
295-6, 297-8, 309,
310, 315, 317, 319,
321, 326, 335
Michaelis, Colonel John
86
Middlesex Regiment 20,
55
MIG Alley 280
Mike Targets 5, 6, 168
Milburn, General Frank
46, 56, 68, 90, 105,
114, 127, 193, 202,
215, 258, 259, 310,
311(fn), 313
Militis, Major Jean 120-
1
Miller, Major Dickie
160, 235
Miller, Ron 309
Millet, Allan R. 296(fn),
314(fn)
Mills bomb
(fragmentation
grenade) 305
Milward, Major Colin
77, 81
mine-clearance tanks
120
mines 120, 265, 266
box mines 243
Mitchell, Major Charles
79, 81, 98, 233, 234,
312, 313
Mitchell, Major Jack
180(fn)
Mole, Lieutenant John
31, 70, 72, 74, 121,
185, 225, 229, 230,
322, 335
Mongols 9

Morgan, Private 172
*Morning Post* 321
mortars 37-8, 105
Chinese 229(fn)
movies xv
Moxley, Robert 54
Muccio, John 92
'Muddy Paddy'
competition 117, 265
Munsan 259
Munsan Corridor 311
Murphy, Byron 132
Murray, Captain Gavin
61, 62, 163, 228, 240

NAAFI 116
napalm 55, 73-4, 101,
123, 163, 169, 213,
214, 273, 292
Napoleonic wars 30, 32
Nelson, Lord 209
*New York Times* 18
*New Yorker* 255
Newcombe, Captain
Michael 58, 161, 168-
9, 170(fn), 178,
180(fn), 181, 183, 262
Newhouse, Dorothy 281
Newhouse, Private
George 27-8, 156,
210, 211, 217(fn), 335
*News of the World* 281
newsreels 255
Nicholls, Gunner Bob 38,
39, 41, 42, 47-8, 61,
78, 92, 94-5, 100-1,
116, 133, 142, 144,
146, 194, 230, 234,
318, 320, 324-5, 335-6
Nicholls, Lieutenant
Max 230
night blindness 277, 278
Nixon, Sir Christopher
115
Norman, Major Mike
318

Norris, Captain 168
North Korea *see*
Democratic People's
Republic of Korea
(DPRK)
North Korean People's
Army (NKPA) 15,
20-1, 22, 43, 44, 47,
49, 50, 261, 291
atrocities 96
casualties 296(fn)
invasion of South
Korea (1950) 15-17,
19-21
strength 21
units
63rd Army 258-9
64th Army 258-9
North Korean People's
Committee 13
North Korean police
292, 293
nuclear weapons 17

O'Flaherty, Captain
Dennis 36, 52
Ojeda, Lieutenant-Colonel
Dionisio 202(fn)
O'Kane, Private Henry
32, 57, 76, 271, 272,
273, 278, 281, 282
O'Leary, Corporal
Michael 70(fn)
Oman 332
Operation Big Switch
296-7
Operation Chromite 21
Operation Dauntless
115, 127-8
Operation Killer 109
Operation Little Switch
295-6
Opium Wars 19
Ormrod, Captain Peter
33, 48, 59, 61, 106,
110, 125, 163, 170,

173, 188(fn), 193, 227, 228, 235, 239-40, 241-2, 245, 247, 251, 267, 336
Orton, Sergeant Reg 239
Osan 11, 19
Oxford Bren gun carriers 34, 64, 73, 139

Paegun 255
Paekje 9
Paik Sun-yup, General 16-17, 43, 46, 47, 68, 109, 309, 311(fn), 333, 336
painkillers, natural 269(fn)
Paju City 303
Pangun 220
Panmunjom 296, 326-7
Papworth, Corporal Cyril 155, 156, 157
Park Chung-hee viii, 65(fn)
Park Jong-chol 293(fn)
Patchett, Doug 40, 228, 237, 240, 272
Paul, Lieutenant Ted 34, 60, 61, 98, 99, 186(fn), 187, 188, 189, 190, 227, 244, 245, 246, 247(fn), 336
Peal, Second Lieutenant Arthur 167, 179
Peng Te-huai, Marshal 44, 55, 66, 68, 102, 128, 130, 150, 169(fn), 258-9, 260, 290, 314, 317, 336
Peninsular War 28
People's Liberation Army (PLA) 336
assessment of 45-6
manoeuvrability 45-6
uniforms 45
weaponry 45

see also Chinese People's Volunteer Army (CPVA)
Perkins, Corporal Albert 176, 181, 183
Perrins, Lieutenant Tony 28, 29, 39, 57, 58, 59, 60, 78, 79, 81, 95, 108, 125, 130, 131-2, 224-5, 226, 228, 234, 238, 241, 307, 312-13, 317-18, 320, 321, 326, 337
Philips, Sergeant Armand 119, 120, 123, 136, 137-8, 139, 337, 338
Phillips, Lieutenant Sam 29, 30, 58, 63, 82, 92, 118, 125, 131-2, 144, 163, 164, 267, 319, 326, 337
phosphorus grenades 197, 239, 305
Pickard, Private 172(fn), 184(fn)
Picq, Ardant du 166
Pinchon-ni 274
Plan Golden 199, 225
pole charges 85
police
North Korean 292, 293
ROK 96, 97, 323-4
Polish Parachute Brigade 30
porters 102-3, 201(fn)
Post-Traumatic Stress Disorder 15, 323-4
Poswick, Captain 138
Potts, Lieutenant Gordon 162, 191, 195, 234
Pratt, Major Reggie 142
Preston, Second Lieutenant Tony 172(fn), 214(fn)

Preston-Bell, Cornet John 33, 34, 59, 60-1, 93, 98(fn), 99, 164, 190, 227, 235, 240, 242, 243, 251, 258, 262, 264, 323, 327, 328, 337-8
Princess Patricia's Light Infantry, Canadian 259
prisoners of war 238, 239, 252, 269-300
American 96, 275, 295
bargaining chip in armistice negotiations 295
brainwashing, rumours of 295(fn), 320, 330
captor–prisoner relationships 272
deaths 300
diseases 274, 277-8, 285
escape attempts 288, 290-4
executions 96-7, 265, 316, 323-4, 325(fn)
Filipino 275
'give-up-itis' 275
'ideological re-education' 275-6, 282, 290, 295(fn)
informers 283, 294, 295(fn)
insane 275
interrogation 102, 276, 283, 294
left-wing 276, 277
Lenient Policy 275-6
letter writing 281
local relationships 279
malnutrition 286
march into North Korea 271-4
medical treatment 272, 277, 278, 295

mock executions 285
morale boosters 280, 281
North Korean threats against 274
prisoner exchanges 295-7
'progressives' 275, 282, 283, 289, 295(fn), 298-9
Puerto Rican 275
punishments 284-5, 287-9, 290, 294
racial segregation 284
rations 273, 278, 286
'reactionaries' 276, 282, 283-5, 286-90
reception in the UK 320
repatriation 282, 298-9
resistance 282, 283-5, 286-90, 298
'resisters' 298
show trials 287-8, 290
solitary confinement 285, 288, 289, 290
Turkish 275
weight loss 298
prisoner of war camps 274-80
billets 278
Christmas celebrations 281, 290
daily routine 276, 277, 279
entertainment 279, 283-4
guards 279-80
North Korean-run camps 295, 300
'Peace Fighter' camps 282, 300
propaganda activities 282, 295(fn)
Red Cross parcels 295

religious services 280, 297
sports 281-2
visits from Western leftists 285-6
work details 277
propaganda 123, 281, 282, 295(fn)
prostitution 42, 94-5
Prout, Sergeant Dennis 150
psychological warfare 193(fn)
Puerto Rican POWs 275
Puerto Rican troops 60, 114, 201, 244
Pukch'ang 122, 143, 175
Pulmiji-ri 71, 82, 85, 86, 87-8
Pusan 11, 12, 21, 41, 44, 49, 92, 119
UN War Cemetery xiii, 66, 262(fn), 320
Pusan Perimeter 20, 22, 47
Pyokje pass 111-12
Pyoktong 274, 276, 281
Pyongtaek 11, 116
Pyongyang 10, 11, 43, 47, 53, 55, 82, 111, 274, 327
retreat from 56-8, 95

radar 205
Radcliffe, Sergeant Major 196, 198
Radford, Lieutenant 228
Radio Peking 296
radio reception 54(fn)
Ranger company 109
rations
American 63
British 62-3, 64, 117
liquid 49, 61, 67, 74
prisoners of war 273, 278, 286

rear echelon officers 120
Red Cross 64, 94, 124(fn), 295
Rees, Fusilier Roy 48, 148, 150, 166, 323-4, 325
refugees 56, 68, 89, 91-4, 97
Regimental Aid Posts (RAP) 156, 164, 170, 203, 206
Republic of Korea (ROK, South Korea)
battlefield tours 314, 321
democratic government 325
economic growth 325
establishment of 13
nationalism 16
North Korean invasion of 8
US military occupation (1945) 13
US troops stationed in xv
veterans' visits to 324-7
'zero-to-hero' rise 325, 327
Republic of Korea (ROK)
armed forces 15, 44
atrocities 22, 96-7, 323-4
casualties 261, 296(fn)
and the North Korean invasion (1950) 16, 20, 22
strength 21
units
1st Division 16, 43, 68, 69, 109, 113, 115, 128, 129, 134, 161, 187, 215, 217, 222, 253, 258-9, 259,

260, 261, 310, 311
3rd Division 68
6th Division 16, 43, 46, 68, 161, 226(fn), 259, 260(fn)
7th Division 113
8th Division 68
9th Division 68
12th Regiment 222, 223
25th Division 302
II Corps 54
war memorial 303
Rest and Recreation (R&R) 159
revolvers 25
Rhee Syngman 13-14, 15, 18, 22, 43, 64, 97(fn), 98, 325
Rickord, Major Gerald 103, 160, 162, 185, 194, 225, 226-7, 228, 233, 234(fn), 245, 252(fn), 308, 335, 338
Rickson, John 164(fn)
Riddlington, Sergeant Major 179
Ridgway, Lieutenant-General Matthew Bunker 65, 66, 68, 81, 90, 91, 101, 105, 109, 113, 202, 253, 306, 309, 310, 311, 312
rifles
Garand 269
Kalashnikov AK-47 304
Lee-Enfield 3-4, 25, 304
Simonov 210
Sturmgewehr 44 assault rifle 304
Robertson, Lieutenant-General Sir Horace 215

Route 11 115, 122, 129, 134, 139, 147, 161, 162, 165, 185, 186, 192, 195, 199, 223, 225, 226, 227-52, 257, 271, 303, 323, 327
Route 13 105, 109
Route 33 112-13, 114, 122, 129, 162, 259
Route 57 ('Five Yankee') 115, 122, 162, 171, 172, 186, 187, 189(fn), 204(fn), 302, 303, 308, 312, 314
Royal Army Service Corps 101
Royal Artillery mess, Larkhill 149(fn)
Royal Australian Regiment, 3rd Battalion 259
Royal Engineers 232, 262
Royal Northumberland Fusiliers xiii, 25, 28-30, 41, 83, 92, 94, 96, 97, 98, 100, 102, 103, 104, 105, 108, 109, 114-15, 116, 124, 125, 130, 131, 133, 215, 224, 225, 227, 257, 262, 266, 267, 268, 299, 303, 304, 305, 314, 318(fn), 319, 321, 322, 325(fn), 329, 336, 337, 338
breakout down Route 11 228-44, 245, 247-52
Happy Valley, battle of 69, 76-82, 90
Imjin River, Battle of 134, 141(fn), 142, 144-50, 156, 160,

161, 162-6, 170, 186, 190, 195-9, 305
post-Korean War 329
regimental history 28
sent to Korea 39-41
Sibyon-ni, battle of 51-3
W Company 69, 76, 79, 80, 81, 134, 165, 166, 186, 198, 225, 228, 233, 238
X Company 51, 76, 77, 79, 124, 133, 134, 142, 144, 146, 147, 149, 156, 161, 170(fn), 186, 199, 225, 228, 229, 305
Y Company 29, 51, 76, 77, 78, 92, 134, 144, 147(fn), 161, 163, 164, 165, 166, 170, 186(fn), 198, 199, 228, 262, 334
Z Company 29, 53, 76, 82, 94, 96, 115, 116, 130, 134, 141(fn), 147-9, 161, 162, 164, 165, 170, 173, 195, 196, 198, 199, 228, 229, 303, 305(fn), 330, 339
see also prisoners of war
Royal Northumberland Fusiliers Museum, Alnwick Castle 319
Royal Tank Regiment 69, 79
Royal Ulster Rifles xiii, 25, 30-2, 41, 42, 64, 95(fn), 100, 102, 103, 104, 108, 109, 114, 115, 117, 120, 121, 123, 133, 136, 137, 159, 160, 187(fn), 215, 225, 226, 227, 245, 253,

257, 260(fn), 262, 264, 265, 271, 301, 304, 305, 313, 314, 317(fn), 318(fn), 319, 321, 329, 334, 335, 336, 337
breakout down Route 11 228-44, 247-52
covers US retreat 55, 56-7
Happy Valley, battle of 68-76, 79, 81, 82-90, 91, 313
Imjin River, Battle of 134, 138, 139-41, 147, 162-3, 185-6, 190, 191-2, 193-5, 305, 317
monuments 90
post-Korean War 329
regimental history 30
sent to Korea 39-41
units
  A Company 70, 73, 83, 162, 163, 185, 194, 225, 228
  B Company 70, 73, 74, 83, 84, 159, 162, 185, 225, 227, 228, 232, 234, 235, 239, 304
  Battle Patrol 64, 73, 74, 83, 133, 139, 140, 141, 265
  C Company 83, 185, 194-5, 228, 232
  D Company 73, 83, 84, 162, 194, 195, 225, 228
see also prisoners of war
Rudge, Lieutenant David 198, 262
Rusk, Dean 13(fn)
Russo-Japanese war 12
Ryan, Major Joe 74

St Anne's Cathedral, Belfast 319
St George's Day (1951) 130-1, 159-84
Samsung 90(fn)
samurai 111
Sangbi-ri 122, 143, 175
Sanjom-ni 122, 143, 175
Sansom, Odette 299, 333
Schneider, Pilot Officer Carl 54
School of Infantry, Warminster 28, 29
Schwarzkopf, General Norman 316
scorched-earth policy 56, 91
Scott, Captain Andrew 233
Senterre, Sergeant Lucien 119, 138, 174, 252, 338
Seoul 8, 9, 11, 14-15, 17, 22, 64, 67, 82, 88-9, 91, 109-10, 112, 114, 132, 261, 263, 301-2, 326
  Anglican Cathedral 110, 301-2
  battle scars 114, 301-2
  British Embassy 19(fn), 110, 301
  Capitol Building 22, 301
  Choltusan 10 fn
  Chosun Hotel 17, 64
  CIA building 293(fn)
  cityscapes 325
  communist evacuation (March 1951) 109-10
  and the Fifth Offensive 128

Korean National War Memorial 123(fn), 260(fn), 326
  liberation of (1950) 22, 96
  North Korean invasion (1950) 17
  Toksu Palace 301
  twenty-first century 301-2, 325-6
Shapiro, Michael 285
Sharp, Sergeant David 161, 241, 294, 297, 320(fn), 323
Sharpling, Lance-Corporal Charles 170, 200, 207
Shaw, Major John 30-1, 87-8, 89(fn), 140, 185, 225, 227, 231-2, 262(fn)
Shaw, Sergeant Ted 126
Shaw-Steward, Second Lieutenant Huston 90
shell scrapes 144, 168
Sheppard, Lieutenant 196
Shilla Dynasty 9, 115
Shorthouse, Ted 80, 81
Sibyon-ni 11, 50, 51-3, 64, 306
Sidney, Sir Philip 185
signalling methods 54
Sino-Japanese Wars 12
Sino-Soviet Friendship Treaty (1950) 18
Sinuiju 11, 47
Sinwon-ni 263
Sixth Offensive 260(fn)
Slim, Field-Marshal Sir William 267
slit trenches 116, 191
Smith, Ben 163
smoke generators 35, 37, 45, 54, 128
snakes 62

Sokchangsang-ni *122, 143, 175*

Soldiers of Gloucestershire Museum 187(fn), 189(fn)

Solma-ri 118, *122, 143, 175*

Somme 30, 316

Songchu-dong *75, 76, 77*

Sop'yonch'an *122, 143, 175*

Soule, General Robert 114, 172-3, 187, 201-3, 215, 224(fn), 244(fn), 308, 310, 311(fn), 312, 313

South Korea *see* Republic of Korea (ROK)

Soviet Union 9, 13, 18
   Berlin Blockade 17
   military aid to North Korea and China 15, 128, 296(fn)
   nuclear weapons 17
   occupation of North Korea 13

spam 302

Special Air Service (SAS) 288(fn), 334

Special Operations Executive (SOE) 120, 245(fn)

Speer, Major Miles 199, 228, 235(fn)

spies 119-20

springtime, Korean 118

Stalin, Joseph 13, 15, 18(fn), 44

Stalingrad 135(fn)

Sten submachine-guns 25

Steward, Sergeant 230

Strachan, Captain George 100, 301

Strachan, Fusilier David 30, 60, 77-8, 82, 93, 96-7, 130, 147, 148, 197, 199, 324, 326-7, 338

Strong, Sergeant 40

Sturgeon, Sergeant Tommy 84-5, 103

Suez Crisis (1956) 318

Sun Tzu 47(fn), 111, 231

Suwon *11*

Sweetlove, Corporal Norman 31, 100, 118, 123, 195, 233, 248, 321, 338

Sykes, Sergeant Bill 283-4

T-34 tanks 15, 17, 19, 34

Taedong River 10, 56, 58

Taedong River bridges 56, 57

Taedong Valley 273

Taegu *11*

Taejeon *11*, 20, 96

Tagamp'o *122, 143, 175*

Taiwan 43, 45, 54

tall stories 256-7

Tanggogae *122, 143, 175*

tanks
   Centurions 34, 35-6, 62, 69, 99, 100, 104, 105, 114, 123, 125, 188(fn), 193, 237, 240, 264
   Churchills 69, 79
   Cromwells 69, 73, 83, 85, 86, 100
   M-24s 186
   mine-clearance tanks 120
   Panthers 34-5

Taraktae *122, 143, 175*

Task Force Smith 19

Task Force Walker 314

Taylor, Lance Corporal 177

Teale, Trooper 99

Temple, Second Lieutenant Guy 1-2, 3, 4, 5-7, 26, 27, 28, 57, 61, 100, 134, 137, 142(fn), 151, 179-80, 203, 208, 210, 216, 217, 218, 219, 275, 277-8, 282, 283, 290-1, 297, 298-9, 303, 305-6, 320-1, 322-3, 326, 338-9

Thackery, Colin 101

Thanksgiving dinners 47, 93-4

Tharp, Lieutenant-Colonel Steve viii

Thermopylae 256

Thirkettle, Doug 53, 81

38th parallel xi, 13, 15, 59, 113, 296

Thompson, Corporal Joe 29, 52-3, 60, 61, 79, 80, 81, 101, 323, 324, 327, 339

Tibet 45

*The Times* 257

Tokchong *122, 143*, 225

Tokyo 159-60, 266

Toledo Infantry Academy 256

Tomenson, Fusilier Stan 78, 81, 116-17, 147, 148, 195-6, 198, 199, 339

Tongduchon 112, *122, 143, 175*, 302

toothache 277

*Toronto Telegram* 256

tracer ammunition 151(fn)

Trevor, Major Ken 160

trip flares 116, 127

Truell, Lieutenant George 27, 36, 37(fn), 39, 61, 110, 120, 132,

148-9, 150, 165, 215, 216(fn), 217, 250, 301, 303, 318, 339
Truman, Harry 15, 18, 59, 113, 239(fn), 256
Truth and Reconciliation Commission 96(fn)
Tunjan *122*, *143*, *175*
Turkish Brigade 54, 55, 128, 132, 161, 259, 310
Turkish POWs 275
25-pounders 37, 51, 61, 105, 190
typhus 87(fn), 98, 274

Uijongbu xv, *11*, 16, 112, 114, 115, 186, 259, 261, *263*
'Uijongbu Corridor' 112-13, 302, 311, 317
Ungría, General José 256
United Nations (UN) 16, 39, 320
  resolution calling for ceasefire 59
  resolution calling for military aid to South Korea 18
  Soviet boycott of 18
  supply lines 49-50
  UN Command *see* Belgian Battalion; British Army; Commonwealth forces; French Battalion; Greek Battalion; Princess Patricia's Canadian Light Infantry; Republic of Korea (ROK) armed forces; Royal Australian Regiment; Turkish Brigade; US Army

UN Security Council 18
United States xv, 17-18
  military occupation of South Korea 13
  response to South Korean invasion (1950) 18
  *see also* US Army
Unmaurhan *122*, *143*, *175*
Unsan *11*, 46
US Army
  casualties 261, 296, 314(fn)
  and NKPA invasion of South Korea 19-22
  strength 21
  units
    I Corps 7, 56, 68, 101, 114, 127, 132, 161, 167, 199, 215, 258, 260, 261, 308, 311, 311(fn), 317
    IX Corps 259
    1st Cavalry 46, 103, 104
    2nd Infantry Division 54, 55, 302
    3rd Infantry Division 7, 109-10, 114, 128, 129, 172, 186, 226(fn), 249, 259, 307, 308, 310, 311, 317
    7th Infantry Regiment 173, 226(fn), 260, 261, 310, 311(fn)
    10th Field Artillery Battalion 201, 310
    15th Infantry Regiment 259, 310, 311(fn)
    23rd Regimental Combat Team 109

    24th Infantry Division 19-20, 76, 128, 133, 161, 259, 260, 261
    24th Infantry Regiment 161
    25th Infantry Division 54, 68, 82(fn), 128, 161, 259, 260, 261
    27th Infantry Regiment 82(fn), 86, 90
    35th Infantry Regiment 310
    64th Tank Battalion 201, 310
    65th Infantry Regiment 114, 201, 202, 244, 249, 261, 309, 310, 311(fn)
    73rd Tank Battalion 223, 259, 310
  winter retreat (1950) 54-9, 82(fn)
US Marine, 1st Marine Division 161, 259
USAF 21, 47, 54, 213-14, 273, 295
  *see also* air operations

Valley of the Water Dragon 112-35, *122*
  *see also* Imjin River, Battle of
Van Fleet, General James 113, 187, 202, 253, 254, 259, 261, 301, 310, 314
Vance, Martin 83
VanDamme, Sergeant André 119, 120, 137, 174, 176, 339
venereal diseases 95(fn)

Verhaegen, Lieutenant Benoit 137
Vietnam 43
Vietnam War xiv-xv, 314(fn), 316
Viverio, Major 245

'Wag's Truckers' 84
Walker, Corporal 183-4
Walker, Sergeant 'Hooky' 84
Walker, General Walton 20, 40, 46, 47, 56, 64-5, 91, 99
Walsh, Lieutenant Paul 138
Walwyn, Major Charles 104, 105, 106, 299
war correspondents 90, 117, 133, 140
War Graves Commission (WGC) 265
Ward, Major Guy 205
Washbrook, Captain Ronnie 205, 212, 217
'Washy-Washy' 67, 94
water torture 293
Wateridge, Corporal 172(fn)
Waterloo 316
Waters, Second Lieutenant Terry 131, 211, 299-300, 303
weaponry
    British 25, 304-5
    CPVA 108, 315
    see also bayonets; grenades; machine guns; rifles; tanks
Wear, Fusilier Vic 29, 41, 51, 61, 229, 325, 340
Webster, Brigadier Dick 98(fn), 302(fn)
Weller, Major Sam 205, 216

Wellington, Duke of 159
wells, poisoned 63(fn)
Whatmore, Second Lieutenant Denys 123, 132, 151-3, 154, 157, 189(fn), 203, 209, 214, 221, 222, 256-7, 264-5
Whitamore, Lieutenant Peter 31, 39, 123, 194, 195, 230, 232-3, 234, 237, 239, 241, 271, 272, 276, 282, 283, 284, 285, 294, 298, 306, 320, 340
Whitchurch, Private Ben 171, 207, 209, 257(fn), 270, 304-5, 324, 340
Whybro, Trooper Denis 34, 36, 42, 49, 106, 190, 193, 240-1, 241, 247, 251, 257, 258, 264
Wilcox, David 5(fn)
Wilson, Captain 'Jumbo' 205
Wingate, Major-General Orde 27
'winkle groups' 154, 155
Winn, Major John 29, 78, 96, 164, 195-6, 198, 199
Winn, Captain the Honourable Roland 245
Winnington, Alan 285
winter 1950-51 59-62
'The Witch' 191, 193, 198
Withers, Googie 39
Withers, Major Harry 39
Wolfe, General James 26
Wolfs, Second Lieutenant Henri 119, 120, 121, 138-9, 173-

4, 176(fn), 244, 246, 328, 340
Women's Institute food parcels 64
Wonsan 11, 12
Wood, Major 'Lakri' 151(fn), 160
World War I 28, 30, 32
World War II xiv, xv, xvi, 12-13, 17, 18, 28, 29, 30, 31, 32, 34, 65, 135(fn), 318
worms 277, 278
Wragg, Ben 77

Yalta Conference (1945) 13
Yalu River 43, 45, 47, 53, 54, 294
Yang Teh-chih, General 129, 169
Yangp'yong 263
Yellow Sea 59, 112, 301
Yi Dynasty 9
Yi Song-gye 9
Yongch'on 122, 143, 175
Yongdungpo 63, 100, 254
Yongjong-ni 122, 143, 175
Yongmun-san 260
Yongsan 123(fn), 293(fn)
Young, Lieutenant-Colonel Maris 36, 37, 109-10, 116, 204, 212(fn), 216, 262
Younger, Major Tony 41, 61, 88-9, 93, 117, 132-3, 165, 225, 239(fn), 247, 251, 265, 268

Zhang Shu-guang 315
Zippo petrol lighters 63